D0872092

# The Early Works of John Dewey

## 1882–1898

# John Dewey

## The Early Works, 1882–1898

## 5: 1895–1898

## *Early Essays*

*Carbondale and Edwardsville*

SOUTHERN ILLINOIS UNIVERSITY PRESS

FEFFER & SIMONS, INC.

*London and Amsterdam*

The Early Works of John Dewey, 1882–1898, *is the result of a co-operative research project at Southern Illinois University.*

*Jo Ann Boydston is the General Editor. Fredson Bowers is Consulting Textual Editor.*

*The Editorial Advisory Board consists of Lewis E. Hahn, Chairman; George E. Axtelle, emeritus; Joe R. Burnett; S. Morris Eames; Wayne A. R. Leys; William R. McKenzie; and Francis T. Villemain.*

*Polly V. Dunn is Staff Assistant.*

CENTER FOR EDITIONS OF
AMERICAN AUTHORS
*AN APPROVED TEXT*
MODERN LANGUAGE
ASSOCIATION OF AMERICA
®

Copyright © 1972 by Southern Illinois University Press
All rights reserved
Printed in the United States of America
Designed by Andor Braun
Frontispiece drawing of John Dewey by Herbert L. Fink
International Standard Book Number 0-8093-0540-2
Library of Congress Catalog Card Number 67-13938

# Contents

**36810**

# Preface

WITH THE ASSISTANCE of many scholars and friends we began, in 1961, to collect and prepare for publication all of the extant published works of John Dewey. During the six years between 1961 and the issuance of the first volume in the series, the magnitude and difficulty of the undertaking confirmed the need for ready access by the public to this important philosopher's forty books and nearly eight hundred articles published in some one hundred fifty journals. Students had found it increasingly difficult to examine Dewey's thought, both because of the inaccessibility of materials and the size of the corpus of Dewey's writings. As work on the texts progressed and news of our project spread, we received numerous requests for copies of hard-to-locate materials for identification of items, and for information about revisions. The varied sources of these requests indicated that the collected works will be useful to students in a number of specialized disciplines; and, of course, many readers will be interested in the reactions of a great mind to seventy years of tumultuous events. Americans will be able to follow Dewey's interpretation of and his growing concern with the global scene. Readers in other countries will have a basis for estimating the extent to which Dewey's thought transcends national boundaries and is viable for the twentieth century.

We decided that the extraordinary effort and expense of publishing the collected works would be best justified if we developed definitive texts. Therefore, in this edition we have applied the principles and techniques of modern textual criticism. This approach, developed primarily in connection with editing the works of such American literary figures as Hawthorne, has been used here for the first time in editing the writings of an American philosopher.

Those familiar with Dewey's essays will appreciate the reasons for our decision to print most of his works in approximately chronological order. (The exceptions are those in which Dewey's participation was limited or questionable—*The Psychology of Number* [1895], the Chinese lectures, and a few other items—all scheduled for late volumes in the series.) Many of

Dewey's insights were reflections upon the interrelations of such fields as philosophy, education, law, and the social sciences. To have identified a book or an article with only one particular discipline would have been to ignore its relevance to both the history and the continuing inquiries in other disciplines. It was decided that the disadvantages of a chronological order would be offset by two special features of the edition: (1) a complete analytical index; and (2) a guide to the works of John Dewey, presenting, in one volume, surveys by outstanding scholars of Dewey's contributions to such subjects as logic, psychology, and æsthetics. Included in that volume is a listing of the works classified in each of the selected fields, with cross-references to major works in other fields.[1]

The first five volumes, *The Early Works*, present most of the writings published in Dewey's "formative period," beginning in the year 1882 and ending in 1898. In addition to the articles, reviews, and other short pieces, the five volumes of *The Early Works* include the *Psychology*, *Leibniz's New Essays Concerning the Human Understanding*, *Outlines of a Critical Theory of Ethics*, and *The Study of Ethics*.

Each volume has the following parts: Table of Contents, Preface, Introduction, Texts, Checklist of References, various kinds of textual apparatus—Textual Principles and Procedures, A Note on the Texts, Emendations in the Copy-Texts, Textual Notes, Correction of Quotations, special emendations lists—and an Index.

We are grateful to all those, and there were many, who helped in the work of preparing and publishing these volumes. Some of them are mentioned in the paragraphs that follow.

The administrative officers of Southern Illinois University most directly involved in our work were: Delyte W. Morris, former President; Charles D. Tenney, formerly Vice-President; John E. Grinnell, formerly Vice-President for Operations, now retired; Robert W. MacVicar, former Chancellor of the Carbondale Campus; John S. Rendleman, formerly Vice-President for Business Affairs, now President of the Edwardsville Campus; Elmer J. Clark, Dean, College of Education; Arthur E. Lean, former Dean of the College of Education; Ronald G. Hansen, Associate Dean of the Graduate School and Co-ordinator of Research and Projects; John O. Anderson, former Co-ordinator of Research and Projects; C. Richard Gruny,

1    *Guide to the Works of John Dewey*, ed. Jo Ann Boydston (Carbondale: Southern Illinois University Press, 1970).

Legal Counsel; William E. Simeone, former Dean, Graduate School; Jacob O. Bach, former Chairman of the Department of Educational Administration.

The Chairman of the Advisory Committee throughout the history of this undertaking was Willis Moore, Chairman of the Department of Philosophy, who deserves special thanks for his perceptive and able leadership. Members of the Advisory Committee not mentioned in other connections were: Henry Dan Piper, former Dean of the College of Liberal Arts and Sciences; Roger E. Beyler, Dean of the College of Liberal Arts and Sciences; and the late Robert D. Faner, former Chairman of the Department of English. In the Office of Research and Projects, Webster Ballance, Wayne Stumph, and Larry Hawse were of special help.

Many persons consulted with the Editorial Board on a variety of aspects of the work. We are indebted to all of them. Among those who helped with the design and advancement of the project were: John L. Childs, George S. Counts, George Dykhuizen, George R. Geiger, James H. Hall, Harry W. Laidler, Corliss Lamont, Charles A. Madison, Richard P. McKeon, Charles Morris, the late Donald A. Piatt, George Kimball Plochmann, Paul A. Schilpp, and Horace Kallen. In addition, the scholars involved in preparing the *Guide to the Works of John Dewey* have made outstanding contributions: William W. Brickman, Max H. Fisch, Horace L. Friess, Gail Kennedy, Bertram Morris, Tsuin-Chen Ou, Darnell Rucker, and Herbert W. Schneider. Professor Schneider contributed to almost every aspect of our work.

We are profoundly indebted to M. Halsey Thomas, whose excellent bibliography[2] saved us years of work. For suggestions about materials and where to find them, we owe thanks to many of the persons mentioned in other connections as well as to Karl Andrén, James W. Merritt, Sidney Ratner, Paul G. Kuntz, R. D. Archambault, William S. Minor, Robert L. McCaul, Lewis S. Feuer, Charles A. Lee, the late Archibald W. Anderson, Erwin V. Johanningmeier, Burton Raimer, Hensley C. Woodbridge, James Collins, and Francis Sparshott. For invaluable help on the Chinese materials, we thank Robert W. Clopton, Cho-Yee To, and Barry Keenan.

For the specialized help that only experienced and enthusiastic library personnel can give, we thank: Ralph E. McCoy,

[2]    M. H. Thomas, *John Dewey: A Centennial Bibliography* (Chicago: University of Chicago Press, 1962).

Dean of Library Affairs of Southern Illinois University; Ferris S. Randall, Director, Morris Library; Elizabeth O. Stone, formerly Assistant Director, Morris Library, now retired; Harold J. Rath and Maxine E. Walker in the Special Services Division. Bill V. Isom and Thomas L. Kilpatrick, former and present staff members of the Education Library, and the Humanities Librarian, Alan M. Cohn, gave assistance far beyond the call of duty. Kenneth Duckett, Curator of Special Collections, contributed valuable insights and materials in the course of his work on oral history.

We are grateful to Peter Draz, Robert H. Land, Joseph E. Hall, and Waldo H. Moore of the Library of Congress; Alice Bonnell, Carole Carlson, the late Roland Baughman, and Kenneth A. Lohf of Columbia University Library; and the late Hilmar A. Sieving, who was Education Librarian, University of Chicago. Although we cannot acknowledge them by name, many other librarians in the United States, Formosa, Germany, England, and Hawaii co-operated in helping us obtain materials.

The continuing support and co-operation of the College of Education of the University of Illinois, Champaign-Urbana, have played an important role in numerous aspects of this work.

We are indebted in several ways to the textual consultants who worked with us in the initial stages to suggest procedures for our work: Matthew J. Bruccoli, Neal Smith, and Bruce Harkness.

For the outstanding role he played in this work in its beginning and for his continued interest, our gratitude goes to Harold Taylor. Ernest Nagel, Mason W. Gross, and the late Agnes E. Meyer were also very helpful.

The following, who were members of the staff at various times, were instrumental in the successful launching of this publishing venture: Aldona Johnson, Alimae Persons, Marilee Kuehn, Joan Lash, Kathleen Poulos, Helen Wilfinger, David L. Miller, Edward F. McClain, Robert Andresen, Deems Brooks, and Elizabeth Evanson.

In this the concluding volume of *The Early Works of John Dewey, 1882–1898*, we acknowledge with deepest gratitude the vision and support of Delyte W. Morris, former President of Southern Illinois University.

                                                        *The Editors*

# Introduction
## *Toward Unity of Thought and Action*

THE YEARS 1895 to 1898 were for John Dewey a season of increasing achievement and recognition. While still considerably less than forty years of age, he was chairman of a philosophy department which included not only philosophy and psychology but also, at his insistence, pedagogy as well. He held a professorship in all three fields and was acknowledged for his contributions to each of them. It would be difficult to say which of these roles he preferred: the systematic philosopher, the scientific psychologist, or the experimental educator. Actually, he saw them as intimately related, and they culminated in what he may well have considered his major achievement of the period, the establishment of a laboratory primary school under his own direction.

This volume contains the complete published production of John Dewey for that four-year period, throughout which he remained at the University of Chicago. There he pursued a great variety of scholarly interests, as the scope of his writings reveals. The works of this period may, for the purposes of analysis, be put into the following categories: philosophy, philosophy of education, psychology, psychology of education, psychology of selected educational subjects, child-study, elementary education, secondary education, laboratory schools, pedagogy as a university discipline, and other miscellaneous matters.

The literary means by which these interests were expressed are also quite varied. They may be grouped into the following types: contributions to journals, papers presented to scholarly audiences, remarks made at association discussions, book reviews and other comments on the works of others, rebuttals to the comments of others upon his own works, public lectures, articles for the local university publication, prospectuses for educational ventures, syllabi for university courses, letters to editors, and a personal credo.

His efforts were frequently in response to the views of such contemporary giants as James Mark Baldwin, Paul Carus, G. Stanley Hall, William Torrey Harris, Thomas Henry Huxley, William James, Herbert Spencer, and Wilhelm Wundt, as well as many other important, although lesser, figures. He also reacted to many of the intellectual currents and social movements of the time. To mention but a few: in philosophy he reacted to the prevailing idealism in its many forms and to a nascent pragmatism; in psychology, to faculty psychology, associationism, and an emerging scientific empiricism; in education, to the child-study movement, "traditional" pedagogy, the use of Pestalozzi's "gifts," Herbart's methodology, the "culture-epoch" curriculum, and the "new education." And pervading every consideration was the conflict between the old world-view of a static nature, society, and man and the newer concept of a dynamic universe, which had been so recently and dramatically illustrated in the development of Charles Darwin's theory of organic evolution.

At first glance, and even after a second look, Dewey's writings of these years seem to represent an alarming diffusion, a scattering of effort in too many directions. They present so many reactions to so many influences on so many subjects expressed in so many forms that one looks almost in desperation for some element which ties them all together.

Yet, a closer study of the material will reveal a thread that does run through the material, touching almost everything he published during this period. Stated briefly, from philosophy the thread runs in two strands, through sociology and through psychology, to education. In the material of the period, Dewey seemed to assert that the only proper procedure of philosophy is the method of modern science. For the most part, he restricted his interests in philosophy to ethics, which he tended to identify with social ethics, and often referred to as sociology. His interests in psychology at this time were largely confined to what he called the development of powers, frequently characterized as self-expression or growth, which he seemed to take as the essence of learning. These two, a sociology which contributed the subject-matter and a psychology which provided the method, met in education, the function of which was given as "self-realization" from the individual point of view and "civilization" from the social.

The connecting thread may be identified as a search for unity, the outlines of which can now be stated more explicitly. It was an attempt to unite philosophy with sociology and psychology, through the use of the scientific method, and with education, for the attainment of the best life. This procedure seems to represent his effort to meet his own philosophical objective: to arrive at the proper relation between philosophy and practice.

The unity he sought was, in the broadest sense, the unity of thought and action.

The unity he sought in the larger sense, however, required that he pursue it also in the smaller detail. This he did repeatedly in the material of this period. The following will serve as a few highly selective examples.

Knowledge, he concluded in *The Significance of the Problem of Knowledge*, is a statement of action, and the proper means for creating such a statement is to be found in the method of modern science. In philosophy, he thought, this should mean a shift in interest from metaphysics and epistemology to psychology and social ethics. "Psychology is the attempt to state in detail the machinery of the individual considered as the instrument and organ through which social action operates" (p. 23), while social ethics is "an inquiry of the *particular* values which ought to be realized in the life of everyone, and of the conditions which shall render possible this realization" (p. 23). Although the terminology is slightly different, the idea was further elaborated in "Ethical Principles Underlying Education."

All ethical theory is two faced. It requires to be considered from two different points of view, and stated in two different sets of terms. These are the social and the psychological. We do not have here, however, a division, but simply a distinction. Psychological ethics does not cover part of the field, and then require social ethics to include the territory left untouched. Both cover the entire sphere of conduct. Nor does the distinction mark a compromise, or a fusion, as if at one point the psychological view broke down, and needed to be supplemented by the sociological. Each theory is complete and coherent within itself, so far as its own end or purpose is concerned. But conduct is of such a nature as to require to be stated throughout from two points of view. How this distinction happens to exist may perhaps be guessed at by calling to mind that the individual and society are neither opposed to each other nor separated from each other. Society is a society of individuals and the individual is always a social individual. He has no existence by himself. He lives in, for, and by society, just as society has no existence excepting in and through the individuals who constitute it. But we can state one and the same process (as, for example, telling the truth) either from the standpoint of what it effects in society as a whole, or with reference to the particular individual concerned. The latter statement will be psychological; the former, social as to its purport and terms (pp. 54–55).

The psychological point of view deals with the "how" of conduct, the sociological with the "what" (pp. 55–56).

When Thomas Henry Huxley became a spokesman for those who held that ethical and cosmic processes are different, indeed opposed to each other, Dewey responded with the essay "Evolution and Ethics." In it he undertook to show that the key concepts of the theory of organic evolution, such as "fittest," "selection," and "struggle for survival," are as appropriate to human social life as they are to other realms of nature. They are found in the ethical process, he concluded, as they are in the cosmic, and they operate the same way. "Man in his conscious struggles, in his doubts, temptations, and defeats, in his aspirations and successes, is moved on and buoyed up by the forces which have developed nature; and . . . in this moral struggle he acts not as a mere individual but as an organ in maintaining and carrying forward the universal process" (p. 53).

In response to the development of a mechanistic psychology, popular at the time partly because it presented a scientific alternative to the traditional dualism, Dewey pointed out in "The Reflex Arc Concept in Psychology" that the "older dualism of body and soul finds a distinct echo in the current dualism of stimulus and response" (p. 96). Facts, he reported, do not support the notion that an organism receives a stimulus and then responds. "The fact is that stimulus and response are not distinctions of existence, but teleological distinctions" (p. 104). An act is a "single concrete whole" (p. 97). "What we have is a circuit" (p. 102).

Dewey published the original *Interest in Relation to Training of the Will* in 1896. For its republication in 1899 he made substantial revisions, the most obvious of which is concerned with the term "self-expression," for which he had received some criticism in the discussion of the original. He used the term less frequently here and at times replaced it with such terms as "growth," "realization," and "direct experience." The basic idea, however, remained the same. "The genuine principle of interest is the principle of the recognized identity of the fact or proposed line of action with the self; that it lies in the direction of the agent's own growth, and is, therefore, imperiously demanded, if the agent is to be himself" (pp. 117–18).

In "Imagination and Expression" he wrote of those who make a sharp distinction between an idea and its expression. He thought they were mistaken. An idea, he indicated, is incomplete until it is realized, and the realization modifies the idea. "Motor expression is not something done with an idea already made in the mind, but is necessary to the appreciation of the idea itself. . . . We cannot speak of an idea *and* its expression; the expression is more than a mode of conveying an already formed idea; it is part and parcel of its formation" (pp. 194–95).

The search for unity John Dewey also took, of course, into his considerations of education. There were those who thought that the function of the school was to serve individual interests primarily, if not exclusively, and others who thought it should serve social needs. In "Ethical Principles Underlying Education" Dewey agreed with neither point of view. "The moral responsibility of the school, and of those who conduct it, is to society" (p. 57). This responsibility, however, is to be interpreted in the proper spirit, which "is equivalent to the training of the child which will give him such possession of himself that he may take charge of himself," but always in a context which is social. "Apart from the thought of participation in social life the school has no end nor aim" (p. 60).

In the same essay he lamented the separation of the intellectual and the moral in education, which he believed must inevitably continue as long as there is a separation between learning and doing.

The child cannot get power of judgment excepting as he is continually exercised in forming and testing judgment. He must have an opportunity to select for himself, and then attempt to put his own selections into execution that he may submit them to the only final test, that of action. Only thus can he learn to discriminate that which promises success from that which promises failure; only thus can he form the habit of continually relating his otherwise isolated ideas to the conditions which determine their value (pp. 81–82).

One gets here some understanding of the basis for his comment in "My Pedagogic Creed" on sentimentalism, "the necessary result of the attempt to divorce feeling from action." "I believe that next to deadness and dullness, formalism and routine, our education is threatened with no greater evil than sentimentalism" (p. 93).

In "The Psychological Aspect of the School Curriculum" Dewey observed the prevalent dualism in pedagogy between mental operations and intellectual content, "between mind and the material with which it operates." He began by making a distinction between a study organized logically and one organized psychologically. The former represents the present completed state of the subject, the understanding of the sophisticated scholar and the understanding it is hoped the student may finally attain. The latter represents the present state of the student's understanding and his interests. "This does not mean that these interests, when discovered, give the ultimate standard for school work, or that they have any final regulative value," but "these native existing interests, impulses, and experiences are all the leverage that the teacher has to work with" (p. 172). Thus, he wrote, we may see what "subject-matter" and "method of instruction" mean. "The subject-matter is the present experience of the child, taken in the light of what it may lead to. The method is the subject-matter rendered into the actual life experience of some individual. The final problem of instruction is thus the reconstruction of the individual's experience" (p. 174).

The final example is Dewey's statement about his experimental school. It is the first and only paragraph under the heading "General Problem and End," published in his "Plan of Organization of the University Primary School."

The ultimate problem of all education is to co-ordinate the psychological and the social factors. The psychological requires that the individual have the free use of all his personal powers; and, therefore, must be so individually studied as to have the laws of his own structure regarded. The sociological factor requires that the individual become acquainted with the social environment in which he lives, in all its important relations, and be disciplined to regard these relationships in his own activities. The co-ordination demands, therefore, that the child be capable of expressing *himself*, but in such a way as to realize *social* ends (p. 224).

It should be admitted that the term "search for unity" used in this introduction is to be considered, in part at least, a literary device. The items of this period suggest that John Dewey had achieved, to a certain extent, a unity of point of view. They also suggest, however, that Dewey was an example of his own thesis that an idea is only completed in its expression and that the expression becomes part of the meaning of the idea. His sensitivity to the thoughts of others, his response to criticism, and most of all his frequent reworking of terms, and consequently concepts, seem to indicate a continuing struggle toward a fundamental unity as yet only partially realized.

Several of John Dewey's works published during this period quickly became popular and eventually became classic. Among them must be mentioned especially "The Reflex Arc Concept in Psychology" and "My Pedagogic Creed."

The publication of "The Reflex Arc Concept in Psychology" probably marks one of the truly important turning points in the study of human behavior. It remained for decades one of the most influential works in the science of psychology and still retains that position among all students not dogmatically committed to some form, by whatever name, of the same mechanistic view that it attempts to correct. The same may be said for disciplines other than psychology. Whenever the study of man rises above the concept of an organic robot as his model, the "Reflex Arc" is studied.

After the fashion of the time, Dewey was asked to publish his personal credo on education. This he did as "My Pedagogic Creed." It was well received immediately and has remained popular. It presents on the whole what one would expect of a credo, declarative statements of belief. Because of this, it is of interest to serious students primarily as a set of very brief conclusions for arguments developed elsewhere. However, for those more interested in what Dewey believed about education than how he came to believe it, it continues to serve, as it has for nearly three quarters of a century, as a source of enlightenment, comfort, and inspiration.

One other subject needs to be especially mentioned. That is the experimental school. John Dewey, who had had a long-standing interest in education, undoubtedly wanted the school very badly. The outline of his reasoning seems rather clear. If sociology and psychology were to be the main lines of investigation for philosophy and science to be its method, education was to be the point of its application. Here, he thought, is where philosophy and practical life, learning and doing, should meet. This is consistent with his insistence that his school be a laboratory, analogous to that of physics and psychology. It was to serve two primarily philosophical purposes. First, it was to be a proving ground for his ideas concerning the relation of thought and action, a testing, in a sense, of his philosophical position. Second, it was to be a resource for the further development of these ideas, a philosophical laboratory in the literal sense of the term. It was not, as it has so often been subsequently identified, a demonstration school. It specifically was not intended as a model for the common school, in any more literal sense than the laboratory discovery of a cure for a disease serves as the mode for its medical treatment. Dewey's concern was to develop fundamental concepts more than pedagogic techniques which could be mechanically transplanted to another learning situation.

In summary, it might be said that this period, 1895 to 1898, was for John Dewey an extraordinarily seminal one. It was a period, brief as it was, in which he spread his thoughts and activities out from philosophy through sociology and psychology to education. Not that he ever left philosophy, in any sense; his interests were still philosophical. His was a philosophical position in the making, and his educational works were directly germane to that development. His many works in the field indicate that it was here, in education, that his philosophy would undergo its application, testing, and revision. In this sense, this collection of items may reasonably be characterized as the first educational volume of this series.

In another sense, moreover, it might be considered the first pragmatic volume. Within this collection of items, one is provided with an early look, when not actually a first glimpse, at ideas with which Dewey was to struggle and labor to develop for the rest of his long life. To trace each of them out to its fullest expression would be a monumental task in itself, for they culminated in such classics of pragmatic philosophy as *Ethics, Democracy and Education, Human Nature and Conduct, Art as Experience, A Common Faith,* and *Logic: The Theory of Inquiry,* to mention but a few. To say more would lead to a consideration of most of his subsequent writings, which continued to represent a persistent creative effort to do himself the task he had attributed to W. T. Harris, "to make philosophy applicable to the guidance of life, and to bring practical life within the grasp of that consciousness of unity which is the essence of philosophic thought" (p. 385), to achieve, in short, a unity of thought and action.

*William Robert McKenzie*

8 June 1971

# EARLY ESSAYS

# THE SIGNIFICANCE

# OF THE PROBLEM

# OF KNOWLEDGE

BY

## JOHN DEWEY

HEAD PROFESSOR OF PHILOSOPHY IN THE UNIVERSITY OF CHICAGO

CHICAGO

The University of Chicago Press

1897

# The Significance of the Problem of Knowledge

It is now something over a century since Kant called upon philosophers to cease their discussion regarding the nature of the world and the principles of existence until they had arrived at some conclusion regarding the nature of the knowing process. But students of philosophy know that Kant formulated the question "how knowledge is possible" rather than created it. As matter of fact, reflective thought for 200 years before Kant had been principally interested in just this problem, although it had not generalized its own interest. Kant brought to consciousness the controlling motive. The discussion, both in Kant himself and in his successors, seems often scholastic, lost in useless subtlety, scholastic argument, and technical distinctions. Within the last decade in particular there have been signs of a growing weariness as to epistemology, and a tendency to turn away to more fertile fields. The interest shows signs of exhaustion.

Students of philosophy will recognize what I mean when I say that this growing conviction of futility and consequent distaste are associated with the outcome of the famous dictum of Kant, that perception without conception is blind, while conception without perception is empty. The whole course of reflection since Kant's time has tended to justify this remark. The sensationalist and the rationalist have worked themselves out. Pretty much all students are convinced that we can reduce knowledge neither to a set of associated sensations, nor yet to a purely rational system of

[*First published by the University of Chicago Press*, 1897, *University of Chicago Contributions to Philosophy*, Vol. I, No. 3, 20 pp. Reprinted *"with slight change" in* The Influence of Darwin on Philosophy (*New York: Henry Holt and Co.*, 1910), *pp.* 271–304.]

relations of thought. Knowledge is judgment, and judgment requires both a material of sense perception and an ordering, regulating principle, reason; so much seems certain, but we do not get any further. Sensation and thought themselves seem to stand out more rigidly opposed to each other in their own natures than ever. Why both are necessary, and how two such opposed factors co-operate in bringing about the unified result of knowledge, becomes more and more of a mystery. It is the continual running up against this situation which accounts for the flagging of interest and the desire to direct energy where it will have more outcome.

This situation creates a condition favorable to taking stock of the question as it stands; to inquiring what this interest, prolonged for over three centuries, in the possibility and nature of knowledge, stands for; what the conviction as to the necessity of the union of sensation and thought, together with the inability to reach conclusions regarding the nature of the union, signifies.

I propose then to raise this evening[1] precisely this question: What is the meaning of the problem of knowledge? What is its meaning, not simply for reflective philosophy or in terms of epistemology itself, but what is its meaning in the historical movement of humanity and as a part of a larger and more comprehensive experience? My thesis is perhaps sufficiently indicated in the mere taking of this point of view. It implies that the abstractness of the discussion of knowledge, its remoteness from everyday experience, is one of form, rather than of reality. It implies that the problem of knowledge is not a problem which has its origin, its value, or its destiny within itself. The problem is one which social life, the organized practice of mankind, has had to face. The seemingly technical and abstruse discussion of the philosophers results from the formulation and stating of the question, rather than the question itself.

I suggest that the problem of the possibility of knowledge is but an aspect of the question of the relation of knowing to acting, of theory to practice. The distinctions which the philosophers raise, the oppositions which they erect, the

[1]    This paper was read at a meeting of the Philosophical Club of the University of Michigan.

weary treadmill which they pursue between sensation and thought, subject and object, mind and matter, are not invented *ad hoc*, but are simply the concise reports and condensed formulæ of points of view and of practical conflicts having their source in the very nature of modern life, and which must be met and solved if modern life is to go on its way untroubled, with clear consciousness of what it is about. As the philosopher has received his problem from the world of action, so he must return his account there for auditing and liquidation.

More especially, I suggest that the tendency for all the points at issue to precipitate in the opposition of sensationalism and rationalism is due to the fact that sensation and reason stand for the two forces contending for mastery in social life: the radical and the conservative. The reason that the contest does not end, the reason for the necessity of the combination of the two in the resultant statement, is that both factors are necessary in action; one stands for stimulus, for initiative; the other for control, for direction.

I cannot hope, in the time at my command this evening, to justify these wide and sweeping assertions regarding either the origin, the work, or the final destiny of philosophic reflection. I simply hope, by reference to some of the chief periods of the development of philosophy, to illustrate to you something of what I mean.

At the outset we take a long scope in our survey and present to ourselves the epoch when philosophy was still consciously, and not simply by implication, human, when reflective thought had not developed its own technique of method, and was in no danger of being caught in its own machinery—the time of Socrates. What does the assertion of Socrates that an unexamined life is not one fit to be led by man; what does his injunction "Know thyself" mean? It means that the corporate motives and guarantees of conduct are breaking down. We have got away from the time when the individual could both regulate and justify his course of life by reference to the ideals incarnate in the habits of the community of which he is a member. The time of direct and therefore unconscious union with corporate life, finding there stimuli, codes, and values, has departed. The development of industry and commerce, of war and politics, has brought face to face communities with different aims and diverse habits; the development of myth and animism into crude but genuine scientific observation and imagination has transformed the physical widening of the horizon, brought about by commerce and intercourse, into an intellectual and moral expansion. The old supports fail precisely at the time when they are most needed—before a widening and more complex scene of action. Where then shall the agent of action turn? The "Know thyself" of Socrates is the reply to the practical problem which confronted Athens in his day. Investigation into the true ends and worths of human life, sifting and testing of all competing ends, the discovery of a method which should validate the genuine and dismiss the spurious, had henceforth to do for man what consolidated and incorporate habit had hitherto presented as a free and precious gift.

With Socrates the question is as direct and practical as the question of making one's living or of governing the state; it is indeed the same question put in its general form. It is a question which the flute player, the cobbler, and the politician must face no more and no less than the reflective philosopher. The question is addressed by Socrates to every individual and to every group with which he comes in contact. Because the question is practical it is individual and direct. It is a question which everyone must face and answer for himself, just as in the Christian scheme every individual must face and solve for himself the question of his final destiny.

Yet the very attitude of Socrates carried with it the elements of its own destruction. Socrates could only raise the question, or rather demand of every individual that he raise it for himself. Of the answer he declared himself to be as ignorant as was anyone. The result could be only a shifting of the centre of interest. If the question is so all-important, and yet the wisest of all men must confess that he only knows his own ignorance as to its answer, the inevitable point of further consideration is the discovery of a method which shall enable the question to be answered. This is the significance of Plato. The problem is the absolutely inevitable outgrowth of the Socratic position; and yet it carried with it just as inevitably the separation of philosopher from shoemaker and statesman, and the relegation of theory to a position for the time remote from conduct.

If the Socratic command, "Know thyself," runs against the dead wall of inability to conduct this knowledge, someone must take upon himself the discovery of how the requisite knowledge may be obtained. A new profession is born, that of the thinker. At this time the means, the discovery of how the aims and worths of the self may be known and measured, becomes, for this class, an end in itself. Theory is ultimately to be applied to practice; but in the meantime the theory must be worked out as theory or else no application. This represents the peculiar equilibrium and the peculiar point of contradiction in the Platonic system. All philosophy is simply for the sake of the organization and regulation of social life; and yet the philosophers must be a class by themselves, working out their peculiar problems with their own particular tools.

With Aristotle the attempted balance failed. Social life is disintegrating beyond the point of hope of a successful reorganization, and thinking is becoming a fascinating pursuit for its own sake. The world of practice is now the world of compromise and of adjustment. It is relative to partial aims and finite agents. The sphere of absolute and enduring truth and value can be reached only in and through thought. The one who acts compromises himself with the animal desire that inspires his action and with the alien material that forms its stuff. In two short generations the divorce of philosophy from life, the isolation of reflective theory from practical conduct, has completed itself. So great is the irony of history that this sudden and effective outcome was the result of the attempt to make thought the instrument of action, and action the manifestation of the truth reached in thinking.

But this statement must not be taken too literally. It is impossible that men should really separate their ideas from their acts. If we look ahead a few centuries we find that the philosophy of Plato and Aristotle has accomplished, in an indirect and unconscious way, what perhaps it would never have effected by the more immediate and practical method of Socrates. Philosophy became an organ of vision, an instrument of interpretation; it furnished the medium through which the world was seen and the course of life estimated. Philosophy died as philosophy, to rise as the set and bent of the human mind. Through a thousand devious and roundabout channels, the thoughts of the philosopher filtered through the strata of human consciousness and conduct. Through the teachings of grammarians, rhetoricians, and a variety of educational schools, they spread in diluted form through the whole Roman Empire and were again precipitated in the common forms of speech. Through the earnestness of the moral propaganda of the Stoics they became the working rules of life for the more strenuous and earnest spirits. Through the speculations of the Skeptics and Epicureans they became the chief reliance and consolation of a large number of highly cultured individuals amid the social turmoil and political disintegration going on. All these influences and many more finally summed themselves up in the two great media through which Greek philosophy finally fixed the intellectual horizon of man, determined the values of its perspective, and meted out the boundaries and divisions of the scene of human action.

These two influences were the development of Christian theology and moral theory, and the organization of the system of Roman jurisprudence. There is perhaps no more fascinating chapter in the history of humanity than the slow and tortuous processes by which the ideas set in motion by that Athenian citizen who faced death as serenely as he conversed with a friend, finally became the intellectually organizing centres of the two great movements which bridged the gulf between ancient civilization and modern. As the personal and immediate force and enthusiasm of the movement initiated by Jesus began to grow fainter and the commanding influence of his own personality commenced to dim, it was the ideas of the world and of life, of God and of man, elaborated in Greek philosophy, which served to transform moral enthusiasm and personal devotion to the redemption of humanity, into a splendid and coherent view of the universe; which resisted all disintegrating influences and gathered into itself the permanent ideas and progressive ideals thus far developed in the history of man.

We have only a faint idea of how this was accomplished, or of the thoroughness of the work done. We have perhaps even more inadequate conceptions of the great organizing and centralizing work done by Greek thought in the political sphere. When the military and administrative genius of Rome brought the whole world in subjection to itself, the most pressing of practical problems was to give unity of practical aim and harmony of working machinery to the vast and confused mass of local custom and tradition, religious, social, economic, and intellectual, as well as political. In this juncture the great administrators and lawyers of Rome seized with avidity upon the results of the intellectual analysis of social and political relations elaborated in Greek philosophy. Caring naught for these results in their reflective and theoretical character, they saw in them the possible instrument of introducing order into chaos and of transforming the confused and conflicting medley of practice and opinion into a harmonious social structure. Roman law, which formed the vertebral column of civilization for a thousand years, and which articulated the outer order of life as distinctly as Christianity controlled the inner, was the outcome.

Thought was once more in unity with action, philosophy had become the instrument of conduct. Mr. Bosanquet makes the pregnant remark "that the weakness of mediæval science and philosophy are connected rather with excess of practice than with excess of theory. The subordination of philosophy to theology is a subordination of science to a formulated conception of human welfare. Its essence is present, not wherever there is metaphysics but wherever the spirit of truth is subordinated to any preconceived practical intent" (*History of Æsthetic*, p. 146).

Once more the irony of history displays itself. Thought has become practical, it has become the regulator of individual conduct and social organization, but at the expense of its own freedom and power. The defining characteristic of mediævalism in state and in church, in political and spiritual life, is that truth presents itself to the individual only through the medium of organized authority.

This was a historical necessity on the external as well as the internal side. We have not the remotest way of imagining what the outcome would finally have been if, at the time when the intellectual structure of the Christian church and the legal structure of the Roman Empire had got themselves thoroughly organized, the barbarians had not made their inroads and seized upon all this accumulated and consolidated wealth as their own legitimate prey. But this was what did happen. As a result, the truths originally developed by the freest possible criticism and investigation became external, and imposed themselves upon the mass of individuals by the mere weight of authoritative law. The external, transcendental, and supernatural character of spiritual truth and of social control during the Middle Ages is naught but the mirror, in consciousness, of the relation existing between the eager, greedy, undisciplined horde of barbarians on one side, and the concentrated achievements of ancient civilization on the other. There was no way out save that the keen barbarian whet his appetite upon the rich banquet spread before him. But there was equally no way out so far as the continuity of civilization was concerned save that the very fullness and richness of this banquet set limits to the appetite, and finally, when assimilated and digested, be transformed into the flesh and blood, the muscles and sinew of him who sat at the feast. Thus the barbarian ceased to be a barbarian and a new civilization arose.

But the time came when the work of absorption was fairly complete. The northern barbarians had eaten the food and drunk the wine of Græco-Roman civilization. The authoritative truth embodied in mediæval state and church succeeded, in principle, in disciplining the untrained masses. Its very success issued its own death warrant. To say that it had succeeded means that the new people had finally eaten their way into the heart of the ideas offered them, had got from them what they wanted, and were henceforth prepared to go their own way and make their own living. Here a new rhythm of the movement of thought and action begins to show itself.

The beginning of this change in the swing of thought and action forms the transition from the Middle Ages to the modern times. It is the epoch of the Renaissance. The individual comes to a new birth and asserts his own individuality and demands his own rights in the way of feeling, doing, and knowing for himself. Science, art, religion, political life, must all be made over on the basis of recognizing the claims of the individual.

Pardon me these commonplaces, but they are necessary to the course of the argument. By historic fallacy we often suppose, or imagine that we suppose, that the individual had been present as a possible centre of action all through the Middle Ages, but through some external and arbitrary interference had been weighted down by political and intellectual despotism. All this inverts the true order of the case. The very possibility of the individual making such unlimited demands for himself, claiming to be the legitimate centre of all action and standard for all organization, was dependent, as I have already indicated, upon the intervening mediævalism. Save as having passed through this period of tremendous discipline, and having gradually worked over into his own habits and purposes, the truths embodied in the church and state which controlled his conduct, the individual could be only a source of disorder and a disturber of civilization. The very maintenance of the spiritual welfare of mankind was bound up in the extent to which the claim of truth and reality to be universal and objective, far above all individual feeling and thought, could make itself valid. The logical realism and universalism of scholastic philosophy simply reflect the actual subjection of the individual to that associated and corporate life which, in conserving the past, provided the principle of control.

But the eager, hungry barbarian was there, implicated in this universalism. He must be active in receiving and in absorbing the truth authoritatively doled out to him. Even the most rigid forms of mediæval Christianity could not avoid postulating the individual will as having a certain initiative with reference to its own salvation. The impulses, the appetite, the instinct of the individual were all assumed in mediæval morals, religion, and politics. The imagined mediæval tyranny took them for granted as completely as does the modern herald of liberty and equality. But the mediæval consciousness knew that the time had not come when these appetites and impulses could be trusted to work themselves out. They must be controlled by the incorporate truths inherited from Athens and Rome.

The very logic of the relationship, however, required that the time come when the individual make his own the objective and universal truths. He is now the incorporation of truth. He now has the control as well as the stimulus of action within himself. He is the standard and the end, as well as the initiator and the effective force of execution. Just because the authoritative truth of mediævalism has succeeded, has fulfilled its function, the individual can begin to assert himself.

Contrast this critical period, finding its expression equally in the art of the Renaissance, the revival of learning, the Protestant Reformation and political democracy, with Athens in the time of Socrates. Then individuals felt their own social life disintegrated, dissolving under their very feet. The problem was how the value of that social life was to be maintained against the external and internal forces that were threatening it. The problem was on the side neither of the individual nor of progress; save as the individual was seen to be an intervening instrument in the reconstruction of the social unity. But with the individual of the fourteenth century, it was not his own intimate community life which was slipping away from him. It was an alien and remote life which had finally become his own; which had passed over into his own inner being. The problem was not how the unity of social life should be conserved, but what the individual should do with the wealth of resources of which he found himself the rightful heir and administrator. The problem looked out upon the future, not back to the past. It was how to create a new order, both of modes of individual conduct and of forms of social life, which should be the appropriate manifestations of the vigorous and richly endowed individual.

Hence it is that the conception of progress as a ruling idea; the conception of the individual as the source and standard of rights; and the problem of knowledge, are all born together. Given the freed individual, who feels called upon to create a new heaven and a new earth, and who feels himself gifted with the power to perform the task to which he is called: —and the demand for science, for a method of discovering and verifying truth, becomes imperious. The individual is henceforth to supply control, law, and not simply stimulation and initiation. What does this mean but that instead of any longer receiving or assimilating truth, he is now to search for and create it? Having no longer the truth imposed by authority to rely upon, there is no resource save to secure the authority of truth. The possibility of getting at and utilizing this truth becomes therefore the underlying and conditioning problem of modern life. Strange as it may sound to say it, the question which was formulated by Kant as that of the possibility of knowledge, is the fundamental political problem of modern life.

Science and metaphysics or philosophy, though often seeming to be at war, with their respective adherents often throwing jibes and slurs at each other, are really the most intimate allies. The philosophic movement is simply the coming to consciousness of this claim of the individual to be able to discover and verify truth for himself, and thereby not only direct his own conduct, but become an influential and decisive factor in the organization of life itself. Modern philosophy is the formulation of this creed, both in general and in its more specific implications. We often forget that the technical problem "*how* knowledge is possible," also means "how *knowledge* is possible"; how, that is, shall the individual be able to back himself up by truth which has no authority save that of its own intrinsic truthfulness. Science, on the other hand, is simply this general faith or creed asserting itself in detail; it is the practical belief at work engaged in subjugating the foreign territory of ignorance and falsehood step by step. If the ultimate outcome depends upon this detailed and concrete work, we must not forget that the earnestness and courage, as well as the intelligence and clearness with which the task has been undertaken, have depended largely upon the wider, even if vaguer, operation of philosophy.

But the student of philosophy knows more than that the problem of knowledge has been with increasing urgency and definiteness the persistent and comprehensive problem. So conscious is he of the two opposed theories regarding the nature of knowledge, that he often forgets the underlying bond of unity of which we have been speaking. These two opposing schools are those which we know as the sensationalist and the intellectualist, the empiricist and the rationalist. Admitting that the dominance of the question of the possibility and nature of knowledge is at bottom a fundamental question of practice and of social direction, is *this* distinction anything more than the clash of scholastic opinions, a rivalry of ideas meaningless for conduct?

I think not. Having made so many sweeping assertions I must venture one more. Fanciful and forced as it may seem, I would say that the sensational and empirical schools represent in conscious and reflective form the continuation of the principle of the northern and barbarian side of mediæval life; while the intellectualist and the rationalist stand for the conscious elaboration of the principle involved in the Græco-Roman tradition.

Once more, as I cannot hope to prove, let me expand and illustrate. The sensationalist has staked himself upon the possibility of explaining and justifying knowledge by conceiving it as the grouping and combination of the qualities directly given us in sensation. The special reasons advanced in support of this position are sufficiently technical and remote. But the motive which has kept the sensationalist at work, which animated Hobbes and Locke, Hume and John Stuart Mill, Voltaire and Diderot, was a human not a scholastic one. It was the belief that only in sensation do we get any personal contact with reality, and hence, any genuine guarantee of vital truth. Thought is pale, and remote from the concrete stuff of knowledge and experience. It only formulates and duplicates; it only divides and recombines that fullness of vivid reality which is got directly and at first hand in sense experience. Reason, compared with sense, is indirect, emasculate, and faded.

Moreover reason and thought in their very generality seem to lie beyond and outside the individual. In this remoteness, when they claim any final value, they violate the very first principle of the modern consciousness. What is the distinguishing characteristic of modern life, unless it be precisely that the individual shall not simply get, and reason about truth, in the abstract, but shall make it his own in the most intimate and personal way? He has not only to know the truth in the sense of knowing about it, but he must feel it. What is sensation but the answer to this demand for the most individual and intimate contact with reality? Show me a sensationalist and I will show you not only one who believes that he is on the side of concreteness and definiteness, as against washed out abstractions and misty general notions; but also one who believes that he is identified with the cause of the individual as distinct from that of external authority. We have only to go to our Locke and our Mill to see that opposition to the innate and the *a priori* was felt to be opposition to the deification of hereditary prejudice and to the reception of ideas without examination or criticism. Personal contact with reality through sensation seemed to be the only safeguard from opinions which, while masquerading in the guise of absolute and eternal truth, were in reality but the prejudices of the past become so ingrained as to insist upon being standards of truth and action.

Positively as well as negatively, the sensationalists have felt themselves to represent the side of progress. In its very eternal character, a general notion stands ready-made, fixed forever, without reference to time, without the possibility of change or diversity. As distinct from this, the sensation represents the never-failing eruption of the new. It is the novel, the unexpected, that which cannot be reasoned out in eternal formulæ, but must be hit upon in the ever-changing flow of our experience. It thus represents stimulation, excitation, momentum onwards. It is a constant protest against the assumption of any theory or belief to possess finality; and it is the ever-renewed presentation of material out of which to build up new objects and new laws.

The sensationalist appears to have a good case. He stands for vividness and definiteness against abstraction; for the engagement of the individual in experience as against the remote and general thought about experience; and for progress and for variety against the eternal fixed monotony of the concept. But what says the rationalist? What value has experience, he inquires, if it is simply a chaos of disintegrated and floating débris? What is the worth of personality and individuality when they are reduced to crudity of brute feeling and sheer intensity of impulsive reaction? What is there left in progress that we should desire it, when it has become a mere unregulated flux of transitory sensations, coming and going without reasonable motivation or rational purpose?

Thus the intellectualist has endeavored to frame the structure of knowledge as a well-ordered economy, where reason is sovereign, where the permanent is the standard of reference for the changing, and where the individual may always escape from his own mere individuality and find support and reinforcement in a system of relations which lies outside of and yet gives validity to his own passing states of consciousness. Thus the rationalists hold that we must find in a universal intelligence a source of truth and guarantee of value which is sought in vain in the confused and flowing mass of sensations.

The rationalist, in making the concept or general idea the all-important thing in knowledge, believes himself to be asserting the interests of order as against destructive caprice and the license of momentary whim. He finds that his cause is bound up with that of the discovery of truth as the necessary instrument and method for action. Only by reference to the general and the rational can the individual insert perspective, secure direction for his appetites and impulses, and escape from the uncontrolled and ruinous reactions of his own immediate tendency.

The concept, once more, in its very generality, in its elevation above the intensities and conflicts of momentary passions and interests, is the conserver of the experience of the past. It is the wisdom of the past put into capitalized and funded form to enable the individual to get away from the stress and competition of the needs of the passing moment. It marks the difference between barbarism and civilization, between continuity and disintegration, between the sequence of tradition which is the necessity of intelligent thought and action, and the random and confused excitation of the hour.

When we thus consider not the details of the positions of the sensationalist and rationalist, but the motives which have induced them to assume these positions, we discover what is meant in saying that the question is still a practical, a social one, and that the two schools stand for certain one-sided factors of social life. If we have on one side the demand for freedom, for personal initiation into experience, for variety and progress, we have on the other side the demand for general order, for continuous and organized unity, for the conservation of the dearly bought resources of the past. This is what I mean by saying that the sensationalist abstracts in conscious form the position and tendency of the Germanic element in modern civilization, the factor of appetite and impulse, of keen enjoyment and satisfaction, of stimulus and initiative. Just so the rationalist erects into conscious abstraction the principle of the Græco-Roman world, that of control, of system, of order and authority.

That the principles of freedom and order, of past and future, of conservation and progress, of incitement to action and control of that incitation, are correlative, I shall not stop to argue. It may be worth while, however, to point out that exactly the same correlative and mutually implicating connection exists between sensationalism and rationalism, considered as philosophical accounts of the origin and nature of knowledge.

The strength of each school is the weakness of its opponent. The more the sensationalist appears to succeed in reducing knowledge to the association of sensation, the more he creates a demand for thought to introduce background and relationship. The more consistent the sensationalist, the more openly he reveals the sensation in its own nakedness crying aloud for a clothing of value and meaning which must be borrowed from reflective and rational interpretation. On the other hand, the more reason and the system of relations which make up the functioning of reason are magnified, the more is felt the need of sensation to bring reason into some fruitful contact with the materials of experience. Reason must have the stimulus of this contact in order to be incited to its work and to get materials to operate with. The reason then that neither school can come to rest in itself is precisely that each one abstracts one essential factor of conduct.

This suggests, finally, that the next move in philosophy is precisely to transfer attention from the details of the positions assumed, and the arguments used in these two schools, to the practical motives which have unconsciously controlled the discussion. The positions have been sufficiently elaborated. Within the past one hundred years, within especially the last generation, each has succeeded in fully stating its case. The result, if we remain at this point, is practically a deadlock. Each can make out its case against the other. To stop at such a point is a patent absurdity. If we are to get out of the cul-de-sac it must be by bringing into consciousness the tacit reference to action which all the time has been the controlling factor.

In a word, another great rhythmic movement is seen to be approaching its end. The demand for science and philosophy was the demand for truth and a sure standard of truth which the new-born individual might employ in his efforts to build up a new world to afford free scope to the powers stirring within him. The urgency and acuteness of this demand caused, for the time being, the transfer of attention from the nature of practice to that of knowledge. The highly theoretical and abstract character of modern epistemology, combined with the fact that this highly abstract and theoretic problem has continuously engaged the attention of thought for more than three centuries, is, to my mind, proof positive that the question of knowledge was for the time being the point in which the question of practice centred, and through which it must find its outlet and solution.

We return, then, to our opening remark: the meaning of the question of the possibility of knowledge raised by Kant a century ago, and of his assertion that sensation without thought is blind, thought without sensation empty. Once more I recall to the student of philosophy how this assertion of Kant has haunted and determined the course of philosophy in the intervening years—how his solution at once seems inevitable and unsatisfactory. It is inevitable in that no one can fairly deny that both sense and reason are implicated in every fruitful and significant statement of the world; unconvincing because we are after all left with these two opposed things still at war with each other, plus the miracle of their final combination.

When I say that the only way out is to place the whole modern industry of epistemology in relation to the conditions which gave it birth and the function it has to fulfill, I mean that the unsatisfactory character of the entire neo-Kantian movement is in its assumption that knowledge gives birth to itself and is capable of affording its own justification. The solution which is always sought and never found, so long as we deal with knowledge as a self-sufficing purveyor of reality, reveals itself when we conceive of knowledge as a statement of action, that statement being necessary, moreover, to the successful ongoing of action.

The entire problem of mediæval philosophy is that of absorption, of assimilation. The result was the creation of the individual. Hence the problem of modern life is that of reconstruction, reform, reorganization. The entire content of experience needs to be passed through the alembic of individual agency and realization. The individual is to be the bearer of civilization; but this involves a remaking of the civilization which he bears. Thus we have the dual question: How can the individual become the organ of corporate action? How can he make over the truth authoritatively embodied in institutions of church and state into frank, healthy, and direct expressions of the simple act of free living? On the other hand, how can civilization preserve its own integral value and import when subordinated to the agency of the individual instead of exercising supreme sway over him?

The question of knowledge, of the discovery and statement of truth, gives the answer to this question; but it *only* gives the answer. Admitting that the practical problem of modern life is the maintenance of the spiritual values of civilization, through the medium of the insight and decision of the individual, the problem is foredoomed to futile failure save as the individual in performing his task can work with a definite and controllable tool. This tool is science. But this very fact, constituting the dignity of science and measuring the importance of the philosophic theory of knowledge, conferring upon them the religious value once attaching to dogma, and the disciplinary significance once belonging to political rules, also sets their limit. The servant is not above his master.

When a theory of knowledge forgets that its value rests in solving the problem out of which it has arisen, viz., that of securing a method of action; when it forgets that it has to work out the conditions under which the individual may freely direct himself without loss of the historic value of civilization—when it forgets these things it begins to cumber the ground. It is a luxury, and hence a social nuisance and disturber. Of course, in the very nature of things, every means or instrument will for a while absorb attention so that it becomes the end. Indeed it is the end when it is an indispensable condition of onward movement. But when once the means have been worked out they must operate as such. When the nature and method of knowledge are fairly understood, then interest must transfer itself from the possibility of knowledge to the possibility of its application to life.

The sensationalist has played his part in bringing to effective recognition the demand in valid knowledge for individuality of experience, for personal participation in materials of knowledge. The rationalist has served his time in making it clear once for all that valid knowledge requires organization and the operation of a relatively permanent and general factor. The Kantian epistemologist has formulated the claims of both schools in defining the judgment as the relation of perception and conception. But when he goes on to state that this relation is itself knowledge, or can be found in knowledge, he stultifies himself. Knowledge can define the percept and elaborate the concept, but their union can be found only in action. The experimental method of modern science, its erection into the ultimate mode of verification, is simply this fact obtaining recognition. Only action can reconcile the old, the general, and the permanent with the changing, the individual, and the new. It is action as progress, as development, making over the wealth of the past into capital with which to do an enlarging and freer business, which alone can find its way out of the cul-de-sac of the theory of knowledge. Each of the older movements passed away because of its own success, failed because it did its work, died in accomplishing its purpose. So also with the modern philosophy of knowledge; there must come a time when we have so much knowledge in detail, and understand so well its method in general, that it ceases to be a problem. It becomes a tool. If the problem of knowledge is not intrinsically meaningless and absurd it must in course of time be solved. Then the dominating interest becomes the *use* of knowledge; the conditions under which and ways in which it may be most organically and effectively employed to direct conduct.

Thus the Socratic period recurs; but recurs with the deepened meaning of the intervening weary years of struggle, confusion, and conflict, in the growth of the recognition of the need of patient and specific methods of interrogation. So, too, the authoritative and institutional truth of scholasticism recurs, but recurs borne up upon the vigorous and conscious shoulders of the freed individual who is aware of his own intrinsic relations to the truth, and who glories in his ability to carry civilization—not merely to carry it, but to carry it on. Thus another swing in the rhythm of theory and practice begins.

How does this concern us as philosophers? For the world it means that philosophy is henceforth a method and not an original fountainhead of truth, nor an ultimate standard of reference. But what is involved for philosophy itself in this change? I make no claims to being a prophet, but I venture one more and final unproved statement, believing, with all my heart, that it is justified both by the moving logic of the situation, and by the signs of the times. I refer to the growing transfer of interest from metaphysics and the theory of knowledge to psychology and social ethics—including in the latter term all the related concrete social sciences, so far as they may give guidance to conduct.

There are those who see in psychology only a particular science which they are pleased to term purely empirical (unless it happen to restate in changed phraseology the metaphysics with which they are familiar). They see in it only a more or less incoherent mass of facts, interesting because relating to human nature, but below the natural sciences in point of certainty and definiteness, as also far below pure philosophy as to comprehensiveness and ability to deal with fundamental issues. But if I may be permitted to dramatize a little the position of the psychologist, he can well afford to continue patiently at work, unmindful of the occasional supercilious sneers of the epistemologist, knowing that the future is with him. It is with him, because the whole cause of modern civilization stands and falls with the ability of the individual to serve as its agent and bearer. And psychology is naught but the account of the way in which conscious life is thus progressively maintained and reorganized. Psychology is the attempt to state in detail the machinery of the individual considered as the instrument and organ through which social action operates. It is the answer to Kant's demand for the formal phase of experience—how experience as such is constituted. Just because the whole burden and stress, both of conserving and advancing experience is more and more thrown upon the individual, everything which sheds light upon how the individual may weather the stress and assume the burden is precious and imperious.

Psychology is the democratic movement come to consciousness. It is the remote and abstract question of how experience in general is possible, translated into the concrete and practical problem of how *this* and *that* experience in particular are possible, and of how they may be actualized.

Social ethics in the inclusive sense is the correlative science. Dealing not with the form or mode or machinery of action, it rather attempts to make out its filling and make up the values which are necessary to constitute an experience which is worth while. The sociologist, like the psychologist, often presents himself as a camp follower of genuine science and philosophy, picking up scraps here and there and piecing them together in somewhat of an aimless fashion—fortunate indeed, if not vague and over-ambitious. But social ethics represents the attempt to translate philosophy from a general and therefore abstract method into a working and specific method; it is the change from inquiring into the nature of value in general to an inquiry of the *particular* values which ought to be realized in the life of everyone, and of the conditions which shall render possible this realization.

There are those who will see in this conception of the outcome of a four-hundred-year discussion concerning the nature and possibility of knowledge a derogation from the high estate of philosophy. There are others who will see in it a sign that philosophy, after wandering aimlessly hither and yon in a wilderness without purpose or outcome, has finally come to its senses—has given up metaphysical absurdities and unverifiable speculations, and become a purely positive science of phenomena. But there are yet others who will see in this movement the fulfillment of its vocation, the clear consciousness of a function which it has always striven to perform; and who will welcome it as a justification of the long centuries when it appeared to sit apart, far from the common concerns of man, busied with discourse of essence and cause, absorbed in argument concerning subject and object, reason and sensation. To such this outcome will appear the inevitable sequel of the saying of Socrates that "an unexamined life is not one fit to be led by man"; and the final response to his injunction "Know thyself."

# The Metaphysical Method in Ethics[1]

In his preface Mr. D'Arcy defines his essential point of view and aim. It is to give *briefly* "an account as well of the metaphysical basis as of the ethical superstructure" of conduct. Referring to Mr. Muirhead's *Elements of Ethics*, Mr. Mackenzie's *Manual of Ethics*, and my own *Outlines of Ethics*, he says of them that their ethical content is much the same as that of his own work, "but all three build without a foundation." This foundation he takes to be Green's method and main results as reached in his *Prolegomena to Ethics*,[2] and he proposes to do in small space what Green did in a more extended way.

It should also be noted that Mr. D'Arcy declares his inability "to accept in its entirety the Hegelian[3] conception of the spiritual principle as presented" by Green. And as matter of fact, Mr. D'Arcy accepts the doctrine of Green only up to a certain point, and then supplements it by quite other considerations, derived, as a rule, from the real or supposed needs of man's religious consciousness, and sometimes from "common sense."

---

[1]   *A Short Study of Ethics*, by Charles D'Arcy. London and New York: Macmillan and Co., 1895.

[2]   As silence is supposed to give consent, it may not be impertinent for me to say that while I have always recognized my own great indebtedness to Green, yet his metaphysical method seems to me far from affording any adequate basis for ethical doctrine; on the contrary, all the serious weaknesses in Green's specifically ethical discussions seem to me to flow from his metaphysical assumptions.

[3]   Mr. D'Arcy seems to accept *in toto*, as does Professor James Seth, Professor Andrew Seth's identification of Green's doctrine with Hegel's. I never have been able to see any basis for this identification. Hegel protests continuously and consistently against the Kanto-Fichtean ethics, and Green's standpoint is essentially the latter. The logic of the identification of Hegel and Green seems to be: Each is "unsound" as to the relation of the human and divine self, and, therefore, both teach the same doctrine.

[*First published in* Psychological Review, III (*Mar. 1896*), 181–88. *Not previously reprinted.*]

It is this effort, then, of Mr. D'Arcy to give the metaphysical foundations of ethical theory, which, affording the distinctive feature of his book, calls for especial attention.

The primary condition of all experience is the relation of the subject and object. The subject eludes our grasp, when approached by itself. The not-self or object is divided into an inner and an outer region, the former including sensations, emotions, thoughts, etc.; the latter contains all the things we know in the world around us. The inner experiences, of course, presuppose the thinking subject. The following course of reasoning shows that the outer region is also dependent. Every *thing* is constituted by relations. The world of things in space and time is simply a vast complex of relations. But it is "of the very nature of a relation to have no existence, no meaning, except for a thinker." A relation is a "unifying of the manifold, and is, therefore, an impossibility apart from a subject, which can pass from one member of the relation to the other, and combine both in a single apprehension." Hence "things exist only so far as they are due to the synthetic activity of the knowing subject." Moreover, since the thing is always constituted by relations to everything else in the universe, it is really a "cosmic object," so that the self is the unifying principle in the whole cosmos of experience.

The self is thus a unifying principle, and it is also the ultimate principle of unity. It is not simply the correlative of object, for it can make itself its own object, being self-conscious. It is a real unit, not a logical principle of a unity.

So far the language and the method remind us of Green, although Green, I think, would hesitate at this extraordinary identification of the self with subject apart from object, and at the ruling out from the self of all sensations, emotions and thoughts. As the method is nominally derived from the Kantian, it is perhaps worth while to note that Kant urged not only the necessity of the synthetic activity of the subject, but equally urged that the subject could be conscious of itself and of its unity only through its synthetic activity upon the manifold. But Mr. D'Arcy knows a better way than that. This theory might lead to the doctrine of the correlativity of the subject and the cosmos of experience—

which appears to be an objectionable doctrine, leading to Pantheism—and consequently having affirmed the synthetic activity of the self in the constitution of the objective world, Mr. D'Arcy affirms that since it is self-conscious, it can also abstract itself wholly from the world which it constitutes. As Mr. D'Arcy simply affirms this as given in the fact of self-consciousness, wholly apart from any examination of the nature or method of self-consciousness, I can only affirm from my standpoint that this way of giving "foundations" for ethics seems to require more foundations for itself than it succeeds in supplying.

Were the doctrine of the correlativity of subject and world affirmed, the self would obviously secure a certain universality; it would not be a merely particular self, if its essential being were found in the constituting of an objective world. But since Mr. D'Arcy holds that the subject exists in essential distinction from this constitutive work, and engages in it as it were only as by play, or as supererogation, the problem comes up: What sort of existence does the constituted world have? Is the universe a private possession of my own? Are we not committed to the doctrine of subjective idealism? Mr. D'Arcy implies, this would be the result if it were intended "to identify the cosmos of the individual experience with Nature. Nature must be accepted as a great fact, a mighty universe." Having thus secured from the simple "common sense" affirmation (see p. 18) a world independent of the subject's consciousness, Mr. D'Arcy has also obtained a basis for the affirmation of an eternal self, free from all the pantheistic leanings of Green's doctrine. Since *our* world of natural things depends upon *our* synthetic activity, then surely this big world of Nature depends upon *its* constituting spirit—God.

I am forced to stop once more in my exposition to raise the question: What founds these foundations? Upon Green's doctrine—no matter what objections may be brought upon other grounds—there is one self and universe. There is no question of subjective idealism, because the subject is defined by reference to the permanent and objective work of constituting a universe; the particular individual knowing is a process of reproducing the eternal constitutive action. But this seems to Mr. D'Arcy pantheistic, and for reasons which he has not explained to the reader (save as indicated in deference to the opinions of Professor Seth and Mr. Balfour) pantheistic implications are to be avoided at all hazards, including those of logic. Hence this sudden break into a cosmos of my experience, and another bigger cosmos, with two spirits, the individual for my cosmos, God for the big one. Two questions can hardly be kept back. If we accept, because we cannot help believing it, the existence of this larger cosmos, it must also be remarked that common sense equally denies the dependence of *our* cosmos upon our subjective activity. Common sense is not particularly alarmed about the existence of the sun, moon and stars in the big cosmos, but objects with great vigor to making the sun, moon and stars which are individually known dependent upon our individual thinking power. I doubt very much if Mr. D'Arcy can satisfy the realist by handing over to him a world, however big, which is unknown, while allowing the subjective idealist complete proprietary rights in the cosmos of individual experience.

But it may be said this is quite unfair to Mr. D'Arcy. Does he not say that the "cosmos of experience must be recognized as identical with a part of the great cosmos of Nature"? This brings me to my second question: Why then is not the individual self-identical with God so far as the identity of worlds goes? How, indeed, do we know there is a bigger unknown world, save as a projection, an extension, out of our present experience? Is it our "own" self,[4] or is it the absolute spirit which really constitutes our cosmos? If the former, how shall we account for its coincidence with the cosmos of the absolute subject, and for the continuity between the two, as the individual cosmos extends itself? How shall we account for this remarkable capacity on the part of a uniquely individual self to construct a world having its own objectivity and relative permanence? But if the latter, then

---

4    Nothing could exceed Mr. D'Arcy's conviction of the "ultimateness" of the individual self. "Self is for every man unique and ultimate. The identification of the self in every man with God involves the identification of all human selves. But since each self is for itself unique and ultimate, this identification amounts to a denial of the essential nature of selfhood" (p. 46).

the whole theory of the ultimate and irreducible distinction of the two selves breaks down.

This same method, viz.: the following of the Kantian analysis of knowledge up to a certain point and then the contradiction of its logical conclusion in the interests of religion and common sense—appears in the discussion of volition and of the common good. Will is treated as self-determination, and as indeed, only the more explicit recognition of the constitutive process found in all knowledge. "Every act of self-determination, every volition, is a determination, not simply of one thing, but of the whole cosmos of experience. Self-determination must be world-determination." This principle of determination recognized from the standpoint of the whole is freedom; while necessity is the principle of the articulation of the parts. They are thus correlative and imply each other, instead of being contradictory. That is to say, each fact or event taken as particular is necessitated; but that it is determined at all and determined in relation to other facts is due to an act of self-determination on the part of the subject (p. 29; pp. 39 and 49 also).

Why the self and the world should not be correlatives, while self-determination and world-determination, freedom and necessity, are correlatives, Mr. D'Arcy does not explain. It is difficult to see why one principle should hold for thought and another for volition; or why, if one is objected to on the ground of pantheistic tendencies, the other is not equally "dangerous." The pressure to make self-determination and world-determination correlatives is obvious. Without this correlativity, self-determination would occur in a purely transcendental, and, so far as we are concerned, empty region; will would have nothing to say or to do with the details of conduct. But the demand for correlativity on the side of knowledge is certainly none the less real although not quite as obvious. What the self-consciousness is which is found neither in consciousness of objects, nor yet in sensations, thoughts or emotions, Mr. D'Arcy does not explain, and we have only his word for it that it is not formal and empty.

The contradiction is still more glaring when we deal with the question of the End or Good. Mr. D'Arcy having settled that the subject is purely individual—for it must not get too closely implicated with the divine self for fear of pantheism—is quite consistent in holding that the end of self is egoistic. "Will is by nature egoistic. . . . No other individual can stand on a level with the self. . . . Reason is essentially anti-social. . . . Self, unless mastered by some superior principle, must wage unceasing war against all who would pretend to equal authority"(pp. 58, 59; the same doctrine also on pp. 124 and 147). Hence every moral system independent of religious ideas breaks down. It cannot explain why a man should love his neighbor as himself; it cannot justify the idea of a common good.[5] On the same line of thought, Mr. D'Arcy questions whether society is really an organic whole, since the individual is so very individual, and refers to it as an "amorphous mass of tissue" (p. 73).[6]

But on the other side, religion is going to help out the egoistic nature of the self. We cannot stop short, after all, with the unity of the self. In this case "God himself would be simply one unit in a multitude and isolated from his creatures. But it is impossible to end in a disconnected multitude." The mind is forced to suppose some principle of unity deeper than the unity of self-consciousness. There is in God a transcendent principle by which he forms the ultimate bond of union among the multitude of persons. The fact of the union of spirits must be assumed as the ultimate basis of all coherence, speculative and practical (pp. 47–48). Hence the common good for all persons. "All persons are naturally exclusive (*i.e.*, they limit one another), yet are they one in God. Hence the good for the whole is the good for every separate member. The true good for every man is a common

---

5    Mr. D'Arcy seems a little hard on the individual self. In the first place, it must be purely individual and unique, since otherwise it will get mixed up in a most pantheistic fashion with God and other selves. On religious grounds, in other words, it is quite shut up in itself. Then the interests of religion being duly secured, the self is gravely rebuked for its self-centred and self-seeking nature, and assured to be greatly in need of the assistance of religion to give it an end common with that of others. It is a little hard, I repeat, to refuse and to demand at the same time participation with other selves to the individual self, and both in the name of religion.

6    Mr. D'Arcy nevertheless holds that there is no other idea save that of organic unity, which can be applied to society, and yet that the truth is not fully represented in that idea (p. 74).

good and an absolute good" (p. 102; see also p. 124). Man and God have a common end. The end of conduct is identified with the end of the universe (p. 126).

We have precisely the contradiction here between the isolated, egoistic end of the self, and the common end of the self through its transcendental union with others in God that we met before as regards the constitutive action of self in *our* cosmos, and of God in *the* cosmos, except that here it is most explicitly recognized that we must not exclude the working of the divine end from the constitution of the human end. Mr. D'Arcy might, indeed, attempt to bridge the gulf by holding that the natural self is wholly given to evil; and that only by supernatural grace, initiated wholly from without, does the natural self come to such social ends; but there are no traces of any such doctrine in him. He seems to hold that in the moral life as such there is the immanence of the common end through the union of all selves in God. Were it not that the contradiction obviously escaped Mr. D'Arcy himself, I should think it wholly unnecessary to point it out. As it is, I must be pardoned for saying that if there is one self, named the divine self, in which all selves are united in a common end which is also the goal of the evolution of the universe, then the doctrine regarding the isolated, exclusive character of each individual self must be radically modified. It certainly is not legitimate to insist on the purely individual character of the self from one point of view; and then, when different considerations are in view, insist upon the community of selves. That the two ends of the contradiction are both set up in the name of religion does not make it any the less a contradiction; although it may make one suspicious of the particular type of religion represented.

Thus far the tendency of our examination has been to make us question whether Mr. D'Arcy's metaphysical foundations do not of themselves require more grounding than any ordinary ethical theory is likely to call for. I shall take space for just one application of his metaphysical to his ethical doctrine, seen in the question of the end, with a view to determining whether the ethical superstructure stands any the more firmly for the foundation put under it.

The ultimate end is the idea of a social universe in which every person's capabilities shall receive their full realization, and in which every person's realization shall contribute to every other person's realization. It is impossible, however, to give any further definition of the ultimate end, because it is impossible to know what are the possibilities of selfhood (pp. 104–5). Whence it is a fair inference that the end though not formal in itself is purely formal for us. "It must be granted at once that the Ideal End, or Ultimate Good, is relative to a set of circumstances at present non-existent" (p. 107).[7]

Mr. D'Arcy then goes on to deal with the proximate end, this ultimate end being obviously useless for the immediate guidance of conduct. "Every collocation of circumstances has its best." "The good is perfectly individualized." "It is no rigid standard." "Its unit is the concrete act" (pp. 108, 112 *passim*). In other words, the real end is always the content of some special act, performed with its own space and time considerations involved in it. This strikes me personally as excellent ethical doctrine; but what demand is there then for the ultimate goal furnished by metaphysics? How does that give foundation in any sense for the concrete ideals with which man is actually concerned? Mr. D'Arcy gives two answers, or two perhaps reducible to one: the thought of the far away goal helps us to read the special instance; and we judge by the *tendency* of the proximate to realize the ultimate end.

As to the first answer, it is of great advantage to the individual to be aware of what he is really about in a special case, and any principle, however formal and abstract, which aids him in doing this is justified thereby. But it is not the *remote* goal, but simply a larger view of the *present*, which thus helps one. It is the reference of an act to the present society which it maintains or furthers that helps one see its

7    To which Mr. D'Arcy adds, "But this is a defect attaching to every ideal"—yes, to every ideal metaphysically established, but to *no* ideal psychologically, or socially, determined, because in the latter case the ideal always is a certain set of present circumstances viewed in certain new relations and therefore no more requiring reference to some ultimate goal of the universe as a whole than does a scientific discovery or an industrial invention

true content; not its reference to a society distant an infinite length of time. So far is the conception of a perfectly realized community at the extreme goal of progress from helping us read the present that, on the contrary, we can only read, or put any meaning into, that conception by reference to the present. As to the other answer, that the present may be conceived as means, it simply removes all value from the present. If the present exists simply as one stage in bringing about an infinitely remote goal, it presents no imperative claims and affords no ends. Such a doctrine simply denies the doctrine that every collocation of circumstances has its *own* best. It makes rainbow chasing the essence of the doctrine of moral ideas. For my own part, I believe that an ethical doctrine with less "foundations" under it is likely to go farther and last longer.

In discussing Mr. D'Arcy's book from this one standpoint of the relation of his metaphysical to his ethical theory, great injustice would be done Mr. D'Arcy if I failed to recognize his own acuteness, subtlety and frequent suggestiveness. No one can read the book without stimulation. Mr. D'Arcy's personal attitude and method as distinct from that of his philosophic position, is straightforward and ingenuous. But the use of religious presuppositions to direct philosophic doctrine, first this way, then that, seems to me essentially disingenuous. Let us either explicitly hold that philosophy has no distinct right to be, but is always a form of theological apologetics; or let us give it the same intellectual freedom that we now yield to mathematics and mechanics. Let us not, even unconsciously, give philosophy the appearance, without the substance, of an independent position. More specifically, the results of Mr. D'Arcy's investigations seem to me to give at least a negative support to the hypothesis that what ethical theory now needs is an adequate psychological and social method, not a metaphysical one.

# *Evolution and Ethics*[1]

To a strictly logical mind the method of the development of thought must be a perplexing, even irritating matter. Its course is not so much like the simple curve described by a bullet as it speeds its way to a mark, as it is like the devious tacking of a sail boat upon a heavy sea with changeable winds. It would be difficult to find a single problem during the whole record of reflective thought which has been pursued consistently until some definite result was reached. It generally happens that just as the problem becomes defined, and the order of battle is drawn, with contestants determined on each side, the whole scene changes; interest is transferred to another phase of the question, and the old problem is left apparently suspended in mid-air. It is left, not because any satisfactory solution has been reached; but interest is exhausted. Another question which seems more important has claimed attention. If one, after a generation or a century, reviews the controversy and finds that some consensus of judgment has finally been reached, he discovers that this has come about, not so much through exhaustive logical discussion, as through a change in men's points of view. The solution is psychologically, rather than logically, justified.

This general reflection is called to mind as I undertake the discussion of the question of the relation of evolution and ethics. A generation ago the entire interest was in the exact relation between man and the lower animals. We had one

---

[1]    This paper was delivered as a public lecture during the Summer Quarter's work of the University of Chicago. This will account for the lack of reference to other articles bearing on the subject. I would call special attention, however, to Mr. Leslie Stephen on Natural Selection and Ethics, in the *Contemporary Review*, and the article by Dr. Carus in *The Monist*, Vol. IV, No. 3, on "Ethics and the Cosmic Order."

[*First published in* Monist, VIII (*Apr. 1898*), 321–41. *Not reprinted during the author's lifetime.*]

school concerned with reducing this difference to the lowest possible limits and urging that the consciousness of man, intellectual and moral, as well as his physical nature, might be considered a direct inheritance through easy gradations from some form of the anthropoid ape. We had another school equally concerned with magnifying the difference, making it, if possible, an unbridgeable chasm. It would be a bold man who would say that this controversy has been settled by the actual weight of concrete detailed evidence, or even that it has been very far advanced. The writings which really throw light on the question, in either direction (so far as the facts are concerned and not merely general considerations), can probably be easily numbered on the fingers of the two hands. Yet suddenly we find that discussion of this question has practically ceased, and that what engages controversy is the relation of what I may call the evolutionary concepts in general to the ethical concepts. Points of agreement and disagreement between the ideas involved in the notion of evolution and those involved in the notion of moral conduct are searched for. It is the state of the imagination and the direction of interest which have changed.

It is the latter question which I purpose to discuss to-day. This particular phase of the problem was precipitated, if not initiated, by the late Professor Huxley in his Romanes Lecture for 1893 on "Evolution and Ethics." It is some points in that address which I shall take as my text,—not for the sake of directly controverting them, but as convenient points of departure for raising the questions which seem to me fundamental. In that lecture, as you will all remember, Mr. Huxley points out in his incisive and sweeping language certain differences between what he terms the cosmic and the ethical processes. Those who recall the discussion following the lecture will remember that many felt as if they had received a blow knocking the breath out of their bodies. To some it appeared that Mr. Huxley had executed a sudden *volte-face* and had given up his belief in the unity of the evolutionary process, accepting the very dualistic idea of the separation between the animal and the human, against which he had previously directed so many hard blows. To some conservative thinkers it appeared that Saul had finally shown himself among the prophets. The lecture was deplored or welcomed according to the way one interpreted it with reference to his own prepossessions.

The position taken by Huxley, so far as it concerns us here, may be summed up as follows: The *rule* of the cosmic process is struggle and strife. The rule of the ethical process is sympathy and co-operation. The *end* of the cosmic process is the survival of the fittest; that of the ethical, the fitting of as many as possible to survive. Before the ethical tribunal the cosmic process stands condemned. The two processes are not only incompatible but even opposed to each other. "Social progress means the checking of the cosmic process at every step and the substitution for it of another, which may be called the ethical process; the end of which is not the survival of those who happen to be the fittest in respect of the whole of the conditions which exist, but of those who are ethically the best. The practice of that which is ethically best —which we call goodness or virtue—involves a course of conduct which in all respects is opposed to that which leads to success in the cosmic struggle for existence. . . . The cosmic process has no sort of relation to moral ends. The imitation by man is inconsistent with the first principles of ethics. Let us understand once for all that the ethical progress of society depends, not on imitating the cosmic process, still less in running away from it, but in combating it" (*Ethics and Evolution*, pp. 81–83, *et passim*).

Even in the lecture, however, Mr. Huxley used certain expressions which show that he did not hold to this opposition in a sense which meant the surrender of his previous evolutionary convictions. Thus he says that the ethical process, "strictly speaking, is part of the general cosmic process, just as the governor in a steam engine is part of the mechanism of the engine" (note 20, p. 115). In a later essay (published as "Prolegomena"), aroused somewhat by the clamour which the lecture had called forth, he makes his position even clearer. Here he illustrates his meaning by referring to the two hands as used in stretching or pulling. Each is opposed to the other, and yet both are manifestations of the same original force (p. 13). It is not that the ethical process is opposed to the entire cosmic process, but that *part* of the cosmic process which is maintained in the conduct of men in society, is radically opposed both in its methods and its aims to that *part* of the cosmic process which is exhibited in the stages of evolution prior to the appearance of socialized man upon the scene.

He makes this point clearer by reference to the analogy of a garden (pp. 9–11). Through the cosmic process, independent of man, certain plants have taken possession of a piece of soil because they are adapted to that particular environment. Man enters and roots out these plants as noxious weeds, or at least as useless for his purposes. He introduces other plants agreeable to his own wants and aims, and proceeds at once to modify the environment; if necessary, changing the soil by fertilization, building walls, altering conditions of sunlight and moisture so as to maintain his garden as a work of art—an artifice. This artificial structure, the one mediated by man's aims and efforts, is so opposed to the natural state of things that if man lets up in the ardor, the continuity, of his labors, the natural forces and conditions reassert themselves, the wall crumbles, the soil deteriorates, and the garden is finally once more overgrown with weeds.

Mr. Huxley is a trenchant writer, and his illustrations hold the mind captive. But possibly further consideration of this very illustration will point to a different conclusion. Illustrations are two-edged swords. There is no doubt in my mind of the justness of the analogy. The ethical process, like the activity of the gardener, is one of constant struggle. We can never allow things simply to go on of themselves. If we do, the result is retrogression. Over-sight, vigilance, constant interference with conditions as they are, are necessary to maintain the ethical order, as they are to keep up the garden. The problem, however, is to locate this opposition and interference,—to interpret it, to say what it means in the light of our idea of the evolutionary process as a whole.

Thus considering the illustration, the thought suggests itself that we do not have here in reality a conflict of man as man with his entire natural environment. We have rather the modification by man of one part of the environment with reference to another part. Man does not set himself against the state of nature. He utilizes one part of this state in order to control another part. It still holds that "nature is made better by no mean, but nature makes that mean." The plants which the gardener introduces, the vegetables and fruits he wishes to cultivate, may indeed be foreign to this particular environment; but they are not alien to man's environment as a whole. He introduces and maintains by art conditions of sunlight and moisture to which this particular plot of ground is unaccustomed; but these conditions fall within the wont and use of nature as a whole.

These may appear as too obvious considerations to be worth mentioning. Surely they could not have escaped Mr. Huxley for a moment. Yet it is possible that their bearing escaped him; for, if I mistake not, when we allow our mind to dwell upon such considerations as these, the entire import of the illustration changes. We are led to conceive, not of the conflict between the garden and the gardener; between the natural process and the process of art dependent upon human consciousness and effort. Our attention is directed to the possibility of interpreting a narrow and limited environment in the light of a wider and more complete one,—of reading the possibilities of a part through its place in the whole. Human intelligence and effort intervene, not as opposing forces but as making this connection. When Huxley says that "the macrocosm is pitted against the microcosm; that man is subduing nature to his higher ends; that the history of civilization details the steps by which we have succeeded in building up an artificial world within the cosmos; that there lies within man a fund of energy operating intelligently and so far akin to that which pervades the universe that it is competent to influence and modify the cosmic process,"—he says to my mind that man is an organ of the cosmic process in effecting its *own* progress. This progress consists essentially in making over a part of the environment by relating it more intimately to the environment as a whole; not, once more, in man setting himself against that environment.

Huxley himself defines the issue in words already quoted in which he contrasts the survival of those who "may happen to be the fittest *in respect of the whole of the condi-*

*tions which exist*, to the survival of those who are ethically the best." The clause italicized sums up the whole problem. It is granted without argument that the fittest with respect to a limited part of the environment are not identical with the ethically best. Can we make this concession, however, when we have in mind the whole of the existing conditions? Is not the extent to which Mr. Huxley pushes his dualistic opposition, are not many of the popular contrasts between the natural and the ethical, results of taking a limited view of the conditions with respect to which the term "fit" is used? In cosmic nature, as Mr. Huxley says, what is fittest depends upon the conditions. If our hemisphere were to cool again, the "survival of the fittest might leave us with nothing but lichens, diatomes, and such microscopic organisms as that which gives red snow its color." We cannot work this idea one way without being willing to work it in the other. The conditions with respect to which the term "fit" must *now* be used include the existing social structure with all the habits, demands, and ideals which are found in it. If so, we have reason to conclude that the "fittest with respect to the whole of the conditions" is the best; that, indeed, the only standard we have of the best is the discovery of that which maintains these conditions in their integrity. The unfit is practically the anti-social.

Loose popular argument—Mr. Huxley himself hardly falls into the pit—is accustomed to suppose that if the principle of the struggle for existence and survival of the fittest were rigorously carried out, it would result in the destruction of the weak, the sickly, the defective, and the insane. An examination of this popular assumption may serve to illuminate the point just made. We are all familiar with Fiske's generalization that civilization is a product of the prolongation of the period of infancy; that the necessity of caring for offspring not able to take care of themselves, during a continually lengthening period, stimulated the affection and care, the moral germs of social life, and required the foresight and providence that were the germs of the industrial arts upon which society depends. Mr. Fiske's contention, whether true or false, is worth putting over against the popular assumption. How far are we to go in the destruction of the helpless and dependent in order that the "fit" may survive? Clearly in this case the infant was one who was "fit," not only in ethical terms but in terms of furthering the evolutionary process. Is there any reason to suppose that the dependent classes are not equally "fit" at present, when measured by the whole of the conditions as a standard?

We may imagine a leader in an early social group, when the question had arisen of putting to death the feeble, the sickly, and the aged, in order to give that group an advantage in the struggle for existence with other groups; — we may imagine him, I say, speaking as follows: "No. In order that we may secure this advantage, let us preserve these classes. It is true for the moment that they make an additional drain upon our resources, and an additional tax upon the energies which might otherwise be engaged in fighting our foes. But in looking after these helpless we shall develop habits of foresight and forethought, powers of looking before and after, tendencies to husband our means, which shall ultimately make us the most skilled in warfare. We shall foster habits of group loyalty, feelings of solidarity, which shall bind us together by such close ties that no social group which has not cultivated like feelings through caring for all its members, will be able to withstand us." In a word, such conduct would pay in the struggle for existence as well as be morally commendable.

If the group to which he spoke saw any way to tide over the immediate emergency, no one can gainsay the logic of this speech. Not only the prolongation of the period of dependence, but the multiplication of its forms, has meant historically increase of intelligent foresight and planning, and increase of the bonds of social unity. Who shall say that such qualities are not positive instruments in the struggle for existence, and that those who stimulate and call out such powers are not among those "fit to survive"? If the deer had never developed his timidity and his skill in running away, the tiger and the wolf had never shown their full resources in the way of courage and power of attack. Again, prevention is better than cure, but it has been through trying to cure the sick that we have learned how to protect the well.

I have discussed this particular case in the hope of enlarging somewhat our conception of what is meant by the term "fit"; to suggest that we are in the habit of interpreting it with reference to an environment which long ago ceased to be. That which was fit among the animals is not fit among human beings, not merely because the animals were non-moral and man is moral; but because the conditions of life have changed, and because there is no way to define the term "fit" excepting through these conditions. The environment is now distinctly a social one, and the content of the term "fit" has to be made with reference to social adaptation. Moreover, the environment in which we now live is a changing and progressive one. Every one must have his fitness judged by the whole, including the anticipated change; not merely by reference to the conditions of today, because these may be gone tomorrow. If one is fitted simply to the present, he is not fitted to survive. He is sure to go under. A part of his fitness will consist in that very flexibility which enables him to adjust himself without too much loss to sudden and unexpected changes in his surroundings. We have then no reason here to oppose the ethical process to the natural process. The demand is for those who are fit for the conditions of existence in one case as well as in the other. It is the conditions which have changed.[2]

Let us turn our attention from the idea of "fitness" to that of the process or method—the "struggle for existence." Is it true that in the moral sphere the struggle must cease, or that we must turn ourselves resolutely upon it, branding it as immoral? Or, as in the case of the idea of fitness, is this struggle as necessary to the ethical as it is to the biological? In reality, the idea of struggle for existence is controlled by the environment in which that struggle is put forth. That which is struggle for life, and successful struggle, at one time, would be inert supineness or suicidal mania at another. This is as true of varying periods in animal development as

[2]    Precisely it may be said, and that is just the reason that Mr. Huxley insists upon the opposition of the natural and the ethical. I cannot avoid believing that this is what Mr. Huxley really had in mind at the bottom of his consciousness. But what he says is not that the form and content of fitness, of struggle for existence, and of selection, change with the change of conditions, but that these concepts lose all applicability. And this is just the point under discussion.

it is of the human contrasted with the animal. The nature of the struggle for existence is constantly modifying itself, not because something else is substituted for it, much less opposed to it; but because as the conditions of life change, the modes of living must change also. That which would count in the Carboniferous period will not count in the Neozoic. Why should we expect that which counts among the carnivora to count with man,—a social animal? If we do not find the same qualities effective (and hence to be maintained) in both cases; or if we find that opposed qualities are called for, what right have we to assume that what was once effected by the struggle for existence has now to be accomplished by another and opposed force?

The term "struggle for existence" seems to be used in two quite different senses by Mr. Huxley. In one case it means practically simply self-assertion. I do not see that the *struggle* for existence is anything more than living existence itself. Life tends to maintain itself because it is life. The particular acts which are put forth are the outcome of the life that is there; they are its expression, its manifestation.

Self-assertion in this sense carries with it no immoral connotation, unless life by its very nature is immoral. But Huxley also uses "struggle for existence" with a distinctly selfish meaning. He speaks of the "ape and tiger promptings" as branded with the name of sins (p. 52). He identifies self-assertion with "the unscrupulous seizing upon all that can be grasped; the tenacious holding of all that can be kept" (p. 51). It is "ruthless." It "thrusts aside or treads down all competitors." It "involves the gladiatorial theory of existence" (p. 82). Hence it is a "powerful and tenacious enemy to the ethical" (p. 85).

Surely, all this is rhetoric rather than philosophy or science. We inherit our impulses and our tendencies from our ancestors. These impulses and tendencies need to be modified. They need to be curbed and restrained. So much goes without saying. The question is regarding the nature of the modification; the nature of the restraint, and its relation to the original impulses of self-assertion. Surely, we do not want to suppress our animal inheritance; nor do we wish to restrain it absolutely,—that is, for the mere sake of restraint. It is not an enemy to the moral life, simply because without it no life is possible. Whatever is necessary to life we may fairly assume to have some relevancy to moral living. More than this is true. That self-assertion which we may call life is not only negatively, but positively a factor in the ethical process. What are courage, persistence, patience, enterprise, initiative, but forms of the self-assertion of those impulses which make up the life process? So much, I suppose, all would grant; but are temperance, chastity, benevolence, self-sacrifice itself, any less forms of self-assertion? Is not more, rather than less strength, involved in their exercise? Does the man who definitely and resolutely sets about obtaining some needed reform and with reference to that need sacrifices all the common comforts and luxuries of life, even for the time being social approval and reputation, fail in the exercise of self-assertion?

The simple fact of the case is of course that these promptings, even the promptings of the "tiger and the ape," are, simply as promptings, neither moral nor immoral; no more sins than they are saintly attributes. They are the basis and material of all acts whatsoever, good and bad. They become good when trained in a certain way, just as they become bad when trained in another way. The man who regards his animal inheritance as evil in and of itself apart from its relation to aims proposed by his intelligence, has logically but one recourse,—to seek Nirvana.[3] With him the principle of self-negation becomes absolute. But with all others, the men and women whom Mr. Huxley is presumably addressing, self-restraint is simply a factor within self-assertion. It relates to the particular ways in which self-assertion is made.

I may appear here to have ignored Huxley's distinction between the struggle for existence and the struggle for happiness (p. 40). The former it will be said, he uses in a definite technical sense as meaning simply the struggle for the perpetuation of life, apart from the kind of life led, and

---

[3]    It is passing strange that Mr. Huxley should not have seen that the logical conclusion from his premises of this extreme opposition are just those which he has himself set forth with such literary power earlier in his essay (pp. 63–68). That he did not shows, to my mind, how much he takes the opposition in a rhetorical, not a practical, sense.

as exhibiting itself in direct conflict with others, leading to the elimination of some. That struggle for existence it may be surely said, is not to be continued within the ethical process. The struggle for existence relates, he says, simply to the "means of living." Besides that we have the struggle for happiness, having to do with the uses to which these means are put,—the values which are got out of them, the ends.

I reply in the first place, that Mr. Huxley contradicts himself on this point in such a way that one would be quite justified in ignoring the distinction; and in the second place, that I am not able to see the validity of the distinction.

As to Mr. Huxley's self-contradiction, he asserts in a number of places that the struggle for existence as such (as distinct from the struggle for happiness) has now come to an end. It held only in the lower social forms when living was so precarious that people actually killed each other, if not for food, at least to secure the scanty store of food available. If it holds now at all it is simply among the small criminal class in society (p. 41). Now Mr. Huxley not only takes this position, but from a certain point of view is bound to take it. If the struggle is still going on, selection is still occurring, and there is every reason to suppose that as heretofore, it is a distinct agent in social progress; and Mr. Huxley is bound to hold that natural selection no longer operates in social progress and that therefore we must have recourse to other means. But if the struggle for existence has thus ceased of itself within any given human society, what sense is there in saying that it is now "a tenacious and powerful enemy with which ethical nature has to reckon"? If it has died out because of the change of conditions, why should the ethical process have to spend all its energy in combating it? "Let the dead bury their dead."[4]

In other words, Mr. Huxley himself is practically unable to limit the meaning of the phrase "struggle for existence" to this narrow import. He has himself to widen it so as to include not only the struggle for mere continuance of

4     Here is his flat contradiction: "Men in society are undoubtedly subject to the cosmic process. . . . The struggle for existence tends to eliminate those less fitted to adapt themselves to the circumstances of their existence" (p. 81). Compare this with pp. 15, 36, 38, and the other passages referred to above.

physical existence, but also whatever makes that life what it is. The distinction between the struggle for existence and the struggle for happiness breaks down. It breaks down, I take it, none the less in animal life itself than it does in social life. If the struggle for existence on the part of the wolf meant simply the struggle on his part to keep from dying, I do not doubt that the sheep would gladly have compromised at any time upon the basis of furnishing him with the necessary food—including even an occasional bowl of mutton broth. The fact is the wolf asserted himself as a wolf. It was not mere life he wished, but the life of the wolf. No agent can draw this distinction between desire for mere life and desire for happy life for himself; and no more can the spectator intelligently draw it for another.

What then is the conflict, the tension, which is a necessary factor in the moral life—for be it remembered there is no difference of opinion with Mr. Huxley upon this point? The sole question is whether the combat is between the ethical process as such, and the cosmic, natural, process as such. The outcome of our previous discussion is that it cannot be the latter because the natural process, the so-called inherited animal instincts and promptings, are not only the stimuli, but also the materials, of moral conduct. To weaken them absolutely, as distinct from giving them a definite turn or direction, is to lessen the efficiency of moral conduct. Where then does the struggle come in? Evidently in the particular turn or direction which is given to the powers of the animal nature making up the immediate content of self-assertion. But once more, what does this turn or direction mean? Simply, I take it, that an act which was once adapted to given conditions must now be adapted to other conditions. The effort, the struggle, is a name for the necessity of this re-adaptation.[5] The conditions which originally called the power forth, which led to its "selection," under which it got its origin, and formation, have ceased to exist, not indeed, wholly, but in such part that the power is now more or less irrelevant. Indeed, it is not now a "power" in the sense of

[5]     I have developed this conception psychologically in the *Philosophical Review* for Jan. 1897, in an article upon "The Psychology of Effort" [*The Early Works of John Dewey*, v, 151–63].

being a function which can without transformation operate successfully with reference to the whole set of existing conditions. Mr. Huxley states the whole case when he says that "in extreme cases man does his best to put an end to the survival of the fittest of former days by the axe and rope." The phrase, "the fittest of *former* days" contains the matter in a nut-shell. Just because the acts of which the promptings and impulses are the survival, were the fittest for by-gone days they are not the fittest now. The struggle comes, not in suppressing them nor in substituting something else for them; but in reconstituting them, in adapting them, so that they will function with reference to the existing situation.

This, I take it, is the truth, and the whole truth, contained in Mr. Huxley's opposition of the moral and the natural order. The tension is between an organ adjusted to a past state and the functioning required by present conditions. And this tension demands reconstruction. This opposition of the structure of the past and the deeds of the present is precisely that suggested in the discussion of the illustrative garden. The past environment is related to the present as a part to a whole. When animal life began on land, water became only one factor in the conditions of life, and the animal attitude towards it was changed. It certainly could not now get along without a water-environment, much less could it turn against it; but its relations to moisture as a condition of life were profoundly modified. An embryonic Huxley might then have argued that the future success of animal life depended upon combating the natural process which had previously maintained and furthered it. In reality the demand was, that which was only a part should be treated as such, and thus subordinated to the whole set of conditions.

Thus when Mr. Huxley says (p. 12) that "nature is always tending to reclaim that which her child, man, has borrowed from her and has arranged in combinations which are not those favored by the general cosmic process," this only means that the environment *minus* man is not the same environment as the one that includes man. In any other sense these "combinations" *are* favored by the general cosmic process,—in witness whereof man through whom that process works has set his sign and seal. That *if* you took man out of this process things would change, is much like saying that if they were different they would not be the same; or, that a part is not its own whole.

There are many signs that Mr. Huxley had Mr. Spencer in mind in many of his contentions; that what he is really aiming at is the supposition on the part of Mr. Spencer that the goal of evolution is a complete state of final adaptation in which all is peace and bliss and in which the pains of effort and of reconstruction are known no more. As against this insipid millennium, Mr. Huxley is certainly right in calling attention to the fact that the ethical process implies continual struggle, conquest, and the defeats that go with conquest. But when Mr. Huxley asserts that the struggle is between the natural process and the ethical, we must part company with him. He seems to assert that in some far century it may be possible for the ape and the tiger to be so thoroughly subjugated by man that the "inveterate enemy of the moral process" shall finally be put under foot. Then the struggle will occur against the environment because of a shortage of food. But we must insist that Mr. Huxley is here falling into the very charges which he has brought against Mr. Spencer's school. The very highest habits and ideals which are organizing today with reference to existing conditions will be just as much, and just as little, an obstacle to the moral conduct of man millions of years from now, as those of the ape and the tiger are to us. So far as they represent the survival of outworn conditions, they will demand re-constitution and re-adaptation, and that modification will be accompanied by pain. Growth always costs something. It costs the making over of the old in order to meet the demands of the new.

This struggle, then, is not more characteristic of the ethical process than it is of the biological. Long before man came upon the earth, long before any talk was heard of right and wrong, it happened that those who clung persistently to modes of action which were adapted to an environment that had passed away, were at a disadvantage in the struggle for existence, and tended to die out. The factors of the conflict upon which Mr. Huxley lays so much stress have been present ever since the beginning of life and will continue to be present as long as we live in a moving, and not a static world. What he insists upon is reconstruction and readaptation,—modification of the present with reference to the conditions of the future.

With the animal it was simply the happy guess,—the chance. In society there is anticipation; with man it is the intelligent and controlled foresight, the necessity of maintaining the institutions which have come down to us, while we make over these institutions so that they serve under changing conditions. To give up the institutions is chaos and anarchy; to maintain the institutions unchanged is death and fossilization. The problem is the reconciliation of unbridled radicalism and inert conservatism, in a movement of reasonable reform. Psychologically the tension manifests itself as the conflict between habits and aims: a conflict necessary, so far as we can see, to the maintenance of conscious life. Without habits we can do nothing. Yet if habits become so fixed that they cannot be adapted to the ends suggested by new situations, they are barriers to conduct and enemies to life. It is conflict with the end or ideal which keeps the habit working, a flexible and efficient instrument of action. Without this conflict with habits, the end becomes vague, empty, and sentimental. Defining it so that the habits may be utilized in realizing it makes it of practical value. This definition would never occur were it not that habits resist it.

Just as habits and aims are co-operating factors in the maintenance of conscious experience, just as institutions and plans of reform are co-workers in our social life, just as the relative antagonism between the two is necessary to their valuable final co-adaptation; so impulse, call it animal if we will, and ideal, call it holy though we may, are mutually necessary in themselves and in their mutual opposition,— necessary for the ethical process. It is well for the ideal that it meet the opposition of the impulse, as it is for the animal prompting to be held to the function suggested by the ideal.

In locating and interpreting this tension, this opposition between the natural and the moral, I have done what I set out to do. There is one other point which it seems worth while to touch upon before leaving the matter. Three terms are always found together in all discussions of evolution,— natural selection, struggle for existence, and the fit. The latter two of these ideas we have discussed in their bearings upon moral life. It remains to say a word or two upon natural selection. Mr. Huxley's position on this point is not quite clear. As has been already suggested, it seems to be varying, if not actually self-contradictory. At times he seems to hold that since the struggle for existence has ceased in the social sphere, selection has ceased also to act, and therefore the work formerly done by it (if we may for the moment personify it as an agent) now has to be done in other ways (see the passages referred to on pp. 43–44). At other times he seems to hold that it is still going on but that its tendency upon the whole is bad, judged from the ethical standpoint, and therefore requires to be consciously counteracted.

Certainly the question of the scope of selection in the sphere of social life is confused. Does it still continue or does it not? If it does operate what are its modes of working? Many seem to suppose that we do not have it excepting where we intentionally isolate those whom we consider unfit, and prevent them from reproducing offspring; or that it is found only if we artificially regulate marriage in such a way as to attempt to select social and animal types considered higher at the expense of the lower. Mr. Huxley naturally considers selection in this sense, not only practically impossible, but intrinsically undesirable. But is this the only or the chief meaning of natural selection? Does it follow that social selection, to use a term employed by late writers, is something radically different from natural selection?

The belief that natural selection has ceased to operate rests upon the assumption that there is only one form of such selection: that where improvement is indirectly effected by the failure of species of a certain type to continue to reproduce; carrying with it as its correlative that certain variations continue to multiply, and finally come to possess the land. This ordeal by death is an extremely important phase of natural selection, so-called. That it has been the chief form in pre-human life will be here admitted without discussion; though doubtless those having competent knowledge of details have good reason for qualifying this admission. However, to identify this procedure absolutely with selection, seems to me to indicate a somewhat gross and narrow vision. Not only is one form of life as a whole selected at the expense of other forms, but one mode of action in the same individual is constantly selected at the expense of others. There is not only the trial by death, but there is the trial by the success or failure of special acts—the counterpart, I suppose, of physiological selection so-called. We do not need to go here into the vexed question of the inheritance of acquired characters. We know that through what we call public opinion and education certain forms of action are constantly stimulated and encouraged, while other types are as constantly objected to, repressed, and punished. What difference in principle exists between this mediation of the acts of the individual by society and what is ordinarily called natural selection, I am unable to see. In each case there is the reaction of the conditions of life back into the agents in such a way as to modify the function of living. That in one case this modification takes place through changes in the structure of the organ, say the eye, requiring many generations to become active; while in the other case it operates within the life of one and the same individual, and affects the uses to which the eye is put rather than (so far as we can tell) the structure of the eye itself, is not a reason for refusing to use the term "natural selection." Or if we have limited that term to a narrower technical meaning, it is certainly no reason for refusing to say that the same kind of forces are at work bringing about the same sort of results. If we personify Nature, we may say that the influences of education and social approval and disapproval in modifying the behavior of the agent, mark simply the discovery on the part of Nature of a shorter and more economical form of selection than she had previously known. The modification of structure is certainly not an end in itself. It is simply one device for changing function. If other means can be devised which do the work more efficiently, then so much the better. Certainly it marks a distinct gain to accomplish this modification in one and the same generation rather than to have to trust to the dying out of the series of forms through a sequence of generations. It is certainly implied in the idea of natural selection that the most effective modes of variation should themselves be finally selected.

But Mr. Huxley insists upon another distinction. Stated

in terms of the garden illustration, it is that: "The tendency of the cosmic process is to bring about the adjustment of the forms of plant life to the current conditions; the tendency of the horticultural process is the adjustment of the needs of the forms of plant life which the gardener desires to raise." This is a very common antithesis. But is it as absolute and sweeping as we generally affect to believe? Every living form is dynamically, not simply statically, adapted to its environment. I mean by this it subjects conditions about it to its own needs. This is the very meaning of "adjustment"; it does not mean that the life-form passively accepts or submits to the conditions just as they are, but that it functionally subordinates these natural circumstances to its own food needs.

But this principle is of especial importance with reference to the forms in which are found the lines of progressive variation. It is, relatively speaking, true of the weeds and gorse of the patch of soil from which Mr. Huxley draws his illustration, that they are adjusted to current conditions. But that is simply because they mark the result, the relatively finished outcome of a given process of selection. They are arrested forms. Just because the patch has got into equilibrium with surrounding conditions progressive variation along that line has ceased. If this were all the life in existence, there would be no more evolution. Something, in other words, did *not* adapt itself to "current conditions," and so development continued.

It would be ungrateful in any discussion of this subject not to refer to Malthus's classic illustration of the feast spread by Nature—not big enough for the invited guests. It is supposed, in its application to struggle for existence and selection, that this means that the life-forms present struggle just to get a share of the food that is already there. Such a struggle for a quota of food already in existence, might result, through selection, in perfecting a species already in existence, and thus in fixing it. It could not give rise to a new species. The selection which marks progress is that of a variation which *creates* a new food supply or amplifies an old one. The advantage which the variation gives, if it tends towards a new species, is an organ which opens up a wider food environment, detects new supplies within the old, or which makes it possible to utilize as food something hitherto indifferent or alien. The greater the number of varieties on a given piece of soil, the more individuals that can maintain a vigorous life. *The new species means a new environment to which it adjusts itself without interfering with others.* So far as the progressive varieties are concerned, it is not in the least true that they simply adapt themselves to current conditions; evolution is a continued development of new conditions which are better suited to the needs of organisms than the old. The unwritten chapter in natural selection is that of the evolution of environments.

Now, in man we have this power of variation and consequent discovery and constitution of new environments set free. All biological process has been effected through this, and so every tendency which forms this power is selected; in man it reaches its climax. So far as the individual is concerned, the environment (the specific conditions which relate to his life) is highly variable at present. The growth of science, its application in invention to industrial life, the multiplication and acceleration of means of transportation and intercommunication, have created a peculiarly unstable environment. It shifts constantly within itself, or qualitatively, and as to its range, or quantitatively. Simply as an affair of Nature, not of art (using these terms in Mr. Huxley's sense) it is a profitable, an advantageous thing that structural changes, if any occur, should not get too set. They would limit unduly the possibility of change in adaptation. In the present environment, flexibility of function, the enlargement of the range of uses to which one and the same organ, grossly considered, may be put, is a great, almost the supreme, condition of success. As such, any change in that direction is a favorable variation which must be selected. In a word, the difference between man and animal is not that selection has ceased, but that selection along the line of variations which enlarge and intensify the environment is active as never before.

We reach precisely the same conclusion with respect to "selection" that we have reached with reference to the cognate ideas—"fit" and "struggle for existence." It is found in the ethical process as it is in the cosmic, and it operates in the same way. So far as conditions have changed, so far as the environment is indefinitely more complex, wider, and more variable, so far of necessity and as a biological and cosmic matter, not merely an ethical one, the functions selected differ.

There are no doubt sufficiently profound distinctions between the ethical process and the cosmic process as it existed prior to man and to the formation of human society. So far as I know, however, all of these differences are summed up in the fact that the process and the forces bound up with the cosmic have come to consciousness in man. That which was instinct in the animal is conscious impulse in man. That which was "tendency to vary" in the animal is conscious foresight in man. That which was unconscious adaptation and survival in the animal, taking place by the "cut and try" method until it worked itself out, is with man conscious deliberation and experimentation. That this transfer from unconsciousness to consciousness has immense importance, need hardly be argued. It is enough to say that it means the whole distinction of the moral from the unmoral. We have, however, no reason to suppose that the cosmic process has become arrested or that some new force has supervened to struggle against the cosmic. Some theologians and moralists, to be sure, welcomed Huxley's apparent return to the idea of a dualism between the cosmic and the ethical as likely to inure favorably to the spiritual life. But I question whether the spiritual life does not get its surest and most ample guarantees when it is learned that the laws and conditions of righteousness are implicated in the working processes of the universe; when it is found that man in his conscious struggles, in his doubts, temptations, and defeats, in his aspirations and successes, is moved on and buoyed up by the forces which have developed nature; and that in this moral struggle he acts not as a mere individual but as an organ in maintaining and carrying forward the universal process.

# Ethical Principles Underlying Education

## I.

It is quite clear that there cannot be two sets of ethical principles, or two forms of ethical theory, one for life in the school, and the other for life outside of the school. As conduct is one, the principles of conduct are one also. The frequent tendency to discuss the morals of the school, as if the latter were an institution by itself, and as if its morale could be stated without reference to the general scientific principles of conduct, appears to me highly unfortunate. Principles are the same. It is the special points of contact and application which vary with different conditions. I shall make no apology, accordingly, for commencing with statements which seem to me of universal validity and scope, and afterwards considering the moral work of the school as a special case of these general principles. I may be forgiven also for adding that the limits of space forbid much in the way of amplification and qualification, and that, so far as form is concerned, the material will therefore be presented in somewhat dogmatic shape. I hope, however, it will not be found dogmatic in spirit, for the principles stated are all of them, in my judgment, capable of purely scientific justification.

All ethical theory is two faced. It requires to be considered from two different points of view, and stated in two different sets of terms. These are the social and the psychological. We do not have here, however, a division, but

[*First published in the* Third Yearbook of the National Herbart Society (*Chicago: The Society,* 1897), *pp.* 7–33. *See* A Note on the Texts *for publishing history.*]

simply a distinction. Psychological ethics does not cover part of the field, and then require social ethics to include the territory left untouched. Both cover the entire sphere of conduct. Nor does the distinction mark a compromise, or a fusion, as if at one point the psychological view broke down, and needed to be supplemented by the sociological. Each theory is complete and coherent within itself, so far as its own end or purpose is concerned. But conduct is of such a nature as to require to be stated throughout from two points of view. How this distinction happens to exist may perhaps be guessed at by calling to mind that the individual and society are neither opposed to each other nor separated from each other. Society is a society of individuals and the individual is always a social individual. He has no existence by himself. He lives in, for, and by society, just as society has no existence excepting in and through the individuals who constitute it. But we can state one and the same process (as, for example, telling the truth) either from the standpoint of what it effects in society as a whole, or with reference to the particular individual concerned. The latter statement will be psychological; the former, social as to its purport and terms.

If, then, the difference is simply a point of view, we first need to find out what fixes the two points of view. Why are they necessary? Because conduct itself has two aspects. On one side conduct is a form of activity. It is a mode of operation. It is something which somebody does. There is no conduct excepting where there is an agent. From this standpoint conduct is a process having its own form or mode, having, as it were, its own running machinery. That is, it is something which the agent does in a certain way; something which is an outcome of the agent himself, and which effects certain changes within the agent considered as an agent or doer. Now when we ask how conduct is carried on, what sort of a *doing* it is, when, that is to say, we discuss it with reference to an agent from whom it springs, and whose powers it modifies, our discussion is necessarily psychological. Psychology thus fixes for us the *how* of conduct, the way in which it takes place. Consideration from this standpoint is necessary because it is obvious that modifications in results or products must flow from changes in the agent or doer. If we want to get different things done, we must begin with changing the machinery which does them.

I hope the term "machinery" here will not be misunderstood by being taken in too dead and mechanical a sense. All that is meant here is that the mode of action of the individual agent controls the product, or what is done, just as the way in which a particular machine works controls the output in that direction. The individual agent has a certain structure, and certain ways of operating. It is simply this which is referred to as machinery.

But conduct has a *what* as well as a how. There is something done as well as a way in which it is done. There are ends, outcomes, results, as well as ways, means, and processes. Now when we consider conduct from this standpoint (with reference, that is to say, to its actual filling, content, or concrete worth) we are considering conduct from a social standpoint—from the place which it occupies, not simply with reference to the person who does it, but with reference to the whole living situation into which it enters.

The psychological view of conduct has to do, then, with the question of agency, of how the individual operates; the social, with what the individual does and needs to do, considered from the standpoint of his membership in a whole which is larger than himself.

We may illustrate by reference to business life. A man starts in a business of manufacturing cotton cloth. Now this occupation of his may be considered from two standpoints. The individual who makes the cloth does not originate the demand for it. Society needs the cloth, and thereby furnishes the end or aim to the individual. It needs a certain amount of cloth, and cloth of certain varying qualities and patterns. It is this situation outside the mere operations of the manufacturer which fixes the meaning and value of what he does. If it were not for these social needs and demands, the occupation of the manufacturer would be purely formal. He might as well go out into the wilderness and heap up and tear down piles of sand.

But on the other side society must have its needs met, its ends realized, through the activities of some specific individual or group of individuals. The needs will forever go unsatisfied unless somebody takes it as his special business to supply them. So we may consider the manufactory of cotton cloth, not only from the standpoint of the position which it occupies in the larger social whole, but also as a mode of operation which simply as a mode is complete in itself. After the manufacturer has determined the ends which he has to meet (the kinds and amounts of cloth he needs to produce) he has to go to work to consider the cheapest and best modes of producing them, and of getting them to the market. He has to transfer his attention from the ends to the means. He has to see how to make his factory, considered as a mode of activity, the best possible organized agency within itself. No amount of reflection upon how badly society needs cloth will help him here. He has to think out his problem in terms of the number and kind of machines which he will use, the number of men which he will employ, how much he will pay them, how and where he will buy his raw material, and through what instrumentalities he will get his goods to the market. Now while this question is ultimately only a means to the larger social end, yet in order that it may become a true means, and accomplish the work which it has to do, it must become, for the time being, an end in itself. It must be stated, in other words, in terms of the factory as a working agency.

I think this parallelism may be applied to moral conduct without the change of a single principle. It is not the mere individual as an individual who makes the final demand for moral action, who establishes the final end, or furnishes the final standards of worth. It is the constitution and development of the larger life into which he enters which settles these things. But when we come to the question of how the individual is to meet the moral demands, of how he is to realize the values within himself, the question is one which concerns the individual as an agent. Hence it must be answered in psychological terms.

Let us change the scene of discussion to the school. The child who is educated there is a member of society and must be instructed and cared for as such a member. The moral responsibility of the school, and of those who conduct it, is to society. The school is fundamentally an institution erected by society to do a certain specific work—to exercise a certain specific function in maintaining the life and advancing the welfare of society. The educational system which does not recognize this fact as entailing upon it an ethical responsibility is derelict and a defaulter. It is not doing what it was called into existence to do, and what it pretends to do. Hence the necessity of discussing the entire structure and the specific workings of the school system from the standpoint of its moral position and moral function to society.

The above is commonplace. But the idea is ordinarily taken in too limited and rigid a way. The social work of the school is often limited to training for citizenship, and citizenship is then interpreted in a narrow sense as meaning capacity to vote intelligently, a disposition to obey laws, etc. But it is futile to contract and cramp the ethical responsibility of the school in this way. The child is one, and he must either live his life as an integral unified being or suffer loss and create friction. To pick out one of the manifold social relations which the child bears, and to define the work of the school with relation to that, is like instituting a vast and complicated system of physical exercise which would have for its object simply the development of the lungs and the power of breathing, independent of other organs and functions. The child is an organic whole, intellectually, socially, and morally, as well as physically. The ethical aim which determines the work of the school must accordingly be interpreted in the most comprehensive and organic spirit. We must take the child as a member of society in the broadest sense and demand whatever is necessary to enable the child to recognize all his social relations and to carry them out.

The child is to be not only a voter and a subject of law; he is also to be a member of a family, himself responsible, in all probability, in turn, for rearing and training of future children, and thus maintaining the continuity of society. He is to be a worker, engaged in some occupation which will be of use to society, and which will maintain his own independence and self-respect. He is to be a member of some particular neighborhood and community, and must contribute to the values of life, add to the decencies and graces of civilization wherever he is. These are bare and formal statements, but if we let our imagination translate them into their concrete details we have a wide and varied scene. For the child properly to take his place with reference to these various functions means training in science, in art, in history; command of the fundamental methods of inquiry and the fundamental tools of intercourse and communication; it means a trained and sound body, skillful eye and hand; habits of industry, perseverance, and, above all, habits of serviceableness. To isolate the formal relationship of citizenship from the whole system of relations with which it is actually interwoven; to suppose that there is any one particular study or mode of treatment which can make the child a good citizen; to suppose, in other words, that a good citizen is anything more than a thoroughly efficient and serviceable member of society, one with all his powers of body and mind under control, is a cramped superstition which it is hoped may soon disappear from educational discussion.

One point more. The society of which the child is to be a member is, in the United States, a democratic and progressive society. The child must be educated for leadership as well as for obedience. He must have power of self-direction and power of directing others, powers of administration, ability to assume positions of responsibility. This necessity of educating for leadership is as great on the industrial as on the political side. The affairs of life are coming more and more under the control of insight and skill in perceiving and effecting combinations.

Moreover, the conditions of life are in continual change. We are in the midst of a tremendous industrial and commercial development. New inventions, new machines, new methods of transportation and intercourse are making over the whole scene of action year by year. It is an absolute impossibility to educate the child for any fixed station in life. So far as education is conducted unconsciously or consciously on this basis, it results in fitting the future citizen for no station in life, but makes him a drone, a hanger-on, or an actual retarding influence in the onward movement. Instead of caring for himself and for others, he becomes one who has himself to be cared for. Here, too, the ethical responsibility of the school on the social side must be interpreted in the broadest and freest spirit; it is equivalent to that training of the child which will give him such possession of himself that he may take charge of himself; may not only adapt himself to the changes which are going on, but have power to shape and direct those changes.

It is necessary to apply this conception of the child's membership in society more specifically to determining the ethical principles of education.

Apart from the thought of participation in social life the school has no end nor aim. As long as we confine ourselves to the school as an isolated institution we have no final directing ethical principles, because we have no object or ideal. But it is said the end of education may be stated in purely individual terms. For example, it is said to be the harmonious development of all the powers of the individual. Here we have no apparent reference to social life or membership, and yet it is argued we have an adequate and thoroughgoing definition of what the goal of education is. But if this definition is taken independently of social relationship we shall find that we have no standard or criterion for telling what is meant by any one of the terms concerned. We do not know what a power is; we do not know what development is; we do not know what harmony is; a power is a power with reference to the use to which it is put, the function it has to serve. There is nothing in the make-up of the human being, taken in an isolated way, which furnishes controlling ends and serves to mark out powers. If we leave out the aim supplied from social life we have nothing but the old "faculty psychology" to fall back upon to tell what is meant by power in general or what the specific powers are. The idea reduces itself to enumerating a lot of faculties like perception, memory, reasoning, etc., and then stating that each one of these powers needs to be developed. But this statement is barren and formal. It reduces training to an empty gymnastic.

Acute powers of observation and memory might be developed by studying Chinese characters; acuteness in reasoning might be got by discussion of the scholastic subtleties of the Middle Ages. The simple fact is that there is no isolated faculty of observation, or memory, or reasoning any more than there is an original faculty of blacksmithing, carpentering, or steam engineering. These faculties simply mean that particular impulses and habits have been co-ordinated and framed with reference to accomplishing certain definite kinds of work. Precisely the same thing holds of the so-called mental faculties. They are not powers in themselves, but are such only with reference to the ends to which they are put, the services which they have to perform. Hence they cannot be located nor discussed as powers on a theoretical, but only on a practical basis. We need to know the social situations with reference to which the individual will have to use ability to observe, recollect, imagine, and reason before we get any intelligent and concrete basis for telling what a training of mental powers actually means either in its general principles or in its working details.

We get no moral ideals, no moral standards for school life excepting as we so interpret in social terms. To understand what the school is actually doing, to discover defects in its practice, and to form plans for its progress means to have a clear conception of what society requires and of the relation of the school to these requirements. It is high time, however, to apply this general principle so as to give it a somewhat more definite content. What does the general principle signify when we view the existing school system in its light? What defects does this principle point out? What changes does it indicate ?

The fundamental conclusion is that the school must be itself made into a vital social institution to a very much greater extent than obtains at present. I am told that there is a swimming school in the city of Chicago where youth are taught to swim without going into the water, being repeatedly drilled in the various movements which are necessary for swimming. When one of the young men so trained was asked what he did when he got into the water, he laconically replied, "Sunk." The story happens to be true; if it were not, it would seem to be a fable made expressly for the purpose of typifying the prevailing status of the school, as judged from the standpoint of its ethical relationship to society. The school cannot be a preparation for social life excepting as it reproduces, within itself, the typical condi-

tions of social life. The school at present is engaged largely
upon the futile task of Sisyphus. It is endeavoring to form
practically an intellectual habit in children for use in a social
life which is, it would almost seem, carefully and purposely
kept away from any vital contact with the child who is thus
undergoing training. The only way to prepare for social life
is to engage in social life. To form habits of social usefulness
and serviceableness apart from any direct social need and
motive, and apart from any existing social situation, is, to
the letter, teaching the child to swim by going through motions outside of the water. The most indispensable condition
is left out of account, and the results are correspondingly
futile.

The much and commonly lamented separation in the
schools between intellectual and moral training, between
acquiring information and growth of character, is simply
one expression of the failure to conceive and construct the
school as a social institution, having social life and value
within itself. Excepting in so far as the school is an embryonic yet typical community life, moral training must be
partly pathological and partly formal. It is pathological inasmuch as the stress comes to be laid upon correcting wrongdoing instead of upon forming habits of positive service. The
teacher is necessarily forced into a position where his concern with the moral life of the pupils takes largely the form
of being on the alert for failures to conform to the school
rules and routine. These regulations, judged from the standpoint of the development of the child at the time, are more or
less conventional and arbitrary. They are rules which have
to be made in order that the existing modes of school work
may go on; but the lack of inherent necessity in the school
work reflects itself in a feeling, on the part of the child, that
the moral discipline of the school is somewhat arbitrary.
Any conditions which compel the teacher to take note of
failures rather than of healthy growth put the emphasis in
the wrong place and result in distortion and perversion. Attending to wrongdoing ought to be an incident rather than
the important phase. The child ought to have a positive
consciousness of what he is about, and to be able to judge
and criticize his respective acts from the standpoint of their

reference to the work which he has to do. Only in this way does he have a normal and healthy standard, enabling him properly to appreciate his failures and to estimate them at their right value.

By saying that the moral training of the school is partly formal, I mean that the moral habits which are specially emphasized in the school are habits which are created, as it were, *ad hoc*. Even the habits of promptness, regularity, industry, non-interference with the work of others, faithfulness to tasks imposed, which are specially inculcated in the school, are habits which are morally necessary simply because the school system is what it is, and must be preserved intact. If we grant the inviolability of the school system as it is, these habits represent permanent and necessary moral ideas; but just in so far as the school system is itself isolated and mechanical, the insistence upon these moral habits is more or less unreal, because the ideal to which they relate is not itself necessary. The duties, in other words, are distinctly school duties, not life duties. If we compare this with the well-ordered home, we find that the duties and responsibilities which the child has to recognize and assume there are not such as belong to the family as a specialized and isolated institution, but flow from the very nature of the social life in which the family participates and to which it contributes. The child ought to have exactly the same motives for right doing, and be judged by exactly the same standard in the school, as the adult in the wider social life to which he belongs. Interest in the community welfare, an interest which is intellectual and practical, as well as emotional—an interest, that is to say, in perceiving whatever makes for social order and progress, and for carrying these principles into execution—is the ultimate ethical habit to which all the special school habits must be related if they are to be animated by the breath of moral life.

We may apply this conception of the school as a social community which reflects and organizes in typical form the fundamental principles of all community life, to both the methods and the subject-matter of instruction.

As to methods, this principle when applied means that the emphasis must be upon construction and giving out, rather than upon absorption and mere learning. We fail to recognize how essentially individualistic the latter methods are, and how unconsciously, yet certainly and effectively, they react into the child's ways of judging and of acting. Imagine forty children all engaged in reading the same books, and in preparing and reciting the same lessons day after day. Suppose that this constitutes by far the larger part of their work, and that they are continually judged from the standpoint of what they are able to take in in a study hour, and to reproduce in a recitation hour. There is next to no opportunity here for any social or moral division of labor. There is no opportunity for each child to work out something specifically his own, which he may contribute to the common stock, while he, in turn, participates in the productions of others. All are set to do exactly the same work and turn out the same results. The social spirit is not cultivated —in fact, in so far as this method gets in its work, it gradually atrophies for lack of use. It is easy to see, from the intellectual side, that one reason why reading aloud in school is as poor as it is is that the real motive for the use of language—the desire to communicate and to learn—is not utilized. The child knows perfectly well that the teacher and all his fellow pupils have exactly the same facts and ideas before them that he has; he is not giving them anything at all new. But it may be questioned whether the moral lack is not as great as the intellectual. The child is born with a natural desire to give out, to do, and that means to serve. When this tendency is not made use of, when conditions are such that other motives are substituted, the reaction against the social spirit is much larger than we have any idea of— especially when the burden of the work, week after week, and year after year, falls upon this side.

But lack of cultivation of the social spirit is not all. Positively individualistic motives and standards are inculcated. Some stimulus must be found to keep the child at his studies. At the best this will be his affection for his teacher, together with a feeling that in doing this he is not violating school rules, and thus is negatively, if not positively, contributing to the good of the school. I have nothing to say against these motives as far as they go, but they are inadequate. The relation between the piece of work to be done and affection for a third person is external, not intrinsic. It is therefore liable to break down whenever the external conditions are changed. Moreover this attachment to a particular person, while in a way social, may become so isolated and exclusive as to be positively selfish in quality. In any case, it is necessary that the child should gradually grow out of this relatively external motive, into an appreciation of the social value of what he has to do for its own sake, and because of its relations to life as a whole, not as pinned down to two or three people.

But unfortunately the motive is not always at this relative best, while it is always mixed with lower motives which are distinctly individualistic. Fear is a motive which is almost sure to enter in—not necessarily physical fear, or of punishment, but fear of losing the approbation of others; fear of failure so extreme and sensitive as to be morbid. On the other side, emulation and rivalry enter in. Just because all are doing the same work, and are judged (both in recitation and in examination, with reference to grading and to promotion) not from the standpoint of their motives or the ends which they are trying to reach, the feeling of superiority is unduly appealed to. The children are judged with reference to their capacity to present the same external set of facts and ideas. As a consequence they must be placed in the hierarchy on the basis of this purely objective standard. The weaker gradually lose their sense of capacity, and accept a position of continuous and persistent inferiority. The effect of this upon both self-respect and respect for work need not be dwelt upon. The stronger grow to glory, not in their strength, but in the fact that they are stronger. The child is prematurely launched into the region of individualistic competition, and this in a direction where competition is least applicable, viz., in intellectual and spiritual matters, whose law is co-operation and participation.

I cannot stop to paint the other side. I can only say that the introduction of every method which appeals to the child's active powers, to his capacities in construction, production, and creation, marks an opportunity to shift the centre of ethical gravity from an absorption which is selfish

to a service which is social. I shall have occasion later on to
speak of these same methods from the psychological side,
that is, their relation to the development of the particular
powers of the child. I am here speaking of these methods
with reference to the relation which they bear to a sense of
community life, to a feeling of a division of labor which
enables each one to make his own contribution, and to produce results which are to be judged not simply as intellectual
results but from the motive of devotion to work, and of usefulness to others.

Manual training is more than manual; it is more than
intellectual; in the hands of any good teacher it lends itself
easily, and almost as a matter of course, to development of
social habits. Ever since the philosophy of Kant it has been
a commonplace in the theory of art, that one of its indispensable features is that it be universal, that is, that it should
not be the product of any purely personal desire or appetite,
or be capable of merely individual appropriation, but should
have its value participated in by all who perceive it.

The divorce between the intellectual and the moral
must inevitably continue in our schools (in spite of the
efforts of individual teachers) as long as there is a divorce
between learning and doing. The attempt to attach genuine
moral consideration to the mere processes of learning, and
to the habits which go along with learning, can result only
in a moral training which is infected with formality, arbi-
trariness, and an undue emphasis upon failure to conform.
That as much is accomplished as actually is done only shows
the possibilities which would go along with the more organic
ethical relationships involved in methods of activity which
would afford opportunity for reciprocity, co-operation, and
mutual service.

The principle of the school as itself a representative
social institution may be applied to the subject-matter of
instruction—must be applied if the divorce between information and character is to be overcome.

A casual glance at pedagogical literature will show
that we are much in need of an ultimate criterion for the
values of studies, and for deciding what is meant by content
value and by form value. At present we are apt to have two,

three, or even four different standards set up, by which different values—as disciplinary, culture, and information values—are measured. There is no conception of any single unifying principle. The point here made is that the extent and way in which a study brings the pupil to consciousness of his social environment, and confers upon him the ability to interpret his own powers from the standpoint of their possibilities in social use, is this ultimate and unified standard.

The distinction of form and content value is becoming familiar, but, so far as I know, no attempt has been made to give it rational basis. I submit the following as the key to the distinction: A study from a certain point of view serves to introduce the child to a consciousness of the make-up or structure of social life; from another point of view, it serves to introduce him to a knowledge of, and command over, the instrumentalities through which the society carries itself along. The former is the content value; the latter is the form value. Form is thus in no sense a term of depreciation. Form is as necessary as content. Form represents, as it were, the technique, the adjustment of means involved in social action, just as content refers to the realized value or end of social action. What is needed is not a depreciation of form, but a correct placing of it, that is, seeing that since it is related as means to end, it must be kept in subordination to an end, and taught in relation to the end. The distinction is ultimately an ethical one because it relates not to anything found in the study from a purely intellectual or logical point of view, but to the studies considered from the standpoint of the ways in which they develop a consciousness of the nature of social life, in which the child is to live.

I take up the discussion first from the side of content. The contention is that a study is to be considered as bringing the child to realize the social scene of action; that when thus considered it gives a criterion for the selection of material and for the judgment of value. At present, as already suggested, we have three independent values set up: one of culture, another of information, and another of discipline. In reality these refer only to three phases of social interpretation. Information is genuine or educative only in so far as it effects definite images and conceptions of material placed in social life. Discipline is genuine and educative only as it represents a reaction of the information into the individual's own powers so that he can bring them under control for social ends. Culture, if it is to be genuine and educative, and not an external polish or factitious varnish, represents the vital union of information and discipline. It designates the socialization of the individual in his whole outlook upon life and mode of dealing with it.

This abstract point may be illustrated briefly by reference to a few of the school studies. In the first place there is no line of demarkation within facts themselves which classifies them as belonging to science, history, or geography, respectively. The pigeonhole classification which is so prevalent at present (fostered by introducing the pupil at the outset into a number of different studies contained in different text-books) gives an utterly erroneous idea of the relations of studies to each other, and to the intellectual whole to which they all belong. In fact these subjects have all to do with the same ultimate reality, namely, the conscious experience of man. It is only because we have different interests, or different ends, that we sort out the material and label part of it science, part history, part geography, and so on. Each of these subjects represents an arrangement of materials with reference to some one dominant or typical aim or process of the social life.

This social criterion is necessary not only to mark off the studies from each other, but also to grasp the reasons for the study of each and the motives in connection with which it should be presented. How, for example, shall we define geography? What is the unity in the different so-called divisions of geography—as mathematical geography, physical geography, political geography, commercial geography? Are these purely empirical classifications dependent upon the brute fact that we run across a lot of different facts which cannot be connected with one another, or is there some reason why they are all called geography, and is there some intrinsic principle upon which the material is distributed under these various heads? I understand by intrinsic not something which attaches to the objective facts themselves, for the facts do not classify themselves, but something in the interest and attitude of the human mind towards them. This is a large question and it would take an essay longer than this entire paper adequately to answer it. I raise the question partly to indicate the necessity of going back to more fundamental principles if we are to have any real philosophy of education, and partly to afford, in my answer, an illustration of the principle of social interpretation. I should say that geography has to do with all those aspects of social life which are concerned with the interaction of the life of man and nature; or, that it has to do with the world considered as the scene of social interaction. Any fact, then, will be a geographical fact in so far as it bears upon the dependence of man upon his natural environment, or with the changes introduced in this environment through the life of man.

The four forms of geography referred to above represent then four increasing stages of abstraction in discussing the mutual relation of human life and nature. The beginning must be the commercial geography. I mean by this that the essence of any geographical fact is the consciousness of two persons, or two groups of persons, who are at once separated and connected by the physical environment, and that the interest is in seeing how these people are at once kept apart and brought together in their actions by the instrumentality of this physical environment. The ultimate significance of lake, river, mountain, and plain is not physical but social; it is the part which it plays in modifying and functioning human relationship. This evidently involves an extension of the term commercial. It has not to do simply with business, in the narrow sense, but includes whatever relates to human intercourse and intercommunication as affected by natural forms and properties. Political geography represents this same social interaction taken in a static instead of in a dynamic way; takes it, that is, as temporarily crystallized and fixed in certain forms. Physical geography (including under this not simply physiography, but also the study of flora and fauna) represents a further analysis or abstraction. It studies the conditions which determine human action, leaving out of account, temporarily, the ways in which they concretely do this. Mathematical geography simply carries the analysis back to more ultimate and remote conditions, showing that the physical conditions themselves are not ultimate, but depend upon the place which the world occupies in a larger system. Here, in other words, we have traced, step by step, the links which connect the immediate social occupations and interactions of man back to the whole natural system which ultimately conditioned them. Step by step the scene is enlarged and the image of what enters into the make-up of social action is widened and broadened, but at no time ought the chain of connection to be broken.

It is out of the question to take up the studies one by one and show that their meaning is similarly controlled by social consideration. But I cannot forbear a word or two upon history. History is vital or dead to the child according as it is or is not presented from the sociological standpoint. When treated simply as a record of what has passed and gone, it must be mechanical because the past, as the past, is remote. It no longer has existence and simply as past there is no motive for attending to it. The ethical value of history teaching will be measured by the extent to which it is treated as a matter of analysis of existing social relations—that is to say as affording insight into what makes up the structure and working of society.

This relation of history to comprehension of existing social forces is apparent whether we take it from the standpoint of social order or from that of social progress. Existing social structure is exceedingly complex. It is practically impossible for the child to attack it *en masse* and get any definite mental image of it. But type phases of historical development may be selected which will exhibit, as through a telescope, the essential constituents of the existing order. Greece, for example, represents what art and the growing power of individual expression stand for; Rome exhibits the political elements and determining forces of political life on a tremendous scale. Or, as these civilizations are themselves relatively complex, a study of still simpler forms of hunting, nomadic and agricultural life in the beginnings of civilization; a study of the effects of the introduction of iron, iron tools, and so forth, serves to reduce the existing complexity to its simple elements.

One reason historical teaching is usually not more effective is the fact that the student is set to acquire information in such a way that no epochs or factors stand out to his mind as typical; everything is reduced to the same dead level. The only way of securing the necessary perspective is by relating the past to the present, as if the past were a projected present in which all the elements are enlarged.

The principle of contrast is as important as that of similarity. Because the present life is so close to us, touching us at every point, we cannot get away from it to see it as it really is. Nothing stands out clearly or sharply as characteristic. In the study of past periods attention necessarily attaches itself to striking differences. Thus the child gets a locus in imagination, through which he can remove himself from the present pressure of surrounding circumstance and define it.

History is equally available as teaching the *methods* of social progress. It is commonly stated that history must be studied from the standpoint of cause and effect. The truth of this statement depends upon its interpretation. Social life is so complex and the various parts of it are so organically related to each other and to the natural environment that it is impossible to say that this or that thing is cause of some other particular thing. But what the study of history can effect is to reveal the main instruments in the way of discoveries, inventions, new modes of life, etc., which have initiated the great epochs of social advance, and it can present to the child's consciousness type illustrations of the main lines in which social progress has been made most easily and effectively and can set before him what the chief difficulties and obstructions have been. Progress is always rhythmic in its nature, and from the side of growth as well as from that of status or order it is important that the epochs which are typical should be selected. This once more can be done only in so far as it is recognized that social forces in themselves are always the same—that the same kind of influences were at work 100 and 1000 years ago that are now—and treating the particular historical epochs as affording illustration of the way in which the fundamental forces work.

Everything depends then upon history being treated from a social standpoint, as manifesting the agencies which have influenced social development, and the typical institutions in which social life has expressed itself. The culture-epoch theory, while working in the right direction, has failed to recognize the importance of treating past periods with relation to the present—that is, as affording insight into the representative factors of its structure; it has treated these periods too much as if they had some meaning or value in themselves. The way in which the biographical method is handled illustrates the same point. It is often treated in such a way as to exclude from the child's consciousness (or at least not sufficiently to emphasize) the social forces and principles involved in the association of the masses of men. It is quite true that the child is interested easily in history from the biographical standpoint; but unless the hero is treated in relation to the community life behind which he both sums up and directs, there is danger that the history will reduce itself to a mere story. When this is done moral instruction reduces itself to drawing certain lessons from the life of the particular personalities concerned, instead of having widened and deepened the child's imaginative consciousness of the social relationships, ideals, and means involved in the world in which he lives.

There is some danger, I presume, in simply presenting the illustrations without more development, but I hope it will be remembered that I am not making these points for their own sake, but with reference to the general principle that when history is taught as a mode of understanding social life it has positive ethical import. What the normal child continuously needs is not so much isolated moral lessons instilling in him the importance of truthfulness and honesty, or the beneficent results that follow from some particular act of patriotism, etc. It is the formation of habits of social imagination and conception. I mean by this it is necessary that the child should be forming the habit of interpreting the special incidents that occur and the particular situations that present themselves in terms of the whole social life. The evils of the present industrial and political situation, on the ethical side, are not due so much to actual perverseness on the part of individuals concerned, nor in mere ignorance of what constitutes the ordinary virtues (such as honesty, industry, purity, etc.) as to inability to appreciate the social environment in which we live. It is tremendously complex and confused. Only a mind trained to grasp social situations, and to reduce them to their simpler and typical elements, can get sufficient hold on the realities of this life to see what sort of action, critical and constructive, it really demands. Most people are left at the mercy of tradition, impulse, or the appeals of those who have special and class interests to serve. In relation to this highly complicated social environment, training for citizenship is formal and nominal unless it develops the power of observation, analysis, and inference with respect to what makes up a social situation and the agencies through which it is modified. Because history rightly taught is the chief instrumentality for accomplishing this, it has an ultimate ethical value.

I have been speaking so far of the school curriculum on the side of its content. I now turn to that of form; understanding by this term, as already explained, a consciousness of the instruments and methods which are necessary to the control of social movements. Studies cannot be classified into form studies and content studies. Every study has both sides. That is to say, it deals both with the actual make-up of society, and is concerned with the tools or machinery by which society maintains itself. Language and literature best illustrate the impossibility of separation. Through the ideas contained in language, the continuity of the social structure is effected. From this standpoint the study of literature is a content study. But language is also distinctly a means, a tool. It not simply has social value in itself, but is a social instrument. However, in some studies one side or the other predominates very much, and in this sense we may speak of specifically form studies. As, for example, mathematics.

My illustrative proposition at this point is that mathematics does, or does not, accomplish its full ethical purpose according as it is presented, or not presented, as such a social tool. The prevailing divorce between information and character, between knowledge and social action, stalks upon the scene here. The moment mathematical study is severed from the place which it occupies with reference to use in social life, it becomes unduly abstract, even from the purely intellectual side. It is presented as a matter of technical relations and formulæ apart from any end or use. What the study of number suffers from in elementary education is the lack of motivation. Back of this and that and the other particular bad method is the radical mistake of treating number as if it were an end in itself instead of as a means of accomplishing some end. Let the child get a consciousness of what the use of number is, of what it really is for, and half the battle is won. Now this consciousness of the use or reason implies some active end in view which is always implicitly social since it involves the production of something which may be of use to others, and which is often explicitly social.

One of the absurd things in the more advanced study of arithmetic is the extent to which the child is introduced to numerical operations which have no distinctive mathematical principles characterizing them but which represent certain general principles found in business relationships. To train the child in these operations, while paying no attention to the business realities in which they will be of use, and the conditions of social life which make these business activities necessary, is neither arithmetic nor common sense. The child is called upon to do examples in interest, partnership, banking, brokerage, and so on through a long string, and no pains are taken to see that, in connection with the arithmetic, he has any sense of the social realities involved. This part of arithmetic is essentially sociological in its nature. It ought either to be omitted entirely or else taught in connection with a study of the relevant social realities. As we now manage the study it is the old case of learning to swim apart from the water over again, with correspondingly bad results on the practical and ethical side.[1]

I am afraid one question still haunts the reader. What has all this discussion about geography, history, and num-

[1]    With increasing mental maturity, and corresponding specialization which naturally accompanies it, these various instrumentalities may become ends in themselves. That is, the child may, as he ripens into the period of youth, be interested in number relations for their own sake. What was once method may become an activity in itself. The above statement is not directed against this possibility. It is simply aimed at the importance of seeing to it that the preliminary period—that in which the form or means is kept in organic relationship to real ends and values— is adequately lived through.

ber, whether from the side of content or that of form, got to do with the underlying principles of education? The very reasons which induce the reader to put this question to himself, even in a half-formed way, illustrate the very point which I am trying to make. Our conceptions of the ethical in education have been too narrow, too formal, and too pathological. We have associated the term ethical with certain special acts which are labeled virtues and set off from the mass of other acts, and still more from the habitual images and motives in the agents performing them. Moral instruction is thus associated with teaching about these particular virtues, or with instilling certain sentiments in regard to them. The ethical has been conceived in too goody-goody a way. But it is not such ethical ideas and motives as these which keep men at work in recognizing and performing their moral duty. Such teaching as this, after all is said and done, is external; it does not reach down into the depths of the character-making agency. Ultimate moral motives and forces are nothing more nor less than social intelligence — the power of observing and comprehending social situations — and social power — trained capacities of control — at work in the service of social interest and aims. There is no fact which throws light upon the constitution of society, there is no power whose training adds to social resourcefulness which is not ethical in its bearing.

I sum up, then, this part of the discussion by asking your attention to the moral trinity of the school. The demand is for social intelligence, social power, and social interests. Our resources are (1) the life of the school as a social institution in itself; (2) methods of learning and of doing work; and (3) the school studies or curriculum. In so far as the school represents, in its own spirit, a genuine community life; in so far as what are called school discipline, government, order, etc., are the expressions of this inherent social spirit; in so far as the methods used are those which appeal to the active and constructive powers, permitting the child to give out, and thus to serve; in so far as the curriculum is so selected and organized as to provide the material for affording the child a consciousness of the world in which he has to play a part, and the relations he has to meet; in so far as these ends are met, the school is organized on an ethical basis. So far as general principles are concerned, all the basic ethical requirements are met. The rest remains between the individual teacher and the individual child.

## II.

I pass over now to the other side of the discussion—the psychological. We have so far been concerned with the principle that the end and standard of the school work is to be found in its functional relation to social life. We have endeavored to apply this principle to some of the typical features of the school in order to give an illustration of what is meant by this statement. We now recur to the counterpart principle: These ends and aims are to be realized in the child as an individual, and by the child as an individual. The social values are abstract until they are taken up and manifested in the life of the individual pupils. We have to ask, therefore, what they mean when translated over into terms of individual conduct. These values are not only to be manifested in individual conduct, but they are to be worked out by individual effort and energy. We have to consider the child as an agent or doer—the methods by which he can reproduce in his own life the constituent values of social life.

The beginning has to be made with the observation of the individual child. We find in him certain dawning powers —instincts and impulses. We wish to know what these stand for—what they represent. This means an inquiry into the ends with respect to which they can function, or become organized instruments of action. This interpretation of the crude powers of the child takes us over into social life. We find there the answers to the questions which the child nature puts to us; we find the completed results which enable us to diagnose the symptoms and indications spontaneously exhibited in the child. Then we have to return again with this interpretation back to the individual in order to find out the easiest, most economical, and most effective points of attachment and relationship between the spontaneous activities of the child, and the aims which we expect these powers to realize. Our business is now to connect the two. This can be done only through the medium of the child himself; the teacher cannot really make the connection. He can only form the conditions in such a way that the child may make it for himself. Moreover, even if the teacher could make the connection, the result would not be ethical. The moral life is lived only as the individual appreciates for himself the ends for which he is working, and does his work in a personal spirit of interest and devotion to these ends. Consequently we are again thrown back upon a study of the individual; upon psychology in order to discover the means which are available to mediate the spontaneous and crude capacities of the child over into habits of social intelligence and responsiveness.

Now, it is psychology which reveals to us the nature and the working of the individual as such. Accordingly psychological study is absolutely required in education to help determine its ethical import and conduct in two specific directions. (1) In the first place, all conduct springs ultimately and radically out of native instincts and impulses. We must know what these instincts and impulses are, and what they are at each particular stage of the child's development, in order to know what to appeal to and what to build upon. Neglect of this principle may give a mechanical imitation of moral conduct, but the imitation will be ethically dead because it is external and has its centre without not within the individual. We must study the child, in other words, to get our indications, our symptoms, our suggestions. The more or less spontaneous acts of the child are not to be thought of as giving moral forms to which the efforts of the educator must conform—this would result simply in spoiling the child, but they are to be thought of as symptoms which require to be interpreted; as stimuli which need to be manifested in directed ways, as material which, in however transformed a shape, is the only ultimate constituent of future moral conduct and character.

(2) Our ethical principles need also to be stated in psychological terms because the child supplies us with the only means or instruments at command with which moral ideals are to be realized. The subject-matter of the curriculum, however important, however judiciously selected, is empty

of conclusive moral content until it is made over into terms of the individual's own activities, habits, and desires. We must know what history, geography and mathematics mean in psychological terms, that is, as modes of personal experiencing, before we can get out of them their moral potentialities.

The psychological side of education sums itself up, of course, in a consideration of the nature of character, and of how character best grows. Some of the abstractness of the previous discussion may be relieved, if not removed, if we state it with reference to character.

It is a commonplace to say that this development of character is the ultimate end of all school work. The difficulty lies in the execution of this idea. And an underlying difficulty in this execution is the lack of any conception of what character means. This may seem an extreme and uncalled-for statement. If so, the idea may be better conveyed by saying that we conceive of character simply in terms of results; that we have no clear conception of it in psychological terms—that is, as a process, as working or dynamic. We know what character means in terms of the kinds of actions which proceed from character, but we have not a definite conception of it on its inner side, as a piece of running, psychical machinery.

I propose, then, to give a brief statement of the nature of character from this point of view. In general, character means power of social agency, organized capacity of social functioning. It means, as already suggested, social insight or intelligence, social executive power, and social interest or responsiveness. Stated in psychological terms, it means that there must be a training of the primary impulses and instincts, which organizes them into habits which are reliable means of action.

(1) Force, efficiency in execution, or overt action, is the necessary constituent of character. In our moral books and lectures we may lay all the stress upon good intentions, etc. But we know practically that the kind of character we hope to build up through our education is one which not only has good intentions, but which insists upon carrying them out. Any other character is wishy-washy; it is goody,

not good. The individual must have the power to stand up and count for something in the actual conflicts of life. He must have initiative, insistence, persistence, courage and industry. He must, in a word, have all that goes under a term, "force of character." Undoubtedly, individuals differ greatly in their native endowment in this respect. None the less, each has a certain primary equipment of impulse, of tendency forward, of innate urgency to do. The problem of education on this side is that of discovering what this native fund of power is, and then of utilizing it in such a way (affording conditions which both stimulate and control) as to organize it into definite conserved modes of action—habits.

(2) But something more is required than sheer force. Sheer force may be brutal; it may override the interests of others. Even when aiming at right ends it may go at them in such a way as to violate the rights of others. More than this, in sheer force there is no guarantee for the right end itself. It may be directed towards mistaken ends, and result in positive mischief and destruction. Power, as already suggested, must be directed. It must be organized along certain channels of output or expression in such a way as to be attached to the valuable ends.

This involves training on both the intellectual and emotional side. On the intellectual side we must have judgment —what is ordinarily called good sense. The difference between mere knowledge, or information, and judgment is that the former is simply held, not used; judgment is ideas directed with reference to the accomplishment of ends. Good judgment is a sense of respective or proportionate values. The one who has judgment is the one who has ability to size up a situation. He is the one who can grasp the scene or situation before him, ignoring what is irrelevant, or what for the time being is unimportant, and can seize upon the factors which demand attention, and grade them according to their respective claims. Mere knowledge of what the right is in the abstract, mere intentions of following the right in general, however praiseworthy in themselves, are never a substitute for this power of trained judgment. Action is always in the concrete. It is definite and individualized. Except, therefore, as it is backed and controlled by a knowledge of the actual concrete factors in the situation demanding action, it must be relatively futile and waste.

(3) But the consciousness of end must be more than merely intellectual. We can imagine a person with most excellent judgment, who yet does not act upon his judgment. There must not only be force to insure effort in execution against obstacles, but there must also be a delicate personal responsiveness—there must be an emotional reaction. Indeed good judgment is impossible without this susceptibility. Unless there is a prompt and almost instinctive sensitiveness to the conditions about one, to the ends and interests of others, the intellectual side of judgment will not have its proper material to work upon. Just as the material of objects of knowledge is related to the senses, so the material of ethical knowledge is related to emotional responsiveness. It is difficult to put this quality into words, but we all know the difference between the character which is somewhat hard and formal, and that which is sympathetic, flexible, and open. In the abstract the former may be as sincerely devoted to moral ideas as the latter, but as a practical matter we prefer to live with the latter, and we count upon it to accomplish more in the end by tact, by instinctive recognition of the claims of others, by skill in adjusting, than the former can accomplish by mere attachment to rules and principles which are intellectually justified.

We get here, then, the ethical standard upon the psychological side, by which to test the work of the school. (*a*) Does the school as a system, at present, attach sufficient importance to the spontaneous instincts and impulses? Does it afford sufficient opportunity for these to assert themselves and work out their own results? Omitting quantitative considerations, can we even say that the school in principle attaches itself, at present, to the active constructive powers rather than to processes of absorption and learning, acquiring information? Does not our talk about self-activity largely render itself meaningless because the self-activity we have in mind is purely intellectual, out of relation to the impulses of the child which work through hand and eye?

Just in so far as the present school methods fail to meet the test of these questions we must not be surprised if the ethical results attained are unsatisfactory. We cannot secure the development of positive force of character unless we are willing to pay the price psychologically required. We cannot smother and repress the child's powers, or gradually abort them (from failure to permit sufficient opportunity for exercise), and then expect to get a character with initiative and consecutive industry. I am aware of the importance attaching to inhibition, but mere inhibition is valueless. The only restraint, the only holding-in that is of any worth is that which comes through holding all the powers concentrated in devotion to a positive end. The end cannot be attained excepting as the instinct and impulses are kept from discharging at random and from running off on side tracks. In keeping the powers at work upon their relevant ends, there is sufficient opportunity for genuine inhibition. To say that inhibition is higher than power of direction, morally, is like saying that death is worth more than life, negation worth more than affirmation, sacrifice worth more than service. Morally educative inhibition is one of the factors of the power of direction.

(*b*) We must also test our school work as to whether it affords the conditions psychologically necessary for the formation of good judgment. Judgment as the sense of relative values involves ability to select, to discriminate, by reference to a standard. Acquiring information can therefore never develop the power of judgment. Whatever development the child gets is in spite of, not because of, those methods of instruction which emphasize simple learning. The test comes only when the information acquired has to be put to use. Will it do what we expect of it? I have heard an educator of large experience say that in her judgment the greatest defect of instruction today, on the intellectual side, is found in the fact that children leave school without a mental perspective. Facts seem to them all of the same importance. There is no foreground nor background. There is no instinctive habit of sorting out our facts upon any scale of worth, and of grading them accordingly. This may be an exaggerated statement, but in so far as there is any truth in it, it points to moral evils as serious as the intellectual ones.

The child cannot get power of judgment excepting as

he is continually exercised in forming and testing judgment. He must have an opportunity to select for himself, and then to attempt to put his own selections into execution that he may submit them to the only final test, that of action. Only thus can he learn to discriminate that which promises success from that which promises failure; only thus can he form the habit of continually relating his otherwise isolated ideas to the conditions which determine their value. Does the school, as a system, afford, at present, sufficient opportunity for this sort of experimentation? Excepting in so far as the emphasis of the school work is upon the doing side, upon construction, upon active investigation, it cannot meet the psychological conditions necessary for the judgment which is an integral factor of good character.

(c) I shall be brief with respect to the other point, the need of susceptibility and responsiveness. The informal, social side of education, the æsthetic environment and influences, are all-important here. In so far as all the work is laid out in regular and formulated ways, in so far as there are lacking opportunities for casual and free social intercourse between the pupils, and between the pupils and the teacher, this side of the child's nature is either being starved or else left to find haphazard expression along more or less secret channels. When the school system under plea of the practical (meaning by the practical the narrowly utilitarian) confines the child to the three R's and the formal studies connected with them, and shuts him out from the vital sources of literature and history, and deprives him of his right to contact with what is best in architecture, music, sculpture and picture, it is hopeless to expect any definite results with respect to the training of this integral element in character.

What we need in education more than anything else is a genuine, not merely nominal faith in the existence of moral principles which are capable of effective application. We believe that, so far as the mass of children are concerned, if we keep at them long enough we can teach reading and writing and figuring. We are practically, even if unconsciously, skeptical as to the possibility of anything like the same sort of assurance on the moral side. We believe in moral laws and rules, to be sure, but they are in the air. They are something set off by themselves. They are so *very* "moral" that there is no working contact between them and the average affairs of everyday life. What we need is to have these moral principles brought down to the ground through their statement in social and in psychological terms. We need to see that moral principles are not arbitrary, that they are not merely transcendental; that the term "moral" does not designate a special region or portion of life. We need to translate the moral into the actual conditions and working forces of our community life, and into the impulses and habits which make up the doing of the individual.

All the rest is mint, anise, and cummin. The one thing needful is that we recognize that moral principles are real in the same sense in which other forces are real; that they are inherent in community life, and in the running machinery of the individual. If we can secure a genuine faith in this fact, we shall have secured the only condition which is finally necessary in order to get from our educational system all the effectiveness there is in it. The teacher who operates in this faith will find every subject, every method of instruction, every incident of school life pregnant with ethical life.

# My Pedagogic Creed

## Article One.  What Education Is

I believe that all education proceeds by the participation of the individual in the social consciousness of the race. This process begins unconsciously almost at birth, and is continually shaping the individual's powers, saturating his consciousness, forming his habits, training his ideas, and arousing his feelings and emotions. Through this unconscious education the individual gradually comes to share in the intellectual and moral resources which humanity has succeeded in getting together. He becomes an inheritor of the funded capital of civilization. The most formal and technical education in the world cannot safely depart from this general process. It can only organize it; or differentiate it in some particular direction.

I believe that the only true education comes through the stimulation of the child's powers by the demands of the social situations in which he finds himself. Through these demands he is stimulated to act as a member of a unity, to emerge from his original narrowness of action and feeling and to conceive of himself from the standpoint of the welfare of the group to which he belongs. Through the responses which others make to his own activities he comes to know what these mean in social terms. The value which they have is reflected back into them. For instance, through the response which is made to the child's instinctive babblings the child comes to know what those babblings mean; they are transformed into articulate language and thus the child is introduced into the consolidated wealth of ideas and emotions which are now summed up in language.

[*First published in* School Journal, LIV (*Jan. 1897*), 77–80. *See A Note on the Texts for publishing history.*]

I believe that this educational process has two sides—one psychological and one sociological; and that neither can be subordinated to the other or neglected without evil results following. Of these two sides, the psychological is the basis. The child's own instincts and powers furnish the material and give the starting point for all education. Save as the efforts of the educator connect with some activity which the child is carrying on of his own initiative independent of the educator, education becomes reduced to a pressure from without. It may, indeed, give certain external results but cannot truly be called educative. Without insight into the psychological structure and activities of the individual, the educative process will, therefore, be haphazard and arbitrary. If it chances to coincide with the child's activity it will get a leverage; if it does not, it will result in friction, or disintegration, or arrest of the child nature.

I believe that knowledge of social conditions, of the present state of civilization, is necessary in order properly to interpret the child's powers. The child has his own instincts and tendencies, but we do not know what these mean until we can translate them into their social equivalents. We must be able to carry them back into a social past and see them as the inheritance of previous race activities. We must also be able to project them into the future to see what their outcome and end will be. In the illustration just used, it is the ability to see in the child's babblings the promise and potency of a future social intercourse and conversation which enables one to deal in the proper way with that instinct.

I believe that the psychological and social sides are organically related and that education cannot be regarded as a compromise between the two, or a superimposition of one upon the other. We are told that the psychological definition of education is barren and formal—that it gives us only the idea of a development of all the mental powers without giving us any idea of the use to which these powers are put. On the other hand, it is urged that the social definition of education, as getting adjusted to civilization, makes of it a forced and external process, and results in subordinating the freedom of the individual to a preconceived social and political status.

I believe each of these objections is true when urged against one side isolated from the other. In order to know what a power really is we must know what its end, use, or function is; and this we cannot know save as we conceive of the individual as active in social relationships. But, on the other hand, the only possible adjustment which we can give to the child under existing conditions, is that which arises through putting him in complete possession of all his powers. With the advent of democracy and modern industrial conditions, it is impossible to foretell definitely just what civilization will be twenty years from now. Hence it is impossible to prepare the child for any precise set of conditions. To prepare him for the future life means to give him command of himself; it means so to train him that he will have the full and ready use of all his capacities; that his eye and ear and hand may be tools ready to command, that his judgment may be capable of grasping the conditions under which it has to work, and the executive forces be trained to act economically and efficiently. It is impossible to reach this sort of adjustment save as constant regard is had to the individual's own powers, tastes, and interests—say, that is, as education is continually converted into psychological terms.

In sum, I believe that the individual who is to be educated is a social individual and that society is an organic union of individuals. If we eliminate the social factor from the child we are left only with an abstraction; if we eliminate the individual factor from society, we are left only with an inert and lifeless mass. Education, therefore, must begin with a psychological insight into the child's capacities, interests, and habits. It must be controlled at every point by reference to these same considerations. These powers, interests, and habits must be continually interpreted—we must know what they mean. They must be translated into terms of their social equivalents—into terms of what they are capable of in the way of social service.

## Article Two.    *What the School Is*

I believe that the school is primarily a social institution. Education being a social process, the school is simply that form of community life in which all those agencies are concentrated that will be most effective in bringing the child to share in the inherited resources of the race, and to use his own powers for social ends.

I believe that education, therefore, is a process of living and not a preparation for future living.

I believe that the school must represent present life— life as real and vital to the child as that which he carries on in the home, in the neighborhood, or on the playground.

I believe that education which does not occur through forms of life, forms that are worth living for their own sake, is always a poor substitute for the genuine reality and tends to cramp and to deaden.

I believe that the school, as an institution, should simplify existing social life; should reduce it, as it were, to an embryonic form. Existing life is so complex that the child cannot be brought into contact with it without either confusion or distraction; he is either overwhelmed by multiplicity of activities which are going on, so that he loses his own power of orderly reaction, or he is so stimulated by these various activities that his powers are prematurely called into play and he becomes either unduly specialized or else disintegrated.

I believe that, as such simplified social life, the school life should grow gradually out of the home life; that it should take up and continue the activities with which the child is already familiar in the home.

I believe that it should exhibit these activities to the child, and reproduce them in such ways that the child will gradually learn the meaning of them, and be capable of playing his own part in relation to them.

I believe that this is a psychological necessity, because it is the only way of securing continuity in the child's growth, the only way of giving a background of past experience to the new ideas given in school.

I believe it is also a social necessity because the home is the form of social life in which the child has been nurtured and in connection with which he has had his moral training. It is the business of the school to deepen and extend his sense of the values bound up in his home life.

I believe that much of present education fails because it neglects this fundamental principle of the school as a form of community life. It conceives the school as a place where certain information is to be given, where certain lessons are to be learned, or where certain habits are to be formed. The value of these is conceived as lying largely in the remote future; the child must do these things for the sake of something else he is to do; they are mere preparation. As a result they do not become a part of the life experience of the child and so are not truly educative.

I believe that moral education centres about this conception of the school as a mode of social life, that the best and deepest moral training is precisely that which one gets through having to enter into proper relations with others in a unity of work and thought. The present educational systems, so far as they destroy or neglect this unity, render it difficult or impossible to get any genuine, regular moral training.

I believe that the child should be stimulated and controlled in his work through the life of the community.

I believe that under existing conditions far too much of the stimulus and control proceeds from the teacher, because of neglect of the idea of the school as a form of social life.

I believe that the teacher's place and work in the school is to be interpreted from this same basis. The teacher is not in the school to impose certain ideas or to form certain habits in the child, but is there as a member of the community to select the influences which shall affect the child and to assist him in properly responding to these influences.

I believe that the discipline of the school should proceed from the life of the school as a whole and not directly from the teacher.

I believe that the teacher's business is simply to determine on the basis of larger experience and riper wisdom, how the discipline of life shall come to the child.

I believe that all questions of the grading of the child and his promotion should be determined by reference to the same standard. Examinations are of use only so far as they test the child's fitness for social life and reveal the place in which he can be of the most service and where he can receive the most help.

## *Article Three. The Subject-Matter of Education*

I believe that the social life of the child is the basis of concentration, or correlation, in all his training or growth. The social life gives the unconscious unity and the background of all his efforts and of all his attainments.

I believe that the subject-matter of the school curriculum should mark a gradual differentiation out of the primitive unconscious unity of social life.

I believe that we violate the child's nature and render difficult the best ethical results, by introducing the child too abruptly to a number of special studies, of reading, writing, geography, etc., out of relation to this social life.

I believe, therefore, that the true centre of correlation of the school subjects is not science, nor literature, nor history, nor geography, but the child's own social activities.

I believe that education cannot be unified in the study of science, or so-called nature study, because apart from human activity, nature itself is not a unity; nature in itself is a number of diverse objects in space and time, and to attempt to make it the centre of work by itself, is to introduce a principle of radiation rather than one of concentration.

I believe that literature is the reflex expression and interpretation of social experience; that hence it must follow upon and not precede such experience. It, therefore, cannot be made the basis, although it may be made the summary of unification.

I believe once more that history is of educative value in so far as it presents phases of social life and growth. It must be controlled by reference to social life. When taken simply as history it is thrown into the distant past and becomes dead and inert. Taken as the record of man's social life and progress it becomes full of meaning. I believe, however, that it cannot be so taken excepting as the child is also introduced directly into social life.

I believe accordingly that the primary basis of education is in the child's powers at work along the same general constructive lines as those which have brought civilization into being.

I believe that the only way to make the child conscious of his social heritage is to enable him to perform those fundamental types of activity which make civilization what it is.

I believe, therefore, in the so-called expressive or constructive activities as the centre of correlation.

I believe that this gives the standard for the place of cooking, sewing, manual training, etc., in the school.

I believe that they are not special studies which are to be introduced over and above a lot of others in the way of relaxation or relief, or as additional accomplishments. I believe rather that they represent, as types, fundamental forms of social activity; and that it is possible and desirable that the child's introduction into the more formal subjects of the curriculum be through the medium of these activities.

I believe that the study of science is educational in so far as it brings out the materials and processes which make social life what it is.

I believe that one of the greatest difficulties in the present teaching of science is that the material is presented in purely objective form, or is treated as a new peculiar kind of experience which the child can add to that which he has already had. In reality, science is of value because it gives the ability to interpret and control the experience already had. It should be introduced, not as so much new subject-matter, but as showing the factors already involved in previous experience and as furnishing tools by which that experience can be more easily and effectively regulated.

I believe that at present we lose much of the value of literature and language studies because of our elimination of the social element. Language is almost always treated in the books of pedagogy simply as the expression of thought. It is true that language is a logical instrument, but it is fundamentally and primarily a social instrument. Language is the device for communication; it is the tool through which one individual comes to share the ideas and feelings of others. When treated simply as a way of getting individual information, or as a means of showing off what one has learned, it loses its social motive and end.

I believe that there is, therefore, no succession of studies in the ideal school curriculum. If education is life, all life has, from the outset, a scientific aspect; an aspect of art and culture and an aspect of communication. It cannot, therefore, be true that the proper studies for one grade are mere reading and writing, and that at a later grade, reading, or literature, or science, may be introduced. The progress is not in the succession of studies but in the development of new attitudes towards, and new interests in, experience.

I believe finally, that education must be conceived as a continuing reconstruction of experience; that the process and the goal of education are one and the same thing.

I believe that to set up any end outside of education, as furnishing its goal and standard, is to deprive the educational process of much of its meaning and tends to make us rely upon false and external stimuli in dealing with the child.

## Article Four. The Nature of Method

I believe that the question of method is ultimately reducible to the question of the order of development of the child's powers and interests. The law for presenting and treating material is the law implicit within the child's own nature. Because this is so I believe the following statements are of supreme importance as determining the spirit in which education is carried on:

1. I believe that the active side precedes the passive in the development of the child nature; that expression comes before conscious impression; that the muscular development precedes the sensory; that movements come before conscious sensations; I believe that consciousness is essentially motor or impulsive; that conscious states tend to project themselves in action.

I believe that the neglect of this principle is the cause of a large part of the waste of time and strength in school work. The child is thrown into a passive, receptive or absorbing attitude. The conditions are such that he is not permitted to follow the law of his nature; the result is friction and waste.

I believe that ideas (intellectual and rational processes) also result from action and devolve for the sake of the better control of action. What we term reason is primarily the law of orderly or effective action. To attempt to develop the reasoning powers, the powers of judgment, without reference to the selection and arrangement of means in action, is the fundamental fallacy in our present methods of dealing with this matter. As a result we present the child with arbitrary symbols. Symbols are a necessity in mental development, but they have their place as tools for economizing effort; presented by themselves they are a mass of meaningless and arbitrary ideas imposed from without.

2. I believe that the image is the great instrument of instruction. What a child gets out of any subject presented to him is simply the images which he himself forms with regard to it.

I believe that if nine-tenths of the energy at present directed towards making the child learn certain things, were spent in seeing to it that the child was forming proper images, the work of instruction would be indefinitely facilitated.

I believe that much of the time and attention now given to the preparation and presentation of lessons might be more wisely and profitably expended in training the child's power of imagery and in seeing to it that he was continually forming definite, vivid, and growing images of the various subjects with which he comes in contact in his experience.

3. I believe that interests are the signs and symptoms of growing power. I believe that they represent dawning capacities. Accordingly the constant and careful observation of interests is of the utmost importance for the educator.

I believe that these interests are to be observed as showing the state of development which the child has reached.

I believe that they prophesy the stage upon which he is about to enter.

I believe that only through the continual and sympathetic observation of childhood's interests can the adult enter into the child's life and see what it is ready for, and upon what material it could work most readily and fruitfully.

I believe that these interests are neither to be humored nor repressed. To repress interest is to substitute the adult for the child, and so to weaken intellectual curiosity and alertness, to suppress initiative, and to deaden interest. To humor the interests is to substitute the transient for the permanent. The interest is always the sign of some power below; the important thing is to discover this power. To humor the interest is to fail to penetrate below the surface and its sure result is to substitute caprice and whim for genuine interest.

4. I believe that the emotions are the reflex of actions.

I believe that to endeavor to stimulate or arouse the emotions apart from their corresponding activities, is to introduce an unhealthy and morbid state of mind.

I believe that if we can only secure right habits of action and thought, with reference to the good, the true, and the beautiful, the emotions will for the most part take care of themselves.

I believe that next to deadness and dullness, formalism and routine, our education is threatened with no greater evil than sentimentalism.

I believe that this sentimentalism is the necessary result of the attempt to divorce feeling from action.

## *Article Five.  The School and Social Progress*

I believe that education is the fundamental method of social progress and reform.

I believe that all reforms which rest simply upon the enactment of law, or the threatening of certain penalties, or upon changes in mechanical or outward arrangements, are transitory and futile.

I believe that education is a regulation of the process of coming to share in the social consciousness; and that the adjustment of individual activity on the basis of this social consciousness is the only sure method of social reconstruction.

I believe that this conception has due regard for both the individualistic and socialistic ideals. It is duly individual because it recognizes the formation of a certain character as the only genuine basis of right living. It is socialistic because it recognizes that this right character is not to be formed by merely individual precept, example, or exhortation, but rather by the influence of a certain form of institutional or community life upon the individual, and that the social organism through the school, as its organ, may determine ethical results.

I believe that in the ideal school we have the reconciliation of the individualistic and the institutional ideals.

I believe that the community's duty to education is, therefore, its paramount moral duty. By law and punishment, by social agitation and discussion, society can regulate and form itself in a more or less haphazard and chance way. But through education society can formulate its own purposes, can organize its own means and resources, and thus shape itself with definiteness and economy in the direction in which it wishes to move.

I believe that when society once recognizes the possibilities in this direction, and the obligations which these possibilities impose, it is impossible to conceive of the resources of time, attention, and money which will be put at the disposal of the educator.

I believe it is the business of every one interested in education to insist upon the school as the primary and most effective interest of social progress and reform in order that society may be awakened to realize what the school stands for, and aroused to the necessity of endowing the educator with sufficient equipment properly to perform his task.

I believe that education thus conceived marks the most perfect and intimate union of science and art conceivable in human experience.

I believe that the art of thus giving shape to human powers and adapting them to social service, is the supreme art; one calling into its service the best of artists; that no insight, sympathy, tact, executive power is too great for such service.

I believe that with the growth of psychological science, giving added insight into individual structure and laws of growth; and with growth of social science, adding to our knowledge of the right organization of individuals, all scientific resources can be utilized for the purposes of education.

I believe that when science and art thus join hands the most commanding motive for human action will be reached; the most genuine springs of human conduct aroused and the best service that human nature is capable of guaranteed.

I believe, finally, that the teacher is engaged, not simply in the training of individuals, but in the formation of the proper social life.

I believe that every teacher should realize the dignity of his calling; that he is a social servant set apart for the maintenance of proper social order and the securing of the right social growth.

I believe that in this way the teacher always is the prophet of the true God and the usherer in of the true kingdom of God.

# The Reflex Arc Concept in Psychology

That the greater demand for a unifying principle and controlling working hypothesis in psychology should come at just the time when all generalizations and classifications are most questioned and questionable is natural enough. It is the very cumulation of discrete facts creating the demand for unification that also breaks down previous lines of classification. The material is too great in mass and too varied in style to fit into existing pigeon-holes, and the cabinets of science break of their own dead weight. The idea of the reflex arc has upon the whole come nearer to meeting this demand for a general working hypothesis than any other single concept. It being admitted that the sensori-motor apparatus represents both the unit of nerve structure and the type of nerve function, the image of this relationship passed over into psychology, and became an organizing principle to hold together the multiplicity of fact.

In criticizing this conception it is not intended to make a plea for the principles of explanation and classification which the reflex arc idea has replaced; but, on the contrary, to urge that they are not sufficiently displaced, and that in the idea of the sensori-motor circuit, conceptions of the nature of sensation and of action derived from the nominally displaced psychology are still in control.

The older dualism between sensation and idea is repeated in the current dualism of peripheral and central structures and functions; the older dualism of body and soul finds a distinct echo in the current dualism of stimulus and response. Instead of interpreting the character of sensation,

[*First published in* Psychological Review, III (*July 1896*), 357–70. *See A Note on the Texts for publishing history.*]

idea and action from their place and function in the sensori-
motor circuit, we still incline to interpret the latter from our
preconceived and preformulated ideas of rigid distinctions
between sensations, thoughts and acts. The sensory stimulus
is one thing, the central activity, standing for the idea, is
another thing, and the motor discharge, standing for the
act proper, is a third. As a result, the reflex arc is not a comprehensive, or organic unity, but a patchwork of disjointed
parts, a mechanical conjunction of unallied processes. What
is needed is that the principle underlying the idea of the reflex arc as the fundamental psychical unity shall react into
and determine the values of its constitutive factors. More
specifically, what is wanted is that sensory stimulus, central
connections and motor responses shall be viewed, not as
separate and complete entities in themselves, but as divisions
of labor, functioning factors, within the single concrete
whole, now designated the reflex arc.

What is the reality so designated? What shall we term
that which is not sensation-followed-by-idea-followed-by-
movement, but which is primary; which is, as it were, the
psychical organism of which sensation, idea and movement
are the chief organs? Stated on the physiological side, this
reality may most conveniently be termed co-ordination. This
is the essence of the facts held together by and subsumed
under the reflex arc concept. Let us take, for our example,
the familiar child-candle instance (James, *Psychology*, I,
25). The ordinary interpretation would say the sensation of
light is a stimulus to the grasping as a response, the burn
resulting is a stimulus to withdrawing the hand as response
and so on. There is, of course, no doubt that is a rough practical way of representing the process. But when we ask for
its psychological adequacy, the case is quite different. Upon
analysis, we find that we begin not with a sensory stimulus,
but with a sensori-motor co-ordination, the optical-ocular,
and that in a certain sense it is the movement which is primary, and the sensation which is secondary, the movement
of body, head and eye muscles determining the quality of
what is experienced. In other words, the real beginning is
with the act of seeing; it is looking, and not a sensation of
light. The sensory quale gives the value of the act, just as

the movement furnishes its mechanism and control, but both sensation and movement lie inside, not outside the act.

Now if this act, the seeing, stimulates another act, the reaching, it is because both of these acts fall within a larger co-ordination; because seeing and grasping have been so often bound together to reinforce each other, to help each other out, that each may be considered practically a subordinate member of a bigger co-ordination. More specifically, the ability of the hand to do its work will depend, either directly or indirectly, upon its control, as well as its stimulation, by the act of vision. If the sight did not inhibit as well as excite the reaching, the latter would be purely indeterminate, it would be for anything or nothing, not for the particular object seen. The reaching, in turn, must both stimulate and control the seeing. The eye must be kept upon the candle if the arm is to do its work; let it wander and the arm takes up another task. In other words, we now have an enlarged and transformed co-ordination; the act is seeing no less than before, but it is now seeing-for-reaching purposes. There is still a sensori-motor circuit, one with more content or value, not a substitution of a motor response for a sensory stimulus.[1]

Now take the affair at its next stage, that in which the child gets burned. It is hardly necessary to point out again that this is also a sensori-motor co-ordination and not a mere sensation. It is worth while, however, to note especially the fact that it is simply the completion, or fulfillment, of the previous eye-arm-hand co-ordination and not an entirely new occurrence. Only because the heat-pain quale enters into the same circuit of experience with the optical-ocular and muscular quales, does the child learn from the experience and get the ability to avoid the experience in the future.

More technically stated, the so-called response is not merely *to* the stimulus; it is *into* it. The burn is the original seeing, the original optical-ocular experience enlarged and transformed in its value. It is no longer mere seeing; it is seeing-of-a-light-that-means-pain-when-contact-occurs. The

---

1    See *The Psychological Review* for May, 1896, p. 253, for an excellent statement and illustration, by Messrs. Angell and Moore, of this mutuality of stimulation.

ordinary reflex arc theory proceeds upon the more or less tacit assumption that the outcome of the response is a totally new experience; that it is, say, the substitution of a burn sensation for a light sensation through the intervention of motion. The fact is that the sole meaning of the intervening movement is to maintain, reinforce or transform (as the case may be) the original quale; that we do not have the replacing of one sort of experience by another, but the development (or as it seems convenient to term it) the mediation of an experience. The seeing, in a word, remains to control the reaching, and is, in turn, interpreted by the burning.[2]

The discussion up to this point may be summarized by saying that the reflex arc idea, as commonly employed, is defective in that it assumes sensory stimulus and motor response as distinct psychical existences, while in reality they are always inside a co-ordination and have their significance purely from the part played in maintaining or reconstituting the co-ordination; and (secondly) in assuming that the quale of experience which precedes the "motor" phase and that which succeeds it are two different states, instead of the last being always the first reconstituted, the motor phase coming in only for the sake of such mediation. The result is that the reflex arc idea leaves us with a disjointed psychology, whether viewed from the standpoint of development in the individual or in the race, or from that of the analysis of the mature consciousness. As to the former, in its failure to see that the arc of which it talks is virtually a circuit, a continual reconstitution, it breaks continuity and leaves us nothing but a series of jerks, the origin of each jerk to be sought outside the process of experience itself, in either an external pressure of "environment," or else in an unaccountable spontaneous variation from within the "soul" or the "organism."[3] As to the latter, failing to see the unity of activity,

---

[2]    See, for a further statement of mediation, my *Syllabus of Ethics*, p. 15 [*The Early Works of John Dewey*, IV, 237].

[3]    It is not too much to say that the whole controversy in biology regarding the source of variation, represented by Weismann and Spencer respectively, arises from beginning with stimulus or response instead of with the co-ordination with reference to which stimulus and response are functional divisions of labor. The same may be said, on the psychological side, of the controversy between the Wundtian "apperceptionists"

no matter how much it may prate of unity, it still leaves us with sensation or peripheral stimulus; idea, or central process (the equivalent of attention); and motor response, or act, as three disconnected existences, having to be somehow adjusted to each other, whether through the intervention of an extra-experimental soul, or by mechanical push and pull.

Before proceeding to a consideration of the general meaning for psychology of the summary, it may be well to give another descriptive analysis, as the value of the statement depends entirely upon the universality of its range of application. For such an instance we may conveniently take Baldwin's analysis of the reactive consciousness. In this there are, he says (*Feeling and Will*, p. 60), "three elements corresponding to the three elements of the nervous arc. First, the receiving consciousness, the stimulus—say a loud, unexpected sound; second, the attention involuntarily drawn, the registering element; and, third, the muscular reaction following upon the sound—say flight from fancied danger." Now, in the first place, such an analysis is incomplete; it ignores the status prior to hearing the sound. Of course, if this status is irrelevant to what happens afterwards, such ignoring is quite legitimate. But is it irrelevant either to the quantity or the quality of the stimulus?

If one is reading a book, if one is hunting, if one is watching in a dark place on a lonely night, if one is performing a chemical experiment, in each case, the noise has a very different psychical value; it is a different experience. In any case, what precedes the "stimulus" is a whole act, a sensori-motor co-ordination. What is more to the point, the "stimulus" emerges out of this co-ordination; it is born from it as its matrix; it represents as it were an escape from it. I might here fall back upon authority, and refer to the widely accepted sensation continuum theory, according to which the sound cannot be absolutely *ex abrupto* from the outside, but is simply a shifting of focus of emphasis, a redistribution of tensions within the former act; and declare that unless the sound activity had been present to some extent in the prior co-ordination, it would be impossible for it now to come to prominence in consciousness. And such a reference would be

and their opponents. Each has a *disjectum membrum* of the same organic whole, whichever is selected being an arbitrary matter of personal taste.

only an amplification of what has already been said concerning the way in which the prior activity influences the value of the sound sensation. Or, we might point to cases of hypnotism, mono-ideism and absent-mindedness, like that of Archimedes, as evidences that if the previous co-ordination is such as rigidly to lock the door, the auditory disturbance will knock in vain for admission to consciousness. Or, to speak more truly in the metaphor, the auditory activity must already have one foot over the threshold, if it is ever to gain admittance.

But it will be more satisfactory, probably, to refer to the biological side of the case, and point out that as the ear activity has been evolved on account of the advantage gained by the whole organism, it must stand in the strictest histological and physiological connection with the eye, or hand, or leg, or whatever other organ has been the overt centre of action. It is absolutely impossible to think of the eye centre as monopolizing consciousness and the ear apparatus as wholly quiescent. What happens is a certain relative prominence and subsidence as between the various organs which maintain the organic equilibrium.

Furthermore, the sound is not a mere stimulus, or mere sensation; it again is an act, that of hearing. The muscular response is involved in this as well as sensory stimulus; that is, there is a certain definite set of the motor apparatus involved in hearing just as much as there is in subsequent running away. The movement and posture of the head, the tension of the ear muscles, are required for the "reception" of the sound. It is just as true to say that the sensation of sound arises from a motor response as that the running away is a response to the sound. This may be brought out by reference to the fact that Professor Baldwin, in the passage quoted, has inverted the real order as between his first and second elements. We do not have first a sound and then activity of attention, unless sound is taken as mere nervous shock or physical event, not as conscious value. The conscious sensation of sound depends upon the motor response having already taken place; or, in terms of the previous statement (if stimulus is used as a conscious fact, and not as a mere physical event) it is the motor response or attention which constitutes that, which finally becomes the stimulus to another act. Once more, the final "element," the running away, is not merely motor, but is sensori-motor, having its sensory value and its muscular mechanism. It is also a co-ordination. And, finally, this sensori-motor co-ordination is not a new act, supervening upon what preceded. Just as the "response" is necessary to constitute the stimulus, to determine it as sound and as this kind of sound, of wild beast or robber, so the sound experience must persist as a value in the running, to keep it up, to control it. The motor reaction involved in the running is, once more, into, not merely to, the sound. It occurs to change the sound, to get rid of it. The resulting quale, whatever it may be, has its meaning wholly determined by reference to the hearing of the sound. It is that experience mediated.[4] What we have is a circuit, not an arc or broken segment of a circle. This circuit is more truly termed organic than reflex, because the motor response determines the stimulus, just as truly as sensory stimulus determines movement. Indeed, the movement is only for the sake of determining the stimulus, of fixing what kind of a stimulus it is, of interpreting it.

I hope it will not appear that I am introducing needless refinements and distinctions into what, it may be urged, is after all an undoubted fact, that movement as response follows sensation as stimulus. It is not a question of making the account of the process more complicated, though it is always wise to beware of that false simplicity which is reached by leaving out of account a large part of the problem. It is a question of finding out what stimulus or sensation, what movement and response mean; a question of seeing that they mean distinctions of flexible function only, not of fixed existence; that one and the same occurrence plays either or both parts, according to the shift of interest; and that because of this functional distinction and relationship, the supposed

---

[4]    In other words, every reaction is of the same type as that which Professor Baldwin ascribes to imitation alone, viz., circular. Imitation is simply that particular form of the circuit in which the "response" lends itself to comparatively unchanged maintenance of the prior experience. I say comparatively unchanged, for as far as this maintenance means additional control over the experience, it is being psychically changed, becoming more distinct. It is safe to suppose, moreover, that the "repetition" is kept up only so long as this growth or mediation goes on. There is the new-in-the-old, if it is only the new sense of power.

problem of the adjustment of one to the other, whether by superior force in the stimulus or an agency *ad hoc* in the centre or the soul, is a purely self-created problem.

We may see the disjointed character of the present theory, by calling to mind that it is impossible to apply the phrase "sensori-motor" to the occurrence as a simple phrase of description; it has validity only as a term of interpretation, only, that is, as defining various functions exercised. In terms of description, the whole process may be sensory or it may be motor, but it cannot be sensori-motor. The "stimulus," the excitation of the nerve ending and of the sensory nerve, the central change, are just as much, or just as little, motion as the events taking place in the motor nerve and the muscles. It is one uninterrupted, continuous redistribution of mass in motion. And there is nothing in the process, from the standpoint of description, which entitles us to call this reflex. It is redistribution pure and simple; as much so as the burning of a log, or the falling of a house or the movement of the wind. In the physical process, as physical, there is nothing which can be set off as stimulus, nothing which reacts, nothing which is response. There is just a change in the system of tensions.

The same sort of thing is true when we describe the process purely from the psychical side. It is now all sensation, all sensory quale; the motion, as psychically described, is just as much sensation as is sound or light or burn. Take the withdrawing of the hand from the candle flame as example. What we have is a certain visual-heat-pain-muscular-quale, transformed into another visual-touch-muscular-quale—the flame now being visible only at a distance, or not at all, the touch sensation being altered, etc. If we symbolize the original visual quale by v, the temperature by h, the accompanying muscular sensation by m, the whole experience may be stated as vhm-vh*m-vhm'*; *m* being the quale of withdrawing, *m'* the sense of the status after the withdrawal. The motion is not a certain kind of existence; it is a sort of sensory experience interpreted, just as is candle flame, or burn from candle flame. All are on a par.

But, in spite of all this, it will be urged, there is a distinction between stimulus and response, between sensation and motion. Precisely; but we ought now to be in a condition to ask of what nature is the distinction, instead of taking it for granted as a distinction somehow lying in the existence of the facts themselves. We ought to be able to see that the ordinary conception of the reflex arc theory, instead of being a case of plain science, is a survival of the metaphysical dualism, first formulated by Plato, according to which the sensation is an ambiguous dweller on the border land of soul and body, the idea (or central process) is purely psychical, and the act (or movement) purely physical. Thus the reflex arc formulation is neither physical (or physiological) nor psychological; it is a mixed materialistic-spiritualistic assumption.

If the previous descriptive analysis has made obvious the need of a reconsideration of the reflex arc idea, of the nest of difficulties and assumptions in the apparently simple statement, it is now time to undertake an explanatory analysis. The fact is that stimulus and response are not distinctions of existence, but teleological distinctions, that is, distinctions of function, or part played, with reference to reaching or maintaining an end. With respect to this teleological process, two stages should be discriminated, as their confusion is one cause of the confusion attending the whole matter. In one case, the relation represents an organization of means with reference to a comprehensive end. It represents an accomplished adaptation. Such is the case in all well developed instincts, as when we say that the contact of eggs is a stimulus to the hen to set; or the sight of corn a stimulus to peck; such also is the case with all thoroughly formed habits, as when the contact with the floor stimulates walking. In these instances there is no question of consciousness of stimulus *as* stimulus, of response *as* response. There is simply a continuously ordered sequence of acts, all adapted in themselves and in the order of their sequence, to reach a certain objective end, the reproduction of the species, the preservation of life, locomotion to a certain place. The end has got thoroughly organized into the means. In calling one stimulus, another response we mean nothing more than that such an orderly sequence of acts is taking place. The same sort of statement might be made equally well with reference to the succession of changes in a plant, so far as these are considered with reference to their adaptation to, say, producing seed. It is equally applicable to the series of events in the circulation of the blood, or the sequence of acts occurring in a self-binding reaper.[5]

Regarding such cases of organization viewed as already attained, we may say, positively, that it is only the assumed common reference to an inclusive end which marks each member off as stimulus and response, that apart from such reference we have only antecedent and consequent;[6] in other words, the distinction is one of interpretation. Negatively, it must be pointed out that it is not legitimate to carry over, without change, exactly the same order of considerations to cases where it is a question of *conscious* stimulation and response. We may, in the above case, regard, if we please, stimulus and response each as an entire act, having an individuality of its own, subject even here to the qualification that individuality means not an entirely independent whole, but a division of labor as regards maintaining or reaching an end. But in any case, it is an act, a sensori-motor co-ordination, which stimulates the response, itself in turn sensori-motor, not a sensation which stimulates a movement. Hence the illegitimacy of identifying, as is so often done, such cases of organized instincts or habits with the so-called reflex arc, or of transferring, without modification, considerations valid of this serial co-ordination of acts to the sensation-movement case.

The fallacy that arises when this is done is virtually the psychological or historical fallacy. A set of considerations which hold good only because of a completed process, is read into the content of the process which conditions this completed result. A state of things characterizing an outcome is regarded as a true description of the events which led up to this outcome; when, as a matter of fact, if this

---

[5]    To avoid misapprehension, I would say that I am not raising the question as to how far this teleology is real in any one of these cases; real or unreal, my point holds equally well. It is only when we regard the sequence of acts *as if* they were adapted to reach some end that it occurs to us to speak of one as stimulus and the other as response. Otherwise, we look at them as a *mere* series.

[6]    Whether, even in such a determination, there is still not a reference of a more latent kind to an end is, of course, left open.

outcome had already been in existence, there would have been no necessity for the process. Or, to make the application to the case in hand, considerations valid of an attained organization or co-ordination, the orderly sequence of minor acts in a comprehensive co-ordination, are used to describe a process, viz., the distinction of mere sensation as stimulus and of mere movement as response, which takes place only because such an attained organization is no longer at hand, but is in process of constitution. Neither mere sensation, nor mere movement, can ever be either stimulus or response; only an act can be that; the *sensation* as stimulus means the lack of and search for such an objective stimulus, or orderly placing of an act; just as mere movement as response means the lack of and search for the right act to complete a given co-ordination.

A recurrence to our example will make these formulæ clearer. As long as the seeing is an unbroken act, which is as experienced no more mere sensation than it is mere motion (though the onlooker or psychological observer can interpret it into sensation and movement), it is in no sense the sensation which stimulates the reaching; we have, as already sufficiently indicated, only the serial steps in a co-ordination of *acts*. But now take a child who, upon reaching for bright light (that is, exercising the seeing-reaching co-ordination) has sometimes had a delightful exercise, sometimes found something good to eat and sometimes burned himself. *Now the response is not only uncertain, but the stimulus is equally uncertain; one is uncertain only in so far as the other is.* The real problem may be equally well stated as either to discover the right stimulus, to constitute the stimulus, or to discover, to constitute, the response. The question of whether to reach or to abstain from reaching is the question what sort of a bright light have we here? Is it the one which means playing with one's hands, eating milk, or burning one's fingers? The stimulus must be constituted for the response to occur. Now it is at precisely this juncture and because of it that the distinction of sensation as stimulus and motion as response arises.

The sensation or conscious stimulus is not a thing or existence by itself; it is that phase of a co-ordination requiring attention because, by reason of the conflict within the co-ordination, it is uncertain how to complete it. It is doubt as to the next act, whether to reach or no, which gives the motive to examining the act. The end to follow is, in this sense, the stimulus. It furnishes the motivation to attend to what has just taken place; to define it more carefully. From this point of view the discovery of the stimulus is the "response" to possible movement as "stimulus." We must have an anticipatory sensation, an image, of the movements that may occur, together with their respective values, before attention will go to the seeing to break it up as a sensation of light, and of light of this particular kind. It is the initiated activities of reaching, which, inhibited by the conflict in the co-ordination, turn round, as it were, upon the seeing, and hold it from passing over into further act until its quality is · determined. Just here the act as objective stimulus becomes transformed into sensation as possible, as conscious, stimulus. Just here also, motion as conscious response emerges.

In other words, sensation as stimulus does not mean any particular psychical *existence*. It means simply a function, and will have its value shift according to the special work requiring to be done. At one moment the various activities of reaching and withdrawing will be the sensation, because they are that phase of activity which sets the problem, or creates the demand for, the next act. At the next moment the previous act of seeing will furnish the sensation, being, in turn, that phase of activity which sets the pace upon which depends further action. Generalized, sensation as stimulus is always that phase of activity requiring to be defined in order that a co-ordination may be completed. What the sensation will be in particular at a given time, therefore, will depend entirely upon the way in which an activity is being used. It has no fixed quality of its own. The search for the stimulus is the search for exact conditions of action; that is, for the state of things which decides how a beginning co-ordination should be completed.

Similarly, motion, as response, has only a functional value. It is whatever will serve to complete the disintegrating co-ordination. Just as the discovery of the sensation marks the establishing of the problem, so the constitution of the response marks the solution of this problem. At one time, fixing attention, holding the eye fixed, upon the seeing and thus bringing out a certain quale of light is the response, because that is the particular act called for just then; at another time, the movement of the arm away from the light is the response. There is nothing in itself which may be labelled response. That one certain set of sensory quales should be marked off by themselves as "motion" and put in antithesis to such sensory quales as those of color, sound and contact, as legitimate claimants to the title of sensation, is wholly inexplicable unless we keep the difference of function in view. It is the eye and ear sensations which fix for us the problem; which report to us the conditions which have to be met if the co-ordination is to be successfully completed; and just the moment we need to know about our movements to get an adequate report, just that moment, motion miraculously (from the ordinary standpoint) ceases to be motion and becomes "muscular sensation." On the other hand, take the change in values of experience, the transformation of sensory quales. Whether this change will or will not be interpreted as movement, whether or not any consciousness of movement will arise, will depend upon whether this change is satisfactory, whether or not it is regarded as a harmonious development of a co-ordination, or whether the change is regarded as simply a means in solving a problem, an instrument in reaching a more satisfactory co-ordination. So long as our experience runs smoothly we are no more conscious of motion as motion than we are of this or that color or sound by itself.

To sum up: the distinction of sensation and movement as stimulus and response respectively is not a distinction which can be regarded as descriptive of anything which holds of psychical events or existences as such. The only events to which the terms stimulus and response can be descriptively applied are minor acts serving by their respective positions to the maintenance of some organized co-ordination. The conscious stimulus or sensation, and the conscious response or motion, have a special genesis or motivation, and a special end or function. The reflex arc theory, by neglecting, by abstracting from, this genesis and this function give us one disjointed part of a process as if it were the whole. It gives us literally an arc, instead of the circuit; and not giving us the circuit of which it is an arc, does not enable us to place, to centre, the arc. This arc, again, falls apart into two separate existences having to be either mechanically or externally adjusted to each other.

The circle is a co-ordination, some of whose members have come into conflict with each other. It is the temporary disintegration and need of reconstitution which occasions, which affords the genesis of, the conscious distinction into sensory stimulus on one side and motor response on the other. The stimulus is that phase of the forming co-ordination which represents the conditions which have to be met in bringing it to a successful issue; the response is that phase of one and the same forming co-ordination which gives the key to meeting these conditions, which serves as instrument in effecting the successful co-ordination. They are therefore strictly correlative and contemporaneous. The stimulus is something to be discovered; to be made out; if the activity affords its own adequate stimulation, there is no stimulus save in the objective sense already referred to. As soon as it is adequately determined, then and then only is the response also complete. To attain either, means that the co-ordination has completed itself. Moreover, it is the motor response which assists in discovering and constituting the stimulus. It is the holding of the movement at a certain stage which creates the sensation, which throws it into relief.

It is the co-ordination which unifies that which the reflex arc concept gives us only in disjointed fragments. It is the circuit within which fall distinctions of stimulus and response as functional phases of its own mediation or completion. The point of this story is in its application; but the application of it to the question of the nature of psychical evolution, to the distinction between sensational and rational consciousness, and the nature of judgment must be deferred to a more favorable opportunity.

SECOND SUPPLEMENT

TO THE

# HERBART YEARBOOK

FOR 1895

_____

## INTEREST AS RELATED TO WILL

BY

### DR. JOHN DEWEY

OF THE UNIVERSITY OF CHICAGO

_____

EDITED BY

### CHARLES A. McMURRY

SECRETARY OF THE SOCIETY

_____

REPRINTED 1899 BY THE SOCIETY

## Prefatory Note to Second Edition

IN THIS second edition considerable change has been made. In the first place, I have tried by excision and rewriting to state the underlying psychology in somewhat less abstract and formal fashion. In the second place, some portions, especially of Part III, were originally called out by the state of discussion when this article was first written. The only excuse for controversy is to make itself unnecessary, and I believe there is sufficient advance in mutual understanding to make possible considerable omission here. The space thus saved has been given to a fuller discussion of the more distinctly educational aspects. I would suggest to those specially interested in the educational side to read Parts I and IV first, and more thoroughly; Parts II and III afterward, and more casually.

Dr. Charles De Garmo has supplied this second edition with topical headings to bring out more distinctly the significant points under discussion.

# Interest in Relation to Training of the Will

## Introduction

There is much the same difficulty in isolating any educational topic for discussion that there is in the case of philosophy. The issues are so interdependent that any one of them can be selected only at the risk of ignoring important considerations, or else of begging the question by bringing in the very problem under discussion in the guise of some other subject. Yet limits of time and space require that some one field be entered and occupied by itself. Under such circumstances about all one can do is to pursue a method which shall at least call attention to the problems involved, and to indicate the main relations of the matters discussed to relevant topics. The difficulty is particularly great in the discussion of interest. Interest is in the closest relation to the emotional life, on one side; and, through its close relation, if not identity, with attention, to the intellectual life, on the other side. Any adequate explanation of it, therefore, would require the development of the complete psychology both of feeling and of knowledge, and of their relations to each other, and the discussion of their connection or lack of connection with volition.

Accordingly, I can only hope to bring out what seem to me to be the salient points, and if my results do not command agreement, help at least define the problem for further discussion.

[*First published as* Second Supplement *to the* First Yearbook of the National Herbart Society (*Bloomington, Ill.: Pantagraph,* 1896), *pp.* 209–46; *revised and reprinted* (*Chicago: University of Chicago Press,* 1899), *40 pp. See A Note on the Texts for publishing history.*]

While it would be sanguine to anticipate agreement upon any important educational doctrine, there is perhaps more hope of reaching a working consensus by beginning with the educational side. If we can lay down some general principle regarding the place and function of interest in the school, we shall have a more or less sure basis from which to proceed to the psychological analysis of interest. At all events, we shall have limited the field and fixed the boundaries within which the psychological discussion may proceed. After this we shall proceed to the discussion of some of the chief attitudes assumed toward the problem of interest in historic and current investigations. Finally, we may return with the results reached by this psychological and critical consideration to the educational matter with more definite emphasis upon the question of moral training.

I.

### Interest vs. Effort—an Educational Law-suit

At first sight the hope of gaining a working consensus regarding interest on the educational side seems futile. The first thing that strikes us is the profound contradiction in current educational ideas and standards regarding this matter of interest. On the one hand, we have the doctrine that interest is the keynote both of instruction and of moral training, that the essential problem of the teacher is to make the material presented so interesting that it shall command and retain attention. On the other hand, we have the assertion that the putting forth of effort from within is alone truly educative; that to rely upon the principle of interest is to distract the child intellectually and to weaken him morally.

In this educational law-suit of interest *versus* effort let us consider the respective briefs of plaintiff and defendant. In behalf of interest it is claimed that it is the sole guarantee of attention; that, if we can secure interest in a given set of facts or ideas, we may be perfectly sure that the pupil will direct his energies towards mastering them; that, if we can secure interest in a certain moral train or line of conduct, we are equally safe in assuming that the child's activities are responding in that direction; that, if we have not secured interest, we have no safeguard as to what will be done in any given case. As matter of fact, the doctrine of discipline has not succeeded. It is absurd to suppose that a child gets more intellectual or mental discipline when he goes at a matter unwillingly than when he goes at it with complete interest and out of the fullness of his heart. The theory of effort simply says that unwilling attention (doing something which is disagreeable and because it is disagreeable) should take precedence over spontaneous attention.

Practically the theory of effort amounts to nothing. When a child feels that his work is a task, it is only under compulsion that he gives himself to it. At the least let-up of external pressure we find his attention at once directed to what interests him. The child brought up on the basis of the theory of effort simply acquires marvelous skill in appearing to be occupied with an uninteresting subject, while the real heart and core of his energies are otherwise engaged. Indeed, the theory contradicts itself. It is psychologically impossible to call forth any activity without some interest. The theory of effort simply substitutes one interest for another. It substitutes the impure interest of fear of the teacher or hope of future reward for pure interest in the material presented. The type of character induced is that illustrated by Emerson at the beginning of his essay on "Compensation," where he holds up the current doctrine of compensation as virtually implying that, if you only sacrifice yourself enough now, you will be permitted to indulge yourself a great deal more in the future; or that if you are only good now (goodness consisting in attention to what is uninteresting) you will have, at some future time, a great many more pleasing interests—that is, may then be bad.

While the theory of effort is always holding up to us a strong, vigorous character as the outcome of its method of education, practically we do not get this character. We get either the narrow, bigoted man who is obstinate and irresponsible save in the line of his own preconceived aims and beliefs; or else we get a character dull, mechanical, unalert, because the vital juice of the principle of spontaneous interest has been squeezed out of it.

We may now hear the defendant's case. Life, says the other theory, is full of things not interesting, but which have to be faced none the less. Demands are continually made, situations have to be dealt with which present no features of interest. Unless the individual has had previous training in devoting himself to uninteresting work, unless habits have been formed of attending to matters simply because they must be attended to, irrespective of the personal satisfaction gotten out of them, character will either break down, or avoid the issue, when confronted with the more serious matters of life. Life is too serious to be degraded to a merely pleasant affair, or reduced to the continual satisfaction of personal interests. The concerns of future life, therefore, imperatively demand such continual exercise of effort in the performance of tasks as to form the habit of recognizing the real labors of life. Anything else eats out the fibre of character and reduces the person to a wishy washy, colorless being; or else to a state of moral dependence, with over-reliance upon others and with continual demand for amusement and distraction.

Apart from the question of the future, continually to appeal even in childhood days to the principle of interest is eternally to excite, that is, distract the child. Continuity of activity is destroyed. Everything is made play, amusement. This means over-stimulation; it means dissipation of energy. Will is never called into action at all. The reliance is upon external attractions and amusements. Everything is sugar-coated for the child, and he soon learns to turn from everything which is not artificially surrounded with diverting circumstances. The spoiled child who does only what he likes is the inevitable outcome of the theory of interest in education.

The theory is intellectually as well as morally harmful. Attention is never directed to the essential and important facts. It is directed simply to the wrappings of attraction with which the facts are surrounded. If a fact is repulsive or uninteresting, it has to be faced in its own naked character sooner or later. Putting a fringe of fictitious interest around it does not bring the child any nearer to it than he was at the outset. The fact that two and two make four is a naked fact which has to be mastered in and of itself. The child gets no greater hold upon the fact by having attached to it amusing stories of birds or dandelions than he would if the simple naked fact were presented to him. It is self-deception to suppose that the child is being interested in the numerical relation. His attention is going out to and taking in only the amusing images associated with this relation. The theory thus defeats its own end. It would be more direct and straightforward to recognize at the outset that certain facts have to be learned which have little or no interest, and that the only way to deal with these facts is through the power of effort, the internal power of putting forth activity wholly independent of any external inducement. Moreover, in this way the discipline, the habit of responding to serious matters, is formed which is necessary to equip the child for the life that lies ahead of him.

## The Verdict

I have attempted to set forth the respective claims of each side as we find them, not only in current discussions but in the old controversy, as old as Plato and Aristotle. A little reflection will convince one that the strong point in each argument is not so much what it says in its own behalf as in its attacks on the weak places of the opposite theory. Each theory is strong in its negations rather than in its position. It is a common, though somewhat surprising, fact that there is generally a common principle unconsciously assumed at the basis of two theories which to all outward appearances are the extreme opposites of each other. Such a common principle is presupposed by the theories of effort and interest in the one-sided forms in which they have already been stated.

This identical assumption is the externality of the object or idea to be mastered, the end to be reached, the act to be performed, to the self. It is because the object or end is assumed to be outside self that it has to be *made* interesting, that it has to be surrounded with artificial stimuli and with fictitious inducements to attention. It is equally because the object lies outside the sphere of self that the sheer power of "will," the putting forth of effort without interest, has to be appealed to. The genuine principle of interest is the principle of the recognized identity of the fact or proposed line of action with the self; that it lies in the direction of the agent's own growth, and is, therefore, imperiously demanded, if the agent is to be himself. Let this condition of identification once be secured, and we neither have to appeal to sheer strength of will, nor do we have to occupy ourselves with making things interesting to the child.

## Divided Attention

The theory of effort, as already stated, means a virtual division of attention and the corresponding disintegration of character, intellectually and morally. The great fallacy of the so-called effort theory is that it identifies the exercise and training of will with certain external activities and certain external results. It is supposed that because a child is occupied at some outward task and because he succeeds in exhibiting the required product, he is really putting forth will, and that definite intellectual and moral habits are in process of formation. But as a matter of fact, the moral exercise of the will is not found in the external assumption of any posture, and the formation of moral habit cannot be identified with the ability to show up results at the demand of another. The exercise of the will is manifest in the direction of attention, and depends upon the spirit, the motive, the disposition in which work is carried on.

A child may be externally entirely occupied with mastering the multiplication table, and be able to reproduce that table when asked to do so by his teacher. The teacher may congratulate himself that the child has been so exercising his will power as to be forming right intellectual and moral habits. Not so, unless moral habit be identified with this ability to show certain results when required. The question of moral training has not been touched until we know what the child has been internally occupied with, what the predominating direction of his attention, his feelings, his disposition has been while engaged upon this task. If the task has appealed to him merely as a task, it is as certain, psychologically, as the law of action and reaction is, physically, that the child is simply engaged in acquiring the habit of divided attention; that he is getting the ability to direct eye and ear, lips and mouth, to what is present before him in such a way as to impress those things upon his memory, while at the same time getting his mental imagery free to work upon matters of real interest to him.

No account of the actual moral training secured is adequate unless it recognizes this division of attention into which the child is being educated, and faces the question of what the moral worth of such a division may be. External mechanical attention to a task conceived as a task is the inevitable correlate of an internal random mind-wandering along the lines of the pleasurable.

The spontaneous power of the child, his demand for realization of his own impulses, cannot by any possibility be suppressed. If the external conditions are such that the child cannot put his spontaneous activity into the work to be done, if he finds that he cannot express himself in that, he learns in a most miraculous way the exact amount of attention that has to be given to this external material to satisfy the requirements of the teacher, while saving up the rest of his mental powers for following out lines of imagery that appeal to him. I do not say that there is absolutely no moral training involved in forming these habits of external attention, but I do say that there is a question of moral import involved in the formation of the habits of internal inattention.

While we are congratulating ourselves upon the well-disciplined habits which the pupil is acquiring, judged by his ability to reproduce a lesson when called upon, we forget to commiserate ourselves because the deeper intellectual and moral nature of the child has secured absolutely no discipline at all, but has been left to follow its own caprices, the disordered suggestions of the moment, or of past experience. I do not see how anyone can deny that the training of this internal imagery is at least equally important with the development of certain outward habits of action. For myself, when it comes to the mere moral question and not a question of practical convenience, I think it is infinitely more important. Nor do I see how anyone at all familiar with the great mass of existing school work can deny that the greater part of the pupils are gradually forming habits of divided attention. If the teacher is skillful and wide-awake, if she is what is termed a good disciplinarian, the child will indeed learn to keep his senses intent in certain ways, but he will also learn to direct the fruitful imagery, which constitutes the value of what is before his senses, in totally other directions. It would not be wholly palatable to have to face the actual psychological condition of the majority of the pupils that leave our schools. We should find this division of attention and the resulting disintegration so great that we might cease teaching in sheer disgust. None the less, it is well for us to recognize that this state of things exists, and that it is the inevitable outcome of those conditions which require the simulation of attention without requiring its essence.

## Making Things Interesting

The principle of making objects and ideas interesting implies the same divorce between object and self as does the theory of "effort." When things have to be *made* interesting, it is because interest itself is wanting. Moreover, the phrase is a misnomer. The thing, the object, is no more interesting than it was before. The appeal is simply made to the child's love of pleasure. He is excited in a given direction with the hope that somehow or other during this excitation he will assimilate something otherwise repulsive. There are two types of pleasure. One is the accompaniment of activity. It is found wherever there is self-expression. It is simply the internal realization of the outgoing energy. This sort of pleasure is always absorbed in the activity itself. It has no separate existence in consciousness. This is the type of pleasure found in legitimate interest. Its stimulus is found in the needs of the organism. The other sort of pleasure arises from contact. It marks receptivity. Its stimuli are external. We take interest; we get pleasure. The type of pleasure which arises from external stimulation is isolated. It exists by itself in consciousness as a pleasure, not as the pleasure of activity.

When objects are made interesting, it is this latter type of pleasure that comes into play. Advantage is taken of the fact that a certain amount of excitation of any organ is pleasurable. The pleasure arising is employed to cover the gap between self and some fact not in itself arousing interest.

## Division of Energies

The result here also is division of energies. In the case of disagreeable effort the division is simultaneous. In this case it is successive. Instead of having a mechanical external activity and a random internal activity at the same time, there is oscillation of excitement and apathy. The child alternates between periods of over-stimulation and of inertness. It is a condition realized in some so-called kindergartens. Moreover, this excitation of any particular organ, as eye or ear by itself, creates an abiding demand for such stimulation. It is as possible to create an appetite on the part of the eye or the ear for pleasurable stimulation as it is on the part of the taste. Some kindergarten children are as dependent upon the recurrent presence of bright colors or agreeable sounds as the drunkard is upon his dram. It is this which accounts for the distraction and dissipation of energy so characteristic of such children, and for their dependence upon external suggestion.

## Summary

Before attempting a more specific psychological analysis, the discussion up to this point may be summarized as follows: Genuine interest in education is the accompaniment of the identification, through action, of the self with some object or idea, because of the necessity of that object or idea for the maintenance of self-expression. Effort, in the sense in which it may be opposed to interest, implies a separation between the self and the fact to be mastered or task to be performed, and sets up an habitual division of activities. Externally, we have mechanical habits with no psychical end or value. Internally, we have random energy or mind-wandering, a sequence of ideas with no end at all because not brought to a focus in action. Interest, in the sense in which it is opposed to effort, means simply an excitation of the sense organ to give pleasure, resulting in strain on one side and listlessness on the other.

But when we recognize there are certain powers within the child urgent for development, needing to be acted upon, in order to secure their own due efficiency and discipline, we have a firm basis upon which to build. Effort arises normally in the attempt to give full operation, and thus growth and completion, to these powers. Adequately to act upon these impulses involves seriousness, absorption, definiteness of purpose, and results in formation of steadiness and persistent habit in the service of worthy ends. But this effort never degenerates into drudgery, or mere strain of dead lift, because interest abides—the self is concerned throughout.

## II.

### *The Psychology of Interest*

We come now to our second main topic, the psychology of interest. It should be obvious from the preceding educational discussion that the points upon which we particularly need enlightenment are its relation to desire and pleasure on one side, to ideas and effort on the other.

I begin with a brief descriptive account of interest. Interest is first active, projective, or propulsive. We take interest. To be interested in any matter is to be actively concerned with it. The mere feeling regarding a subject may be static or inert, but interest is dynamic. Second, it is objective. We say a man has many interests to care for or look after. We talk about the range of a man's interests, his business interests, local interests, etc. We identify interests with concerns or affairs. Interest does not end simply in itself as bare feelings may, but always has some object, end, or aim to which it attaches itself. Third, interest is subjective; it signifies an *internal* realization, or feeling, of worth. It has its emotional, as well as its active and objective sides. Wherever there is interest there is response in the way of feeling.

These are the various meanings in which common sense employs the term interest. The root idea of the term seems to be that of being engaged, engrossed, or entirely taken up with some activity because of its recognized worth. The etymology of the term *inter-esse*, "to be between," points in the same direction. Interest marks the annihilation of the distance between the person and the materials and results of his action; it is the instrument which effects their organic union.[1]

1    It is true that the term interest is also used in a definitely disparaging sense. We speak of interest as opposed to principle, of self-interest as a motive to action which regards only one's personal advantage; but these are neither the only nor the controlling senses in which the term is used. It may fairly be questioned whether this is anything but a narrowing or

We have now to deal more in detail with each of the three phases mentioned:

## The Propulsive Phase of Interest

(1) The active or propulsive phase of interest takes us back to the consideration of impulse and the spontaneous urgencies or tendencies of activity. There is no such thing as absolutely diffuse, impartial impulse. Impulse is always differentiated along some more or less specific channel. Impulse has its own special lines of discharge. The old puzzle about the ass between two bundles of hay is only too familiar, but the recognition of its fundamental fallacy is not so common. If the self were purely passive or purely indifferent, waiting upon stimulation from without, then the self illustrated in this supposed example would remain forever helpless, starving to death, because of its equipoise between two sources of food. The error is in the supposition of this balanced internal condition. The self is always already doing something, intent on something urgent. And this ongoing activity always gives it a bent in one direction rather than another. The ass, in other words, is always already moving toward one bundle rather than the other. No amount of physical cross-eyedness could induce such psychical cross-eyedness that the animal would be in a condition of equal stimulation from both sides.

In this primitive condition of spontaneous impulsive activity, we have the basis for natural interest. Interest is no more passively waiting around to be excited from the outside than is impulse. In the selective or preferential quality of impulse we have the basis of the fact that at any given time, if we are psychically awake at all, we are always interested in one direction rather than another. The condition of total lack of interest, or of absolutely impartially distributed interest, is as mythical as the story of the ass in scholastic ethics.

An equally great fallacy is the oft-made assumption of some chasm between impulse and the self. Impulse is spoken

degrading of the legitimate sense of the term. However that may be, it appears to me certain that much of the controversy regarding the moral use of interest arises because one party is using the term in the larger, objective sense of recognized value or engrossing activity, while the other is using it as equivalent to selfish motive.

of as if it were a force swaying the self in this direction or that; as if the self were an indifferent, passive something waiting to be moved by the pressure of impulse; in reality, impulse is simply the impetus or outgoing of the self in one direction or other. This point is mentioned now because the connection of impulse and interest is so close that any assumption, at this point, of impulse as external to self is sure to manifest itself later on in the assumption that interest is of the nature of an external inducement or attraction to self, instead of being an absorption of the activities of the self in the object that allows these activities to function.

## The Objective Side of Interest

(2) Every interest, as already said, attaches itself to an object. The artist is interested in his brushes, in his colors, in his technique. The business man is interested in the play of supply and demand, in the movement of markets, etc. Take whatever instance of interest we choose and we shall find that, if we cut out the factor of the object about which interest clusters, interest itself disappears, relapsing into mere subjective feeling.

Error begins in supposing the object already there, and then calling the activity into being. Canvas, brushes, and paints interest the artist, for example, only because they help him find his existing artistic capacity. There is nothing in a wheel and a piece of string to arouse a child's activity save as they stimulate some instinct or impulse already active, and supply it with the means of its execution. The number twelve is uninteresting when it is a bare, external fact; it has interest (just as has the top or wheelbarrow or toy locomotive) when it presents itself as an instrument of carrying into effect some dawning energy or desire—making a box, measuring one's height, etc. And in its difference of degree exactly the same principle holds of the most technical items of scientific or historic knowledge—whatever furthers one, helps mental movement, is of necessary and intrinsic interest.

## Emotional Phase of Interest

(3) We now come to the emotional phase. Value is not only objective but subjective. That is, there is not only the thing

which is projected as valuable or worth while, but there is also the feeling of its worth. It is, of course, impossible to define feeling. We can only say that it is the purely individual consciousness of worth, and recognize that wherever we have interest there we have internal realization of value.

The gist of the psychology of interest may, accordingly, be stated as follows: An interest is primarily a form of self-expressive activity—that is, of growth through acting upon nascent tendencies. If we examine this activity on the side of the content of expression, of what is done, we get its objective features, the ideas, objects, etc., to which the interest is attached, about which it clusters. If we take into account that it is self-expression, that self finds itself, is reflected back to itself, in this content, we get its emotional or feeling side. Any account of genuine interest must, therefore, grasp it as outgoing activity holding within its grasp an intellectual content, and reflecting itself in felt value.

## *Mediate* vs. *Immediate Interest—Work* vs. *Drudgery*

There are cases where self-expression is direct and immediate. It puts itself forth with no thought of anything beyond. The present activity is the only ultimate in consciousness. It satisfies in and of itself. The end *is* the present activity, and so there is no gap in space nor time between means and end. All play is of this immediate character. All purely æsthetic appreciation approximates this type. The existing experience holds us for its own sake and we do not demand of it that it take us into something beyond itself. With the child and his ball, the amateur and the hearing of a symphony, the immediate engrosses. Its value is there, and is there in what is directly present.

We may, if we choose, say that the interest is in the object present to the senses, but we must beware how we interpret this saying. The object has no conscious existence, at the time, save *in* the activity. The ball to the child is his game, his game is his ball. The music has no existence save in the rapt hearing of the music—so long as the interest is immediate or æsthetic. It is frequently said to be the object which attracts attention, which calls forth interest to itself by its own inherent qualities. But this is a psychological impossibility. The bright color, the sweet sound, that interest the child are themselves phases of his organic activity. To say the child attends to the color does not mean that he gives himself up to an external object, but rather that he continues the activity which results in the presence of the color. His own activity so engrosses him that he endeavors to maintain it.

On the other hand, we have cases of indirect, transferred, or, technically, mediated interest. That is, things indifferent or even repulsive in themselves often become of interest because of their assuming relationships and connections of which we are previously unaware. Many a student, of so-called practical make-up, has found mathematical theory, once repellent, lit up by great attractiveness when he studied some form of engineering in which this theory was a necessary tool. The musical score and the technique of fingering, in which the child can find no interest when it is presented as an end in itself, when it is isolated, becomes fascinating when the child realizes its place and bearings in helping him give better and fuller utterance to his love of song. It is all a question of relationship, whether it appeals or fails to appeal; and while the little child takes only a near view of things, as he grows he becomes capable of extending his range, and seeing an act, or a thing, or a fact, not by itself, but in its value as part of a larger whole. If this whole belongs to him, if it is a mode of his own movement, then the particular gains interest too.

Here, and here only, we have the reality of the idea of "making things interesting." I know of no more demoralizing doctrine—when taken literally—than the assertion of some of the opponents of interest that *after* subject-matter has been selected, *then* the teacher should make it interesting. This combines in itself two thoroughgoing errors. On one side, it makes the selection of subject-matter a matter quite independent of the question of interest—and thus of the child's own native urgencies and needs; and, further, it reduces method in teaching to more or less external and artificial devices for dressing up the unrelated materials, so that it will get some hold upon attention. In reality, the principle of "making things interesting" means that subjects shall be selected in relation to the child's present experience, powers, and needs; and that (in case he does not perceive or appreciate this relevancy) the teacher shall present the new material in such a way as to enable the child to appreciate its bearings, its relationships, its necessity for him. It is *this bringing of the child to consciousness in new material* which constitutes the reality of what is so often perverted, both by friend and foe, in the idea of "making things interesting."

In other words, the problem is one of the degree of intrinsic connection furnished as a motive for attention. The teacher who tells the child he will be kept after school if he doesn't recite his geography lesson better[2] is appealing to the psychology of mediate interest. The former English method of rapping knuckles for false Latin quantities is one way of arousing interest in the intricacies of Latin. To offer a child a bribe, or a promise of teacher's affection, or promotion to the next grade, or ability to make money, or to take a position in society, are other modes. They are cases of transferred interest. But the criterion of judging them lies just here: How far is one interest externally attached to another, or substituted for another? How far does the new appeal, the new motive, serve to interpret, to bring out, to *relate* the material otherwise without interest? It is a question, again, of *inter-esse*, of interaction. The problem may be stated as one of the relations of means and end. Anything indifferent or repellent becomes of interest when seen as a means to an end already related to self, or as an end which will allow means already at command to secure further movement and outlet. But, in normal growth, the interest in one is not simply externally tied on to the other; it suffuses, saturates, and thus transforms it. It interprets or revalues it—gives it a new significance in consciousness. The man who has a wife and family has thereby a new motive for his daily work—he sees a new meaning in it, and takes into it a steadiness and enthusiasm previously lacking. But if he does his

---

[2]     I have heard it argued in all seriousness that a child kept after school to study has often got an interest in arithmetic or grammar which he didn't have before, as if this proved the efficacy of "discipline" *versus* interest. Of course, the reality is that the greater leisure, the opportunity for individual explanation afforded, served to bring the material into its proper relations in the child's mind—he "got a hold" of it.

day's work as a thing intrinsically disagreeable, as drudgery, simply for the sake of the final wage-reward, the case is quite different. Means and end remain remote; they do not permeate one another. The person is no more really interested in his work than he was before; it, in itself, is a hardship to be escaped from. Hence he cannot give full attention to it; he cannot put himself unreservedly into it. But to the other man every stroke of work may mean literally his wife and baby. Externally, physically, they are remote; mentally, in consciousness, they are one; they have the same value. But in drudgery means and end remain as separate in consciousness as they are in space and time. What is true of this is true of every attempt in teaching to "create interest" by appeal to external motives.

At the opposite scale, take a case of artistic construction. The sculptor has his end, his ideal, in view. To realize that end he must go through a series of intervening steps which are not, on the face of it, equivalent to the end. He must model and mould and chisel in a series of particular acts, no one of which is the beautiful form he has in mind, and every one of which represents the putting forth of personal energy on his own part. But because these are to him necessary means for the end, the ideal, the finished form is completely transferred over into these special acts. Each moulding of the clay, each stroke of the chisel, is for him at the time the whole end in process of realization. Whatever interest or value attaches to the end attaches to each of these steps. He is as much absorbed in one as in the other. Any failure in this complete identification means an inartistic product, means that he is not really interested in his ideal. A genuine interest in the ideal indicates of necessity an equal interest in all the conditions of its expression.

### Relation of Interest to Desire and Effort

We are now in position to deal with the question of the relation of interest to desire and to effort. Desire and effort in their legitimate meaning are both of them phases of mediated interest. They are correlatives, not opposites. Both effort and desire exist only when the end is somewhat remote. When energy is put forth purely for its own sake, there is no question of effort and equally no question of desire. Effort and desire both imply a state of tension. There is a certain amount of opposition existing between the ideal in view and the present actual state of things. We call it effort when we are thinking of the necessity of a decided transformation of the actual state of things in order to make it conform to the ideal—when we are thinking of the process from the side of the idea and interested in the question how to get it realized. We call it desire when we think of the tendency of the existing energies to push themselves forward so as to secure this transformation, or change the idea into a fact—when we think of the process from the side of the means at hand. But in either case, obstacles delaying us, and the continued persistence of activity against them, are implied. The only sure evidence of desire, as against mere vague wishing, is effort, and desire is aroused only when the exercise of effort is required.

In discussing the condition of mediate interest we may emphasize either the end in view, the idea, or we may start with the consideration of the present means, the active side urgent for expression. The former is the intellectual side, the latter the emotional. The tendency of the end to realize itself through the process of mediation, overcoming resistance, is effort. The tendency of the present powers to continue a struggle for complete expression in an end remote in time is desire.

## Impulse, Emotion

We often speak of appetite as blind and lawless. We conceive it as insisting upon its own satisfaction, irrespective of circumstances or of the good to the self. This means that the appetite is only felt; it is not known. It is not considered from the standpoint of its bearings or relationships. It is not translated over into terms of its results. Consequently, it is not made intelligent. It is not rationalized. As a result energy is wasted. In any strong appetite there is an immense amount of power, physical and psychical, stirred up; but where the agent does not anticipate the ends corresponding to this power, it is undirected. The energy expends itself in chance channels or according to some accidental stimulus. The organism is exhausted, and nothing positive or objective is accomplished. The disturbance or agitation is out of proportion to any ends reached. All there is to show for such a vast excitation of energy is the momentary satisfaction felt in its stimulation and expenditure.

Even as regards this blind appetite, there is, however, a decided difference of type between the lower animals and man. In the animals, while the appetite is not conscious of its own end, it none the less seeks that end by a sort of harmony pre-established in the animal structure. Fear serves the animal as a stimulus to flight or to seeking cover. Anger serves it for purposes of attack and defense. It is a very unusual occurrence when the feeling gets the better of the animal and causes it to waste its powers uselessly. But of the blind feelings in the human being, it is to be said that most of them require adjustment before they are of any regular permanent service. There is no doubt that fear or anger may be rendered useful to the man as they are to the animal. But in the former case they have to be trained to this use; in the latter they originally possess it. The ultimate function of anger is undoubtedly to do away with obstacles hindering the process of realization, but in a child the exhibition of anger is almost sure to leave the object, the obstacle, untouched and to exhaust the child. The blind feeling needs to be rationalized. The agent has to become conscious of the end or object and control his aroused powers by conscious reference to it.

For the process of self-expression to be effective and mechanical, there must, in other words, be a consciousness of both end and means. Whenever there is difficulty in effecting adjustment of means and ends, the agent is thrown into a condition of emotion. Whenever we have on one side the idea corresponding to some end or object, and whenever we have on the other side a stirring up of the active impulses and habits, together with a tendency of the latter to focus themselves at once upon the former, there we have a disturbance or agitation, known on its psychical side as emotion. It is a commonplace that as fast as habit gets definitely formed in relation to its own special end the feeling element drops out. But now let the usual end to which the habit is adapted be taken away and a sudden demand be made for the old habit to become a means towards a new end, and emotional stress at once becomes urgent. The active side is all stirred up, but neither discharges itself at once, without any end, nor yet directs itself towards any accustomed end. The result is tension between habit and aim, between impulse and idea, between means and end. This tension is the essential feature of emotion.

## Function of Emotion

It is obvious from this account that the function of emotion is to secure a sufficient arousing of energy in critical periods of the life of the agent. When the end is new or unusual and there is great difficulty in attending to it, the natural tendency would be to let it go or turn away from it. But the very newness of the end often represents the importance of the demand that is being made. To neglect the end would be a serious, if not fatal, matter for the agent. The very difficulty in effecting the adjustment sends out successive waves of stimuli, which call into play more impulses and habits, thus reinforcing the powers, resources at the agent's command. The function of emotion is thus to brace or reinforce the agent in coping with the novel element in unexpected and immediate situations.

The normal moral outcome is found in a balance between the excitation and the ideal. If the former is too weak or diffused, the agent lacks in motor power. If it is relatively too strong, the agent is not able to handle the powers which have been stirred up. He is more or less beside himself. He is carried away by the extent of his own agitation. He relapses, in other words, into the phase of blind feeling.

## Function of Desire

Desire cannot be identified with mere impulse or with blind feeling. Desire differs from the appetite of the animal in that it is always conscious, at least dimly, of its own end. When the agent is in the condition known as desire, he is conscious of some object ahead of him, and the consciousness of this object serves to reinforce his active tendencies. The thought of the desired object serves, in a word, to stimulate the means necessary to its attainment. While desire is thus not a purely impulsive state, neither, of course, is it a purely intellectual one. The object may be present in consciousness, but it is simply contemplated as an object; if it does not serve as stimulus to activity, it occupies a purely æsthetic or theoretic place. At most, it will arouse only a pious wish or a vague sentimental longing, not an active desire.

The true moral function of desire is thus identical with that of emotion, of which, indeed, it is only one special phase. Its place in the moral life is to arouse energy, to stimulate the means necessary to accomplish the realization of ends otherwise purely theoretic or æsthetic. Our desires in a given direction simply measure the hold which certain ends or ideas have upon us. They *exhibit* the force of character, the *Drang* in that direction. They *test* the sincerity of character. A produced end which does not awaken desire is a mere pretension. It indicates a growing division of character, a threatening hypocrisy.

The moral treatment of desire, like that of emotion, involves securing a balance. Desire tends continually to overdo itself. It marks energy stirred up to serve as means; but the energy once stirred up tends to express itself on its own account independently of the end. Desire is greedy, lends itself to over-hastiness, and unless watched makes the agent over-hasty. It runs away with him. It is not enough that the contemplation of the end stir up the impulses and habits; the consciousness of the end must also abide, after they are excited, to direct the energy called into being.

## Relation of Pleasure to Desire

We thus get a criterion for the normal position of pleasure in relation to desire. There can be no doubt that desire is always more or less pleasurable. It is pleasurable in so far as the end of self-expression is present in consciousness. For the end defines satisfaction, and any conception of it awakens, therefore, an image of satisfaction, which, so far as it goes, is itself pleasurable. The use of this pleasure is to give the end such a hold upon the agent that it may pass over from its ideal condition into one of actualization. Normal pleasure has a strictly instrumental place. It is *due* to the thought of the end on one side, and it *contributes* to the practical efficiency of the end on the other. In the case of self-indulgence the end is used simply to excite the pleasurable state of consciousness, and having done this, is thereafter denied. Pleasure, instead of serving to hold the mind to the end, is now made itself the end.

## Bearing of Desire on Interest

What, it may be asked, is the connection of this with the question of interest? Precisely this: In the analysis of desire we are brought back exactly to the question of mediate interest. Normal desire is simply a case of properly mediated interest. The problem of attaining the proper balance between the impulses on one side and an ideal or end on the other is just the question of getting enough interest in the end to prevent a too sudden expenditure of the waste energy — to direct this excited energy so that it shall be tributary to realizing the end. Here the interest in the end is taken over into the means. Interest, in other words, marks the fact that the emotional force aroused is functioning. This is our definition of interest; it is impulse functioning with reference to an idea of self-expression.

Interest in the end indicates that desire is both calmed and steadied. Over-greedy desire, like over-anxious aversion, defeats itself. The youthful hunter is so anxious to kill his game, he is so stimulated by the thought of reaching his end, that he cannot control himself sufficiently to take steady aim. He shoots wild. The successful hunter is not the one who has lost interest in his end, in killing the game, but the one who is able to translate this interest completely over into the means necessary to accomplish his purpose. It is no longer the killing of the game that occupies his consciousness by itself, but the thought of the steps he has to perform. The means, once more, have been identified with the end; the desire has become mediate interest. The ideal dies as bare ideal to live again in instrumental powers.

## Analysis of Ends

So far we have been discussing the process of mediated self-expression from the standpoint of the means. We have now to consider the same process, throwing the emphasis of intellectual analysis on the side of the end. Because of the length of the foregoing discussion we may here briefly consider the end or ideal, on the sides, respectively, of its origin and its function.

First, its origin. The ideal is normally a projection of the active powers. It is not generated in a vacuum nor introduced into the mind from outside impulses and habits actually striving for expression. It is simply these active powers getting off and looking at themselves to see what they are like; to see what they are upon the whole, permanently, in their final bearings, and not simply as they are at the moment and in their relative isolation. The ideal, in other words, is the self-consciousness of the impulse. It is its self-interpretation; its value in terms of possible realization.

Second, hence its function. If the ideal had its genesis independent of the active powers, it is impossible to see how it could ever get to work. The psychical machinery by which it should cease to be barely an ideal, and become an actuality, would be wanting. But just because the ideal is normally the projection of the active powers into intellectual terms, the ideal inevitably possesses active quality. This dynamic factor is present to stay. Its appearance as motive is not anything different in kind from its appearance as ideal. Motivation is just the realization of the active value originally attaching to it.

## Conflict of Ideals

In other words, when the ideal has the function of motive (a power inducing to activity), we have precisely the same fact, viewed from the standpoint of the end, that we have just now considered as the passing over of desire into mediate interest when viewing it from the side of the means. So long as the ideal does not become a motive, it indicates that the ideal itself is not yet definitely formed. There is conflict of ideals. The agent has two possible ends before him, one corresponding to one set of his active powers and another to another set of impulses or habits. Thought, reflection, is not focused, accordingly, in any single direction. The self has not yet found itself. It does not know what it really wants. It is in process of tentative self-expression, first trying on one self and then another to see how they fit. The attainment of a single purpose or the defining of one final ideal indicates the self has found its unity of expression. At this exact point the ideal, having no longer any opposition to hold it back, begins to show itself in overt action. The ideal has become a motive. The interest in the end is now taken over into the impulses and habits, and they become the present ends. Motive is the interest in the ideal mediated into impulse and habit.

## Meaning of Normal Effort

Normal effort is precisely this self-realizing tendency of the ideal—its struggle to pass over into motive. The empty or formal ideal is the end which is not suggested by, or does not grow out of, the agent's active powers. Lacking any dynamic qualities, it does not assert itself; it does not become a motor, a motive. But whenever the ideal is really a projection or translation of self-expression, it must strive to assert itself. It must persist through obstacles, and endeavor to transform obstacles into means of its own realization. The degree of its persistency simply marks the extent to which it is in reality and not simply in name a true ideal or conceived form of self-expression.

The matter of good intentions or "meaning well" affords a good illustration of this principle. When a person who has outwardly failed in his duty offers his good intentions as a justification or palliation of conduct, what determines whether or no his excuse shall be accepted? Is it not precisely whether he can or not show effort on the part of his intention, his ideal, to realize itself, and can show obstacles intervening from without which have prevented its expression up to the point of overt realization? If he cannot show overwhelming interference from without, we have a right to conclude either that the agent is attempting to deceive us or else is self-deceived—that his so-called good intention was in reality but a vague sentimental wish or else a second-handed reference to some conventional ideal which had no real hold upon him. We always use the persistence of an end against obstacles as a test of its vitality, its genuineness.

## Effort as Strain

On the other hand, effort in the sense of strain because of lack in interest is evidence of the abnormal use of effort. The necessity of effort in this sense indicates that the end nominally held up is not recognized as a form of self-expression —that it is external to the self and hence fails in interest. The *conscious* stirring up of effort marks simply the unreal strain necessarily involved in any attempt to reach an end which is not part and parcel of the self's own process. The strain is always artificial; it requires external stimulation of some sort or other to keep it going and always leads to exhaustion. Not only does effort in its true sense play no part in moral training, but it plays a distinctly immoral part. The externality of the end as witnessed in its failure to arouse the active impulses and to persist towards its own realization makes it impossible that any strain to attain this end should have any other than a relatively immoral motive. Only selfish fear, the dread of some external power, or else purely mechanical habit, or else the hope of some external reward, some more or less subtle form of bribery, can be really a motive in any such instance.

## Summary

We thus see how the theories of pleasure as a motive and artificial effort as a motive have the same practical outcome. The theory of strain always involves some reference to either pleasure or pain as the real controlling motive. And the theory of pleasure, because of its lack of an intrinsic end which holds and directs the powers, has continually to fall back upon some external inducement to excite the flagging powers. It is a commonplace in morals that no one puts forth more effort with less avail than the habitual seeker after pleasure.

The outcome of our psychological analysis is thus identical with the results reached by consideration of the practical educational side. There we found that the appeal to making things interesting, to stirring up pleasure in things not of themselves interesting, leads as a matter of common experience to alternation of over-stimulation and dull apathy.

Here we find that the desire for pleasure as an end leads necessarily to the stirring up of energies uselessly on one side, and the undirected, wasteful expenditure of energies on the other.

On the educational side we saw that the appeal to the sheer force of "will," so-called, apart from any interest in the object, means the formation of habits of divided attention—the mechanical doing of certain things in a purely external way on the one side and the riotous, uncontrolled play of imagery on the other. On the psychological side we find that interest in an end or object simply means that the self is finding its own movement or outlet in a certain direction, and that consequently there is a motive for effort, for putting forth energy, in realizing the desirable end.

On the educational side we were led to assume that normal interest and effort are identical with the process of self-expression. We have now through the process of mediated self-expression secured a fairly adequate psychological justification for that practical postulate of education.

III.

## *Kantian* vs. *Herbartian Theories of Desire and Will*

Current discussions as to the relation of interest to moral training have centred largely about the relative merits of the Kantian and Herbartian theories of desire and will. So far as I can see, as between the two theories it is a case of six of one and half a dozen of the other. Judged by the outcome of the previous discussion, neither theory has an adequate conception either of interest or of moral volition.

The criticisms of the Kantian theory have been so thoroughly worked out by Hegel and Schleiermacher in Germany, and recently by Bradley, Green, and Caird, in England, that we need here give only a very brief summary. Kant holds that the sole end or object of desire is pleasure; that desire, in other words, is always self-seeking in the bad sense of that term. The end set up by desire must, therefore, be excluded from any share in moral motivation. The agent must take the moral law, the end laid down by reason, not only as his end but also as his motive. But all special ends are excluded from the end of reason because they are empirical and not adequate to the necessity and universality of reason. Reason thus becomes purely formal. It is empty, having no content.

It should hardly be necessary to dwell upon the inadequacy of a theory which excludes all specific concrete ends from forming the content of the moral motive. Such a theory would have, as its practical outcome, only the deification of mere good intentions on one side, or else the setting up of hard and fixed rules on the other. The inefficiency of such a theory for the purpose of the educator also goes without saying. It is not the work of the educator of children to fix their attention upon abstract morality or to induce them to act with the formal law of duty as their controlling motive. It is rather his business to get the children to realize what the general abstract demands of morality require in very special and concrete instances and to give them such an interest in these specific moral ends as will endow them with motor power. Kant's theory absolutely fails to supply any guidance as to method in this respect. The teacher who attempted to work by it would inevitably, so far as he influenced pupils at all, make them into either sentimentalists or prigs. He would make them self-conscious in the bad sense of that term, concerned, that is to say, with their own attitude towards morality rather than with conduct itself.

One or two points in Kant's psychology are, however, perhaps worth remark. On the one hand we have his assumption that the whole impulsive, appetitive, desiring nature of man works toward moral evil, is selfish. The dualism between sense and reason, which is the essence of his theory of knowledge, re-appears also in his critique of will. The self is split in two. It has one phase which is only particular and another phase which is merely universal. All this is assumption without justification from either the biological, or psychological, or the logical point of view. Biologically, impulse and appetite represent, not a striving for pleasure, but a striving to maintain and further the life process. Psychologically, impulse is always a means, an instrument, for realizing an end. Pleasure arrives, not as its animating and intended aim, but as an accompaniment of the putting forth of activity. Logically, the particular has to be conceived as one specified mode of activity of an organic whole; the universal as the principle which organizes particulars into the unified whole.

Moreover, when we take the particular kind of interest which Kant does finally admit, its inadequacy to the needs of the educator is glaring. Reverence for the moral law is the one form of emotion which Kant admits. But this interest is of necessity a late one in the process of development. Observation, both of the race and of the individual, justifies this statement. Given a moral character already formed, an appeal to this interest undoubtedly has value—especially in critical periods of moral stress; for it may be questioned whether in the great mass of the acts even of the mature character it would be advisable to bring in distinct consciousness of moral law, rather than to trust to the value lying in the ends themselves. But the problem for the educator is not how to reach the formed character in which reverence for the moral law as such has any meaning. The problem for him is how to utilize present interests and special ends so that there may grow out of them in due time such a sense of law and of the claims of law as to hold and reinforce character in critical periods of temptation.

We find the Herbartian claiming the following things: First, interest is psychical activity. It is an inner animation of the self, a stirring up of the self. In the satisfaction of interest, pleasure is felt and mental ease of operation is furthered. Second, it is attached to the object for its own sake and not because of what the object may do in serving further ends. Genuine interest, according to the Herbartians, is always immediate; absorbed, that is, in the value of the object. It is involuntary, that is, precedes, and is independent of, the awakening of any desire. Mediate interest is what is usually termed an impure interest, attaching not to the object for its own sake, but for its usefulness in reaching more remote ends of pleasure or of success. Third, interest is the means by which certain ideas and certain connections between ideas can be so established and reinforced as to become practically influential in directing the child's conduct.

All this seems to me sound educational sense. Make allowance for the different use of the terms immediate and mediate interest, and it agrees substantially with the analysis already given. But when we go to the psychology of interest we find an account which not only does not justify previous statements but actually contradicts them.

According to this psychological view, interest is not psychical activity, but is a product of the actions and reactions of ideas. Interest is simply one case of feeling, and all the feeling depends upon the mechanism of ideas. In his desire to get rid of the "faculty" psychology, Herbart denies any original or primitive character to either impulse or feeling. Interest from this point of view is an outcome, a result only. It may be said to be the end of education, but it cannot possibly be a means, a motive. Instead of directing ideas, it is their passive reflex.

When some idea (*Vorstellung*) is crowded below, or down towards, the threshold of consciousness, it strains against the counteracting ideas. The idea, having no force *per se*, becomes a force through pressure, and through the resistance of self-preservation it exerts against such pressure. In this forward and backward striving of the ideas some ideas fuse; the new and the old join hands. This fusion (the essence of apperception) gives a certain pleasure, the sense of ease. Hence a peculiar kind of feeling, known as interest. The demand, not for any special *Vorstellung*, but for the repetition of the apperceptive process, for the repetition of this junction between new and old (because of its peculiar pleasure?), is interest. It is the need to occupy itself further with the same activity.

In other words, interest is attached in no sense to the *content* of the ideas, aiming at appreciating their intrinsic values, but depends wholly on the formal interaction of the ideas; it accompanies the apperceptive process as such, independently of the particular set of ideas apperceived.

The weakness both of Herbartian psychology and pedagogy seems to me to lie just here—in giving the idea a sort of external existence, a ready-made character, an existence and a content not dependent upon previous individual activity. It abstracts the idea from impulses and the activity that results from them, just as does the Kantian theory. The Kantian ideas have the advantage on the side of scope, of comprehensiveness; the Herbartian *Vorstellungen* have it on the side of definiteness, of immediate availability. But both doctrines fail to recognize the genesis of the ideas, the conceived ends, out of concrete spontaneous action; and equally fail to recognize their function as being the guides and directors of the instinctive tendencies to action.

Herbartianism seems to me essentially a schoolmaster's psychology, not the psychology of a child. It is the natural expression of a nation laying great emphasis upon authority and upon the formation of individual character in distinct and recognized subordination to the ethical demands made in war and in civil administration by that authority. It is not the psychology of a nation which professes to believe that every individual has within him the principle of authority, and that order means co-ordination, not subordination. It would be folly not to recognize to the full all the Herbartians say about the moral importance of forming certain ideas and certain relationships among ideas, and the extent to which character may be formed or disintegrated through the right and wrong use of the intellectual side of instruction in both its form and content. But just as our psychology shows us that ideas arise as the definition of activity, and serve to direct that activity in new expressions, so we need a pedagogy which shall lay more emphasis upon securing in the school the conditions of direct experience and the gradual evolution of ideas in and through the constructive activities; for it is the extent in which any idea is a projection of natural tendencies that measures its weight, its motor power, its interest.

We are not bound up to the one-sidedness of either Kant or Herbart, on the historical, any more than on the psychological, side. We may go back to Plato and Aristotle, with their assertion that "the particular training in respect to pleasure and pain which leads one to take pleasure in, to love, what demands love, and to feel pain in, to hate, what deserves hate, is education." Or, we may go ahead to Hegel, who could say that the "actual rationality of heart and will can only be at home in the universality of intellect," and yet write as follows: "The impulses and inclinations are sometimes contrasted, quite to their disadvantage, with the morality of duty for duty's sake. But impulse and passion are the very life blood of all action; they are necessary if the individual is to be really concerned in his end and its execution. The aim, the ideal, with which 'morality' has to do, is, as such, bare content, the universal—an inactive thing. It finds its actualizing in the agent; finds it only when the aim is immanent in the agent, is his *interest*, and—should it claim to engross his whole efficient subjectivity—his passion."

IV.

It only remains briefly to summarize from the educational side the whole discussion.

### INTEREST IN RELATION TO THE TEACHER AND TO THE CHILD

*Summary*

We are often told that the doctrine of interest in education means that the undeveloped, crude, and capricious capacity and insight of the child are substituted for the matured, trained, and wider outlook and experience of the adult. Our previous discussion should enable us to set this matter to rights. There are existing natural interests on the part of the child, due in part to the stage of development at which he is arrived, in part to his habits previously formed, and to his environment. These *are* relatively crude, uncertain, and transitory. Yet they are all there is, so to speak, to the child; they are all the teacher has to appeal to; they are the starting points, the initiatives, the working machinery. Does it follow that the teacher is to accept them as final; to take them as a standard; to appeal to them in the sense of arousing them to act for their own satisfaction just as they are? By no means. The teacher who thus interprets them is the only serious enemy the idea of interest really has. The significance of interest is in what *it leads to*; the new experiences it makes possible, the new powers it tends to form. The impulses and habits of the child must be *interpreted*. The value of the teacher is precisely that with wider knowledge and experience he may see them, not only as beginners, but also in their outcome, in their possibilities, that is, in their ideals. Here is Herbart's many-sided interest with its fivefold classification. Here is the interest of the child to talk about himself and his wonderful experiences, and his friends and their remarkable doings. What may it lead to? What is its possible outcome? Here is his interest in scribbling, in making houses and dogs and men. What does it *amount* to, *come* to? And so on to the end of the chapter. To answer such questions as these is not only to know the psychology of the child. It is to tax to the utmost the wisdom of the adult, knowledge of history, science, and the resources of art. Subject-matter, in all its refinements and comprehensiveness, is one name for the answer to the question: What shall these dawning powers amount to?

But it is a long road from the beginning to the end, from the child's present needs and tastes to his matured growth. The ground must be traveled step by step. It is always *today* in the teacher's practice. The teacher must be able to see to what *immediate and proximate use* the child's interests are to be put in order that he may be moving along the desired line, in the desired direction. The interest to scribble must be taken advantage of *now*, not in order that ten years from now he shall write beautiful letters, or do fine book-keeping, but that he may get some good of it now; may effect something which shall open another step in advance, and draw him on from his own crudity. This utilizing of interest and habit to make of it something fuller, wider, something more refined and under better control, might be defined as the teacher's whole duty. And the teacher who always utilizes interest will never merely indulge it. Interest in its reality is a moving thing, a thing of growth, of richer experience, and fuller power. Just how to use interest to secure growth in knowledge and in efficiency is what defines the master teacher. Here is no place to answer. But it is obvious from previous discussion that there will be a distinction according as children are mainly in the stage of direct interest, when means and end lie close together, or have reached a capacity for indirect interest, for consciously relating acts and ideas to one another, and interpreting one in terms of the other. The first, the period of elementary education, evidently requires that the child shall be taken up mainly with direct, outgoing, and positive activity, in which his impulses find fulfillment and are thereby brought to conscious value. In the second, the time of secondary education, there is basis for reflection, for conscious formulation and generalization, for the back-turned activity of the mind which goes over and consciously defines and relates the elements of its experience. Here the teacher can bring the child to consciousness of the larger meaning of his own powers and experiences, not simply through giving them such outlet that the child perceives the bearings, but indirectly and vicariously through reflection upon and absorption of the experiences of others.

### INTEREST AND DISCIPLINE

Just because interest is an outreaching thing, a thing of growth and expansion in the realization of impulse, there can be no conflict between its genuine utilization and the securing of that power and efficiency which mark the trained mind—which constitute real "discipline." Because interests are something that have to be *worked out* in life and not merely indulged in themselves, there is plenty of room for difficulties and obstacles which have to be overcome, and whose overcoming forms "will" and develops the flexible and firm fibre of character. To *realize* an interest means to *do* something, and in the doing resistance is met and must be faced. Only difficulties are now intrinsic; they are significant; their meaning is appreciated because they are felt in their relation to the impulse or habit to whose outworking they are relevant. Moreover, for this reason, there is motive to gird up one's self to meet and persistently to deal with the difficulties, instead of getting discouraged at once, or half-consciously resorting to some method of evasion, or having to resort to extraneous motives of hope and fear—motives which, because external, do not train "will," but only lead to dependence upon others.

The absurdity in much of the current conception of discipline is that it supposes (1) that unrelated difficulties, tasks that are only and merely tasks, problems that are made up to be problems, give rise to educative effort, or direction of energy; and (2) that power exists and can be trained at large apart from its application. (1) A problem is a mental thing, a psychical thing; it involves a certain mental attitude and process on the part of the one to whom it presents itself. Nothing is made really a problem by being labeled such, or because it presents itself as such to a teacher, or even because it is "hard" and repulsive. To appreciate a problem as such, the child must feel it as his own difficulty, which has arisen within and out of his own experience, as an obstacle which he has to overcome, in order to secure his own end, the integrity and fullness of his own experience. But this means that problems shall arise in and grow out of the child's own impulses, ideas, habits, out of his attempts to express and fulfill them—out of his efforts to realize his interests, in a word. (2) There is discipline or trained power only when there is power to use. Any other conception of "discipline" reduces it even below the level of the professional gymnastic performer—to a level of monkey tricks. If there be anyone who gives up his whole life to getting skill in the solution of charades and enigmas in the puzzle columns of magazines, puzzles which are invented *ad hoc*, just to be puzzles, he is the one who answers to much in the current notion of mental discipline. But such a conception does not need to be argued against. There is only discipline when one can put his powers economically, freely, and fully at work upon work that is intrinsically worth doing. The failure of mathematics to fulfill its boasted function of discipline is largely due precisely just to this isolation from application. The child who juggles glibly with complex fractions may easily fail utterly at running across the simplest sort of case in actual life. He "never had that kind before"; or he doesn't know "what rule to use." Discipline at large he has plenty and to spare; discipline in capacity to adjust his own knowledge and habits to the difficulties that arise in the natural course of experience he has little of. It would be ludicrous were it not pathetic—and often tragic. But this separation of school power and school discipline from the everyday work and requirements of the world is inevitable when it is thought to secure discipline by making up intellectual problems *per se*, instead of securing the conditions which compel them to arise in the working out of the child's own nature experience.

### CONCLUSION

In conclusion we may say that little can be accomplished by setting up interest as an end in itself. As it is said about happiness, so with interest—it is best got when it is least consciously aimed at. The thing to do is to get at the conditions that lie back of and compel interest—the child's own powers and needs, and the instruments and materials of their realization. If we can find the child's urgent impulses and habits, if we can set them at work in a fruitful and orderly way, by supplying proper environment, we shall not need to bother much about his interests; they will mostly take care of themselves. And so, I am most firmly convinced, with the training of his "will." The fact is this supposed divorce of interest and will has its roots and its vitality in a man-made psychology, which has erected the distinctions due to its own analytic abstractions into independent entities and faculties. Anyway we take it, there is only person—man or child—at the bottom of it all, and whatever really trains that person, which brings order and power, initiative, and intelligence into his experience, is most certainly training the will. We may safely leave it to those who believe there is a distinct somewhat named will in the human individual, outside of and apart from the active make-up and balance of the individual, to invent ways of training that will. For those who believe that will is the name given to a certain attitude and process of the whole being, to power of initiative, of persistent and intelligent adjustment of means to end, training of the will means whatever tends to growth in independence and firmness of action conjoined with sincere deliberation and reasoned insight.

## The Discussion at Jacksonville

THE Herbart Round Table meeting at Jacksonville, Florida, February 20, 1896, was attended by a considerable company of those who had read the paper, and were much interested in the discussion. Dr. Charles De Garmo presided.

Dr. Dewey being absent on account of sickness, C. A. McMurry was asked to introduce the discussion by a brief statement of the points. Afterward the discussion moved on without interruption for an hour and a half. The following is a brief statement of some of the arguments offered in the discussion. This statement was submitted to Dr. Dewey, who adds a short rejoinder at the close.

The first principal criticism raised against Dr. Dewey's paper by Dr. Everest and others was that some of the terms used, such as self-activity, self-expression, and interest, are not clearly defined. It is impossible to tell just what they mean. Mr. George P. Brown suggested that a knowledge of the terminology used by Dr. Dewey in his psychology was necessary to understand this paper. Self-activity and self-expression are familiar terms in this field of thought. The child, for example, desires to realize himself in his play. The flower and the plant are the self-realization of the vital forces in the seed. Self-expression is the natural product of the activities at work in the plant and animal. Dr. Everest noticed that self-realization might be bad. A boy seeks to realize himself in evil directions, as in reading bad books.

Dr. Harris was called upon by Mr. Brown, and answered somewhat as follows: Dr. Dewey's paper was a very able production. He had read it, but was not yet fully satisfied as to its meaning. It well deserves several readings, as do all Dr. Dewey's works. He was inclined to think that Dr. Dewey had forced the situation by his interpretation of interest. He seems to have taken his standpoint from Hegel's *Philosophie des Rechts*. Will is the centre and core of the highest pure being. God makes a universe of freedom and evolution.

This is the interpretation of the artist's work in the God who looks down from the Sistine Chapel. Will wills will. Dr. Dewey emphasizes self-expression, and has modified this to point toward interest. But interest points toward pleasure. Kant's criticism of Hedonism is correct forever as against interest. Pleasure is an ambiguous term, good or bad. Behind this uncertainty you can masquerade *ad libitum*. You can masquerade behind interest as an equally ambiguous term. Interest is a low thing, a high thing, and a middle thing. It is a hat that covers too many things. The good and the bad are brought together under one term. The advocates of interest should specify just what they mean under that term. Self-activity itself is a law of development only when man wills to promote the best self-activity in the world at large. Dr. Dewey is wrong in this interpretation of Kant. When the materials of instruction have been selected, it is the proper thing for the teacher to make them interesting to the children.

Dr. White thought that interest is a vague and indefinite term. Interest does not lead up to desire and motive. If interest determines the deed, how shall we dodge the conclusion that all morals break down? It is easier to act in the direction of interest, but duty sets its heel on interest in the highest concerns. This idea of interest is a soup theory. Children should not be allowed to run in the direction of their interests. In all the real efforts of life and of experience, at least, we are called upon to sacrifice pleasure to duty.

Dr. Harris remarked that Dr. White's idea was based upon the ambiguity of the meaning of interest. We should fasten on to the real aims of the child. Frank McMurry called attention to the fact that love prompts to action. Dr. White wanted to know if love had anything to do with interest. The reply was that love and interest are of the same kind, love being a more intense form of the other. Mr. Gillan wished to know if interest was present in the painful; in toothache, or in the amputation of one's arm. Mr. Powell thought the effort to get rid of pain was a mediate interest. Mr. Sutton called attention to the sentence, beginning as follows: "The fact that they are repulsive indicates that we do not consider them intrinsically connected with the desired end," etc. It was further remarked that pain itself is not the source of motive. The desire for health, for the removal of pain, or any obstacle, is the real source of interest.

Mr. Treudley and Dr. Harris were drawn into a discussion of the will of man as related to the will of God, and how far the finite will is a form or expression of the infinite. Toward the close of the discussion, Charles McMurry raised the question as to the pedagogical value of interest. Those who advocate interest as a vital element in teaching are charged with ambiguity, good interests and bad interests. The opponents of interest, however, reject both the good and the bad. They deny the value of interest *in toto.* They are at least as much at fault as the supporters of the theory of interest. The defenders of this theory are in no doubt as to what interests they wish to cultivate. It is the genuine, the high interests, the ideals, which they wish to promote. No one doubts this. Herbart, as a philosopher, attempted to point out six great sources of true interest, so that no one can be in doubt as to what is meant, essentially, by the advocates of interest. Moreover, all the most important terms are subject to the same ambiguity which is charged to the term interest. Will-training may be good or bad; self-activity may be good or bad; education may be good or bad; and yet we use these terms, and we understand what we mean by them.

We need an answer to this question: Shall we accept Dr. Dewey's analysis of the psychology of interest? He has given a full and masterly analysis of the natural movement involved in ideas, interest, desire, motive, and effort. Shall we accept the place and value given by Dr. Dewey to interest in the process of learning? The pedagogical problem is a simple and direct one.

Dr. Dewey, not having been able to be present at the discussion, desires to add the following to the foregoing report. "Of course, the term interest, taken without explanation or discussion, is ambiguous. If it had a meaning which was fully elaborated and universally recognized, no scientific interest would attach to further discussion. All terms which at a given time are centres of discussion have a like ambiguity. The discussion occurs precisely to clear up this ambiguity. The entire preceding paper is an attempt to discover what the genuine meaning is which must be attached to the term, on psychological grounds, and what the corollary is as to the proper educational use of interest. The analysis given and the application made may be quite out of the way, but I see no way to advance matters except to formulate and then criticize such statements. Discussions of interest, based on purely arbitrary definitions of the term, underived from any psychological analysis, are of no help; and mere complaints of the ambiguity of the word, disconnected from examination of an attempt to give its true import, leave the ambiguity just where they find it. As a basis of discussion any detailed formulation must be of use, no matter how erroneous, and I hope the foregoing discussion may receive enough examination and criticism to help us on to a true conception of the psychical nature and educational use of interest. Cut and dried definitions are to be avoided rather than sought for in psychology; what we need is thorough analysis preceding such definitions. It may be remarked, however, that such summarizing definitions occur in the previous paper."

## References

"The best Herbartian discussion I have found is Walsemann, *Das Interesse*; with this may be compared Grössler, *Das vielseitige*

*Interesse*, and Viedt, *Vielseitiges Interesse*. Kern, *Grundriss der Pädagogik*, is also quite explicit. Hegel's criticisms on Kant are scattered all through his works, as Sec. 135 of his *Philosophie des Rechts*, but are best summed up in his *Works*, II, 304 ff. The quotation from Hegel is found in *Philosophie des Geistes*, Sec. 475. He also says in this same paragraph that the agent never acts without interest."

# The Psychology of Effort

There are three distinguishable views regarding the psychical quales experienced in cases of effort. One is the conception that effort, as such, is strictly "spiritual" or "intellectual," unmediated by any sensational element whatever; it being admitted, of course, that the expression or putting forth of effort, in so far as it occurs through the muscular system, has sensational correlates. This view shades into the next in so far as its upholders separate "physical" from "moral" effort, and admit that in the former the consciousness of effort is more or less sensational in character, while in the latter remaining wholly non-sensuous in quality. The third view declines to accept the distinction made between moral and physical effort as a distinction of genesis, and holds that all sense of effort is sensationally (peripherally) determined. For example, the first theory, in its extreme or typical form, would say that when we put forth effort, whether to lift a stone, to solve a refractory problem, or to resist temptation, the sense of effort is the consciousness of pure psychical activity, to be carefully distinguished from any sense of the muscular and organic changes occurring from the actual putting forth of effort, the latter being a return wave of resulting sensations. The second view would discriminate between the cases alluded to, drawing a line between effort in lifting the stone, which is considered as itself due to sense of strain and tension arising from the actual putting forth of energy (and hence sensuously conditioned), and the two other cases. Various writers, would, however, apparently draw the line at different places, some conceding the sense of effort in intellectual attention to be sensational, mediated through feeling the contraction of muscles of forehead, fixa-

[*First published in* Philosophical Review, VI (*Jan. 1897*), 43–56. *Not reprinted during the author's lifetime.*]

tion of eyes, changes in breathing, etc. Others would make the attention, as such, purely spiritual (*i.e.*, in this use, non-sensational), independently of whether the outcome is intellectual or moral in value. But the third view declares unambiguously that the sense of effort is, in any case, due to the organic reverberations of the act itself, the "muscular," visceral, and breathing sensations.[1]

In the following paper I purpose, for the most part, to approach this question indirectly rather than directly, my underlying conviction being that the difference between the "sensational" and "spiritual" schools is due to the fact that one is thinking of a distinctly psychological fact, the way in which the sense or *consciousness* of effort is mediated, while the other is, in reality, discussing a logical or moral problem, —the interpretation of the category of effort, the value which it has as a part of experience. To the point that the distinction between "physical" and "spiritual" effort is one of interpretation, of function, rather than of kind of existence, I shall return in the sequel. Meantime, I wish to present a certain amount of introspective evidence for the position that the sense of effort (as distinguished from the fact or the category) is sensationally mediated; and then to point out that if this is admitted, the real problem of the psychology of effort is only stated, not solved; this problem being to find the sensational *differentia* between the cases in which there is, and those in which there is not, a sense of effort.

The following material was gathered, it may be said, not with reference to the conscious examination of the case in hand, but in the course of a study of the facts of choice; this indirect origin makes it, I believe, all the more valuable. The cases not quoted are identical in kind with those quoted, there being no reports of a contrary sense. "In deciding a question that had to be settled in five minutes, I found myself turned in the chair, till I was sitting on its edge, with the

[1]     Professor James, to whom, along with Ferrier, we owe, for the most part, the express recognition of the sensational quales concerned in effort, appears to accept the second of these three types of views. I do not know that the question has been raised as to how this distinction is reconcilable with his general theory of emotion; nor yet how his ground for making it—the superiority of the spiritual over the physical—is to be adjusted to his assertion (*Psychology*, II, 453), that the sensational theory of emotions does not detract from their spiritual significance.

left arm on the back of the chair, hand clenched so tightly that the marks of the nails were left in the palm, breathing so rapid that it was oppressive, winking rapid, jaws clenched, leaning far forward and supporting my head by the right hand. The question was whether I should go to the city that day. When I decided to go I felt more like resting than starting."

The next instance relates to an attempt to recall lines of poetry formerly memorized. "There is a feeling of strain. This I found to be immediately dependent upon a hard knitting of the brows and forehead,—especially upon a fixing and converging of the eyes. At the same time there is a general contraction of the system as a whole. The breathing is quiet, slow, and regular, save where emotional accompaniments break it up. The metre is usually kept by a slight movement of the toes in the shoes or by a finger of the hand. As the recollection proceeds, there is a sensation of peering, of viewing the whole scene. The fixation exhausts the eyes much more than hard reading."

The succeeding instance relates to the effort involved in understanding an author. "First, I am conscious of drawing myself together, my forehead contracts, my eyes and ears seem to draw themselves in and shut themselves off. There is tension of the muscles of limbs. Secondly, a feeling of movement or plunge forward occurs. My particular sensations differ in different cases, but all have this in common: First, a feeling of tension, and then movement forward. Sometimes the forward movement is accompanied by a muscular feeling in the arms as if throwing things to right and left, in clearing a road to a desired object. Sometimes it is a feeling of climbing, and planting my foot firmly as on a height attained."[2]

Now of course I am far from thinking that these cases, or any number of such cases, prove the sensational character of the consciousness of effort. Logically, the statements are all open to the interpretation that we are concerned here with products or incidental *sequelæ* of effort, rather than with its

[2] A number of cases, on further questioning, reported a similar rhythm of contraction and movement accompanying mental effort. This topic would stand special inquiry.

essence. But I have yet to find a student who, with growing power of introspection, did not report that to him such sensations seemed to constitute the "feel" of effort. Moreover, the cumulative force of such statements is very great, if not logically conclusive. Many state that if they relax their muscles entirely it is impossible to keep up the effort. Sensations frequently mentioned are those connected with breathing,—stopping the respiration, breathing more rapidly, contracted chest and throat; others are contraction of brow, holding head fixed, or twisting it, compression of lips, clenching of fist, contraction of jaws, sensations in pit of stomach, goneness in legs, shoulders higher, head lower than usual, fogginess or mistiness in visual field, trying to see something which eludes vision, etc.

But upon the whole I intend rather to assume that the sense of effort is, in all its forms, sensationally conditioned. We have in this fact (if it be a fact) no adequate psychology of effort, but only the preliminary of such theory. The conception up to this point has, for theoretical purposes, negative value only; it is useful in overthrowing other theories of effort, but throws no positive light upon its nature. The problem of interest, as soon as the rival theories are dismissed, comes to be this: Granted the sensational character of the consciousness of effort, what is its specific *differentia*? What we wish now to know is what set of sensory values marks off experiences of effort from those closely resembling, but not felt as cases of effort. So far as I know this question has not been raised.

How then does, say, a case of perception with effort differ from a case of "easy" or effortless perception? The difference, I repeat, shall be wholly in sensory quale; but in *what* sensory quale?

At this point a reversion to a different point of view, and the introduction of a different order of ideas is likely to occur. We may be told, as an explanation of the difference, that in one case we have a feeling of activity, a feeling of the putting forth of energy. I found that persons who in special cases have become thoroughly convinced of the sensational quality of all consciousness of effort, will make this answer. The explanation is, I think, that the point of view unconsciously shifts from effort as a psychical fact, as fact of direct consciousness, to effort as an objective or teleological fact. We stop thinking of the sense of effort, and think of the reference or import of the experience. Effort, as putting forth of energy, is involved equally in all psychical occurrences. It exists with a sense of ease just as much as with a sense of strain. There may be more of it in cases of extreme absorption and interest, where no effort is felt, than in cases of extreme sense of effort. Compare, for example, the psychophysical energy put forth in listening to a symphony, or in viewing a picture-gallery, with that exercised in trying to fix a small moving speck on the wall; compare the energy, that is, as objectively measured. In the former case, the whole being may be intensely active, and yet there may be, at the time, absolutely no consciousness of effort or strain. The latter may be, objectively, a very trivial activity, and yet the consciousness of strain may be the chief thing in the conscious experience. In some cases it seems almost as if the relation between effort as an objective fact, and effort as a psychical fact, were an inverse one. If a monotonous physical movement be indefinitely repeated, it will generally be found that as long as "activity" is put forth, and accomplishes something objectively (as measured in some dynametric register), there is little sense of effort. Let the energy be temporarily exhausted and action practically cease, then the sense of effort will be at its maximum. Let a wave of energy recur, and there is at once a sense of lightness, of ease. And in all cases, the sense of effort and ease follows, never precedes, the change in activity as objectively measured.[3]

We are not concerned, accordingly, with any question of the existence or non-existence of spiritual activity, or even of psycho-physical activity. The reference to this, as furnishing the *differentia* of cases of consciousness of effort from those of ease, is not so much false as irrelevant.

Where, then, shall we locate the discriminative factor? Take the simplest possible case: I try to make out the exact form, or the nature, of a faint marking on a piece of paper a few feet off, at about the limit of distinct vision. What is the

[3]    Lombard, *Journal of Physiology*, 1892.

special sensation-carrier of the sense of effort here? Intro-
spectively I believe the answer is very simple. In the case of
felt effort, certain sensory quales, usually fused, fall apart in
consciousness, and there is an alternation, an oscillation, between them, accompanied by a disagreeable tone when they
are apart, and an agreeable tone when they become fused
again. Moreover, the separation in consciousness during the
period when the quales are apart is not complete, but the
image of the fused quale is at least dimly present. Specifically, in ordinary or normal vision, there is no distinction
within consciousness of the ocular-motor sensation which
corresponds to fixation, from the optical sensations of light
and color. The two are so intimately fused that there is but
one quale in consciousness. In these cases, there is feeling
of ease, or at least absence of sense of effort. In other cases,
the sensations corresponding to frowning, to holding the
head steady, the breathing fixed—the whole adjustment of
motor apparatus—come into consciousness of themselves on
their own account. Now we are not accustomed to find satisfaction in the experience of motor adjustment; the relevant
sensations have value and interest, not in themselves, but
in the specific quales of sound, color, touch, or whatever
they customarily introduce. In at least ninety-nine one-
hundredths of our experience, the "muscular" sensations are
felt simply as passing over into some other experience which
is either aimed at, or which, when experienced, affords satisfaction. A habit of expectation, of looking forward to some
other experience, thus comes to be the normal associate of
motor experience. It is felt as fringe, as "tendency," not as
psychical resting-place. Whenever it persists as motor, whenever the expectation of other sensory quales of positive value
is not met, there is at least a transitory feeling of futility,
of thwartedness, or of irritation at a failure. Hence the disagreeable tone referred to. But in the type of cases taken as
our illustration, more is true than a failure of an expected
consequent through mere inertia of habit. The image of the
end aimed at persists, and, through its contrast with the
partial motor quale, emphasizes and reinforces the sense of
incompleteness. That is to say, one is continually imaging
the speck as having some particular form,—an oval or an

angular form; as having a certain nature,—an ink-spot, a fly-speck. Then this image is as continually interfered with by the sensations of motor adjustment coming to consciousness by themselves. Each experience breaks into, and breaks up, the other before it has attained fullness. Let the image of a five-sided ink-spot be acquiesced in apart from the motor adjustment (in other words, let one pass into the state of reverie), or let the "muscular" sensations be given complete sway by themselves (as when one begins to study them in his capacity as psychologist), and all sense of effort disappears. It is the rivalry, with the accompanying disagreeable tone due to failure of habit, that constitutes the sense of effort.

It will be useful to apply the terms of this analysis to some attendant phenomena of effort. First, it enables us to account for the growing sense of effort with fatigue, without having to resort to a set of conceptions lying outside the previously used ideas. The sense of fatigue increases effort, just because it marks the emergence into consciousness of a distinct new set of sensations which resist absorption into, or fusion with, the dominant images of the current habit or purpose. Upon the basis of other theories of effort, fatigue increases sense of effort because of sheer exhaustion; upon this theory, because of the elements introduced which distract attention. Other theories, in other words, have to fall back upon an extra-psychical factor, and something which is heterogeneous with the other factors concerned. Moreover, they fail to account for the fact that if the feeling of fatigue is surrendered to, it ceases to be disagreeable, and may become a delicious languor.

In a similar way certain facts connected with sense of effort, as related to the mastery of novel acts, may be explained. Take the alternation of ridiculous excess of effort, with total collapse of effort in learning to ride a bicycle. Before one mounts one has perhaps a pretty definite visual image of himself in balance and in motion. This image persists as a desirability. On the other hand, there comes into play at once the consciousness of the familiar motor adjustments,—for the most part, related to walking. The two sets of sensations refuse to coincide, and the result is an amount of stress and strain relevant to the most serious problems of the universe. Or, again, the conflict becomes so unregulated that the image of the balance disappears, and one finds himself with only a lot of "muscular" sensations at hand; the effort entirely vanishes. I have taken an extreme case, but surely every one is familiar, in dealing with unfamiliar occupations, of precisely this alternation of effort, out of all proportion to the objective significance of the end, with the complete mind-wandering and failure of endeavor. If the sense of effort is the sense of incompatibility between two sets of sensory images, one of which stands for an end to be reached, or a fulfillment of a habit, while the other represents the experiences which intervene in reaching the end, these phenomena are only what are to be expected. But if we start from a "spiritual" theory of effort, I know of no explanation which is anything more than an hypostatized repetition of the facts to be explained.

It probably has already occurred to the reader, that when the theory of the sensational character of the consciousness of effort is analyzed, instead of being merely thrown out at large, the feeling that it deals common-sense a blow in the face, disappears. If we state the foregoing analysis in objective, instead of in psychical terms, it just says that effort is the feeling of opposition existing between end and means. The kinæsthetic image of qualitative nature (*i.e.*, of color, sound, contact) stands for the end, whether consciously desired, or as furnishing the culmination of habit. The "muscular" sensations[4] represent the means, the experiences to which value is not attached on their own account, but as intermediaries to an intrinsically valuable consciousness.

Practically stated, this means that effort is nothing more, and also nothing less, than tension between means and ends in action, and that the sense of effort is the awareness of this conflict. The sensational character of this experience, which has been such a stumbling to some, means that this tension of adjustment is not merely ideal, but is actual (*i.e.*,

---

4      Perhaps it would be well to state that sensations of tendons, joints, internal contacts, etc., are what is meant by this term, — the whole report of the motor adjustment.

practical); it is one which goes on in a struggle for existence. Being a struggle for realization in the world of concrete quales and values, it makes itself felt in the only media possible,—specific sensations, on the one hand, and muscular sensations, on the other. Instead of denying, or slurring over, effort, such an account brings it into prominence. Surely what common-sense values in effort, is not some transcendental act, occurring before any change in the actual world of qualities, but precisely this readjustment within the concrete region. And if one is somewhat scandalized at being told that the awareness of effort is a sense of changes of breathing, of muscular tensions, etc., it is not, I conceive, because of what is said, but rather because of what is left unsaid—that these sensations report the state of things as regards effective realization.

It is difficult to see, upon a more analytic consideration than common-sense is called upon to make, what is gained for the "spiritual" nature of effort by relegating it to a purely extra-sensational region. That "spiritual" is to be so interpreted as to mean existence in a sphere transcending space and time determinations, is, at best, a piece of metaphysics, and not a piece of psychology; and as a piece of metaphysics, it cannot escape competition with the theory which finds the meaning of the spiritual in the whole process of realizing the concrete values of life. I do not find that any of the upholders of the non-sensational quality of effort has ever made a very specific analysis of the experience. Professor Baldwin's account, however, being perhaps the most thoroughgoing statement of effort as preceding sensation, in "physical" as well as "spiritual" effort is, perhaps, as explicit as any. In one passage, effort is "distinct consciousness of opposition between what we call self and muscular resistance." Now a consciousness of muscular resistance, whatever else it may or may not be, would seem to involve sensations, and the consciousness of effort to be, so far forth, sensationally mediated—which is contrary to the hypothesis. Moreover, it is extremely difficult to see how there can be any consciousness of opposition between the self in general, and the muscles in general. Until the "self" actually starts to do something (and then, of course, there are sensations), how can the muscles offer any opposition to it? And even when it does begin to do something, how can the muscles, as muscles, offer opposition? If because the act is unfamiliar, then certainly what we get is simply a case of difficulty in the having of a unified consciousness—the kinæsthetic image of the habitual movement will not unify with the proposed sensory image, and there is rivalry. But this is not a case of muscles resisting the self; it is a case of divided activity of the self. It means that the activity already going on (and, therefore, reporting itself sensationally) resists displacement, or transformation, by or into another activity which is beginning, and thus making its sensational report.

But Professor Baldwin gives another statement which is apparently different. "In all voluntary movement, therefore, there is an earlier fiat than the will to move, *i.e.*, the fiat of attention to the particular idea of movement" (p. 342). And it is repeatedly intimated that the real difficulty in effort is, not in the muscular execution, but in holding a given idea in consciousness. (In fact, on the same page, it is distinctly stated that, even in muscular effort, the real effort is found in "attending" to the idea.) Now, this statement is certainly preferable to the other, in that it avoids the appearance of making the muscles offer resistance to the self. But now, what has become of the resistance, and, hence, of the effort? Is there anything left to offer opposition *to* the self? Can an idea, *qua* pure idea, offer resistance and demand effort? And is it the self, as barely self, to which resistance is made? Such questions may, perhaps, serve to indicate the abstractness of the account and suggest the fact that effort is never felt, save when a *change of existing activity is proposed*. In this case, the effort may be centred in the introduction of the new idea as against the persistence of the present doing, or it may be to maintain the existing habit against the suggested change. In the former, the new activity will probably be categorized as duty; in the latter case, as temptation or distraction. But in either alternative, effort is felt with reference to the adjustment of factors in an action. Neither of these is exclusively self, neither the old nor the new factor; and the one which happens to be especially selected as self varies with the state of action. At one period, the end or aim is regarded as self, and the existing habit, or mode of action, as the obstruction to the realization of the desired self; at the next stage, the end having been pretty well defined, the habit, or existing line of action, since the only means or instrument for attaining this end, is conceived as self, and the ideal as "beyond," and at once as resisting and as soliciting the self.

I do not suppose any one will question this account, so far as relates to the fact that the sense of effort arises only with reference to a proposed change in the existing activity, and that at least the existing activity has its sensational counterpart. Doubt is more likely to arise as regards the proposed end, or the intruding distraction. This, it may be said, is pure idea, not activity, and, hence, has no sensational report. But whoever takes this position must be able to explain the *differentia* between instances of logical manipulation of an idea, æsthetic contemplation, and cases of sense of effort. I may take the idea of something I ought to do, but which is repulsive to me; may say that I ought to do it, and may then hold the idea as an idea or object in consciousness, may revolve it in all lights, may turn it over and over, may chew it as a sweet or a bitter cud, and yet have absolutely no sense of effort. It is only, so far as I can trust my own observation, when this idea passes into at least nascent or partial action, and thus comes head up against some other line of action, that the sense of effort arises.

In other words, the sense of effort arises, not because there is an activity struggling against resistance, or a self which is endeavoring to overcome obstacles outside of it; but it arises within activity, marking the attempt to coordinate separate factors within a single whole. Activity is here taken not as formal, but as actual and specific. It means an act, definitely doing something definite. An act, as something which occupies time, necessarily means conflict of acts. The demand for time is simply the result of a lack of unity. The intervening process of execution, the use of means, is the process of disintegrating acts hitherto separate and independent, and putting together the result, or fragments, into a single piece of conduct. Were it not for the division of acts and results in conflict, the deed, or co-ordination, would be accomplished at once.

One of the conflicting acts stands for the end or aim.

This, at first, is the sensory image which gives the cue and motive to the reaction or response. In the case previously cited, it is the image of the colored speck, as determining the movements of the head and eye muscles.[5] That we are inclined to view only the motor response as act, and regard the image, either as alone psychical, or as pure idea, is because the image is already in existence, and, therefore, its active side may be safely neglected. Being already in possession of the field, it does not require any conscious activity to keep it in existence. The movement of the muscles, being the means by which the desired end may be reached, becomes the all-important thing, or *the* act; in accordance with the general principle that attention always goes to the weakest part of a co-ordination in process of formation, meaning by weakest, that part least under the immediate control of habit. This being conceived alone as act, everything lying outside of it is conceived as resistance; thus recognition is avoided of the fact, that the real state of things is, that there are two acts mutually opposing each other, during their transformation over into a third new and inclusive act.

We have here, I think, an adequate explanation of all that can be said about the tremendous importance of effort, of all that Professor James has so conclusively said. This importance is not due to the fact that effort is the one sole evidence of a free spiritual activity struggling against outward and material resistance. It is due to the fact that effort is the critical point of progress in action, arising whenever old habits are in process of reconstruction, or of adaptation to new conditions; unless they are so readapted, life is given over to the rule of conservatism, routine, and over-inertia. To make a new co-ordination the old co-ordination must, to some extent, be broken up, and the only way of breaking it up is for it to come into conflict with some other co-ordination; that is, a conflict of two acts, each representing a habit, or end, is the necessary condition of reaching a new act which shall have a more comprehensive end. That sensations

[5]    It must not be forgotten that both sensory stimulus and motor response are both in reality sensori-motor, and, therefore, each is itself an act or psychical whole. On this point, see my article in the *Psychological Review* for July, 1896, entitled "The Reflex Arc Concept" [*The Early Works of John Dewey*, v, 96–109].

of the bodily state report to us this conflict and readjustment, merely indicates that the reconstruction going on is one of acts, and not mere ideas. The whole prejudice which supposes that the spiritual sense of effort is lost when it is given sensational quality, is simply a survival of the notion that an idea is somehow more spiritual than an act.

Up to this time I have purposely avoided any reference to the attempt to explain effort by attention. My experience has been that this mode of explanation does not explain, but simply shifts the difficulty, at the same time making it more obscure by claiming to solve it. There is some danger that attention may become a psychological pool of Bethesda. If we have escaped the clutch of associationalism, only to fall into attentionalism, we have hardly bettered our condition in psychology. But the preceding account would apply to any concrete analyses of effort in terms of attention. The psychological fallacy besets us here. We confuse attention as an objective fact, attention for the observer, with attention as consciously experienced. During complete absorption an onlooker may remark how attentive such a person is, or after such an absorption one may look back and say how attentive one was; but taking the absorption when it occurs, it means that only the subject-matter is present in consciousness, not attention itself. We are conscious of being attentive only when our attention is divided, only when there are two centres of attention competing with each other, only when there is an oscillation from one group of ideas to another, together with a tendency to a third group of ideas, in which the two previous groups are included. The sense of strain in attention, instead of being coincident with the activity of attention, is proof that attention itself is not yet complete.

To establish the identity of attention with the formation of a new act, through the mutual adaptation of two existing habits, would take us too far away from our present purpose; but there need be no hesitation, I believe, in admitting that the sense of attention arises only under the conditions of conflict already stated.

# The Psychological Aspect of the School Curriculum

There is a rough and ready way, in current pedagogical writing, of discriminating between the consideration of the curriculum or subject-matter of instruction and the method. The former is taken to be objective in character, determined by social and logical considerations without any particular reference to the nature of the individual. It is supposed that we can discuss and define geography, mathematics, language, etc., as studies of the school course, without having recourse to principles which flow from the psychology of the individual. The standpoint of method is taken when we have to reckon with the adaptation of this objective given material to the processes, interests, and powers of the individual. The study is there ready-made; method inquires how the facts and truths supplied may be most easily and fruitfully assimilated by the pupil.

Taken as a convenient working distinction, no great harm is likely to arise from this parceling out of the two phases of instruction. When pressed, however, into a rigid principle, and made the basis for further inferences, or when regarded as a criterion by reference to which other educational questions may be decided, the view is open to grave objections.

On the philosophic side it sets up a dualism which, to my own mind, is indefensible; and which, from any point of view, is questionable. Moreover, many of the writers who hold this distinction on the practical or pedagogical side would certainly be the last to admit it if it were presented to them as a philosophic matter. This dualism is one between

[*First published in* Educational Review, XIII (*Apr. 1897*), 356–69. *Not previously reprinted.*]

mental operation on one side, and intellectual content on the other—between mind and the material with which it operates; or, more technically, between subject and object in experience. The philosophic presupposition is that there is somehow a gap or chasm between the workings of the mind and the subject-matter upon which it works. In taking it for granted that the subject-matter may be selected, defined, and arranged without any reference to psychological consideration (that is, apart from the nature and mode of action of the individual), it is assumed that the facts and principles exist in an independent and external way, without organic relation to the methods and functions of mind. I do not see how those who refuse to accept this doctrine as good philosophy can possibly be content with the same doctrine when it presents itself in an educational garb.

This dualism reduces the psychological factor in education to an empty gymnastic. It makes it a mere formal training of certain distinct powers called perception, memory, judgment, which are assumed to exist and operate by themselves, without organic reference to the subject-matter. I do not know that it has been pointed out that the view taken by Dr. Harris in the *Report of the Committee of Fifteen* regarding the comparative worthlessness of the psychological basis in fixing educational values is a necessary consequence of the dualism under discussion. If the subject-matter exists by itself on one side, then the mental processes have a like isolation on the other. The only way successfully to question this condemnation of the psychological standpoint is to deny that there is, as a matter of fact, any such separation between the subject-matter of experience and the mental operations involved in dealing with it.

The doctrine, if logically carried out in practice, is even less attractive than upon the strictly theoretical side. The material, the stuff to be learned, is, from this point of view, inevitably something external, and therefore indifferent. There can be no native and intrinsic tendency of the mind toward it, nor can it have any essential quality which stimulates and calls out the mental powers. No wonder the upholders of this distinction are inclined to question the value of interest in instruction, and to throw all the emphasis upon the dead lift of effort. The externality of the material makes it more or less repulsive to the mind. The pupil, if left to himself, would, upon this assumption, necessarily engage himself upon something else. It requires a sheer effort of will power to carry the mind over from its own intrinsic workings and interests to this outside stuff.

On the other side, the mental operation being assumed to go on without any intrinsic connection with the material, the question of method is degraded to a very low plane. Of necessity it is concerned simply with the various devices which have been found empirically useful, or which the ingenuity of the individual teacher may invent. There is nothing fundamental or philosophical which may be used as a standard in deciding points in method. It is simply a question of discovering the temporary expedients and tricks which will reduce the natural friction between the mind and the external material. No wonder, once more, that those who hold even unconsciously to this dualism (when they do not find the theory of effort to work practically) seek an ally in the doctrine of interest interpreted to mean the amusing, and hold that the actual work of instruction is how to make studies which have no intrinsic interest interesting—how, that is, to clothe them with factitious attraction, so that the mind may swallow the repulsive dose unaware.

The fact that this dualistic assumption gives material on one hand such an external and indifferent character, while on the other it makes method trivial and arbitrary, is certainly a reason for questioning it. I propose, accordingly, in the following pages, to examine this presupposition, with a view to showing that, as a matter of fact, psychological considerations (those which have to deal with the structures and powers of the individual) enter not only into the discussion of method, but also into that of subject-matter.

The general tone of Dr. Harris's criticism of my monograph on *Interest as Related to Will* is so friendly and appreciative that it would be hypercritical and controversial for me to carry on the discussion longer without raising some deeper problem. I am convinced that much of the existing difference of opinion as regards not only the place of interest in education, but the meaning and worth of correlation, is due to failure to raise the more fundamental question which I have just proposed; and that the thing needed in the present state of discussion is, as it were, to flank these two questions by making articulate the silent presupposition which has been so largely taken for granted.

What, then, do we mean by a study in the curriculum? What does it stand for? What fixes the place which it occupies in the school work? What furnishes it its end? What gives it its limitations? By what standard do we measure its value? The ordinary school-teacher is not, of course, called upon to raise such questions. He has certain subjects given to him. The curriculum is, as we say, laid out, and the individual teacher has to do the best he can with the studies as he finds them. But those who are concerned theoretically with the nature of education, or those who have to do practically with the organization of the course of study—those who "lay out" the course—cannot afford to ignore these questions.

On the whole, the most philosophic answer which has as yet been given to these questions in America is that worked out by Dr. Harris in his deservedly famous St. Louis reports, and more recently formulated by him in the *Report of the Committee of Fifteen*, as well as in the articles which he has written opposing the Herbartian conception of correlation. In substance, we are told that a study is the gathering up and arranging of the facts and principles relating to some typical aspect of social life, or which afford a fundamental tool in maintaining that social life; that the standard for selecting and placing a study is the worth which it has in adapting the pupil to the needs of the civilization into which he is born.

I do not question this statement, so far as it goes, on the positive side. The objectionable point is the negative inference that this social determination is exclusive of the psychological one. The social definition is necessary, but is the psychological one less pressing? Supposing we ask, for example, *how* a given study plays the part assigned to it in social life? What is it that gives it its function? How does the study operate in performing this function? Suppose we say not simply that geography does, as a matter of fact, occupy a certain important position in interpreting to the child the structure and processes of the civilization into which he is born; suppose that, in addition, we want to know how geography performs this task. What it is that intrinsically adapts it to this and gives it a claim to do something which no other study or group of studies can well perform? Can we answer this question without entering into the psychological domain? Are we not inquiring, in effect, what geography is on the psychological side—what it is, that is to say, as a mode or form of experience?[1]

Moreover, we must ask how the given study manages to do the work given it before we can get any basis upon which to select the material of instruction in general; and much more before we can select the material for pupils of a certain age or of a certain social environment. We must take into account the distinction between a study as a logical whole and the same study considered as a psychological whole. From the logical standpoint, the study is the body or system of facts which are regarded as valid, and which are held together by certain internal principles of relation and explanation. The logical standpoint assumes the facts to be already discovered, already sorted out, classified, and systematized. It deals with the subject-matter upon the objective standpoint. Its only concern is whether the facts are really facts, and whether the theories of explanation and interpretation used will hold water. From the psychological standpoint, we are concerned with the study as a mode or form of living individual experience. Geography is not only a set of facts and principles, which may be classified and discussed by themselves; it is also a way in which some actual individual feels and thinks the world. It must be the latter before it can be the former. It becomes the former only as the culmination or completed outgrowth of the latter. Only when the individual has passed through a certain

---

[1]    I note that many critics have objected to the title of the book, *The Psychology of Number*, on the ground that, as one objector put it, "Psychology is the science of mind, and hence this title virtually reads, 'The science of the mind of number,' which is absurd." Do these critics mean that quantity, number, etc., are not modes of experience? That they are not specific intellectual attitudes and operations? Do they deny that from the educational, as distinct from the scientific standpoint, the consideration of number as a mode of experience, as a mental attitude and process of functioning, is more important than the definition of number from a purely objective standpoint?

amount of experience, which he vitally realizes on his own account, is he prepared to take the objective and logical point of view, capable of standing off and analyzing the facts and principles involved.

Now, the primary point of concern in education is beyond question with the subject as a special mode of personal experience, rather than with the subject as a body of wrought-out facts and scientifically tested principles. To the child, simply because he is a child, geography is not, and cannot be, what it is to the one who writes the scientific treatise on geography. *The latter has had exactly the experience which it is the problem of instruction to induce on the part of the former.* To identify geography as it is to the pupil of seven or fifteen with geography as it is to Humboldt or Ritter is a flagrant case of putting the cart before the horse. With the child, instruction must take the standpoint not of the accomplished results, but of the crude beginnings. We must discover what there is lying within the child's present sphere of experience (or within the scope of experiences which he can easily get) which deserves to be called geographical. It is not the question of *how* to teach the child geography, but first of all the question *what* geography is for the child.

There is no fixed body of facts which, in itself, is eternally set off and labeled geography, natural history, or physics. Exactly the same objective reality will be one or other, or none of these three, according to the interest and intellectual attitude from which it is surveyed. Take a square mile of territory, for example; if we view it from one interest, we may have trigonometry; from another standpoint we should label the facts regarding it botany; from still another, geology; from another, mineralogy; from another, geography; from still another standpoint it would become historical material. There is absolutely nothing in the fact, as an objective fact, which places it under any one head. Only as we ask what kind of an experience is going on, what attitude some individual is actually assuming, what purpose or end some individual has in view, do we find a basis for selecting and arranging the facts under the label of any particular study.

Even in the most logical and objective consideration,

we do not, therefore, really escape from the psychological point of view. We do not get away from all reference to the person having an experience, and from the point of how and why he has it. We are simply taking the psychology of the adult (that is to say, of the one who has already gone through a certain series of experiences), of one who has, therefore, a certain background and course of growth, and substituting the mature and developed interest of such a person for the crude and more or less blind tendency which the child has. If we act upon this distinction in our educational work, it means that we substitute the adult's consciousness for the child's consciousness.

I repeat, therefore, that the first question regarding any subject of study is the psychological one, What is that study, considered as a form of living, immediate, personal experience? What is the interest in that experience? What is the motive or stimulus to it? How does it act and react with reference to other forms of experience? How does it gradually differentiate itself from others? And how does it function so as to give them additional definiteness and richness of meaning? We must ask these questions not only with reference to the child in general, but with reference to the specific child—the child of a certain age, of a certain degree of attainment, and of specific home and neighborhood contacts.

Until we ask such questions the consideration of the school curriculum is arbitrary and partial, because we have not the ultimate criterion for decision before us. The problem is not simply what facts a child is capable of grasping or what facts can be made interesting to him, but what experience does he himself have in a given direction. The subject must be differentiated out of that experience in accordance with its own laws. Unless we know what these laws are, what are the intrinsic stimuli, modes of operation and functions of a certain form of experience, we are practically helpless in dealing with it. We may follow routine, or we may follow abstract logical consideration, but we have no decisive educational criterion. It is the problem of psychology to answer these questions; and when we get them answered, we shall know how to clarify, build up, and put in order the content of éxperience, so that in time it will grow to include the systematic body of facts which the adult's consciousness already possesses.

This is a distinctly practical question—a question which concerns the actual work of the schoolroom and not simply the professorial chair. Upon the whole, I believe that the crying evil in instruction today is that the subject-matter of the curriculum, both as a whole and in its various stages, is selected and determined on the objective or logical basis instead of upon the psychological. The humble pedagogue stands with his mouth and his hands wide open, waiting to receive from the abstract scientific writers the complete system which the latter, after centuries of experience and toilsome reflection, have elaborated. Receiving in this trustful way the ready-made "subject," he proceeds to hand it over in an equally ready-made way to the pupil. The intervening medium of communication is simply certain external attachments in the way of devices and tricks called "method," and certain sugar-coatings in the way of extrinsic inducements termed "arousing of interest."

All this procedure overlooks the point that the first pedagogical question is, How, out of the crude native experience which the child already has, the complete and systematic knowledge of the adult consciousness is gradually and systematically worked out. The first question is, How experience grows; not, What experience the adult has succeeded in getting together during his development from childhood to maturity. The scientific writer, having a background of original experience, and having passed through the whole period of growth, may safely assume them and not get lost; the subject-matter standing to him in its proper perspective and relation. But when this adult material is handed over ready-made to the child, the perspective is ignored, the subject is forced into false and arbitrary relations, the intrinsic interest is not appealed to, and the experience which the child already has, which might be made a vital instrument of learning, is left unutilized and to degenerate.

The genuine course of procedure may be stated as follows:

We have first to fix attention upon the child to find out

what kind of experience is appropriate to him at the particular period selected; to discover, if possible, what it is that constitutes the special feature of the child's experience at this time; and why it is that his experience takes this form rather than another. This means that we observe in detail what experiences have most meaning and value to him, and what attitude he assumes toward them. We search for the point, or focus, of interest in these experiences. We ask where they get their hold upon him and how they make their appeal to him. We endeavor by observation and reflection to see what tastes and powers of the child are active in securing these experiences. We ask what habits are being formed; what ends and aims are being proposed. We inquire what the stimuli are and what responses the child is making. We ask what impulses are struggling for expression; in what characteristic ways they find an outlet; and what results inure to the child through their manifestation.

All this is a psychological inquiry. It may be summed up, if I am permitted to use the word, under the head of "interest." Our study is to find out what the actual interests of the child are; or, stated on the objective side, what it is in the world of objects and persons that attracts and holds the child's attention, and that constitutes for him the significance and worth of his life. This does not mean that these interests, when discovered, give the ultimate standard for school work, or that they have any final regulative value. It means that the final standard cannot be discovered or used until this preliminary inquiry is gone through with. Only by asking and answering such questions do we find out where the child really is; what he is capable of doing; what he can do to the greatest advantage and with the least waste of time and strength, mental and physical. We find here our indicators or pointers as to the range of facts and idea legitimate to the child. While we do not get the absolute rule for the selection of subject-matter, we do most positively get the key to such selection. More than this, we here have revealed to us the resources and allies upon which the teacher may count in the work of instruction. These native existing interests, impulses, and experiences are all the leverage that the teacher has to work with. He must connect with them or fail utterly. Indeed, the very words leverage and connection suggest a more external relation than actually exists. The new material cannot be attached to these experiences or hung upon them from without, but must be differentiated from them internally. The child will never realize a fact or possess an idea which does not grow out of this equipment of experiences and interests which he already has. The problem of instruction, therefore, is how to induce this growth.

The phenomena of interest, then, are to be studied as symptoms. Only through what the child does can we know what he is. That which enables us to translate the outward doing over into its inner meaning is the ability to read it in terms of interest. If we know the interest the child has, we know not simply what he externally does, but why he does it; where its connection with his own being can be found. Wherever we have interest we have signs of dawning power. Wherever we have phenomena of a lack of interest, wherever we have repulsion, we have sure tokens that the child is not able to function freely, is not able to control and direct his own experience as he would; or, if I may use what Dr. Harris calls a "glib and technical term," does not "*express himself*" easily and freely. Once more, these phenomena of interest are not final. They do not say to the teacher: We are your final end, and all your energies are to be devoted to cultivating us just as we are. None the less, they are indices and instruments; they are the only clues which the instructor can possibly have to what experiences are such really, and not simply in name. They reveal the general standpoint from which any subject must be presented in order to lay hold on the child. The problem of the teacher is to read the superficial manifestations over into their underlying sources. Even "bad" interests, like that of destruction, are the signs of some inner power which must be discovered and utilized.

In the second place, in saying that these psychical phenomena afford opportunities, give clues, and furnish leverages, we are virtually saying that they set problems. They need to be interpreted. They have the value of signs, and, like all signs, must be interpreted into the realities for which they stand. Now it is the province of the subject-matter on its logical and objective side to help us in this work of translation. We see the meaning of the beginning through reading it in terms of its outcome; of the crude in terms of the mature. We see, for example, what the first babbling instincts and impulses mean by contemplating the articulate structure of language as an instrument of social communication, of logical thought, and of artistic expression. We see what the interest of the child in counting and measuring represents, by viewing the developed system of arithmetic and geometry. The original phenomena are prophecy. To realize the full scope of the prophecy, its promise and potency, we must look at it not in its isolation, but in its fulfillment.

This doctrine is misconceived when taken to mean that these accomplished results of the adult experience may be made a substitute for the child's experience, or may be directly inserted into his consciousness through the medium of instruction, or, by any external device whatsoever, grafted upon him. Their value is not that of furnishing the immediate material or subject-matter of instruction, any more than the phenomena of interest furnish the final standards and goals of instruction. The function of this ordered and arranged experience is strictly interpretative or mediatory. We must bear it in mind in order to appreciate, to place, the value of the child's interests as he manifests them.

Thus we come, in the third place, to the selection and determination of the material of instruction, and to its adaptation to the process of learning. This involves the interaction of two points of view just considered. It is working back and forth from one to the other. The transitory and more or less superficial phenomena of child life must be viewed through their full fruitage. The objective attainments of the adult consciousness must be taken out of their abstract and logical quality and appreciated as living experiences of the concrete individual. Then we may see what both subject-matter and method of instruction stand for. The subject-matter is the present experience of the child, taken in the light of what it may lead to. The method is the subject-matter rendered into the actual life experience of some individual. The final problem of instruction is thus the reconstruction of the individual's experience, through the medium of what is seen to be involved in that experience as its matured outgrowth.

We have two counterpart errors: one is the appeal to the child's momentary and more or less transitory interest, as if it were final and complete, instead of a sign of nascent power; as if it were an end instead of an instrument; as if it furnished an ideal instead of setting a problem. The other is taking the studies from the scientific standpoint, and regarding them as affording the subject-matter of the curriculum. As the phenomena of interest need to be controlled by reference to their fullest possibility, so the scientific content of the studies needs to be made over by being "psychologized," seen as what some concrete individual may experience in virtue of his own impulses, interests, and powers. It is the element of control which takes us out of the region of arbitrary tricks and devices into the domain of orderly method. It is the making over and psychological translation of the studies which renders them a genuine part of the *Lehrstoff* of the pupil. It is because of the necessity of this operation, the transfiguring of the dead objective facts by seeing them as thoughts and feelings and acts of some individual, that we are justified in saying that there is a psychological aspect to the curriculum.

In applying this to the actual studies which make up the present curriculum, no one would deny, I suppose, that language, literature, history, and art, being manifestations of human nature, cannot be understood in their entirety, nor yet fully utilized in the work of instruction, until they are regarded as such manifestation. But we must go a point further, and recognize that in education we are not concerned with the language that has been spoken, the literature that has been created, the history that has been lived, but with them only as they become a part of what an individual reports, expresses, and lives. Even in the sciences, where we appear to be dealing with matters that are more remote from the individual, we need to remember that educationally our business is not with science as a body of fixed facts and truths, but with it as a method and attitude of experience. Science in the sense in which we can find it stated in books, or set forth in lectures, is not the subject-matter of instruction. Anything that can be found in these forms is simply an index and instrument. It sets before us our goal—the attitude of mind and kind of experience which we wish to induce; when it is read over, into psychological terms, it helps us reach our goal; but without the psychological rendering, it is inert, mechanical, and deadening.

Because the actual, as distinct from the abstract or possible, subject is a mode of personal experience, not simply an ordered collection of facts and principles, the curriculum as a whole, and every study in detail, has a psychological side whose neglect and denial lead to confusion in pedagogic theory; and in educational practice to the dead following of historic precedent and routine, or else to the substitution of the abstract and the formal for the vital and personal.

# Some Remarks on the Psychology of Number

In the October, 1897, number of *The Pedagogical Seminary* Mr. D. E. Phillips has presented a very considerable bulk of data bearing upon the question of the development of the number sense, from the standpoints both of experimentation and collection of illustrative material from child life. He has also presented a theory in interpretation of these facts. This theory, as I understand it, separates the counting process, in which number undoubtedly has its origin and development, from the consciousness of quantity, holding that the number idea in the form of a series, is a distinct process psychologically and pedagogically from the ratio idea; or, as it is stated in the summary on page lxxxiv, "Number as measurement is not the whole of the development of number but only the complimentary side of the series idea; number as measurement can by no means explain all the mental phenomena of numbers."

The matter has, I think, sufficient psychological interest of its own to justify further consideration; and this consideration is specially urgent when we note that according as we separate the counting or series idea from the quantity idea, or connect it organically with the latter, we get two quite different educational procedures indicated. I propose, accordingly, a further discussion of the matter, based for the most part upon Mr. Phillips's own data and treatment.

The first point which appears to require examination is the question of the origin and development of the series idea, both in the concrete and the abstract. At the outset I

[*First published in* Pedagogical Seminary, v (*Jan. 1898*), 426–34. *Not previously reprinted. See "Number and Its Application Psychologically Considered,"* The Early Works of John Dewey, v, *to which page references in the article above have been keyed.*]

experience considerable embarrassment in interpreting Mr. Phillips's statement (p. xli) that "nearly all children, no matter how taught, first learn to count independently of objects, in which the series idea gets ahead," or again (p. xliii) that "the naming of the series generally goes in advance of the application to things." My difficulty is in understanding what Mr. Phillips means by the "naming of the series." His argument demands that this naming of the number series be genuine counting or enumeration; the facts which he educes in support of his proposition relate to the mere repetition or rattling off of a series of number *names*. I find it difficult to convince myself that Mr. Phillips has not distinguished between two such totally different matters as naming a number series and repeating a series of names of numbers: but careful reading of his paper has not assured me that he is free from this confusion. For example on page xxxviii it is said: "M knew number names long before numbers themselves, and applied them to anything indiscriminately, the numbers seldom agreeing with the number of objects." Page xxxix: "Have children of the kindergarten count, and you will find that they leave out the difficult names and carry on the series the same, often repeating without being conscious of it. . . . M—— when learning to count things or impressions, would count eight, nine, for one object. The number series always get ahead." "This child learned the figures in order; *i.e.*, 1, 2, 3, 4. He could tell them in this way up to forty, but if they were changed around he would not know but what it meant the same. He associated number with place or order only." "Most children I have taught," says an experienced teacher, "*will* learn the names independent of things. For sometimes they do not associate them as how many of anything, but merely the name of the series. . . . Children learn number names as they learn other words, by hearing them repeated. They use them without knowing their respective values. They apply them promiscuously calling three objects ten as the case may be. Very frequently they have the idea that the number name belongs *to the object in whatever order among others* it is placed" (italics mine). A number of other instances could be quoted, but it is probably enough to refer to the summary of data on page lvii, where it is stated that three hundred and fourteen out of three hundred and forty-one returns say that children learn *number names by rote as an abstract word* (italics mine).

While, I repeat, it hardly seems credible that Mr. Phillips could confuse counting with the repetition of number names, yet the foregoing quotations, which might be largely multiplied, point in this direction. It must be borne in mind that these statements are not isolated, but are the substance of the evidence educed by Mr. Phillips to show that the formation of the number series precedes the application of number to objects. It is hardly necessary, I suppose, to argue that since this supposed evidence refers in reality only to the learning of certain words, it is just as irrelevant to the proof of Mr. Phillips's proposition, as would be the evidence that children learn to say the alphabet before they count objects. The repetition of number names is no more counting than is the saying of counting out rhymes like: "Eeny, meeny, miny, mo," etc., in fact, hardly as much so, for in the latter there is a genuine pairing off, or crude equating which approaches the number concept. It is barely conceivable that Mr. Phillips does not mean to attribute any numerical significance to this saying of number terms (though if such is the case, I utterly fail to see why it should be exhibited as indicating that counting goes in advance of application of number to things), but merely means to indicate the satisfaction which the child takes in any series or succession. I do not doubt this latter fact at all, nor do I doubt that interesting psychological results could be got from a careful study of the child's delight in successive recurrences. One group of Chicago kindergartners, for example, has been making a careful study of this matter and finds the child's interest in statements of: "This is the house that Jack built" type, so strong that a large number of rhymes and stories along similar lines have been constructed to the children's eminent satisfaction. Nor do I doubt that such phenomena are indirectly relevant to the psychology of number; but it must be clearly recognized that such facts have absolutely no power in support of the statement that genuine counting or formation of a real number series precedes the application of number to things, which is the point in question. Moreover, so far as these facts have any connection with the number sense at all, the essential thing is to see under what circumstances the mere interest in seriality of repetition becomes transformed into an interest in that particular form of seriality which we term counting. To confuse series interest in general with the series interest in its counted off form, is about as flagrant a case of the fallacy of accident as one could imagine.

This brings us to the question which is of fundamental importance. What is the origin and significance of the interest in series and succession? Secondly, under what circumstances does this assume the numerical form? I begin with the first point. Mr. Phillips's Psychology of Succession seems to me somewhat unnecessarily crude. On page xxxviii he says: "Succession of some kind is the earliest and most continuous thing in consciousness. Series of innervations, touches, sounds, sights, etc., are the constant things in consciousness; one series only gives way to another." Page xxxv: "Changes in consciousness are continually taking place produced by the varying impressions from all the senses. Consciousness is not one continuous impression, but an innumerable multitude of successive changes. . . . As already stated, without doubt different senses contribute to these ideas." Page xxxvi: "The series idea is established by a multitude of successive and rhythmical sensations conveyed through the different senses."

I call this psychology crude because it seems to confuse the *de facto* occurrence of changes in consciousness with a consciousness of such changes, this latter being necessary to any consciousness of a series; and because it implies that sensations, simply as sensations, come to us, individualizing themselves, and also arranged in series. Now one cannot, intelligently, watch a baby for fifteen minutes without seeing that there is a very great difference between distinctness and orderly sequence in sense *stimuli* and definiteness and sequence in *conscious* sensation. It is a matter of great difficulty, requiring several months of infant life to secure ability to pick out a distinct sound, color, touch, or taste at all. The child's consciousness certainly begins with a sense blur or confusion into which specification is only gradually introduced.

Instead, then, of taking for granted the existence of a series, supposing that it is adequately motivated by the mere occurrence of different sensations, we have to discover the principle through which the original blur is specified into definite states of consciousness, and these serially ordered with reference to each other. Of course an adequate discussion of this point is out of the question here, but, in order that we may have an idea of the origin of succession to put beside Mr. Phillips's, I would make the following statement: It is the motor reaction or process of adjustment which breaks up the sensory blur into definite states, and it is the continuity of motor adjustment (corresponding to habit) which arranges these into a series. Fortunately for our discussion all the evidence that Mr. Phillips brings up points in this direction. For example, page xxxvi: The cases given of "reproducing or following a series" are all motor. It is not mere having of sensations; it is throwing, repeating strokes with the clock, rolling mud balls, nodding the head, arranging pebbles, etc. On page xli, it is expressly stated: "A movement of some muscle, as the toe or finger, or nodding of the head, can be observed in nearly all children when counting at first." On page xli, instances of such motor reaction are given; also on page lvi, under the caption of "Tallying by Beats"; on page lvii, in Miss Shinn's valuable record, things were enumerated by touching them, taking nuts out of a box, transferring objects: and once more on page lix; so also page lxi. So striking is the evidence, that Mr. Phillips himself, in his final summary of conclusions on page lxxxiv, says: "Some movement is perhaps unavoidable in the early stages of counting. If the motor element be a necessity of all thought it is even more so in following an abstract series." The term "following" perhaps throws some light on Mr. Phillips's confusion. It seems to indicate that the series is already there and that the movement simply parallels the members of the series as they come and go. But this confuses the adult standpoint with the child's. The child *makes* the series *by* the movements: that is to say, by movement he interrupts the vague continuum and introduces definiteness or individuality.

We thus get a basis for interpreting the importance (which Mr. Phillips does well in emphasizing) of rhythm in the formation of an orderly series. This subject is also of course too large to go into, but Dr. Bolton's important investigations may be referred to. One passage given on page xxxi may be quoted: "The subjects were found to be unconsciously keeping time by tapping, nodding, etc., at every second or fourth click. When movement was restrained in one muscle it was likely to appear elsewhere. These *movements* are the condition of rhythmical grouping." It is the grouping of minor movements within a larger whole of movement which marks off a mere on-going series into those regular recurrences of stress and slur which make up what we call rhythm.

When interpreted, Mr. Phillips's own data confirm the statement quoted by him from McLellan and Dewey's *Psychology of Number* "That number is to be traced . . . back to *adjustment of activity*" (p. xxxiv). This is the point worked out in considerable detail in Chapter 3, pages 35 to 44 of that book. Perhaps this is as fitting a place as any to say something about the rational factor in number. Mr. Phillips objects to the doctrine of the *Psychology of Number* (see his pp. l–li) on the ground that it makes altogether too much of the rational processes of abstraction and generalization, and altogether too little of the instinctive, unreflective side. I shall not charge Mr. Phillips with lack of candor; but either the statement in the book is so confused and obscure that the point is not plainly made, or else Mr. Phillips has read it somewhat carelessly. He certainly is bound, in making his objection, to use the terms abstraction and generalization in the same sense in which they are used by the authors in question. However defective the statement may be, the point is certainly insisted upon that *practical* activity precedes the rational in the *conscious* sense of the latter term; it is pointed out that abstraction first exists practically in simple selection or preference as to ends and means, and that generalization is of the same practical sort, consisting in the adjustment of means to ends; and that only at a later period does this practical selection and adjustment come to consciousness in explicit rational form. The whole moral of the book pedagogically, so far as primary number is concerned, might be said to be this: "Do not teach number either merely mechanically or merely rationally. Give the child something to do which involves the use of numerical considerations in a reasonable related way. Thus he will gain practical familiarity with them, by using them for some purpose and end, instead of in a meaningless, haphazard way, will be forming orderly practical habits of relating, which afterwards will become conscious in real generalization." I quote from page 30 of the book referred to: "The child may and should perform many operations and reach definite results by *implicitly using the ideas* they (that is numbers) involve, long before these ideas can be explicitly developed in consciousness. If facts are presented in their proper connection, as stimulating and directing the primary mental activities, the child is slowly but surely feeling his way towards a conscious recognition of the nature of the process. This unconscious growth towards a reflective grasp of number relations is seriously retarded by untimely analysis."

In view of these facts, and in view of the fact that Mr. Phillips himself, finds the origin of the series in a purely objective basis—the occurrence of sensations, while McLellan and Dewey find it in a practical basis—motor reactions, it seems to me that I am not unreasonable in feeling that Mr. Phillips ought to have welcomed these authors as allies, and as providing a scientific support for his own contention (otherwise unproved) regarding the relation between the spontaneous and the conscious phases of number processes, instead of turning his guns upon them to the extent of two or three of his valuable pages.[1]

We now turn from the consideration of the series in general to that particular form of the series which we call

---

[1] There seems to be reason for supposing that Mr. Phillips has been led astray by identifying the principles of these authors with that of Mr. Speer—a procedure which is not just on either side. Mr. Speer is entitled to full claim to originality of method as far as Dewey and McLellan are concerned. It is not just to him to consider his book simply an application of the theory of the *Psychology of Number*, nor is it just to the authors of that book to interpret their theory simply in the light of Mr. Speer's practice. There is one fundamental point, I am happy to say, upon which we are in complete accord, that is the correspondence between the number idea and the quantity idea. But both the theory and practice of handling this point are very different. Mr. Speer's method, comparatively speaking, emphasizes the how much or continuity side at the expense of the discrete or how many side; and the two books interpret the conception of relation

counting. We have already disposed of the confusion between counting process and the mere repetition of number names and hence are ready to deal with the former question proper. In order to define the problem I may refer to an apparent misconstruction by Mr. Phillips of the doctrine of the *Psychology of Number*. On pages xxxiv, l, lxxiv, lxxx, lxxxi, he implies or states that the ratio idea is insisted upon in that book to the exclusion of the series idea, or at least to the very great subordination of the counting process. Nothing could be further from the mark. The doctrine of that work is that the counting process (the series idea) and the quantitative or magnitude idea, are logically correlative; *hence* the ratio idea. To subordinate the series (how many) to magnitude idea (how much) would destroy ratio, not exalt it. On page 145 of that book it is stated that counting is the fundamental process of arithmetic. On pages 163 to 165 the necessity of the counting process proceeding from the mechanical to the intelligent counting, is expressly insisted upon. So again on pages 44 to 51. In fact it is hardly worth while to give specific quotations. The characteristic theory of the book is the emphasis laid upon the principle that counting, the formation of the series, and measuring go together. More than this it is expressly stated both in the theoretical and the practical part that the numbering process or formation of a series, *comes to consciousness* first, and that ratio, *as a conscious idea*, is a later outcome (here, once more, is a difference between Speer's method and that of the book in question).

I do not mention this for the sake of justifying the book, although if Mr. Phillips has gone so far astray in understanding it, it is possible that others have also. I mention it for its value in helping define the real question. This

---

in very different ways. To Mr. Speer, relating means (upon the whole) intellectual comparison; to the authors of the *Psychology of Number* relating means, primarily, practical adjustment. On pp. li–lii, Mr. Phillips quotes a sentence from the *Psychology of Number* and in the same connection, as if it bore upon its interpretation, makes the following quotation: "Reasoning in arithmetic establishes equality of relation. Reasoning in any subject, equality or likeness of relations." This latter sentence is quoted from Mr. Speer. It would be pedantic to make a moral issue of this, but I should like to know by what rule of criticism one is justified in quoting from one author to interpret another. As matter of fact, this statement is quite unlike the doctrine of *Psychology of Number*.

is not whether counting precedes or follows the ratio idea; but what is the *use* or value of the counting process? What is its *motive*? *Why* do we count? I doubt if anybody would go to the point of absurdity of developing an arithmetical method which omitted the counting side. Number *as* number *is* enumeration. Certainly Mr. Speer, with all the emphasis thrown upon conscious comparison of magnitudes and the statement of result in ratio form, has used counting in the definition of the ratio—my objection being simply that he does not emphasize sufficiently this counting or discrete factor. But the important question, both psychologically and pedagogically is: How shall we *utilize* the counting process? Shall we isolate it, or shall we treat it as having a function in the definition of value? This is all there is to the whole question.

I will now state my conception of the origin and development of the counting process, comparing this statement from time to time with that given by Mr. Phillips. My general conception is as follows: At the outset the child learns to count (in the genuine sense as distinct from the mere repetition of a mere lot of words) by *reference* to separate things making up a vague totality. If we take the facts preceding conscious counting, this is evident. The child keeps tally by some movement of his own with some objective fact or event; he equates, so to speak, an action of his own with some action outside of himself. All the evidence that can be educed with reference to the formation of system to number names points the same way—the connection between counting and the toes, fingers, hands, etc. So also does the connection of number with space—noted by Mr. Phillips himself. It is equally evidenced by observation of children in cases of learning to count as distinct once more, from saying number names. I am glad to refer to Miss Shinn's record which completely bears out (though in considerably greater detail than my own) observations which I have made upon three children. For a considerable period there is interest in marking off objects by pairs, one against the other. During this period the idea of two is understood, that of one and the other, but nothing beyond. While this pairing off was marked from sixteen months onward as late as the twenty-eighth month, three could not be counted. **Mr. Phillips** gives a good deal of concrete data bearing out the statement made in the *Psychology of Number* that counting involves the *ordinal* idea as well as the cardinal, evidence taking the form that the child will identify a given number like three or four with a particular stick or object. In one of my own observations in teaching a girl of three to count upon her hands, in beginning with the thumb it was numbered one. The next time beginning with the little finger the thumb was called five, whereupon she insisted that it was one. This confusion continued for a few days, when the child spontaneously remarked: "Why, you can begin at either end." Up to this time she had never been certain with reference to three; after this she counted intelligently up to ten.

But it hardly seems worth while to go over the specific evidence. The moment one ceases to confuse counting with repetition of number names the proposition that we learn to count, irrespective to application to things, becomes absolutely meaningless. When we count we surely count something. The difficulty in learning to count is the difficulty of distinguishing relations of order from those of mere place or form (see for example the cases on p. xlix of Mr. Phillips's article, in which cases of the confusion of form and number are given; so also pp. lv, lvi). So great is this demand for something to count, that I have known of a number of children who have reached the period of spontaneous counting who insisted upon saying one one, two ones, three ones, four ones, and so on, and were quite confused when the number was given to them simply as an aggregate. In one case I remember a child of four, who, when something was said to her about seven, was at first confused, and then spontaneously said: "O, I suppose you mean seven ones." Both the positive evidence, then, and the negative (that is, the difficulties which children have in learning to count) show that counting arises in connecting, not merely with a series succession, with the *successive ordering of units in a series*, such units being represented by fingers or objects with which the child is familiar. The abstraction previously referred to, necessary to counting, consists in the fact that the child must be able to grasp relative place or order in a series as distinct from absolute place, from spatial form, or other purely qualitative considerations: a fact adequately proved by Mr. Phillips's own data.

I come now to the period of spontaneous delight in counting—in which counting *is* free from all *explicit* reference to objects. The data collected by Mr. Phillips on this point are wholly in agreement with my own observation and with reminiscences which I have collected of adults regarding the counting period in their own lives (the point referred to on p. 26 of the *Psychology of Number*). This is in no wise in contradiction to what has already been said concerning the original connection of learning to count with some spatial reference and distinction. *After* the child has learned to count, the power acquired becomes temporarily an end in itself. The power is set free and manifests itself spontaneously. This is simply in accordance with the general principle of play. This delight in counting comes in the play period of the child's life, as a rule, and evidences the same general principle. Powers originally acquired under some practical (not merely sensible nor merely intellectual) stress, when acquired, run free or on their own account for awhile. The child takes similar delight in walking, running, talking, on their own account, doing them for the mere sake of doing them. It would be futile to deny this. It is folly not to take sufficient account of them pedagogically, and I quite agree with what Mr. Phillips says about the usual failure to utilize this spontaneous delight pedagogically. The child is hampered by being made to work in a formal way upon small numbers and counting by ones, when, if left to himself, he would spontaneously occupy himself with larger numbers and count by twos, fours and fives, almost as easily as by ones. This is as mischievous and cramping as it would be to keep the child going through exercises in learning to walk after he has learned. But theoretically it would be equally futile to deny that this spontaneous interest in counting for its own sake was preceded by a somewhat slow and tedious process in which the child was learning to count (just as to walk) through ordering or adjusting things to each other in a succession of acts.

We now come to the next step, both intellectually and

pedagogically. The average child who enters school at six or seven is emerging from this counting period. What he now needs is some further use to which his ability to count may be put, in order to gain new power. Otherwise there is arrested development. Nothing has interested me more in Mr. Phillips's article than his statement that numerical precocities and prodigies are connected with a too protracted dwelling in the counting stage. Now, unless some arrest, similar in principle though less in extent, is to occur in every child when he goes to school, some function must be found with reference to which the child may utilize his ability to count. My contention is that the number sense becomes vitalized and truly educative at this point by being largely directed towards the definition of values in the form of measurement. It is referred to things again, but not for the sake of merely counting the things—that is a relapse to an outgrown stage of development and is an error which is responsible for much of the benumbing, cramping grind of our school work. The reference to things is now in the sense of defining magnitude, measuring area, using scales to determine weight, enumerating the value of commodity with reference to money units, etc., etc. Here the power of counting is used as a tool of control and construction and so becomes truly educative.

Now a word, more definitely, as to the relationship of the series idea to the ratio idea. In the first stage, learning to count, there is always somewhat which is counted off. This *somewhat* limits the process of counting; and in turn the counting definitely marks out the somewhat counted. This "somewhat" may be illustrated by the fingers of the hand, by a pile of sticks or stones or whatever. The moment the child begins to count, this totality presents itself as vaguely quantitative. Through the counting, this vagueness is transformed into relative definiteness. Mr. Phillips says: "It is absurd to think of a savage attempting to measure a given quantity without any concept of number." I should say it was. Number is absolutely essential to the measurement of quantity. It is by counting or enumerating the number of units that we find out how much of a quantity there is. The point is simply that the savage and the child begin with vague concepts of plurality, corresponding to the series, and with an equally vague sense of the totality or unity (quantity) which is split up into this plurality. By the application of one factor to the other *each* is defined. It is absurd to suppose that any one measures without a concept (vague that is) of number; but it is equally absurd to suppose that the savage or the child has a perfectly clear, definite, and ready-made concept of number before he ever counts up any quantity, and then proceeds to measure the quantity or find out how much there is. We begin with an equally vague "many" and an equally vague "much." Each clears the other up through mutual application. It hardly seems consistent in Mr. Phillips to insist so much upon the child's primitive, crude consciousness of plurality in the form of a series, and not to bring out with equal clearness the part played by intensive concepts of degree—little, much, more, less, light, heavy, hotter, colder, etc.,—in the child's experience. It certainly is misleading in the outcome, because it throws the factor of plurality out of perspective and out of its bearings, and hence narrows and distorts the pedagogical province of number.

Of course, one cannot avoid reflecting his own attitudes and prepossessions in any series of questions which may be sent out. But it must equally be borne in mind that the data received in reply to such questions have value just in proportion to the extent in which the questions have covered the whole ground or only a part of it. It is accordingly exceedingly unfortunate, to say the least, that not a *single* one of the questions in the syllabus given by Mr. Phillips has to do with the child's spontaneous experiences and expressions with *reference to questions of quantity and magnitude.* If one cared for one-sided results, I would agree to get up a syllabus bearing on what children say and do regarding questions of more and less, and instinctive comparison of values and amounts, the replies to which would throw into as great relief the quantitative side as Mr. Phillips's data do the strictly numerical side. But this would not be well balanced. The investigation should cover *both* points. I should be very glad if Mr. Phillips would supplement his present inquiry by another along this line; for, till this be undertaken, his present data are necessarily so one-sided as to lend themselves to false interpretations. It would take up, not only such questions as children's spontaneous interest in measurements, but also in formal comparison of amounts. I suggest merely one line which I think would be instructive. Many children in the same family are given to comparing the amount of food given them, particularly when it is a dainty or a luxury. Comparisons of amounts of candy, cake, dessert, and the use of counting to find out who has the most, would, I think, be quite fruitful in showing the way in which the child spontaneously uses number. (This point was suggested to me by Superintendent Ames, of Riverside.)

In the second period, that of counting as spontaneous play, the reference to quantity is, of course, not so obvious. It reappears, however, in a somewhat subtle form. I am glad to be able to refer again to Mr. Phillips's own data. It is seen in the interest of children in the "last" number—an interest I think which is almost universal. Mr. Phillips refers to the child who wanted to know all the numbers there are, page xxxviii. In general I think it will be found, moreover, that when children are spontaneously counting, they generally set up in advance the amount to which they are going to count up—as a hundred, a thousand, a million, or in extreme cases a child sets out to count clear up to the "last number." Here the magnitude conception recurs as at once setting a limit to and motivating the counting process.

In the third stage the relation between counting and magnitude is so obvious that nothing further need be said. I may say, however, one word more about the ratio idea in itself. The theory and practice of the *Psychology of Number* are that when counting is used by the child to value some amount or other, the ratio idea is *implied* or involved. It need *not*, therefore, be consciously, or explicitly stated. In fact, I should say that for a considerable period it should not be. It is enough that the child gets a sense for the use and application of number for purposes of evaluation, without his consciously formulating the factors involved. Familiarity through use must precede conscious formulation. But our point further is that when number is so used the transition to the conscious ratio idea, whether in the form of ratio proper, or percentage of fractions, is natural, and inevitable. The child is saved that break which is almost uniform in present school practice—and a questionnaire upon this point would be instructive. I mean the break between whole numbers and fractions; and between the four fundamental processes and ratio and percentage. When number is used to value quantity, this idea is practically implied from the outset; and when conditions require, and the child is sufficiently mature, he passes without mental friction to conscious recognition. In closing I wish to say that this is not a mere doctrinaire statement, but that it rests upon continuous experimenting and observation in a school where the child's number sense is developed strictly in connection with construction operation in manual training, cooking, sewing, and science work, where number relations are introduced as instrumental to practical valuations.

In conclusion, the discussion may be thus summarized: A conscious series arises through a process of motor adjustments. This is rhythmical, and the rhythm facilitates at counting by making regular breaks and groupings. The series becomes numerical when its parts are *ordered* with reference to place and value in constituting the whole group. Along with this goes a vague recognition of muchness or magnitude (corresponding to the whole group) which is made definite through counting. Then the power of counting becomes an end in itself; *what is* counted is now simply some total amount or numerical magnitude set as limit. Finally (unless there is to be arrested development), this counting power is reapplied to magnitudes of value in order to measure or define them. This *implies* ratio, which comes to *consciousness* as need demands.

# Imagination and Expression

It is obvious that the teaching of artistic expression will start along the lines of least resistance, and be effective as to both external output and as to the educator of the individual pupil just in the degree in which it bases itself upon the psychical impulse which furnishes the motive to expression. But something more is required than a right start. If the education is to be effective, this impulse must be directed, must be utilized to the full. You will pardon me accordingly if I engage in a somewhat technical psychological discussion of what the motive to expression is, and what occurs in the realization of this motive. We have plenty of glorification of art, and of the importance of artistic training, but we have almost no definite scientific attempts to translate the artistic process over into terms of its psychical machinery—that is, of the mental processes which occasion and which effect such expression. In entering upon the attempt to make such a translation I shall select as basis of the discussion, for reasons which require no explanation, drawing as the type of artistic expression.

We may begin our analysis with the familiar distinction of idea and technique. Every mode of expression, no matter how mechanical, no matter how fantastic, how impressionistic, has these two sides. The architect's drawing of the plan of a house, the engineer's working plan for the construction of a machine must have an idea to be expressed, or else any series of lines drawn with a ruler would serve as well. And the crudest attempt of a child to illustrate "Hickory-Dickory-Dock" has also its technique[1]—its mode of

1    This is to be interpreted in the light of the distinction hereafter made between unconscious and conscious technique.

[First published in part in the Western Drawing Teachers' Association Third Annual Report (n.p., 1896); first published in full in Kindergarten Magazine, IX (Sept. 1896), 61–69. Not previously reprinted. See A Note on the Texts for publishing history.]

realization. It is also clear that in this process of expression the primary function belongs to the idea, the secondary to the technique; they are related as content and form, as material to be conveyed or delivered and as mode of conveyance, as what and as how. But lest this statement should be misinterpreted, as it seems to me it often is misinterpreted, it must be added that to say that one is final and the other subservient, one is end, the other means, does not of necessity mean that attention is to be concentrated upon the one and the other is to be neglected. What we derive from this statement of the subservience of technique to idea is not a criterion for the amount of attention to be given to each, but a criterion for the reason of directing attention to one or the other; we get a motive for attending. If one is thoroughly interested in the idea as something to be expressed, he must, on that account, be interested in the mode of expression. An insufficient interest in the form or process always marks something crude, hazy, or unreal in the content. We must be interested in the expression just in proportion to the intensity, the controlling character of our interest in the idea. But, on the other hand, this interest in the idea, in the story to be told, the thought to be realized, is the only basis for an artistic interest in the technique. A mode of expression separated from something to express is empty and artificial; it is barren and benumbing.

I make this point at the outset because it seems to me to define both the practical and the theoretical problem of drawing instruction. It is comparatively simple to abstract the technique, to make command of certain tools, physical and mental, the end and aim; it is comparatively easy to start from the image, the story, and allow that to find its own unaided outlet, and under claim of the superiority of idea to technique, allow not simply a crude and unformed result to pass—that is a matter of no importance in itself—but to encourage crude and slovenly habits of expression to grow up—which is an exceedingly important matter. The *via media* which is such a difficult path to find—the straight and narrow path which makes for artistic righteousness—goes in neither of these directions, but attempts on the one hand to make the interest in the idea, the vital image to extend itself to the mode of conveyance, to make the entire interest in technique a functional not an isolated one, while on the other it recognizes the necessity of having the mode of expression react back into the idea, to make it less cloudy, more definite, less haphazard, more accurate, less the product of the momentary undeveloped interest and thought, more the outcome of mature reflection and comprehensive interest.

So much for our practical problem in general. Now for its psychological equivalence. What corresponds to idea, what corresponds to technique in the natural psychical process; how are these related to each other; how do they interact in a mutually helpful way? We cannot accept one apparently simple way of answering this question. We cannot say that the idea is imaginative, is spiritual, while what corresponds to the technique is physical, mechanical. The simplicity of this answer is at the cost of reality. The mental occurrence which represents the form or mode of expression is just as much an image as is the idea itself. It is not the problem of the relation of a spiritual image to a physical organ of expression but of one sort of imagery to another. And while this is perhaps an unusual putting of the matter, we must recognize that after all it is because the whole process is one of imagery that the problem is a soluble one in an educative sense. If one side, the idea, were alone a matter of the imagination, and the technique were simply a matter of delicate and accurate physical control of the eye and muscle, we could never get a genuine harmonizing of the two factors in the problem; we should be compelled simply to alternate from one side to the other or to make the best compromise we could.

In saying that the side of technique is itself a matter of imagery, I refer to what the psychologists term motor imagery, and to the well known fact that imagery of all kinds has a tendency to overflow in the motor channels, and that thus there is a tendency to reproduce through action and experience, or to put forth in expression whatever has been gained in impression and assimilated into an idea. I refer moreover, to the fact that such motor expression is not something done with an idea already made in the mind, but is necessary to the appreciation of the idea itself. If there is one principle more than another upon which all educational practice, not simply education in art, must base itself it is precisely this: the realization of an idea in action through the medium of movement is necessary to the vividness, the definiteness, the fullness of that idea itself. We cannot speak of an idea *and* its expression; the expression is more than a mode of conveying an already formed idea; it is part and parcel of its formation. The so-called mechanical phase is necessary to the integrity of the spiritual. Education, like philosophy, has suffered from the idea that thought is complete in itself, and that action, the expression of thought, is a physical thing. We are learning to know that thought is thought only in and through action.

Here we have the natural psychical origin of drawing, as well as of all other forms of expression. There is a natural tendency for every image to pass into movement; an inert image, an image which does not tend to manifest itself through the medium of action is a non-existence. In later life, we have learned to suppress so many suggestions to action, and have learned to delay the expression of so many others, that this fundamental law has become somewhat obscured, but a study of child life and growth reveals it in its purity and intensity, and reveals also that the suppression of manifestation of an image or delay in its passage into action is an acquired habit, a later acquisition. In the early period, the tendency of every image to secure realization for itself in the medium of action is witnessed in play and in the incessantly urgent desire of the child for conversation; his impulse to tell everything, to communicate. A complete discussion of play would take us apart from our present purpose, but certainly its fundamental meaning is the proof it furnishes that mere absorption or accumulation or impression does not suffice; that it is never a complete or self-sufficing mental condition, but requires to be fulfilled in expression, by translation into activity. It requires comparatively little observation of a child to reach the conclusion that the child does not get hold of any impression or any idea until he has *done* it; the impression is alien, is felt as inadequate, as unsatisfactory until the child makes it his own by turning it over into terms of his own activities. He gains his ideas and makes them truly his own, a part of himself, by reproducing them—and this reproduction is literal and not metaphorical. He acts an idea *out* before he really takes it *in*. In infancy this manifests itself in the continual handling, pulling, punching, throwing of all objects with which the child comes in contact; in the continual imitation of the child. How are we to account for this instinct of imitation except on the basis that it is not enough for him to see or hear as an observer; that the child gets hold of what he sees and hears as he himself reproduces, which from his standpoint is creation! Later on this principle manifests itself in the fact that every object stimulates him to use it in some way; he cannot see a hat without trying to put it on; a drawer without wanting to shut and open it; a poker without wanting to poke, etc., etc. Later still, this realization through action is manifested in play, ordinarily so-called—the appropriation to himself in terms of his own constructive activities of the world of nature and society in which he finds himself.

Before making the transition in the discussion to the mode of expression called drawing, two principles should be noted. One of these points is the complete absorption at this stage of what later on we term image and technique respectively. In all these earlier reproductive activities it is clear that there are not two sides to the child, an image and its expression; the image *is* only in its expression, the expression is only the image moving, vitalizing itself. The technique is unconscious; it has no separate value in consciousness. There is no interest in the *how*, distinct from the *what*.

The spontaneous grace and beauty of child life is precisely that the balance between image and expression is unbroken; the period of analysis, of distinction between the end to be reached, and the mode of reaching it, with its consequent effort and reflection, has not arrived. The other point is most closely connected with this. It is that the animating idea has no objective existence to the child; it is not something which he thinks about or looks at; it is something in which he lives. In other words, it is his whole self, his whole life, for the time. This complete absorption *in* the image is the test and sign of genuine play. Any marking off of the idea by itself, putting it, as it were, outside of the totality of life, shows either that the child is being forced and is going through the form without the reality of play, or else, if it is natural, that he is emerging from the play into the work period. These two related points, the unconsciousness of technique or the lack of any consciousness of the mode of doing, apart from what is being done, and the complete absorption of the agent in his action, we must take with us to the consideration of the beginnings of instruction in artistic expression of a more formal kind than is play.

Drawing as a development of play marks, however, a growing inhibition or control. The *whole* image at first moves in the *whole* organ by the principle of radiation or expansion. Drawing marks the limitation to certain channels; moreover it is directed more immediately by the eye image, not the experience as a whole; it marks therefore, *relatively* an *analysis*. However, even here we must recognize the principle of integrity; it is only relatively that there is distinction.

Drawings then at first are means of reinforcing and continuing some interesting life experience of the child, through giving it back to the eye by means of the hand. The start *must* be imaginative, not simply ought to be. Even in drawing objects the child will draw from his image, not from the object itself. There is no road from the object to the child's motor nerves and hand, but only from his mental picture of the object. The use of the object must be therefore simply to help the construction of the image; anything else merely creates dependence upon the external. It not only leads to servility, but by disintegrating imagery makes the product mechanical. Moreover, the child is interested in objects simply from the standpoint of the part they play in his life, their use, the value they have for him, not as objects, but as factors in some life scene. Thus objects at first are seen, not so much in terms of their visual appearance as in terms of touch, because touch represents more adequately the immediate experience values of the object, what can be done directly with it, while sight represents more indirect, and as it were, symbolic values. In any case, the object is apperceived as function, as service, as purpose, never as mere object. It is on this account that the picture, judged as itself an object, is so crude. It lacks proportion, definiteness of spatial form and structure. The child is unconscious of all these defects, because he sees not the mere external product before him, but the whole mental picture which interests and holds him.

Correction of this crudity, perfection of the picture considered as an object means the gradual development of conscious technique—the power of seeing the picture produced by itself as it is to the eye, not simply as it is to the whole of experience; and the power to control the movements of the hand and eye by this visual picture as a standard. This involves a certain separation and abstraction. The eye activities and their resulting values, have to be set free from their close unification with the sense of touch. A new language, the visual language has to be substituted for the visual-touch-action language.

Psychologically what takes place is a return upon an experience to see how it occurs, and the reconstruction of that experience, the making it over on the basis of the method thus brought to consciousness. The uniform law is, first the doing; then the consciousness of the how of doing; then the return of this mode into the experience to enrich and develop it, a fuller, more interesting doing.

Hence we may lay down with practical psychological certainty the following principles regarding the relation of technique to pictorial image in drawing instruction. The beginning must always be with some imaginative free expression in which both the experience represented and the process of expression have their own adequate value to the child. The consciousness of technique must grow up out of and within this expression, having its own meaning within itself. Every gain in technique must be at once utilized for a further and richer imaginative expression.

It is with reference to these principles that current methods of instruction in drawing would receive most criticism from the psychologist. It is perhaps natural that the drawing teacher, the author of text-books should be most interested in the production of a good picture, viewed from the standpoint of results or the object as an object, and hence should isolate the technique, or method of reaching such good external products, fixing his attention upon that to the comparative neglect of the psychical condition of the pupil, or to the conditions which will give free play of imagery. But those who are interested in drawing, not as an end in itself, but because of its place in education as a whole, must insist upon the proper psychological correlation of this study; must insist upon the function of technique, as subordinate to imaginative expression, and as effecting the transition from one such expression to another.

The following means of developing technique in its proper place may be indicated.

First, foremost and all the time: Incidental criticism of products of imaginative expression. The crude picture does not adequately represent the child's own image. It comes far short in some directions; it distorts in others. Questions and suggestions will bring the child to realize the discrepancy between what he meant to do, and what he has actually done. This makes him turn around upon his image, reflect upon it, define it more accurately, and makes him alert for the differences between false and adequate expression. When the child comes to have the habit of looking at his own products, of comparing them with his original image and of criticizing one by reference to the other (without being unduly discouraged and thus paralyzed) the battle for technique is, in principle, won.

Second: Drawing in connection with nature study affords excellent means for development in technical definiteness and accuracy. It is necessary to image parts in definite, not in haphazard relations, in order that the idea of the whole may be realized. But even here, especially with younger children, it is necessary to bear in mind that the primary interest is not in the external appearance of the object as an object, but in function, use, æsthetic quality and relation to life.

Third: Drawing in connection with history, architectural reproductions, marks a similar normal and intrinsic demand for the correction of crudity and vagueness.

Fourth: The æsthetic interest is strong in the child and may be taken advantage of in connection with decorative design and construction. But this principle is often conformed to in name and denied in fact. It is not enough that the teacher knows that there is a decorative *motif* involved. It must be real decoration to the child. The mere objective pattern will not appeal to him nearly as much as the pattern used as decoration on the cover of his own portfolio.

Fifth: Wherever there is any kind of manual training, there is a necessary demand, in the development of the activity itself, for correct technique.

Sixth: The child may learn much from the incidental and mainly unconscious imitation of the methods used by others. There is all the difference in the world educationally between that unconscious assimilation of the mode of handling used by another better trained person, and the mechanical and set copying of that person's work. One imitates the process and tends to set free the child's powers; the other imitates the product and tends toward slavishness. Drawing is a language; there is much which, if not exactly conventional, must yet be learned by seeing how others manipulate the material and tools in order to get certain results. Hence the great value of good drawing done *before* the children, their conscious attention, however, being upon the picture itself and not upon the teacher. Much might be accomplished, I feel sure, by simplified reproductions of great landscapes showing how great artists have obtained certain effects. The landscape itself is an exceedingly complex thing. Help is needed in seeing it, in imaging it. Good pictures afford this aid, just as good literature helps in interpreting the complex scene of life. If some one would reproduce these pictures, simplifying their outline, their shading, and yet retaining their salient points and characteristic spirit, that one would perform a great service for our schools.

Now there is nothing new in any of these suggestions. But what the psychologist would urge is the need of using any one and all of them in the proper place. The crying evil is the abstraction of the technique, making it in reality only a means toward the true end—free expression—an end in itself. What psychology urges is, that attention be fixed upon the one thing needful, the presentation and construction by the mind of a complete image, and having its own value and meaning in itself, and that technique be treated as an aid in this construction and presentation, and not as a thing by itself.

# *The Æsthetic Element in Education*

I interpret this title to mean a certain phase of all education, rather than a particular group of studies.

I. Responsiveness, an emotional reaction to ideas and acts, is a necessary factor in moral character.

II. It is also a necessary element in intellectual training, as supplying a delicacy and quickness of recognition in the face of practical situation.

III. The significance of the æsthetic element is that it trains a natural sensitiveness and susceptibility of the individual to usefulness in these directions. The individual has a natural tendency to react in an emotional way; but this natural disposition requires training. In some, who are naturally obtuse or thick-skinned, it requires to be brought out; in others, who are naturally more sensitive, it may assume a morbid and exaggerated form, unless made to function in definite ways.

IV. The factors in æsthetic experience which are especially adapted to afford the right training are balance and rhythm. Balance implies control or inhibition which does not sacrifice a fullness and freedom of the experience. It is opposed both to random, undirected action and to repressed, or undeveloped, action. Rhythm involves regularity and economy in the sequence of actions. Both balance and rhythm are forms of variety in unity: rhythm being temporal, balance spatial.

V. The æsthetic element thus should combine freedom of individual expression and appreciation with the factor of law and regularity in what is expressed. It is possible to extend the idea of artistic production to all kinds of work.

VI. Modern theory and practice in education have laid

[*First published in* Addresses and Proceedings *of the National Educational Association*, 1897, *pp.* 329–30. *Not previously reprinted.*]

relatively too much stress upon the volitional training in practical control and intellectual training in the acquisition of information, and too little upon the training of responsiveness. We need to return more to the Greek conception, which defined education as the attaching of pleasure and pain to the right objects and ideals in the right way. This ideal over-emphasized the emotional element, but we have now gone to the opposite extreme.

# Results of Child–Study Applied to Education

[*What principles, methods, or devices for teaching, not now in common use, should in your opinion be taken as fundamental and authoritative, and be applied in school work?*]

In stating the following principles it is taken for granted that there are no results which are "foregone" in the sense of being beyond further investigation, criticism, or revision; but that what is wanted is a statement of results sufficiently assured to have a claim upon the parent and teacher for consideration as working hypotheses.

1. The radical error which the application of results of Child-Study would inhibit is, in my judgment, the habit of treating the child from the standpoint of teacher or parent; *i.e.*, considering child as something to be educated, developed, instructed, or amused. Applications of this particular principle will be found in connection with the positive statement following.

2. The fundamental principle is that the child is always a being with activities of his own, which are present and urgent and do not require to be "induced," "drawn out," or "developed," etc.; that the work of the educator, whether parent or teacher, consists solely in ascertaining, and in connecting with, these activities, furnishing them appropriate opportunities and conditions.

[*First published in* Transactions of the Illinois Society for Child-Study, I (*Jan. 1895*), *18–19. Reprinted in Appendix* II, "*The Theory of the Chicago Experiment,*" *by John Dewey, in* The Dewey School, *by Katherine Camp Mayhew and Anna Camp Edwards (New York: D. Appleton-Century Co., 1936), pp. 474–76.*]

More specifically:

(a) Sensory and motor activities are always connected.

(b) Ideational activity is perverted and cramped unless it has a motor object in view and finds a motor outlet.

(c) The sensori-motor and idea-motor co-ordinations tend to ripen in a certain order.

(d) The larger, coarser and freer co-ordinations always mature before the finer and more detailed ones.

(e) All normal activities have a strong emotional coloring,—moral (personified characters, dramatized deeds and situations) and æsthetic.

(f) Curiosity, interest and attention are always natural and inevitable concomitants of the ripening of a given co-ordination.

(g) Finally and fundamentally, a child is a social being. Hence, educationally, the following methods:

(1) Reading, writing, drawing and music should be treated as ways in which a given idea, under the influence of its own emotional coloring, finds its own expression. The work of the teacher is to see that the mental image is formed in the child and opportunity afforded for the image to express itself freely along lines of least resistance, in motor discharge. Reading is psychologically dependent upon writing and drawing, needs observation for stimulus, and the stirring of the social instinct—the demand for communication—for object.

(2) Number arises in connection with the measuring of things for purposes of constructive activity; and hence arithmetic should be so taught, and not in connection either with figures or with the observation of objects.

(3) Nature study, geography, and history are to be treated as extensions of the child's own activity; *e.g.*, there is no sense (psychologically) in studying any geographical fact except as the child sees that fact entering into and modifying his own acts and relationships.

(4) Minute work is to be avoided, whether it is (i) mainly physical, as in some of the Kindergarten exercises, in many of the methods used in drawing and writing, or (ii) mainly intellectual, as starting with too much analysis, with

parts rather than wholes, presenting objects and ideas apart from their purpose and function, what they will do.

(5) The intellectual and moral discipline, the total atmosphere, is to be permeated with the idea that *the school is to the child and teacher the social institution in which they, for the time, live,* and that it is not a mere means for some outside end.

# The Kindergarten and Child-Study

While the child-study movement in name is a recent affair, and while in many of its superficial features it deserves the name sometimes given it—that of a fad—in its underlying reality it represents the culmination of educational and social forces which have been at work for generations, and presents itself as a factor which must be permanently reckoned with. It is a part of the psychological movement. It represents the attempt to state experience in terms of the individual instead of the class, and to adopt training in individual needs and powers of service.

Special opportunities for study of child psychology under unusually favorable circumstances offer themselves in the kindergarten. The following directions may be singled out:

1. There is the study of the motor and constructive activities of the child. In the adult the conventionalities of life and long periods of past training conspire to suppress most of the outward signs of mental activity. In childhood the normal relationship between feeling and idea on one side and expressive activity on the other is most obvious. And the kindergarten, by the sort of work which prevails in it, gives peculiarly valuable occasions for studying this connection. The time is ripe for restudying the gifts and occupations from the standpoint of what is now known regarding the laws of development of motor activity in childhood.

2. The kindergarten has always laid much emphasis upon the conception of play as an educational factor. Psychologists have now taken up the study of play, and are relating it both to the general principles of mental evolution and to the facts of structure of the nervous and muscular systems. Sociologists are also studying play from the stand-

[*First published in* Addresses and Proceedings *of the National Educational Association*, 1897, *pp.* 585–86. *Not previously reprinted.*]

point of the inheritance and modification of social customs and habits. Here, too, the hour has come for reconsidering kindergarten practice in the light of the theory of play and the facts gathered from a study of the spontaneous plays of children. It needs to be looked at in the light of difference of age, of sex, of nationality, of social environment, as well as of individual temperament.

3. Much is now said regarding the artistic and æsthetic factor in education. Both because the kindergarten has from the outset laid more emphasis on the artistic than have the succeeding periods of our school, and because of the comparative freedom of expression in the kindergarten it is highly important that the manifold opportunities which present themselves along this line should be utilized.

In conclusion, the study of the kindergarten theory and practice from the psychological standpoint is important, because it enables the teachers to translate the abstract and general propositions of philosophic theory into terms of the concrete living individual, and because it is psychology which controls the adaptation of all materials and occupations to the capacities and aims of the individual child. To put psychology into kindergarten practice means to make it more vital and more personal.

# Criticisms Wise and Otherwise on Modern Child-Study

The features of child-study against which criticisms have been justly directed are the results partly of the exaggerations incident to all large movements in their inception, partly of the misdirected gyrations of those camp-followers who, hanging about education as about all other progressive forces, attempt to use child-study for their own advertising and aggrandizement, and partly of the unwise zeal of those who, lacking in stability, are blown about by every new wind of doctrine and lose the just perspective.

Many of the criticisms which have justification are caused by the premature assertion on the part of some that the child-study movement was to afford a new, certain, positive, and scientific basis for education, replacing all the supposedly tentative and speculative foundations hitherto built upon. When the proposed revolution failed to materialize, and teachers found that, as hitherto, they had to rely upon good judgment, personal experience, and a knowledge of the ideas and practices of others, many felt that they had been fooled, and turned from an indiscriminate worship at the shrine of child-study to a condemnation equally indiscriminate.

Many of the criticisms proceed from a failure to draw the lines carefully between those aspects of child-study which belong to the province of the scientific investigator and those which interest the educator. It takes time to develop scientific method, to collect and sift facts, to derive theoretic conclusions. There is no more sense in attacking the scientific investigator in this line because he doesn't provide on demand usable recipes, ticketed and labeled for

[*First published in* Addresses and Proceedings *of the National Educational Association,* 1897, *pp.* 867–68. *Not previously reprinted.*]

all pedagogical emergencies, than there would have been in attacking the early pioneers in electricity because they worked quietly in the laboratory upon seemingly remote and abstruse subjects instead of providing us off-hand with the telegraph, telephone, electric light, and transportation.

Another source of criticism has been the undue isolation of child-study from the sciences upon which it is dependent. The only excuse for making child-study a thing by itself and attributing to it a unity of its own is not that the child is a unique fact separate from others, but simply because it presents a focus to which principles of physiology and psychology may be directed. When those ignorant of or disregarding these larger sciences plunge directly into child-study and expect to get valuable results, the method is quackery, and the outcome confusion. As Professor James is reported as saying: "You could get a great many interesting anecdotes and peculiar facts together by starting out upon an indiscriminate study of adults. It would have just as much and just as little scientific and practical value as similar child-study. I may add there is a fear of theory, of speculation, of hypothesis, which is as absurd as pure speculation divorced from fact. The mere collection of facts, uncontrolled by working hypothesis, unenlightened by generalization, never made a science and never will. I plead for a closer union of child-study with general psychological theory." In conclusion, the speaker said that child-study interpreted simply as one direction of general physiology and psychology had two things to do for education. One is furnishing certain generalizations regarding the order of growth, etc., a line well illustrated by Dr. Halleck's paper of yesterday. This is of general use in determining the whole scheme of education, but to the average teacher it will be of use in giving insight into individual children and ability to interpret their individual needs and temperaments. Its final value for the great mass of teachers will be measured by the extent to which it enables a teacher to see more accurately and adequately into the different individual pupils that present themselves. Mere general theories and mere facts *about* children are no substitutes for insight *into* children.

# The Interpretation Side of
# Child-Study

In the succeeding sessions of this Society, you will have
presented to you many of the more detailed methods and
results of the investigations which are being carried on in
child life in all its various phases. It seemed to me that it
might be worth while, this evening, to raise a somewhat
different aspect of the question, and not attempt to give you
any of the methods by which experts are engaged in investi-
gating children, any of the results in their pedagogical or
psychological bearings which have grown out of the application of these methods, or any of the popular phases which are
perhaps of equal, and in some respects superior, importance.
It seems to me that it might be worth while to raise the
question which lies back of such a congress as this, such a
meeting as we have here tonight, back of all this enthusiasm, back of this enthusiastic study, search for methods and
attempts to apply them.

What is the source of this interest in child life? What
is the meaning of the fact that at the close of the century
these investigations carried on here and there in more or less
technical ways have gathered such momentum? Is it not
significant that such a society could be organized, could
create such an interest at large, and attract such a representative audience as is here tonight? How are we to interpret this new interest and this new kind of interest in the
child? Where did it come from? What is it for? What may
we expect of it? These are questions which I think any one
who is curious about social phenomena must raise as he sees
the wonderful growth of this Child-Study movement. It con-
fronts us as a fact, and it led me to inquire first out of curi-

[*First published in* Transactions of the Illinois Society for Child-
Study, II (*July 1897*), 17–27. *Not previously reprinted.*]

osity, to see if I could formulate any reasons that would answer the questions. Such results as I have obtained for myself, I will endeavor to present to you this evening.

There are three great sources, or three great movements, in the development of interest in the child. These I term, respectively, political, æsthetic, and scientific.

The political interest in the child began to develop, that is, attention was directed to the child on this basis, in the time of Plato and Aristotle. There have always been educational systems where there have been people of any degree of social organization. There have always been precepts and rules regarding conduct and education. We find no people which have counted at all in the civilization of the world which have not gone beyond education in some way or other to formulate its rules. But there is a distinct difference between formulating the precepts for education, and consciously raising the question of what the end, the object, of education is, and, upon the basis of that end as a standard, attempting to formulate the methods and principles of educational work. That inquiry began, I repeat, with Plato and Aristotle. Of course, people have always observed children, given attention to them, have been interested in them. But again there is a great difference between mere recognition of the child, mere adaptation of one's self to the child, and the conscious reflection upon what the child means, what he stands for, and how that child is to be treated if he is to attain to that for which he stands. Once more, it was Plato and Aristotle who first consciously brought to light that point of interest in child life. The first source of conscious interest in the child was the position of the child as a factor in social organization. All these three interests of which I shall speak this evening, the practical or political, the æsthetic, and the scientific, came at times of great agitations of life—at times when old institutions were being transformed, when there was a conflict between civilizations and races previously separated, when life was in a ferment, and when it was necessary for persons to reflect upon the meaning of life and to attempt to settle for themselves some well-defined and established principles which would afford a basis for holding life together, for organizing it. The time of Plato and Aristotle was precisely such a period, a period of contact of the Oriental and Western civilizations; it was a period of the breaking down of the old religious faith. All bases of life, political, moral, and religious, were being questioned, and that led such men as Plato and Aristotle to question regarding the nature of life itself, whether it could be organized and what the principles were which made it capable of organization. It was that problem, the question of how, in the breaking down of the older traditions, older habits and older principles upon which life had been organized, through reflection and discussion to find a safe and sure standard upon which to proceed in reconstruction, reorganization, of society, which led to the interest in education. Plato's great treatise on education is also a treatise on metaphysics, ethics, principles of art, and so on. It is impossible to draw a line, saying, this part is metaphysical, another part political, and another part educational. He realized that all these questions were one. The philosophy dealt with the question of discovering the principles; the question of education was the question of applying these principles; the question of social organization was the question of the way in which society should be built up after the discovery and application of these principles; so *there* was a source of conscious interest in the child.

If social life is to be what it should be, if the state is once more to be organized, then the beginning must be with the child, and the shaping and directing—in short the conducting—of the child must be from the first consciously undertaken with a view of reaching this idea. Plato, in short, realized that the foundation in any established political organized life was the child and the shaping and directing of the life of the child through educational instruments from his birth up to his full emergence into civic life. There must always be some reason, however. People do not give attention to any subject, even such a subject as children, unless there is some urgent motive for it. The child was such a factor in the reorganization of society that he must receive *definite* attention. Not the child, however, *as* a child, not the child in himself, but the child as a factor, as an instrument, as an element, in political organization, was what received attention at this time. Not, I repeat, the child in himself, but the child as an instrument, as a part of the social structure. There was a great advance here, because there was a systematic end in view, a training, an education, based on principles reflectively established and not on mere routine or tradition such as all the older types of education up to the time of Plato and Aristotle had represented. It was systematic in its end, systematic in its scope, systematic in its use of means, in the observation of children from this one point of view. Children must be trained and observed from the start to see what position in the social life-structure they are best adapted to fit into. This interest in the child and this interest in education as a means of shaping children for the social structure became imbued into civilization early; but mediæval Christianity changed the form of interest because it changed the type of social ideal, of social structure, which was held in view. Education still had the same motive back of it, and attention to children was on the same basis, still aiming to direct the child for this fitting of himself into the ideal social structure in view.

In this movement, then, it was recognized that society is not the work either of chance or of fate, but that society is in some sense, a work of art. Not of art as distinct from nature, but of nature coming to consciousness in man, and through man's own nature assuming more perfect forms because having an end in view. The interest in education and in the child originated, then, because man recognized that social life was capable of intelligent direction. The first step in getting at this direction was to begin with the child and prepare him from the first for the type of social life held in view. As this was the first, so it is today still the deepest and best organized motive in popular consciousness both for education and for attention to the child. If it is asked, whether in a popular, or in a more technical way, what the justification of the public school system is, what the justification of the denominational religious type of education is, the answer, ninety-nine cases out of a hundred, will come back to us in this form—the child is to be a member of a certain form of social life, and he must be trained from the start to make him a capable and efficient member of that social order, and that can be done only as we attend to him through these educational means. It takes shape in the statement that the supreme consideration controlling the whole curriculum of the school lies in the demands of the civilization into which the child is born. While this basis requires attention to the child, while it makes it necessary to think of him, while it makes it necessary to attend to him in a way which otherwise would have been impossible to attain, it cannot be said to be complete. The mere fact that he is not taken in himself, but as a type of society, is dangerous. It tends to rigidity, mechanism, arbitrary schemes. Many of the most routine features of the educational life of our children, both in the family and in the school, are due precisely to the fact that the child has been considered not as himself, but from the standpoint of the mere political organization into which he is to be fitted. If we have an end set up in advance for the child, if we make up our mind beforehand where and how he is to fit in, then once more we have the conditions of attending to the child for a definite end. We do not attend to these things for the mere luxury of attending; it is the end in view which will determine what we shall see. If we have in view a fixed end to which the child is to be adapted, the things in the child which relate to that end are the only things which we are capable of seeing. The child has always been with us. Child-Study may be a new thing; organizations for it may be new. He has been with us ever since humanity has been here. How are we to account for the fact that these most wonderful facts of child life have not been seen before? How are we to account for the fact that the scales on our eyes are only now beginning to fall off, unless we concede that we have not been seeing the child, we have not been observing him as he is, but simply seeing him from the standard of his relation to some goal which we set up in advance?

We can say of each of these typical movements of interest in child life, that its source came at times of great expansion, or even conflict, of traditions, habits, ideals—moral, religious, artistic—which have previously been distinct and separate. The second of these great types came at the time of the Renaissance, at the time of the contact between mediæval Christianity and the revival of Hellenic learning, when Europe began to be one socially, and not merely as a physical fact of geography. The great source of interest in the child which was born at that time was the æsthetic aspect. No longer was the child simply a necessary element in social life, and therefore to be shaped for that life, but he was looked upon as having a symbolic, an ideal and prophetic significance. The child was born again in the painting of this period. Else why all this interest in the Holy Family, this interest in child life and mother life, and the centering not only of religious energy, but practically of the whole tendency of art, itself, upon the child? I take it that the child was recognized now as having this prophetic value; the child life was recognized as somehow pointing forward not simply to some particular form of social life, but rather as a dream of some social life which as yet they could not formulate, which lay either too far beyond or too far behind. The child was taken as a prophetic type of the ideal fate of the unrealized social order, and then got the religious and æsthetic value. The interest on one hand was retrospective. In looking at childhood, men seemed to see their own lost innocence, lost promises, that which they might have been and once promised to be, had given an earnest of being but failed in becoming. In looking at the child, and those things which centre about the thought and life of the child, humanity thought to escape the limitations which it felt pressing upon it; as if men had said, "we cannot be what we want to be, we are filled with limitations; but in the child we see the freedom, the spontaneity, the ideal, which with us has become so dim, so wretched."

The interest was not only retrospective, but was also perspective; not merely looking back to a lost estate, but truly seeing if we once have been this that our children are now, then under some conditions humanity may be that again. In the domain of faith, the child is evidence of things not seen. He is moving in and towards the world yet unrealized. In the Sistine Madonna we certainly have these values; this consciousness of looking backward and forward is summed up in motherhood and childhood, the germinating forces, the forces which make for continuity, for openness, and for movement.

Now here again there is a distinct advance from that earlier type of interest which took the child from the standpoint of his use in some social order. The child is still conceived of as a member of the social order, but the order is not fixed but moving; he is not so much to be fitted into it as he gives a clue to it, what it should be, and what it may become. The difficulty was that the gulf after all between the real, the actual, limitations of life, and the ideal set up, remained, so that the interest tended to become sentimental, or the source of what afterwards in literature became romantic. The position of the child as ushering in a new and better life is taken to satisfy the emotions of the adult rather than as a stimulus to action on the part of adult. The child is taken as affording consolation, as a relief from the ideal, for the adult, and there is no easier or cheaper way of deceiving ourselves than by setting up something as an ideal in order to free ourselves from the responsibility of realizing it. The child is a symbol to an adult, rather than a fact himself, a symbol of unfulfilled hope of his own nature, a symbol of what an adult wanted to be, what he would be if he could, rather than a sign of what the child himself should be, and what all the forces should be directed to make him. So at best this lifts itself to the motive of art in all its forms, and it does help humanity to find its ideal; but, at the worst, the child becomes the plaything of the adult, still under the name of being his ideal—something to make home pleasant. Gradually the evil tendencies of the interest which has its source in the æsthetic point of view, tend to reinforce, or rather correct, the other; each emphasizes and sets the other off. The school only too often stands for the mechanical routine side, while the home stands for the child as a plaything, a symbol, something to make life more agreeable, more happy for the adult.

The third source and type of interest has been the scientific movement of our present century. This interest also comes at the time of expansion, the new development of life; it comes when old habits and traditions—physical, national, social, industrial, moral and religious—are breaking down; when the world, and not simply one part of the world, is being made one. This scientific interest focused itself upon the child as a phase of the general interest in growth in the beginning of things, therefore as a factor in growth, and as a key to the nature of growth. The great sciences of the present century have been the historical and social sciences, taken from a historical point of view. The great scientific work, proper, of the century is summed up in the term "evolution," again the movement, growth, from the simple beginning.

While this is generally recognized, we often overlook the fact of the accidental way in which this historical interest grew out of the interest I have just referred to—the æsthetic. The historical interest in science and philosophy of the present century were born of the German romanticism of the last century. The ideal of the literary and artistic romanticists of the eighteenth century was a return to nature, to the childhood of the race. The childhood of humanity, if not of the individual, was idealized; it was made the source and expression of everything that was free, beautiful, ideal, spontaneous. Whether we find it in cruder forms in Rousseau or in more refined classic forms in Schiller, there is still the same idea that somehow there is a lost Garden of Eden, that the early history of the race was a time of poetry, a time of imagination and fancy, and now we are simply in the clutches of hard, unrelenting, real prose. This was the time to escape these conditions, to get back to poetic conditions. Out of that romantic ideal of the return to childhood of humanity and the return to primitive conditions, to nature, developed, not simply as a matter of theory, but as a matter of demonstrable fact, the interest in history as such, that new born interest which marks the present century, which does not see its interest limited to what is about it at present, but realizes that the whole past is, with the present, an organic part of human life and progress. In this return we have the idea that the primitive is the unspoiled.

This scientific interest, as all such movements, has moved from the mass to the particular, from the bulk to the parts which are contained in it, from the race to the individual, from the childhood of humanity to the childhood of the individual. Psychology, baffled, working on a purely formal basis, betakes itself to the beginnings, to the germs.

Now the question which meets us is, what is the relation between these three movements? What is the relation of the last movement to the two others spoken of, the practical or political interest, and the æsthetic? Is it simply a third interest added upon the other two, or is it a substitute for the other two? Does it possibly reinforce, correct and vivify the other two? A distinguished psychologist has made an argument, within a year or two, to the effect that there is an opposition between science and personality; that the question of personality is a question of nature, that science takes not natures but objects, and therefore the attempt to have a scientific study of children means that we are losing the social and sentimental interest, that we are losing our spontaneous sympathy in a large measure, and reducing the child to an object to be looked at, poked at and felt of. What are we to say of this? Is it true that it reduces the child from a living being to an object, and therefore reduces our interest in the child from the vital, sympathetic, to the curious? Science certainly does make us view the child as an object, but that does not settle the question; it still remains. As what kind of an object does the child present himself to our investigation? The question is not, what may a given scientific man do, but what does the scientific attitude itself demand and require? Does the scientific point of view destroy, pervert and suppress the intrinsic significance of object study? Or does it do that only in so far as it fails to be scientific? In other words, when we substitute the universal point of view of science for our own prejudices, do we reduce the child from a person to a thing, or do we see him for the first time more truly as a person? Take the scientific question in relation to the æsthetic. Is not the question simply this, are we to take the child as he is in himself, or as an expansion of our ideals? Are science and sympathy antithetical? Certainly there is no discovery, no observation, no profound explanation in the way of theories where there is not close and continuous attention. To what shall we give our best attention? The personal and æsthetic interest is the crowning motive for scientific study. The return to nature, in other words, must be literal and not sentimental. We ought to go to the little child, in fact. The symbolism of the child must be taken as genuine, as intrinsic, as having meaning for the child himself and not simply for us. Science, in a word, gives us a basis for transforming the emotional idealism which has clustered about the child into practical idealism and working forces.

Just a word about the relation of the scientific to the political. Do we have here again opposition or superimposition of one interest upon another? Again, I think we have the most fruitful interaction. Is it not social interest which gives to the scientific interest its motive? As long as social life was comparatively stable, as long as it was fixed in narrow groups, based upon tradition, it was not relatively, from a practical standpoint, a matter of much importance that the child was taken in a comparatively fixed way. But now the whole world is practically one because of increased range, containing side by side all kinds of types, and we do not and cannot know what a child's life will be either industrially or in its social quality. To attempt to educate him means to educate him for the present, and then when the future comes upon him leave him either stranded or wrecked. The only way to educate him for the flexible future is to give him the utmost command of himself and of the methods of civilization. Only, in other words, by giving the child command of himself now, and by giving him command of that self through the command of the fullest, most complete existing tools by which civilization makes progress, can we prepare the child for his future place, his future work.

What is the relation of this to the question in hand? The scientific type to the practical type? Simply this: We cannot, whether we approve the fact or regret it, educate the child for special membership on the basis of habit, routine, or tradition. The society for which the child, today, is to be educated, is too complex, makes too many demands upon personality to be capable of being based upon custom and routine without the utmost disaster. We must educate him by giving him the widest powers and most complete tools of civilization. Only a study, only the knowledge, of what those powers are and how to master them, and what would instrumentally aid or hinder in their development, and how, is in any way adequate to this task.

For the practical interest, as we have said of the æsthetic, the scientific type is not a substitute; neither, again, is it superimposed upon the other two. It is these other interests which set the problem, which furnish the end, which make the demand for science, and it is science and science alone which can respond to these demands and can solve the problems which the emotional idealistic interest and practical or political interest made. The extension of science to the child means that he has embodied in his own structure, laws. That great saying, "Come, then, let us live with our children," means all these things; it means the co-operation and mutual interaction and reinforcement of these types of interest.

# PLAN OF ORGANIZATION

## OF THE

# UNIVERSITY PRIMARY SCHOOL

# Plan of Organization of the University Primary School*

## General Problem and End

The ultimate problem of all education is to co-ordinate the psychological and the social factors. The psychological requires that the individual have the free use of all his personal powers; and, therefore, must be so individually studied as to have the laws of his own structure regarded. The sociological factor requires that the individual become acquainted with the social environment in which he lives, in all its important relations, and be disciplined to regard these relationships in his own activities. The co-ordination demands, therefore, that the child be capable of expressing *himself*, but in such a way as to realize *social* ends.

## Sociological Principles

i.] The school is an institution in which the child is, for the time, to live — to be a member of a community life in which he feels that he participates, and to which he contributes. This fact requires such modification of existing methods as will insure that the school hours are regarded as much a part of the day's life as anything else, not something apart; and the school house, as for the time being, a home, and not simply a place to go in order to learn certain things. It requires also that the school work be so directed that the child shall realize its value for him at the time, and not simply as a preparation for something else, or for future life.

ii.] As an institution, it is intermediate between the family and other larger social organizations. It must, there-

* This is privately printed, not published, and is to be so treated. It will be understood to define the general spirit in which the work is undertaken, not to give a rigid scheme. [1895(?). Not reprinted during author's lifetime.]

fore, grow naturally out of the one, and lead up naturally to the other.

1. As the family is the institution with which the child is familiar, the school life must be connected as far as possible with the home life. The child should be led to consider and to get some practical hold of the activities which centre in the family—*e.g.*, shelter, the house itself and its structure; clothing, and its construction; food, and its preparation; as well as to deepen and widen the ethical spirit of mutual service.

2. A consideration and command of these same activities take the child out into the larger relations upon which they depend—*e.g.*, the consideration of wood, stone, and food takes in a large sphere of existing social activities, and takes one back to previous states of society out of which the present has grown.

III.] The school, as an institution, must have a *community* of spirit and end realized through *diversity* of powers and acts. Only in this way can it get an organic character, involving reciprocal interdependence and division of labor. This requires departure from the present graded system sufficient to bring together children of different ages, temperaments, native abilities, and attainments. Only in this way can the co-operative spirit involved in division of labor be substituted for the competitive spirit inevitably developed when a number of persons of the same presumed attainments are working to secure exactly the same results.

IV.] The end of the institution must be such as to enable the child to translate his powers over into terms of their social equivalencies; to see what they mean in terms of what they are capable of accomplishing in social life. This implies:

1. Such *interest* in others as will secure responsiveness to their real needs—consideration, delicacy, etc.

2. Such *knowledge* of social relationships as to enable one to form social ideas or ends.

3. Such volitional command of one's own powers as to enable one to be an economical social agent.

## Psychological Principles

i.] The child is primarily an acting, self-expressing being, and normally knowledge and feeling are held within the grasp of action, growing from it and returning into it. This activity is neither purely psychical, nor purely physical; but involves the expression of imagery through movement.

ii.] The child, being socially constituted, his expressions are, normally, social. The child does not realize an activity save as he feels that it is directed towards others and calls forth a response from others. Language, for example, whether speech, writing, or reading, is not primarily expression of *thought*, but rather social *communication*. Save as it realizes this function, it is only partial (and more or less artificial) and fails, therefore, of its educative effect, intellectually, as well as morally; its complete, or organic, stimulus being absent.

iii.] The intellectual dependence upon expressive activity may be indicated as follows:

*1. Sense-perception.*

(a) Sensation. Save as a sensation of color, sound, taste, etc., is functionally required in order to carry on, assist, or reinforce some outgoing or expressive activity, appeal to sense means either a deadening, a dulling, of the sense activity, rendering it mechanical because its organic stimulus is lacking; or else means distraction, dissipation, a continued demand for stimulation for its own sake, apart from its use or function. It is often forgotten that to stimulate the ear or eye without demand, must either require the organ to protect itself by stimulating response in a purely mechanical way, or else must create an appetite for such stimulus—as much in principle in case of the eye or hand as of the taste for alcohol.

(b) Observation. The mind naturally selects or discriminates material with reference to expression or maintenance of its own activity. It picks out the means, the clues, the signals to carrying its own imagery. Separated from this function, observation becomes dead, and results in making mere distinctions for their own sake, a practice which is mentally disintegrating, and results in accumulating material which is either forgotten, or else carried by sheer force of memorizing.

2. *Ideas.* Separated from their stimulus by their function in action, ideas degenerate from knowledge, or appreciated significance, and become mere information, necessarily second-handed and conventional. Symbols, which have their value as economical guides to and instruments of action, become, when severed, meaningless and arbitrary, and serve to confuse and distract. A consecutive expressive activity is always logical, having its own method, and demands judgment in selection of relevant material.

Summing up, we may say that the regular relationship is that sense-observation selects the *material* for further self-expression, while the reasoning process determines the *method* for utilizing this material in expression. Hence the psychological principle that the mind always begins with a *whole*, expressing function, use, activity, and proceeds from this to matters of form, objective quality and abstract relations.

iv.] The emotional dependence upon expressive activity may be illustrated as follows:

1. The *direct* appeal to feeling, in any form, whether moral or æsthetic, inevitably leads to isolating that feeling from its proper function—that of valuing and reinforcing action—and makes it sentimental.

2. The important part played by *interest* in education is generally recognized. Normal interest accompanies all self-expression; indeed, it is only the internal individual realization of activity. Unless the child appreciates the *end* of what he is doing, unless there is some *motive* or reason realized by him for the activity, and for mastering the facts presented, real interest and attention are elsewhere, no matter how thoroughly the external appearances of interest are simulated. Moreover, the child detects by instinct whether the end or motive present is genuine, or whether it is made up as an excuse for getting him to do something. It is the

absence of genuine motives, actual demands inherent in the given situation, which so often makes training of emotion and interest partial. It is, therefore, important that not only the principle of construction should be utilized, but utilized in producing things which appeal to the child as needed, as necessary.

3. In connection with this, it is important that *real wholes* should be constructed if there is to be educative interest. Interest goes along with sense of power, of accomplishment. When (as in some of the manual training systems) a child is kept making a sequence of geometrical forms, having no relevancy to his other activities, or is kept at a certain tool or certain principle of structure till he has mastered it, irrespective of producing some actual completed whole—interest (relatively) flags. It is more important that, at the outset, the child should realize he is accomplishing something, and something needed, even if the product, externally viewed, is crude, than that an external perfection should be aimed at in such a way as to keep the child at a long series of activities meaningless to him. In other words, normal interest requires that *technique*, both intellectual and practical, be mastered *within* the process of active expression, or construction of wholes, and relative to the recognized necessities of such construction. (It is not only necessary that the child should get a sense of power, of mastery, but also should realize his own limitations and weaknesses. This feeling also results when the principle mentioned is adhered to. In the recognition of the non-adaptation of his product to its intended purpose or function, the child has put before him the objectification of his own defects, and also receives the stimulus to remedy them. No such standard of judgment exists when genuine and necessary wholes are not produced as the child's own self-expression.)

4. The principle of interest is often abused by being reduced to the concept of amusement, or making something interesting. Complete, or organic interest, is realized only when the child puts his entire self into his activity. His activity, even if comparatively trivial, objectively considered, must appeal to the child as worth while, as genuine work.

(1) Work does not mean labor in the sense of disagreeable effort, but energies directed to something recognized as necessary. (2) Work in this sense is incompatible with "play" in the sense of conscious "make believe," but not in the sense of free expression, the principle of all artistic activity. When the child is *conscious* that he is only playing, he ceases to play, because interest dies out. (3) Expression, in a word, unites the ideas of an end which manifests the self, and thus is free (principle of play) and of the complete devotion of all energies to realizing this end (principle of work).

v.] Psychology of learning. Learning is the process intermediate between ignorance and comprehension in self. It arrives normally when an image in process of expression is compelled to extend itself and to relate itself to other images, in order to secure proper expression. The expansion or growth of imagery is the medium of realization, and this is obtained when the materials of expression are provided, and the end to which these are the means is recognized by the child. The process of learning, in other words, conforms to psychological conditions, in so far as it is *indirect*; in so far that is, as attention is not upon the *idea of learning*, but upon the accomplishing of a real and intrinsic purpose—the expression of an idea.

## Educational Applications

The problem, as already stated, is the co-ordination of the social and psychological factors. More specifically this means utilizing the child's impulses towards, and powers of, expression in such a way that he shall realize the social ends to which they may be made serviceable, and thus get the wish and capacity to utilize them in this way. The starting point is always the impulse to self-expression; the educational process is to supply the material and provide (positively and negatively) the conditions so that the expression shall occur in its normal social direction, both as to content and form or mode. This gives the standard for determining the entire school operation and organization, both as to the whole and as to its details.

Consequently the beginning is made with the child's

expressive activities in dealing with the fundamental social materials—housing (carpentry), clothing (sewing), food (cooking). These *direct* modes of expression at once require the derived modes of expression, which bring out more distinctly the factors of social communication—speech, writing, reading, drawing, moulding, modelling, etc.

Both by themselves and in connection with the derived modes of expression they (1) lead back to *science*, the study of the materials used, and of the processes by which these materials are produced and controlled; (2) and lead on to *culture*, the recognition of the part these activities, and others bound up in them, play in society. This leads at once into the study of history—the realization of these various activities in their development from the simple to the complex. It is obvious that this movement once initiated, whether on the scientific or the historical side, demands recognition of the relations between the natural materials and processes on one side, and the human activities on the other. This brings the analysis to that set of facts usually called "geography." This gives the materials and method of the problem of correlation. It becomes obvious that the only adequate *basis* of correlation, whether upon the social or the psychological side, is the child's own activities of primary expression—*his constructive powers*. To take either "science" on one side, or "history and literature" on the other, as the basis of correlation is psychologically to attempt the impossible task of getting a synthesis in terms of knowledge, when only action really unifies; and, sociologically, it abstracts either *materials* or else *results*, neglecting, or relegating to a subordinate position, the *process* which unites and explains both materials and outcome.

The theory of correlation to be worked out in the school involves, therefore, the following features:

1. Finding the basis of unity always in a *constructive* activity, involving an image or idea (intellectual), the coordination of movements required to execute this idea (volitional), and the interest in the process of adjustment (emotional).

2. The three typical activities of cooking, carpentry, and sewing (taken in a broad sense) are taken as affording

adequate opportunity, on the psychological side, for constructive work, while socially they represent the fundamental activities of the race.

3. The method is to analyze these activities, so far as required to give value to the work, into a knowledge of the materials and processes. Animal, vegetable life, soil, climate, etc., are studied not as mere *objects* (a psychological unreality), but as factors in action. So the *processes*, arithmetical, physical, and chemical, are studied not in themselves, but as the forms in which these materials are controlled. The knowledge of nature, or "science," results from this analysis of the *modus operandi* and the materials of individual constructive activity.

4. Further, the method is to follow out these activities into their social ramifications. Present social life, on one hand, is too complex for realization by the child, while past life, taken as *past*, is remote and psychologically inert. But through his interest in his own activity of cooking, and primitive building, the child is interested in the different forms this activity has assumed at different times. He can be led to analyze the existing complex social structure by following up the growth of the homes, foods, etc., of men, from the pre-historic cave-dweller through the stone and metal ages up to civilization, etc.

5. As the analysis of activity on the side of its materials leads to a knowledge of the environment, and consideration of its various forms leads to knowledge of history, we are taken at each point to a consideration of the relation of environment to modes of human activity—geography, whether in its simplest local features or in its broadest physical aspects.

6. Both the original construction and the consideration of materials and modes of activity call, at every point, for expression in the form of *communication*. There is, then, everywhere the demand for artistic expression—drawing, coloring, modelling, etc., speech, written records, etc. "Literature" itself is simply one form of this process of communication or artistic expression.

Moreover, we have here also a new phase of correlation. Literature, etc., while not the basis of co-ordination (that being found only in personal construction), affords the opportunity for bringing together in a common focus the variety of interests and facts which develop out of the original unity. (The ordinary theory of co-ordination fails in taking its different subjects or facts ready-made, instead of differentiating them from a unity.) The images which are expressed in an artistic whole are, of necessity, intimately fused together, no matter how diverse before.

Other distinguishing features of the school have probably been sufficiently indicated. Attention may again be called to that of having the school represent a genuine community life; and to that of a study of the individual child, with a view of having his activities properly express his capacities, tastes and needs. Attention may again be called to the principle of *indirect* training, and the consequent necessary emphasis upon initiating the proper *process* rather than securing any immediate outward *product*, in the faith that the proper process, once obtained, will determine, in its due season, its own products; while any attempt to force the result apart from first securing the proper psychological process can result only in undue forcing and gradual disintegration of power.

## A. House-keeping

Study house and premises.

Discuss means and methods for management.

Form committees which shall be changed at regular intervals.

| | |
|---|---|
| Floors | Animal pets |
| Blackboards | Supplies |
| Plumbing | Reception of visitors |
| Ventilation and heating | Marshal and lieutenants |
| Linen | Order of yard |
| Wardrobe | Games |
| Clock | Tools |
| House plants | |

Buy materials needed.

Engage service needed.

Learn prices and qualities.

Draw simple map of vicinity showing relation of homes to school.

Learn the industries and shops, workers, prices, etc., of the neighborhood and city through relation to the school work. University. Museum.

Mineralogy, geology, geography and history of the region as far as possible through study of soil, climate, etc., in their relation to our school life of cooking, gardening, etc.

## B. Wood-Work

### WOOD

Sandpaper block
Thread-winder
Yard stick
Pencil sharpener
Meter stick
Chicken coop
Plant trellises
Triangle
Paper cutter
Stools
Modelling tool (1)
Bread board
Test-tube holder
Towel racks
Trays for dishes
Trays for minerals
Tool racks
Baker's shovel
Boxes for thread and needles

Boxes for matches
Disks for holding hot dishes
Modelling tools (2 and 3)
Plant stick
Barrel cover
Ladle
Trays for handling materials
Boxes for pencils
Boxes for knives and forks
Boxes for minerals
Boxes for seeds
Plate rack
Book stand
Toys
Houses, boats, etc., to illustrate history

### PASTEBOARD AND PAPER

Boxes
Trays
Envelopes
Book-covers

Circle-maker
Toys
Models, etc.

Study teacher's model or invent one.

Discuss materials.

Study woods.

Collect woods.

Label and arrange specimens.

Visit carpenters and wood-workers.

Study growth of wood in the tree. Life of the tree. Observe trees of the locality. Read of trees valuable in commerce —geography of the regions. Trees in pictures—interesting through use, form, or history.

Markets for lumber. Prices. Transportation. Fossilized wood.

Cost of labor connected with lumber.

Study of lumber as building material compared with stone, brick, etc.

Architecture—historically evolved from the tree dwelling.

Architecture—influenced by geographical conditions.

Study homes of people—in history and at present. Study fine architectural pictures. Make models and designs.

Write and read records of observations made.

Write and read stories and descriptions of subjects related to work.

Keep records in book form—design covers.

Draw and paint illustrations for these records.

Picture with pencil, crayon, sand, clay, etc., the stories and inventions and places talked about.

Draw working plans for articles needed.

Draw simple maps indicating routes of transportation, etc.

Make exact estimates of work to be done and statement of work that has been done. Cost—to one child—for class. Keep accounts and bills. Order and buy materials.

Learn prices of woods—causes of difference.

Learn cost of labor—reasons.

Learn cost of transportation—reasons.


*Arithmetic:*

Measurements and estimates of articles made. Linear measure—area—cubic measure.

Prices of materials used. Prices of raw materials. Cost of

labor needed to prepare materials. Amounts produced in different countries.

Measurements of trees. Exact growth of different parts. Comparison of different trees; different parts of the same tree. Weight of ash in different woods. Metric system.

Cost of labor-saving machines studied about. Amount of labor saved. Financial gain.

Distances over which goods are transported. Cost of transportation.

Accounts of expense involved in articles made. Bills made, kept, receipted, etc. Buying of materials.

Measurements and weights of soils and their constituents, absorptive power, etc.

*Botany:* Life of the tree.

Select individual trees and watch their changes through the seasons. Compare.

Study structure of tree with the purpose of knowing the parts and the work of each part. Roots and rootlets, trunk, bark, green layer, sap, wood, fruit, branches, twigs, leaves, stems, blades, veins, etc. Adaptation to environment. Comparison of woods as to use and usefulness, beauty, habitat, history.

Æsthetic effects of trees, individuals, groups, masses. Characteristics of trees of different countries.

*Chemistry:*

Constituents of wood—ash, carbon and water.

Assimilation of food in living tissues.

Combustion of woods as compared with other building materials.

*History:*

Uses that have been made of these woods by other people and in other times.

What we should do without these tools and materials.

Argue growth of knowledge and invention of primitive man through the rough and polished stone and metal ages.

Some famous buildings of history and the people who made them.

Men who have become famous through discoveries or inventions in buildings.

Lines of people now engaged in forestry, logging, milling, carpentry, etc., brick-making, plastering, masonry.

Paint and draw: Trees and their parts as records, woods of different countries, homes of people talked about, buildings studied. Illustrate industries connected with buildings and building material. Study pictures, whenever practicable, which show architectural development in history, also treatment of foliage by good artists.

Model in clay or sand or pasteboard: Forms of life and invention which can properly be expressed in those ways, caves, rude implements, etc.; countries or regions from which various woods are brought.

*Physics:*

Effect of heat and cold on materials studied; influence of that force in building.

Use of wedge—through its place in work done.

Use of lever—through its place in work done.

Use of screw—through its place in work done.

Equilibrium and centre of gravity in handling materials and modelling buildings.

Water power and as much machinery as practicable, in connection with visits to planing mills, etc.

Models of inventions as often as possible.

*Zoology:*

Protection of man against adverse elements in his environment.

Adaptation and methods compared with those of plants and animals.

Effect of change of seasons, etc., on the building instinct of animals.

Dormant plant life.

Hibernation.

*Geography:*

Homes of the trees which we use or study, especially those near us.

Geographical conditions upon which the growth of wood depends. Irrigation—the life of a stream and its relation to trees. Temperature. Soil.

Geographical conditions which affect the building industries. Water-ways. Railways. Water power, etc.

*Geology and Mineralogy:*

Soils—formation and qualities; effects on vegetation; one compared with others.

Fossilized woods—coal, etc. Observation of conditions, inference as to history. Story of Geological Ages.

Stones and rocks used in building. Their use to the earth, to man. Tests. History.

Materials of mortars, brick, glass, etc.

## C. Foods

| | | |
|---|---|---|
| Boil rice | Porridges | Beans and peas —baked |
| Boil potatoes | Unfermented | Beans and peas —in soup |
| Bake potatoes | breads—with | Cook milk |
| Crush wheat | water and | Cook eggs |
| Bake with water | milk—with | Cook meats |
| Bake cornmeal with water | eggs | |
| Bake oatmeal with water | Fermented bread | |
| | Yeasts | |
| | Beans and peas —boiled | |

Study of any food to commence with the cooked dish.

Science and history will help in showing the uses of food and best means of preparation.

Method will be to discover through experiment best processes.

Elementary physiology of eating and digestion.

Elementary hygiene of eating and digestion.

Simple chemistry in study of food elements—carbonaceous,

albuminous, mineral—and changes effected through heat, combination, digestion, etc.

Physics through application of forces such as heat, light, machinery, etc.

Botany: Production of foods—leading to gardening, farming, marketing, etc.

History: How other people use, or have used, these foods—and how they produced them.

Geography related to history and botany.

Mineralogy and geology through relation of soil to growth.

Visit to markets, store-houses, etc.

Visit to farms, gardens, dairies, bakeries, mills, chemists.

Learn qualities and prices of foods.

Learn value of labor connected with the production of the foods.

Read of men famous for work done relating to these studies.


*Botany:*

Study plants used as food.

Plant gardens and record growth. Compare our own plants with those of other regions.

Elementary study of microbes.


*Chemistry:*

Constituents of the foods used—albumen, carbon, mineral matter—and effect produced upon them by different modes of cooking.

Effects of combining food elements.

Digestion and assimilation—elementary principle.

Fermentation.

Combustion of different fuels. Study of flames.


*Physics:*

Study machinery and utensils for cooking.

Effect of heat on *air, water, metals, gas.*


*Arithmetic:*

Transportation of foods—distances, etc., quantities of food imported and exported at different times.

Exact measurement of effect of heat on foods; evaporation, expansion.

Time as an element of cooking. Study of the clock. Different modes of recording and telling time.

Exact measurements of children's physical strength and proportions.

Prices of foods—wholesale and retail—imported and domestic.

Weights and measures. Arithmetical processes taught whenever needed. Fractional parts whenever involved.

Avoirdupois weights.

Dry measure.

Liquid measure.

Metric system of measures and weight.

Gardening—area—square measure.

Exact growth of plants and their parts. Comparison.

Exact weights of soil, water, etc., and relation to growth.

Comparison of measure of growth in our plants with those of other countries.

Time as an element of growth. Study of Table of Time.

*Zoology:*

Physiology of eating and digestion. Elementary hygiene.

Nutrition of man compared with that of animals and plants. Organs of prehension and digestion compared. Adaptation.

Animal movements necessary to getting of food. Adaptation of parts of the body to their uses. Animal tissues, growth and hygiene.

*History:*

Uses made of these foods by other people. Their modes of preparation.

Inventions in cooking.

History from primitive conditions to civilization. From cannibal life through hunting, etc., to present society.

Plan followed as in "Wood-Work."

Races and individuals famous for physical strength—courage.

Stories of heroism. Greek ideals of physical perfection.

Visits to museums.

*Geography, Geology and Mineralogy*, as in "Wood-Work."

## D. Clothing

| | | |
|---|---|---|
| Hem towels | Aprons | Book bags |
| Holders | Work bags | Costumes, etc. |
| Dust-cloths | | |

Observe materials. Learn prices. Buy.

Collect materials—raw and manufactured.

Study utensils necessary.

Fibres of cotton, wool, silk, hair.

Visit mill, spinners, weavers, etc.

Invent devices for working and using materials.

History of these materials and their use by other people.

Evolution of inventions.

Visit museums for anthropological relics.

Industrial uses of the materials. Adaptability to different uses. Combustibility—conductivity compared with paper and metals.

History of clothing—developed from primitive conditions.

Animal coverings—animal types compared. Adaptability.

Hygiene of clothing. Circulation of blood—respiration. Story of the life of Harvey. Costumes of people of other times.

Fabrics—oriental means—colors—designs.

Design patterns for fabrics and garments; cut and make—distributing whenever practicable.

Careful attention to business details involved.

Write, read, model, paint, draw, etc., as in plan for "Wood-Work."

*Botany, Geography, Geology and Mineralogy*, according to plan for "Wood-Work."

Special study of wool, silk, cotton growing regions. Manufacturing regions. Commercial centres.

*Zoology:*

Coverings of man compared with those of animals and plants.

Adaptation to environment.

Animal movement in relation to getting clothing. Specialization of parts.

Special study of the animals which furnish us clothing.

*History:*

Plan followed as in "Wood-Work" and "Foods."

*Physics:*

Study of sewing machine, spinning wheel, looms, etc., as far as possible.

Inventions made by children as often as can be.

Adaptation of utensils to use.

Application of power to work to be done.

Force controlled.

*Arithmetic:*

Problems of machines worked out as they present themselves—if possible.

Prices, etc., as in "Foods" and "Wood-Work."

Exact measurements of special parts of animals studied—comparisons and ratios as data for conclusions in biology.

## Suggested Program—Two Months

*January—second week:*

Inspect school-house and premises, suggesting work to be done.

Divide children into committees for work.

Buy and sell supplies for year's work.

Hem towels and dust-cloths.

Make pasteboard box.

Make paper envelope.

Measure heights of children.

History: How other people sew. Primitive man. Eskimo.

Geography: Elementary ideas of *caves*.

Arithmetic: Use of yard and foot-rule. Prices of supplies, accounts, etc. (addition and subtraction, etc.).

Write and read record of work done, history discussed, observations made.

*January—third week:*

Continue hemming of towels and dust-cloths.

Cook rice.

Make sandpaper blocks.

Continue measurements of heights.

> History: Work along the line of evolving clothing.
>
> Botany: Study of starch-cell. Observation of woods, grain, hardness.
>
> Arithmetic: Use of measures, cost of wood. "Long measure."
>
> Physics: Effect of heat on water.

*January—fourth week:*

Make thread-winder.

Continue study of rice.

Make holders for hot dishes.

> History: Continue second week's plan. People who live chiefly upon rice.
>
> Botany: Study trees and woods. Planting of rice.
>
> Geography: Of rice countries.
>
> Zoology: Silk and wool fibres compared with cotton and flax.
>
> Arithmetic: Quantities of water evaporated at different temperatures. Liquid measure.

*February—first week:*

Make yard stick.

Continue study of rice.

Making cooking-aprons.

> History: Of clothing continued—also of cooking and building, from primitive people to more civilized as children discover the need of inventions.
>
> Botany: Starch-cells, trees.
>
> Arithmetic: Estimate quantities of materials needed. Prices. Buy.
>
> Physics: Observation of force directed and energy saved through sewing machine.
>
> Geography: Distribution of trees valuable for wood.
>
> Zoology: Foods, simple principles of physiology and hygiene.

*February—second week:*

Make pencil sharpener.

Make meter stick.

Make work bag.

Make boxes of pasteboard.

Boil potatoes.

Botany: Continue study of starch-cell—potato—woods and trees.

Arithmetic: Metric system of linear measurement. Prices of materials, quantities needed, etc.

Physiology: Foods.

History: Of clothing, building, foods, continued.

Geometry: Circle.

# A Pedagogical Experiment

The Pedagogical Department of the Chicago University has opened in connection with its theoretical work a small primary school. It is located at 389 Fifty-seventh Street, in the neighborhood of the University. The school has two sides, which of course are the obverse and reverse of the other — the one for the children, the other for students in the University taking up pedagogical work. The school is not a school of practice in the ordinary sense; nor is the main object of the Pedagogical Department to train teachers. It rather takes teachers who have already considerable experience, and who now wish to acquaint themselves more thoroughly with the rational principles of their subject, and with the more recent of educational movements. Former superintendents and normal school teachers make up, accordingly, a large part of the graduate students in pedagogy. The primary school serves the purpose of a focus to keep the theoretical work in touch with the demands of practice, and also makes an experimental station for the testing and developing of methods which, when elaborated, may be safely and strongly recommended to other schools. It is believed that there is nothing which our common schools need more than wise guidance in this respect — the presentation of methods which are the offspring of a sound psychology, and have also been worked out in detail under the crucial tests of experience.

The actual work of the school is proceeding along three converging lines. One is the attempt to grade the work to the individual pupil, rather than to grade rigidly the children themselves. Pupils just out of the kindergarten work side by side with those of two years' school experience, each profit-

[First published in Kindergarten Magazine, VIII (June 1896), 739–41. Not previously reprinted.]

ing from the contact with those of diverse years and attainments and interests. Much of the selfishness of childhood and after seems to be due to the enforced segregation of a rigidly graded system. Not only do children gain morally from the more rational and freer relations, but also intellectually. The presence of less advanced children makes natural a motive to reading and to telling observations or things learned very different from the artificial one of simply "reciting" before one's equals.

Secondly, the school is being conducted on the belief that the "studies" of the elementary school may best be mastered by being treated not as studies, but as factors in the child life. The child comes to school to *do*; to cook, to sew, to work with wood and tools in simple constructive acts; within and about these acts cluster the studies—writing, reading, arithmetic, etc. Nature study, sewing, and manual training, so-called, are by no means new features in education; what perhaps is the novel and distinctive feature of the primary school of the University is that these things are not introduced as some studies among others, but as the child's activities, his regular occupations, and the more formal studies are grouped about these occupations, and, as far as possible, evolved naturally from them. The measuring and weighing in cooking, sewing and carpentry afford ample opportunity for number work; they draw the child's attention to the ways in which other people have lived, how the inventions and tools arose, and thus give a basis for history; they lead out to the sources of the material, etc.—geography; they involve principles of chemistry, physiology, physics, and cannot be truly mastered without reference to these principles; they touch plants and animals and the modes in which they live and grow—biological studies. In fact, it is found that the child learns most easily along the lines of least resistance, and most effectively along the lines of greatest germinal power, when his problems grow out of his practical work, as either involved in it or enrichments of it. Along the latter direction it is sought to introduce the artistic element as much as possible into the work. The foregoing may be summed up in terms of current phrases of pedagogy by saying that the child's own life (as repeating within itself the familiar activities of food and shelter which centre in the home) gives the best basis for both correlation and apperception.

The third may be more briefly spoken of, as it is virtually involved in the second. It is the question of giving material of instruction that has an *intrinsic* worth, and making the formal and mechanical side strictly subservient, instead of, as too often, teaching anything, however trivial, on the basis that the chief aim is to learn the formal studies —the three R's. Nature study is now, fortunately, not so unknown as once; perhaps the distinctive feature of the science work in the primary school is the effort made to organize the scientific material into related wholes, instead of presenting isolated facts or going in a scrappy manner from one thing to another. It is not necessary to present either isolated facts nor to force children prematurely into consciousness of relations—the *related fact* is what holds the child's interest, and the great scientific generalizations regarding growth are all of them principles of relation. In some respects such work can best be undertaken at a university, so far as the first working out of methods is concerned. It must be a co-operative work; no one person can possibly be a specialist in all directions or have a sufficient and accurate hold upon facts and sources. The large number of graduate students at the University affords a body to draw from who are interested in the adaptation of the more *important* and *reliable* facts of their branches, and the primary school expects to draw in a constantly increasing degree from such students, both for directions as to materials and methods, and actual teaching.

It is expected that the work will be enlarged another year, so as to include children from six to twelve. A new and specially built schoolhouse is not out of the question if the friends of the University and of elementary education testify practically to their belief in the wisdom of uniting the two in a co-operative educational work. The term fees have been placed at a low figure ($12 for twelve weeks) in order that the school might be in spirit a common school. All interested are invited to call and see the school community at work. There is only one session, from 9:15 to 12:15.

# Interpretation of the Culture-Epoch Theory

I find considerable difficulty in defining to myself just what part the representatives of this theory expect it to play *educationally*, and just *how* they expect it to play that part. The fact or non-fact of the correspondence of development in the race and in the child is one thing; the educational *interpretation* of that fact is another; and the practical use to be made of it in the school room is a third thing, though one in the closest dependence upon the second. As definite a statement as any I have come across is that of Professor Van Liew, on page 116 of the First Herbart *Yearbook*: (1) The need is for a principle that will give correspondence between child and subject-matter; (2) this is supplied in the culture-epoch theory; (3) hence,[1] the cultural products of each epoch will contain that which appeals most sympathetically and closely to the child at that epoch.

Now, there are two questions which I wish to raise here. First, what is the criterion or standard employed? Is it the succession of epochs in the race, or is it the development of instincts, of interests in the child? This may seem, to the wise, an unnecessary or a foolish question, but I have read the recent literature on the subject, and I cannot decide that the writers have fairly asked this question of themselves. As long as we are dealing with the establishment of the correspondence as a *fact*, it is quite legitimate to shift from one side to the other, now taking the race, now taking the child.

---

[1]   This "hence" is my own interpolation. It is not stated as *inference* in the text. But, otherwise, I see no relevancy.

[*First published in* Public-School Journal, xv (*Jan. 1896*), 233–36. *Reprinted in* Second Yearbook of the National Herbart Society (*Bloomington, Ill.: The Society*, 1896), *pp.* 89–95.]

But when we come to the *educational* interpretation of this fact, not so! Only if these held an *exact* parallelism would this be possible. And the *exact* parallelism is confessedly absent.[2]

It does not seem to me that the upholders of the theory have clearly recognized that if the correspondence is not exact, the standard, educationally, is the sequence in the child, not in the race. It is a question of psychology, of child-study, not of race history. To study first the race side, and finding certain epochs then to conclude to the same in the child is unjustifiable. Pressing the analogy with biological recapitulation as far as it can be pressed, two points stand out: (1) The process of recapitulation takes place biologically during the embryonic period, and many of the phases are exceedingly transitory. They are without any practical import at all, being of value simply to the scientific student— say, the "fish" phase. The analogy then would indicate that it is quite possible that the race-culture gamut is now, say, within the first two or three years of child life, and that many or most of its phases are of no educational significance at all, however interesting they may be to the anthropologist. No one proposes that the mother shall modify her diet when the human embryo has reached the "fish" phase, or take any practical note of it. Why should we not follow the same principle in the social recapitulation? Is there not danger of arresting development at that point by making too much of it? Now, I do not go to this extent myself, but there is nothing in the principle, *from the side of the race development*, why we should not. (2) When the analogy is used, it must be with a profound recognition of the extent to which "short cuts" have developed in the human being (see Baldwin, *Mental Development*, pp. 21–28, and the extent to which these have modified the nature of the recapitulation).

The exceptions are, in many cases, more important than the rule. In all cases, it may fairly, even if roughly, be said that whenever an earlier structure is recapitulated in post-embryonic human structure, it is simply as a factor, as

---

[2]    It will be noted that I do not question the fact of correspondence in a general way.

a contributor, and is modified by the new function to which it contributes.

Now, in the foregoing I am not questioning the correspondence "in general"; I am simply pointing out considerations which absolutely forbid us to begin from the side of race development, and infer to child development. We must, in all cases, discover the epoch of growth independently in the child himself, and by investigation of the child himself. All the racial side can do is to suggest questions. Since this epoch was passed through by the race, it is possible we shall find its correlate in the child. Let us, then, be on the look-out for it. Do we find it? But the criterion comes back in all cases to the child himself. If this is admitted by the upholders of the theory, many who have thought they did not agree will find themselves agreeing. But to admit this, is to come near, dangerously near, to making the child the centre.

Moreover, if we keep in mind the modification of the inherited structure to make it subservient to new function, still further changes must be introduced. Just as the visual centre of the lower animals is represented in man, but no longer as a complete visual centre, so the hunting social epoch is represented in the child, but no longer as the dominant, complete activity, but simply as one impulse among many, having a certain relative urgency.

This fact alone is enough to condemn giving one year out of eight years (one out of five to many) to the hunting epoch of social life—or anything but an incidental reference to it on a higher scale; here is the nomadic epoch and some (hypothetical) interest now corresponding. Shall we then make this interest supreme and study that epoch? Or, shall we recognize the *relative* part played by pastoral activities in *present* society—the grazing in Texas, in Dakota, etc., and *then* call attention to the fact that whole peoples once lived in that way? The biological analogy—to say nothing of common sense—would require the latter.

The second question I would ask is this: Admitting the correspondence in general, *and as verified and controlled by study of present* child life, how is the inference justified that it is the cultural *products* which are to be made the objects of study? This inference is simply taken for granted by the upholders of the theory—it does not seem to have even occurred to them that *this* point needed discussion; but it is the nerve of the whole matter. The interpretation of the fact of correspondence, as meaning necessarily or even primarily, study of cultural *products*, in history and literature, seems to me to rest upon confusion theoretically, and to be practically misleading. Let me state what seems to be the true conception, using first the words of Professor Felmley (Supplement to Herbart *Yearbook*, pp. 195–96) and then modifying them to bring out my idea more definitely. "The appropriate food for each of our spontaneous interests is the mass of *ideas* that engaged the ancestors to whom the instinctive interest is due." The modification I suggest is to substitute the term activities for ideas, or, better yet, to conjoin the two terms.

Whatever words be used, the point is that the interest and instinct correspond not primarily to the *products* of a given age but to the psychical conditions which originated those products; these conditions secured for the child, then he is prepared to deal educatively with the products. When the child is in the "agricultural" stage, it is sheer assumption to suppose that this chief interest is in the literary or institutional products of that epoch; it is also sheer assumption to suppose that this agricultural interest is *adequately* met on the educational side by allowing it to feed at first on the "cultural products" of this epoch. It is an interest *which demands primarily its own expression*, and not simply an acquaintance, second-handed, with what that interest effected at some remote period. The agricultural instinct requires, according to the true analogy, to be fed in just the same way in the child in which it was fed in the race—by contact with earth and seed and air and sun and all the mighty flux and ebb of life in nature. It requires to be fed by knowledge of how agriculture is *now* carried on, what its products are, how these reach the market, etc. Then the child may be brought into contact with the historic cultural products, and will have some "apperceptive organs" for them and will be able to utilize them vitally. I do not say that to give him contact with these products before his interests have found some expression of their own is to give him a stone instead of bread, but it is not too much to say that it is giving him, relatively, a toy instead of reality.[3]

The idea that history and literature are the basis of concentration has been assumed to be a necessary consequence of the culture-epoch theory. I hope the foregoing remarks have made it clear that they are not so connected; while, undoubtedly, they do follow at once from that interpretation of the theory which assumes that the parallelism is not between the life and interest of the epoch and the life and interest of the child, but between the life of the child and the products, or results, of the life of the epoch.

It seems strange to me that one can clearly recognize that *beginning* reading and writing are formal, dependent upon a content requiring expression, and then give to literature any other position. Literature is certainly not an entity by itself; it is expression, as much so, as beginning reading, and educative contact with it means first initiation into the activities and ideas which are expressed. It is as hopeless to get a real vital concentration to centre about "literature" as it would be to get it to gather about drawing. Neither study is central, but each is radial, expressive of some core, some content which is not drawing, nor yet literature.

I may run the risk of shocking my readers still more, perhaps, by saying that a *direct* interest in history is also impossible. Children like stories, but stories are histories brought up to date—regarded as part of present life. Children are interested directly in present life, in the social conditions which exist all about them and with which they come in contact; and any genuine, any educative historic interest is simply a reflex of this interest in the *existing* social structure. If there be such a thing in the child as the nomadic interest, it finds its natural and direct prey not in the shifting hordes of semi-barbaric tribes as they wandered with the flocks over a half-barren territory, but in the railway and steamboat before his eyes, with their cargoes of oxen, and their migratory tribes from Germany and Ireland and the isles of the seas. Let this movement be realized and then

---

[3]    It does not seem to me that Mr. Galbreath's remarks about the intrinsic relation between idea and effort to execute it (pp. 163–65, 167 of Supplement to *Yearbook*) were adequately met. Their bearing is wide.

there is a basis for considering other modes of movements, and other relationships between ox and man!

One word by way of illustration about the myth. It seems to be assumed in the discussions that the myth is a primitive, simple product which the mind sheds by a sort of direct radiation, or, to mix the metaphor, by spontaneous combustion termed fancy. And that, therefore, there is some special, almost pre-ordained fitness in it for the child. But naïveté belongs rather to this view of the myth than to the myth itself. The myth is a complete social product, reflecting in itself the intellectual, the economic and the political condition of a certain people. Most of the classic myths are still more complicated by containing in themselves records of the conflict of one form of civilization, one type of economic life, one political régime with another. Now these myths, the best of them, told as *stories*, are a very excellent thing; I have a great respect for the educative value of the right story at the right time, but it is self-deception to suppose that they have a value other than that of a story—that by some inner affinity to the child's nature, he is being morally introduced into the civilization from which the myth sprung, and is receiving a sort of spiritual baptism through "literature." No, the story is an occasional stimulation, an occasional diversion, an occasional awakener; and its permanent value is in the degree in which the child realizes for himself the elements of experience finding expression in the story—a condition more often met by the tales of historic heroes in the struggles of historic progress than in myths. And the myth itself is of permanent value as a story in just the degree in which the child has been led for himself first to appreciate the natural facts and the social conditions which are reflected in it. If he has been led in his nature study to realize the part played by the sun in the economy of life, if he has been led to appreciate the historic condition of people with a precarious relationship to fire, myths of the sun and fire may play a serious and a worthy part. Let us treat the intellectual resources, capacities, and needs of our children with the full dignity and respect they deserve, and not sentimentalize nor symbolize the realities of life, nor present them in the shape of mental toys.

I have endeavored to point out that accepting the correspondence theory in general, it requires in its educational interpretation and bearings, first, to be investigated, verified, and controlled absolutely from the side of child life; and, secondly, to be utilized primarily from the side of the activities and ideas in society which now correspond to the dawning interest, and only secondarily from that of the historical products of these activities and ideas. Even if the last point is not admitted, I think it must be confessed that there is a gap in the existing argument, from the fact of corresponding epochs, to the study of the *products* of the race epoch; and that this gap needs to be filled before the theory is relieved of ambiguity and confusion and stands justified.

# The Primary-Education Fetich

It is some years since the educational world was more or less agitated by an attack upon the place occupied by Greek in the educational scheme. If, however, Greek occupies the place of a fetich, its worshippers are comparatively few in number, and its influence is relatively slight. There is, however, a false educational god whose idolaters are legion, and whose cult influences the entire educational system. This is language study—the study not of foreign language, but of English; not in higher, but in primary education. It is almost an unquestioned assumption, of educational theory and practice both, that the first three years of a child's school life shall be mainly taken up with learning to read and write his own language. If we add to this the learning of a certain amount of numerical combinations, we have the pivot about which primary education swings. Other subjects may be taught; but they are introduced in strict subordination.

The very fact that this procedure, as part of the natural and established course of education, is assumed as inevitable, —opposition being regarded as captious and revolutionary,— indicates that, historically, there are good reasons for the position assigned to these studies. It does not follow, however, that because this course was once wise it is so any longer. On the contrary, the fact, that this mode of education was adapted to past conditions, is in itself a reason why it should no longer hold supreme sway. The present has its claims. It is in education, if anywhere, that the claims of the present should be controlling. To educate on the basis of past surroundings is like adapting an organism to an environment which no longer exists. The individual is stultified, if not disintegrated; and the course of progress is

[*First published in* Forum, xxv (*May 1898*), 315–28. *Reprinted in* Education Today, *ed. Joseph Ratner* (*New York: G. P. Putnam's Sons, 1940*), *pp. 18–35.*]

blocked. My proposition is, that conditions—social, industrial, and intellectual—have undergone such a radical change, that the time has come for a thoroughgoing examination of the emphasis put upon linguistic work in elementary instruction.

The existing status was developed in a period when ability to read was practically the sole avenue to knowledge, when it was the only tool which insured control over the accumulated spiritual resources of civilization. Scientific methods of observation, experimentation, and testing were either unknown or confined to a few specialists at the upper end of the educational ladder. Because these methods were not free, were not capable of anything like general use, it was not possible to permit the pupil to begin his school career in direct contact with the materials of nature and of life. The only guarantee, the only criterion of values, was found in the ways in which the great minds of the past had assimilated and interpreted such materials. To avoid intellectual chaos and confusion, it was necessary reverently to retrace the steps of the fathers. The régime of intellectual authority and tradition, in matters of politics, morals, and culture, was a necessity, where methods of scientific investigation and verification had not been developed, or were in the hands of the few. We often fail to see that the dominant position occupied by book-learning in school education is simply a corollary and relic of this epoch of intellectual development.

Ordinary social conditions were congruent with this intellectual status. While it cannot be said that, in the formative period of our educational system in America, authority and tradition were the ultimate sources of knowledge and belief, it must be remembered that the immediate surroundings of our ancestors were crude and undeveloped. Newspapers, magazines, libraries, art-galleries, and all the daily play of intellectual intercourse and reaction which is effective today were non-existent. If any escape existed from the poverty of the intellectual environment, or any road to richer and wider mental life, the exit was through the gateway of books. In presenting the attainments of the past, these maintained the bonds of spiritual continuity, and kept our forefathers from falling to the crude level of their material surroundings.

When ability to read and write marked the distinction between the educated and the uneducated man, not simply in the scholastic sense, but in the sense of one who is enslaved by his environment and one who is able to take advantage of and rise above it, corresponding importance attached to acquiring these capacities. Reading and writing were obviously what they are still so often called—the open doors to learning and to success in life. All the meaning that belongs to these ends naturally transferred itself to the means through which alone they could be realized. The intensity and ardor with which our forefathers set themselves to master reading and writing, the difficulties overcome, the interest attached in the ordinary routine of school life to what now seems barren,—the curriculum of the three R's,—all testify to the motive-power these studies possessed. To learn to read and write was an interesting, even exciting, thing: it made such a difference in life.

It is hardly necessary to say that the conditions, intellectual as well as social, have changed. There are undoubtedly rural regions where the old state of things still persists. With reference to these, what I am saying has no particular meaning. But, upon the whole, the advent of quick and cheap mails, of easy and continuous travel and transportation, of the telegraph and telephone, the establishment of libraries, art-galleries, literary clubs, the universal diffusion of cheap reading-matter, newspapers and magazines of all kinds and grades,—all these have worked a tremendous change in the immediate intellectual environment. The values of life and of civilization, instead of being far away and correspondingly inaccessible, press upon the individual—at least in cities—with only too much urgency and stimulating force. We are more likely to be surfeited than starved: there is more congestion than lack of intellectual nutriment.

The capital handed down from past generations, and upon whose transmission the integrity of civilization depends, is no longer amassed in those banks termed books, but is in active and general circulation, at an extremely low rate of interest. It is futile to try to conceal from ourselves the fact that this great change in the intellectual atmosphere —this great change in the relation of the individual to accumulated knowledge—demands a corresponding educational readjustment. The significance attaching to reading and writing, as primary and fundamental instruments of culture, has shrunk proportionately as the immanent intellectual life of society has quickened and multiplied. The result is that these studies lose their motive and motor force. They have become mechanical and formal, and out of relation—when made dominant—to the rest of life.

They are regarded as more or less arbitrary tasks which must be submitted to because one is going to that mysterious thing called a school, or else are covered up and sugar-coated with all manner of pretty devices and tricks in order that the child may absorb them unawares. The complaint made by some, that the school curriculum of today does not have the disciplinary value of the old-fashioned three R's, has a certain validity. But this is not because the old ideal has been abandoned. It is because it has been retained in spite of the change of conditions. Instead of frankly facing the situation, and asking ourselves what studies can be organized which shall do for today what language study did for former generations, we have retained that as the centre and core of our course of study, and dressed it out with a variety of pretty pictures, objects, and games, and a smattering of science.

Along with this change in the relation of intellectual material and stimulus to the individual there has been an equally great change in the method and make-up of knowledge itself. Science and art have become free. The simplest processes and methods of knowing and doing have been worked out to such a point that they are no longer the monopolistic possessions of any class or guild. They are, in idea, and should be in deed, part of the social commonwealth. It is possible to initiate the child from the first in a direct, not abstract or symbolical, way, into the operations by which society maintains its existence, material and spiritual.

The processes of production, transportation, consumption, etc., by which society keeps up its material continuity, are conducted on such a large and public scale that they are obvious and objective. Their reproduction in embryonic form through a variety of modes of industrial training is entirely within the bounds of possibility. Moreover, methods of the discovery and communication of truth—upon which the spiritual unity of society depends—have become direct and independent, instead of remote and tied to the intervention of teacher or book. It is not simply that children can acquire a certain amount of scientific information about things organic and inorganic: if that were all, the plea for the study of the history and literature of the past, as more humanistic, would be unanswerable. No; the significant thing is that it is possible for the child at an early day to become acquainted with, and to use, in a personal and yet relatively controlled fashion, the methods by which truth is discovered and communicated, and to make his own speech a channel for the expression and communication of truth; thus putting the linguistic side where it belongs—subordinate to the appropriation and conveyance of what is genuinely and personally experienced.

A similar modification, almost revolution, has taken place in the relation which the intellectual activities bear to the ordinary practical occupations of life. While the child of bygone days was getting an intellectual discipline whose significance he appreciated in the school, in his home life he was securing acquaintance in a direct fashion with the chief lines of social and industrial activity. Life was in the main rural. The child came into contact with the scenes of nature, and was familiarized with the care of domestic animals, the cultivation of the soil, and the raising of crops. The factory system being undeveloped, the home was the centre of industry. Spinning, weaving, the making of clothes, etc., were all carried on there. As there was little accumulation of wealth, the child had to take part in these, as well as to participate in the usual round of household occupations. Only those who have passed through such training, and, later on, have seen children reared in city environments, can adequately realize the amount of training, mental and moral, involved in this extra-school life. That our successful men have come so largely from the country, is an indication of the educational value bound up with participation in this practical life. It was not only an adequate substitute for what we now term manual training, in the development of hand and eye, in the acquisition of skill and deftness; but it was initiation into self-reliance, independence of judgment and action, and was the best stimulus to habits of regular and continuous work.

In the urban and suburban life of the child of today this is simply a memory. The invention of machinery, the institution of the factory system, the division of labor, have changed the home from a workshop into a simple dwelling-place. The crowding into cities and the increase of servants have deprived the child of an opportunity to take part in those occupations which still remain. Just at the time when a child is subjected to a great increase in stimulus and pressure from his environment, he loses the practical and motor training necessary to balance his intellectual development. Facility in acquiring information is gained: the power of using it is lost. While need of the more formal intellectual training in the school has decreased, there arises an urgent demand for the introduction of methods of manual and industrial discipline which shall give the child what he formerly obtained in his home and social life.

Here we have at least a *prima facie* case for a reconsideration of the whole question of the relative importance of learning to read and write in primary education. Hence the necessity of meeting the question at closer quarters. What can be said against giving up the greater portion of the first two years of school life to the mastery of linguistic form? In the first place, physiologists are coming to believe that the sense organs and connected nerve and motor apparatus of the child are not at this period best adapted to the confining and analytic work of learning to read and write. There is an order in which sensory and motor centres develop,—an order expressed, in a general way, by saying that the line of progress is from the larger, coarser adjustments having to do with the bodily system as a whole (those nearest the trunk of the body) to the finer and accurate adjustments having to do with the periphery and extremities of the organism. The oculist tells us that the vision of the child is essentially that of the savage; being adapted to seeing large and somewhat remote objects in the mass, not near-by objects in detail. To violate this law means undue nervous strain: it means putting the greatest tension upon the centres least able to do the work. At the same time, the lines of activity which are hungering and thirsting for action are left, unused, to atrophy. The act of writing—especially in the barbarous fashion, long current in the school, of compelling the child to write on ruled lines in a small hand and with the utmost attainable degree of accuracy—involves a nicety and complexity of adjustments of muscular activity which can be definitely appreciated only by the specialist. As the principal of a Chicago school has wittily remarked in this connection, "the pen is literally mightier than the sword." Forcing children at a premature age to devote their entire attention to these refined and cramped adjustments has left behind it a sad record of injured nervous systems and of muscular disorders and distortions. While there are undoubted exceptions, present physiological knowledge points to the age of about eight years as early enough for anything more than an incidental attention to visual and written language-form.

We must not forget that these forms are symbols. I am far from depreciating the value of symbols in our intellectual life. It is hardly too much to say that all progress in civilization upon the intellectual side has depended upon increasing invention and control of symbols of one sort or another. Nor do I join in the undiscriminating cry of those who condemn the study of language as having to do with mere words, not with realities. Such a position is one-sided, and is as crude as the view against which it is a reaction. But there is an important question here: Is the child of six or seven years ready for symbols to such an extent that the stress of educational life can be thrown upon them? If we were to look at the question independently of the existing school system, in the light of the child's natural needs and interests at this period, I doubt if there could be found anyone who would say that the urgent call of the child of six and seven is for this sort of nutriment, instead of for more direct introduction into the wealth of natural and social forms that surround him. No doubt the skillful teacher often succeeds in awakening an interest in these matters; but the interest has to be excited in a more or less artificial way, and, when excited, is somewhat factitious, and independent of other interests of child life. At this point the wedge is introduced and driven in which marks the growing divorce between school and outside interests and occupations.

We cannot recur too often in educational matters to the conception of John Fiske, that advance in civilization is an accompaniment of the prolongation of infancy. Anything which, at this period, develops to a high degree any set of organs and centres at the expense of others means premature specialization, and the arrest of an equable and all-round development. Many educators are already convinced that premature facility and glibness in the matter of numerical combinations tend toward an arrested development of certain higher spiritual capacities. The same thing is true in the matter of verbal symbols. Only the trained psychologist is aware of the amount of analysis and abstraction demanded by the visual recognition of a verbal form. Many suppose that abstraction is found only where more or less complex reasoning exists. But as a matter of fact the essence of abstraction is found in compelling attention to rest upon elements which are more or less cut off from direct channels of interest and action. To require a child to turn away from the rich material which is all about him, to which he spontaneously attends, and which is his natural, unconscious food, is to compel the premature use of analytic and abstract powers. It is wilfully to deprive the child of that synthetic life, that unconscious union with his environment, which is his birthright and privilege. There is every reason to suppose that a premature demand upon the abstract intellectual capacity stands in its own way. It cripples rather than furthers later intellectual development. We are not yet in a position to know how much of the inertia and seeming paralysis of mental powers in later periods is the direct outcome of excessive and too early appeal to isolated intellectual capacity. We must trust to the development of physiology and psychology to make these matters so clear that school authorities and the public opinion which controls them shall have no option. Only then can we hope to escape that deadening of the childish activities which led Jowett to call education "the grave of the mind."

Were the matter not so serious it would be ludicrous, when we reflect how all this time and effort fail to reach the end to which they are specially consecrated. It is a common saying among intelligent educators that they can go into a schoolroom and select the children who picked up reading at home: they read so much more naturally and intelligently. The stilted, mechanical, droning, and sing-song ways of reading which prevail in many of our schools are simply the reflex of the lack of motive. Reading is made an isolated accomplishment. There are no aims in the child's mind which he feels he can serve by reading; there is no mental hunger to be satisfied; there are no conscious problems with reference to which he uses books. The book is a reading-lesson. He learns to read not for the sake of what he reads, but for the mere sake of reading. When the bare process of reading is thus made an end in itself, it is a psychological impossibility for reading to be other than lifeless.

It is quite true that all better teachers now claim that the formal act of reading should be made subordinate to the sense of what is read,—that the child has first to grasp the idea, and then to express his mental realization. But, under present conditions, this profession cannot be carried out. The following paragraph from the *Report of the Committee of Fifteen on Elementary Education* states clearly enough the reason why; though, as it seems to me, without any consciousness of the real inference which should be drawn from the facts set forth: —

The first three years' work of the child is occupied mainly with the mastery of the printed and written forms of the words of his colloquial vocabulary,—words that he is already familiar enough with as sounds addressed to the ear. He has to become familiar with the new forms addressed to the eye; and it would be an unwise method to require him to learn many new words at the same time that he is learning to recognize his old words in their new shape. But as soon as he has acquired (before three years) some facility in reading what is printed in the colloquial style, he may go on to selections from standard authors.

The material of the reading-lesson is thus found wholly in the region of familiar words and ideas. It is out of the question for the child to find anything in the ideas themselves to arouse and hold attention. His mind is fixed upon the mere recognition and utterance of the forms. Thus begins that fatal divorce between the substance and the form of expression, which, fatal to reading as an art, reduces it to a mechanical action. The utter triviality of the contents of our school "Primers" and "First Readers" shows the inevitable outcome of forcing the mastery of external language-forms upon the child at a premature period. Take up the first half-dozen or dozen such books you meet with, and ask yourself how much there is in the ideas presented worthy of respect from any intelligent child of six years.

Methods for learning to read come and go across the educational arena, like the march of supernumeraries upon the stage. Each is heralded as the final solution of the problem of learning to read; but each in turn gives way to some later discovery. The simple fact is, that they all lack the essential of any well-grounded method, namely, relevancy to the child's mental needs. No scheme for learning to read can supply this want. Only a new motive—putting the child into a vital relation to the materials to be read—can be of service here. It is evident that this condition cannot be met, unless learning to read be postponed to a period when the child's intellectual appetite is more consciously active, and when he is mature enough to deal more rapidly and effectively with the formal and mechanical difficulties.

The endless drill, with its continual repetitions, is another instance of the same evil. Even when the attempt is made to select material with some literary or historic worth of its own, the practical outcome is much like making *Paradise Lost* the basis of parsing-lessons, or Cæsar's *Gallic Wars* an introduction to Latin syntax. So much attention has to be given to the formal side that the spiritual value evanesces. No one can estimate the benumbing and hardening effect of this continued drill upon mere form. Another even more serious evil is the consequent emptiness of mind induced. The mental room is swept and garnished—and that is all. The moral result is even more deplorable than the intellectual. At this plastic period, when images which take hold of the mind exercise such suggestive motor force, nothing but husks are provided. Under the circumstances, our schools are doing great things for the moral education of children; but all efforts in this direction must necessarily be hampered and discounted until the school-teacher shall be perfectly free to find the bulk of the material of instruction for the early school-years in something which has intrinsic value,—something whose introduction into consciousness is so vital as to be personal and reconstructive.

It should be obvious that what I have in mind is not a Philistine attack upon books and reading. The question is not how to get rid of them, but how to get their value,—how to use them to their capacity as servants of the intellectual and moral life. The plea for the predominance of learning to read in early school life because of the great importance attaching to literature seems to me a perversion. Just because literature is so important, it is desirable to postpone the child's introduction to printed speech until he is capable of appreciating and dealing with its genuine meaning. Now, the child learns to read as a mechanical tool, and gets very little conception of what is worth reading. The result is, that, after he has mastered the art and wishes to use it, he has no standard by which to direct it. He is about as likely to use it in one way as in another. It would be ungrateful not to recognize the faithfulness and relative success with which teachers, for the last ten or fifteen years, have devoted themselves to raising the general tone of reading with their pupils. But, after all, they are working against great odds. Our ideal should be that the child should have a personal interest in what is read, a personal hunger for it, and a personal power of satisfying this appetite. The adequate realization of this ideal is impossible until the child comes to the reading-material with a certain background of experience which makes him appreciate the difference between the trivial, the merely amusing and exciting, and that which has permanent and serious meaning. This is impossible so long as the child has not been trained in the habit of dealing with material outside of books, and has formed, through contact with the realities of experience, habits of recognizing and dealing with problems in the direct personal way. The isolation of material found in books from the material which the child experiences in life itself—the forcing of the former upon the child before he has well-organized powers of dealing with the latter—is an unnatural divorce which cannot have any other result than defective standards of appreciation, and a tendency to elevate the sensational and transiently interesting above the valuable and the permanent.

Two results of our wrong methods are so apparent in higher education that they are worth special mention. They are exhibited in the paradox of the combination of slavish dependence upon books with real inability to use them effectively. The famous complaint of Agassiz, that students could not see for themselves, is still repeated by every teacher of science in our high schools and colleges. How many teachers of science will tell you, for example, that, when their students are instructed to find out something about an object, their first demand is for a book in which they can read about it; their first reaction, one of helplessness, when they are told that they must go to the object itself and let it tell its own story? It is not exaggerating to say that the book habit is so firmly fixed that very many pupils, otherwise intelligent, have a positive aversion to directing their attention to things themselves,—it seems so much simpler to occupy the mind with what someone else has said about these things. While it is mere stupidity not to make judicious use of the discoveries and attainments of others, the substitution of the seeing of others for the use of one's own eyes is such a self-contradictory principle as to require no criticism. We only need recognize the extent to which it actually obtains.

On the other hand, we have the relative incapacity of students to use easily and economically these very tools— books—to which most of their energies have been directed. It is a common experience with, I will not say only the teachers of undergraduate students, but of graduate students,—candidates for advanced degrees,—to find that in every special subject a large amount of time and energy has to be spent in learning how to use the books. To take a book and present an adequate, condensed synopsis of its points of view and course of argument, is an exercise not merely in reading, but in thinking. To know how to turn quickly to a number of books bearing upon a given topic, to choose what is needed, and to find what is characteristic of the author and important in the subject, are matters which the majority of even graduate students have to learn over again for themselves. If such be the case,—and yet attention to books has been the dominant note of all previous education,—we are surely within bounds in asking if there is not something radically wrong in the way in which books have been used. It is a truism to say that the value of books consists in their relation to life, in the keenness and range which they impart to powers of penetration and interpretation. It is no truism to say that the premature and unrelated use of books stands in the way. Our means defeat the very end to which they are used.

Just a word about the corresponding evils. We have to take into account not simply the results produced by forcing language-work unduly, but also the defects in development due to the crowding out of other objects. Every respectable authority insists that the period of childhood, lying between the years of four and eight or nine, is the plastic period in sense and emotional life. What are we doing to shape these capacities? What are we doing to feed this hunger? If one compares the powers and needs of the child in these directions with what is actually supplied in the regimen of the three R's, the contrast is pitiful, tragic. This epoch is also the budding-time for the formation of efficient and orderly habits on the motor side: it is pre-eminently the time when the child wishes to do things, and when his interest in doing can be turned to educative account. No one can clearly set before himself the vivacity and persistency of the child's motor instincts at this period, and then call to mind the continued grind of reading and writing, without feeling that the justification of our present curriculum is psychologically impossible. It is simply a superstition: it is a remnant of an outgrown period of history.

All this might be true, and yet there might be no subject-matter sufficiently organized for introduction into the school curriculum, since this demands, above all things, a certain definiteness of presentation and of development. But we are not in this unfortunate plight. There are subjects which are as well fitted to meet the child's dominant needs as they are to prepare him for the civilization in which he has to play his part. There is art in a variety of modes—music, drawing, painting, modelling, etc. These *media* not only afford a regulated outlet in which the child may project his inner impulses and feelings in outward form, and come to consciousness of himself, but are necessities in existing social life. The child must be protected against some of the hard and over-utilitarian aspects of modern civilization: positively, they are needed, because some degree of artistic and creative power is necessary to take the future worker out of the ranks of unskilled labor, and to feed his consciousness in his hours of contact with purely mechanical things.

Those modes of simple scientific observation and experiment which go under the name of "nature study" are calculated to appeal to and keep active the keenness of the child's interest in the world about him, and to introduce him gradually to those methods of discovery and verification which are the essential characteristics of modern intellectual life. On the social side, they give the child an acquaintance with his environment,—an acquaintance more and more necessary, under existing conditions, for the maintenance of personal and social health, for understanding and conducting business pursuits, and for the administration of civic affairs. What is crudely termed manual training—the variety of constructive activities, which, begun in the Kindergarten, ought never to be given up—is equally adapted to the characteristic needs of the child and to the present demands of associated life. These activities afford discipline in continuous and orderly application of powers, strengthen habits of attention and industry, and beget self-reliant and ingenious judgment. As preparation for future social life, they furnish insight into the mechanical and industrial occupations upon which our civilization depends, and keep alive that sense of the dignity of work essential to democracy. History and literature, once more, provide food for the eager imagination of the child. While giving it worthy material, they may check its morbid and chaotic exercise. They present to the child typical conditions of social life, they exhibit the struggles which have brought it into being, and picture the spiritual products in which it has culminated. Due place cannot be given to literature and history until the teacher is free to select them for their own intrinsic value, and not from the standpoint of the child's ability to recognize written and printed verbal symbols.

Here we have the controlling factors in the primary curriculum of the future,—manual training, science, nature study, art, and history. These keep alive the child's positive and creative impulses, and direct them in such ways as to discipline them into the habits of thought and action required for effective participation in community life.

Were the attempt suddenly made to throw out, or reduce to a minimum, language-work in the early grades, the last state of our schools would undoubtedly be worse than the first. Not immediate substitution is what is required, but consideration of the whole situation, and organization of the materials and methods of science, history, and the arts, to make them adequate educational agencies. Many of our present evils are due to compromise and inconsistency. We have neither one thing nor the other,—neither the systematic, all-pervasive discipline of the three R's, nor a coherent training in constructive work, history, and nature study. We have a mixture of the two. The former is supposed to furnish the element of discipline and to constitute the standard of success; while the latter supplies the factor of interest. What is needed is a thoroughgoing reconciliation of the ideals of thoroughness, definiteness, and order, summed up in the notion of discipline, with those of appeal to individual capacities and demands, summed up in the word "interest." This is the Educational Problem, so far as it relates to the elementary school.

Change must come gradually. To force it unduly would compromise its final success by favoring a violent reaction. What is needed in the first place is, that there should be a full and frank statement of conviction with regard to the matter from physiologists and psychologists and from those school administrators who are conscious of the evils of the present régime. Educators should also frankly face the fact that the New Education, as it exists today, is a compromise and a transition: it employs new methods; but its controlling ideals are virtually those of the Old Education. Wherever movements looking to a solution of the problem are intelligently undertaken, they should receive encouragement, moral and financial, from the intellectual leaders of the community. There are already in existence a considerable number of educational "experiment stations," which represent the outposts of educational progress. If these schools can be adequately supported for a number of years they will perform a great vicarious service. After such schools have worked out carefully and definitely the subject-matter of a new curriculum,—finding the right place for language-studies and placing them in their right perspective,—the problem of the more general educational reform will be immensely simplified and facilitated. There will be clear standards, well-arranged material, and coherent methods upon which to proceed. To build up and equip such schools is, therefore, the wisest and most economical policy, in avoiding the friction and waste consequent upon casual and spasmodic attempts at educational reform.

All this amounts to saying that school reform is dependent upon a collateral wider change in the public opinion which controls school board, superintendent, and teachers. There are certain minor changes, reforms in detail, which can be effected directly within the school system itself. But the school is not an isolated institution: it is one of an organism of social forces. To secure more scientific principles of work in the school means, accordingly, clearer vision and wiser standards of thought and action in the community at large. The Educational Problem is ultimately that society shall see clearly its own conditions and needs, and set resolutely about meeting them. If the recognition be once secured, we need have no doubts about the consequent action. Let the community once realize that it is educating upon the basis of a life which it has left behind, and it will turn, with adequate intellectual and material resources, to meet the needs of the present hour.

# The Influence of the High School upon Educational Methods

The high school is between two fires. More than any other portion of our educational system its work is marked by divided aims, and this through no fault of its own, but through opposed demands made upon it. About the function of the primary school at one end and of the university at the other, there is no dispute. Questions there may be, and are, about the best ways of realizing the end, or just how much the end shall include; but there is no question as to what the school in its main features shall stand for. But the high school occupies no such assured place. I do not refer to those who deny its utility completely. I wish to treat all opinions respectfully, yet I do not think that this question before this body[1] needs discussion or would suffer it. Carlyle says that a final question about every society is whether or no it possesses *lungs*; whether or no it can take capacity, talent, power for service, born in any section or stratum of society, and bring it to the place where it can do its work. Even though statistics should indicate that a much smaller percentage of pupils than is the case reach and pass through the high school, so long as that institution selects some choice youth and brings them forth to larger opportunity and more efficient service, it shall stand justified.

No, I refer to the opposed aims actually set before the high school by the conditions under which it exists. It must, on the one hand, serve as a connecting link between the lower grades and the college, and it must, upon the other,

---

[1]    This paper was read at the School and College Conference, at the University of Chicago, November 15, 1895.

[*First published in* School Review, IV (*Jan. 1896*), *1–12. Not previously reprinted.*]

serve not as a stepping-stone, but as a final stage, as itself the people's college, to those who do not intend to go, or who do not go to college. The academy which is distinctly a preparatory school does not have to contend with this difficulty. While we are thankful for the increasing number and the increasing efficiency of our distinctive preparatory schools, we must also be thankful that the split is not wholly between schools which prepare for college alone and those which do not; but that the division of energies exists within one and the same institution. However difficult the problem for those in charge of the high school, they have the consolation of knowing their sufferings are vicarious—that both primary and university education are reaping the benefits of their struggles. It is a helpful thing for the lower schools, and for the colleges that this conflict has to be faced and fought out within the limits of one and the same school.

It is of these interactions of the high school that I wish to speak—the influence it has exercised upon the rest of the educational system because of the peculiar place it occupies: not so much formally as informally, not so much of conscious purpose as through the conditions it has created. The proposition I wish to put before you is that the high school has been an intermediary in a very real sense; it has been the intermediary between the college, and the non-college business and professional public.

As this intermediary, it has operated to reflect back into the lower grades as much as possible of college ideal and method, thus solidifying and elevating the intellectual possessions of the public which never sees the college doors. There has been university extension by unconscious permeation, by indirect radiation. On the other hand, by practically compelling the college to adjust itself to the conditions of its preparatory constituency, it has served to break down the monastic and scholastic survivals in education, and to so modify the college aims and means as to bring them into much closer contact with everyday life. There are those who regret this as a departure from the self-included literary aims and spirit of the college, but to them I do not address myself. It is not necessary to be a spiritual recluse in order to escape being a Philistine.

First, as to the effect upon the university. As long as the academy existed primarily as a mere preparatory school for the college, its influence upon the college was of necessity slight. Action and reaction did not appear to be equal. But given a high school having other aims than those supplied by the college, another constituency to which it is responsible, and the college faces a serious problem. It must adjust itself more or less to the conditions thus created; it must meet the competition of this other environment of the high school, and so modify its courses and methods as to offer equal or superior attractions. It is led out into the struggle for existence and must exhibit its fitness to survive.

The fact is that certain changes in the policy, curriculum and methods of the college were initiated more promptly in the West than in the East, and were carried out with less discussion, almost from necessity, and with little consciousness of their radical nature. In the East these changes came, if at all, only as the results of long discussion, and often of the strong will of some educational reformer. The difference is due, I think, more than to anything else, to this fact; in the West the college was dependent upon a high school to whose independent volition it had to adjust itself; while the eastern college was in relation to a preparatory school which had to follow, almost blindly, the lead of the college.

As the outcome, the logic of the situation brought on certain changes in the West as a matter of practical wisdom, as a matter, it might be said, of obvious business prudence. These changes grew out of the educational soil. In the East, these changes had to be tenderly matured and skillfully grafted by some university gardener. The main changes in the college curriculum of the West during the last twenty-five years, changes in which the West preceded the East, were precisely those required by the status and needs of the high school. I refer to such matters as the co-education of the sexes, which in the West corresponded to the mixed high school, just as the separate colleges of the East were the logical complements of the boys' preparatory school and the young ladies' seminary; to the diversification of courses; the introduction of Latin, modern language and science courses into the curriculum upon the same level with the

Greek course, instead of in side schools, or as temporary concessions to the weakness of the human mind. That this diversification is not yet ended is evident from the fact that the university, within whose walls we are gathered, made provision, in its original statement, for a course in commercial and political science. When this precedent is generally followed, it may be said that the action of the high school upon the college, in the way of securing a complete outlet for itself, will be complete. Add to these things the introduction of greater range of selection of studies, and, in a less formal way, the introduction of consultation and co-operative methods between high school and college, and we have a broad, if sketchy, picture before us of the great changes wrought in the college curriculum and methods, in virtue of the conditions created by the high school. It is not empty conceit for the high school representative to congratulate himself upon having been an important factor in bringing these changes about.

But the high school has been an intermediary in another direction. It has not only brought a pressure upon the college, which has turned the latter to walk more closely parallel with life, but it brought pressure from the college and discharged it upon the lower grades. This reflex influence upon primary and intermediate work has arisen upon its face, through the need of securing a better preparation for college, doing more work in the same time and doing it better. But the outcome has been to give a deeper and a higher preparation for life to those who never see or think of college—who never even reach the high school.

The weakest point in our school system has been the grades from the fourth to the eighth, whether tested by methods used or results reached. Before this time the child has had a sense of power in learning to read and write; after this, instead of using his powers to master new fields, he goes on reading and writing. He has been gaining skill in drawing, in mastering numbers—he now goes on drawing and figuring. At the outset he has had the delight of an introduction to a new and expanding world; suddenly, the horizon walls shut down, and the child is confined to filling in his narrowed world with more or less repugnant details.

From the satisfaction that comes by contact with the new, he has been switched off into the dissatisfaction that comes with the endless turning over of the old. The benumbing, mechanical influence which is the serious evil of the average American school today is in full operation.

But a change has been occurring, and evidences multiply that the demand for the change is reaching an acute point. Within a dozen years, the university has thrown back an additional year's work upon the high school; within twenty, it has probably thrown back almost two years, besides demanding better work in quality. The high school has been able to meet this demand, and will be able to meet further demands which the college is likely to make, only by turning back and demanding better work, and work different in spirit and newer in method, from the lower grades. Much of this movement is in promise, rather than in evidence. But the signs are many and multiplying. There is the introduction into the lower grades of geometry and algebra, taught by rational methods, in place of the numerical contortions of the average arithmetic; the substitution of literary masterpieces as wholes for the grind of continuing to learn to read broken off fragments after one has already known how to read several years;[2] the acquaintance with history at something like second-hand, at least, instead of the memorizing of text-books; the extension of science work and the introduction of simple experimental and observational methods; finally, the introduction of foreign language work (whether ancient or modern, I will not dogmatize) to that degree found to be advisable to give any child command of his own powers, whether he go to college or not.

Now all this intensification and enriching, past, present, and especially prospective, is very largely the outcome of the pressure of the university upon the high school, reflected down and back. No other influence, save the introduction of manual training, has compared with this; and that has been largely induced and fostered by the introduction of

---

2    It is a common statement (and a common fact) that the child, upon entering the eighth grade does not read aloud with as much ease and effectiveness as upon entering the fourth.

engineering courses in the college, and the founding of higher technological schools.

Is the influence of the high school upon educational methods exhausted in the lines already spoken of? There is one great possibility, as yet unrealized, so far as any systematic effort is concerned. This is the preparation by the high school of teachers for the lower grades. The simple fact is that this *is* one of its chief functions at present, but the high school is doing it only incidentally and unsystematically. My query is whether the high school must not awaken to consciousness of what it is already doing by the way, and make that one of its chief functions. The query is whether the high school stands quite justified before the community, until it shall recognize and equip itself for this task; whether the performance of this function would not do away with the last vestige of grumbling about, and attack upon, the high school.

Certain facts stand out beyond any peradventure. Fact one, there is not a sufficient recognition of the need of professional training to send all would-be teachers to the normal school; fact two, the normal schools are not numerous enough nor well enough endowed at present to fit all possible teachers; fact three, the normal schools have at least half their time taken up, at present, with high school, non-professional work; fact four, the average school board will rarely go outside its own town and school system for a teacher in the "grades." Conclusion: the high school is the chief source of supply, and, therefore, *must be the chief hope and mainstay*, in the matter of furnishing teachers for the lower grades.

This being the case, the only cause for surprise is, not to hear put forth the idea that the high school should consciously assume this responsibility, but that the public has so long tolerated the fact that it has not assumed it. It is true that many of the high schools now have training classes, as graduate courses, annexed to them. This is undoubtedly a great help. But this is not precisely what I have in mind. I mean that the high school, in its own organization, should regularly provide for the training of capable teachers for the lower grades.

Now I suppose the feeling of many of you in sympathy with the general trend of these remarks is that, under existing circumstances, such an undertaking is impracticable. The curriculum is already overcrowded; we want fewer courses, rather than more; fewer studies rather than more. We are already at our wits' end because of the pressure from the university, on one side, and that of the business sense of our community on the other; and lo and behold! here is a proposition to add still more to our burdens. I reply "amen" to the spirit of this response. But I believe that when anything really requires doing, the attempt to do it will introduce order and ease rather than confusion and hardship. I believe we are bound to assume this even if we cannot see our way clearly through in detail. But there are certain suggestions which may be made in the line of indicating where the principle of order and economy will be found.

1. In the first place, the introduction of a training course would give a practical motive for doing much work now done without any sense of its bearings. We all agree— or almost all—with great cheerfulness to the proposition that character, not information, is the end of education, and then tamely submit to, or wilfully create conditions which make it impossible that the school should be an active force in character building. But the greatest of these conditions is that the information gained does not find outlet in action. Absorption, income is the rule—and then we wonder whether learning tends to selfishness! I do not believe any more helpful inspiration could come into any school than the conviction that what is being learned must be so learned that it may be of service in teaching others.[3] This is not the place to discuss ways and means of practice work, but I believe the solution of this difficult problem will be in the discovery that it is stupidity to suppose that there is no alternative between no practice teaching, and the turning over of whole classes to the pupil-teacher at the outset. The latter method of ne-

---

[3]    I hope I may be pardoned for repeating what an instructor of one of our best high schools said to me in private conversation—it went so much beyond what I dared say. It was that *no* person ought to be allowed to graduate from the high school until he had put to use his knowledge in teaching; that this was the best test and the best guarantee for sure assimilation.

cessity throws the teacher into a mechanical attitude, it not only does not tend to, but it hinders, the development of sympathy and psychological insight. The proper place of the pupil-teacher is as a helper, here, there and anywhere that he can discover something to do, dealing with a few individuals in their personal difficulties, rather than with the "teaching" of a class *en masse*. This personal relationship once secured, the pupil-teacher will be in a healthy attitude when dealing with a class as a whole. Moreover this method would go far to relieve that congestion where one teacher deals with from forty to sixty pupils.

2. A training course does not mean so much new subjects for study as a new interest in, and a new point of view for existing subjects. I do not think physiology would be any the less well learned as physiology if emphasis were thrown upon questions of ventilation, of hygienic seats and postures, of the importance of correct muscular attitudes and gymnastic exercises, of the use and education of the senses of touch, sight and hearing, and a thousand other points. What is true of physiology is true in kind, even if in less degree, of all the sciences. It is not so obviously true of the languages and of history, but even here contact with the needs and methods of younger children would serve to fertilize rather than to deaden the material. What is required in any case is a selection and adjustment of subjects already taught, rather than a large number of new studies.

3. Two new studies however are required. These are psychology and social ethics. If asked eight or even five years ago about the admissibility of introducing the subject of psychology into the high school, I hesitated and doubted its wisdom save under very exceptional circumstances. For various reasons, the danger was great that psychology would be made a formal thing, the study of a text-book, with its definitions and classifications, rather than of psychical life itself; a study pursued by memorizing very largely. There was a possibility, if not a probability, that the text-book used would be a rehash of the state of the subject as it was fifty years ago. But this is now changed. One can have these out-of-date books and follow dead and mechanical methods if he will, but other and fresher possibilities are

easily open. There are plenty of new books, new in material and methods; there are simple experimental appliances and methods to be utilized; the whole subject of child-study has grown up. Psychology, for the high schools, has undergone a change from a mechanical thing fossilized and mummified in out-of-date books, and pigeon-holed to rigidity, into a living human thing.

None the less, it will be said, this means the introduction of a new study into a crowded curriculum. I won't suggest that certain things might give way and that the study of the human nature which lies in us, and in whose expressions we live and have our deepest contacts and relations, has claims equal to various and sundry subjects which I will not mention. Such a suggestion might seem extreme and utopian, and I'll not make it.

But a few facts may be selected indicating that this new study would serve to relieve rather than congest the course of study. In the first place the period covered by the high school is the age of adolescence. This is the natural age of introspection. There is no time of life when the interest in self, and in the relations and adjustments of self to others is so pressing and conscious as at this time. If metaphysics is a disease, like mumps and measles, then this is the time when it is epidemic. The failure to utilize this interest is a pedagogic blunder. It is a blunder in the economy of the school; it is a blunder from the standpoint of the pupil, who has one of the most educative of all interests left without direction and so liable to perversion and distortion. So far is it from true that psychology would lead to morbid self-consciousness, that in many cases the tendency to morbidness both in one's self and in relation to others is a harassing and grievous fact; and the conscious direction of this tendency in a scientific channel would be one of the greatest, if not the greatest, means for purging it of its morbidness. Moreover many of the studies of the high school would be greatly reinforced in interest and greatly lessened in difficulty by the judicious introduction of the right sort of psychology. If we take literature on its formal side, rhetoric and grammar, it *is* psychology, and logic allied to psychology; a failure to recognize this psychological basis and import means the erection of artificial difficulties. Of literature in its content, its æsthetic and moral values, much the same is true. The teaching of literature is continually swinging from a sentimental and falsely philosophic standard on one side to the dwelling upon merely technical matters of information, etc., on the other. The student is either required to descant upon the moral lessons conveyed, to formulate appreciations of the various kinds of beauties presented (formulations of necessity conventional and second-hand), or the text becomes a peg upon which to hang the dictionary and encyclopædia. A rational introduction of some of the recent methods and results regarding the imagination and the emotions would do more, I think, than all else put together to give both freshness and substance to the study of literature. History affords the same opportunity for discussions of questions of habit and character, purpose and motive. The study of the sciences demands some account of the processes of observation and reasoning and the main types of inference, etc.[4]

By social ethics, I mean, again, not a study of a formal text-book but the observation and discussion of certain obvious phases of actual social life. The adult's interest in social life has become so specialized and so technical, and also so much a matter of course, that he continually fails to realize the force and vividness with which social interests and problems press upon the inquiring and observing child.

Political economy has had much the same history as psychology in the high school; first introduced, and then, upon the whole, discredited, and both rightly so, without doubt, under the circumstances. But there is a study of economic forces and interactions actually at work which is highly interesting and important as well as of ethical content, and which forms the basis for unifying work in history, geography and the sciences—as the numerous points where physics and chemistry touch processes of manufacture and distribution.

---

[4] Professor Münsterberg says (p. 19, of an address before the Massachusetts Schoolmasters' Club): "The chief facts of seeing and hearing, attention and memory, perception and imagination, feeling and will, dreams and illusions, could become an extremely important and suggestive part of the school education, not as a special branch of the school curriculum, but sprinkled into the whole school work."

To sum up the matter in terms of the current agitation of the correlation of studies, psychology as a concrete study of human nature in the individual, and sociology as the concrete study of human nature in its organized forms, are the natural bases for unification of studies in the high school, whether we look at the dominant interests and impulses of the pupil at this age, or at the material studied.[5] This seems to me to constitute a fair basis for the claim that these studies would introduce order rather than confusion, work for ease rather than for hardship in the high school economy.

The schools already have a certain running machinery, a certain prescribed and acquired *modus operandi*; teachers have their acquired tastes and habits. It is not easy to re-adjust these. I do not propose what I have said as a model to be at once and everywhere conformed to. But I believe the high schools must soon face the question of affording a course of training for would-be teachers in the lower grades, and that it behooves those who have any responsibilities in the shaping of the educational structure to give serious attention to this matter, and to shape the modifications which continually occur in this direction. When this function shall be taken in by the high school, I believe the influence of the high school upon educational methods will be at its full tide—a tide which will never ebb.

[5]    It will be noticed that I have said nothing of the separate study of systematic pedagogy. The omission is not accidental, but the reasons cannot be given here. There is a certain division of labor in the training of teachers with reference to which I hope to write in the future.

# Pedagogy as a University Discipline

## I.

A distinct division of labor is indicated as regards training in the science and art of education. There must be some schools whose main task is to train the rank and file of teachers— schools whose function is to supply the great army of teachers with the weapons of their calling and direct them as to their use. It must be the province of such schools to give discipline along lines already well established rather than to undertake experiment along new lines. They must, indeed, be awake to the reception of new ideas, but in undertaking the primary preparation of teachers for the school room, it will rarely be advisable to undertake their initiation into ideas or methods not having some guarantee of time and experience back of them.

Parallel to such training schools must be those which direct their energies to the education, not of the rank and file, but of the leaders of our educational systems—teachers in normal and training schools, professors of pedagogy, superintendents, principals of schools in our large cities, many of whom have under them more teachers than a superintendent in smaller towns. Such persons are not in need of introduction to the rudiments of their work; they have already served their apprenticeship in practice and learned the elements of the theory. They are, moreover, as a rule persons who have already had a college training, and who know what disciplined scientific work is. Such students are necessarily repelled if they find work adjusted to a lower intellectual level than they have become familiar with, or carried on by less orderly intellectual methods than they

[*First published in* University [*of Chicago*] Record, 1 (*Sept. 1896*), 353–55, 361–63. *Not previously reprinted. See Appendix 3*, The Early Works of John Dewey, v.]

have mastered. Because of these facts college graduates very rarely seek a normal or training school after having had a college education; if they become dissatisfied with their pedagogical horizon, there is, at present, very little resource save a journey to some German university which has recognized the need of advanced as well as elementary pedagogics.

Training schools of this type should and may, moreover, devote themselves more directly to the work of pedagogical discovery and experimentation. Dealing with those who know what has already been accomplished, what the existing status is, who are mature and have the balance of learning and experience, such work can be safely undertaken. There is no danger of confusion, of premature introduction to a range of truth lying beyond capacity for successful application. Such students are not only capable of initiation into the region of discovery and testing of new truths, but require it; since, as a rule, they seek after this higher type of training just because they are dissatisfied with the existing régime, or their educational environment.

It is obvious, without argument, that this higher type of training must be undertaken for the most part, if it is to be done in America at all, by universities and to a considerable extent as graduate work.

An additional, urgent reason for attempting such work in an American university may be found in our social and political traditions. These are all against any close, systematic and centralized direction and supervision of education on the part of a governmental authority. Extreme local self-government has been the rule in education even more, if anything, than in any other part of the American system. It makes little practical difference, for present purposes, whether one regret or laud this tendency. It is clear that our educational systems are in need of some kind of direction and systematization from expert sources. If the government does not furnish this, so much the greater the necessity for its being undertaken on a voluntary basis. It must be assumed with the authority of science, if without that of bureaucratic control. The universities are the natural centres of educational organization, unless the chaos of extreme centrifugal force is to continue indefinitely. It is for them to gather together and focus the best of all that emerges in the great variety of present practice, to test it scientifically, to work it out into shape for concrete use, and to issue it to the public educational system with the imprimatur, not of governmental coercion, but of scientific verification. Organization on the basis of co-operation, of free and full interaction of the various parts of our educational system is a necessity. It must accomplish what the central educational departments of Germany and France accomplish under the conditions prevailing in those countries.

One other fact may be mentioned as marking the university as the destined place assuming the responsibility of this higher training. A reorganization of the educational system is already occurring. It is impossible to undertake, here, a complete statement of the conditions meeting fulfillment in this reconstructive movement. One of these, however, is the great intellectual advance of the present century, an advance equally great in the regions of history and of science. The accumulation of knowledge has become so great that the educational system is disintegrating through the wedges of new studies continually introduced. While there is an almost constant cry that the curriculum is being too diversified, that students are distracted and congested by the wealth of material forced upon them, the demand for more studies and for more time for each of these studies never ceases. The pressure began in the college and high school. It is now finding its way into the primary grades, partly from social infiltration, partly from the continued pressure from above for such training below as will relieve the difficulties of the situation above. It is as nearly certain as any educational expectation may be that if the increased demands, as regards number of languages, range of literary study, of history and of the physical and biological sciences are to be met, even half way, in the college and high school, the response must proceed from changing the methods in the lower grades, and by beginning work along these lines in the primary school—yes, and in the kindergarten. It is not a mere question of local expedience, whether it is advisable here and there to modify the traditional "three R's" curriculum. It is a question of the right organization and balance of our entire educational system, from kindergarten to university, both in itself as a system and in its adjustment to the existing social environment.

This reconstruction may go on in a haphazard, an empirical, way, now trying this scheme, now abandoning it for that, without consciousness of the ends to be reached, without utilization of the manifold failures and successes and with all the waste of time, money and human life involved in such change. Or it may go on with some clear, if flexible, consciousness of the nature of the problem, of the ends to be met; and with some adaptation of means to these ends the latter conditions ought to be most clearly met at a university, where psychology and sociology are most systematically pursued, where scientific inquiry is at its height and where methods of work are most fully developed. In addition, it is at the university where there is the accumulation of the quantity and quality of knowledge which is trying to break through into the secondary and primary school systems. That is to say, the experiment of the introduction of science or history into lower education is a matter of subject-matter as well as of method. It is reasonable to suppose that it can most fruitfully and efficiently be attempted where this subject-matter is most adequately and accurately represented. One of the difficulties in introducing scientific methods and materials into lower grades is that "facts" are taught which are not facts; or facts are brought in in an unrelated, relatively incoherent way; methods are used which are out of date. The child should be started on the most advanced plane, with the least to unlearn and to correct as regards both particular things and methods; with the maximum of attainable accuracy and with a selection of ideas and principles in some ratio to their importance and future fertility. Where specialists abound, where investigations are continually in progress, where the laboratory and the library are thoroughly equipped, is, if anywhere, the place where such requirements are met. On the other side, the necessity of applying a specialized range of considerations to the purposes of education is the best way of preventing the specialist from becoming narrow. Such a task necessitates looking at the special material in the light of both its adaptation to other studies and to human nature. For one danger of higher education, from the point of view of broad human interests, is that with high specialization there is increasing likelihood of the centre of scholarship getting removed from the mass of men, and the things of daily life. Culture becomes tangential to life, not convergent. The problem of the application of the results of special research to educational ends compels a generalization both of subject-matter and of interest.

## II.

A complete organization of the discipline of pedagogy is still lacking. There is no German university in which the subject is presented in a way at once detailed and systematic. So far as can be determined in advance of trial, such an organization of the subject for university purposes would include four main lines of discussion and research, all correlated and focused in a laboratory of a school of practice, experiment and demonstration.

Of these four lines, two are mainly concerned with the administrative, two with the scholastic side of education.

From one point of view the school must be regarded as a social and political institution, having its own special relationships to other institutions within some particular state, and having its own internal organization and administrative machinery. From this point of view arise those phases of pedagogical science which deal both with the history and the theory of school systems. Historically, we must know how every people that has made a contribution to civilization has administered its educational forces; what practical ideals it has held in view and how it has shaped its means to realize these ideals. Hebrew, Egyptian, Greek, Roman, each has had a certain type of character in mind, a certain sort of social and political service to be rendered; partly by instinct, partly by conscious design, each nation has adapted its system to satisfy these requirements. The school system has always been a function of the prevailing type of organization of social life.

Just as the contemporaneous systems are of chief importance, so the study of these systems, English, French, German, and American, connects most closely with the other phase of this institutional study—the theory of the best attainable organization and administration in our own country under existing conditions.

Such a theoretical study includes such topics as the following: The relation of the general government to education; the various state systems and their relation to county and township direction; study of the conditions of supervision and control in both the rural districts and the larger cities, with the various problems thus presented, to the relation of the school system to the other parts of our political machinery; the various methods for the training of the teachers; special questions of school superintendency and supervisorship. Another type of question, falling under this same general head, is that connected with the school building as the practical centre of school work. Here are involved problems of economics, of financial control, of the proper division of labor between the scholastic and the business side of the school system; of sanitation and hygiene with relation to site, plumbing, seats, blackboards, etc.; of æsthetics in architecture and internal arrangement and decoration; questions of laboratories, museums, libraries and the entire working equipment of the school.

Those who are skeptical as to claims of pedagogy to a position in the sisterhood of university studies overlook both the vast amount of positive knowledge at hand here and the necessities of having this knowledge collected and organized. It is not a matter of crude speculation nor of doling out arbitrary empiric devices, but of getting together a definite sphere of historical, sociological and economic facts; and of combining these facts with others drawn from physiology, hygiene and medicine, etc., and of effecting a working synthesis of this great range of scientific data.

When we turn from the administrative to the scholastic side, the needs are no less urgent and the material no less specific and no less open to scientific method. Parallel to the historical development of the school as a social institution is the historic development of ideas concerning education. Just as the history of the institution correlates with the history of other institutions, so this relates to the history of reflective thought, of philosophy and of religion. It is an organic part of the record of the intellectual development of humanity, as the other is of its institutional development. No reason can be given for neglecting this that would not apply with equal, or greater, force to the history of science or philosophy. The theoretical study involves the generalization of this historic material, the various systems of pedagogy which have emerged, together with a thorough discussion of psychology and sociology in their bearings upon the selection, arrangement and sequence of the studies of the curriculum and the methods required to give them their full efficiency. If we call the corresponding study on the institutional side that of the educational plant, the problem that meets us here is how to utilize this plant, how to get the maximum of value for human life out of it.

There is no more reason for limiting the range of pedagogy to a part of the last problem mentioned—that of the methods required in teaching a subject—than there would be in limiting physiology to the most uncertain and empirical aspects of medicine. The question of subject-matter and method is indeed of supreme importance because it is the question of how the machinery of the institution is to touch human life, how it is to get its translation from machinery into human activity. But backed and surrounded by the disciplines of history, sociology, political science, physiology and psychology, such a study is no more a dealing in certain devices for making certain studies palatable than the pharmacopœia of cod-liver oil exhausts scientific hygiene and medicine. The question of method is impossible of divorce from that of subject-matter; it is simply a question of the relation one subject bears to another and bears to the human mind. It is the subject-matter taken out of the abstractness forced upon it for purposes of its own convenient study and put into its concrete connections with the rest of the world of knowledge and culture and with the life of man in society. There is opportunity and demand here for the most progressive psychology in determining the relation of studies to the mind in its various stages of development. There is need for a comprehensive philosophy in systematizing the relations of sciences to one another, in determining their correlations, and for widest knowledge of the sciences themselves in their details.

So much for the lecture and book side of university

instruction in pedagogy. But every university discipline now has its side of research, of investigation, of addition to the resources of the world. Its function is not exhausted in gathering together, systematizing and perpetuating the accomplishments, theoretical and practical, of the past. There remains the responsibility of testing the attainments of the past with reference to the needs of the present; there is imposed the duty of positive contribution of new facts, new principles. The heart of university work resides more and more in the laboratory and in the working equipment of the seminary.

Where is this equipment to be found in the case of a department of pedagogy? Clearly in a school which shall test and exhibit in actual working order the results of the theoretical work. Experience has confirmed what might have been expected *a priori*, that pedagogical instruction, whether in universities or normal schools, is effective in proportion as the theory of the class room is accompanied by actual school work. Only in this way can the student get the real force of what is advanced in the lecture or text-book; only in this way can there be assurance that the teaching of the class room is not vague and impracticable. Moreover, if there is a science of education it is an experimental science, not a purely deductive one. All well-ordered experiment presupposes two things: a working hypothesis, an idea to be put to the test, and adequate facilities for making the test. There must be a continual union of theory and practice; of reaction of one into the other. The leading idea must direct and clarify the work; the work must serve to criticize, to modify, to build up the theory.

But just as the teaching side of pedagogical work in a university is differently directed and constituted from that of the normal school, so also the accompanying laboratory. The former is a school of practice in the sense that in it the future teachers get such practical exercise in the weapons of the calling as to prepare them for the actual work of teaching. But "practice" in a university school of practice is a word of enlarged sense. It refers not so much to individual pupils as to the principles which are tested and demonstrated. Such a school is, in the strictest sense, a laboratory. Without it the instruction in pedagogy is in relatively as disorganized and crippled a condition as chemistry and physics would be with only lectures and books to depend upon.

That this fact is hardly recognized nominally, and next to not at all practically, simply indicates in how backward a condition the whole scientific organization of education is — how little society is as yet awakened to the possibility of applying scientific methods of inquiry and organization to educational matters. It is not over-sanguine to anticipate a transformation in education similar to that of chemistry when there is consciousness of the possibilities in this direction, and men are as willing to spend time and money in one direction as in the other. The sole hindrance is the skepticism, latent rather than expressed, passive rather than active, as to whether education is capable of intellectual organization, whether it really falls within the realm of scientific method and is subject to the intelligent application of law.

Let this inertia of conviction once be shaken, and just in proportion to the importance of education, and the extent to which it touches human life, will the response to the claims of pedagogy, as scientific theory of the practical organization of educational forces, be ready and ample. There is no doubt that a laboratory of chemistry might be made self-supporting by devoting itself, say, to work in dyes or drugs of direct commercial import. Whether the ultimate utilitarian output, to say nothing of chemical truth, would be as great is quite another matter. It is inconceivable that, in the long run, the needs of the theory of education should be grasped in any less generous and complete a fashion. In many respects the response of the American public to the needs of the highest education is the most striking fact of the day. There is no parallel in history to the lavishness with which means have been put at the disposal of educational interests in the last two decades. It is inconceivable that devotion to the problem of scientific investigation and organization of educational resources should be less than that or different from that in the more direct and obvious phases of education. What is needed is a sufficient beginning to exhibit the importance and the practicability of the work.

Te University of Chicago
THE UNIVERSITY EXTENSION
THE LECTURE-STUDY DEPARTMENT

# EDUCATIONAL ETHICS

## SYLLABUS OF A
## COURSE OF SIX
## LECTURE-STUDIES

BY JOHN DEWEY, PH.D.,
HEAD PROFESSOR OF PHILOSOPHY
AND PEDAGOGY

CHICAGO
The University of Chicago Press
1895

# Lecture I.   Ethical Problem of the School

*WHAT IS A SCHOOL?*

    I. A Social Institution.
        1. Place among other institutions.
        2. Preparatory function.
            (*a*) Legal concept; (*b*) political concept; (*c*) industrial concept.
        3. Social membership in democracy.
    II. Realized in Individuals.
        1. What individuality implies.
        2. Function as non-preparatory, or self-included.
    III. Problem of School Organization: Present Power *vs.* Future Vocation.
        1. Psychological and sociological standpoints.
        2. Extent and limitation of each.
        3. True definition: psychology gives means, sociology aim.
    IV. The Ethic of the School.
        1. Ideal is development of social consciousness.
        2. This definition complete, because
            (*a*) Recognizing social end.
            (*b*) Recognizing individual means.
            (*c*) Means and end not external, but (i) only end enables us to *interpret* means; and (ii) only means give any *content* to end.
    V. This Ethical Standard Must Be Applied.
        1. To form, or *method.*
        2. To content, or subject-matter (studies).
        3. To school life as whole, vital unity of method and studies.
    VI. The Ethical Hypothesis or Postulate; Unity of Development of Individuality and of Social Service.

*References:*
    For this ethical postulate, see
    Dewey, *Outlines of Ethics*, pp. 127–32 [*The Early Works of John Dewey*, III, 320–23].

[*First published by University of Chicago Press, 1895, for the Lecture-Study Department, University Extension, University of Chicago. Not previously reprinted.*]

Dewey, *Study of Ethics*, pp. 9–12 [*The Early Works of John Dewey*, IV, 231–34].

Literature upon the school as a social institution, and the moral problems and principles arising therefrom is largely significant from its absence. Material will be found in

Parker, *Concentration*, Ch. 14, and Ch. 16.

Jones, in Indianapolis School Reports.

Tompkins, *School Management*.

## Exercises

1. How do you account for the prevailing absence in sociological treatises of any discussion of the school as an institution?
2. What is the theoretical justification of the remark attributed to Leibniz, that if he could order the schools of Europe for a generation he could revolutionize the civilization of Europe?
3. If the school reflects community life, and community life depends upon the habits acquired in school, can we get out of a hopeless circle?
4. Point out phases of excessive individualism in existing social life that seem to you to be developed or reinforced by existing school methods. State these methods and how they operate in this direction.
5. Point out facts in the existing school life that positively corroborate the postulate.
6. Give negative instances; that is, show where methods which fail in realizing present powers also hinder or prevent realization of social service.

## Lecture II.   The Ethics of Method

The question of method is the individual (psychological) side of the whole ethical question, as the question of subject-matter is of the social. *Reverence for child* its motto.

I. Psychology, as Revealing to Us the Normal Individual Process, Gives Standard for Methods.

   1. Is not formal, save in sense in which form means norm.

2. Is considered formal
    (*a*) Because of separation of mind and body in psychology.
    (*b*) Because of a psychology of powers or faculties in general.

II. The Normal Psychological Process.
  1. Instinctive expression of impulse.
  2. Consciousness of the induced experience, results, or new values.
  3. Absorption of these into original impulse, (*a*) enlightening, (*b*) deepening and (*c*) correcting it.
    This analysis agrees with practical sense, which has for ideal a character possessing (*a*) *good judgment*, (*b*) *force*.

III. The Normal Educational Process Bases Itself upon the Psychological. The Abnormal Departs from It.
  1. Failures upon the side of purpose, or of educating judgment.
    (*a*) Setting up remote and external ends.
      (i) Failure to have end developed out of impulse; set up authoritatively, instead of experimentally. Functions of success and of failure.
      (ii) So remote as to be no ends at all, save objectively. The moral fallacy. Illustrated in learning to read, write, etc.
    (*b*) Setting up isolated and narrow ends.
      (i) Purely intellectual ends, discrimination, analysis *per se*, are isolated. Illustrations in current methods.
      (ii) Failure to bring out social content of activity narrows end. Illustrations.
  2. Failures upon side of impulse, or of educating force.
    (*a*) Failing to connect sense activity with its full motor discharge.
    (*b*) Artificially stimulating impulses, thus destroying continuity.
    (*c*) Forcing an impulse—neglect of principle of gradual maturing.
    (*d*) Continuing an impulse unduly—neglect of prin-

ciple that an impulse tends to become factor of larger activity.

3. Results are
- (*a*) Breaking down of force; listlessness, disintegration, openness to external suggestion (hypnotism), caprice, and either undue self-distrust or conceit.
- (*b*) Lack of sense of relative values; no standard for discriminating important, permanent from trivial and temporary.

*References:*

Dewey, *Study of Ethics*, pp. 13–24 [*The Early Works of John Dewey*, IV, 235–46].

McLellan and Dewey, *Psychology of Number*, Ch. 1.

## *Exercises*

1. Discuss the criticism of the psychological or "subjective" basis in *Report of Committee of Fifteen.*
2. Discuss the statement that instruction, being intellectual, needs to be supplemented by distinct moral training.
3. Do the methods necessarily employed in right instruction in geography or literature lead more readily to good character than those in arithmetic or grammar?
4. What ethical philosophy is involved in the plea of a child to be excused because he "didn't mean to" do it? Discuss the philosophy of the proper treatment of him.

## Lecture III.   The Ethics of the Curriculum, or Subjects of Study

The child has to interpret his powers in terms of their social function, his own social membership. Hence *reverence for society* is the motto.

I. Educational Values.
1. Necessity of standard of measurement.
2. Fallacy of fixed classification. Each study represents a certain *interest* in the whole.

    3. Social life alone furnishes standard.

II. The Social Process.
1. The material or conditions of social activity are *nature*.
2. Nature is realized or expressed in life. Meaning of *art*.
3. Knowledge of energies and their adjustments to one another the connecting link.

III. The Normal Educational Process as Based upon the Social.
1. The value of nature study (biological sciences, geography, etc.).
2. The value of modes of expression (reading, writing, etc.).
3. The value of studying mechanism of process (mechanics, chemistry, arithmetic).

IV. Departures from the Normal.
1. Isolation of nature study; taking knowledge of *objects* or *law* as standard. "Realism."
2. Isolation of means of expression; form without content, symbols taken as reality. "Humanism."
    (*a*) Literary or scholastic education.
    (*b*) Disciplining *vs.* discipline.
3. Isolation of mechanical side.

V. Results.
1. Ethical materialism—failure to interpret objects and laws in terms of their functions.
2. Ethical individualism. The powers having simply a formal training are not educated to work with reference to the whole.
3. The right and wrong "Commercialism"; the right and wrong "practical."

*Exercises*

1. Discuss the ethical value of manual training (*a*) upon the individual or psychological side, and (*b*) upon the social.
2. Is the correlation of arithmetic closer with nature study or with study of industrial activities of society?
3. What are the *ethical* reasons for teaching tables of weights and measures from the beginning?

4. Discuss the kindergarten gifts and occupations from standpoint of lecture.
5. Why do the defects of the "realistic" and the "literary" types of education increase, instead of offsetting each other?

# Lecture IV. The Herbartian Theory of Unification

## *ITS ADVANTAGES.*

1. Does not separate intellectual and moral training.
2. Aims at unification (organization) both in method, and in curriculum.
3. Developed into a definite, coherent system, not merely truistic generalities.

## *DEFICIENCIES.*

I. Method. Theory of Apperception.
  1. Neglect of intrinsic activity, impulse, instinct.
      (*a*) Overemphasis upon objects as *presented*.
      (*b*) Overemphasis upon ideas—formalism in methods, exaggeration of conscious formulation.
      (*c*) Excess of principle of "formation," of "culture" upon ethical side. Psychology of child as *pupil*, rather than as human being.
  2. No organic unity among ideas.
      (*a*) Ideas separate and hence apperception formal. Theory of interaction, not of organization.
      (*b*) Hence no *true* correlation, or co-ordination. Unity a teacher's device, not principle intrinsic in subject-matter.
      These defects supplemented by "Culture-Epoch" doctrine as supplying standard.
II. Subject-Matter. Theory of Stages of Development.
  1. Exaggeration. Many past stages reduced to passing, often trivial incidents.
  2. Not fundamental. *Fact* of development in certain order not sufficient; must know its principle.
  3. Inverts true state of case.

      (*a*) Psychologically—historical analysis is of interest simply as throwing light on child's present powers.

      (*b*) Socially—historical stages are of interest not *as historical*, but as *factors* in *present* civilization.

III. Results. German and American Educational Ideals and Methods. Forming *vs.* Freeing Powers.

*References:*

    De Garmo, *Herbart and the Herbartians*.

    Lange, *Apperception*.

    Herbart's *Psychology* (in International Educational Series).

    *First Yearbook of the Herbart Society*, articles by McMurry and Van Liew.

    Rein.

## *Exercises*

1. Is it true that Herbart's practical pedagogy is not affected in its value by his metaphysics?

2. Discuss his distinction between "government" and "training."

3. Discuss question of how far education of child's color sense should follow historical development.

4. Give criteria for determining amount of attention to be given to North American Indians in primary education.

5. Is there any intrinsic connection between the Herbartian principles and the "Robinson Crusoe"[1] kind of correlation?

6. Why does Herbartianism make history or literature rather than science basis of correlation?

## Lecture V.   Epochs of Child Development

I. Negative. No Successive Development of Mental Faculties or Powers.

II. Positive. Growth Is

    1. In complexity of activity, or range of content.

---

1    See *Report of Committee of Fifteen*.

    2. In interest, or point of view from which activity is carried on.

III. Stages.

    1. Period of mastery of body as organ—working out main co-ordinations.
    Educational bearings, (*a*) Social sympathies; (*b*) Imitation.

    2. Period of ideal co-ordinations. Free imaginative activities. Play period.
    Educational bearings, (*a*) Idealization of types of social activities; (*b*) Play as regulated—educational processes (writing, number, form, etc.) taught as ends in themselves, not as means.

    3. Period of interest in ordering of activity—rise of distinct intellectual interest. Mechanical period.
    Educational bearings, (*a*) Interest in tools, mechanism of activity; (*b*) Interest in symbols.

    4. Period of interest in oneself as related to others and to the world. Reflective period.
    Educational bearings, (*a*) Interest in reflective analysis and why; (*b*) Introspective interest; (*c*) Conscious æsthetic interest.

IV. Result. There Is, Normally, No *Succession* of Studies, But Only the Same Material Lived Through, with Different Types of Interest, and Deepened Consciousness of Meaning. Illustrations.

## *Exercises*

    1. Discuss doctrine: "First form faculty, then furnish it."

    2. Criticize doctrine: "First, plenty of observations, then reasoning about them."

    3. Observe workings of spontaneous recollection in child with reference to principle that it is not "faculty" which grows but interest.

    4. Observe growth of imagination in child from 2 to 4, noticing concomitant growth of sense of before and after, of purpose, etc.

    5. What is the psychological and the pedagogical meaning of the interest in personal adornment during period of adolescence?

# Lecture VI.    The School and Moral Progress

*THE PROBLEM OF SOCIAL PROGRESS.*

I. The Two Traditionally Opposed Principles.
   1. Reform the individual.
   2. Change the institution.
II. The School Is the Place Where These Two Principles Are One, *i.e.*, Where Reform Is Neither Purely Individual nor Purely Institutional.
   1. Society reflects itself in purified form in the school.
   2. Possibility of application of science and philosophy to social organization. Scientific interest of teacher.
   3. Social legislation. Social interest of teacher.
      (*a*) Formative *vs.* formal: self-executing legislation.
      (*b*) Regulative *vs.* corrective.

*RELATION OF SCHOOL TO OTHER INSTITUTIONS.*

I. To the Family.
   1. Home, when isolated, is a fetich. Family a social organ.
   2. In performing its function, it needs from the school
      (*a*) Supplementing.
      (*b*) Direction.
II. To Industrial Society.
   1. School must supply sufficient technical training, manual and otherwise to enable its members
      (*a*) To participate effectually in industrial callings.
      (*b*) To adjust themselves to great changes. Origin of social wreckage.
   2. It must afford a social consciousness which will enable individual to interpret industrial movements.
      (*a*) Otherwise, he becomes either a slave or a dupe.
      (*b*) Prevention of social collisions.
III. To Political Institutions.
   Their importance generally maximized in theory, and minimized in practice.
   1. School must afford habit of organization and co-operation for common ends. This implies

2. Faculty of both (*a*) subordination, and (*b*) leadership.

3. Must afford knowledge of conditions, (*a*) physical, (*b*) historical.

IV. To Church.

1. Both school and church suffering from lack of active co-operation.

2. Church's privilege to become more and more educative, continuing work of school.

3. The religious function of the school.

## Exercises

1. How does the school deal with the problem of freedom and authority?

2. The place of (*a*) industrial training, (*b*) of trade schools in public school system.

3. How do you account, upon the moral and social side, for the great exaggeration at present, among practical men, of the value of the *book* features of primary education?

4. Mention specific ways in which school and church are now supplementing each other. Give suggestions as to further ways.

The University of Chicago
THE UNIVERSITY EXTENSION
THE LECTURE-STUDY DEPARTMENT

# EDUCATIONAL PSYCHOLOGY

## SYLLABUS OF A
## COURSE OF TWELVE
## LECTURE-STUDIES

BY JOHN DEWEY
HEAD PROFESSOR OF PHILOSOPHY
AND PEDAGOGY

CHICAGO
The University of Chicago Press
1896

## Lecture I.    The Psycho-physic Organism, or the Body as Instrument of the Psychical Life

I.  The Organism in General.
1.  *Utilization* of environment; storing up and setting free its energies. Function as uniting environment and organs.
2.  Its primary quality; movement as self-sustaining through selection and assimilation of environment. Various forms assumed in movement.

II.  Place of Nervous System in Organism.
1.  The specialization of structure and division of labor in the organism. Its economy. Resulting interdependence.
2.  Consequent need of interrelating or co-ordinating structure: a clearing house and arbitrator. Specialization and co-ordination correlative. Differences in lower and higher organisms.
3.  The connecting structure not only is necessitated by specialization, but also favors further specialization. Examples.

III.  Specific Functions and Structures of the Nervous System.
1.  Necessity for valuing activities of special organs and activities.
    (1)  Sensory system (peripheral) performs this function.
    (2)  Differentiation of values. Assimilation through *contact* the primary immediate form; other sensory values as mediations of touch; special sense-organs.
    (3)  Sense functions are to be regarded primarily as differentiations of organic *activity*, not as *simply* receptive. Physical receptivity or passivity means liability to destruction; functional

[*First published by University of Chicago Press, 1896, for the Lecture-Study Department, University Extension, University of Chicago. Not previously reprinted.*]

receptivity means a highly specialized activity; that is, a high grade of receptivity means a high grade of sensitiveness. Biological evidence.

2. Necessity for balancing these special activities. That is, these specialized activities must report to a common centre.
   (1) The central (spino-cerebral) system.
   (2) Can strike a balance of values only as it has a *cumulative* power which enables it to *load*, or even up certain activities temporarily deficient, and to reduce those temporarily in excess. That is, adjusts present claims on basis of past registration. Evidence from normal and pathological physiology.

3. Necessity for connections between various central and peripheral structures, and between various central structures.
   (1) It is the latter which makes the centres into a centre. Commissural and associative fibres. Connections in the spinal cord.
   (2) The former have naturally two *directions*:
      *a.* From sense-organ to brain, sensory or afferent.
      *b.* From brain to that motor organ (muscular unit) relevant to the sense-organ, efferent.

4. The functional and structural unit of organization:
   (1) The primitive nervous structure unites reporting, discharging and connecting functions in itself.
   (2) The reflex arc unit: developed into the organic circuit through recognition of the reciprocal connection between muscular movement and sense-activity, whether (*a*) direct or (*b*) indirect.

*Literature:* (Covers Lecture II also.)

Donaldson, *Growth of Brain.*

James, *Psychology*, I, Chs. 2, 3.

Baldwin, *Feeling and Will*, pp. 1–83.

Wundt, *Human and Animal Psychology.*

Carus, *Soul of Man.*

Ladd, *Elements of Physiological Psychology.*

Hering, *Memory and Specific Energies of the Nervous System* (Open Court Co.).

Exner, *Physiologische Erklärung der psychischen Erscheinungen* (Leipzig, 1894).

Foster, *Physiology*, Sections on Nervous System.

# Lecture II.   The Psycho-physic Organism (continued)

### A. *THE PRINCIPLES OF DEVELOPMENT AND ORGANIZATION.*

1. The Principle of Specialization, or Continued Differentiation.
    1. Have already noted differentiation into reporting, centralizing and connecting structures.
    2. Differentiations within reporting structures.
        (1) Various sense-organs — skin organs, hearing, sight. Respective functions.
        (2) Within one and the same organ, as eye.
            a. Protecting mechanism.
            b. Adjusting.
            c. Refinement of qualities. All these subserve utmost possible differentiation of the sensory activity.
    3. Differentiation of central system.
        (1) Great main distinction into "higher" and "lower" centres; structure of cord and basal ganglia, on one side; of cortex and related structures on the other.
        (2) Two theories regarding this distinction.
            a. The "projection" and "representation" theory. According to this the automatic and mechanical functions evolve first, "higher" functions are simply adjustments of these.
            b. The "contemporaneous growth" theory. According to this, the "upward" and "downward" growths are correlative; that is, reflex action as well as the highest cortical

activity represents a complex, differentiated acquisition.

    *c.* Reasons for accepting the latter view, (*i*) biological (*ii*) anatomical.

  (3) Localization of function within the brain.

    *a.* Facts.

    *b.* These facts interpreted as particular instance of specialization: indifference and substitution.

    *c.* The physiological correlate of an *idea*; of attention.

4. Differentiation of connecting system. Disputed point: (*a*) indifference *vs.* (*b*) specific-nerve energy. That is, does specialization take the form of susceptibility to certain stimuli only, or of increased conductivity for any stimulus?

II. The Principle of Co-ordination.

1. Every specialization involves a corresponding *grouping* of central elements and related connecting fibres. The end is specialized, the means to end co-ordinated.

2. Co-ordination of movements with each other.

  (1) Massive or trunk.

  (2) Finer or towards extremities. Order of development from former to latter. (Educational applications.)

3. Co-ordination of movements with sensory activities.

  (1) Gradual ripening (see Lecture III).

  (2) Increase in range of co-ordination.

    (*a*) Reflex action, (*b*) instinct, (*c*) formed habit, (*d*) deliberative activity.

III. The General Principle of Habit.

Using habit, in its broadest sense, as a generic line of activity, it is equivalent to co-ordination of movements with one another and with sense-activities in reference to a specific end or movement. In other words, it is a specialized co-ordination. As uniting these two factors, a study of habit affords a basis for review. Habit involves

1. Integration, or modification of central structure,

through use; a *disposition* of stored energy corresponding to previous activities. Co-ordination as consecutive or involving continuity in time.

2. Selection of paths of discharge; increased facilitation in certain lines. Co-ordination as simultaneous, or definite adjustment.

3. The unit of co-ordination is functional rather than mechanical: evidence.

    (1) Anatomical—the relation of cells and fibres.

    (2) Biological—the assumption of new activities in the race and individual.

IV. Educational Application.

1. Success, *i.e.*, reaching an end (gaining a definite *unified* outlet) is the primary factor.

2. Repetition, the secondary factor. Consequences of reversing the order.

## B. THE FUNDAMENTAL FUNCTIONS OF NERVOUS SYSTEM.

Summarizing the preceding, we may say, the nervous system has one primary, inclusive function: co-ordination of specialized activities to a common end. This function of co-ordination has two phases.

I. Stimulation.

Because of the whole which functionally unites the various parts, each special activity tends to arouse another, and this not by mere general diffusion, but by specific stimulation.

1. Stimulation of movement by relevant activity.

2. Reinforced stimulation by indirectly related activity.

    (1) Experimental evidence—Knee-kick; dynamometer; one sense-activity affects others; extreme cases; colored hearing, etc.

    (2) Pathological evidence—Hypnotism, etc.; "compulsory ideas"; epilepsy, pathological anger and fright.

II. Inhibition or Control.

1. No evidence of special mechanism, save in exceptional cases.

2. Inhibition is *functional*, *i.e.*, through interaction of

related activities. By itself, each activity tends to exhaust itself—law of inertia. Held in check by demands made upon it. That is, inhibition is *not* of activity as such but only of *direction* of activity. Occurs by means of

(1) Loading of central organ, its acquired habit—
  (*a*) influence of fatigue, (*b*) of removing higher centres.
(2) Simultaneous stimuli acting as competitors.

3. Inhibition evidenced in
  (1) Delay of response.
  (2) Increased content (co-ordinated range) of response (increase of non-coördinated range is evidence of lack of inhibition).
  (3) Unusual channel as mode of response.

III. Phases of Co-ordination.

1. Neither stimulation nor inhibition represents a special power, but only one phase of the interaction of factors in a co-ordination.
2. Stimulation stands for intensity and thus for extent —for alertness. The new, or progressive factor.
3. Inhibition stands for economy in expenditure and thus for limitation—for control. The old, or conservative factor.
4. The interaction of stimulation and inhibition is seen in phenomena
  (1) Of *Summation*.
  (2) Of *Rhythm*. The fundamental rhythms and their economy. Evidences of rhythm in the central nervous system.

*Literature:*

In addition to references of Lecture I see
Butler, *Unconscious Memory.*
James, *Psychology*, I, Ch. 4.
Mercier, *Nervous System and Mind.*

# Lecture III.   Epochs of Psychical Development

I. General Principle.

Motion alone can be *observed*. Problem is that of interpreting movements. Idea of co-ordination gives clue. What are the typical co-ordinations of a period; what co-ordinations are in process of forming?

II. Early Infancy; Mastery of Main Physical Co-ordinations.

    1. Primary instincts, or inherited co-ordinations. Differences in animals and man.

    2. Gradual acquisitions on basis of inherited tendencies.

        (1) Order of evolution of sense-activities.

        (2) Co-ordination of sight, touch and muscular sensation. (*a*) Following with eye and head; (*b*) winking; (*c*) reaching or following with body and hand; (*d*) grasping and throwing; (*e*) maintenance of equilibrium, at rest; (*f*) maintenance of equilibrium in motion.

        (3) Co-ordination of these co-ordinations with auditory sensations; (*a*) responding to language; (*b*) acquisition of articulate language; (*c*) relation of speech to action; (*d*) to thought.

        (4) Part played by imitation:

            *a*. Imitation as immediate, mechanical.

            *b*. Mediate, plastic, beginning of play.

        (5) Social nature of child.

III. Later Infancy; Period of Free Use of Formed Co-ordinations.

    1. Dawn of imagination. Ability to see a whole of an activity in a part. Stimulus to action less immediate.

    2. Play—the spontaneous exhibition of imagery in action is play. Co-ordinations run off for mere sake of utilizing them. Inventiveness, play and art. The social aspects of play.

IV. Symbolic Period.

The use of a formed co-ordination as means to a co-ordination involving a serial adjustment in time. Difference from play. Mechanical. True and false mechanical.

    1. The interest in symbols. Distinction between existence of image and what it stands for or suggests.

    2. Interest in tools. Activity of self realized in power to

make adjustments. Significance of love of a tool.

v. Reflective Interest. The Co-ordination of One's Activity as a Whole with That of Others in Society. The Period of Adolescence.

1. The race in the individual, self-consciousness, true and false. Healthy is accompaniment of conscious readjustment to others; morbid comes from isolation.

2. Various manifestations of this reflective interest. Changed attitude regarding one's manners, chance for new moral motive; changed attitude towards history and literature.

vi. Conclusion.

No serial growth of faculties, but development of types of interest and complexity of activity. The corresponding pedagogical conclusion is no serial order of subjects, but one world lived through with increase of comprehension and change of interest.

*Literature:*

Tracy, *Psychology of Childhood.*

Baldwin, *Mental Development.*

Illinois Society for Child-Study; *Pedagogical Seminary*, especially on adolescence and detailed studies of many special points.

On Imitation, see also Royce, *Psychological Review*, and *Century*, May 1894.

See also Baldwin, *Century*, Dec. 1894, for impulses and instincts, prayer, mind of child, etc.

Warner, *Mental Faculty*, Chs. 3, 4.

*Exercises*

1. Do you find differences in the kinds of games played by boys and girls? Give as many games as possible, classed distinctively as boys' or girls', describing the less familiar, and bringing out salient points of difference—if you find decided differences of type, give any reasons that suggest themselves to you.

2. Report cases of spontaneous imitation noted in one or more children during a week. Give sex and age of child. N.B. Is the imitation a direct copy, or freely manipulated? Length of time intervening between model or imitation. Discriminate cases of physical

and normal imitation, *e.g.*, gait, posture, manner of speech, or general spirit. Notice children playing school; what school happenings and expressions do they imitate, etc.

3. One of the present greatest needs is systematic observation of one and the same child from the age of six to that of nine inclusive. Will you undertake such an observation of one child as continuously as possible for one month? Give, if possible:

    (1) Predominant type of imagery; see Lecture IV.

    (2) Emotional type—how does child manifest his satisfactions and dissatisfactions, *e.g.*, buoyant, noisy, calm, emotional signs, prominent or repressed; sudden anger, pouts, sulks; how does he manifest his desire for reconciliation after a breach?

    (3) Interests. What plays does he prefer, what part does he take, leader or follower, does he like to "boss," what occupations does he take up spontaneously when left to himself? What kind of incidents in literature or history awaken response, what subjects does he do best in, what worst in? What do you consider his strongest point, his weakest point, both intellectually and morally? (It will be understood these questions are meant to be suggestive only; the more points covered, the better.)

## Lecture IV.  The Psychical Unity and Its Main Distinctions

I. Importance of General Map.

  1. Importance of seeing unity below all differences— avoiding fixed separations.

  2. Of getting bearings in discussing details. Why educational psychology is often no more helpful.

II. The Unity Found in the Organic Circuit Involved in Co-ordination. The Distinctions Are Divisions of Labor within the Co-ordination.

  1. Every co-ordination brought to consciousness in-

volves expression, impression and the adjustment of one of these to the others, outgo, income and the balance.

2. In most general terms, the outgo (when conscious) is will; the income is feeling, which when differentiated constitutes sensations; while striking the balance is thought, or intellection.

III.

1. The beginning and the end is volitional; volitional being used in its broad sense as spontaneous activity; in its narrow sense as activity so mediated by feeling and thought as to realize ends felt as valuable.

2. The outgo is apperception; the income, organized as capital for further use is retention.[1]

IV. The Divisions of Labor.

1. Feeling is the sense of value, the realization of spontaneous activity in general. The indefinite sense of value, when defined and made objective, constitutes sensations. Sensations

   (1) Are to be distinguished from the mere sensory stimuli or nervous shocks.

   (2) Are the specific *qualities* reported in experience, or definite values of conscious activity. As definite, they mark selection, or preference, with regard to further activity,[2] and hence

   (3) *Arise* through specialized activities, and *serve* as warnings from continuing activity or as signals to direct, or to reinforce (impulsive and emotional quality).

2. Thought is correlative to sensation (as sensation is to thought); that is, the *meaning* of a sensation is always in strict ratio to its conscious *relations*, and these relations constitute *thought* values. *Ideas* measure the value of sensations, and *sensations* are the material valued. A judgment is the organic unity of sensation (as subject) and idea (as predicate).

   (1) Meaning or significance in thought is the ac-

---

[1]   Dewey, *Psychology* [*The Early Works of John Dewey*, II], pp. 77–81; 130–32.

[2]   See Lecture IX for further account of discrimination.

tivity pointed to or indicated by a sensation.

(2) Thought arises in conflict of activities, through the need of striking a balance, that is, of discovering the course of action which will reconcile a number of conflicting minor activities. Hence, thought means delay (inhibitory function).

(3) The logical processes accordingly always relate to the management of a certain material as means to an end, and consist in harmonizing this material, *i.e.*, giving it a single line of discharge in which the various factors reinforce one another. Conscious and unconscious logic.

3. Volition.

(1) Sensation, as stated, never loses its primary impulsive quality; it is impulse objectified, defined. Hence it tends to action—Sensori-motor functions.

(2) Ideas, as adjusting various values, or thought as co-ordinate sensory qualities, simply brings the meaning of impulse to consciousness and thus frees it. It inhibits only the *immediate* tendency of impulse, not impulse itself.

(3) Hence, will is no new or separate faculty. It is the whole self realized in action; that is, it is impulsive, or spontaneous, activity translated into specific values, or sensations, which serve as means to execute some *idea*, or proposed co-ordination. Volition is the defined and idealized impulses: in other words

a. It marks the translation of feeling into interest.

b. The judgment into an intuition.

c. Into conscious deed.

It is the conscious organic circuit.

v. Educational Applications.

1. Breaks in the circuit.

(1) Presenting a sensory quality when there is no felt demand for it in activity.

(2) Forming ideas which do not find expression, or motor discharge.

(3) Motor activities having no idea back of them.

2. Positive—all true education maintains the circuit and thus forms character, which involves

(1) On the side of feeling (and sensation) responsiveness, susceptibility;

(2) On the side of intellect, a sense of relative values, *i.e.*, good judgment;

(3) On the side of impulse, force.

## Literature:

Dewey, *Psychology*, and *Study of Ethics*; the former for the general relations between feeling, knowledge and will, the latter for relations of emotion and thought to concrete volition.

Stanley, *Evolutionary Psychology of Feeling*, gives an exhaustive study of that subject.

Carpenter, *Mental Physiology*, is most excellent for motor power of ideas.

## Exercises

1. Give some illustrations of the organic circuit, taken from your own everyday experience.

2. Give instances of intuition (in the practical sense of that term) and show how it is correlative to interest and skill.

3. Give instances, from your own experience, of the motor power of sensations, on both the negative and stimulating sides.

4. Give instances, from your own daily experience, of the motor power of ideas.

## Lecture V.   Imagination: Descriptive

1. Imagination.

Specific imagery, not faculty in general. A power of realization, not of making real artificial. Hence its importance: Mean term between ignorance and realization, between alien material and comprehension in self. It is the mental machinery.

II. Galton's Investigations.

Questions upon visualization, its frequency, mode of occurrence, etc. Completeness of object, definiteness of form and detail; vividness of coloring; degree of illumination. Results; "freaks" in imagery.

III. Brief Study of Forms of Imagery.

1. Visual.
2. Auditory.
3. Tactile.
4. Gustatory and olfactory.
5. Motor. Problem: Is this a distinct type, co-ordinate with others, or is there motor imagery connected with each of the previous forms? Educational bearings of this question.

IV. Economy of Mental Imagery.

1. Why adults have less varied forms of imagery than children, scientific thinkers than laymen.
2. Practical problem: How to secure economy of select type, representing line of least resistance, without sacrificing richness of mental life.

V. Function of Various Types of Imagery.

1. Touch: Close connection with feeling; primitive form, great emotional and moral significance; sensitiveness in criminals. Intellectually, or as quality gives depth, solidity; is a continual check to others; tends to become common denominator.
2. Visual: On the emotional side, gives vividness. On side of presentation, fullness, multiplicity, co-existence.
3. Auditory: On emotional side, gives emphasis, intensity, stress. On intellectual side, rhythm, sequence, concentration.
4. Motor: Slight immediate emotional quality, smoothness and jar its main features; serves, therefore, all the better for abstract intellectual purposes, schemes, relationships, the "fringe."[3] It also gives limitation, definiteness of form.

---

[3]    James, *Psychology*, I.

*Literature:*

> Galton, *Human Faculty*, synopsized in James, *Psychology*, II.
> Queyrat, *L'Imagination*.
> Dewey, *Psychology*.

## Exercises

Take familiar objects like your breakfast table, and the face of your watch and note carefully how well you can visualize it; noting

1. *Completeness*: How much can you see at once? Does it come as a whole, or by parts? Can you hold the parts together if you try, or does one go as another comes, etc.?
2. *Definiteness* of outlines, and details of patterns, etc. *Vividness* of colors and degree of illumination.
3. Do you image involuntarily, or does it take effort? Where do you place yourself? Does the image change unless you try to hold it? Do you keep your attention fixed upon one part of it, or do you go from one part to another of it?

## Lecture VI.   Imagination: Its Position in Psychical Life

I. Realization and Imagination.
  1. Imagination the medium of realization.
  2. A personal, organic activity.
  3. Differs in degree of completeness only.
  4. Tends towards realization.
II. Organic Circuit.
  Hence is sole internal instrument of instruction. Learning as medium between knowledge and ignorance corresponds to imagination. Involved, therefore, in all mental operation where any new, or hitherto foreign, element is assimilated.
III. Imagination in Sense-Perception.
  1. Mere presence of object not enough. Fallacy in instruction.

2. Mere presence of sensation not enough. Fallacy in instruction.

3. *Meaning* of a sensation: What is not sensuously present. Supplied as imagery. Hallucination and real perception. Meaning of apperception. Building up of objects and world of objects.

IV. Imagination in Memory.

    1. Memorizing is image of certain definite sensory qualities, isolated from others which interpret them. The danger in appealing much to this kind of imagery.

    2. Good memory depends on vividness and content of original imagery. Relevancy more important than mere sensuous vividness, more important than number or repetition. Repetition is of value when introducing greater scope of relationship, or when selective in character. Fertility of imagery induced, its expansive, assimilative power, the educational test. Bearing upon question of examinations.

V. Imagination in Thinking.

    1. Image and thought not exclusive. Error of substituting an abstract logical analysis for a concrete psychological one.

    2. Thought the related *movement* of image; differs from "association of images" in being movement towards a conceived end.

        (1) A concept is the *way* of movement.

        (2) Inference the movement of diverse images or trains of images to a common, harmonizing or comprehensive focus.

        (3) Judgment the placing of an image in a movement.

VI. Conclusion.

Imagery is the mechanism through which growth in knowledge is maintained. It is the medium of learning and hence of teaching.

*Exercises*

1. Give analysis of perception of Sistine Madonna, showing the imagery involved.

    2. Same for perception of object through telescope or microscope.

    3. Give illustrations of use of imagination in scientific hypotheses.


# Lecture VII. Imagination: Its Movement

I. Imagery, as Expanding, Moving.
    1. Its physiological aspect.
    2. Its basis and aim.

II. Movement in Relation to End—Realization.
    1. Spontaneous movement—poetry, art.
        (1) Largest possible coherent whole. Principle of integration. Means by which whole is maintained. Emotional phase.
        (2) Richness of detail. Principle of suggestion, or redintegration. Means of reinforcing.
        (3) Application to some forms of artistic construction.
    2. Reflective movement.[4] Prose. Science.
        (1) Reduction of image—symbol.
        (2) Manipulation of image.

III. Failures of Movement of Imagery.
    1. Natural: idiocy, etc.
    2. Induced.
        (1) Arrested imagery.
            *a.* Minute and cramped co-ordinations. Mechanical products. Kindergarten plays; reading, writing, etc.
            *b.* Over-analysis and excessive formulation. The process *vs.* the product; unconscious and conscious.
        (2) Disintegrated imagery.
            (N.B.—All arrest leads to disintegration, because it isolates.)
            *a.* Overstimulation. Lack of continuity, of growth. Meaning of thoroughness.

---

[4] This process is discussed in more detail in connection with attention and reasoning.

   *b.* Failure to supply outlet. Lack of material, of opportunity. Lack of aim, of object.

IV. Moral Aspects of Movement.

  1. Imagery and interest. Why and when image is interesting. Focusing *vs.* dissipation. Two types of pleasure; energy, distraction. The normal tension of the spontaneous and the reflective.

  2. Imagery and desire. Apperceptive organs, *i.e.*, dominant types of imagery. Urgency of mental demand corresponds to force of image.

  3. Responsibility for furnishing conditions for healthy, moving imagery. Morbidness, impurity, etc.

## Lecture VIII.   Attention and Interest

I. Recapitulation.
Image as moving and redintegrating allied imagery. When in some special direction, to a point, this movement constitutes attention.

II. Movement of Imagery Not Impartial, or at Large, or Vague, but Specialized, Preferential in Character. Why —Necessity to Life. "Pay Attention."

  1. Adjustment of habit (representing the past) to demand (representing the future). At-tention. Nature of tension.

  2. Absence of mind. Loss of presence of mind.

  3. Emotional agitation accompanying this adjustment. Types of interest.

III. Phases of This Movement or Adjustment.

  1. End corresponds to demand.

   (1) This unifies process by imposing limit. The organic circuit. Reverie. Dreams.

   (2) Is the phase of *concentration* in attention.

   (3) Fixity of attention; limit of movement *vs.* rigidity.

   (4) Requires selection.

  2. Means correspond to habits.

   (1) Define process by supplying reinforcement.

   (2) Are adaptation of selected material—relevancy and irrelevancy. Testing.

(3) Preparatory activity.

3. Whole process one of relation; analysis and synthesis.[5]

IV. Stages in Development of Movement. Value of Adjustment of Habit to Demand Depends upon Possibility of Anticipation. Hence Two Stages.

1. Non-voluntary.
   (1) Exists where there is little anticipation—little tension.
   (2) Found with *immediate* interest.

2. Voluntary.
   (1) Exists when there is consciousness of end to be reached; considerable tension, effort.
   (2) Found with mediate interest.
   (3) The practical problem. Spontaneity and effort in character.

*Literature:*

Dewey, *Psychology*, Ch. 7.
James, *Psychology*, I, Ch. 17.
Baldwin, *Handbook of Psychology*, I, Ch. 5.
Carpenter, *Mental Physiology*, Ch. 3.

## Lecture IX. Judgment with Special Reference to Observation

I. Recapitulation.

1. Adjustment of habit to demand constitutes act of relating.

2. Has two sides.
   (1) Analysis, de-fining, marking off the limits.
   (2) Synthesis, taking together, adaptation.

3. Hence the standard of knowledge or truth.
   (1) Unity of form, generality of comprehension, and
   (2) Definiteness of detail, range of extension.

II. Judgment: Adjustment of Perception and Conception.

1. These distinctions *functional* only. Same *existence*, an image at basis of each. Galton's illustration.

2. Nature of good judgment.

[5] This point is discussed in connection with the judgment. Lecture IX.

III. Judgment as Observation.
  1. Discrimination.
    (1) Relation to movement. Illustrated in origin and development of spatial distinctions.
    (2) Function is preference or selection of necessary means. Pedagogy of analysis, its right and wrong use.
      *a.* Information *vs.* wisdom. Scholasticism.
      *b.* Illustrated in "object-lessons," in Kindergarten work. "Sensationalism."
      *c.* Illustrated in reading, writing, drawing. Isolation from function.
      *d.* Effect upon memory.
  2. Observation as a logical process.
    (1) A general principle or standard implied. Involved rationale. Observation is comprehension.
      *a.* Illustrated in practical life.
      *b.* In scientific discovery.
    (2) Accuracy of observation; measurement, *i.e.,* specific reference to standard. Number as the formal manifestation of all logical operations.
    (3) Observation and comparison. Comparison involved in observation. Illustrated in grammar and biology.
  3. Observation as a mental habit.
    (1) Requires keenness, alertness. This means responsiveness, sympathy.
    (2) Results in intuitive power. Ability to seize situation as whole.

*Literature:*
  Dewey, *Psychology*, Ch. 8.
  James, *Psychology*, I, Ch. 13.


## Lecture X.  Judgment as Thought

  I. General Nature of Inference; Not Opposed to Observation. "Unconscious Inference." Conscious Use of Symbols.
  II. Formation of Concept.

1. Abstraction. Taking a point of view. Specialization of aim.
2. Reduction of imagery. Loss of concrete detail and affective quality. Process of exclusion. Process of forming symbols illustrated in written language. Symbol as economical device.

III. Function of Concept: to Afford Method or Plan of Action. Leads to Organization of Experience.
  1. Empirical and rationalistic fallacies arise from neglect of function.
  2. Illustrations in numerical concepts.
  3. Illustrations in geometrical concepts.

IV. Induction and Deduction.
  1. Correlative growth of the specific and the generic. Not *from* the particular to the general.
  2. Use of induction in scientific work; in laboratory work: definiteness of realization. Opposite not deduction, but conventional, or second-handed knowledge. Misinterpretation of the inductive principle.
  3. Use of deduction. Principle of control through limitation; principle of organization. Opposite is aimless, random work. Working hypothesis.

V. Reasoning and Intuition.
  1. Inference as a coherent movement of diverse images to a common focus, to a comprehensive result.
  2. An intermediate stage between one intuition, or concrete realization, and another. The individual is the goal as well as the beginning of knowledge.
  3. Knowledge and moral action. The Socratic principle.

## Lecture XI. The Emotions in Their Moral Significance

I. Emotion and Attention.
  The tension between habit and aim (or object), appears as an excitation, disturbance of self. This tension, as felt, is emotion. Hence, three phases of emotion.
  1. Volitional.—Emotion as disposition, as tendency to action. Marks an active attitude, a readiness in a

certain direction. Race habits in the individual. Darwin's theory.

2. Intellectual.—Object or end to which action refers itself. Corresponds to purpose.

3. Affective, or feeling.—James's theory. Follows upon, does not precede, active side. Suggested modification of James's theory; the idea, or object equally follows active side, so that feeling and idea are correlative.

II. The Emotion and Action.

The emotion marks check in activity, temporary inability to adjust habit to object, and consequently the stirring up of larger areas, hence:

1. The normal function of emotion is to call in reinforcements which will brace the activity.

2. The abnormal emotion arises from isolation and arrest; that is, the feeling is not attached to activity, does not *function*. Thus the feeling comes to be an end in itself; assumes either of two forms:

   (1) Sensuality.

   (2) Sentimentality. This distinction is in the kind of feeling, and not in the psychological or moral principle concerned.

III. The Interpretation of Emotions.

Emotions, before they can be dealt with on *moral* grounds, need to be observed and interpreted on *psychological* grounds.

1. All emotion expressed in movements: gesture, posture, etc.

2. How to interpret these movements, the problem of child-study; the image seeking to complete itself in action.

3. Illustrations in anger, fear, vanity, disposition to bully or meddle.

IV. The Treatment of Emotion.

1. No emotion can be dealt with in itself; only indirectly or through action. Failures to observe this principle lead to sentimentality through isolating the feeling side.

2. Emotion and imagination.

   (1) Imagery as the partial or incomplete activity involves emotion. To cultivate certain imagery

is to cultivate a certain emotion and thus disposition.

(2) Place of indirect imitation or examples. Danger of too many examples which cannot be exemplified by pupil. Dangers of symbolism.

3. The development of emotion into interest.

(1) When the tension between habit and end is overcome so that habit is attached to end (when adjustment is made so that we have *co-ordination*), emotion becomes interest.

(2) Interest less exciting, but steadier and more permanent than emotion.

(3) Kind of interest displayed marks character; exhibits an habitual direction of activity. Development of right interest thus equivalent to development of right character. Interest equals moral motive.

4. Two types of interest. Interest may be either

(1) Intrinsic, or

(2) Extrinsic. The former belongs to activity, because of its own quality; latter belongs to it because of some more or less artificial attachments or associations. Bribery; "making" a thing interesting. Amusing a child *vs.* child's play. Extrinsic interest means distraction, irrelevant stimulation, and hence mental and moral disintegration. Test of whether an appeal to interest is genuine or artificial.

a. Does it serve to reveal some interest, hitherto latent, in the subject-matter itself? or

b. Does it contract that interest by substituting another for it? The test illustrated in cases of punishment and of appeal to affection for parent or teacher.

*Literature:*

Darwin, *Expression of Emotions.*

James, *Psychology,* II, Ch. on Emotion.

Dewey, "Theory of Emotion" [*The Early Works of John Dewey,* IV, 155–88]; M'Lennan, *Psychological Review,* Sept. 1895.

*Exercises*

1. Give as many facts as you can gather in your experience, bearing (in either direction), upon James's theory of the priority of action to emotion, *e.g.*, fright, timidity, bashfulness (do you first feel abashed and then blush, or do you first blush?).
2. Describe as fully as you can your complete bodily condition in any one strong emotion, including state of muscular system, breathing, circulation, disturbances in digestive tracts, etc.
3. Give instances of different types of expression of anger in different children, showing connection, if possible, with temperament of child.
4. Give half a dozen instances of concrete difficulties in dealing with emotions of children, methods employed and results.

## Lecture XII.   The Nature of Character

I. Description of Good Character. A Good Character, as the Term Is Practically Used, and as an Object to Be Reached in Education, Involves
   1. Efficiency, force. To be good is to be good for something, not simply to mean well.
   2. Responsiveness. Susceptibility to demands, unexpressed as well as formulated. Responsiveness insures reponsibility.
   3. Good judgment. Sense. This means a definite comprehension of relative values.
      Anyone who has force, openness and sense is educated.
II. Psychology of Character. These Factors Are All Found in the Normal Psychological Processes as a Unity, in the Organic Circuit.
   1. The impulse, primary and spontaneous.
   2. The experiences (feelings and sensations) which come about in the expression of the impulse.
   3. The organic reaction of these experiences into the original impulse.

(1) *Differentiating* it.

(2) *Enlightening* or informing it.

III. Normal Training of Character Recognizes and Builds upon This Natural Psychological Process.

    1. Must allow impulse to reveal itself, to express itself in action. Failure to provide this condition weakens and exhausts force. Impulse is suppressed and thus destroyed or distorted, or it is factitiously stimulated, and thus thoroughness (continuity) and genuineness are lost.

    2. Must provide conditions so that child can realize end or aim which corresponds to (functions) his powers; sense of vocation, or power; self-consciousness. Failure found when

        (1) Ends are set up externally, authoritatively.

        (2) When very remote ends are set up. Learning to read, write and accumulating information.

        (3) When isolated or partial ends only are recognized. Excessive analysis. Failure to recognize social quality of action.

    3. Must provide conditions so that child shall have practice.

        (1) In selecting means corresponding to ends.

        (2) In arranging means for these ends. Moral value of so-called "manual training." Of observation and interpretation of nature. Moral defects of book education.

IV. The Experimental Method as to Truth and as to Goodness.

    1. Method, spirit, more important than any particular result.

    2. It alone will insure the desiderata of force, openness, and sense, in character.

*Literature:*

Dewey, *Study of Ethics*, pp. 13–34; 50–56; 81–88 [*The Early Works of John Dewey*, IV, 228–56, 271–76, 299–305].

# Pedagogy I B 19.
# Philosophy of Education
## 1898–1899 — Winter Quarter

### A. THE NATURE AND PROCESS OF EDUCATION.

I. Its Conditions.
1. An educable being. See Fiske, "The Meaning of Infancy," in *Excursions of an Evolutionist*, also *Destiny of Man*, pp. 35–76; N. Butler, *The Meaning of Education*, pp. 3–34.
2. A social standard, or determining habits.

II. Informal Education.
1. A process: (1) of growth; (2) of adjustment. Possible conflicts.
2. Modes of informal education: (1) stimulation; (2) imitation, James Mark Baldwin, *Mental Development*, pp. 81–91, 263–366; Harris, *Psychologic Foundations of Education*, pp. 295–305, and N.E.A. *Proceedings*, 1894, p. 637; Royce, "The Imitative Functions, and Their Place in Human Nature," *Century*, Vol. XLVIII; (3) suggestion, James Mark Baldwin, *Mental Development*, Ch. 6; M. Small, "The Suggestibility of Children," *Pedagogical Seminary*, Vol. IV; Thomas, *La Suggestion*; (4) influence of environment; (5) conscious communication.
3. Types in stationary and progressive communities.

III. Formal Education.
1. Relation to informal.
2. Education and instruction—place and function of knowledge, Brunetière, *Éducation et Instruction*;

[First published by the University of Chicago, 1898. Not reprinted during the author's lifetime.]

Herbart, *Science of Education*, Chs. 1 and 2, and Bk. II, Ch. 4; Seth, "The Relation of Knowledge to Will and Conduct," in *Fourth Yearbook of the National Herbart Society.*

IV. Resulting Conceptions.

1. Definition: (1) two aspects: individual and social; (2) one-sided definitions from this standpoint; (3) break-down of individualistic definitions; (4) of sociological; (5) current practice a compromise.

2. Elements in definition: (1) discipline or training; (2) information; (3) culture, one-sided definitions again. Elements united in idea of socialized growth. Ideals of humanism and realism, etc.

3. Education as growth involving reconstruction: (1) beginning; (2) process; (3) result; (4) significance from this standpoint of (a) school, (b) subject-matter, (c) method; (5) ideal of reconstruction *vs.* (a) development of faculty, interpretation of faculties; and *vs.* (b) preparation.

V. The School as a Social Institution.

1. Its organization and administration: (1) relation to community life at large; (2) relations to special institutions as (a) family, (b) church, (c) state and city. Harris, "The Church, the State, and the School," *North American Review*, Vol. CXXXIII, and *Psychologic Foundations of Education*, Chs. 31 and 32; Vincent, *Social Mind and Education*, esp. Ch. 4; Rosenkranz, *Philosophy of Education*, pp. 143–49; E. Barnes, "Child as Social Factor," in *Studies in Education*; Plato, *Republic*; Aristotle, *Politics*, Bk. I; Ward, *Dynamic Sociology*; Fouillée, *Education from National Standpoint*; Hinsdale, "Social Factors in Popular Education in the United States," in *Studies in Education*, p. 313; Meyer, *Die soziale Frage und die Schule*; Dewey, "My Pedagogic Creed" [*The Early Works of John Dewey*, V, pp. 84–95]; A. Small, *The Demands of Pedagogy upon Sociology*; Monroe's *Bibliography*, p. 162; Rosenkranz, *Philosophy of Education*, Part Three (historical); E. Barnes and M. Barnes, "Education among

the Aztecs" and "Historical Ideals and Methods of Chinese Education," in *Studies in Education*, pp. 13 and 112 (historical).

2. Internal administration: (1) significance of order and government, authority, self-government, punishment; (2) the positive and negative in the ethical resources of the school; general social ideals, motives and habits *vs.* specialized school virtues; school an organized community life.

On *Moral Education*: Hall's *Bibliography*, pp. 178–83; Harris, St. Louis Superintendent's Annual Report for 1871; Malleson, *Early Training of Children*; Adler, *Moral Instruction of Children*; H. Spencer, *Education*, Ch. 3; Bain, *Education as a Science*, pp. 99–119, and Ch. 12; Dewey, "Ethical Principles Underlying Education" [*The Early Works of John Dewey*, v, pp. 54–83]; Laurie, *Institutes of Education*, pp. 219–38; Hall, "Moral Education and Will Training," *Pedagogical Seminary*, Vol. II, pp. 72–89; Herbart, *Science of Education*, pp. 200–252.

On *School Discipline*: White, *School Management*, pp. 114 and 190; Wickersham, *School Economy*, Ch. 4; Joseph Baldwin, *School Management*; Laurie, *The Training of Teachers*, p. 309; Rosenkranz, *Philosophy of Education*, Ch. 2; for Inductive Studies, see E. Barnes, "Discipline at Home and in the School," in *Studies in Education*, pp. 26, 71, 110, 149, 190, 228, 270, and "Punishment as Seen by Children," *Pedagogical Seminary*, Vol. III, p. 235; Darrah, "Children's Attitude Toward Law," in *Studies in Education*, pp. 213, 254; Frear, "Class Punishment," in *Studies in Education*, p. 332; Snedden, "Children's Attitude Toward Punishment for Weak Time Sense," in *Studies in Education*, p. 344.

## B. INTRINSIC ORGANIZATION OF SCHOOL LIFE.

1. Content and Form of School Life. Content Is Curriculum or Course of Study; Form Is Method.

   1. Organic relation to school life.

2. Organic relations to each other.
3. Organic relations of psychical and social. On psychology in reference to education: see Harris, *Report of Committee of Fifteen*; Dewey, "The Psychological Aspect of the School Curriculum" [*The Early Works of John Dewey*, v, 164]; Bain, *Education as a Science*, pp. 1–10; Findlay, "The Scope of Science of Education," *Educational Review*, Vol. XIV, p. 236; Royce, "Is There a Science of Education?" *Educational Review*, Vol. I, pp. 15 and 121; Sully, "The Service of Psychology to Education," *Educational Review*, Vol. IV, p. 313; Münsterberg, "Psychology and Education," *Educational Review*, Vol. XVI, p. 105; see also McLellan and Dewey, *Psychology of Number*, Ch. 1.
4. Relation of pupil and teacher; of interest and aims; significance of information, discipline and culture from this point of view; utility and self-development.

II. Factors in Problem.
1. Organization involves: (1) differentiation, or division of labor; (2) interaction or mutual responsibility.
2. It is organization for life-process or growth; a problem involving order in continuity as well as at any given time; starting point and aims.

III. Characteristic Epochs in Growth.
1. Direct experience—outgoing, spontaneous, *i.e.*, unreflective.
2. Consciousness of means and ends as distinct—of skill and rules as necessary.
3. Consciousness of organization itself: (1) generalization conscious; (2) specification conscious.
4. Consciousness of calling or function in life.

IV. Educational Equivalents.
1. Home and beginning elementary.
2. Later elementary, so-called grammar or intermediate.
3. Secondary.
4. Higher training for vocation and profession; characteristic subject-matter.

v. Practical Problems Involved.

  1. Significance of grades and grading; promotions, etc.; examinations, etc.

  2. Adjustment of established subdivisions to one another: (1) kindergarten; (2) intermediate; (3) high school and college; (4) college to university and professional school; practices in various countries; line of movement and solution.

  3. Class organization and individual growth: (1) the tutor *vs.* class, see Newman, on *Idea of a University*; (2) uniform *vs.* elective curriculum; (3) specialized *vs.* general instructing force.

  Upon *Examinations*: Seth, "The Educational Value of Examinations," *Educational Review*, Vol. XII, p. 133; Paulsen, "Examinations," *Educational Review*, Vol. XVI, p. 166; Fitch, *Lectures on Teaching*, Ch. 6; Latham, *Action of Examinations*.

  Upon *Gradation*: Harris, *Psychologic Foundations of Education*, Ch. 36; Jackman, "The School Grade a Fiction," *Educational Review*, Vol. XV, p. 456; Prince, "Grading and Promoting of Pupils," *Educational Review*, Vol. XV, p. 231; Laurie, *Occasional Addresses*, p. 1; Pickard, *School Supervision*, Ch. 10.

  Upon "*Electives*": Palmer, *The New Education* (college); see also Ladd, "Education, New and Old," *Andover Review*, Vol. V; Garnett, "The Elective System of the University of Virginia," *Andover Review*, Vol. V; Gilman, "The Group System of College Studies in The Johns Hopkins University," *Andover Review*, Vol. V; Denison, "Individualism in Education," *Andover Review*, Vol. V; Howison, "The Harvard 'New Education'," *Andover Review*, Vol. V; Eliot, *Educational Reform*, pp. 125, 273, 303, 375; Hinsdale, *Studies in Education*, p. 6; Thurber, "Election of Studies in Secondary Schools," *Educational Review*, Vol. XV, p. 418; E. Goodwin, "Electives in Elementary Schools," *Educational Review*, Vol. X, p. 12; Hall's *Bibliography*, p. 204.

  On *Promotions*: Shearer, "The Lock-Step of the Public Schools," *Atlantic Monthly*, Vol. LXXIX; N.E.A. *Proceedings*, *1898*, pp. 442–48, *Proceedings*, *1893*,

p. 83, and *Proceedings*, *1895*, p. 459; Harris, St. Louis Superintendent's Annual Report for 1873; Pickard, *School Supervision*, Ch. 11; N. Butler, Editorial, *Educational Review*, Vol. VII, p. 515.

On *Class and Individual Instruction*: Parker, "Departmental Instruction," *Educational Review*, Vol. VI, p. 342; also N. Butler, Editorial, *Educational Review*, Vol. VI, p. 410; Fitzpatrick, "Departmental Teaching," *Educational Review*, Vol. VII, p. 439; Search, "Individual Teaching," *Educational Review*, Vol. VII, p. 154; see also N. Butler, Editorials, *Educational Review*, Vol. VII, pp. 305 and 515; Harper, *N.E.A. Proceedings*, *1895*, pp. 990–93.

## C. ORGANIZATION OF SUBJECT-MATTER.

I. Theories of Selection.

 1. Application of previous principles: (1) differentiation of experience leading to efficiency and content in function; (2) the working out of this principle (a) standard of value, (b) significance of types of study; science and humanities.

 2. Theory of isolated values and their co-ordination; curriculum a composite; Dr. Harris's view.

 3. Culture-epoch theory: (1) stated; (2) criticized; true significance of history and literature.

II. Theories of Interaction—"Correlation."

 1. Application of previous principles: (1) direct experience: communication, construction, expression and inquiry; (2) evolution into indirect. Consequent interrelation (a) mastery and relationships of technique of communication—so-called form studies, (b) of construction and expression—manual training and art, (c) of inquiry—method in science and history; (3) motive and application the basis of "correlation" at this stage; (4) specialized values in final stage; (5) confirmation from history of science; (6) genetic and static classifications.

 2. Logical co-ordination; theory stated and criticized; value in recognition of objective relationships.

 3. Herbartian correlation; theory stated and criticized.

*Values in Education* (general): H. Spencer, *Education*, Chs. 1, 2; N. Butler's *Meaning of Education*, and "What Knowledge Is of Most Worth?" *Educational Review*, Vol. x; W. H. Payne, *Contributions to Science of Education*, Ch. 3; Bain, *Education as a Science*, Ch. 5; Holman, *Education*, Ch. 3; Laurie, *Institutes of Education*, esp. pp. 211–26; Patten, "The Educational Value of College Studies," *Educational Review*, Vol. I, p. 105 (college); Jenks, "A Critique of Educational Values," *Educational Review*, Vol. III, p. 1; Hanus, "Educational Aims and Educational Values," *Educational Review*, Vol. IX, p. 323; W. Goodwin, "The Educational Value of the Ancient Classics," *Educational Review*, Vol. IX, p. 335; Norton, "The Educational Value of the History of the Fine Arts," *Educational Review*, Vol. IX, p. 343; Hill, "The Educational Value of Mathematics," *Educational Review*, Vol. IX, p. 349; Thompson, "The Educational Value of History," *Educational Review*, Vol. IX, p. 359; Woodhull, "The Educational Value of Natural Science," *Educational Review*, Vol. IX, p. 368; Browne, "The Educational Value of English," *Educational Review*, Vol. IX, p. 377; Schilling, "The Educational Value of the Modern Languages," *Educational Review*, Vol. IX, p. 385; Baker, "Educational Values," *Educational Review*, Vol. x, p. 209; Hinsdale, "Dogma of Formal Discipline," in *Studies in Education*; Youmans, "Discipline," in *Culture Demanded by Modern Life*, pp. 1–56; Arnold, *Culture and Anarchy*.

*Curriculum in General*: Dewey, "The Psychological Aspect of the School Curriculum" [*The Early Works of John Dewey*, v, pp. 164–76]; Bain, *Education as a Science*, Chs. 6 and 7 on Sequence, Ch. 11, "The Renovated Curriculum"; Hinsdale, "Sources of Human Cultivation," in *Studies in Education*; Maxwell, "Grammar School Curriculum," *Educational Review*, Vol. III, p. 472; Prince, in *Report of* [Mass.] *Board of Education*, 1897 and 1898; Hanus, "Attempted Improvements in Course of Study," *Educa-*

*tional Review*, Vol. XII, p. 435; Eliot, *Educational Reform*, pp. 151, 253 and 197; N.E.A. *Report of Committee of Ten*; Dutton, "The Relation of Education to Vocation," *Educational Review*, Vol. XII, p. 335; Laurie, *The Training of Teachers* (primary), p. 121, (secondary), p. 187; Laurie, *Occasional Addresses* (secondary), p. 59; Aber, *An Experiment in Education*; Beale *et al.*, *Work and Play in Girls' Schools*; F. Spencer, *Aims and Practices of Teaching*; Barnett, *Teaching and Organization*, all give detailed statements regarding the theory and practice of the course of study in English schools.

*Curriculum, Herbartian*: Rein *et al.*, *Theorie und Praxis des Volksschulunterrichts*, 8 vols., Culture-Epochs, I, 16–62; Concentration, I, 63–87; Formal Steps of Method, I, 88–131; Value of Myths, Tales, etc., I, 132–50; Geometry in Grades, IV, 214–63, and VIII, 124–68; History, V, 28 ff.; Geography, III, 165–87, and VII, 63–96; Science, IV, 143–99, VII, 98–137, and VIII, 51–118; see also De Garmo, *Herbart and the Herbartians*; Rein, *Outlines of Pedagogics* (trans. by Van Liew); Dodd, *Introduction to the Herbartian Principles of Teaching*; Ufer, *Pedagogy of Herbart*.

A book entitled *Herbart und die Herbartianer* contains full bibliography of Continental Herbartian Litera-ature; Culture-Epochs, p. 61; Concentration, p. 61; Formal Stages, p. 63; Myths, Tales, p. 64.

Upon *Values of Various Subjects in Curriculum*: Besides references under Values [in Education] (General), Herbartian Curriculum and Correlation, see Harris, St. Louis Superintendent's Annual Reports for 1868 (Three R's), 1869, 1871, 1872.

*Correlation, etc.*: See references under Herbartian Curriculum; also *First Yearbook of the Herbart Society* and *Second Yearbook of the Herbart Society*; Vincent, "Integration of Studies," in *Social Mind and Education*; Parker, *Talks on Pedagogics*; Fitch, *Lectures on Teaching*, Ch. 15; Harris, *Psychologic Foundations of Education*, pp. 321–32, and "The Necessity for Five Co-ordinate Groups of Studies in the Schools," *Educational Review*, Vol. xi, p. 323; see also *Report of Committee of Fifteen*; Lukens, "The Correlation of Studies," *Educational Review*, Vol. x, p. 364; Jackman, "Mr. Lukens on the Correlation of Studies," *Educational Review*, Vol. xi, p. 72; De Garmo, "German Contributions to the Co-ordination of Studies," *Educational Review*, Vol. iv, p. 422, and "A Working Basis for the Correlation of Studies," *ibid.*, Vol. v, p. 451; F. McMurry, "Concentration," *Educational Review*, Vol. ix, p. 27; Gilbert, "Practicable Correlations of Studies," *Educational Review*, Vol. xi, p. 313; Jackman, "Correlation of Science and History," *Educational Review*, Vol. ix, p. 464; Hinsdale, "The Laws of Mental Congruence and Energy Applied to Some Pedagogical Problems," *Educational Review*, Vol. x, p. 152; see also N.E.A. Index Titles: Studies, correlation of, and isolation.

*Culture-Epoch Theory*: In addition to Herbartian references, see *First Yearbook of the Herbart Society* and *Second Yearbook of the Herbart Society*; Vanderwalker, "The Culture-Epoch Theory from an Anthropological Standpoint," *Educational Review*, Vol. xv, p. 374; Vincent, *Social Mind and Education*, Ch. 12.

*Language*: Bain, *Education as a Science*, Ch. 9, "Mother Tongue," Ch. 10, "The Value of the Classics"; Jacobi, *Primary Education*, Ch. 4; Collins, *Study of English Literature* (college, literature *vs.* philology), also "Language Versus Literature at Oxford," *Nineteenth Century*, Vol. xxxvii; Lavisse, *Étude et Étudiants* (classics), p. 35; Laurie, *Training of Teachers* (Latin), p. 213; Hinsdale, *Teaching the Language Arts*; C. McMurry, *Special Method for Literature and History* (pp. 3–54 on myths and tales), and *Special Method in Reading*; Laurie, *Lectures on Language and Linguistic Method in the School*; Farrar, *Essays on Liberal Education*; Price, "Language and Literature: Their Connection in Practical Education," *Educational Review*, Vol. xi, p.

12; and *N.Y. Teacher's Monographs*, Vol. 1, No. 3.

*Mathematics*: Whewell, *Thoughts on Study of Mathematics*; Hamilton, "On the Study of Mathematics, as an Exercise of Mind," in *Dissertations on Philosophy and Literature* (reply to Whewell); Bain, *Education as a Science*, p. 288; Cajori, *Teaching and History of Mathematics in the United States*; Fitch, *Lectures on Teaching*, Ch. 11; McLellan and Dewey, *Psychology of Number*; Indices of *Educational Review*, Vols. II, IV, VI, X; Peirce, "The Logic of Mathematics in Relation to Education," *Educational Review*, Vol. XV; Harris, *Psychologic Foundations of Education*, Ch. 37.

*History*: Hall (ed.), *Methods of Teaching History*; H. Adams, Johns Hopkins Studies, *Methods of History Study*; M. Barnes, *Studies in Historical Method*; Hinsdale, *How to Study and Teach History*; Kemp, *Outline of Method in History*; Lorenz, *Der moderne Geschichtsunterricht*; Hinsdale, *Studies in Education*, p. 206; Fitch, *Lectures on Teaching*, Ch. 12; Smith, *Lectures on the Study of History*; Freeman, *Methods of Historical Study*; Droysen, *Principles of History*; Salmon, "The Study of History in Elementary Schools," *Educational Review*, Vol. I, "Unity in College Entrance History," *ibid.*, Vol. XII, and "History in the German Gymnasia," *ibid.*, Vol. XV; Rice, "History in the Common Schools," *Educational Review*, Vol. XII, also Outlines of *Course of Study in History and Literature*.

*Art in Education*: Bain, *Education as a Science*, Ch. 13; Waldstein, *Study of Art in Universities*; N.E.A. *Proceedings* Index; Harris, *Psychologic Foundations of Education*, Ch. 38; Crane, *Relations of Art to Education*; Langl, *Modern Art Education*; Clarke, *Art and Industry: Education in the Industrial and Fine Arts in the United States*.

*Manual Training*: Ham, *Manual Training*; MacArthur, *Education in Relation to Manual Industry*; Love, *Industrial Education*; Stetson, *Technical Education*; N.E.A. *Proceedings*, 1889, p. 417, and

N.E.A. *Proceedings*, 1897, p. 742, see also Index.

*Sciences*: Youmans, *Culture Demanded by Modern Life*; Preyer, *Naturforschung und Schule*; *N.Y. Teachers' Monographs*, Vol. I, No. 2; Huxley, *Science and Education*; J. Payne, *Lectures on Education*, p. 253; Fitch, *Lectures on Teaching*, Ch. 14; Jackman, on Nature Study, also "Relation of Arithmetic to Elementary Science," *Educational Review*, Vol. v, "Correlation of Science and History," *ibid.*, Vol. ix, and "Representative Expression in Nature-Study," *ibid.*, Vol. x; Harris, *Psychologic Foundations of Education*, Ch. 39.

*Geography*: Geikie, *The Teaching of Geography*; C. McMurry, *Special Method in Geography*; Parker, *How to Study Geography*; Mill, *Hints on Geographical Books*, Chs. 1 and 2; Laurie, *Occasional Addresses*, p. 83; Davis, "The Teaching of Geography," *Educational Review*, Vols. iii and iv, "Governmental Maps in Schools," *ibid.*, Vol. vii; Redway, "Text-books of Geography," *Educational Review*, Vol. v, "The Status of Geography Teaching," *ibid.*, Vol. vii, "Some Applications of Physiography to History," *ibid.*, Vol. viii, "What Is Physiography?" *ibid.*, Vol. x; C. McMurry, "Geography as a School Subject," *Educational Review*, Vol. ix; *Fourth Yearbook of the National Herbart Society*; King, *Methods and Aids in Geography*.

### D. ORGANIZATION OF METHOD—SUMMARY AS TO SIGNIFICANCE OF METHOD.

I. General Psychology of Method.

    1. In direct stage: (1) learning by experience (a) organic circuit, immediate attention and interest, play, apperception, (b) implicit generalization, habit the principle of organization, (c) implicit specializations, variation in growth and use; (2) consequent standpoint in practice, examples.

    2. In indirect or reflective stage: (1) consciousness of end—practical, theoretical—control of problem, mediate attention and interest, origin and function of

imagery; process of learning one of direction of inquiry; (2) corresponding school practice, examples.

II. Method in Recitation.
1. Herbartian formal steps stated, advantages.
2. Criticized: (1) preparation—conscious and unconscious; real significance of consciousness of end—a point, topic, unifying centre; (2) presentation: value of presented material, sensations; objects, books and talks; significance of particulars; (3) generalization, conscious and unconscious, an organizing principle; (4) application, also an attitude, not a distinct step or function; (5) types and method-units; correct practice but not in line with theory.
3. Growth an organic process. Dangers of too great formalization. Neglect of the instinctive, the habitual, the motor generally in Herbartianism.

### E. CONCLUSION AND SUMMARY.

I. Education a Growth—as Reconstruction.
II. The Original and the Acquired. The Individual and the Social. Utility and Culture. The Natural and the Spiritual. The Intellectual and the Ethical. False Dualism in Each Case. A Unified Conception.

*Method in General*: C. McMurry, *General Method*, and C. and F. McMurry, *Method of the Recitation*; De Garmo, *Essentials of Method*; Tompkins, *Philosophy of Teaching*; J. Adams, *Herbartian Psychology Applied to Education*; Lange, *Apperception*; McLellan, *Applied Psychology*, pp. 167–76, 180–86, and Chs. 9 and 10; Harris, *Psychologic Foundations of Education*, Chs. 4, 22, 28, 30 and 35; Fitch, *Art of Questioning*.

*Interest*: Dewey, "Interest in Relation to Training of the Will" [*The Early Works of John Dewey*, v, 111–50]; Harris, "Herbart's Doctrine of Interest," *Educational Review*, Vol. x, p. 71, "Professor John Dewey's Doctrine of Interest as Related to Will," *ibid.*, Vol. xi, p. 486, and "In What Does Spiritual Evolution Consist?" *Education*, Vol. xvi, p. 413; F.

McMurry, "Interest: Some Objections to It," *Educational Review*, Vol. XI, p. 146; J. Adams, *Herbartian Psychology*, Ch. 10; Wilson, "The Doctrine of Interest," *Educational Review*, Vol. XI; De Garmo, "Is Herbart's Theory of Interest Dangerous?" *Public-School Journal*, Vol. XIV; Harris, Reply to De Garmo's "Is Herbart's Theory of Interest Dangerous?" *Public-School Journal*, Vol. XIV; Brown, "Educative Interests," *Public-School Journal*, Vol. XV; C. McMurry, "Correlation of Studies," *Public-School Journal*, Vol. XV.

## Topics

1. Adjustment of the parts of educational system to one another.
2. Grading and promotions; class-work and individuality.
3. Uniform curriculum and electives above the elementary school.
4. Specialized or departmental teaching.
5. Preparation of teachers and the normal school problem.
6. Problems of superintendency.
7. Moral education, direct and indirect, in the school.
8. The place and relations of technical and professional education.
9. The shortening of the curriculum (involving comparison with French and German schools).
10. The enriching of the curriculum.
11. Correlation, co-ordination and concentration of studies.
12. Culture-epoch theory.
13. Humanities and science.
14. History of educational practices as affected by social conditions.
15. The growth of the curriculum as affected by social conditions.
16. The conflict of studies in high school and college.
17. Values of school subjects.
18. Literature and language in elementary education.
19. Literature and language in secondary education.
20. Literature and language in higher education.

21. History—educational value and methods.
22. Geography—educational value and methods.
23. Mathematics—educational value and methods.
24. The natural sciences—educational value and methods.
25. Significance of play in education.
26. Significance of art in education.
27. Significance of "manual training" in education.
28. Development of will.
29. The interpretation of the Pestalozzian maxims.
30. The formal steps of instruction.
31. Adaptation of method at various stages of growth.
32. Theories of classification of sciences—Spencer, Comte, etc.
33. Problem of rural education.
34. Study of civics, sociology and political economy in elementary and secondary education.

In working up special topics the student should consult special Bibliographies in Hall and Monroe; also the General Index to Reports of the N.E.A. and to Barnard's School Journal. He should be familiar with *Poole's Index to Periodical Literature*, and with the Yearly Indices (Cumulative) since its issue. The *Educational Review* should be consulted. The *School Review* and the *Proceedings* of the North Central Association are indispensable for topics having to do with secondary and higher education. Upon many topics, the subject index in the Pedagogical Library is very full. See also Buisson's *Dictionnaire*, and Rein's and Schmid's Encyclopædias.

# *Book Reviews*

## The Philosophic Renascence in America[1]

The nine books lying before me are an interesting sign of the times. Drifting together from various quarters, and finally tied up in one packet and calling for notice in one review, they present at once an extraordinary diversity and an extraordinary unity. The diversity is in the various methods of approach to philosophy which they represent in contemporary thought; the unity is in a certain underlying trend and aim which, disguised by differences in terminology and of school attachment, is none the less real and assured—even though some of the authors represented might horroresce at the thought of kinship with some of the others. It accordingly seems better worth while for the nonce to take this casual collection of books as an index of the present di-

[1]    *The Elements of Metaphysics*: Being a Guide for Lectures and Private Use, by Dr. Paul Deussen; trans. by C. M. Duff. New York: Macmillan Co.
    *Three Lectures on the Vedanta Philosophy*, Delivered at the Royal Institution in March, 1894, by F. Max Müller, K.M. New York: Longmans, Green, and Co.
    *Genetic Philosophy*, by David J. Hill. New York: Macmillan Co.
    *Hegel's Philosophy of Mind*. Trans. from the Encyclopædia of the Philosophical Sciences, with Five Introductory Essays, by William Wallace, M.A. New York: Macmillan Co.
    *Our Notions of Number and Space*, by Herbert Nichols, Ph.D., and William E. Parsons, A.B. Boston: Ginn and Co.
    *The Diseases of the Will*, by Th. Ribot; trans. by Merwin-Marie Snell. Chicago: Open Court Publishing Co.
    *The Psychic Factor*: An Outline of Psychology, by Charles Van Norden, D.D. New York: D. Appleton and Co.
    *Basal Concepts in Philosophy*: An Inquiry into Being, Non-Being, and Becoming, by Alexander T. Ormond, Ph.D. New York: C. Scribner's Sons.
    *A Primer of Philosophy*, by Paul Carus, Ph.D. Chicago: Open Court Publishing Co.

[*First published in* Dial, XVIII (*Feb. 1895*), 80–82. *Not previously reprinted.*]

rection of thought, than to subject each severally to an exhaustive analysis.

At the outset the collection is characteristic in this: it has within it five books by American writers, including one by a thinker of German birth, but now at home in America and conducting two of its most thoughtful periodicals; it has within it two translations from the German, and one from the French, and one book by a German acclimated in England rather than in the United States. It does not take a very long look backward to realize the significance of the possibility of any such collection. It marks at once the extent to which English and American thought is breaking loose from its long-time local prepossessions and insulation, and is endeavoring to assimilate the thought of continental Europe; and it marks also the vigor of the philosophic renascence— for such we may fairly term it—in the United States. Add to this that one of the books (Professor Müller's) deals expressly with an old philosophy of India, while another (Dr. Deussen's) is pretty well saturated with the same Vedantic lore, though attempting to adjust it (*via* Schopenhauer) more closely to modern thought, and we see that the existing ferment of thought is cosmopolitan.

An equal variety meets us if we attempt to classify the books from the standpoint of their subject-matter. The collection is not fairly representative on the ethical side, but apart from that it contains four books which deal expressly with constructive philosophical work, three with psychological inquiry, while Professor Müller and Dr. Deussen again stand for that craving for something beyond either the rationally philosophical or the experimentally demonstrable which is so marked a feature of the present; for though we may conventionally ignore the matter, yet occultism and Orientalism in one form or another are most emphasized traits of the existing popular consciousness.

Of the translations, not much need be said. The Ribot has so long been familiar to students of psychology that it is only necessary to welcome its appearance in English, and express thanks to the translator for his satisfactory work; indeed, all of the translations issuing from the Open Court Press reach a satisfactory standard of workmanship. Mr.

Wallace has been known for years by his translation of
Hegel's *Logic*, and his attempt with the *Philosophie des
Geistes* is equally successful, while it will introduce Hegel to
many in a new aspect—as among other things a psychologist,
and, according to his lights and the state of knowledge when
he wrote, a physiological psychologist. Mr. Wallace's introductory essays are suggestive, ingenious, and literary; they
represent that phase of the Oxford philosophical tradition
which delights in philosophy for its culture value (to use the
current cant phrase), and sits very easily to its severer and
more scientific sides—the tradition which found its culmination in Jowett's Introductions to the Platonic dialogues. Mr.
Wallace is more serious and thorough-going in his methods
than Jowett was; but there is the same occasional complete
inconsequence, the same occasional sacrifice of ideas to the
needs of clever statement, and the same undercurrent of
feeling that it is hardly worthy of an English gentleman and
scholar to be too anxious about definiteness and precision in
thought. Mr. Wallace has probably carried the art of translating Hegel as far as it can be carried upon present methods. It is quite possible that a translator may sometime arise
who will give up the attempt to find technical terminology to
correspond to Hegel's philosophical dialect, and set about
doing in English what Hegel himself did in German (as
Aristotle had done before him in Greek)—hunting up pregnant words of idiomatic speech, and squeezing the philosophic meaning out of them. As for Dr. Deussen's work,
what shall we say? The translation is well done; but was the
original worth translating? The form is largely a *quasi* geometrical method; definitions abound, which, like all philosophic definitions that precede, instead of summing up discussion, beg the question; disjunctions, which ingeniously
conceal the problem while appearing to simplify it, are
numerous. And through it all is the gospel of the Vedanta,
with Schopenhauer as its prophet and expounder. Those
who already know their Spinoza and Kant and Schopenhauer will hardly get much out of the book; those who want
a philosophy not for philosophic but for æsthetic and emotional purposes may easily turn from, say, theosophy to Dr.
Deussen's constructions of the universe. Speaking of the

Indian philosophy brings me to Professor Müller's book, which, like all his recent work, is pedantically popular in style, written largely, if not *ad captandum*, at least *ad audiendum*, and yet manages to convey in a wonderfully easy way a large amount of useful information to him who can separate that information from its graceful entwinings with Mr. Müller's own opinions and feelings about a great variety of subjects.

Mr. Van Norden's title, *The Psychic Factor*, covers an attempt to state the more elementary facts of psychology with especial reference to many of the more recent biological investigations, and with some emphasis on the phenomena of dreams, hypnotism, etc. Mr. Van Norden is a long way from being a systematic thinker, but he has a keen eye for salient facts, and a power of lucid expression. His book may serve as a popular summary of many of the points of chief interest in current psychology. Mr. Nichols gives the method and results of the application of experimental psychology to the problems of number and space. The work is really a laboratory monograph, and will appeal to the specialist. It is symptomatic of the courage and energy of the modern psychologist, that he completely ignores the attempt of the metaphysician to shut off a little enclosure of concepts, like number and space, warning all experimental methods to keep off. Mr. Nichols's treatise on *Notions of Number and Space* shows that experimental methods may be applied with some hope of fruit to the "metaphysical" categories, but strikes me as suggestive rather than as conclusive. The book in form has a way—irritating to me—of stating on one side a high general and vague conclusion, and then one hundred and nine very specific conclusions, but with none of the *media axiomata* which are most helpful to other workers.

There are left for consideration three attempts to deal constructively with philosophy. Mr. Ormond, in his *Basal Concepts in Philosophy*, attempts the deepest flight. He takes up seriously and earnestly the problem of the relation of God to the finite world, and hopes to add something to its solution by a reconstruction of the triad of Hegelian categories of Being, Non-Being, and Becoming, through a conception of Non-Being as that which the Absolute Being or

Spirit continually wars against and suppresses, but which never, as it does in Hegelianism, becomes a moment of Being. It is obviously out of the question to discuss Mr. Ormond's argument in a brief review, but I cannot refrain from pointing out two things. One is that, to many, Mr. Ormond's entire problem will seem self-made, factitious. This problem is, how an absolute can give rise to a finite, the perfect to an imperfect. There will be many who will want to know whence Mr. Ormond gets his definition of an absolute, and his standard of perfection; who will inquire, what is the ground of the assumption that the absolute is absolute apart from what he terms the "finite," and how Mr. Ormond is so certain of the nature of perfection as to assume, without discussion, that "perfection" can get along without having as factors of itself those things which Mr. Ormond labels imperfection. There are some who prefer a world with night as well as day, of pain as well as pleasure, of temptation as well as of a goodness which to them would seem tedious without the struggle of conquest. This may be very poor taste on their part, but it represents a standpoint which is not so much rejected as ignored by Mr. Ormond. My other remark is that to many Mr. Ormond's solution of the problem of evil will appear in unstable equilibrium between what he would term, I suppose, a pantheistic optimism or monism, and the old-fashioned orthodox dualism of personal God and personal Devil. The mind can formally follow the idea of an Absolute Being which in thinking itself has to exclude all taint of Non-Being, and so keeps up at once the thought of Non-Being, and the warfare to exclude it. But the mind will have a feeling that a genuine Absolute would not have to spend time in contending with what, after all, is but its own shadow. I do not wish to seem to deal flippantly with a serious effort to think out a fundamental problem, but one can hardly escape the conclusion that Mr. Ormond's Absolute is engaged in setting up a man of straw, and then—never *quite* knocking the straw man down, because in that case it would lose this negative exercise of exclusion through which it maintains its own positive identity. Mr. Ormond does not appear to realize how essentially one his position is with that of Fichte.

Mr. Hill's *Genetic Philosophy* deals amiably and readably with a large number of questions of genesis and evolution, bringing to bear upon problems of the origin of life, feeling, consciousness, art, morality, etc., a considerable range of reading, and an easy style. Unfortunately, the book is marred by a certain pretentiousness, manifest even in its title. The work is in no sense itself a philosophy of genesis, or genetic in the sense of using a thorough-going evolutionary method. It simply discusses lucidly and with considerable discrimination certain specific genetic questions. The claim is even more emphatic and offensive in the Introduction, where the book is offered as affording a way out of existing philosophic confusion.

Mr. Carus in his *Primer of Philosophy* has put before us in a thoughtful, yet easily grasped form, an attempt to combine the data and methods of modern science with certain metaphysical concepts, resulting, as he says, in a reconciliation of philosophies of the types of Mill's empiricism and Kant's apriorism. This spirit of synthesis and mediation is prominent throughout the book, which is thoroughly worth reading and study. It is doubtful, however, if it will fulfill the pious wish of the author and set the stranded ship of philosophy afloat again; indeed, were the ship of philosophy stranded, I doubt the ability of the united efforts of the whole race to get it afloat. It is wiser to think of the ship of philosophy as always afloat, but always needing, not, indeed, the impetus of any individual thinker, but the added sense of direction which the individual can give by some further, however slight, interpretation of the world about.

*Johnson's Universal Cyclopædia.* Vols. I–V (A–Mozambique). New York: Johnson Co., 1894.

The striking feature of the philosophic content of this *Cyclopædia* compared, not simply with former editions of itself, but also with other cyclopædias, is the much more adequate attention given to psychological topics. This may

[*First published in* Psychological Review, II (*Mar. 1895*), 186–88. *Not previously reprinted.*]

not unreasonably be attributed, I suppose, to the presence among its editors of Professor Baldwin; just as the editorial care of Dr. Harris had previously made the metaphysical side of philosophy more prominent in Johnson's than in any other save the *Britannica*. There seems to be particularly good reason for ascribing the difference to the interest of Professor Baldwin in the fact that it is only in the fourth and fifth volumes, after Professor Baldwin is well installed in the editorial chair, that the psychological articles become numerous. Some of the psychological topics which are so unfortunate as to begin with $A$ or $B$, are in quite striking contrast to the accuracy and fullness of the later articles. The article on Association of Ideas, for example, gives a fair descriptive statement, but is quite innocent of modern problems and methods, to say nothing of results. In contrast with the definitely experimental tone pervading the later articles, it is somewhat startling to read regarding association, that the search for a physiological solution is in vain, and to find the following proposition set forth as an explanation: "This wonderful power of the human mind is part of the perfection which it owes to the Great Being who is its author."

The letters $G$, $H$ and $I$ are fortunately very rich in psychological captions and the comparative barrenness of the earlier pages is more than made good. I know of no better way to give an idea of the variety of topics treated than to give a running list of the more important subjects: Genetic Psychology, Genius, Habit, Hedonism, Hypnotism, Ideal Feelings, or Emotions, Ideals, Illusion, Imagination, Imitation, Impulse, Innervation, Instinct, and Insanity, all by Professor Baldwin; Generalization, Hegel, Hindu Philosophy, Idea, Idealism, Identity, Immortality, Infinite, by Dr. Harris, and Intuitionalism, by the present writer. The article on Histology by Dr. Piersol should also be mentioned. In general, it may be noted that the neurological side is quite carefully looked after.

To go into as much detail regarding all the letters would render this notice a catalogue, not a review, but the articles on Localization (in space and of brain functions) and upon Motive by Professor Baldwin, and that by Dr.

Cattell upon Memory should be noted. It is in no way invidious to any of the other articles to say that the article upon Memory is in respect to its objectivity, lucidity and presentation of current scientific problems and method, a model of what cyclopædia information should be.

Several of Professor Baldwin's articles seem to me a distinct advance upon his own statement of the same subject in his *Psychology*. The idea is more definitely put, and the style more precise. There are many of these articles to which not only the "general reader," but the psychological specialist will turn with interest, and, judging from my own case (if I may venture for the nonce to pose as a specialist) with profit. The article, for example, on Impulse is highly suggestive; the reference of impulse to the central apparatus as representing the growth of the whole system, rather than to a specific stimulus, appears to be a very decided advance upon previous efforts to discriminate impulse from reflex action. The article upon Imitation is excellent, as we should expect from one who has made the psychology of that subject peculiarly his own. The article upon emotion (under the caption of Ideal Feelings) is admirable, save the attempt to state the theories offered in explanation. Of course not everything can be given in such an account; and yet surely the contribution of James-Lange is too important, whether accepted or rejected, to be so briefly summed up. The attempt of Darwin to explain emotional expressions might well have received some attention. The article on Imagination would have been helped by reference to the concrete investigations in imagery; but aside from that it is well done. (There is a heading Generic Image, referring one to Image, but the latter does not appear as a distinct topic; it may also be noted in this connection that a *q.v.* to Insistent Ideas is found in the article upon Illusion, but no such caption occurs.) The article upon Genetic Psychology is too short to give Professor Baldwin a fair opportunity, but fortunately we shall soon have a chance to read a fuller expression of his views. This present account is clear and full within its limits. But I wonder when I read the following: "Suppose we say, with many psychologists, that volition is necessary to all adaptive muscular efforts; an appeal to the child shows us so many facts to the contrary that we are able to bring genetic psychology to refute the position." I do not wonder at Professor Baldwin's saying this; on the contrary, it is true enough to immediate facts. But I wonder if the final outcome of the appeal to the child will not be to change the ready-made concept of volition which serves as the standard in the above instance, and to generalize the idea of volition by making it equivalent to all acquired co-ordination.

However, I might go on indefinitely commenting upon points of interest. I shall fulfill my duty better if I divert the attention both of psychologists and the general public to the unusually full and suggestive discussion of psychological topics to be found in this last edition of *Johnson's Cyclopædia*. Teachers will find its great value for reference further increased by the generally good and up-to-date bibliographies.

*Studies in Character*, by S. Bryant. New York: Macmillan Co., 1894, and *Hedonistic Theories from Aristippus to Spencer*, by John Watson. New York: Macmillan Co., 1895.

Mrs. Bryant's essays are grouped under the heads "Ethical" and "Educational." None the less there is a decided unity of method and point of view running through all of them. The ethical essays carry educational implications throughout, and it is the ethical side of education which commands Mrs. Bryant's attention. It is to be hoped that the book will attain a wide reading in the educational community. It is a book that does not shock one's intellectual self-respect, which is more than can be said of many professedly pedagogical treatises; and it utilizes in an unobtrusive, but none the less effective, way very much that is best in current ethical and psychological writings. Mrs. Bryant is at home in what is being said and discovered in the vital places of current discussions—another mark of eminent distinction from much of what passes as pedagogical contributions. Systematic in outer form, being a

[*First published in* Psychological Review, III (*Mar. 1896*), *218–22. Not previously reprinted.*]

collection of essays, the book is not; systematic in unity of conception and method the book is, much more so than many more pretentious treatises.

In dealing with such topics as "My Duty to My Neighbor," "Friendship," "Soundness of Intellect," etc., one perhaps could be brilliant only at the expense of sanity, and original only by leaning towards eccentricity, and the originality of sincerity (which, as Mrs. Bryant quotes Carlyle is the real originality), Mrs. Bryant possesses. However this may be, there is a tendency at times to fall into a certain explicitness of classification and definition that makes long continued reading an impossibility. A few pages are suggestive; two or three chapters of it load one with the feeling of assisting in the laying out of the corpse of the moral universe. As Professor James has remarked about too much descriptive psychology there are many things which it is highly interesting to experience, but a little tedious to be reminded of in too much detail and with too explicit a touch after we have been through them. Perhaps only Aristotle at his best, and the French moral essayists with their capacity for unexpected epigram and their ability to flash upon the reader the ironical reverse of their own definitions, have ever been at home in this region of moral description.

As to the implied ethical doctrine of the book, it is upon the whole, the idealistic interpretation of the conception of self-realization, vitalized for educational purposes with considerable concrete psychology regarding the motor tendencies of ideas and concrete insight into individual temperaments and types. I cannot forbear from pointing out that while in her ethical doctrine Mrs. Bryant conceives the "ideal" to be perfection located at a remote goal; for practical purposes, she, like all other perfectionists, gets down to approximate ideal, which is the right functioning of present powers, or the relating of conditions of a present situation. The same contradiction occurs when Mrs. Bryant is getting at ideals from a psychological standpoint. The theory implied in practice is so certain to be more adequate than theory set up as theory of practice.

There appears to me also to be a regrettable tendency in Mrs. Bryant to over-emphasize the personal or immediate, direct side of conduct—devotion to persons, whether one's self or somebody else, instead of devotion to work, to action and to persons, whether one's self or others, indirectly through their implications in activity. But so far as there is any consensus of ethical doctrine on this point, I suppose it is with Mrs. Bryant rather than with the reviewer; and, as the point is too big for discussion in a review, the matter must go as a personal regret and dissent. All this direct moral devotion to persons, I believe can end only in useless complications, weariness of flesh and spirit and contradictions between our aspirations and our accomplishments, both in theory and in practice.

Professor Watson publishes his criticism of hedonism "as a needful supplement to the ethical part of his [my] Outlines of Philosophy." His method of criticism is, as indicated in his title, historic. It is historical types, rather than actual historic continuity, however, which Mr. Watson deals with; his authors being Aristippus, Epicurus, Hobbes, Locke, Hume, Bentham, John Stuart Mill and Spencer; about one-fourth of the book being devoted to the last named.

After discussing the influence of the Sophists, Aristippus is considered as the type of naïve and, in one sense, the only consistent hedonism—the seizure of the pleasure of the present moment. Professor Watson points out a psychological contradiction contained in the idea of seeking momentary pleasure; *seeking* for pleasure introduces struggle and pain; pleasure as pleasure comes and is enjoyed without being sought. The doctrine is also shown to involve an essential misreading of human nature, ignoring the simple fact of experience that men seek active ends in which undoubtedly they anticipate and find pleasure, rather than pleasure as such. Epicurus enlarges and, in an objective sense, rationalizes the momentary, transitive end of Aristippus in introducing the idea of the greatest pleasure on the whole as an end; but as Professor Watson points out, at the expense of hedonism, virtually substituting a state of contentment for the ideal of pleasure; and contentment, in turn, involves its own peculiar self-contradiction, since to make the attainment of individual contentment the ideal is to throw everything back upon individual temperament, and thus deify lawlessness. Hobbes generalizes the hedonistic conception still further; Aristippus simply ignored the state; Epicurus was for getting along with it with the least possible trouble; Hobbes will turn the whole social organization into a means of bringing pleasure to the individual.[1]

Locke represents a consistent inconsistency—a philosophy of compromise. His intentions are good; his performance poor. He intends to assert freedom, but he holds that the strongest uneasiness determines the will, and uneasiness is simply the desire for the pleasure that is strongest. He intends to uphold the objectivity of moral distinctions, and defines the good as that which is conformable to law; but when he states how law lays hold on the individual he falls back on the pleasures got by obedience and the pains suffered through disobedience. Hume is as uncompromising as Locke the reverse. Pleasure is the sole motive, and reason can never be a motive; its sole office is to serve the feelings. With Hume the hedonistic logic may be said to have become explicit and self-conscious. The self being only a bundle of feelings, there is naught but feeling to seek or avoid, or by which to seek or avoid.

With Hume the logical evolution of hedonism ceases; since him we have only recurrences to earlier types, or else its ennobling through the introduction of ideas non-hedonistic in character. Bentham in a way went back to Hobbes, only with great practical interest in social reform which led him to introduce elements irreconcilable with hedonism, while Stuart Mill can be made consistent only by interpreting his practical views from the standpoint of an idealistic theory. The examination of Mr. Spencer takes up his ethical doctrine both in its hedonistic psychology, its evolutionary aspects and the relation of one of these to the other, with a view to showing that Mr. Spencer's general formula of evo-

[1]    While I hesitate to differ from Professor Watson on a historical point, this statement as regards Hobbes seems doubtful. Perhaps Hobbes ought in logical consistency to have taken this view; but as matter of fact he seems to me to throw all the emphasis on the *substitution* of the end of the sovereign for that of the individual; and his whole political reasoning to be a back-handed way of saying that *since* men live in society they must regard the social end before the individual end; and that *if* they lived in a state of nature, while each might then follow his own selfish end, yet such a state would be self-contradictory. In other words, Hobbes's psychology and his sociology contradict each other flagrantly, instead of the latter being an instrument as regards the former.

lution throws no light on moral conduct; that his psychology destroys the reality of obligation, and does not justify the transition from egoism to altruism; while the idea of a completed life and completed society held up as the goal from the side of evolution have no special coherence with the ideal of pleasure set up on the analytic side.

Philosophic exposition is at its best as to style in this book of Professor Watson's. I could with difficulty name another book which might at once command so thoroughly the respect of the specialist and receive comprehension by the layman as does this lucid, direct piece of exposition and criticism. It may be of service to teachers of ethics to point out that the expositions of the various authors, mainly in the authors' own words, are well proportioned, condensed and accurate, and, in some cases, the best available substitutes for a perusal of the original texts, and in all cases a helpful accompaniment of such perusal.

The book seems to me to close the case, on the polemic side, as regards hedonism. Undoubtedly we shall go on having arguments both for and against hedonism, but the interest seems about done with. The rise of a new psychological method and of a new sociological point of view and body of facts have presented new problems and shifted the focus of attention. These indirect influences have probably done quite as much as more direct criticism in making hedonism a played-out standpoint. Just because Professor Watson's book has accomplished its task so thoroughly, one lays it down with a feeling of what has not been accomplished, and of what constitutes the next task—the discussion of hedonism from the historic standpoint, in the evolutionary sense. We do not need longer to contend with hedonism as a present foe, and consequently we want to comprehend it more thoroughly as a manifestation—comprehend it not in terms of itself, but in terms of the social and intellectual conditions which have given birth to it, to see what it really means when so interpreted. From the historic evolutionary standpoint, there has been the same inner necessity, in the logic of growth, for the appearance of these hedonistic systems as there has been for that of any transcended animal or political form of life. What is that inner necessity?

*The Number Concept: Its Origin and Development*,
by Levi L. Conant, Ph.D. New York and London:
Macmillan and Co., 1896.

Only one exception can be taken to this book—as to its
title. The book is not upon the origin of the number concept nor yet upon its development. The book deals with
primitive methods of counting and with modes of expressing
or registering the results of such counting. The true title
would be: "Numeral Systems (or Number Words), Their
Origins and Various Forms." Since the work actually undertaken is thoroughly and accurately carried out, this matter
of title is, perhaps, of little account; yet one who approaches
the book expecting to have light thrown upon the psychology
of the numerical idea will be struck by the discrepancy between the title and the contents.

This discrepancy is worth insisting upon, because there
is possible a psychological inquiry upon an anthropological
basis which would agree with the title. The author insists
(on pp. 2–4) that the question of the origin of number is
outside the limits of inquiry, with his title page still staring
him in the face! "Philosophers have endeavored to establish
certain propositions concerning this subject, but, as might
have been expected, have failed to reach any common
ground." The context shows that Dr. Conant understands by
this subject the old controversy as to whether numerical
judgments are *a priori* or the result of experience. He is
quite right in ruling out this topic from an anthropological
investigation, and confining himself to the simple statement
that all primitive societies reveal that they have some, however crude, sense of number. But this is not the point from
which the psychologist is interested in the problem. The
sense of number is a historical, an evolutionary development.
It arises in the race and in the individual. The psychological
(and the pedagogical) problem is: Under what circumstances, in response to what stimuli or needs, in what psy-

[*First published in* Psychological Review, III (*May 1896*), 326–29.
*Not previously reprinted.*]

chical context, does this sense arise? It would be impossible to say, in advance, just how much light anthropological investigation would throw upon this problem; but it may safely be said that it will throw some light; and it is a pity that Dr. Conant, through confusing the metaphysical and the psychological problems of origin, should not have contributed what his learning and thorough research fit him to contribute. The book would then have been as useful to the psychologist as it now is to the philologist.

The following points of psychological interest may be gleaned from the philological data: 1. The numerical systems are *rhythmical*. The count proceeds up to a certain point (sometimes only 2; sometimes 3, joints of a finger; sometimes 5, fingers of one hand; sometimes 10, both hands; sometimes 20, fingers and toes; then a knot is tied, a notch cut, etc., and the count repeated. With further developments, compound words are formed, making it possible to dispense, more or less, with the notch or knot, a definite base of reference being formed. 2. While the origin of many number names is from the fingers, many denote *activities* performed upon the fingers. For example, 1 may mean "used to start with," or "the end is bent." 3. The rhythms of the system show reference *ahead* and also *backwards*. For example, 9 may mean "almost done," "that which has not its 10," "there is still one more," "hand next to complete," "keep back one finger," etc. The reference to the starting point, however, is much more common. Nine will more often mean "4 of the *other* hand," or "hand with 4" or "end and 4." It is undoubtedly true, as Dr. Conant remarks (p. 72) that the savage does not discriminate the numerical idea from the concrete image of fingers or whatever with which it is bound up, *i.e.*, does not consciously abstract. But it is equally true that this continual thought of reference forwards or backwards in the larger number, is, psychologically considered, an abstracting movement. When, for instance, in the Zuni scale, 3 means "the equally dividing finger," instead of simply the biggest finger, it must be acknowledged that abstraction is pretty well along. While it is not true to the same extent of the verbal form in which 6 means "1 on the other," still the element of relation is obviously prominent in the latter. While a careful study of the actual circumstances under which savages use number would be necessary to justify the statement that the ratio element in number early comes to consciousness, the philological material collected by Dr. Conant points in that direction. 4. The fact that the "student is struck with the prevalence of the dual number" in the grammatical structure of the earlier languages is an important fact. Mind first dichotomizes the universe; the world is "this and that," "this" and "the other one." Observations which I have made on such small children as have come within my scope bear out this principle for the individual. There was not, at first (with these children at least), a plural number, but conscious selection or preference. Two denoted not a couple, but a contrast, something left out or ruled out. Two was not used in an aggregative or enumerative sense until an effort was made also to recognize aggregates larger than 2, which at first (agreeing here also with the philological record) took the form of "a lot"— many. I cannot, however, agree with Dr. Conant that the difficulty which the savage met in attempting "to pass beyond 2, and to count 3, 4, 5, is, of course, but slight." On the contrary, it seems to me the *essential* difficulty, marking a distinct advance in consciousness. It is one thing to mark off the mental universe into this and not this; it is quite another to assume the attitude of *ordering* things within the universe, and this is what occurs when numbers develop into a row or sequence. At all events, in the observation of children just referred to, I found that the attaching of any meaning to 3 was a much later accomplishment (often a year intervening) than in the case of 2; and that when the idea of 3 was grasped there was no difficulty in getting the child to count intelligently to 10; thus indicating that the idea of 3 is not simply cumulative, but marks a different psychical attitude. Till a child can grasp the idea of 3, numbers like 3, 4, 5, etc., are taken by him to be the absolute names of certain individuals.

An incidental psychological contribution, which will not fail of catching the attention of those psychologists and sociologists who are dwelling upon the importance of imitation, is found on page 11. Experiments were made upon five different primary rooms in Worcester, Massachusetts, to determine the "natural" place of beginning in counting off on the fingers. In two cases the teacher allowed one child to count while the other children watched. In both cases every other child followed exactly the example of the leader.

It is to be hoped that Dr. Conant, or some other equally competent student, will supplement this book with another, in which the anthropological data concerning the circumstances and motives with relation to which savages count will be collected so as to extend and to justify the philological data and conclusions; and will also take up the matter of systems of *measurement*, upon both a philological and anthropological basis. In this case the contributions to psychology will be direct and not simply incidental.

*Studies in the Evolutionary Psychology of Feeling*, by H. M. Stanley. New York: Macmillan Co., 1895.

Mr. Stanley has given us a book of about four hundred solidly thought out and solidly written octavo pages; and he has done his work so conscientiously that a reviewer who wishes to give an account of its contents cannot have recourse to compression by means of squeezing out padding and useless repetitions. It is quite out of the question, therefore, that the account should be adequate as to extent. The recourse must be to give, if possible, some representative samples; premising that, from the point of view of method and general scope as well as of specific content (especially in the way of frequent shrewd and apt observations, in no wise trite or shop-worn, about feeling and feelings), the book demands the attention of every psychologist interested in this intricate and obscure side of his work.

The pure psychology of feeling, as Mr. Stanley remarks, is advanced but little. Is there any way out of the confusion and darkness? "If the study of feeling is to become scientific, we must, I think, assume that all feeling is a biological function, governed by the general laws of life and

[*First published in* Philosophical Review, v (*May 1896*), 292–99. *Not previously reprinted.*]

subject in origin and development to the law of struggle for existence" (p. 3). The difficulty of applying the biological method is not, however, underrated. "No amount of objective physiological research can tell us anything about the real nature of feeling" (p. 6), and again, "Mind can be for us only what mind is in us" (p. 5). With the assurance, then, that Mr. Stanley recognizes to the full the difficulties inherent in his subject-matter,[1] let us see what the biological point of view can tell us.

Assuming consciousness as a purely biological function, as a mode for securing favorable reactions, we are brought to the point of view of self-conservation. Mental function must have originated in some very simple form, as demanded for self-conservation at a critical point in the organism's career. Hence an origin in cognitive consciousness may fairly be ruled out. "Mere apprehension would not serve the being any more than the property of reflection the mirror." The organism reacts through pain. This pain, at the outset, must have been bare, undifferentiated pain without particular quality. With this primitive act of blind, formless pain is associated the will act of struggle and effort. "The first consciousness was a flash of pain, of small intensity, yet sufficient to awaken struggle and preserve life" (p. 14). Pleasure is not an accompaniment of pain; it does not follow from it at first. Pleasure, perhaps, came after two modes of pain had differentiated, pain of lack and pain of excess, and came in as intermediary between them (p. 16). Mr. Stanley endeavors to reinforce this view of feeling as primitive from certain considerations derived from the present mature consciousness, and also by rebuttals of certain ideas of Ward and Höffding. The general line taken is that "centrality of response" (identified with feeling) is the initial element still, even in every developed psychosis, preceding cognitive discrimination and purposive action. "A bright color gives pleasure before we see it, and this pleasure

---

[1]  As we shall see, the objection which may be brought against Mr. Stanley is not that he has unduly magnified the biological region as against that of introspection, but rather that he has not, his problem granted, utilized the biological data enough. There is practically no discussion of biological detail in the book.

incites to the seeing it" (p. 19). "It is pain-pleasure which forces all action" (p. 29).[2]

Personally, I have not found Mr. Stanley's argument convincing. If we are to have any ideas at all upon such hypothetic matters as the character of primitive consciousness, I remain of the belief that the simplest possible consciousness always shows itself to reflection to possess the threefold phases; and that, on *a priori* grounds, every consciousness which is to be serviceable in the struggle for self-conservation must possess something corresponding to these phases. I utterly fail to see how pure, bare pain can be (1) a stimulus at all, or (2) a stimulus to any serviceable action. Pain, as it approaches sheer pain, seems to me always paralyzing, inhibitory as to action. It marks loss of some sort; and the sense of loss, taken *per se*, is anything but stimulating. The doctrine that pain has some specially useful function is due, I think, to the ascetic phases of Christian teaching, and remains as a harmful survival of the Puritanic consciousness,—a sort of offset to the hedonistic phases of Christianity. When pain is stimulating to action, it is so, I think, not immediately, but through the medium of thought or some sensory *quale*. Loss may stop a man in full flood of action, and by causing him to readjust his mental perspective, his sense of values, affect his subsequent action—but not as direct stimulus.

However, it may be said that pain is notoriously associated with writhing movements to relieve it, to escape the painful object, etc. I do not think we are in position to say whether these movements *follow* pain naturally; or whether pain is naturally associated with certain forms of dis-coordinated movements; or whether, again, we have simply found in experience that pain is more bearable as we effect alterations in its quality, and have also found that we can effect this alteration through change of position. A combination of the two latter hypotheses seems to me more likely, but I would not dogmatize. But in any case, where is the evidence that such movements as are "stimulated" by pain are

2    Mr. Stanley's views are the absolute, or generalized, opposite of the James-Lange theory. The latter, however, hardly receives the attention it would seem to require.

serviceable? Blind, formless pain (admitting that it gives rise to action at all) would be bound, we must say, to give rise to blind, formless movements, which, if useful, would be so purely by chance. To rule out all discriminative character from the feeling, while allowing it to the consequent action, is certainly illegitimate. An animal, I should say, had much better trust to the sheer mechanism of his organization in a crisis than have the additional problem of pain to wrestle with; if his actions are to be a matter of chance anyway, I think the chances are more in his favor if he does not have a pain seizure. Introduce differential features into the pain, and the case undoubtedly changes; one pain may be one kind of a signal, and another pain, another kind. But the introduction of this differential *quale* means, of course, something of the same nature as that which in our developed consciousness we call knowledge; differentia falling within content of feeling being the closest analogue we can imagine to our "objective" consciousness. But in this case, the primitive character of mere feeling goes.

It must be remembered that the one phase which has the floor at any or all periods of development, is action corresponding to present volitional consciousness. The organism which can have a "flash of pain" is an organism which already seeks and assimilates food and reproduces its kind. There is not even a question of whether pleasure-pain determines function or *vice versa*; some functional activity, that of the food process, *must* be predicated at the outset, or there is no organism to feel, and no biological point of view to take. It appears much more natural, then, to build up our hypothetic consciousness by reference of feeling to actions performed with reference to food and reproduction, than *vice versa*, especially as this method requires a correlative and contemporaneous "intellectual" development. This, moreover, is quite consonant with what Mr. Stanley says (pp. 62–72) regarding sensations being not original and simple elements of mind, but rather developed forms of some general undifferentiated cognitive state, as apprehension of bodily disturbance. This point of view is one certainly reinforced by all biological considerations, and is fatal to the tendency recently decadent but now very prominent in the

Wundtian school, to build up mind out of sensations as elements.

The type of reaction first discussed by Mr. Stanley deals with feeling due to injury actually experienced. It marks a distinct advance in the evolutionary scale, when the animal can act from feeling which anticipates actual injury. When this stage arrives, there is emotion. Its essential *rationale* is, therefore, its anticipatory function. I remarked before that it is possible to object to Mr. Stanley, not by any means on the ground of his too great use of the evolutionary method, and of biological data, but because he uses them too little. The account of the *rationale* of the origin of emotion just given is obviously biological in type; the account which follows of the mental mechanism involved in this anticipatory function seems to me based wholly on the analysis of a complex and mature human experience. It not only does not grow out of any consideration of biological data, but, for myself, I confess inability to make it square with any image of any type of animal consciousness, unless possibly the just sub-human.

The account runs as follows. Anticipation involves representation. This is something more than mere revival of past experience. It is not simple re-presentation, for that is only presentation over again. It involves *sense* of return. It must be appreciated *as* revival. This would not avail as anticipation, unless there were also *sense* of value for future experience. It is an experience *of* (past) experience and *for* (future) experience. That is, the objectifying of the past experience is not self-contained, but conveys a meaning for experience. Besides, there must be not simply representation of object, but re-feeling of some previous feeling; the representation of object is only subsidiary. But we have not the complete analysis of emotion yet. It is not the revival of feeling, but a new feeling, *sui generis*, created by this complex of revivals, which constitutes emotion. "However we may be puzzled to see how mere cognition of experienceable pain develops a peculiar pain which is the essence of fear, yet we must acknowledge its production to be a fact" (p. 102). An emotion, in fine, is a "feeling reaction from the representation of the feeling potency of the object" (p. 107).

As an analysis of emotion in the human consciousness, this seems to me not only a painstaking, but—barring a criticism now to be made—a fairly successful one. As regards emotion in its present developed state, Mr. Stanley seems to me to fall into the psychologist's fallacy,—he introduces into the emotional experiencing, as its own distinctions, different elements which come out only in the psychologist's reflection. "Object," "feeling of object," and "feeling of this feeling" are differences which we mark out when we look at the emotion critically, not distinctions falling in any sense within its own content. Object is always an ambiguous term; it may mean either the total psychical object, *i.e.*, the content of the entire experience, or it may mean the intellectual, or knowledge-giving, phase of this experience discriminated in afterthought. Surely the real psychical object is not object, cognitive function, *plus* feeling, but is sensory *quale* felt as having such and such a worth, the marking off of subjective and objective sides coming in only as one looks back and retrospectively analyzes the experiencing previously had. The problem of "how cognition of experienceable pain develops a peculiar pain," fear, is, if not settled, at least much simplified by recognizing the difference of these two points of view. It now becomes simply one case of the general problem of the emotional setting attaching to any *quale* of experience.

Taking the problem in this way, and considering the matter not from the standpoint of full-fledged emotion in an adult human being, but from that of early stages of development, Mr. Stanley fails to recognize that the James-Lange theory, taken together with Darwin's theory, affords a complete account of what, on the basis of his own theory, remains an ultimate and inexplicable pure fact. If fear, as feeling, is subsequent to action, the problem is simply to discover the particular differentia of the type of activity under which fear arises.[3] The emotion is accounted for by being placed. But if one feeling arouses another directly, and not through the mediation of action, the genesis of the

[3]    See, for example, my article in the *Psychological Review*, January, 1895 ["The Theory of Emotion," *The Early Works of John Dewey*, IV, 169–88].

particular qualitative experience of fear remains a mystery. We can only bow to the fact. The ultimate contradiction in Mr. Stanley's method, here as elsewhere, is giving a teleological function to psychical values having only a purely blind origin. The feelings continually become more and more important, on one side, as affording the whole evolutionary *nisus*, while, on the other side (that of origin) they become more and more meaningless. The emotion, *after* it is there, has great evolutionary significance; but it has no evolutionary origin.

More in detail, what ground is there for assimilating the animal type of emotional experience to the human? Is not Mr. Stanley's account unduly anthropomorphic? If we are to define emotion as distinctly representative in character, must we not ascribe emotion to all the lower animal forms only by heteronomy? That animals are afraid and angry, etc., in the practical sense of those terms, admits of no doubt: *i.e.*, they *act* afraid, etc. But to insist that the lower animals have not only a revival of a previous object, but in addition a *sense* of revival, and a *sense* of value for future experience in the revival, seems to me to break down all distinctions, in the evolutionary process, between lower and higher stages. Of course an animal which can recognize a re-presentation *as* representation is capable of discriminating image from reality, psychical event from objective function. How an animal can make this conscious distinction between appearance and reality here, and not make it elsewhere and thus build up the whole critical apparatus of science for accurately discriminating between the two, I do not see. In other words, I see no reason whatever (and a good many reasons to the contrary) for supposing any of the animal's revivals are of another type than those which Mr. Stanley calls "hallucinatory." A revival of a past experience can function as a directive or monitory stimulus for the future, simply as a psychical event. All we need is the principle of habit. That this principle sometimes means getting cheated, and is not economical to the fullest degree, is, no doubt, a fact. But certainly the emergence of the human animal has some evolutionary significance, marks some great gain in economy, and the reasonable supposition is that it marks the ability to discriminate between image as psychical occurrence and the reality which that image indicates. I should not dwell upon this point at such length were it not for its connection with the matter of the evolutionary significance of feeling. It is by no means simply a matter of individual preference that Mr. Stanley ascribes this complex character to comparatively primitive emotion. Holding, as he does, the evolutionary *nisus* to be always in feeling, he must find a great change in type of feeling for every great evolutionary advance. That he is compelled to give a representative or consciously ideal character to feeling so far down in development, seems to me perilously near a *reductio ad absurdum* of the part attributed to feeling. Leaving the lower animals out of account, we know enough of emotion in child and savage life to say that all primitive emotion is based on what Mr. Stanley calls the hallucinatory type of revival, and that this type is tremendously effective in action even in relatively complex human societies.

I have covered only a little over one-third of Mr. Stanley's work. The rest of the book discusses desire, attention, self-feeling, feeling and the logical development, the æsthetic and ethical emotions. I need hardly say that one finds careful observation and thoughtful analysis throughout. When one fails to agree, he still receives a valuable service: he is forced to think out reasons for differing, and to define his own position.

I have tried to fulfill the pleasant task of giving a sample of the method and of the conclusions reached, and the less pleasant one of indicating why both seem to me suggestive of the need of another view. I may resume by saying that, as to method, Mr. Stanley appears to me to have attempted to defend, upon the basis of an analysis of a complex adult consciousness, a certain view of the part played by feeling in evolution, rather than an evolutionary discussion of feeling as such; while, as to conclusion, the origin of the different types of feeling is left inexplicable, a teleological function being ascribed to them which it is quite impossible they should possess, severed from connection with discriminative quality and from relation to habits of life. The book suffers throughout, it also appears to me (though I freely admit I may be led astray here by my own special interests and attempted investigations), by failure to recognize the meaning, to say nothing of the claims, of the James-Lange theory taken in connection with Darwin's. This theory, it may be recalled, accounts for the evolution of feelings by reference to habits of use in maintaining life, whether getting food, attack and defense in relation to enemies, or reproduction; and holds that the emotional stress of feeling emerges, when formed habits conflict with the line of action demanded by a changed situation,—when, accordingly, it is necessary to readjust the habit.

In conclusion, I may point out that Mr. Stanley's position pushes the tension, already urgent enough, between the biologist and the psychologist to the breaking point. That pain-pleasure determines function (p. 47); that an animal is not fierce because he possesses claws, but possesses claws, etc., because he is fierce (p. 128); that feeling, indirectly if not directly, produces nerve-structure (p. 376),—these and similar statements, in their present unmediated form, seem to me to make impossible any understanding between the psychologist and the biologist, no matter how open-minded the latter may be. The problem of the place of consciousness in evolution is a hard enough one at best; to assume that mere feeling, as feeling, has been the primal, persistent, and essential factor of evolution, on the biological as well as the psychological side, introduces simplicity only at the expense of an irreconcilable quarrel between the sciences. It is not simply that the individual biologist will not be inclined to accept the doctrine: it means that, as a biologist, he cannot. It is simply to say that the biological process cannot be stated in biological terms. Start with the priority of action, not feeling, and ultimate agreement is at least conceivable. Life-preserving actions being objectively teleological (*i.e.*, in result) it is at least conceivable that *consciousness* of this teleological element should be a distinct advantage. The difficulties in this view are those of detail, not of principle; *i.e.*, it is theoretically possible to state it in biological as well as in psychological terms. Moreover, it is difficult to avoid the conclusion that there is an ambiguity in Mr. Stanley's own treatment. At times we have such statements as the following: "Evolutionary psychology bases itself on the idea that mental development originates and is continued through struggle, or will-effort." First, this is ambiguous, because it is not easy to tell in what relation it stands to the doctrine of the primitive character of feeling. It is one thing to say that will-effort comes first and is painful, and another to say that pain initiates will-activity. Second, it is not possible to tell what is meant by will-effort, when the term is used in this unanalyzed way. If it is set up as a faculty by itself, the statement needs very close scrutiny. If it means that the nodal points of psychical development come when life habits which are objectively useful have to be readjusted, and are thus differentiated or mediated, the doctrine appears to be identical with that which I have already positively stated; but such a doctrine demands a large reconstruction of many other positions taken in the book.

*Studies of Childhood*, by James Sully. New York: D. Appleton and Co., 1896.

This book is a series of topical or classified studies of certain phases of the psychology of child life, covering, upon the whole, the period of life from two to six years of age, with quite a marked preference for those phenomena which dawn or are at their height in the second and third years. The topics covered are: The imagination of childhood; its reasonings, including a study both of the process and the more marked and characteristic processes; the beginnings of language; the emotion of fear; some phenomena of morality, including a study of children's egoism, altruism, lies, and an account of their reactions to the moral injunctions of their elders; and a study of the child's æsthetic nature as manifested in his instinctive expressions and in his primitive drawings. The book concludes with a detailed individual study (covering about 100 pages) of one of his own children; and a very interesting study of the childhood of George Sand, drawn from the latter's autobiography. In

[*First published in* Science, *n.s.* IV (*Oct.* 1896), 500–502. *Not previously reprinted.*]

this connection it may be remarked that a distinct feature of the book is not only the author's own style, which is literary rather than "scientific," but his wide acquaintance with auto-biographical allusions to childhood and his apt use of such reminiscences. Ruskin, Dickens, Quinet, Tolstoi, Stevenson and many others figure in these pages.

This topical character of the treatment practically makes any synopsis of the book, beyond such a bare scheduling of headings, out of the question. An immense number of relevant observations of childhood, gathered from practically all available sources, supplemented by Mr. Sully's own observations, and enlivened by judicious remarks upon the salient qualities of childhood, make the book what it is. The hypercritical will probably conceive that the running commentary is sometimes discursive, occasionally dangerously near the padding point, and frequently of no great importance. But I confess myself sufficiently grateful in finding a book to review which is interesting to read as well as technically instructive.

The impossibility of summarizing the material content of the book makes it advisable to direct attention to the method, both what Mr. Sully himself says about method and that which he actually employs. As to the former, Mr. Sully devotes considerable space in his introduction to the objects and difficulties of child-study, and to an account of the equipment necessary for observation and interpretation. The interest in child-study he finds to be partly due to the general development of natural science and partly to specifically psychological needs. The infant is, so to speak, more obviously a natural phenomenon than the adult; and the evolutionist in particular finds in him obvious signs of close kinship with the animal world, both in the fœtal and early post-fœtal stages. The ethnologist also finds in the child a summary of the prehistoric development of the race. To the psychologist the opportunities of escape from the interwoven complexities of the adult consciousness make this a promised land of science. Yet the difficulty even with the reference to the outward phenomenon is very great; witness the difficulties in identifying the first smile of the child, his first sign of recognition, his first conscious attempt in any direction. And, of course, the difficulty is still greater when we come to interpret these movements into their psychical equivalents. These difficulties are so great that the author "confesses that in spite of some recently published highly hopeful forecasts of what child-psychology is going to do for us, I think we are a long way off from a perfectly scientific account of it"; a remark to which no one will take exception if there is much emphasis upon the "perfectly."

There are two qualities necessary for good work. The first is the "divining power," sympathetic insight, tact or fineness of spiritual insight. This is required both for such rapport with children as to establish the conditions for natural, unconstrained exhibition of genuine phenomena, and for interpretation. (Mr. Sully's own work, I remark in passing, shows a very unusual amount of such native divining tact and personal sympathy.) There is danger, however, that the very liveliness of this touch with child life will take off the edge from close, objective, systematic study of the bare, cold facts. Hence the second requirement, good psychological training. Fathers, Mr. Sully thinks, are more apt to come short as regards the first of these qualifications; mothers as regards the second.

As concerns method in general most is to be expected from the prolonged observation of individual children such as is represented by the work of Preyer and Miss Shinn. Mr. Sully's remarks here are so much to the point as to justify quotation in full. "No fact is really quite simple, and the reason why some facts look so simple is that the observer does not include in his view all the connections of the occurrence which he is inspecting. . . . It is only when the whole fact is before us, in well-defined contour, that we can begin to deal with its meaning." And of course, this wholeness of the fact presupposes knowledge of the individual child, his environment, history, temperament, etc. When we come to older children this specific individual study may be supplemented by more general and statistical collections.

All this seems to me well and judiciously put. Mr. Sully's own work in the pages which follow bears evidence throughout that he realizes practically, as well as theoretically, the limitations, the problems and the needs of which he has been talking. Nevertheless, there are reasons for holding that this book will be to the psychologist, at least, rather "raw materials to serve" than a contribution to psychology as such.

It is possible to go at the study of the child with the purpose of arranging the observed phenomena under the customary rubrics of psychology, laying emphasis upon extreme exhibitions of principles which are discernible only feebly or subtly in the adult, or upon the phenomena which mark departures from the forms which are familiar in the adult consciousness. Here, however, unconsciously, *the adult consciousness as already analyzed is taken as the standard.* Another method treats the child consciousness as, if I may use the expression, perfectly good consciousness on its own account, just as good consciousness as the adult. The interest is wholly in the light which such consciousness may throw upon psychical principles in general. The aim is not to classify the phenomena under principles already accepted, but to reconstruct those principles from the study of facts hitherto neglected. Mr. Sully's actual procedure seems to me to adopt the first named course. He rarely uses the new facts to criticize and modify the customary classifications and explanations, but rather takes these latter for granted and crowds the observations under them—with some projecting edges.

As an example, we may take his theoretical treatment of imagination in childhood. After making a good beginning by remarking that "imagination in an active, constructive form takes part in the very making of what we call sense-experience," he goes on to give cases of the personification of inanimate objects in perception, and takes up the argument as follows: "Now, it may be asked whether all this analogical extension of imagery to what seem to us such incongruous objects involves a vivid and illusory apprehension of these as transformed. . . . A conjectural answer can be given. In this imaginative contemplation of things the child but half observes what is present to his eyes, one or two points only of supreme interest in the visible thing, whether those of form, as in assimilating the piano-hammer to the owl, or of action as the *falling* of the leaf, being selectively alluded to, while assimilative imagination overlaying the visual impression with the image of a similar object does the rest. In this way the actual field of objects is apt to get veiled, transformed by the wizard touch of a lively fancy."

Now, from the standpoint of a certain psychology, the customary one, this is very well said. But it merely assumes, without questioning, two things which the facts discussed are well adapted to make us question: the "actual field of objects," "what is present to the eyes" on one side and the imagination or fancy, as some sort of distinct power on the other. But is not this somewhat naïve? Is this reference to the "actual field of objects" anything more than making the special constructions of the adult consciousness, made from the standpoint of its supreme interests, the fixed standard? Is the problem how and why the child overlays the things present to his eyes with fanciful unrealities one of his own inner being? Or is it why and how the growing consciousness gradually shears down the original experience, inhibiting the larger part of the interests which determined it, and gradually confines itself to one or two definite ends and habits in selecting the qualities which shall constitute the world of things? In a word, is the child object the adult ("or real") object with an overplus of fanciful fringe, or is the adult object the child object pared down and rearranged to meet the dominant needs of mature life—one being just as "real" as the other in an abstract or metaphysical sense?

I do not mean to affirm that Mr. Sully is wrong in choosing the former alternative. But the fact that he has adopted it without considering there is an alternative, indicates to my mind that, for the most part, he is just classifying the new scientific material under the old headings, instead of remaking the point of view.

From the standpoint of the scientific psychologist this is an important qualification regarding Mr. Sully's work. Quite probably, however, it fits the book all the better for the task of mediating between the psychologist and the public of parents and teachers into whose hands the book will fall; and, as there are many signs that this is the end the book has in view, it is a pleasure to add that it fulfills this particular purpose better than anything as yet published upon child psychology. A good index adds materially to the usability of the book.

## Harris's *Psychologic Foundations of Education*[1]

The title of **Dr.** Harris's new book, *Psychologic Foundations of Education*, taken apart from its sub-title and from the Preface, is perhaps liable to misinterpretation—such a misinterpretation as, giving one a false impression of its purpose, might lead to misconception of its contents. The title perhaps most naturally suggests an attempt to derive education as an organized system of discipline, of subject-matter, and of methods of instruction, from certain psychological premises. But this is not what **Dr.** Harris attempts. The aim of the book is better indicated in the following quotation from its Preface: "It is an attempt to show the psychological foundation of the more important *educational factors* in civilization and its schools." It is the psychology, then, of the factors which are presupposed by education and which enter into it, rather than the psychology of the educational process as such, which is the chief concern of **Dr.** Harris.

These factors are of two chief types. On the one hand, since the great thing in education is growth or development of the individual, it is important to be able to see how the lower powers of knowing and acting develop into the higher activities. Hence the sub-title: "An Attempt to Show the Genesis of the Higher Faculties of the Mind." If one is ignorant "of the way in which higher faculties re-enforce the lower, he will attempt to cultivate them isolatedly, and he will generally produce arrested development of the mind in the lower stages of its activities or faculties and prevent the further intellectual growth of his pupils during their lives." The other type of factors is concerned with the psychology of civilization, particularly with such relations of the individual to society as enable the individual to participate in the spiritual life of the race. With relation to the first sort of

1      New York: D. Appleton and Co., 1898.

[*First published in* Educational Review, XVI (*June 1898*), 1–14. *Not previously reprinted.*]

factors, Dr. Harris contrasts his view with that of the "faculty psychology," which inventories certain mental powers regarded as ultimate and independent, and which conceives of educational psychology as a series of prescriptions for cultivating these separate powers—failing to see the continued genesis of the higher out of the lower and the reaction of the higher to transform the lower. With regard to the second type of factors, he contrasts his view with that purely individualistic psychology which ignores the educative agency of institutions of art and religion, of play and work, of national life, etc., upon the individual.

It is obvious accordingly that teachers should go to Dr. Harris's book for culture and enlargement of spirit rather than for specific psychological analysis of correct modes of educational procedure. What they should expect to get from it is a deeper insight into the underlying forces and principles which make education what it is in aim and spirit. Its value consists in the avenues of insight which it opens into the larger issues of life both individual and social. Those acquainted with the past multifarious activities of its distinguished author will see that it combines the two main lines of thought to which Dr. Harris has for so long a time devoted himself. It gives us on one side the ripe fruits of his continuous study of speculative philosophy under the guidance of the great German masters; and on the other, the net results of the study of education as an administrative system and its relations to other social institutions, as practically participated in by the author. It would not be difficult for one to trace the development of part of the book from the earlier thought of Dr. Harris as published in the *Journal of Speculative Philosophy*, and of another part from the reports, almost simultaneously issued, of Dr. Harris as superintendent of the St. Louis school system.

The author himself divides the book into three parts, the first termed: Psychologic Method; the second, Psychologic System; and the third, Psychologic Foundations; but since Dr. Harris explains that Parts I and II go over practically the same ground, first unsystematically, simply to develop the various points of view involved, and then in a more rigid and complete system, it will be found practically convenient to disregard this order and arrange the exposition and criticism under the following heads: first, his general psychologic presuppositions and standpoint; second, his social psychology, and, third, the application to education.

Dr. Harris's fundamental and all-pervasive principle is that of self-activity or self-determination. Self-activity involves the idea of a real totality or systematic whole. It is marked off from things or objects as isolated, and also from the causal connections of interaction which bind various objects together. The conception of such a whole is bound up in both the common-sense knowing of particular objects and the scientific knowing of causal connections. Both things and relations presuppose the whole to which they belong and within which they have existence and efficacy. Since this ultimate principle is the total, it must be conceived of as the originator of the action and interaction going on between the beings which constitute it. The change which is found in the parts can be accounted for only with reference to the causal and creative energy which resides in the whole. Such an original source of energy forms what we call will, personality, or self-consciousness. A self-active whole can be defined only as a subject which is its own object and thus as reason.

Such a self-conscious personality acts under the law of freedom. The principle of causation in the sense of external determination, necessity, or fate, holds only between the various parts and phenomenal manifestations which enter into the total. Their lack of freedom is simply the exhibition of their dependence; a thing, as distinct from a person, is simply a transmitter, not a source of energy. It is the very nature of absolute personality to manifest itself in finite personalities, which reproduce its form and participate in its content and thus tend toward similar creative freedom. The lowest stage of such self-activity is found in plants; for plants attack and assimilate the environment and in all their activities aim at the realization of their own type as an end. The animal exhibits a still higher form of self-activity; for locomotion is a more adequate mode of subordinating the environment than is mere nutritive appropriation. Moreover in feeling, the end, self-development, comes in a crude way to consciousness of itself; and in feeling the environment is ideally reproduced or made over from the standpoint of the needs and interests of the animal organism. The feeling is both intellect and will in germ. The principle of self-activity as it emerges in more adequate form out of feeling, at the same time elevating the latter, gives rise to memory, to language and conception, and finally to reason, which not merely objectively manifests the principle of self-activity, but consciously recognizes it as the essence both of the soul and of the world of reality. In evolution to this point of self-recognition we have the human personality with its distinguishing characteristics of will and intellect. Its power of knowing itself or of seizing upon self-activity in any of its manifestations, Dr. Harris calls introspection.

This is, then, the philosophical basis of psychology which consists, through the method of introspection, in tracing the involution and evolution of the mental powers from the lowest form of self-activity, feeling, up to the highest, reason and will. To facilitate this evolution is the aim of education. Hence the close connection between the psychology of the genesis of the higher powers and an insight into the nature of education. Besides this pure, or introspective, psychology, we have, however, in addition, the so-called new psychology which studies the relations of mind and body, termed physiological psychology, and child-study. While rational psychology studies the constitution of mind as such, and is thus intrinsically an investigation of self-consciousness, the latter deals with the natural and animal conditions within which the spiritual being operates, tending to enthrall or arrest him in his development. Child-study, in particular, is said to find its most profitable field of investigation in the study of arrested development, because it will reveal the danger of fixing in rigid habit any form of activity which belongs to a lower stage. Physiological psychology simply studies the correlation of mental phenomena with bodily changes. In this connection Dr. Harris gives a *résumé*, occupying two chapters, of some results of this science concerning localization of function in the brain—a summary in which he has unfortunately relied too much upon the ingenious but doubtful speculations of Luys and which do not, as they stand, appear to serve any particular purpose.

If I may be allowed a word of criticism, I should say that this position suffers quite materially from an almost total ignoring of what is most characteristic in the great psychological renaissance now going on. Take the matter of child-study, for example: why should it be limited largely to the negative and pathological sides, to arrested development? Why is not this in reality quite secondary to the positive side, the study of the facts and principles of mental growth? The more we agree with Dr. Harris that the chief matter, both in psychology and in education, is growth in rational insight and in power of volitional control, the more genetic psychology, as a study of the actual normal facts of such growth, becomes a necessary means to any adequate psychological statement. Genetic psychology, instead of being set over against rational psychology, thus becomes a necessary instrument for translating the more or less vague, abstract, and nominal propositions of the latter, into concrete and realizable form. Of course we are far enough from an attainment of this ideal, but surely this is the point of view from which to regard it. The same is true in principle of physiological psychology. Those who conceive this as simply an effort to correlate physical and psychical phenomena are certainly now few in number. Its interest lies rather in its affording a method of approach to the investigation and interpretation of psychical phenomena for their own sake. Here too, then, the barrier which Dr. Harris seems inclined to set up between rational psychology as an account of the development of spiritual being, and physiological psychology as merely an account of the material conditions of this development, breaks down. Physiological psychology, so-called, becomes simply a definite and controllable method of getting at psychical development itself.

What shall be said of the great field of modern psychology as pursued by contemporary exponents, a field certainly falling within neither physiological psychology nor child-study in any limited sense of these terms? How shall we account for Dr. Harris's complete ignoring of this field? It is certainly neither empirical in the old sense of that term, occupied simply with observing and inventorying a mass of mere facts, nor yet is it rational in the sense of being simply a logical analysis of the general concepts of self-activity, soul, feeling, reason, will, etc. Indeed its essential characteristic is that it attempts to combine the two points of view, to get rid of the abstract dualism involved in setting it up. It is an effort to determine, from the standpoint of the concrete examination of a tremendous variety and complexity of material, the essential principles of the development of psychical life. At one moment the biological, at another the physiological, or the experimental, or the child-study, or the pathological, or the "empirical" (in the old sense) aspect may be uppermost; but in any case these are simply methods or modes of approach to the central principle of origin and growth. All this industry, which is really the distinguishing characteristic of psychology as pursued today, whether in Germany, France, England, or this country, cannot be lightly waved one side. It is indeed quite true that some of its followers here and there—but these much less numerous and influential than one might suppose—conceive of their method and results in a more or less materialistic and mechanical way, and oppose them to the interests of a spiritual philosophy. But I am willing to venture the prophecy that in the long run the concerns of the latter may be entrusted most safely to the hands of psychological science as it is now developing itself; that this will be the great means of translating the chief points of view and results of the former into specific, clearly realizable forms, capable of being set forth in terms of our common language without recourse to the technical terminology of transcendentalists; and that, excepting as the idealistic philosophy does reinforce and vivify itself in this way, it will become more and more scholastic and arbitrary, degenerating into the barren explication of certain formal general categories. And particularly for an educator, would I suggest that this translation and interpretation are necessary. The perception of merely general principles remains comparatively barren and inert for practice. It is only too easy to yield a pious assent to the principles in their general form and at the same time in matters of practice to adhere to empirical rule of thumb and purely traditional routine, or be at the mercy of the catch devices of the educational sciolist. What is most needed in education is, I take it, the connecting links, the intermediate terms lying between the formal general principles and the specific details—a connection which will make the former workable while it illuminates and emancipates the latter. And I do not believe that these connecting links can be found except in a psychology conceived in a somewhat more experimental and less purely rationalistic form than that of Dr. Harris.

Limits of space compel me now to pass on to Dr. Harris's social psychology and to the matter of educational application, omitting unfortunately the specific psychology of Dr. Harris's treatment of perception and the various forms of the syllogism involved in it, of recollection and memory, conception, etc. It is community life, participation in the organized and continuous resources of civilization, which alone enables the individual to realize the high capacities which are latent in him. As mere individual, man cannot ascend above savagery. As an individual he is an insignificant affair, as social whole he constitutes a living miracle. It is through social relations that the individual emerges from his animal and natural state and becomes really a spiritual being. In social combination the individual recognizes and comes to work for the aims which he has in common with others. Every such co-operative effort eliminates something of the exclusiveness and selfishness embodied in the natural constitution of man, and brings him nearer recognition of, and communion with, the true personality which is universal. Family, school, civil society, state, and the Church are exemplifications of such common aims and labors, and so each has its distinctively ethical and educative reaction into the development of the individual.

Dr. Harris conceives family, civil society, and the state as secular forms of combination, while æsthetic art, religion, and science, embodied in the invisible Church, are the spiritual. The secular institutions provide man with the means of living and protect and defend him against physical violence and suffering. The spiritual have for their end the evolution of man's absolute ideal and the elevation of the natural individual into participation in the life of the social whole, so that he achieves independence of the temporal and finite and comes to live a divine life. This distinction, both in terminology and in substance, seems to mark a somewhat unfortunate relapse into the dualism between the natural and the spiritual characteristic of the Middle Ages. When we consider either the facts or the theory of the matter, it certainly seems forced to deny spiritual content and function to the family. And while, superficially considered, industrial society might be regarded simply as a mechanism for contributing to the physical comfort and well-being of man; more deeply considered, invention and commerce are chief instrumentalities which spiritual culture has had to rely upon for its general propagation and diffusion. It is, I think, Dr. Harris himself who has spoken of the newspaper, which certainly arises in the play of industrial life, as an organ of the spirit, in bringing home to each individual the consciousness of the larger life in which he plays a part. If we were to eliminate from man's present consciousness of social interdependence and interaction all that has been put there through development of industry and commerce, we certainly should have a great hole left. But it is difficult to tell how far Dr. Harris means to have this dualism pressed. He tells us that the ethical element must be regarded as essential to all institutions; and that the forms of spiritual combination—art, religion, and science—are to be looked upon as underlying and conditioning even the secular institutions of man. If this thought were worked out, it seems to me the distinction made between the secular and the spiritual would largely disappear.

In his historic psychology of nations, Dr. Harris finds a spiritual factor in present civilization derived from Greece, Rome, and Judea respectively. Greece educates all modern nations in forms of art and literature. Rome educates men on the side of will in the limitations of its modes of expression so as to prevent collision of the individual with the social whole. We owe to the Hebrew insight into the nature of the Absolute as a person and as essentially out-going love in nature, being interested in all finite personalities and in lifting them up toward his own absolute truth and righteousness.

We then have a chapter on the psychology of play and crime considered as reactions against the social order. Education is the process of adoption of the social order in place of one's mere animal caprice. In work and in political organization, the individual surrenders his particular nature to the social order, but in play full reign is given to individual caprice, whim, and private inclination. Festivals and games are to be considered as reversals of the movement from the individual to the social; they are methods of recovering the sense of particular freedom. In play, however, the serious recognition of social order remains as something substantial underneath the mass. But when the reaction against the social order is fixed it becomes crime.

We come now to the more specific educational application. Each institution has its own educative function, in that it lifts the individual out of his animal condition toward a realization of a spiritual potentiality, by filling the latter with the content elaborated and conserved in the development of humanity as a whole. The school is to be considered simply as one of these educative institutions. It arises when the child's interest centres on learning the ways of society outside of the family. Its object is to initiate him into the technicalities of intercommunication with his fellow-men and to familiarize him with the ideas that underlie civilization, and which he must use as tools of thought if he would observe and understand the phases of human life around him. This idea is amplified through application to the various stages of school life and through the study of the materials of the course of study.

As the child passes out of the imitative period of his development and gets the use of language and has acquired a certain amount of knowledge of the external world, he arrives at the capacity of seeing universals, of feeling ideal possibilities, and of acting for their realization. The child now passes into the symbolic period, where objects and images are used to embody and convey thoughts and values not capable of being imaged in themselves. It marks, as it were, the transition of the sense period to the thought period. Educationally speaking, this is the kindergarten period.

After the symbolic period comes the conventional, generally reached at the age of seven. The child is now conscious of himself as an individual having special duties and labors of his own. He thus needs the instruments of self-help; he needs to master the conventionalities of human learning, he needs to learn how to read and write and how to record the results of arithmetic. Here we have the elementary stage of school education, whose purpose is to gain command of the conventionalities of intelligence—the various instrumentalities which enable the child to get access to the intellectual conquests of the race. Its course of study deals chiefly with giving the child a mastery over the symbols of reading, writing, and arithmetic, and the technical words in which are expressed the distinctions of arithmetic, geography, grammar, and history. Moreover, this stage of education takes the child mainly at the first stage of knowing; that is, when he can perceive, for the most part, only isolated things or objects, not relations or causal principles. Hence it takes the world of human learning in fragments; it fails to give insight into the interrelation of things.

Secondary education, beginning about fourteen, begins to see things and events as parts of processes, to deal with more essential relations and with forces and laws. The child turns from occupation with dead results and comes to the investigation of the living process of production. Higher education is based on the third stage of knowing. It teaches the unity of human learning. It shows how all branches form a connected whole, and what each contributes to the explanation of others. It enables him to see the function of each study, then, in the totality of spiritual experience. In doing this it makes learning really ethical; it shows the bearing of the study on the conduct of life, thus converting knowledge into wisdom.

As regards the subject-matter, we must recognize five co-ordinate groups of studies. All of these groups must be represented at each stage of education. The psychology of these five groups of study is found in the somewhat metaphorical concept of five windows to the soul, opening out on five great divisions of the life of man. Through two of these windows the soul looks out upon nature: one including mathematics and physics, the formal or time-and-space aspect of nature; the other, upon the actual scene of nature, the world in its forms—natural history, or biology and geography. The other three windows look out upon various aspects of human life. History surveys the exhibition of the will of mankind. Language and grammar embody the structural framework of the intellect. Literature sums up all the inner life of the people, the identity between its aspirations and ideals, and its acts, whether in overt deeds, or in its interpretations of life.

In conclusion, I can only suggest certain doubts and queries which arise in my mind, both with reference to this philosophy of the stages of the school system, and of the various groups of study. I should not question that, upon the whole, Dr. Harris's theory of elementary, secondary, and higher education is a fair statement of existing practice. Indeed, I should say that it displays a very remarkable insight and power of formulation (characteristic of Dr. Harris in all his dealings with concrete subject-matter) in laying bare the inner rationale of our present organization. But when laid bare with such succinctness, its inherent defects appear only the more clearly revealed. That the period of elementary education shall long continue to be regarded as centering about the technical symbols of intercommunication, eked out with fragmentary bits of information concerning the world of nature and of man, seems to me incredible. All that is most vital and progressive in existing elementary education is moving away from these traditions, in the direction of introducing positive and first-hand contact with the realities of experience, as distinct from the mere symbols of knowledge, and toward more positive spiritual content. Under these circumstances, I deplore greatly that Dr. Harris should throw his deservedly great authority in the direction of what seems unduly conservative or even reactionary.

I doubt very much if the psychological justification which Dr. Harris lays down for his doctrine, that of the three stages of knowledge, will hold as it is here applied. It is very doubtful, both as matter of theory and of observable fact, whether the first attitude and interest of the mind are in things as isolated, or in unrelated detail. As Dr. Harris himself frequently recognizes, the act of isolation is essentially one of abstraction. It involves the beginnings of reflection. As he says about the child in the symbolic period, the early phase of mind is synthetic rather than analytic. The interest at this period is decidedly in wholes as wholes; the fragment as such, the isolated, is decidedly repellent and irritating. It is the scene, the situation, the story that attracts and holds. Details are ignored save as they carry out the meaning and spirit of the whole. The early mental attitude of the child is in a way closely akin to philosophic interest. It is of course crude and naïve; but the natural bent of attention is toward function, aim, moving spirit, rather than toward particulars. Observation of particulars as particulars, the movement toward isolation and definition, is a counterpart of the movement of the mind toward the discovery of interrelation and mutual dependence. Interest in seizing the particular as such, and interest in grasping the universal process as such, are two poles of the same operation of reflection. Instead of going from particulars through interrelation up to wholes, the mind moves from the apprehension of vague wholes, through correlative specification and generalization, to systematized wholes. The first period of education would therefore have for its aim to bring the child, not in contact with fragments, but with typical large experiences of humanity, taken in outline and with reference to their pervasive spirit. It is fortunate that the congruence between theory and right practice is so great; but if there were not this natural agreement, one might almost say that the purpose of the elementary school would be to counteract the tendency toward isolation and premature specialization upon technical symbols. It would be intolerable in a democratic country to have ninety-five per cent of children shut off for the most part from ethical content and from the influences which tend to convert information into wisdom, reserving this latter just for the élite who are able to go to college.

A few words now regarding the classification of school studies. Does not co-ordination involve systematic interrelation? Is it co-ordination to set up five groups of study in a row, side by side; or does co-ordination mean that a functional unity is present with reference to which any of the particular groups represents simply a division of labor which can be fulfilled only as it is kept in the most organic relations with every other? Or, from the practical side, how can geography and history be separated from each other, without depriving the former of its main source of interest, and the latter of its articulating framework? In elementary education at least, are not mathematics and physics comparatively barren abstractions excepting as related not simply to each other, but to the constructive processes of the individual and of society? Is it not somewhat artificial to make grammar and language studies the chief repository of the structure of the intellect, to the neglect of that magnificent logical apparatus exhibited in modern scientific modes of investigation and verification? Can the average child best lay hold of and realize the laws of reason through a study of a relatively dead product in language, or through their constant personal use in the discovery and statement of truth? While it is impossible to overestimate the spiritual dependence of the individual upon society, does not Dr. Harris somewhat ignore the extent to which democratic society, with the resources of modern science at command, can put into the hands of the individual the *methods* by which the spiritual interests of society are conserved, and thus emancipate him very largely from the necessity of immediate dependence upon its *products*? If this be true, would not practical acquaintance with processes, even from the very first, demand relatively a larger sphere of importance as compared with information about products? These questions will indicate some of the directions from which it seems to me the educational theory and practice of the future will tend to modify and revise, not only Dr. Harris's valuation of the respective subjects, but his conception of their relationships to each other.

More than any other one person who could be named in our educational world, Dr. Harris stands for the doctrine laid down in his book that philosophy, as a "view of wholes," and practical action stand in the most intimate relations to each other; that every science must put on a philosophic form before it becomes useful in practical life. This combination of philosophy and practice is the key to Dr. Harris's work. This book is itself a monument to this conviction which has found expression with **Dr.** Harris not simply in theoretic form, but in his continued endeavor in all directions to make philosophy applicable to the guidance of life, and to bring practical life within the grasp of that consciousness of unity which is the essence of philosophic thought.

*Social and Ethical Interpretations in Mental Development: A Study in Social Psychology*, by James Mark Baldwin. New York: Macmillan Co., 1897.

Professor Baldwin's book is extraordinarily ample in the range of ground covered and extremely full of incidental observation and reflection in each particular point. The impossibility of adequate notice of all features, as well as the intrinsic importance of the concepts of the individual and society in relation to each other, compel me accordingly to confine attention to the latter point. In order to be as succinct as possible, as well as to give the reader command of what seems to me the keys to both the strong and the weak points of Mr. Baldwin's discussion, I will reverse the ordinary procedure, and commence by stating what I have found to be the chief difficulty in his position, and the general character of the confusion which seems to me to be bound up in his statement of it.

In an examination of the sort attempted by Professor Baldwin, there are two possible points of view. One examines the individual from the standpoint of psychical process and determines how far this process is social in its genesis and function. The point of interest here is in the quality of the process as psychical; in itself as psychical it is individual; indeed, it *is* the individual as conscious. The social aspect of the question is found in determining whether the significance, the import of this process, judged with reference to the conditions which initiate it and the results which it effects, is social or not. This seems to me the most natural interpretation (as well as the most legitimate and fruitful

[*First published in* Philosophical Review, VII (*July 1898*), 398–409. *Not previously reprinted.*]

point of view intrinsically) of Mr. Baldwin's statement that his method "inquires into the psychological development of the human individual in the earlier stages of his growth for light upon his social nature, and also upon the social organization in which he bears a part" (p. 2).

The other point of view would examine, not into the process, but into the content of the individual's experience, and would endeavor to discover what elements in this content he has in common with other individuals, what factors seem to be characteristically his own, and what the import of these two groups of contents may be. There is no doubt of the importance of this latter inquiry, but it seems to me a sociological rather than a psychological one. Its worth is in throwing light upon the particular type of social organization or institution which is under discussion. In any event the two sorts of problems, that concerning process and that concerning content, are quite distinct, and the failure to put clearly to one's self which problem it is he is endeavoring to solve, can result only in confusion. Mr. Baldwin seems to me to take the latter point of view when he says that his thesis "falls into two main inquiries: What are the principles which the individual shows in his mental life . . . and what additional principles, if any, does society exhibit?" (p. 1). This seems also to be what he has in mind when he speaks of the "psychological development of the individual examined for light upon the social elements and movements of his nature" (p. 2). The latter phrase, however, seems to contain just the ambiguity in mind. So far as one is simply looking for social elements in the individual, I do not see any particular sense in the qualifying phrase "psychological."

The bearing of the distinction may be seen from the following considerations. From the standpoint of content as the final criterion, we should be obliged to say that the social nature of the individual ceased as soon as the elements in his experience ceased to be identical with those of his fellows. The common elements would define his sociality; the unlike elements, his individuality. But from the standpoint of process all this would be a matter of relative indifference; it is conceivable that the whole process simply as such is individual, while in its *raison d'être*, genesis, and outcome it is social. Moreover, if we take the standpoint of content, the question arises: What is the import of the consciousness of personality, and how does the sense of personality differentiate into consciousness of self on one side and of others on the other? The mere presence of identical and unlike elements is quite a different thing from the sense of community, and from the sense of individual selfhood as attributed to one's self or to others. This is clearly recognized when Mr. Baldwin says that the question is: "What is in consciousness when one thinks of himself or of another person?" And again: "To get such inquiries down to a psychological basis the first requisite to be reached is the concept of the person. Not the person as we look at him in action, alone, or chiefly; but the person as he thinks of himself" (p. 13). I do not see that this inquiry has anything to do with the matter of common content as between different individuals. It is simply a question of discovering the conditions which determine the sense of personality. The criterion for the social or non-social character of the latter will consist in the detection of the situation under which it arises and the part which it plays. I do not find anywhere in Mr. Baldwin's book a clear recognition of the two possible meanings of "sense of personality"; the one sense in which it means awareness of the particular contents which as matter of fact make up the person at a given time, and the other, the sense of personality *qua* personality. The former is a matter which will concern simply the onlooker, the scientific observer and investigator. The latter alone is personality to the individual himself, and hence is alone strictly psychological.

I do not mean that Mr. Baldwin does not recognize and take account of both these points of view; I mean simply that his results seem to be vague, ambiguous, and often flatly contradictory, because of unconscious shifting about from one to the other. From the point of view which I have termed that of content, there is no psychological derivation of the concepts of conscious personality, of conscious sociality, or of conscious placing of the one with reference to the other. Society is regarded as there; the individual is regarded as there; and the inquiry is simply into the give and take between the two. Such an inquiry is interesting and important, but, I must repeat, it is not in so far a psychological inquiry at all. When we want to know how the sense of individuality develops psychically, it is no answer to say: through the assimilation of social elements, that is, of contents derived from other personalities. This would give us the social or objective differences between John Smith and Peter Robinson, but it throws absolutely no light on the other question of how the sense of personality and of individuality originate and grow. On the other side, we want to know about the process of social growth and are told that social factors constitute and influence the individual; here society is taken for granted. In other words, when we want to know about the individual we are referred to society; when we want to know about society we are referred to the individual. Both concepts are assumed, not explained or derived.

It may be said that this does Mr. Baldwin injustice, because he insists upon precisely this point himself: "I do not see in short how the personality of this child can be expressed in any but social terms; nor how, on the other hand, social terms can get any content of value but from the understanding of a developing individual. This is a circle of definition of course, and that is just my point. On the one hand we can get no doctrine of society, but by getting the psychology of the socius with all its natural history; and, on the other hand, we can get no true view of the socius at any time without describing the social conditions under which he normally lives with the history of their action and reaction upon him" (p. 21).

Apart from the fact that an author's recognition of the circle into which he has fallen, while it does credit to his candor, does not eliminate the contradiction, such a statement does not modify the conclusion that while we set out to learn something about the structure and growth of society through studying the individual, we arrive simply at a statement that society is already there influencing the individual who is also equally taken for granted. As a negative result on the sociological side, that is, as against those who would assert individuals independent of society or society independent of psychical individuals, the discovery of this interdependence is of value. But once more, I do not see that we know any more of the psychology of the sense of personality and of society than we did before.

More, however, is true than this. Mr. Baldwin's method in simply sending us from society to the individual, and from the individual to society, fails as matter of fact to establish even this interdependence. It leaves us where we began with society *and* individual, *and* a reciprocal influence of each on the other.

This comes out first very clearly in his statement of the relation of social "matter" and "process" to each other. Mr. Baldwin says (pp. 478, 479) that while imitation is the true type of social function, it fails signally as a complete explanation of society, since it gives no answer to the question of matter. "The case of imitation at its purest is just the case in which the social vanishes." But when we come to discuss the "matter" (pp. 487–88) we are told that this consists of thoughts which originate in the mind of the individuals of the group. "At their origin there is no reason for calling them social matter, since they are particular to the individual. They become social only when society—that is the other members of the social group, or some of them—also thinks them."[1] This occurs through imitation. How a matter which is not itself social can become socialized through a process which is not social either, I do not see. The denial of sociality to the individual as such (that is, as distinct from certain elements of content which he finally takes on) is even more explicit in the following quotation: "The child must grow up to be an individual. That is incumbent on him at all hazards, what more he may attain in the way of being a good or wise or social individual, is based on this first presupposition" (p. 290).

Yet (p. 507) it is stated that the thought of self is dependent upon a twofold imitation; in one of which the individual understands the social copy by imitation; and by the other of which "he confirms his interpretation by another

[1] Notice here the unconscious postulating of the very thing to be explained, namely, society, the social group with its members, etc. Were it not for this unconscious assumption, we should have an absolutely numerical individualistic view. The thought of the individual in itself is not social; but other individuals come to think in the same way and then there is society!

imitative[2] act by which he ejectively reads his self-thought into the persons of others." And (pp. 494, 495) it is expressly stated that the thought which is available for purposes of social organization (*via* the broad gauge track of imitation), is not thought as private or particular at all; but "the sort of thought which the individual thinks when he reaches his sense of social situations as functions of his thought of himself"—which would seem to mean that the only thought-material which becomes content for social organization is thought which already is a social interpretation! The verbal, or even the logical, contradiction is a comparatively slight matter; what is important for us is that this contradiction arises from the shifting about of two points of view. According to one, the individual is non-social till some identity of content can be set up between him and other non-social individuals. According to the other, we have an individual already socialized in a social group or situation of which his thoughts are interpretations. According to the former point, it is difficult to see how there can be any *sense* of sociality at all. Identity of content in intrinsically different persons is certainly a different matter from sense of personality as social. From the latter point of view, this difficulty vanishes, simply because society as constituted of individuals, and individuals as constituting society, are taken as already there; the thoughts of the individual, in so far as legitimate interpretations, are already social.

In the final summary, after stating again the circle, social sanctions and institutions being generalizations from individual thoughts, while these are received from society, he goes on to say (pp. 542, 543): "It cannot be absolutely true that the examination of society gives rules and sanctions adequate for private life; since only the generalized part of human life is embodied in institutions. The individual must have his *private* rules of conduct for the situations *which are particular to his knowledge and action*." The dependence equally fails on the other side, because "the strictly average

---

2    This act by which one "imitatively" reads himself into others is an example of the loosely magnificent way in which the concept of imitation gets to be used. The same occurs on p. 418. How one can imitate himself *into* others passes understanding.

individual *who would correspond to the generalizations which society embodies is mythical.*"[3]

But in this case the problem is not solved at all, for it does not arise when there is objective agreement, identity of content between individual and society. It is located in the search for an explanation or statement of the psychology of the individual in social terms—his social construction—or, if not that, then for some psychology of the individual as non-social. But we get neither. We are simply told that there is the individual who is not social, and the society which is not capable of determination in individual terms. We are told to be sure that they "tend" to come together. But we are also told they tend to fall apart.[4] What then have we but a restatement of the original data of the problem: there is society, there are individuals; partly they can be stated in terms of identical content, and partly they cannot. I cannot make out that this "conclusion" has forwarded an understanding of the matter one whit.

In this statement, moreover, we have taken the matter at Mr. Baldwin's own valuation. But, if we turn to the facts (suggested, indeed, in his own statement that the individual corresponding to social generalizations is *mythical*), the case is still worse. If sociality of personality is dependent upon identity of content, is there ever any such thing in any case of self-conscious action? Is it found anywhere except in cases of action so customary that the individual never dreams of referring either to himself or to others? The psychical individual (that is, the individual conscious of individuality) is *always* "particularizing." As such he never barely repeats or assimilates a given situation as it is, but specifies it in terms of his own capacity and function. He thinks it over again in terms of his specific implication in it. Hence, if identity of content is criterion, it is only in an objective (not conscious) sense that the individual is *ever* identified with society. We have not then even a restatement

---

[3]    Italics mine in both cases.
[4]    "Society solves it, only to renew it" (p. 544). Just what can be meant, however, by "society" solving this and renewing it, when it is just the bond between society and the individual which is in question, is not clear to me.

of the original dualisms; they have been emphasized to the extreme of refractoriness.

As usual, Mr. Baldwin recognizes all this in another place. What really constitutes the individual a particularizing force is his inventions, and the essence of an invention is precisely that it is *not* imitation (pp. 100–109). Mr. Baldwin first recognizes that bare imitation gives nothing new (p. 102), since the child is simply acting out his own habits on the basis of reinstating an old mental content. But he makes a valiant attempt to connect invention (as the individualizing principle) with imitation on the basis of "persistent imitation," which is commonly known as effort.[5] But, granting for the sake of argument (and only for that sake) that effort is adequately characterized as persistent imitation, two facts still stand out. One is that it is not the imitation of others as such, but difficulty in this imitation, resistance to it, which brings out the self-sense. The phenomenon may arise in an attempt to imitate, but when it arises, it is just *not* imitative. And the second fact is that the final outcome is not imitative either. "He learns a great number of combinations which are *not* those he is after" (p. 103, italics mine). He thus learns that he can invent, can vary (p. 104). And these two great lessons are much more important, as Mr. Baldwin justly remarks, "than the mere acquisition of the single thing he sets out to do" (p. 104). "The outcome, that is new" (p. 105). One may still persist in calling invention (the consciousness of the new and its worth) imitation; but whether naming it this does more than expose a self-contradiction, I am not so sure. The manifest fact is, that *qua* imitator, the child would feel dissatisfied with all these new elements as extraneous and misleading, as failures; would insist, if possible, upon eliminating them and getting back to the simple, "reinstated" content. This would be imitation—but hardly learning. But once more, I

5    Another example of Mr. Baldwin's large use of the category of imitation comes out here. He starts out to show that all learning is through imitation (p. 101); this, too, in spite of the definition of imitation as reinstatement of an old content! When this latter point becomes obvious, he says: "How can the *imitative situation* [italics mine] instruct the child?" (p. 102). Then, when the situation, in which imitation plays a minor part, is shown to teach the child, the result is triumphantly accredited to "imitation."

am not interested in detecting a merely personal contradiction. This confusion is inherent in any theory which makes a certain identity of content between persons the criterion of sociality.

The same contradictions turn up in another form in the discussion of the origin of sense of personality. We begin with a projective sense of personality; this is made subjective; then this is "ejected" in turn. At first, the subjective sense of personality is said to arise by imitation of the projective.[6] But the "projective" is *not* personal as such (see *Mental Development*, pp. 18, 119, 335). Hence no amount of imitative reproduction, or absorption of this as "copy" would ever give a sense of personality. So the ground shifts, and it is through effort that sense of subjective agency arises (p. 8; *cf.* p. 231, but particularly p. 337 of *Mental Development*: "the first germinating nucleus of selfhood over against objecthood"). In other words, personality is here referred to a certain psychical process, not to content-identity. It is conceivable that a thorough analysis of the conditions and nature of effort would reveal this process as having a social import, but this Mr. Baldwin does not give beyond trying to attach effort to imitation—thus coming back to that, after all, as the only guarantee of sociality.

Hence the "subjective" self is still non-social and some way must be found to socialize it. Mr. Baldwin tries to work this out along at least three different and incompatible lines. One has already been referred to: others imitate in turn. Of this, nothing more need be said. Mr. Baldwin's allusion to parrots and tuning forks seems to me quite sufficient (p. 479). The second is that the agent does not feel sure of himself, does not complete his thought of himself, until his self-thought has received the acceptance and confirmation of others—an acceptance which he eagerly attempts to get, the need for the integration of himself being so great. (See the discussion, pp. 112–20: the child's sense of reality "involves social confirmation," etc.) This means, in turn, that the child's thought is *already*, tentatively and partially at least, social, and that it enacts itself to secure completion by

[6]     P. 9; see also pp. 31, 87, 99, 417, 503, 505.

social confirmation or else revision and criticism. It is the precise counterpart of the discussion already referred to in which "particularization" is treated not as merely personal, or private, but as a certain construing of a social situation. I am far from objecting to this doctrine; but we must note, in the first place, that it now assumes society as given in order to explain the social nature of the individual, and, in the second, that it is in flat contradiction not merely to what is said about the subjective sense of personality elsewhere, but to other statements regarding the ejective process itself. While here the ejective process is the fulfillment, the guarantee of the child's social nature, at other places (pp. 19–20) the ejective self is the habitual; it "despises" others, practices superior activities upon them, is "unsocial, aggressive, and self-centred" (see also p. 231). This is the legitimate, the only consistent, development of that view which regards the "subjective" self as itself barely subjective, or exclusively individual. To read this out, to act this out, would, of course, be to assert it as against others, and when Mr. Baldwin wants to account for the "egoistic" self, this is his basis of explanation, while at other times the ejective process is that of generalization which extends the social content.

But the third path followed is an attempted fusion of these two. According to it, the sense of personality at first is *general*; it is unspecified as regards reference to ego and alter, and is afterwards differentiated. (This would seem to mean that personality at first projective, is "subjected" and "ejected" at the same time under stress of the same situation; but this is my own statement purely, Mr. Baldwin does not make it.) Thus, on page 80, we are told there is "only *one* body of personal data" which shifts its locus upon occasion; on pages 14–16, that there is one self-thought (see also pp. 29, 49); on page 491 that there are not "two different thoughts for himself and the other—the *ego* and the *alter*— but one thought common in the main for both." From this point of view ego and alter are repeatedly declared to be simply emphasized poles of the common underlying thought of personality. The aggressive, habitual self, already spoken of, from this point of view is nothing but the tipping up the social or general personality at one end.

The worth of this contention is not the point at issue. It not only stands in flat contradiction to the other official doctrine of Professor Baldwin, that all progress is first by particularizing the thoughts of others into oneself, and then generalizing them back again, but is in equally flagrant opposition to Mr. Baldwin's other express theory of the general self, which emerges when he comes to discuss the ethical self. According to the group of statements just referred to, the general sense of personality underlies the distinction of ego and alter selves; but when Mr. Baldwin wants to get an ethical self, in order to ground obligation, this general self tends to become a later growth, the unification of just the two disparate selves, which a few short pages before were not disparate, but simply poles of a relationship (pp. 34–55). The contradiction appears most clearly when Mr. Baldwin says (p. 51) that this ethical self "is a slow social attainment on the part of the child. He gets it only by getting certain other thoughts of self first." But from the other point of view, be it remembered, the general self (and the ethical is simply the general) *preceded* differentiation into ego and alter.[7]

The same contradiction comes out in Mr. Baldwin's treatment of the relation of publicity to ethical sense and sanction. Here, too, we have three incompatible views. The

---

[7]     Limits of space prevent further detailed examination. But I will suggest that a careful reading of the discussions, pp. 34–55, will reveal no less than three differing concepts of the general self. According to one, it is distinctly a psychical process; it represents motor synthesis, or integration, of a variety of partial tendencies. This is in harmony with Mr. Baldwin's professed psychology of the "general" as equivalent to motor attitude. It seems to be highly suggestive and valuable. It is admirably stated on p. 266. It locates generality of personality in *process* of a certain sort, not in content. But it finds no application. Another point of view comes out in the insistence on *obedience*—the consciousness of law is the general, and this consciousness is reached through having to obey *other* personalities. Here the general is quantitative. But Mr. Baldwin evidently feels the arbitrary and external character of such a general, and so, in turn, the father who imposes law does it because this *is* the law of the whole social situation—its generality lies in its being an interpretation of the family group as such. (On p. 54 there is the confusion between "general" because *common* to a number—a quantitative conception—and general because involved in the group as such.) The crucial question is this: Is the idea which, as thought, is peculiar to the father, but which he insists upon having obeyed, general or not? If not, does it become general simply *because* others obey? Or, in so far as it is an interpretation of the interests of the group as such, is it, perforce, general from the start?

extreme, on one side, is found in the statement that "the developed ethical sense needs less and less to appeal to an alter self, an authority . . ." (p. 52). But this view stands alone till we come to the question of final ethical conflict. The chief confusion is between the concept of publicity in a quantitative sense, a matter of content, and as a process of interpretative construction of a social situation. That the ethical self must be, in my consciousness of it, a public self, is the proposition (p. 315). The quantitative interpretation comes out when Mr. Baldwin says "in case I know the action is quite private, quite secret, absolutely unknown to anybody else, then the full reinstatement of the conditions of an ethical judgment, is, *ipso facto*, not present" (p. 315). And, again, "the thought that the judgment passed *is actually in the mind of some other* is necessary to a full ethical judgment as such" (p. 318, italics mine).[8] In spite of the undoubted help in both reinforcement and enlightenment, that we get from confession, or even from imagination of others as knowing of our proposed deed, this seems to me extraordinary doctrine as matter of fact—particularly as often our surest token that an intention is wrong, is our shrinking from having anybody else know of it; while according to these statements we could not really judge it wrong until we knew somebody else did know of it. But its correctness is not so much in question as its contrast with another view of publicity. This view emerges upon pages 498, 499 (as well as pp. 438, 517, 532). According to this the appeal is to a "higher self already formed in my breast through social experience," through which I "anticipate." Its publicity is in its *ideal reference*, and this reference is accordingly to *every* agent; the quantitative generality follows *from* the quantitative; while, from the other point of view, publicity consists in actual possession of the same content by *two* or more agents. The doctrine now propounded is that just because the ethical self *as such* is general, its thought must be accepted and ratified by any self, whether you or me.

Naturally, when we come to ethical growth, the latter

---

8     See also p. 425. The passage on p. 435 is open to either interpretation.

point of view dominates. According to the first conception, a thought originally not ethical becomes such when one knows somebody else accepts it—a process of moral legislation by majorities that leaves Hobbes nowhere. But he now learns that "the growth of society is but the generalization of the individual's ethical ought into society's conventional ought" (p. 534). Hence ethical rules are "capable" of being embodied in the sanctions of society; "they *are to have* the publicity which attaches to the ethical sanction as such" (p. 535). The contradiction is obvious enough when we recall that at the outset the judgment could not be ethical unless it *already* had such publicity. Add that Mr. Baldwin finds the final and most significant conflict between individual and society to be precisely in the cases where the individual opposes his ethical judgment to those of others (see pp. 539–40 and p. 544), and we see how completely Mr. Baldwin has shifted his statement of the interpretation of the nature of publicity and generality.[9]

All these various contradictions summarize themselves in Mr. Baldwin's varying conceptions of the socius or social personality. There seem to be no less than three independent and incompatible views on this point. One of these goes back to identity of content, established by imitation. Any self is in so far a socius as it is built up by imitative appropriations from others. But on a more organic basis, the community self, or spirit, the sense of common interest, of a community of situation, in which all live, and of which their thoughts are interpretations, is the socius (pp. 30, 32, 47).

[9]    Limits of space compel me to relegate to a footnote the fact that Mr. Baldwin has precisely the same contradiction concerning the relation of intelligence and the ethical. On one hand, the very nature of intelligence is to generalize, and hence to usher in the ethical, especially since the general as such is motor or dynamic. On the other, the intelligence occupies a lower plane, is "private," "personal," or, when named "social," is so named simply because it uses social forces for personal advantages, and is finally displaced by the ethical sentiment. I cannot work this out in detail; but the reader is referred to pp. 250, 397, 398, for the first position; and to pp. 321, 323, 327, 382, 527 for the second. On p. 515, both views are stated—one that intelligence tends toward selfish use, the other, that intelligence, as such, is generalizing process; and be it remembered, the "general" is the only psychological criterion afforded for the ethical—a fact which does not prevent Mr. Baldwin from remarking that one cannot give reasons "for pronouncing conduct right" (p. 395; see also p. 535). Mr. Baldwin, indeed, appears to reconcile the genetic and the intuitive views by taking them both by turns.

The third view serves as a bridge to pass over from the first individualistic notion to the second highly socialized one. According to this, the socius is the common element in ego and alter. This is like the first view in that it begins with separate selves. It differs in that neither self as such is the socius, but simply the identity of content. It is like the second view in that the concept of the "common" is used, but differs in that it is one of abstract content, instead of a principle of organization. On pages 53 and 55 the socius is respectively public opinion, the relationships existing between members of a family, and another person whom the child obeys. On page 24, all three conceptions get happily stated in sequence. ( *a* ) "He thinks of the other, the alter, as his *socius*, just as he thinks of himself as the other's *socius*; and the only thing that remains more or less stable, throughout the whole growth is the fact that there is ( *b* ) a growing sense of self which includes both terms, the ego and the alter. In short ( *c* ) *the real self is the bipolar self*, the social self, *the socius*."[10]

I should be glad to speak upon the more strictly psychological side of Mr. Baldwin's conception of the relation of thought-content and action, and of its specific application to the problem of the nature of desire, and also to say something about the psychology of imitation as such, and the psychology of the relation of habit and accommodation. But I have used an intolerable amount of space in following the concepts of the relations of the individual and the social through the various forms in which they appear, and must abstain. It would be a grateful task not only to acknowledge the suggestiveness, the thought-provoking and thought-compelling quality of Mr. Baldwin's book—that goes without saying—but to point out the richness of the details of many of the various discussions which have just been criticized as regards their coherency in fundamental concepts. More particularly should I like to refer to the value of the discussions of the social aids to invention (language, play, and art); to the clear and judicious summing up under the

[10]    The letters interjected are my own, of course. ( *a* ) gives the individualistic view; ( *c* ) the social organization, or community view; ( *b* ) the identity of content view.

second head; to the original contribution to the theories of art which adds the factor of "showing off," at once psychical and social, to the ordinary play-concept; to the admirable conception of the genius, so free both from the attempt to explain away his significance, by losing him in the social mass, and from the attempt on the other side to isolate him upon a mysterious non-social pedestal; to the discussion of the development of bashfulness and shame, etc. I should regret very much to have my failure to call attention to these matters interpreted as failure to recognize their positive value. But I chiefly desire to acknowledge the indebtedness, on the part of all interested in the relations of psychology and sociology, to Mr. Baldwin for his courage in attacking at first hand problems which most steer clear of, or simply repeat well-worn conventionalities concerning, and for the fresh, varied, and vigorous way in which he has opened up new problems and new points of view.

## Rejoinder to Baldwin's Reply

If Professor Baldwin really means that he made no attempt "to say what either the individual or society is," I probably did take him too seriously, and my criticisms do not touch even a "knob on his harness." I confess I thought he *was* trying to throw light upon the nature of the individual and of society by use of the genetic method—not their metaphysical nature, but their psychological and empirical nature. Just as the evolutionary zoölogist attempts to say what the horse is—not the metaphysical horse (if perchance there be such), but the horse of our common knowledge. If I have gone astray in supposing that Professor Baldwin really had such a serious scientific purpose in view, I cannot take all the blame to myself. Having been told that the "first requisite" is "the concept of the person," that current discussion has often failed from lack of determining this concept, and that Professor Baldwin was about to fill the void, I naturally looked for something of the sort. I still am un-

[*First published in* Philosophical Review, VII (*Nov. 1898*), 629–30. *Not previously reprinted. See* "Social Interpretations: A Reply," *by* J. M. Baldwin, The Early Works of John Dewey, v.]

able to see how any one can fruitfully discuss "the law of their [individual and society] evolution, and by what relation of fact or of implication of each by the other, this law of evolution proceeds," without some determination of the concepts of society and of personality. Indeed, if left to myself (not being sufficiently familiar with Aristotle and Hegel), I confess I should have thought that the chief value of the genetic method was that it enabled us to *substitute* a scientific statement of the nature of personality and society, and their relations to each other, for a metaphysical one.

Professor Baldwin, in his reply, furnishes some confirmation that my judgment as to the looseness of his writing, is not overdrawn. In his book he said: "He thinks of the other, the alter, as his socius, just as he thinks of himself as the other's socius; and the only thing that remains more or less stable, throughout the whole growth is the fact that there is a growing sense of self which includes both terms, the ego and the alter. In short, the real self is the bi-polar self, the social self, the socius" (p. 24). This is one of the passages that confused and confounded me—where I had the sense of assisting at an elusive and shifting scene. Afterwards I thought I found a key to the shifting; I found evidence of three modes of interpretation of sociality running more or less consistently in their inconsistency throughout the whole book. In my review, I pointed these out. Professor Baldwin now admits, so far as this passage is concerned, that three distinct phases of self-development are involved; but dismisses the matter with the remark that, "while the passages might be better expressed, there is essentially no inconsistency in these three aspects of development." Well, is there anything whatsoever in the passage, or in its context, to suggest, even remotely, that it is not exactly the same body of fact which is under description throughout? If Mr. Baldwin had realized at the time that he was referring to three stages of growth, would a mere change of phraseology have sufficed? It is precisely the lack of clear analysis of different phases and stages, the slippery and easy identification of them, the failure to face the exact conditions under which each phase arises and passes into another—it is this to which my criticism refers as his contradictions. I cannot suppress my conviction that a closer contact with, and grip upon, these problems would involve not only considerable rewriting, but considerable rethinking.

In reading Professor Baldwin's book, I was continually confused and perplexed by what (to me) were continually recurring contradictions, as well as vaguenesses. After many readings, I thought I got the key to them. In order to simplify and unify my critical notice (expressly stating at the outset that I should reverse the ordinary procedure of such reviews), I gave my general criticism before my detailed ones. The former, of course, is simply an inference, a hypothesis of my own, to account for the multitude of specific contradictions found. Be it correct or incorrect, the particular ones still remain. Such a method seemed to be desirable, because Professor Baldwin apparently writes *currente calamo*; and, as I read him, whatever is uppermost for the moment is said without much reference to what is said elsewhere, in spite of his multitude of references to his own writings. Such writing is almost certain to be suggestive; it is not easy to combine it with a *systematic* discussion of such an ambitious topic as the evolution of society and the individual and their mutual implications. So in spite of the fact that Professor Baldwin finds my criticisms largely "verbal and logical" (not that to be logical is such a bad thing), my method of statement was due to an attempt to penetrate below the surface of the contradictions, and find, if possible, the key to them. Neither Professor Baldwin nor myself is, of course, the final judge of the success of this attempt.[1]

[1]    Of course I am pleased that Professor Baldwin finds my *New World* criticism more satisfactory. I confess that, if possible, I should like to avoid the conclusion that I could spend so much time and thought upon a book, and then almost completely miss its point. As the materials for both reviews were collected at the same time, as in writing the later I did not refer to the book save to verify a few references, and as, in my mind, they were two lines of development of the same fundamental criticism (of the idea, ultimately, that repetition or multiplication of a private or individual mental content will give sociality), I am not without hopes that in time Professor Baldwin will allow more relevancy to my criticism in this *Review*.

## Social and Ethical Interpretations in Mental Development

Professor Baldwin's important book[1] may be termed either a sociological psychology or a psychological sociology. Various attempts at social psychology, as a psychology of corporate or community action, thought and sentiment, in their various manifestations, we already have. Mr. Baldwin's purpose is rather to show how social factors and relations enter into and determine the consciousness of the individual, so that any psychological account which ignores the social influences and proceeds to evolve the individual out of himself, so to speak, is necessarily defective and "abstract." Put positively, and in Mr. Baldwin's own words, "A man is a social outcome rather than a social unit" (p. 87). On the sociological side, Mr. Baldwin's determination to find psychological considerations the important ones is equally marked. As he says: "It seems to me to be a permanent advance that the biological analogy is giving place to a psychological analogy, and that this is leading the writers in so-called 'sociology' to examine the psychological processes which lie wrapped up in the activities and responsibilities called social" (p. 475). The conclusion is that, since society is really the organization of thoughts, "the true analogy is not that which likens society to a physiological organism, but rather that which likens it to a psychological organization" (p. 544).

This two-faced aspect of the work reflects itself in the arrangement and treatment of the topics. Book I discusses "the person" in order to find out what social constituents make him up, and how; Book II discusses "society," to discover the personal elements and processes which form and control it. In detail, the book on Personality considers the

---

1    *Social and Ethical Interpretations in Mental Development: A Study in Social Psychology*, by James Mark Baldwin. New York: Macmillan Co., 1897.

[*First published in* New World, VII (*Sept. 1898*), *504–22. Not previously reprinted.*]

various dominant stages in its development: its equipment of instinct, intelligence and sentiments, and its sanctions or controlling motives in conduct. And in each case the object is the same—to reveal the persistent and important presence of social data and relationships. On the social side, there is a discussion first of the social forces, showing the directions of growth which are parallel to the moments in the development of the person; secondly, a discussion of the process and matter of social organization and the direction of social progress; and thirdly, a summing up in terms of applications of the conclusions reached to rules of conduct—rules of conduct, by the necessity of the case, looking to a synthesis of individual initiative with social application and reference.

I shall here make no attempt to follow the exact order of this discussion, and for two reasons. In the first place, the variety of particular topics discussed is so great that omission and condensation are a necessity, especially as the importance of many of these topics is such as to tempt one into discursiveness. And, in the second place, there is a certain single movement, termed by Mr. Baldwin "the dialectic of personal growth," which gives the key to the variety of topics. As the book now stands, the reader is more or less confused, and even annoyed, by the multiplicity of references back and forth. The same topic is discussed over and over again, and in many cases it is difficult, if not impossible, to see either that any essentially new point of view has been reached or that any intrinsically new material is introduced. It would add to the intelligibility and the effectiveness of the volume if there were such a redistribution of material as would centralize the variety of treatments we now have—as for example, the five separate discussions of the ethical—about their common principle.

Since, as just indicated, this fundamental principle is found in the theory of the moments and stages of personal growth, I shall begin with a somewhat extended summary of Professor Baldwin's views on this subject. The prevailing popular view isolates the ego from the alter. One's own self is considered as quite a distinct entity, and the selves of other people are of course equally independent. Moreover, each self is something pretty definitely fixed once for all. Just as one person may come into external relation to another, so, of course, changes in the outward manifestations of the self are recognized. But the essential self remains after all practically identical—it matures, it gains additional habits, but that is about all. Professor Baldwin questions radically both phases of the popular assumption. The self is not something fixed, it is rather a growth, and any examination of it is futile which is not based upon the salient epochs of this growth. Moreover, the content of the self, as it exists in consciousness, is by no means an isolated, separate matter. The thought of self, whether as referred to the ego or the alter, is to a very considerable extent a common thought. What one attributes to the self, what one wants for the self, he wants equally for his own self and for other selves because of this identity of content. And even when the thought of ego is consciously marked off from the thought of alter, it is not because it has an original independent content of its own; it is rather an attitude assumed in the presence of the other. It is therefore intrinsically conditioned upon consciousness of the other. As Mr. Baldwin puts it in general terms: "My thought of self is in the main, as to its character as a personal self, filled up with my thought of others distributed variously as individuals; and my thought of others as persons is mainly filled up with myself."

I have spoken of two factors in the conception of the self. But it is not to be understood that Mr. Baldwin makes any separation here. On the contrary, the consideration of the stages of the personal growth of the self is at the same time the key to the relationship between ego and alter. There are three stages of the thought of self. The first is projective. Here the child does not discriminate consciously between himself and others. He does apparently distinguish between selves and things. The thing stands for relatively mechanical regularity. The behavior of persons is irregular, unstable; it cannot be anticipated. It brings in continually novel and surprising factors. It thus introduces an element which lies decidedly in advance of present achievement. It is apparently for this reason that it is termed projective, but Mr. Baldwin is by no means as full and explicit on the nature of the projective self as one could wish.

As the child begins to imitate these novel unmastered features, he makes them his own, he transfers them over into himself. Thus he enters upon the subjective stage. He becomes a subject to himself, distinct from others. While psychologically this only occurs through the introduction of effort into his attempts at imitation, yet, since the material is derived imitatively from others, the content of the subject is clearly nothing peculiar or unique.

Now the child begins to utilize his new thought of self. He does it in two ways. In the first place he sees that others, those who up to this time have been simply projects, are also subjects to themselves. He realizes them, too, as persons like himself. In other words, the ordinary dualism between ego and alter breaks down here, because just as one conceives his ego only through material derived from others, so he appreciates them as others only by transferring or reading out his own accomplishments. In the second place, he insists that others shall be like him. He does not simply intellectually ascribe personality to them, but in and through his acts he insists practically upon this identity of personality content—for, psychologically, action is always the motor functioning of a thought-content. This third stage is the ejective.

If this view is correct, popular conceptions must, as Mr. Baldwin insists, be greatly revised. Not only do we get a common element underlying the distinction of ego and alter, but we cannot understand any exhibition in which ego or alter is clearly differentiated excepting as we inquire after the other term in the relationship. Each, in Mr. Baldwin's language, is a pole; polarization is obviously a phenomenon of reciprocity, of correlation. Just what makes up the content of the child's thought of himself at a given time will depend upon whether he is in the projective, subjective or ejective stage; and which stage he is in is simply a matter of the type of relation assumed towards others. We cannot say that the child is selfish or generous in any fixed sense of those terms —not in the meaning of developed social significance which they possess for adults. If the other person is uncertain, dominating, presenting novel features, the child is thrown into the learning, imitative attitude; he is compliant, docile, servile. Such will be the case with his elders in general, and with his father in particular. But others will be ejects to the child. He has mastered their modes of action. There is nothing in them excepting what the child reads in. So he is aggressive, superior, apparently egoistic in dealing with them. The practical attitude, in a word, changes with the change in the thought-content. The child to whom others are projects, who is imitative, may be said psychologically to be subject to suggestion and to be in the attitude of accommodation. The child to whom others are ejects is the person of habit. Accommodation and habit—these are the two typical and alternating modes of personal activity.

We now have the data for the explanation of the ethical self. Neither the docile, imitative, accommodating self, nor yet the aggressive, assertive, habitual self, is the whole or true self. The true self is the self in the whole process of development with the full circuit of social relationships involved—the "Socius" in Mr. Baldwin's terminology. Now if we can find the circumstances under which the child becomes conscious of the inadequate and partial character of the "habitual" and the "accommodating" self, and becomes aware of the socius as their bond of union, we shall understand the genesis of the ethical sense. This sense of inadequacy arises through the requirement of obedience, of conformity to the will of others. Where one has to face an ethical problem, it means precisely that one cannot follow either his natural sympathetic accommodating impulses or yet his self-assertive, habitual tendencies. He has the consciousness of an ideal self conforming to a law in which these opposed tendencies are reconciled. Now "whenever he obeys, the boy has forced in upon him a situation which his thoughts of himself are not adequate to interpret." He is not responding to his habitual self because his private preferences may be directly violated. He is not acting out his accommodating self because he may be very unwilling to do what he is doing. There is a new self there, the law-giving personality. It is this which, by representing a common interest, a family propriety, the mass of accepted tradition, brings home to him what the socius means. In one sense it is projective, it is ideal, beyond him, but as it is conformed to, and its meaning learned, it becomes ejective, it is realized as a common principle which all must observe. Moreover, this law is always the realized self of some one. It is an achieved personality. It is this sense of a person which is real for itself and yet ideal for the agent, but as ideal a law which must be realized through him, which constitutes the essence of conscience.

The ethical self is thus essentially a social self. (The discussion up to this time is a synopsis of Chapter 1. What is now said is derived from Chapter 8). Its social quality is, of course, obvious from both points of view, the subjective and the ejective. On the one hand, the sense of this higher personality arises through the presence of other personalities from whom the demand for obedience proceeds and in whom the model of goodness is embodied. On the other side, the child continually reinforces and guides himself in his obedience by expecting the approval of others; and then, more actively, he insists that the law he obeys become also a law for others. What he has learned to obey he insists that others obey also. There is thus in reality but one application of the "ought"—it is to the common content or "socius" which is assumed to be present both in ego and alter. Because of this continual play back and forth, this give-and-take, there is a solidarity in the ethical realm of the individual and his social fellows. The individual learns his ethical lessons from society. The ethical accomplishment or attainment of one generation is handed on to the next, and thus becomes not only a standard for a particular individual, but also a matter of common and united attainment for all—social heredity. It is in the ethical sphere that we find the highest expression of the real bond between the social whole and the individual.

That the ethical self is essentially a social self appears also in the sphere of emotion and sentiment. Publicity is a controlling factor in this sphere. Self-condemnation is associated with the image of some one else who disapproves. There is no lively emotional reaction as long as the sin is simply private. It is in actual or imagined awareness on the part of others of his own doing that the individual gets the purchase on his act which brings out remorse and repentance —his reaction against it. So, too, the sense of moral approval is never at its best excepting when accompanied with the knowledge or belief that it is socially shared. The ethical self is thus social both objectively, that is, as to its content; and subjectively, or as to our own feeling towards conduct. It is so objectively, because, by its very nature, it is a thought which assimilates and combines the partial thoughts of self and eliminates all merely private traces and references. It is so subjectively, because we cannot really judge our own conduct ethically, and get the proper emotional reaction to it, unless we realize that others are passing the same sort of judgment that we pass, or would judge in the same way if they only knew of it. (I put in the two alternatives because Mr. Baldwin does not seem quite certain on this point. Sometimes publicity is found in the fact that others actually know of the act; in other cases the requirement of publicity is fulfilled imaginatively.) On the ejective side, the individual's sense of the generality, the publicity of his ethical ideas and beliefs, makes him a legislator for others. He is always, in so far forth, a reformer or prophet— that is to say, he must insist, that as ethical, his ideas are of necessity valid for every one. Thus, the measure of his own sincerity and depth of conviction will be found in his efforts to secure similar recognition from others.

Mr. Baldwin uses the same dialectic to explain the nature and value of religious sentiments (Chs. 8 and 10). The ethical sense is derived through contact with personalities who impose laws, and in turn it finds embodiment in the concept of the ideal personality. There is the tendency to make the ideal person real, "a separate corporate personality." As all the ideal elements are gradually concreted in this one great ejective personality, the moral ideal takes shape in the God-idea. Corresponding to this on the social side, with reference to the sanctions which act upon the individual, we find a public religious institution with its accompanying content of religious doctrine. If we consider, not the ejective side, but the relation of the subject to the projective aspects of personality, we have an explanation of the sense of something transcendent, something infinite and incapable of adequate embodiment in any positive form, constituting the other great factor in religious sentiment—a feeling of awe and of mystery. The ejective attitude may be summed up in the sense of dependence, finding expression in faith; the projective in the feeling of mystery expressed in reverence for a person. While the religious sentiment thus grows out of the ethical, religion in turn represents such realization of its essential factors as to react upon it and give it a necessary support. It is through this reaction that religious forces become legitimate factors in social progress. Here Mr. Baldwin makes the very important point that religious institutions ought to affect social progress and in course of historical development have actually come to do so *indirectly*; that is, through inspiring and reinforcing the ethical sanction in the individual rather than directly or through immediate social pressure and enforcement. This point, which may not unfairly be termed a psychological rendering of the notion of the separation of church and state, seems to me of great suggestiveness.

I turn now to some of the points which Mr. Baldwin brings out in discussing the matter from the social side. He points out that it is customary to put physical heredity and social environment in marked antagonism to each other, as when it is asked which is the more important in the development of the individual. The real solution of the question lies in the discovery of the falsity of the antithesis. Physical heredity must itself have some social functioning and social control. It is quite out of the question that it should work in any large sense either contrary to, or independently of, the forces in the social environment which are continually playing on the individual. Physical heredity, in other words, will be effective just in the degree in which it co-operates with the social environment—this, if I understand it, is the idea which Mr. Baldwin expresses in the term "social heredity." More specifically, it finds expression in the statements that the individual must be born to learn and that all the individuals must be born to learn the same things. Physical heredity must, on the negative side, not be of a sort to throw the individual into antagonism beyond a certain point with the interests of the community; positively, it must lend itself, must have an active trend, towards just the sort and variety of relationships which the social tradition imposes. The real identity of physical heredity and social environment comes out also from the other side, when we call to mind that the social environment can be only the sphere of the exercise of the collective heredities of individuals.

The consideration of invention and of the nature of genius involves points of so much importance that a more extended statement is required. The principle which Mr. Baldwin is most concerned with is that invention, while proceeding through the medium of the thought of the individual, cannot be considered as arbitrary and uncontrolled from the social point of view. Whether we take it at its origin or in its outcome, its nature and value are socially determined and estimated. The novel, which is introduced in invention, always arises from the platform or level of attainment which has been socially constituted through imitation. It is a variation of elements within this content, so as to adapt it to the action required by new conditions, rather than an abrupt introduction from without. Invention is selection, emphasis, and thus readjustment, on the platform of the attained. Psychologically the originality of the child is found in the way he imitates, in the new combinations which he hits upon, and in the new sense of his own powers gained while he is engaged in imitating: it is not a process set over against imitation. In previous terminology, it is a phase of the operation by which the projective becomes subjective. It is thus a social variation rather than an individualistic creation. But we must go further. We have still to reckon with the ejective process. The child not only acts upon his own original conception, but demands that others do so too. He reads his new thought outward; he makes it a factor in his construing of other personalities, in what he demands and expects of them. He endeavors to make his invention socially valid, to get recognition for it. Moreover, this demand reacts upon the novel thought itself to revise and purify it. The child changes his idea of his new invention and of himself in relation to it according as others approve or disapprove, according as he can or cannot utilize it as a means of directing their action. In a word, the child's sense of the value of his invention depends upon the amount and kind of social recognition which it receives. We all use this criterion of availability for social assimilation as a standard by which to judge of the significance and the validity of our new thoughts, which are tentative and hypothetical excepting as we anticipate their social reception. In this connection Mr. Baldwin gives an interesting discussion of language, play and art as social aids to invention, in originating and testing the new elements.

The application to the discussion of genius may be briefly indicated. The sane man, the average good social member, is the one who instinctively utilizes the social standard of value in measuring his own ideas. The genius is the one who unites with this faculty the power of unusual variation. The crank, the visionary, the fanatic, shares with him this capacity for variation, but lacks essentially the power to view his own thoughts from the standpoint of the social judgment. We may say that many inventions are tested simply by time. The original novelty is more or less of an accident. If it is imitated, adopted, assimilated, it becomes organized into the social traditions; it is given validity through social acceptance. But the genius unites to his power of great variation the power of anticipating the social reaction. He is, so to speak, more social in his judgment than existing society itself. He can take the standpoint of a later, more developed society, and from its standpoint can estimate and select the variations that occur to him. It is through the scientific and æsthetic inventions of the genius that social progress is largely determined. Considering great discoveries from this point of view, we find what has already been shown to be true of inventions and the individual is true of them. They are rooted in the knowledge already possessed by society. The content of the discovery, if it far transcends the working level of existing society, is of necessity inert and futile. It represents a centre of crystallization, a nucleus of social habits. But while it is thus a precipitate, a condensation of existing social interests, it is also a locus of social accommodation. Existing institutions must readjust themselves in order to be adapted to the new factor.

This idea finds further development in Mr. Baldwin's distinction of social forces as particularizing and as generalizing. The individual, *qua* individual, is the variation, the new thought, the invention in social matter. There is no need to say once more that these variations all fall within certain limits of social attainment, nor that they function with reference to a future society. It is perhaps necessary to recognize that the initiative of all progress is found in the individual. Society never changes *en masse*; it changes first in the new conception born in the mind of some individual. The generalizing social force is correlative. It is assimilation, through imitation, of this idea on the part of others. The thought must cease to be simply the individual's thought and become valid by being made into a social habit. Through this process, elements of too extreme variation from the current level are eliminated, and permanence is secured. While the particularization represents the initiation of social progress, generalization represents its carrying out, its actual realization. Hence it is that society is conceived as the organization of "thoughts, intellectual states, such as imaginations, knowledges and informations."

We have here the key to both the agreements and the conflicts, particularly in the ethical sphere, of the individual and society. Upon the whole there must be agreement. All ethical conduct must have a public social reference; and even when the individual is an ethical reformer he must start from the existing platform of social sentiment. On the other hand, the ethical rules and criteria found in society are simply generalizations of what once was the deeper insight of the individual. But a final conflict is possible. The individual may govern himself by an ethical principle in advance of social attainment and may insist, in opposition to the established order, that others obey it also. Apparently, according to Mr. Baldwin, there is no common standard nor umpire in this final and irreducible antinomy. The individual cannot argue; morality is not a thing of logical sanction, and society must stand with equal blindness to its own rules, and insist upon them against the individual who would change its ethical order. It seems to be a sheer case of arbitrary moral intuition on one side, *versus* positive established convention on the other. And apparently (apparently, I say, for Professor Baldwin is so brief on this point that there is danger of misunderstanding) the only appeal is to results; one or the other does ultimately come out ahead.

Fragmentary and schematic as is the above summary, I hope it will not entirely fail of two purposes: first, to suggest some of the main lines of thought, particularly with reference to ethical application, where probably the interest of most lies; and, secondly, to induce the reader to turn to the book for himself. It remains to state certain criticisms which have occurred to me during my study of Mr. Baldwin's book. At the outset, let me say that I am in hearty sympathy with the type of results reached by Mr. Baldwin. His insistence upon the social character of the self, upon the development of individuality through social give-and-take; his conception of the ethical self as the organized or integrated unity which takes up into itself attitude and tendencies otherwise partial; his conception of social influences in giving form and content to conscience—all these points seem to me in line with what is most healthy and most fertile in contemporary thought. From the standpoint of the reader who is interested in results rather than in methods, and who must be helped by Mr. Baldwin's work out of the too prevalent individualism into a more adequate social point of view, there is nothing to express save acquiescence and gratitude. But the student, as distinct from the general reader, is of necessity interested not merely in results, but also in the methods by which they are reached. From this point of view I find certain questions, certain doubts, continually intruding. From limitation of space, I can only state salient points quite dogmatically, and cannot undertake to prove what I have to say. But the dogmatic statement may at least serve to put the reader in possession of a point of view which is a possible alternative.

Upon the social side, with all due sympathy for the reaction from a too exclusively biological conception of society, it may be questioned whether society can be adequately conceived as an "organization of thoughts." If one accepts the evolutionary point of view at all (which, of course, Mr. Baldwin does), one cannot fail to recognize that "thoughts" are relevant, if not merely relative, to the life process—to functioning activities. Thought comes in to interpret, to control, to mediate, to evaluate these activities. So does feeling, of course. (It is difficult to account for Mr. Baldwin's slighting of feeling.) Any view which disregards the transfiguring capacity of the psychical in general, and of thought in particular, in relation to the sphere of vital activities, is certainly inadequate. Society is not merely biological. But it does not follow that we must go to the other extreme, and set thoughts and knowledges up as a substitute for activities. *Conscious activities*, vital functions which are valued in both feeling and thought, *interests*, in a word, these seem to me the real "matter" of social organization. "Community of interests" is definitely more fundamental than uniformity of thought. The conception of society as an organization of imaginations and informations is pale, faded and academic, unreal, when we look at that instinctive, uneasy, boiling cauldron of tendencies, desires and ends which comes to the mind's eye when we think of society as a concrete fact.

Nor does Mr. Baldwin's theoretical justification for his position seem adequate. Briefly stated, it is that imitation is the method of "give-and-take" which makes society, and that imitation must be of thought-contents. Desire and belief are motor functions of the ideas to which they attach—hence we must have identity of ideas before we can get identity of belief and desire. If we set feeling and impulse up as material for imitation, we should get only a society where habit, fixity, is all, and in which no accommodation, and hence no progress, is possible. So we find, in the dialectic of personality-growth, all the emphasis thrown upon effecting similar thought-contents.

There seem to me three very doubtful psychological assumptions here. The statement that imitation of impulse and feeling would give only a rigid society is merely an assertion, no proof is offered. "Impulse," at least, would seem to move in just the other direction—to be a break in an established habit.[2]

---

2    It is interesting to note that the only passage to which Mr. Baldwin refers in his justification of his statement is a discussion of suggestibility in case of "mob action," where the trait insisted upon, however, is not fixity of habit, but capriciousness, explosiveness, frenzy, volatility!

Secondly, fixing upon imitation as, *par excellence*, the social process seems to me either very arbitrary, or else to involve such an extensive and loose use of the term as to take away its significance. I cannot fully discuss this problem here; but the following questions and considerations occur. Can "thought" be imitated at all? Can anything but action, in one form or another, be imitated? Does not Mr. Baldwin very much exaggerate the part played by conscious imitation in the child? I should say that conscious imitation is rare, and relatively late. The little child does not imitate *me* (I mean in *his* consciousness, as distinct from an observer's) or even *my* acts. When the other person is consciously "copy," then precisely the child is engaged in "monkey shines," or is offensively "smart." Mr. Baldwin seems not free from the psychologist's fallacy here. The observer calls a result imitative because he sees both persons concerned; but the *process*, to the infant, is not imitation. It is a case of the adjustment of a response to a stimulus—that is, his eye-activity stimulates his hand; it directs it in its doing. And if we ask why the response is, as a matter of fact, imitative, the answer is, because we have here a co-ordination which has been of great importance to the race, and which the child is even now trying to build up. In all directions, his hand is following the lead of the eye, is getting its cues from it. There is a period before which the child is inaccessible to a given form of imitative suggestion. There is a later period when he is cold to it. The interval, in which the child is open, must be precisely the period when the child is instinctively urgent in this direction, as sounds are imitated when the babbling impulse is strongest in him. Thus, imitation comes in to mediate the child's natural tendency, not to set him off on a new and "social" track.

Finally, taking imitation as a social phenomenon, I should say that it is, upon the whole, a social effect rather than a social cause. Persons have, through the necessities of common conditions of life, formed certain habits in common, and the structural adaptations for these habits have been "selected," or fixed. That a stimulus, which is a fragment of one of these habits, should serve to set off the other portions of it, is not a matter of surprise. But if this is the case, persons imitate one another because of previous com-

mon modes of living, because of a companionship or sociality
previously established. It is a mark, a sign of sociality, but
not to any considerable extent a cause.

Again, while I agree with all Mr. Baldwin says about
an act considered as a motor function of an ideal content, so
far as it means that some other activity does not supervene
upon the idea from without, he appears to me to go only
halfway. The idea, the knowledge content, grows out of,
as well as leads up to, action. It represents a meeting place,
a nodal point, in two or more habits, giving rise to conflict,
temporary inhibition. The idea is all the time developing *as
an idea*. It is not fixed, clear and self-contained from the
start. The intellectual side of desire and belief grows in and
through actions, instead of being a finished antecedent. The
idea is intermediary, in other words. It has a motor function
only because it has a motor origin and a motor quality intrinsically and throughout. This involves a modification not
only of Mr. Baldwin's theory of desire, of the relation of intelligence to impulse, and to ethical sentiment, but also of
the relation of imitation to thought. "Reinstatement" of any
previous content, or of a content exhibited by another, ceases
to be the main thing; reconstruction, readjustment, becomes
the function of knowledge.

Upon the social side, this change of psychology would
carry with it many other important changes. It would not
be necessary any longer to rule out or ignore the part played
in social organization and development by the physical environment. The emphasis being upon interaction and mutuality of interest, any stimulus which operates in this direction is relevant. It would not be necessary to rule out or
ignore the part played by competition, struggle and survival
of the fittest. The real test of the social work done by the
inventor of the telegraph is not the number of people who
imitate either his act or his thought, it is the readjustment
of actions, and of the exercise of interests that he makes necessary. It is the new stimulus he gives, the new mode of
control he introduces. The invention changes the price of
daily bread, makes the daily newspaper, compels new methods of doing business—all of which affect me profoundly
as a social being, even though I use the telegraph but once

a year. And in making itself valid in this interplay of forces, there is plenty of room for struggle, for existence and for selection. The psychological is no longer set over against the biological.

The same general line of consideration applies also to the "irreducible" ethical antinomy between the individual and society. If a "thought" arising in the individual is the fundamental matter, and if it simply remains for society to imitate or not to imitate, as it sees fit, the case is certainly hopeless. But if an idea, a thought, arises with reference to the redirection it gives action, then there is already a social criterion for the worth of the idea: its power of social solution and synthesis. On the other side, the social reaction is not left a brute, arbitrary thing. Just in proportion as the idea represents, and provides a method for, more effective and more harmonious activity, in so far it must come to recognition—not by imitation, nor yet necessarily through any uniform intellectual assent, but through the medium of the social reorganization it effects. Doubtless there is tension here. The ideal or insight of the individual can be elaborated and tested only through its application; its function is to afford a method for organizing action and it remains to see if it will perform that office. But this is no more an irreducible conflict between the individual and society, than is the precisely analogous reciprocal action that goes on between the scientific hypothesis advanced by some individual thinker and the received body of knowledge at a given time.

In its fundamental aspects, I do not find Professor Baldwin's account of the ethical personality on the individual side more convincing. At first, the scheme seems attractive: an imitative self, in relation to a novel, dominating personality, and accordingly "accommodating," compliant, generous; a personality, in relation to "ejective" personalities, who, having mastered his lessons, is aggressive and self-assertive, because habitual; finally, the ethical self which subjects both of these to a generalized law-giving and law-abiding ideal personality. What I question in this scheme involves substantially the same principle already discussed on the social side: the substitution, as it seems to me, of connection between distinct personalities through the medium of intellectual contents, for distinctions and identifications of interest within a unity of action, a unity of reciprocal adjustments effected by stimuli and responses. The child, I should say, defines himself and others all the time in terms of this larger whole of interaction, in terms of the particular part played by each in maintaining and developing it. It is primarily this whole of "give-and-take" in action, and only derivatively in ideas, which makes the real "socius," and which, as it is gradually brought to consciousness in its organizing, and therefore controlling, relations to its members, appears as the ethical self. I can only briefly suggest the reasons for this change of conception.

In the first place, the identification of the "projective" self, in relation to the imitative, as the irregular, the uncertain, seems to me very doubtful. At first, as Mr. Baldwin recognizes, the "other," the parent or nurse, is the one whose movements bring satisfaction. It is not necessary, I think, to give this any conscious hedonic coloring. The bringing of satisfaction is the fulfilling of the child's wants, providing conditions for the fulfillment of his own active tendencies, organically responding in a word. This union of demand and satisfaction is the infant's first world—there is no distinction of subject ego which needs, and object alter which supplies. But, as the child begins to recognize and to anticipate (generally in the seventh month), he begins also to suffer disappointment and loss. He begins now consciously to mark himself off as the one who demands, who incites, and some one else as the one in whose power his satisfaction or discomfort lies. Then begin to develop all those facts which Mr. Baldwin truly and vividly describes (pp. 123–24 of *Mental Development*), of the child's watchfulness, his acute attention to all changes in countenance, gesture, and movement. Not, however, merely as strange intellectual presentations to be made one's own through imitation, but as signs of actions performed or to be performed in relation to the infant's own activities—as completing them, arousing them, directing them. And, of course, the corresponding growth in self-sense is of the activities that call forth those of the parent, or that in turn answer to them. Imitation appears at this time because, as already suggested, it is an important case (only a case however) of the general principle of adjustment of stimulus and response. One learns by imitation, because imitation is a mode of acting, of co-ordinating.

As these adjustments are made, habits are formed—rather, the adjustment effected *is* the habit. The child proceeds to utilize the habit as a power with which he makes new and more complex co-ordinations—arousing new and interesting activities in others, replying in new and valuable ways to what they do. In terms of this development of an inclusive whole of action, he continues to define himself and others—conscious definition being most acute at times of greatest tension, that is, at times when there is the greatest difficulty in maintaining or securing easy and full interplay.

If we turn to the facts, we shall find good reason to question the division into an imitative accommodating self in relation to parents, and an habitual, assertive self, in relation to dolls and smaller children. It would be as near the truth to say that when the child is with his parents he is not imitating; and that when he is imitating them he is not compliant; or, on the other side, that when the child is "habitual," he is not aggressive, and he is with his elders. It is impossible to make any general statements at all based on the supposed presentations or relations of intellectual contents. The child is certainly as apt to imitate his elders when he is not with them; in many cases, such imitation would be considered impertinent and at once rebuked. In many, perhaps most, cases the child learns from his parent not by imitating, but rather by responding, by following the lead of some question or direction. He utilizes his habits to carry the suggestion into effect. The child is compliant, not when he does not know what to expect, not when he feels a domineering power over him (except in cases of terrorism, which I am sure is far from what Mr. Baldwin means); but when he has some idea of the probabilities of the case, and so of what is expected of him. Moreover, as to the moral implications, the child may be compliant from prudential calculation, or as a mode of deceit, as well as from generosity or sympathy; and certainly rudeness and discourtesy lend themselves as easily to imitation as do their opposites. It is only in logical form that imitation is identical with the accommodating attitude. On the other side, what does the "trying on," the experimenting of the "ejective" period mean but just that habits are still forming—the child is learning himself and others? It is poor pedagogy and poor psychology particularly to associate learning with the receptive, compliant attitude. On the moral side, his "bossing," tyrannizing tendencies are just as much efforts to imitate and his efforts to discover himself, as they are merely to assert fixed habits. But the child is also sympathetic in this attitude. He "loves," pets, protects, and nurses dolls and younger children, as well as manipulates them.

So lacking, indeed, are we in any criterion for personality, sense, and social attitude, on the basis of the attempt to define them in terms of reactions to intellectual contents, that Mr. Baldwin himself frequently shifts his ground. Sometimes, it is the assimilating process which makes one the "subject"; by taking things into one's personality, they become new, different, inventive in quality. This is the particularizing process. Then the "ejective" process is the imitative one. This is no longer the generalizing process, but habit is private. Sometimes it is the development on the "subject" side, which makes the "contrary" boy, the boy of marked individuality, while the ejective process is the one which gives social dependence and distrust of self!

That the ethical self is precisely the self as the whole self seems to me the keynote to ethical psychology. But, here again, two modes of interpretation are open to us. Are we to find this wholeness primarily on the static or on the dynamic side? That is, is it found first in a thought, which then passes into action; or is the organization of habits and tendencies into a functioning whole the primary thing? Mr. Baldwin seems ambiguous as to the import of this "whole" self. There are traces, to my mind, of two incompatible views. One of these, in line with his professed theory, throws all the emphasis upon the influence of one personality directly upon another, through the medium of the content presented for obedience. The other, and, to me, better theory throws the emphasis upon the social whole, upon the organized unity of interests through action. This theory seems to me much the truer; but it involves a wide departure from the doctrine which makes sociality consist in the transfer of a given intellectual content from one person to another. Upon the first alternative, the law-giving personality is all, upon one side; the merely conforming personality receiving into himself, he knows not why, some idea from the other, is all, upon the other side. But what makes the command of the superior personality ethical? Certainly, it is not the mere fact that it is command. And what makes conformity, on the part of the inferior personality, ethical? Certainly not the mere fact that it has the form of obedience. This leads to the second position—the "other" personality is not the source of moral law, but simply the mediator who, through deeper insight and greater power of interpretation and expression, reveals to the child the reality of the situation, the organized action, in which as agent he is implicated. The moral law is the law of this situation, and the moral self is the one which organizes its various powers into unity through functioning them in reference to the situation.

The individualistic conception is emphasized in such sayings as this: "The sense of this my self of conformity to what *he* [father, brother, friend, God] teaches and would have *me* do—this is once for all, my conscience" (pp. 50–51, italics mine). It is implied in making obedience of one person to another the chief instrument of moralization—a superstition which seems to me to originate in just that individualistic philosophy against which Mr. Baldwin's book is a valiant and successful protest. When he says: "We appeal to some one else in whom we trust, as having arrived at deeper insight or better information of the conditions of the social life of the neighborhood than we have" (p. 39); while the interpretation is a little ambiguous (depending upon how much we take it *merely* on trust), the implication is that the conditions of social life are the really controlling ethical considerations, and that the "other" personality has fallen into his proper ethical place—not a law-giver, but a translator, an interpreter. This view comes out more unambiguously in the following: "The parents themselves are usually the source of family law over against the rest of the family. But that they are held to the actual socius and *to the relationships existing between them and the others*—is seen in any attempts they make to transcend these relationships" (p. 53). The words I have italicized have meaning only on the basis of an organic unity of action and interest, consciousness of which, as an organizing principle for the individual, constitutes conscience. Intellectual content, passing from one personality to another, disappears from the scene—or, at least, retreats to its subservient and tributary position.

I fear that in following these criticisms, the reader may have lost sight of the woods for the trees. But they are made as illustrations of one principle—that society, whether from the side of association (sociology) or of individualization (psychology), is to be interpreted with reference to active interests or organized interactions, not with reference to thoughts, intellectual contents. As I have carried criticism about as far probably as any one will be inclined to carry it, I cannot close without expressing my sincere conviction that Mr. Baldwin has opened a new and important field to psychologist and sociologist; that he has introduced us to this field in most generous fashion, through the profusion of his observations and suggestions; and that he has brought to light problems and considerations which must for a long time profoundly influence discussion. My criticism is to be interpreted as evidence of the sincerity of this conviction.

# Miscellany

## Letter to the Editor of the *Chicago Evening Post*

Permit me to express my sense of the great importance of the transfer of the Cook County Normal School to the city, a question coming before the school board Friday evening. The transfer—supposing it to be accomplished—may be a means of either the greatest benefit or the greatest harm to Chicago schools. If the city will contribute liberally to its support, will see that the present time requirement for study and the efficiency of the teaching force are either maintained or increased, and will allow freedom for the best and most progressive methods to be used, I do not believe there is a single step which would do as much for the Chicago schools. This is on the basis that it is kept up in addition to the present training school, and that the graduates with the more advanced and longer training are given preference for places. But if the school is transferred on a basis of personal enmity and false "economy" and narrow insight and sympathy lower the standards of the school as to time, etc., and mechanical methods of teaching and cadetting are introduced, it will be a most lamentable affair for the educational interests of Chicago.

I do not write this in the interests of Colonel Parker. All he needs is fair play and assurance that what on the surface is a public transfer in the interests of public education be not made a handle for consummating private enmities. Infinitely more important than any one man's interest is that justice and fair play be had, and that the city take advantage of the opportunity presented in the line of progress, and not take a step backward educationally.

[*First published in* Chicago Evening Post, *19 Dec. 1895. Not previously reprinted.*]

I have no special plans to formulate, but would suggest that if the school be accepted it be with the assurance that it be continued as at present till July 1, which is certainly only fair to the teachers hired with that moral if not legal understanding; and that meantime the school board consult with educational experts as to the best ways and means of making the school what it can easily be—a resource which will give Chicago the best public-school system in the United States. I feel confident that light and publicity are all that are needed to straighten out the tangles of this matter. I should like to pledge my own efforts in advance, as head of the pedagogical department of the university, to any and every co-operation possible to helping the public schools of Chicago through the instrumentality of a training school.

Permit me in closing this long letter to say that I am emboldened to write because of the thoroughly enlightened and wise course *The Evening Post* and the *Times-Herald* have been taking.

## Psychology of Number

To the Editor of Science—*Sir:* As Professor Fine in his review of McLellan's and Dewey's *Psychology of Number* (January 24, 1896) raised a question of considerable importance to educators and to psychologists, permit me to add a few words to the discussion, first thanking the reviewer for the generally appreciative tone of his article.

1. The question of principle raised is whether or no counting is measuring, whether or no integral number has a metric origin or purpose, and involves the idea of ratio. Now measurement is a word both of a more general and a more technical sense. That, in the most technical mathematical sense, counting is not measurement, is clearly recognized in the book referred to. But as it is held that in the larger sense of the term it is a process of measuring, and that the technical mode of measurement is an outgrowth,

[*First published in* Science, n.s. III (*Feb. 1896*), 286–89. *Not previously reprinted. For the review by H. B. Fine, see* The Early Works of John Dewey, v.]

psychologically, of the broader and looser sense, this disclaimer amounts, perhaps, to little.

Starting from the larger sense, it is held that number has its psychological genesis in the felt need for valuation, and that its function (psychologically once more) is to serve the purposes of valuation. Now counting seems to me indubitably one mode of defining the value of a previously unvalued mental whole, and in that sense to be a mode of measurement. Any process of defining value is, I should say, a form of measurement in the broad sense of that term. Counting implies first a mental whole; secondly, the breaking up of that whole into distinct parts; third, the use of one (any one, not some one) of these parts as a unit; fourth, the measurement of the amount or value of the original whole, through equalizing it to a certain definite number of the selected unit.

But Professor Fine says: "In however loose a sense the word may be used, 'measuring' at least involves the conscious use of a unit of reference. But no one ever did or ever will count a group of horses, for instance, by first conceiving of an artificial[1] unit horse and then matching it with each actual horse in turn—which 'measuring' the group of horses must mean if it means anything."

The whole point here is under what circumstances does one, not a mathematician or for mathematical purposes, count a group of horses. The answer is something of the following sort, it seems to me: One counts when one wishes to find out how many horses he has caught in a day's hunt, whether the same number has been driven back at night that were taken out in the morning; how much money is to be got in selling them, it having been settled that each horse is to fetch the same sum, etc., etc.; how one ranks as a chieftain, or a soldier, compared with others, etc., etc. In other words, one not having arrived at the *abstract* interest of the mathematician (and certainly the child to be educated

---

[1] Whence and wherefore this artificial? The point to be proved involves nothing about an "artificial" unit, but only a unit of reference, and that surely a horse is. But even if the term were relevant in the argument the question would arise whether the use of an artificial unit or of a measured unit is the essence of technical measurement; whether, indeed, a foot is, psychologically, more artificial than a horse.

has not) counts only *when* there is some value to be ascertained, and counts *by* setting off something which, for present purposes is a sample unit of value, *e.g.*, a horse, then equating the total value to the number of such units. Taking the matter in its development then (and not at the stage of the mathematician when abstracts have already become concretes), enumeration is always to define value, *i.e.*, to measure.

If the book referred to did not recognize the distinction between this sort of measuring and the technical sort it should certainly be condemned. But one of the points emphasized is that the former is an imperfect sort of measurement; that we don't really know, *e.g.*, what the possession of 60 horses amounts to till we know what one horse is worth, and so measuring proper (measuring with measured units) is substituted for mere counting, *i.e.*, measuring with undefined units of value.

2. It is said that number is not ratio. If one is using ratio to denote a certain idea, and not a technical abstraction of the mathematicians, I do not see how this statement is to be reconciled with Professor Fine's own account of enumeration: "To count a group of things on the fingers is merely by assigning one of the fingers to each one of the things to form a group of fingers which stand in a *relation of 'one-to-one correspondence to the group of things.'* "[2] And again, "When we say of two groups of things that they are equal numerically, we simply mean that for each in the second there is one in the first, and for each thing in the first there is one in the second, in other words that the groups may be brought into a *relation of one-to-one correspondence.*" What does the phrase italicized mean, save the idea of ratio? If this way of stating it had only been known to me when the book reviewed was written, I should gladly have utilized it to indicate precisely the point we were trying to make—the implicit presence of the ratio idea in every number.

Psychologically there is, of course, a difference in the mental attitude in recognizing a thing as "one," as unity, as

[2]    Italics mine.

a whole, an individual, and recognizing it as "*a* one," a unit. The primary problem the educator has to face, if he is to rationalize the teaching of arithmetic, is the discovery of this difference. The answer given is that "one" (qualitative individuality or unity) becomes "*a* one," a unit when it is *used* to *measure* value; and that, in turn, the need for this use arises when the thing is no longer taken as an adequate end, but as a means to be adjusted to some further end. *E.g.*, once more, when a man is *wholly* occupied in riding or hunting, or feeding a horse, when that absorbs his whole interest, he never takes the numerical view; when he wants to know how much of a horse owner he is, and how far this horse contributes to that end, he necessarily takes it. The question then is whether "one" ever becomes "*a* one," save as it is put into a "relation of one-to-one correspondence."

3. Professor Fine remarks that "the one postulate of arithmetic is that distinct things exist." The mathematician may perhaps be reminded that this postulate is precisely one of the chief problems of the psychologist. Given a certain number of things already recognized as distinct, and it is a very simple matter to go ahead and enumerate them, though even that must have a psychology *motivation*. But the whole tendency of contemporary psychology is to take a psychical continuum as its datum, and find distinctness (the property at the basis of number) as the outcome of a process of differentiation. The identification of this process, the ascertaining of the circumstances under which it arises, the mode of its operation—this is the thing which the psychologist wants to know about number, and is the thing the educator must know to secure the conditions under which the child shall form the number concepts easily and efficiently. The theory of the book, *Psychology of Number*, viz., that the differentiation and enumeration of units arises through the progressively accurate adjustment of means to end, may be right or wrong, but its error can hardly be established, I take it, by a mathematical view which considers number only as it is after it is fully developed, and has become so familiar as to be itself a complete object to the mind. Without pretending to a knowledge of numerical theory which I do not possess, I may say that it seems to me that the work done by Gauss is

at precisely the opposite pole from that which the educator needs from the psychologist, *i.e.*, Gauss was attempting to reduce to its ultimate simple numerical generalizations the developed mathematical structure. Dr. McLellan and myself were engaged upon the much humbler task of finding out what sort of a mental condition creates a demand for number, and how it is that number operates to satisfy that demand.

May I conclude by referring to the practical point involved? The trained mathematician as such is, of necessity, interested in the further use of certain finished psychical products. As a mathematician any reference to the preliminary development of these products can only disturb and divert him. But the problem for the pupil *is how to get the standpoint of the mathematician*; not how to use certain tools, but how to make them; not how to carry further the manipulation of certain data, but how to get meaning into the data. This is ultimately a psychological question, not a mathematical one, although it has to be translated over into mathematical terms and processes; and none is so well fitted to do it as the mathematician, provided only he will project himself far enough backward in the scale of development to realize the problem. The point does not conclude with primary instruction. Our text-books of algebra, geometry and high analysis are almost entirely written from the standpoint of an elegant and logical exposition of the matter as it stands to the trained mathematician. They are very nice for one who doesn't need them any longer. The first books written from the standpoint of one who is still coming to consciousness of the meaning of his concepts will, perhaps, seem foolishness to the trained mathematician, but they will mark the dawn of a new day to the average student. I venture the statement that (putting aside the few with the inborn mathematical instinct) higher and secondary mathematics is to the majority of students a practical riddle with no definite *intellectual* content in itself. What meaning it possesses it has got by way of attained practical facility in solving problems; or through its applications to other sciences or to engineering. It will hardly be denied that the educational value of mathematics is not realized until its concepts and methods have a definite intellectual meaning and content of their own. Can this be secured, save as the methods of instruction follow the evolution of the process out of its cruder psychical forms to the more finished?

I shall be more than satisfied to have made many blunders on the mathematical side if only I do not offer myself up in vain as a spectacle; if only more competent psychologists take up the matter, and if only mathematicians may descend from their acquired mathematical plane and endeavor to rethink the psychical conditions and steps through which their present magnificent apparatus has grown out of primitive, non-mathematical or crudely mathematical forms up to its present high estate. If the psychologist will risk some blundering around among the mathematical concepts, and the mathematician will recognize the relevancy of the psychological demand, and venture a little blundering upon that side, both parties may not only come to an understanding, but mathematical teaching may get what it today so largely lacks, some relationship to the psychical needs and attitudes of those under instruction.

# On the Study of History in the Schools

There is one suggestion to be emphasized. That is that the course might be extended downwards. If there is to be any solution of the congestion in the secondary schools it must be in breaking down the rigid barrier between the so-called higher education and primary education. There are primary schools in existence that have eight years of historical work—schools which begin history in the first grade and keep it up. This introduction of history into the primary grades has come almost entirely without help or pressure from the higher grades. It has come because the teachers in those grades felt the need of getting something more adjusted to the needs of the pupils, something more vital than the usual formal three R's. I think it will be found that the interests of the high school and college would be furthered

[*First published in a symposium in* School Review, IV (*May 1896*), 272. *Not previously reprinted.*]

by devoting a part of their energies to seeing what can be done towards introducing history as a part of the regular work of the lower grades and in improving the methods of teaching history in the lower grades. We can't pile everything into the secondary school; we must find relief farther back.

## The Sense of Solidity

To THE EDITOR OF SCIENCE: Having had frequently the following experience, I record it with the hope that it may call forth either analogous experiences from others or some explanation.

On falling asleep with any weight in my arms I have noticed that on waking at a certain stage of drowsiness the feeling of solidity has entirely vanished. It is not only that the sensation of weight is very much dulled, but the sense of continuity in the held body is gone. Indeed, it often seems as if the hole between the parts whose contact is actually experienced could be felt. The contrast with ordinary experience is so great that it serves to bring out very effectually the fact that ordinarily in holding an object we have not only a sense of contact and of weight, but also a sense of "filling-in," of tactile solidity or continuous extension. In the experience referred to, the contact sensations also appear to have a granular rather than a continuous character.

[*First published in* Science, *n.s.* VIII (*Nov. 1898*), *675. Not previously reprinted.*]

# APPENDIXES

# 1

## The Need for a Laboratory School

There is, at present, in the U.S. besides the beginning made in this University, no opportunity provided for graduate work in Pedagogy, in a systematic and well balanced way. This means that college professors in Pedagogy, normal school teachers, heads of training schools, city supervisors and superintendents have either to take up their work without adequate preparation or else must study in Germany where educational conditions are different. This fact in turn means that whole primary and secondary educational staffs, upon whom rests the responsibility of organizing, directing and supervising the foundations of our entire system, are being left unduly to the mercy of accident, caprice, routine or useless experiment from lack of scientific training. In these facts we have given both the problem and the opportunity for the work in Pedagogy at this University. It is not to compete with training and normal schools in the preparation of grade teachers, nor yet with other colleges in giving a certain amount of instruction in the theory and history of education; it is to organize its forces with reference to giving advanced instruction and direction to the class referred to. The first university to undertake this work will, in my judgment, secure the recognition, and, indeed, the leadership of the educational forces of the country. Here lies the greatest opportunity as yet unutilized in American education: —this whether judged from the greatness of the demand, the intrinsic importance of the work, or the attention the institution first organizing this department will receive. That other institutions are beginning to see the situation is evidenced

[*Statement to President William Rainey Harper*, n.d. 1896 (?). Not previously published.]

in the last report of President Schurman of Cornell (pp. 47–52) in which he at length discusses the state of affairs just referred to, and makes a plea for the organization of a graduate college of Pedagogy at Cornell to undertake precisely this line of work. I could take considerable of your time in detailing letters and oral expressions of satisfaction that the University of Chicago is beginning in this line—received from city superintendents and normal school teachers who realize the present needs. In such response to our present modest beginnings there is prophecy of the possibilities of the future.

The conduct of a school of demonstration, observation and experiment in connection with the theoretical instruction is the nerve of the whole scheme. Without this no pedagogical department can command the confidence of the educational public it is seeking to lay hold of and direct; the mere profession of principles without their practical exhibition and testing will not engage the respect of the educational profession. Without it, moreover, the theoretical work partakes of the nature of a farce and imposture—it is like professing to give thorough training in a science and then neglecting to provide a laboratory for faculty and students to work in. Such a school, in addition, is by all odds the most effective means for securing the necessary endowment of a department to undertake, in a systematic way, this training of the directors of our educational system. It would be the work almost of chance to find in advance persons of means who realized the importance of this new line sufficiently to endow it. The school itself furnishes the required demonstration. Moreover it tends of itself to arouse the interest needed for its own development. As a matter of policy, it would be hard to suggest any way in which the University could so easily get such a strong hold upon the interests of a number of persons as by affording their children with as nearly as possible an ideal education.

It is quite obvious that for such a school to stand still is for it to go backwards. It must grow as rapidly as possible to cover the whole period up to preparation for college. This is necessary to get the full advantage of our position before the educational public, and to reach the parents interested as well as to furnish a thorough training for our students in Pedagogy.

With means already furnished by your Body the model school now covers about the first two and a half years of the primary course. The appropriation made was for six months and for a sum of $1250. If your honorable Body can see its way simply to maintain the same rate, viz., appropriate $2500 for the year from July '96 to July '97 (including the maintenance of the school for six weeks in the summer when an unusually large number of teachers will be in residence) it will be possible to extend the work upwards, so as to cover four and a half years of the primary curriculum and downwards to take in the Kindergarten grades. This extension without increase of relative cost will be possible because of the greater economy attaching to larger numbers in connection with the greater returns from tuition; because of the permanent plant already secured; because of the growing possibility of utilizing students in the University for assistants at slight cost, and because the interest aroused is such as to justify the raising of a sum of money from friends of the schools and of the University.

Respectfully submitted,

*John Dewey*
Head professor of philosophy and pedagogy.

# 2

# *The University School**

The attention of those interested in educational experiments is called to the school conducted under the auspices of the Pedagogical Department of The University of Chicago. The school is located at 5714 Kimbark Avenue, and there are at present thirty-two pupils enrolled, their ages ranging from six to twelve years. There are two regular teachers employed, Miss Clara Mitchell, a graduate of and former teacher in the Chicago Normal School, and Miss Katharine Camp, a graduate of the University of Michigan and recently in charge of the science in the Normal Department of Pratt Institute. Miss Camp will have charge of the science work, and Miss Mitchell of the history and literature particularly. There is also a regular instructor in carpentry and woodwork, and one in music, and in addition there are some assistants from the classes in pedagogy.

Especial attention is paid to matters of health. The children have the use of the University gymnasium and the advantage of instruction by Miss Anderson of the women's gymnasium, who also undertakes a careful study of the physical needs of each child. The prominence of manual training in its different forms secures an ample variety of the activities requisite for physical and mental well-being. When the season is favorable, excursions to the museums, parks, places of geographic or natural interest in the country, and to typical industries in the city are undertaken as often as seems necessary.

---

* Report of an address by Head Professor Dewey before the Pedagogical Club, Saturday, October 31, 1896.

[*First published in* University [*of Chicago*] Record, 1 (*Nov. 1896*), 417–19. *Not previously reprinted.*]

The conception underlying the school is that of a laboratory. It bears the same relation to the work in pedagogy that a laboratory bears to biology, physics, or chemistry. Like any such laboratory it has two main purposes: (1) to exhibit, test, verify, and criticize theoretical statements and principles; (2) to add to the sum of facts and principles in its special line. It is obvious, however, that a laboratory requires a building and an equipment, but this laboratory has as yet few of the facilities needed for the work it has undertaken. It is in the condition in which chemical and other laboratories were some years ago when the need of experimental work was first becoming apparent. Visitors should bear this fact in mind.

As it is not the primary function of a laboratory to devise ways and means that can at once be put to practical use, so it is not the primary purpose of this school to devise methods with reference to their direct application in the graded school system. It is the function of some schools to provide better teachers according to present standards; it is the function of others to create new standards and ideals and thus to lead to a gradual change in conditions. If it is advisable to have smaller classes, more teachers and a different working hypothesis than is at present the case in the public schools, there should be some institution to show this. This the school in question hopes to do, and while it does not aim to be impractical, it does not aim primarily to be of such a character as to be immediately capable of translation into the public school.

The hypothesis underlying this experiment is that of the school as a social institution. Education outside the school proceeds almost wholly through participation in the social or community life of the groups of which one is a member. Through language and personal contact the intellectual and moral resources of the whole group are effectively, if unconsciously, transmitted to each member and put at his disposal. Moreover each individual does certain things (in the way of play and work) along with others, and thereby learns to adjust himself to his surroundings and also gains control of his own special powers.

The work here outlined is based on the assumption that

the more formal education of the school does not depart from the same general course that the unconscious adjustment follows, but organizes it. The school is a special social community in which the too complex social environment is reduced and simplified; in which certain ideas and facts concerning this simplified social life are communicated to the child; in which, also, the child is called upon to undertake not all kinds of activity, but those specially selected on the ground of peculiar adaptation to the child.

This simplified social life should reproduce, in miniature, the activities fundamental to life as a whole, and thus enable the child, on one side, to become gradually acquainted with the structure, materials, and modes of operation of the larger community; while, upon the other, it enables him individually to express himself through these lines of conduct, and thus attain control of his own powers. The fundamental activities (as well as those with which the child has been most in contact) are those connected with the home as the centre of protection, shelter, comfort, artistic decoration, and food supply. Hence the school work aims to centre upon these activities, and, so far as possible, enable the child to reproduce them in a gradual, orderly, and social way, in his own experience. Hence the educational importance attached to manual training, cooking, etc. They are not regarded as special accomplishments to be separately mastered, but rather as the media through which the child may gain social experience, and also as furnishing the most natural centres about which the materials of knowledge may be gathered and communicated to the child. It is intended to apply this same general idea to each branch of instruction. With the activities of the home as a point of departure, the different subjects taught in the ordinary school are the necessary products of this working out of the fundamental forms of social action. A large part of the educational waste comes from the attempt to build a superstructure of knowledge without a solid foundation in the child's relation to his social environment. In the language of correlation, it is not science, or history, or geography that is the centre, but the group of social activities growing out of the home relations. It is beginning with the motor rather than with the sensory side.

Since so much is said about sense training in the new education, it is well to ask under what stimulus the senses act. Attention itself is selective. The eye of the animal is alive to those things only which have a relation to its activities,—the getting of food or the escape from danger. The child, too, is attentive to what relates to his activities,—in other words, to what interests him, hence the senses get their stimulus from the motor side, from what the child wishes to do. It is not necessary to make up a set of stimuli to hold his attention or get him interested when he is using the saw or plane. His senses are on the alert, since he must use them in order to do something. This is the psychological reason for beginning with the child's activities. On the social side they introduce the child to the world of human relations; on the individual side they reveal him to himself as a factor in those relations.

The mode in which the common school studies are developed from these social activities is easily seen. Reading, writing, and spelling are usually taught too soon, since the brain centres called into exercise by these studies are not sufficiently developed to make their use pleasurable and profitable. It is one of the great mistakes of education to make reading and writing constitute the bulk of the school work the first two years. The true way is to teach them incidentally as the outgrowth of the social activities at this time. Thus language is not primarily the expression of thought, but the means of social communication. By its use the child keeps track of his work from day to day; by it he gives to others the results of his own special activity, and his own consciousness is widened by knowing what others have thought and done in the same lines. If language is abstracted from social activity, and made an end in itself, it will not give its whole value as a means of development. When the same reading lesson is given to forty children and each one knows that all the others know it, and all know that the teacher knows it, the social element is effectively eliminated. When each one has something individual to express, the social stimulus is an effective motive to acquisition. It is not claimed that by the method suggested, the child will learn to read as much, nor perhaps as readily in a given period as by the usual method. That he will make more rapid progress later when the true language interest develops, and that the break in the continuity of the child's life will be prevented, can be claimed with confidence.

Number is another of the trinity of fetiches of primary work. With the home activities as the basis of school work there is a constant demand for measurement in carpentry, cooking and sewing. The child may not learn as much of number as by the study of the multiplication table, but he will get an idea of what number really is, instead of the mere technique of number as is the case at present. The children who have been taught abstract relations only cannot translate them into the concrete form required by practical life. If they began with the practical activities, there would be no such difficulty. A teacher in a cooking school stated that it took her adult students nearly a month to get true ideas of measurement. Could any one doubt their knowledge of the multiplication table or fractions? If number is taught not as number, but as a means through which some activity undertaken on its own account may be rendered more orderly and effective, it assumes a different aspect, and affords insight into the ways in which man actually employs numerical relations in social life.

The relation of science to the activities of life is equally vital. In the history of the race, science is the outgrowth of the race activities, and not the result of investigation undertaken for its own sake. Thus the child is repeating the race experience when his activities lead him into the path of knowledge. Cooking leads to botany, chemistry, and the related sciences; the coal used leads to geology and geography, and ultimately to botany also. Carpentry and sewing lead likewise to a knowledge of materials, and the processes of construction, all of which gives a practical insight into the arts of life and their relation to man. All this work will form the avenue of approach to history in its true sense, since history should begin with the conquest of nature by man. Beginning with the life of primitive man living in trees or caves, the additional elements are gradually introduced until the child has the key by means of which he can interpret the complex social life he sees about him. History as simplified social life gives a proper foundation for teaching the literature of any period. *Hiawatha* or the *Iliad* should only be given in connection with a study of the social life of the people represented in the respective poems.

One of the main educational questions under consideration at the present time is the proper organization of the subject-matter of the curriculum, and the relation of the subjects mentioned to other means of expression, such as drawing, coloring and modeling. On the hypothesis given above, it is evident that an organizing principle has been found, and that each study has its essential function in the educational unity. The hypothesis is not to be accepted as proved but needs testing and verifying under different conditions and circumstances. Of the value of careful experiment along this line there can be no question.

## 3

# *Letter and Statement on Organization of Work in a Department of Pedagogy*

Chicago, January 8, 1897

My dear President Harper:

Sometime ago you asked me to prepare and forward to you a statement of what I would consider a fairly full equipment of the Department of Pedagogy. I enclose herewith such a statement. I have not attempted to give the details of courses, assuming that what you wish is rather the general plan of organization and divisions of labor involved.

I enclose also herewith a reprint of the article which I contributed to the University Record upon Pedagogy as a University Discipline, marking the portions which would throw light upon the other document enclosed.

Yours truly,

*John Dewey*

Enc.

[*Letter and statement to President William Rainey Harper, 8 January 1897. Not published during author's lifetime. Marked portions of "Pedagogy as a University Discipline" were: pp. 285.10–287.13,* **The Early Works of John Dewey**, *v.*]

# Plan for Organization of Work in a Fully Equipped Department of Pedagogy

The various lines of work which are naturally included within the scope of a University Department of Pedagogy may be reduced to a few main heads. We have

1. What may be termed for convenience, Educational Physics and Physiology, dealing with the whole plant of educational work and the adaptation of that to the physical being and welfare of the pupils.

2. Educational Sociology which concerns itself with the organization and administration of the educational system, both in relation to other social conditions and institutions and in its own external mechanism and workings.

3. Educational Psychology which deals with all matters appertaining to the adaptation of the school resources and the subject-matter of the curriculum to the child. Its problem is how, out of the plant and school system described above, to get the maximum of result from the standpoint of the individual pupils.

4. We have the subject-matter of general pedagogy occupying itself with the theoretical considerations regarding the nature, ends and aims of educational work and the intellectual organization of curriculum and methods corresponding thereto.

5. Educational History dealing both with the systems which have actually obtained at various times and in various countries, and also with the development of the theory of education as such.

## I. Educational Physics and Physiology

1. School buildings and grounds; city and country; heating, lighting, ventilation and plumbing; laboratories;

school furnishings, desks, black-boards, etc.; school decoration and æsthetics; all this to be inclusive from the Kindergarten to the University. Beside giving courses, the person in charge of this work would be responsible for the collection of plans, drawings, photographs, etc., from all available sources. Summaries should be given in original investigation along these lines, the construction of proper plans, etc. The work should look ultimately to co-operation with school boards in furnishing information upon these points, copies of plans, etc.

2. School Hygiene. The adaptation of the matters mentioned above to the health of children, including the investigation of the normal and abnormal condition of the senses of the muscular system in relation to the physical conditions of school work. The nervous and other diseases of children so far as they act and react upon the work of education, should be included, as also the theory of physical exercise and culture in relation to health. The person in charge of such a course ought to be, if not a physician, one who has had a thorough training in physiology and is in close contact with physicians. The seminar work would involve an examination of the actual school buildings from the standpoint of all their sanitary arrangements. On the practical side there would be such co-operation as occasion might suggest with the City Board of Health and with physicians and others interested. Through the museum and library there should also be formed here a sort of bureau of information to which those engaged in actual school administration might apply.

## II. Educational Sociology

1. Systems of education in their relation to political, economic, religious and intellectual conditions of society, involving such things as a comparative study of the various European systems in their special adaptation to their own surroundings and a study of the various types of the systems found in this country, in their adaptation to their local environments. It would also involve a study of industrial, technical and professional education from the same standpoint.

2. Internal School Organization and Management.

This would include a study of the business side; the raising and expenditure of money for school purposes and the proper divisions of labor involved there. It would take up the functions of school boards: the Superintendent, Supervisors, Principals, etc., and their relations to each other. The question of the methods of preparing teachers for their work and so on, would come under survey also. In fact all the problems which have to deal with the actual administration of the school system. The advanced work would consist in an actual examination of systems of Chicago and other cities near enough to be personally investigated with a view of discovering both the methods actually pursued, the defects and the suggesting of remedies.

## III. Educational Psychology

1. Child-study, both on the side of its methods and the undertaking of actual work, should receive attention.

2. Course or courses should be given in Psychology as applied to instruction. The question of methods in relation to the learning process of the mind.

## IV. General Pedagogy

This is the head which receives most attention, and in some cases, exclusive attention, in the existing status of Pedagogy in colleges. It deals with the philosophy of education as such and the question of educational aims and means. Beside this general work it should include a more special and detailed study of the school curriculum; of the studies actually pursued in the schools, of their respective values and relations to each other; also a study of the various sub-divisions of the educational system, elementary, secondary and higher, from the standpoint of their curricula and their methods.

## V. Educational History

1. The history of educational systems as actually organized, for example, the Chinese, Greek, Roman, Mediæval; the history of the development of the modern common

school system; the history of the development of the curriculum. This is the historical counterpart of what is treated theoretically in III.

2. The history of the theoretical discussions of educational matters. The study of educational classics from Plato down. The study of the epochs of educational reform and the writings which influenced them; the relation of educational thought to philosophical, ethical and religious thought; a consideration of educational theories in their relation to the general culture and intellectual atmosphere of the times.

The above takes up the work of the department from the standpoint of its logical sub-division. From another point of view it may be said that at least four courses should be given as under-graduate courses. These four are general in character and to be taken by those interested in education, apart from specialization along any particular line.

1. The history of educational doctrine.
2. Educational psychology on its theoretical side.
3. Child-study.
4. A synoptic view of school organization; the resources of the school; their administration; the chief contemporary problems in educational administration.

In the above nothing has been said about work in the actual training of teachers as it is assumed that for the most part, at least at the outset, the whole stress must be thrown upon the culture side rather than upon the professional. There are two phases, however, of training work whose comparatively speedy inauguration is worthy of consideration.

I.

When the Manual Training School is definitely annexed to the University, and its location changed so as to be sufficiently in close contact with University work, it would be highly desirable to have it include a special course for training teachers in the direction of manual training. The introduction of this line of work in the public schools is hindered now more by the lack of properly trained teachers than by any other one thing, as public opinion in general is now decidedly in favor of it. The New York Training School for Teachers is the only college of rank now making a specialty of this matter.

II.

We have already begun to have applications for teachers who are trained in the methods in use in our University Primary School. As soon as means are sufficient to give us a good supervising principal (a thing very much needed in itself), we should aim at securing a person who should be able to take oversight of and give direction and criticism to a number of assistants who should, at the same time, be taking theoretical work in the University. Such a move would be economical in more ways than one as it would enable us to derive a revenue from our assistants instead of having to pay anything for their services.

Respectfully submitted:
*John Dewey*

## 4

# *Report of the Committee on a Detailed Plan for a Report on Elementary Education*

In his paper of last year, Dr. W. N. Hailmann indicated the point of view which has controlled the discussions and the considerations of your committee in formulating the following report.[1] As that paper puts it, school instruction and administration must grow out of the pupil's experience; must remember that its object and goal are found, not in itself, but in enriching the child's life experience, and furthering his powers of self-expression and achievement; and that this development must be conceived as social—"the sympathetic co-ordination of individual purpose with that of others in common social endeavor, and in active mutual devotion to worthy universal ideals."

This conception of the relation of school work to individual growth has formed the point of departure of the following report. Such an inquiry obviously rules out investigation of general pedagogical principles on their own account, and equally rules out investigation of the details of school instruction and administration, so far as these operate merely to increase knowledge of such subjects or increased facility in the use of certain school arts. It includes consideration of both details and principles, so far as they have to do with the conduct of the school considered as an intermediary and instrument in the development of the child

[1]   N.E.A. *Proceedings*, 1897, p. 199.

[*First published in* Addresses and Proceedings *of the National Educational Association*, 1898, *pp. 335–43. Not previously reprinted.*]

x

x

himself. This limitation, of course, means no depreciation of the value of the former considerations. It merely states the confines, theoretical and practical, within which the work of this particular committee is contained.

The following report deals:

I. With the general spirit and aim of the proposed investigation;

II. With the general character of the methods to be pursued in reaching this aim; and

III. With suggestions regarding the specific methods to be employed. The latter point is again subdivided into recommendations as to method on the practical or administrative side, and suggestions regarding method on its intellectual side.

## I. Spirit and Aim

Any proposed investigation which requires the expenditure of time and money should grow out of some specific need in the existing situation. If undertaken on merely general principles, it is foredoomed to failure. Moreover, the exact nature of the particular need dealt with determines the peculiar character of the inquiry undertaken. We assume, therefore, that the best introduction to the recommendations which ensue is in the statement of the needs of the present educational situation in this direction.

A word of caution may, however, be in place. It is not for a moment meant to intimate that any conscious knowledge of the conditions and principles to be set forth is possessed, or need be possessed, by the teachers concerned. We wish merely to indicate, from a general standpoint, some educational changes that are going on, together with their reasons; to suggest that these have a deep-seated cause and significance; and to intimate further that, since the main phases of the problem are common to all who are working in educational interests, the experiences of those who have been most successful cannot fail to be serviceable to others. We aim simply to put the educational changes in their general social perspective.

It would undoubtedly be an exaggeration to say that

we are in an educational crisis. But it is within the bounds of sober reason to say that educational materials and methods are undergoing a decided readjustment, and that, along with positive steps in advance, a certain amount of confusion and uncertainty is attendant upon the reconstruction. The change in the educational system is nothing for which educators and teachers are responsible as individuals. It is the reflex of a general social change; it is evidence of the fact that, whenever other social institutions and forces change, the school, as one among many social institutions, must change also. This change, while in part an effect, becomes also in turn a cause. The school does not passively accommodate itself to exigencies forced upon it from without, but has its own social function which requires it to take a position in actively determining the movement of other social forces.

Out of the large number of tendencies which are operative in modifying the conduct of the school, the following may be noted:

1. There has been a tremendous enlargement of the educational equipment, of the resources which are available in the instruction of the young. The last century—yes, almost the last generation—has set free for general use a large number of valuable instruments, formerly only either in the possession of a few, or themselves so crudely developed as not to be educationally available. This increase in equipment is due, in the main, to two reasons: the growth of science, both as pure and, more especially, as applied to life in inventions and industries; and to the democratic development which has brought within the scope of every individual opportunities in art, practical achievement, and scholarship, previously open only to the few.

What some term the enrichment of the curriculum, and others its congestion, is simply the reflex of this social development. History, literature, science in the form of nature study, the arts of music, drawing, painting, various forms of manual training, and now, for the upper grades, elementary algebra, geometry, and one or two foreign languages, have been included within the range of elementary education. They are there either as excrescences, as external attachments, or as organic factors which will not only do their own work, but reinforce the value of all the educational factors. According as the relationship takes one or another form, the so-called "new" education means either congestion of the pupil, his distraction and over-stimulation, or else the orderly development and enrichment of his life.

2. Hand in hand with this increase in the educational tools available has gone, of course, an increase in the demands made upon the school by society. The growth of democracy has furthered the necessity of training, not only social obedience and conformity in ways of good citizenship, but also of active leaders in social and political lines. Moreover, the revolution in the industrial sphere, consequent upon the introduction of machinery and the facilitation of modes of social intercourse and communication, has created a demand for knowledge of the scientific processes and facts involved in modern manufactures and commerce. It requires sufficient practical acquaintance and sympathy with conditions of work to enable the pupil to assume, upon leaving school, an intelligent attitude toward these forces, which are fast becoming controlling ones in life. This response must be active as well as passive. New inventions follow each other so rapidly that the individual who can only passively conform is sure to be left behind in the industrial readjustments consequent upon changes in machinery, and in methods of doing business. Unless he is to sink down to the level of semi-dependent, unskilled laborers, or else become an object of charity, or even a criminal, he must be trained to such power of using his own intelligence as will enable him to keep his own feet, and help determine his own career.

3. The democratic development, once more, has tended to make the child more and more an end in himself. He is now seen to be a personality, not merely in germ or potentially, but actually. The same social movement which has transformed slaves and servile laboring classes into persons who are ends in themselves is affecting also the status and claims of the child. That such a movement is fraught with danger, as well as with responsibilities of higher achievement, there is no need to argue. Unless this tendency is adequately directed, it can mean only still greater disintegra-

tion of the family, and the uprearing of youth who are
undisciplined, demoralized, and who know no law excepting
that of their own whim and momentary interest. But the
growth of the psychological sciences has given an added
means of insight into child nature, so that along with the new
demand there has come the power of meeting it. Upon the
school, however, along with the family, falls the fundamental responsibility for the adjustment of problem and response. Here, or nowhere, must the adjustment be made.
The whole matter of the relationship of school methods and
materials to the positive development and direction of child
life is ripe for consideration.

These various phases of social growth have imposed
upon the school new duties which, partly by instinct and
partly by purpose, it is attempting to meet. It is endeavoring
to see to it that the society which is in process of forming
shall be met by an individual prepared to take his place
actively, as well as passively, within it. To secure this end,
it must use all the instruments put at its disposal, and use
them in such a coherent and definite fashion that they shall
be really serviceable—neither mere fads, nor mere extraneous devices for arousing and stimulating interest in the older
and more routine studies, but intrinsic tools in the development of the whole child nature.

Various communities have felt the demand with varying degrees of force, and, owing to local and variable elements, have met it with varying degrees of success. Some
time or other, however, the demand is sure to become universal. It will have to be met in both country and city, in
both manufacturing and agricultural districts, and in slums
as well as in the sections more favored with wealth and culture.

Here we have the particular problem set for any work
of investigation to be done along these lines. It is to gather
up the results which mark the higher points of achievement
in this direction; and to organize these in such a way that
they will be put at the disposal of other teachers, thus il-
luminating the work of all and economizing their time and
effort by showing channels of successful endeavor.

In certain schools the necessary readjustments are already fairly under way. They have not been made in the light of any general considerations, such as those already set forth, but on account of the immediate requirements of the local situation, through the instinctive tact, sympathy, and good judgment of teachers in perceiving and meeting the concrete wants of children; or, if originally suggested by theory, have long since lost any merely theoretical character through the test of application to working conditions.

The opportunity then, and the demand, is to gather together material of this sort, to sift and compare it so as to see the direction in which it is moving, the principles which are embodied in it; and then to present the results in such fashion that most successful attainments of the few in adapting the work of the school to the needs of child life shall become available for all.

## II.   Method to Be Pursued

1. It follows from this survey of the relation of the proposed investigation to the existing educational situation that the discussion should be inductive and experimental rather than dogmatic or deductive; it should be an inquiry, not a mere exposition. It is no reflection upon the existing science of pedagogy to say that it is very far from being in a perfect condition, even as regards its more general principles. Even these can be assisted in their development by being brought in touch with the experiences which have resulted from the sympathy and practical intelligence of our best teachers. Pedagogy, as a science, cannot afford to despise that direct contact with experience which fructified all other sciences.

Aside from this, general principles may exist, and yet be practically useless through lack of adaptation to the day-by-day work of the school. There is too frequently a yawning chasm between the realm of general principles and the details of school routine. While professedly and officially the latter may be regarded as derived from the former, as matter of fact, they may be, in large measure, survivals due to the mere inertia of custom, or empirical devices having no justification beyond their success in accomplishing some external and temporary result; or they may be evidences of the persistence and energy with which some educator has imposed his particular notions upon the school system—products of one of those waves that periodically roll across the country.

What is needed from the standpoint of general pedagogy is that the routine work should be really illumined and interpreted by organic connection with general principles, while the general principles need to be vitalized, kept fertile and flexible, through adaptation to detail. Our most pressing need is to escape from the current dualism between general principle on one side, and empirical routine and rule of thumb detail on the other. Such an investigation as that here suggested cannot fail to promote this vital interaction of theoretic principle and practical detail.

After the conquests of the inductive method in all spheres of scientific inquiry, we are not called upon to defend its claims in pedagogy. The burden of proof certainly lies with those who would proclaim in advance the sterility of such a mode of procedure. What would be thought of the botanist who should refrain from a study of concrete plants and their parts, on the ground that he could collect merely a multitude of empirical details which would be scientifically and practically valueless? Such a position can only argue a distrust of the general principles which are nominally professed. The more tenaciously one holds to the general principles and their value, the more sure he may be that an investigation of the most successful educational work will bring to light those principles, not in bare abstract form, but clothed with the authority of operative success; not as universals separated from practice, but transfigured through their embodied application in effecting their ultimate purpose—the life development of the child.

2. There need be no hesitation in admitting that it will be a matter of considerable difficulty properly to organize and to present the results attained in this inductive investigation. Two extremes, equally dangerous, would have to be avoided. On one side there is the danger of reading into the collected material *a priori* principles, thus reducing the material until it fits into the rubrics of preconceived ideas. Such a method would give the appearance of organization, but

would be fatal to the whole undertaking. On the other side there is the danger of presenting a crude mass of undigested particulars without reference to principle. This would merely overwhelm teachers by the mere bulk of data amassed; or, if used by them, would be likely to lead only to imitation of the letter without insight into the spirit.

While admitting the possibility of such misuse of the material, the committee by no means thinks this result probable, much less inevitable. Certain principles may be suggested which tend, in the first place, to control the amount and character of the data collected; and, in the second place, to assist in its proper interpretation.

(*a*) With reference to limitation on the side of material collected, the following principles may be laid down. The traditional routine of the school is taken for granted. So far as this is inquired into at all, it is (as will be indicated farther below) simply for the sake of indicating the conditions under which other work is done. The inquiry presupposes the running of the existing school machinery as found in the average, or more than average, American community. In thus taking it for granted, the inquiry is relieved of the necessity either of justifying or of attacking it. The only question is as to the special use of this machinery in the one direction of furthering, instead of restricting, the immediate life experience and vital growth of the child. This limiting principle allows us at once to rule out an immense amount of detail which would otherwise tend to congest the inquiry and obstruct its systematic interpretation. Such material is indeed valuable, but it is not relevant to this particular inquiry.

Another application of this limiting principle may be indicated as follows: The inquiry has nothing to do with school methods or devices from the standpoint of facilitating the mastery of a given subject. Here, for example, is a school which is unusually successful in securing ability to read at an early age. Here is another noted for its success in enabling children to manipulate number with unusual dexterity and accuracy. With such matters the proposed investigation has absolutely nothing to do. Inquiry into the relative merits of the phonic, word, and sentence methods, or of any variation of these, or of this or that particular method in arithmetic, lies quite outside of its view. It is well to have such matters taken account of, and made known to the public through the medium of educational journals, etc.; but the aim of the proposed investigation is to discuss methods from the standpoint of enlarging and enriching the immediate experience of the child, not of furthering the acquisition of knowledge or of school arts. This principle restricts the amount of data available by defining the precise kind wanted. As respects reading and writing, for example, not that is relevant which tells how the child learns to read most rapidly and accurately, but that which indicates how the capacity to read is utilized in the moral development of the child and in enlarging his horizon. What is there in the school life and methods of instruction which promotes the reading of good literature, and which facilitates the application of what is read to the child's own growth? So in arithmetic, not methods of teaching number are important, but the ways in which the child is led to conceive and utilize number relations in enriching his everyday experience.

The same general principle may be applied to any theory. Suppose, for example, it is the matter of correlation. Here the problem for consideration is not success or advisability of correlating one subject with another, but vital connection of the subject with the life of the child as it shows itself at home and on the playground, in his daily, non-scholastic occupations. It is not correlation of geography with history or with arithmetic which is in question, but correlation of geography with the child's daily experience in such a way that the instruction of geography grows out of it and in turn illuminates and interprets it.

( *b* ) There is, moreover, a limiting principle on the side of organization of results. The whole question is that of organic relationship to the development of the child. While we are far from knowing as much about the latter as is desirable, we are, through the development of physiology and psychology, now in possession of certain general principles which will serve as touchstones for the material collected. After it has been found *that* certain methods and materials actually facilitate vital growth of pupils, much can be done in telling *why* they do so. It is quite probable that these psychological principles could not have been applied in advance to prophesy or to deduce such results. But the results, once presented, can be thrown into relief and illuminated by means of psychological principles. The results obtained are, we may repeat once more, largely the immediate outcome of the instinct and sympathy of individual teachers. But once attained, they can be restated and interpreted in the light of larger principles, even though the latter would originally have been quite impotent in obtaining them.

It is not meant, of course, that this work of interpretation is to become a dominant factor in the final presentation. The psychological principles are to be used rather than exhibited. They are to be used in giving the material a coherent and orderly arrangement along lines which will enable the teacher to grasp the salient features of the methods reported upon; and, by getting insight into the reasons for their success, be freed from the necessity of servile imitation. Thus the confusion attendant upon the mere accumulation of data will be avoided; and other teachers, by grasping the results reached in their organic connection with the principles of mental and moral development, will be able to utilize them freely, by making adjustments freely to the needs of their own particular situation.

## III.   Specific Methods to Be Employed

After this survey of the general character of the proposed inquiry, and of the spirit of the method in which it is to be undertaken, your committee would make certain suggestions regarding the practical methods of carrying it out. Under this head we shall have something to say concerning both the administrative conduct of the inquiry and concerning the particular points to be got at upon the educational side.

### A. ADMINISTRATIVE ASPECTS

1. The investigation should be undertaken by a committee possessed of complete discretionary power, under the limitations of the particular task imposed upon it by your

body. This committee should be large enough and varied enough to secure representation to a variety of points of view, not only of pedagogic theory, but of practical experience. Moreover, it should be wide enough to take in the entire country.

2. While a large committee is indispensable in order to meet the needs outlined above, there should be a smaller central committee in order that the inquiry may be prosecuted with system and method. This should serve as a directing body from which instructions could proceed, to which reports could be made, and upon which should fall the responsibility of final collation of results.

Accordingly your committee would suggest some such scheme as the following: A committee of thirteen to be appointed, of whom four shall constitute a central committee, while the other nine shall be district representatives selected from particular geographical units in such a way as to cover the whole country. Each one of these nine district representatives to be regarded as a chairman of a subcommittee, and to be authorized to appoint district conferees to enable him successfully to prosecute the necessary inquiries in the region assigned to him. The central committee should act upon the data thus turned in. The inquiry should occupy at least two years, and the possibility of an extension to three should be definitely contemplated. The inquiry should be prosecuted patiently and persistently, with sufficient time for collection of data and their subsequent collation, or else it will be useless. In order to accomplish this, the National Educational Association should be asked for an appropriation for the expenses of the committee. The sum should be sufficient to cover, for the first year, the services of a stenographer for the central committee, expenditures for printing, postage, etc.; and the second year enough to cover the same items, together with the services of a secretary, who, under the direction of the central committee, should carefully work over the material.

### B. EDUCATIONAL ASPECTS

Your committee has given more time and thought to considering the details of the proposed inquiry with respect to the points upon which information should be sought than to all other things. The committee has been subdivided and various portions of the field assigned to various members. Superintendent Jones has taken the general conduct of the school in relation to child development; Superintendent Dutton, the æsthetic phases of school work and the relation of the school to other educational factors of the community; Miss Arnold, the subjects of the primary curriculum; Mrs. Putnam and Miss Brooks, the general spirit and conduct of kindergarten and primary work, both in themselves and in their vital adaptation to each other. After consultation, it seemed wise to throw the points for investigation into the form of specific inquiries, preceded by a brief statement of the general problems involved. A conspectus of such statements and inquiries will follow. This will constitute the real heart of this report. To this the foregoing statements are preliminary. It will indicate, with as much definiteness as we have been able to attain, in advance of any actual investigation, the main lines along which work should be directed. As developed by any committee your body may further appoint, it will set the main topics for investigation.

## Questions Bearing on the Proposed Inquiry

In current civilization there are growing demands upon the school for increased vital connection of the school work with the requirements of this civilization.

There are evidences that teachers in their work are responding with varying success to these growing demands.

Analyzing in a large way, the efforts of teachers may be grouped as follows:

1. Efforts to base the work of the school upon the pupil's experience.

2. Efforts to systematize the extra-scholastic experience of the pupil, and to supplement this with an ideal experience that shall lead him in his life onward and upward.

3. Efforts to secure the completion of mental acts in actual achievement, thereby fixing them in his organization, building up character, as well as purifying and enriching heredities.

4. Efforts to utilize character so gained and to secure for it attributes of devotion and benevolence by expanding individual purpose into social purpose; directing individual purpose-life deliberately toward healthy co-ordination with the needs and aspirations, the ideals and destinies, of social groups.

The opportunity and the demand are to gather together material of this sort, to sift and compare it in order to find the direction in which it is moving and the principles embodied in it, and to present results in such a fashion that most successful attainments of the few shall become available for all.

This is the purpose of the proposed inquiry, which is to be strictly inductive and experimental.

Such inquiry includes consideration of matters relating exclusively to the traditional school routine, of special methods and devices, of correlation of studies and discussion of psychological principles.

Yet such principles may be used in giving the collected material a coherent and orderly arrangement along lines which will enable the teacher to grasp salient features of the work reported upon, and to get insight into the reasons for their success, thus freeing him from the necessity of servile imitation.

## First Series

1. What is done to ascertain the general knowledge and skill of the child on entering school? the character of his home environment? his tastes, predilections, disposition, hopes, and aspirations?

2. To what extent and in what ways does the school consider, utilize, encourage, modify, or correct these things?

3. What efforts have been made, and with what success, to organize the interests of parents in the school?

4. In what ways does the school utilize the observation of things and phenomena on the part of pupils, in and out of school, in the preparation of lessons and in recitations?

5. How does the school utilize unusual occurrences and interests in the work? How does it utilize public festivals?

6. To what extent are play, and other school exercises

partaking more or less of the character of play, used for idealizing and extending the child's knowledge concerning the industries, commerce, and other phases of community life?

7. What uses are made of school excursions? of travel on the part of individual pupils?

8. Please state your experience with school gardens and window gardens. Are there other opportunities for the care of animals and plants?

9. In what ways does the school consider the child's scope of æsthetic appreciation, and stimulate the same for further extension, in the adjustment of his school environment? in the ornamentation of grounds and buildings? in the selection of photographs and engravings, etc.?

10. What opportunities are afforded, in the school or elsewhere, to hear good music? How does the school utilize these in its work?

11. To what extent do stories told the children rest upon their own actual or probable experience? In what ways are they used to stimulate observation, research, imagination, purpose, and aspiration?

12. In what ways is the child's home, community, and school environment utilized in primary lessons in number? form? nature study? language? drawing? reading and writing?

13. In what ways does the school utilize experiment and more or less independent research in securing data and in the formulation of general facts or laws?

14. What progress has been made in equipping the school with workshops, laboratories, and school gardens?

15. What progress has been made in equipping the school with drawing outfits, musical instruments, libraries, and reading rooms?

16. In what ways do the various studies and exercises, as carried on by you, stimulate original investigation, a spirit of research, æsthetic appreciation, and a healthy imagination? Please answer this question more particularly with reference to reading, form work, and nature study.

17. What is the character of reviews? How often are they held?

18. Please send samples of written records of the pupils' and teacher's work, plans of observation, course of study, time-tables, and specimens of children's work.

## Second Series

1. In what ways are the gains of one lesson utilized in other lessons or exercises? number and form in constructive work? the pencil and brush in nature study, essays and reports, geography and history, etc.? stories, reading, and language in consecutive, orderly narrative, description and report work—oral and written?

2. In what ways do you use kindergarten occupations, devices of "busy work," as well as, later on, the sloyd room and the laboratory, in applying knowledge and skill gained in various subjects to particular ends?

3. In what ways are such occupations used by you in stimulating and educating inventive and creative power? in descriptive and illustrative work?

4. Which of such occupations, as used by you, have a direct bearing on number work, form study, nature study, language, etc.?

5. How far and under what circumstances is it found helpful to correlate singing and instrumental music with games, marches, with other studies and exercises?

6. In what ways does the school utilize in its work special ability on the part of pupils in oral or written expression, as well as in technical skill or art skill, for purposes of instruction, recitation, or other legitimate school work?

7. To what extent are the pupil's creative impulse and his own ideas considered in his progress toward the appreciation and control of conventional art forms?

8. By what means do you associate and stimulate a tendency to read books with a mastery of the art of reading?

9. What specific school festivals are established, and how is the work of the school related to them?

10. How is continuity of progress secured within each class and throughout the school as a whole?

11. What are the tests of advance? How often and under what circumstances are pupils advanced into higher groups or grades?

12. What means have been employed to secure continuity of effort and result between the kindergarten and the school?

13. How are marching, changes of classes, etc., managed so as to secure spontaneous good order, avoiding the establishment of a purely formal routine with arbitrary motives and penalties?

14. How are punctuality, the requisite balance of silence and communication, cleanliness, regard for school property, and other school virtues, secured on a similar basis?

15. What evidences are there that the influence of the school upon the development of the tastes, æsthetic appreciation, disposition, and aspirations of the children is felt in the homes and in the community at large?

## Third Series

1. What is done in the general organization of the school to foster community spirit? to make the children feel at home? to make each child feel that he has a place in the school as a community, not simply with reference to lessons learned?

2. What opportunities are there for responsible leadership and co-ordination on the playground? in the school garden? in the ornamentation and care of the schoolroom, and of other children? on school excursions? on the way to and from school, etc.?

3. How is the recitation conducted so as to furnish motives and opportunities for interchange of experience and knowledge for the benefit of others, instead of serving merely as a test by the teacher of information acquired?

4. Under what circumstances and conditions, both as to pupil and subject, do you teach individually, in groups, or in classes?

5. How and in what exercises are children given an opportunity to enrich individual work through an equitable exchange of products of their labor, more especially in manual work?

6. How and in what exercises are children given opportunity to contribute products of their individual, chiefly manual, work to higher social ends?

7. What opportunities are children given to become actively interested in the work and pupils of lower or higher grades?

8. How and to what extent do children contribute by their art work or otherwise to the ornamentation of the school?

9. In what ways are kindergarten occupation, sloyd, the workshop, or laboratory used for co-operative work?

10. How and in what studies or exercises is division of labor secured, both in the preparation of lessons and in recitations, in research, and in applying knowledge and skill to common ends?

11. How and in what exercises do you utilize independent reading and individually prepared written reports in social school work?

12. When and to what extent are choral and orchestral features introduced in music? What influence do these exert upon the social atmosphere of the school?

13. In what ways are school festivals utilized in developing the social spirit of the school?

14. Are there evidences that attention to social phases of school work exerts a beneficial influence upon the development of strong, self-reliant individuality, coupled with a practically and intelligently benevolent attitude?

15. Are there evidences that the school, by its attention to social training, is exerting a beneficial influence upon the social tastes and tendencies of the community, or, at least, of the younger members of the community?

# Review of *The Psychology of Number and Its Applications to Methods of Teaching Arithmetic*, by James A. McLellan, A.M., LL.D., and John Dewey, Ph.D. International Educational Series. D. Appleton and Co., New York.

H. B. FINE

This book makes a false analysis of the number concept, but advocates methods in teaching arithmetic which are in the main good. The conviction of its authors that the difficulties which children have with arithmetic are due to the neglect of teachers to lay sufficient stress on the metrical function of number has carried them to the extreme of maintaining that number is essentially metrical in its nature and origin. The conviction is well founded, inasmuch as the first serious difficulties of children are with fractions whose primitive function was unquestionably metrical and to which men in general attach no other than a metrical meaning; but there is no reason for drawing the conclusion that because the fraction, which is but a secondary concept of arithmetic, is metrical, its primary concept, the integer, is metrical also, or even that because a child can hardly be made to understand fractions without associating them with measurement, he requires the same help with integers. Nevertheless, the authors of this book maintain, in the most unqualified manner, that the integer is essentially metrical and should be taught accordingly. Thus they account as follows for the origin of number: Man found himself in a world in which the supply of almost everything that he needed was limited. To obtain what he required, therefore, an economy of effort, a careful adjustment of means to an end, was necessary. But the process of adjusting means to an end is valuable in the degree in which it establishes an exact balance between them. "In the effort to attain such a balance, the vague quantitative ideas of smaller and

[*First published in* Science, *n.s.* III (*Jan. 1896*), *134–36. For Dewey's reply see* "Psychology of Number," The Early Works of John Dewey, v.]

greater . . . were transformed into the definite quantitative ideas of just so distant, so long. . . . This demands the introduction of the idea of number. Number is the definite measurement, the definite valuation of a quantity falling within a given limit."

They define counting, the fundamental numerical operation as but measuring with an undefined unit. "We are accustomed to distinguish counting from measuring. Nevertheless, all counting is measuring and all measuring counting. The difference is that in what is ordinarily termed counting, as distinct from measuring, we work with an undefined unit; it is vague measurement because our unit is unmeasured. . . . If I count off four books, 'book,' the unit which serves as unit of measurement, is only a *qualitative*, not a *quantitative* unit."

And they formally define number as "the repetition of a certain magnitude used as the unit of measurement to equal or express the comparative value of a magnitude of the same kind," a definition which, so far as it goes, agrees, it is true, with that given by Newton in his *Arithmetica Universalis*, viz., "the abstract ratio of any quantity to another quantity of the same kind taken as unit," though Newton's purpose having been to formulate a working definition comprehensive enough to include the irrational number, it is anything but evident that this statement represents his analysis of the notion of number in the primary sense.

The immediate objection to all this is that it is much too artificial to be sound. And in fact it requires but a little reflection to be convinced that pure number is not metrical and that counting is not measuring, but something so much simpler that men must have counted long before they knew how to measure in any proper sense.

It is not enough to say that counting is the simplest mathematical operation; it is one of the simplest of intellectual acts. For to count a group of things on the fingers is merely by assigning one of the fingers to each one of the things to form a group of fingers which stand in a relation of "one-to-one correspondence" to the group of things. And counting with numeral words is not a whit more complex. The difference is only that words instead of fingers are attached to the things counted. But, the order of the words being invariable, the last one used in any act of counting is made to represent the result, for which it serves as well as the group of all that have been used would do. The group of fingers or this final numeral word answers as a register of the things by referring to which one may keep account of them as a child does of his marbles or pennies without remembering them individually, and this is the simplest and most immediate practical purpose that counting serves.

The number of things in any group of distinct things is simply that property of the group which the group of fingers—or, it may be, of marks or pebbles or numeral words—used in counting it represents, the one property which depends neither on the character of the things, their order nor their grouping, but solely on their distinctness. Gauss said with reason that arithmetic is the pure science *par excellence*. Even geometry and mechanics are mixed sciences in so far as their reality is conditioned by the correctness of the postulates they make regarding the external world. But the one postulate of arithmetic is that distinct things exist. It is an immediate consequence of this postulate that the result of counting a group of such things is the same whatever the arrangement or the character of the things, and this is the essence of the number-concept.

Counting, therefore, is not measuring and number is not ratio. Pure number does not belong among the metrical, but among the non-metrical mathematical concepts. The number of things in a group is not its measure, but, as Kronecker once said very happily, its "invariant," being for the group in relation to all transformations and substitutions what the discriminant of a quantic, say, is for the quantic in relation to linear transformations, unchangeable. Nor are the notions of numerical equality and greater and lesser inequality metrical. When we say of two groups of things that they are equal numerically, we simply mean that for each thing in the second there is one in the first and for each thing in the first there is one in the second, in other words that the groups may be brought into a relation of one-to-one correspondence, so that either one of them might be taken instead of a group of fingers to represent the other numerically. And when we say that a first group is greater numerically than a second, or that the second is less than the first, we mean that for each thing in the second there is one in the first, but not reciprocally one thing in the second for each in the first. Instead of comparing the groups directly we may count them separately on the fingers, and by a comparison of the results obtain the finger representation of the numerical excess of the one group over the other in case they are unequal. And this is all that is meant when we say that by counting we determine which of two groups is the larger and by how much.

It is therefore obvious, as for that matter our authors themselves urge, that the rational method of teaching a child the smaller numbers is by presenting to him their most complete symbols, corresponding groups of some one kind of thing as blocks, marbles or dots. By such aids he may be taught, with as great soundness as concreteness, not only the numbers themselves and their simple relations, but the meaning of addition, subtraction, multiplication and division of integers and the "laws" which characterize these operations. This accomplished, he is ready to be taught notation and the addition and multiplication tables and to be practised on them until he has attained the art of quick and accurate reckoning. "Measuring with undefined units" is a fiction with which there is no need to trouble him. For in however loose a sense the word may be used, "measuring" at least involves the conscious use of a unit of reference. But no one ever did or ever will count a group of horses, for instance, by first conceiving of an artificial unit horse and then matching it with each actual horse in turn—which "measuring" the group of horses must mean if it means anything. A conception of "three" which makes "three horses" mean in the last analysis "three times a fictitious unit horse" does not differ so essentially as our authors think from the "fixed unit" conception of this number against which they protest so strenuously. And this fictitious operation is no more the essence of multiplication and division than it is of counting. Multiplication of integers is abbreviated addition. The product "three times two" is the sum of three two's not, happily, the measure in terms of a primary undefined unit of something whose measure in terms of a secondary undefined unit is three, when the measure of the secondary unit itself in terms of this primary unit is two.

On the other hand, measuring in the ordinary sense—the process which leads to the representation of *continuous* magnitudes as lines or surfaces, in terms of some unit of measure—deserves all the prominence which our authors would give it in arithmetic. We do not mean measuring in the exact mathematical sense, of course, but the rough measuring of common life, in which the magnitude measured and the unit are always assumed to be commensurable.

Compared with counting, or even addition and multiplication, an operation which involves the use of an arbitrary unit, and the comparison of magnitudes by its aid, is artificial. But this metrical use of number is of immense practical importance and of great interest to any child mature enough to understand it. No doubt a child may use a twelve-inch rule to advantage when practicing multiplication and division of integers. Certainly such an aid is almost indispensable in learning fractions. Without it the fraction is more than likely to be a mere symbol to him, without exact meaning of any kind. "Two-thirds" has a reality for the child who can interpret it as the measure of a line two inches long in terms of a unit three inches long, which it quite lacks for him who can only repeat that it is "two times the third part of unity." Mathematicians now define the fraction as the symbolic result of a division which cannot be actually effected, but that definition will not serve the purposes of elementary instruction. It is as certain that the fraction had a metrical origin as it is that the integer had not, and in learning fractions, as in learning integers, the child cannot do better than follow the experience of the race.

Our authors must, therefore, be credited with doing the cause of rational instruction in arithmetic a real service by laying the stress they do on this proper metrical use of number. Their chapters on the practical teaching of arithmetic, moreover, though unduly prolix, contain many excellent suggestions. It is a pity that a book in the main so sound in respect to practice should be wrong on fundamental points of theory. One can but regret that its authors did not take pains before writing it to read what mathematicians of the present century have had to say on the questions with which they meant to deal. Their conception of number might have been modified by the considerations which have led mathematicians to "arithmetise" the higher analysis itself by replacing the original metrical definition of the irrational number by a purely arithmetical one. At all events their notions of certain mathematical concepts would not have been so crude; they would not have made such a use of mathematical terms as this: "Quantity, the unity measured, whether a 'collection of objects' or a physical whole, is *continuous*, an undefined how *much*; number as measuring value is discrete, how *many*."

# Number and Its Application Psychologically Considered

D. E. PHILLIPS, Clark University

## I.   The Background of Our Number Concept

In the consideration of the subject now to be discussed, I propose to introduce and co-ordinate several phases and considerable work not yet found in any single treatment of the subject; to present a brief digest of the leading lines of thought on Number and Mathematics for primary and secondary schools from the pedagogical and psychological standpoint; and, lastly, to present my original investigations. Whatever merit may attach itself to this article I believe the greatest will consist in bringing together considerable material generally ignored or overlooked in treating the psychology of number, and in the *genetic treatment* of the subject. It appears that the most natural treatment will be to consider (1) the background of our number concept, (2) its development, (3) the original investigations, (4) the special application of the number concept to arithmetic, (5) the conclusion.

I will first review some experimental work which at first thought may appear to have little to do with the question under consideration, but which really underlies the whole psychology of counting. In 1868 Vierordt experimented on time-impressions from the beating of a metronome, reproducing them after the lapse of a short period. The indifference point, the length of interval more easily and accurately judged than any other above or below, was not the same for each individual, but varied between 1.5 sec. and 3.5 sec. For himself this interval was from 2.2 to 2.5 sec., when through the sense of hearing,[1] and twelve impressions could be distinguished if caught in a certain rhythm. Mach performed some experiments by the method of just perceptible differences as to the

---

[1]    Wundt's *Phys. Psych.*, S. 781.

[*First published in* Pedagogical Seminary, v (*Oct. 1897*), 221–78. For Dewey's reply, see "*Some Remarks on the Psychology of Number*," The Early Works of John Dewey, v.]

recognition of the equality of two time intervals. It was found to be most accurate at about .37 sec. and in proportion as one varied from this standard it was necessary to increase the difference between the standard and the interval for comparison in order to recognize their equality.[2] Kollert carried on several similar experiments in Wundt's laboratory, where two metronomes were used; one giving off a constant series, and the other varied intervals for comparison with the standard. Experiments on seven persons for intervals from .4 to .5 sec. showed the indifference point to be between .7 and .8 sec.[3] Estel and Mehner fixed the indifference point at .71 sec., and treated of the multiplication of the indifference point.[4] Dietze performed some experiments to determine the greatest number of metronome beats that could be repeated, and could be recognized to be the same in the repeated as in the original series. The largest series tended to group themselves into rhythmic multiples which he thought could not be suppressed. The largest number was forty and obtained by five groups of eight each.[5] Most of the experiments mentioned above were performed in Wundt's laboratory and under his directions.

Mr. Stevens published in *Mind* the results of 135 experiments on seven different individuals. "Of these, 114 point to this fundamental principle: That there is an interval of time (the value of which varies between .53 and .87 sec.) which can be reproduced with considerable accuracy; but with all other intervals an error is made, which is *plus* for those above and *minus* for those below the indifference point, the average of which was about .71 sec."[6] The direction of the variation as stated here is directly opposite that found in all of the experiments above mentioned, but the methods were different.

Dr. Hall and Prof. Jastrow performed a series of experiments by setting up a number of cogs following no order. One cog was put in as an *avertissement* at the most favorable interval of about .75 sec., and the observer sought to count the clicks. Each series of observations was preceded by a preparatory series of clicks which was arranged so as to exclude any considerable variation, and thereby largely eliminate the element of fatigue. After sufficient revolutions of the drum to satisfy the observer, the record was taken and another number set up. From this work it is concluded that counting objects or impressions is a very complex process, that "impressions in a

[2]   Wundt's *Phys. Psych.*, S. 785.
[3]   *Philosophische Studien*, Bd. i, Heft II, S. 88.
[4]   *Philosophische Studien*, Bd. ii, Heft I, S. 37; and Bd. ii, Heft 4, S. 546.
[5]   Wundt's *Philos. Studien*, II, 362.
[6]   *Mind*, Vol. xv, p. 394.

series must be distinguished from each other, that from 20 to 40 beats per sec. can be distinguished by the average ear without passing into one tone, that 4 or even three clicks must be farther apart than two, that counting requires a series of innervations, if not of actual muscular contractions, and the matching or pairing of the terms in two series in consciousness; that counting is more than tallying by ones; it is giving names to each position in a series. These names are difficult to pronounce, and some become more prominent by means of the greater time or effort they require. This in part accounts for the tendency to count with a system of accents. When the observer is behind in counting and clicks appear to be lost, he has ceased to give attention to the auditory series, having caught the *tempo* in the beginning and perceives only the innervations which expand all short intervals."[7]

Dr. Nichols has made a review of the work on these lines in his article on "The Psychology of Time," and concludes that nearly all persons, under nearly all conditions, find a particular length of interval more easily and accurately judged than any other, that this interval is very variable for different individuals, that the sign of the Constant Error is usually constant in both directions from the Indifference Point, that, when the norm and reproduction are single, the Constant Error is minus for intervals longer, and plus for intervals shorter than the Indifference Point, when the norm and reproductions are multiples, we have exactly the reverse.[8] Later, Dr. Nichols, after some very extensive experiments, asserts this same individual variation, finds the Indifference Point to be about .81 sec., and concludes that "time measurements are memories of certain most striking rhythmical, habit-inducing, and oft-occurring outer occurrences, such as particular watch or clock strokes, the varying lengths and shadows of morning, noon and night, etc."[9]

Dr. Nichols has lately published a small work on *Our Notions of Number and Space*. It is founded on a great number of tests made on the tongue, forehead, abdomen, etc., with pins in a cardboard. From two to five pins were used, arranged in lines, triangles, squares, etc. On the whole four pins were guessed more frequently than 3 or 5. "The more distinct and differentiated the separate terms of a presentation become, the more distinctly do they become numerical presentations. To formulate the genesis of numerical presentation we must determine the laws governing the simultaneous and successive combinations of separate points. The greater the number of

7    *Mind*, Vol. XI, No. 41, pp. 57–61.
8    *American Journal of Psychology*, Vol. III, p. 529.
9    *American Journal of Psychology*, Vol. IV, p. 107.

points in any given distance the less accurate and clear these numerical presentations, and vice versa."[10] Small numbers were overestimated, and large ones under-estimated. "Its origin and foundation must be fundamentally placed in the following law: Presentation of Numbers, of Distance, and of all Spatial Figures, and arrangements in general are alike based, primarily, upon serial events, differing greatly in mode, such as become characteristic of those modes of presentation which we call numerical, external and spatial, but all of them governed by the same fundamental laws of relationship. By reason of this, *all simultaneous presentations are dependent upon, and expressive of, the several modes of serial occurrence out* of which, through life, they have evolved, and become differentiated."[11]

Again, the work on Rhythm, by Dr. Bolton, will be seen to bear strongly on this subject. The preliminary part calls attention to the rhythm in the pulse, respiration, walking, speaking, attention, etc. In respiration the rhythm is about 15 to 20 minutes apart, the simplest voice utterances are primarily rhythmical. Nothing is more striking than the effect of rhythm on children and savages, and no one can avoid the moving of muscles when the rhythm is strong and clear. The instrument gave opportunity for variation in intensity at any place, and intervals of time could be made between 2, 3, 4, 5, 6 or 8 clicks. The rhythmical grouping of sounds was the same *in every case*, and the same was found by Dietze in the work to which I have already referred; and Wundt thought it impossible to *restrain* this grouping absolutely. It is done by intensifying certain sounds and subordinating others. Many say it is the same peculiar periodicity as they observe in the ticking of a clock. Others, when asked to count them, said they counted 4 or 2 as the case might be and began again. The subjects were found to be unconsciously keeping time by tapping, nodding, etc., at every second or fourth click. When movement was restrained in one muscle it was likely to appear elsewhere. These movements are the condition of rhythmical grouping. The accented sounds occupy the first place in the series and the 4-group appears to be composed of two 2-groups. "The conception of a rhythm demands a perfectly regular sequence of impressions within the limits of about 1.0 sec. and 0.1 sec." "When attention is moderate the number of clicks falling into groups vary with the rate. Slower than a certain rate no rhythm is felt. With more rapid 2 clicks form a group. Faster still, 4 clicks form a group."[12]

10  *Our Notions of Number and Space*, p. 184.
11  *Our Notions of Number and Space*, p. 200.
12  *American Journal of Psychology*, Vol. VI, pp. 145–237.

Bechterew found that with two series of strokes, of which one was larger than the other, coming simultaneously at the most favorable rate of 0.3 sec., he could distinguish a group of 18 from one of 18 + 1.[13]

Several tests have been made regarding the eye-span. "If you throw a handful of marbles on the floor," says Hamilton, "you will find it difficult to view at once more than six, or seven at most, without confusion, but if you group them into twos, threes, or fives, you can comprehend as many groups as you can units; because the mind considers these groups as units."[14] Prof. James says: "If a lot of dots or strokes on a piece of paper be exhibited for a moment to a person in *normal* condition, with the request that he say how many are there, he will find that they break into groups in his mind's eye, and that whilst he is analyzing and counting one group in his memory the others dissolve. In short the impression made by the dots changes rapidly into something else. In the trance-subject, on the contrary, it seems to *stick*; I find that persons in the hypnotic state easily count the dots in the mind's eye so long as they do not much exceed twenty in number."[15]

Jevons threw beans into a box and found that 3 and 4 were always guessed correctly, 5 correctly 102 times out of 107, and 6, 120 times out of 147.[16] Mr. Cattell exposed to the eye for .01 sec. cards with short ruled lines, varying from 4 to 15 in number. With 4 or 5 no mistakes were made, but for higher numbers the tendency was to under-estimate rather than over-estimate. He tried similar experiments with letters and figures, with practically the same results.[17]

Schumann made some experiments on memory in which letters were posted at regular intervals on a revolving drum, and observed through a slit. It was observed that when any rate was attended to for sometime, any change in the rate caused errors in judgment that would not have existed had the previous adjustment not occurred. The same was found to be true with metronome beats. He thinks the sensory centers are the seat of these phenomena, that they adjust themselves to a given rhythm, and rather expect excitations at a given time. Similar errors were found in measuring by drawing the fingers along a scale by motion of the arm.[18] Bourdon tested 100 children from 8 to 20 years old by pronouncing random figures, let-

13    James' *Psychology*, Vol. I, p. 407.
14    *Lectures on Metaphysics*, Lecture XIV.
15    *Psychology*, Vol. I, p. 407.
16    *Nature*, Vol. III, p. 281.
17    *Philosophische Studien*, III, 121 ff.
18    "Psychology of Time," by Nichols, *American Journal of Psychology*, Vol. III, p. 522.

ters, and syllables, at the rate of 100 per minute. Ninety-four could reproduce accurately 5 figures. Six, seven, and eight were reproduced by only a few. Figures were much more easily reproduced than letters or syllables, and the power improved a little with age.[19]

Dr. Bolton performed some experiments on the Memory-Span in children, by reading miscellaneously numbers about two-fifths sec. apart. He concludes that the memory-span increases with age rather than with intelligence, that for pupils of public schools it is six, and that the power of visualization plays an important part.[20]

Mr. Johnson has given us the results of similar tests on Feeble-Minded Children in which it appears that some groups surpass the normal children of same age as given above by Bolton and Bourdon, but the average falls below that of normal children. The tables indicate some relation of memory-span to intelligence, yet it is so high that we cannot consider it commensurate with the degree of intelligence. They are ear-minded rather than eye-minded.[21]

In and back of the material that is herein presented we are to seek the proper approach to the whole subject of Numbers if we are ever to treat them in a psychological and pedagogical manner, and to throw light on the most poorly taught subject in our schools. In most treatments on this subject a mistake is made in treating it either from the standpoint of adult psychology, sometimes philosophy, or in considering a concept as having a sudden birth, rather than stages of development. That the concept makes its first appearance in consciousness with the word or language symbol that represents it is a pedagogical misconception once very prevalent, and yet assumed by many who have written on the subject of Number and Mathematics. In Dewey and McLellan's practical part of *The Psychology of Number* one would infer that they believe that the child enters school with a very low, if any, number concept.

Again there is too much tendency to treat certain concepts or ideas as having their origin wholly in a single sense; such as time to the ear, space to muscular movement, and number to the eye. Without doubt the evolution of individual concepts is the proper approach to intellectual evolution, and the concepts now so vivid to man doubtless have a long and interesting history in their development through the lower animals, and in the race, which somewhat corresponds to their continual development in the individual from the dawn to the close of life. Before we can clearly discern the fundamental character that distinguishes one concept from another

[19] Philosophique, août, '94.
[20] *American Journal of Psychology*, Vol. IV, p. 363.
[21] *Pedagogical Seminary*, Vol. III, p. 246.

we must at least consider its evolution in the individual. In most, if not all, of our concepts it will be found that different senses play an important part in their formation, that they are fed, not by a single stream, but by several, and pass through various metamorphic periods. Sight plays such a dominant part in the development of the number concept that most have sought its origin in the observation of things. Dewey and McLellan assert that numbers are not obtained from things, but put into things. "The idea," they continue, "that number is to be traced to measurement and measurement back to adjustments of activity, is the key to the entire treatment of number as presented in these pages."[22] That is to say, our number concept is developed from our necessity to measure things. Civilization imposed upon us this necessity. Had they called the chapter on the *Origin of the Number Concept* the *Development of the Number Concept* it would have more nearly included the facts. But it is absurd to think of a savage attempting to measure a given quantity without any concept of numbers.

Lefevre, whose work is in many respects scholarly and unique, says: "Primary number (the early number concept) is a normal and universal creation of the human mind; it is purely the product of a rational process—an abstraction from a group of objects which represents their individual existence. The concept *one* is only in contrast with the concept *many*. The fundamental concept is prior to, prerequisite for, not derived from, counting."[23] To say that it is a "normal and universal creation of the human mind" is only to drop into the old way of dodging psychological difficulties. In the above quotation we have the inference that recognition of numbers in groups is the necessary stage out of which counting is developed. Most teaching of numbers is now founded on such a supposition, the falsity of which I shall speak later. Concerning the ratio or measuring idea, the *rational process*, on which both of the above works are based, I will show hereafter that such has a place, but that it is a totally different thing from the number series.

"By number," says Schubert, "we understand the result of counting or enumeration, which involves the ordinary or number sign, and the word standing for the thing counted; as five men, seven cities, and to ascend from named to unnamed numbers the notion of addition is necessary."[24]

This is sufficient to present the general drift of most discussions on the origin of the number concept, and before following

---

22      *Psychology of Number*, p. 52.
23      *Number and Its Algebra*, p. 20.
24      *The Monist*, "Notion and Definition of Number," April, '94.

this line further I wish to show the rudimentary stages that are prerequisite to this part of the subject, and then to co-ordinate this in its proper place. They would have done well had they not seized upon a part of the problem as the whole of it.

The first step is surely the formation of a series-idea. Changes in consciousness are continually taking place, produced by the varying impressions from all the senses. Consciousness is not one continuous impression but an innumerable multitude of successive changes. Which one of the senses plays the first and most important part in the series-idea, we are perhaps unable to determine. We cannot go as far as Preyer, who claims that the number concept is derived from the sense of hearing; or Münsterberg, who appears to derive time chiefly from the rhythmic processes of breathing; or Mark, who says that time is the result of the consciousness of continuous metabolic changes; or, like Nichols, find the origin of space and number in touch. As already stated, without doubt different senses contribute to these ideas. The tactile sense very early produces an endless series of changes in consciousness which soon become vaguely recognized as distinct both in time and space; sound continually plays its part after the first few hours of life; random noises, voices, ticking and striking of the clock, all contribute to the formation of the series-idea; the succession of night and day continues to greet the eye, objects come and go before the field of vision; hunger and satisfaction periodically occupy a place in consciousness; functional processes, especially circulation and respiration, play an important part, the movements of a child, first by others, then its own—all these, in process of time, establish firmly the series-idea which exists long before the number-name series. The earliest and most rudimentary form of knowledge in the cognitive sense is a knowledge of a series of changes. This precedes all external knowledge of things.

Since most of the foregoing experiments relate to time, the question as to what this has to do with numbers has naturally arisen. Simply because they have primarily the same origin and are fundamentally the same. Many errors arise simply because such abstract notions are considered under the form in which they occur most frequently in adult life. Although time and number may seem now quite distinct, yet these abstract notions have more in common than is usually supposed. Certain number of clock spaces or of passing events give us a time measure. The hunter or laborer depending upon measuring the distance of the sun from the horizon, is entirely lost if clouds obscure the sun. The power to measure a certain time in hours or days depends upon the power to reproduce the events that have occurred during its lapse. The aged, being unable to remember the passing events, have little sense of time. Some series of succession is the norm by which we judge time. Time is also used to express number; a day's journey once stood for a definite number of miles. Some savages use the seasons and the days of the moon to designate certain numbers. "Representing equal units, and groups of equal units, of any order whatever, and being, as it were, created at any moment for the purpose of calculation, numerical symbols," says Spencer, "seem, at first sight, independent alike of space and time. The fact is, however, exactly the reverse."[25] "The conception of both number and motion," says Ladd, "involves both space and time."[26] Figures or symbols are applied indiscriminately to any series of successions. Later we shall see that some of the strange mental phenomena in the application of numbers, and perhaps the relation of geometry to other mathematics, are traceable to the fact that this series-idea, established by a series of outer existing occurrences, embody the rudiments of the time, space, and number concepts.

This series-idea, established by a multitude of successive and rhythmical sensations conveyed through the different senses, ceases to be symbolized by different touch sensations, circulation, breathing, and movements, by sounds, clock strokes, etc., by varying objects in the field of vision, and becomes a general idea applicable to any series of successions. That this series-idea is the first step, and that it becomes quite abstract, will appear evident when all of the facts are co-ordinated. Long before there is any conscious idea of number, children delight in reproducing or following a series of any kind. I have recorded 91 striking cases of this kind. Watch them throw down a given number of blocks time and time again, repeat a series of sounds; several record cases where children repeat the strokes of the clock, sometimes very accurately. A boy under two years of age rolled, one after another, ten mud balls down an incline, marking one each time until all contained a little cross. The successive nods or motions of the head that children so often go through before any attempt to count, are the same that nearly all children make in counting. Behind such activity the series-idea is manifest. But mathematical prodigies and savages furnish unmistakable proof of this early stage in the origin of our number concept. The former have the series-idea highly abstracted and developed before any names are given to the series. When Mondeux and others spent their early days in arranging and piling up pebbles, they were not forming a

25    *Synthetic Philosophy*, Vol. II, p. 38.
26    *Psychology, Descriptive and Explanatory*, p. 499.

number concept, but simply endeavoring to symbolize the steps in the series-idea. Many of their combinations made without any knowledge of number names are astonishing. Mondeux said: "I did not know there was such a word as multiply, but I made my tables with peas and pebbles."[27] He could neither read nor write, and knew no symbols such as we use, when Jacoby found him. Inaudi, whom Binet has examined very extensively, first used *any* words, then learned the number names from 1 to 100 from his brother, and demanded more. He was then only six.[28] Without number names he performed calculations that to most would appear wholly incredible. At the age of 3 years Gauss is said to have corrected his father who paid his servants at evening and for extra hours. Fuller, Ampère, Bidder, Mondeux, Buxton, Gauss, Whately, Colburn, and Safford learned numbers and their values before figures. Why are children so eager for number symbols? Many want the "last number," but are never satisfied with any number given. Dr. T—— says his little girl has very much annoyed them by asking for the last number. Number names neither mark the origin nor limit the number concept.

Prof. Conant says that no tribes have been discovered to be without some number concept. But it is often limited to the numbers 1 and 2, or 1, 2, and 3.[29] Here we have a work that is a misnomer, since it deals only with the naming of the series. No one has any right to suppose a savage tribe cannot count beyond the current words for numbers. In fact they can and do count further by the gesture language.

I now wish to show that this series-idea becomes abstract, and hence some symbols of representation are necessary. Numerical symbols must be considered as purely representative. So are the fingers, sticks, notches, pebbles, etc., of the savage and the mathematical prodigy. How many other forms of rudimentary representation there may be we cannot tell. One can easily conceive that the difference of the strain of consciousness in grasping two series, or different successions, might roughly stand as a symbol. The child that has never seen but *one* dog cannot, in any sense, have what we call the abstract idea "dog." It is only after many and different kinds have been observed that the idea ceases to represent some particular one or quality. When there is a rapid presentation of many objects belonging to a class the marks are most likely to go unnoticed and an abstract idea is unconsciously formed. Suppose no name is given to these presentations; nevertheless the idea would be gradually

---

[27] Scripture, *American Journal of Psychology*, Vol. IV.
[28] *Psychologie des Grands Calculateurs*, p. 28.
[29] *The Number Concept—Its Origin and Development*.

forming and most likely to be symbolized in its first stages of development. The abstract series-idea has a similar evolution, only much more complex, less conscious, and more highly developed. It may be well to note here that in speaking of the abstract series-idea I do not mean it in the sense in which we speak of the abstract notion of virtue or of God. But such is more in the nascent and unconscious period of development. It is the inheritance of latent experiences, of an infinite repetition of them, implanting the vague idea of an endless succession. It corresponds to the vague abstraction which children show in applying strange names to common objects. Succession of some kind is the earliest and most continuous thing in consciousness. Series of innervations, touches, sounds, sights, etc., are the most constant things in consciousness; one series only gives way to another. Of course we are now speaking in terms of a rudimentary consciousness, and in going back to such a stage one is most likely to carry with him his present mental habits; and, since the eye symbols are so much more convenient now, and have such an irresistible influence over our concepts, it is hard to recognize that it has ever been otherwise and that there has been a gradual substitution. Thought is carried on in substituted symbols almost to the entire exclusion of the original ones, and without recognition that they derive their meaning from other sources at an earlier period. Certainly the prevailing opinion is that the number concept is derived through the sense of sight by the observation of things, or comparison of quantity. To what serious pedagogical and psychological mistakes this may lead is readily observable.

On what other ground than that which has been presented can we explain the facts as we find them in children? Children first name the series without reference to objects of any kind. Every attempt to instruct children in numbers shows that the series-idea is highly abstract. On making a test of 39 children in the kindergarten, I found that 33 of them counted without the slightest reference to the objects to be counted, always running the series far ahead of the objects. Nearly every primary teacher I have consulted says that for sometime children count in this manner, and the same is confirmed in the 616 returns to be considered later. Three hundred and fourteen out of 341 answering this question say the series gets ahead. Of the 39 mentioned above I found that all but two could count 100, yet their teacher said she had no idea they knew any number beyond 10. "M—— knew number names long before numbers themselves, and applied them to anything indiscriminately, the number seldom agreeing with the number of objects; when she was only five she begged to be told 'all the numbers there are.'" Mathematical prodigies, as already pointed out, have the series-idea most firmly fixed, and to them it generally remains a meaningless abstraction. Again children have regard for only the rhythmical order of the number names. "Paul being asked how many puppies the next door neighbor had, replied that he had three. His father said he had four. The child said 'No,' and proceeded to count as follows: 'Tip is naught, Bob is one, Nero is two, and Dandie is three.'" The use of naught for one is not uncommon. Have children of the kindergarten count, and you will find that they leave out difficult names and carry on the series the same, often repeating without being conscious of it. One boy asserted his ability to count 100, but in seven trials he never got beyond 69, always going back to 30. He still thought he counted 100, and appeared to have no idea that he repeated. "M—— when learning to count things or impressions would count eight, nine for one object. The number series always get ahead." "This child learned the figures in order: *i.e.*, 1, 2, 3, 4. He could tell them in this way up to forty, but if they were changed around he would not know but what it meant the same; he associated number with place or order only." "Most children I have taught," says an experienced teacher, "*will* learn the names independent of things. For sometime they do not associate them as how many of anything, but merely the name of the series." A—— writes: "I knew a little girl who was taught the figures in this way because they were easier to make: 1, 4, 7, 9, 10; afterwards, 2, 3, 5, 6, 8. For a long time the child would count 1, 4, 7, 9, 10, 2, 3, 5, 6, 8."

I cite in this connection the following statements collected from experienced teachers: D——. When the objects were beyond his counting series, R—— would look ahead, and finding this to be the case would group two or three objects as one to come out all right. F——. They use them promiscuously. Freddie counted seven sticks; when his mother changed the order, he counted them thus: 3, 4, 1, 2, 5, 6, 7. C——. In nearly all of my experience with little children I find that number names are used as names alone, and thus the third one in a series of objects will be a three to the child, no matter if it be taken from the series or not. L——. I placed little sticks before Willie and told him to touch each stick as he counted, but he was just as liable to touch three when he meant six or any other number. W——. Children learn number names as they learn other words, by hearing them repeated. They use them without knowing their respective values. They apply them promiscuously calling three objects ten as the case may be. Very frequently they have the idea that the number name belongs to the object in whatever order among others it is placed.

The early period at which children learn to count is very significant. They learn to name the series and follow it before they learn letters, to read, or to write. Out of over 1,100 persons, 90% are sure that they learned to count first. The supervisor of one of the large normal kindergartens writes as follows: "The tiniest children in our lowest room could count perfectly as far as eight, giving the names in order, and pronouncing perfectly after the first three or four weeks in school. I was surprised, for I knew that most of these sounds were not associated with any idea of number. I was curious to find out the reason for this occurrence and soon came upon it. The girl teaching in the room counted for gymnastics. The great enjoyment which these little people took in those eight words suggested to me that perhaps it was not so wrong as we have been told to teach children counting. The smaller children often carry on this counting to themselves after being seated, counting over and over. From the movement of their lips I can see that the charm is still upon them." This same delight is manifested until children are 8 or 10 years old.

A passion for counting when children first learn to follow the series is very common; 131 cases are reported, many of which are very interesting. J——. A little girl of seven years seemed to have an absorbing passion for counting everything. One day when at the Township Fair she counted all the chickens. She was once sent on an errand with the injunction to hurry. On the way home she walked on the railroad track and counted the ties. When half way home she forgot the number, so retraced her steps a half mile, and counted them again. M——. Lucy, 6 yrs., having been turning the leaves of a new copy of *Webster's International Dictionary*, turned to me saying— "This dictionary has —— pages." I noticed that she read the number of the last page correctly. "Well, Lucy, how many leaves has the dictionary?" Her answer was a little laugh and "O, don't know, a great many. There are over a thousand." My approval delighted her, and she told me of her self-imposed task of counting a million. "I have counted to seventy thousand." "You have?" "Yes, I am counting a million." "How long will it take you?" "O, I don't believe I ever can, it will take such a long time. I have been counting a long time," she said. An older sister of whom I inquired, thought that she had been counting for nearly a year. In several schools which I have visited, teachers have departed from their usual way of teaching by blocks, etc., just to show what a delight children take in counting. Why is this series named so early? Why such delight in counting? Why should these words be sought and caught so readily? The abstract series is behind it. The child is only keeping up the various activities of following an indefinite series in the various ways before mentioned, by a more convenient series of symbols. But the old signs are not lost at first.

A movement of some muscle, as the toe or finger, or nodding of the head, can be observed in nearly all children when counting at first. In fact many adults consciously or unconsciously do so.

J——. When I was small I always used my fingers to count. In fact am inclined to do it still, so strong is the habit. When the teacher forbade it I used my toes, moving them inside my shoes sometimes; at other times I remember producing a little sound in my throat as a counter. Again, when alone, I was addicted to tapping my fingers in succession. When I wished to remember I always counted off on my fingers in some way that it would be clearly stamped upon my mind. G——. Have seen children who were forbidden to count on their fingers make pressures upon their legs and sides with fingers or elbows. A——. Used to tally with my little finger, but not allowed to do this, I tallied by rubbing two of my back teeth. F——. When counting I tap one foot against the other for every count. L——. When 14 years old was greatly embarrassed upon finding all the boys in school laughing at me. Upon investigation, found that while doing an example I counted everything up on my fingers. This revealed a habit which I was entirely unconscious of. D——. In adding numbers greater than three I would always nod my head first toward one side then the other. I stopped that, for a long time I would think of nodding, but not really do so. In Bolton's work on counting clicks the subjects nodded or moved some muscle. If suppressed in one muscle it was likely to appear in another.

The fact that, at least nearly all children, no matter how taught, first learn to count independently of objects, in which the series-idea gets ahead, that they recognize three or four objects at first as individuals, calling the fourth one four even when set aside by itself, that counting proceeds independently of the order of number names, and often consists in a repetition of a few names as a means of following the series, that children early desire and learn these names; such, taken with the earlier steps presented, furnish unmistakable evidence that the series-idea has become an abstract concept. This is an important fact, the full significance of which will become manifest later.

Before passing to the next step, which is the naming of the series, let us call attention to certain rhythmical processes that must not be ignored, and which all the experiments on counting clicks, etc., show. Whatever fault may be found with these experiments it is evident that there is a favorable rate above and below which error is much more frequent, that it varies somewhat in different individuals and for the different senses, that the multiples are of great importance, that certain grouping is hard to avoid, and that accenting of certain numbers in the series and varying of the rate tend to modify the groups. Again circulation, respiration, etc., are not only continuous series processes, but each has a rhythm of its own. Then the countless modifications of compound rhythms, both organic and locomotive, whose effect may be only dimly perceptible, are never absent and their continual presence may produce an unexpected effect. In listening to the tick of a clock, or any continuous sequence of the kind, we divide it into groups. Several report cases where children have inquired why some "ticks" were longer than others. Number is not the result of any one of these units of consciousness, or rhythmical processes, nor of all of them. They are only a part that contribute to the series-idea; but what they especially do is to stamp, as it were, certain numbers of the series, and give them a dominance over the others.

In all of the returns nothing is more common than the preference children and adults give to certain numbers. Again this preference is often unconsciously manifested. Out of 600 returns Dr. Lancaster observed a decided preference for 18. Many will not give their age, or any other number correctly if it fall on certain ones of the series. There are certain numbers of the series we unconsciously avoid thinking in. Odd numbers are generally disliked. Miss D——has a passion for counting everything to find whether it is even or odd, and is displeased if it is found to be odd. I have before me over 100 expressions similar to the following: "Odd numbers always cause a kind of shrinking, as though some obstacle had arisen, while with even numbers comes a satisfied feeling." "The odd numbers seem to me to have something uncanny about them, and to be of less consequence, fullness, and beauty than the even numbers." Mrs. G——cannot endure having an odd number of anything in the house. Why do merchants price goods $.29, $.47, $.99, etc.? Evidently there is some psychology of number here which is turned to their advantage. We are accustomed, as we say, to think in "round numbers." They appear to be marked "close"; but why should $.47 appear "closer" than $.45? A merchant told me he had sold more of the same article when marked 47 cts. than when marked 45 cts. Cases of dislike for some numbers could be mentioned almost indefinitely where no reason can be observed. Dr. Brown, in relating the incident of the extraordinary precocious girl Marjorie Fleming, gives the following as one of her sayings; "I am now going to tell you the most horrible and wretched plague, the most devilish thing is 8 times 8 and 7 times

7; it is what nature cannot endure." Four is everywhere a favorite number. It is the most important factor in Hindoo arithmetic, all figures and fractions being built upon multiples and fractions of it.[30] Perhaps ten and its multiple stand next, then there is a great variety of choices. I have found nothing to indicate the existence of a number system founded on 6, 7, 8, or 9. Although 12 contains within itself the greatest advantages as a base, it has never been found among savages; notwithstanding civilization has attempted to substitute it for the decimal system, yet it is not likely to prevail. Such is the persistency given to the original system of counting on fingers.

The force of the rhythmical processes may be observed in children's counting, even when counting by 2's, 4's, 5's, etc., which they so much like to do; the rhythm is often very marked, as 5́, 10, 15́, 20, 25, 30́, or 2, 4́, 6, 8́, 10, 12́, etc. Exactly in what order and in what manner these special units of the senses, and rhythmical functions modify the series-idea we do not know, but all observations and experiments tend to show that they do. As I have already pointed out, the compounding of various elements of consciousness in early life, eventually merges into what seems unlike any one of them, yet when such mental activity is analyzed it yields its original component parts.

Let us now consider more fully the naming of the series, several points of which have been mentioned. The naming of the series generally goes in advance of its application to things, and the tendency of modern pedagogy has been to reverse this. This is founded on the false conception that the number concept originates from the observation of things, and the development of number names among savages is sometimes pointed out as proof, but the widely different conditions make such proof of little value. Civilized people have the names to apply to the abstract series, but the savage must invent names or symbols to represent an abstraction that must otherwise remain unexpressed. The fact that the concept is always in advance of the power to name shows that naming is only symbolizing it by means of a corresponding number of things. A few tribes have no word for even one. The Chequitos of Bolivia have none, and use *etama*, meaning alone. Tacanas have only what they borrowed from the Spanish. In the Gudang district only two numerals are used. The original inhabitants of Victoria had no numerals above two, yet they counted, and even recorded the days of the moon. For many years in India "moon" was used for one; "eye," "wing," or "arm," for two; veda, "age," or "ocean," for four, because they considered four oceans; "season," for six, because they

[30]    "Hindoo Arithmetic," *Science*, Vol. xxv, p. 254.

recognized six seasons; but here we see the idea of a recurring series of time must have preceded. A tribe in Australia and some of the Malay race, give names to their children in order of their birth, thus forming a number system extending to nine. The terminations are slightly changed for the girls. I have been told of a district in the U.S. where parents simply number their children according to birth. The moment any series of words is arranged in order in our mind, it becomes a counting machine.[31]

Whewell held that 2 and 2 make 4 is a necessary truth beyond what experience can give. It appears, however, that no such an assumption is necessary, when the concept is fully analyzed. That some number names are among the earliest forms in all languages only strengthens what I have said concerning the very early and in many ways unconscious origin of the series-idea. The use of the names of surrounding objects for numbers among savages gives no evidence that these ideas were derived from *such* objects. Such is but the endeavor of the mind to symbolize ideas gradually evolved as before indicated. The many words which children coin for their own use are not mere babblings, but represent ideas which seek some mode of representation. The adult will frequently fail to see any relation between the name and the object to which it is applied. When a child calls water "guga" and persists in the use of this word for two or three years, it evidently puts into such a word something not conveyed by the general name of the object. For example, a child calls water-melon "bum-bum." Evidently the leading idea conveyed by this word is the thumping common in testing the ripeness of the melon.

In all primitive counting the gesture or sign language comes first. Ah, ah, ah, ah, ah, etc., are natural number words now represented by human machines—striking of clocks, etc. In Livy we read that a nail was driven into the wall of Minerva each year to record its age. The finger method seems to have been the most universal and lasting of all primitive means of counting. Hence the almost universal use of the decimal system, notwithstanding the superior advantages of the duodecimal system, also the prominence given to ten and its multiples. Nearly two-thirds of all number-forms make their first turn at ten, and those that do not almost always do so after reaching the multiples of ten. Sometimes the counting is continued on the toes to twenty and then a man stands for twenty. Most races count to 10, but the exceptions are varied and many. Counting by sticks, pebbles, notches, etc., is second. The Egyptians used simple strokes up to 10, and for the 10's special symbols were used.

[31]    Tylor's *Primitive Culture*, Vol. I, p. 258.

A simple stroke, pebble, or notch elsewhere can represent 10, 20, or 100. Traces of the same system are found in the system of *tallying* at games, etc. In several instances the numbers from 1 to 9 have been represented by the first letters of the alphabet, the 10's by the next nine letters. Again multiplication found an expression by dots over the letters somewhat as we represent variations in vowel sounds. a = 1, ȧ = 10, ä = 100 : o = 8, ȯ = 80, etc. This system was used by the Greeks to 10,000. The Chinese never write 245, but 2-100 4-105. A system of bars separating each order of the number was once common in Europe.[32] Concerning the significance given to symbols and the relation of the number concept to intelligence I will have occasion to discuss later.

This is essentially the counting period, and any words that can be arranged into a series furnish all that is necessary. *Counting is fundamental, and counting that is spontaneous, free from sensible observation, and from the strain of reason.* A study of these original methods shows that multiplication was developed out of counting, and not from addition as nearly all text books treat it. Multiplication is counting. When children count by 4's, etc., they accent the same as counting in gymnastics or music. When a child now counts on its fingers it simply reproduces a stage in the growth of the civilization of all nations.

I would emphasize again that during the counting period there is a somewhat spontaneous development of the number series-idea which Preyer has discussed in his Arithmogenesis; that an immense momentum is given by a systematic series of names; and that these names are generally first learned and applied to objects later. A lady teacher told me that the Superintendent did not wish the teachers to allow the children to count on their fingers, but she failed to see why counting with horse-chestnuts was any better. Her children could hardly avoid using their fingers in counting other objects yet they followed the series to 100 without hesitation or reference to their fingers. This spontaneous counting period, or naming and following the series, should precede its application to objects.

Mathematical prodigies exemplify this period in the highest degree, and in fact it is to this period of mathematical development that they belong. A true theory or presentation of numbers should co-ordinate all such material, but none of our systematic treatments have considered Number-forms, Individualization, or Dramatization, of numbers, Passion for counting, Mathematical prodigies, etc.; in

[32] Number Systems by Conant, *Pedagogical Seminary*, Vol. II, p. 151.

fact the theories exclude any consideration of these facts as well as all the experimental work set forth in the beginning.

Take from the mathematical prodigy the power to manipulate the series in the four operations of Addition, Subtraction, Multiplication, and Division, and you have nothing worthy of attention. They seldom ever make a practical application of their power to things or to business, but, carried away with the delight of counting, they remain in an exaggerated development of this mathematical period. In general they, at least, appear stupid, inactive, having little knowledge of, or interest in, any thing except their ability to make rapid combinations in the abstract series. Gauss presents the greatest exception to this statement, yet his power greatly declined. In spite of opportunity for improvement Colburn, Dase, and Mondeux's talents disappeared. Precocity in calculation commonly appears between the age of 3 and 10 years. Not only do mathematical prodigies belong to the counting period, but we find this period prolonged and highly developed in many who have never attracted attention. Many have a passion for counting which they feel compelled to satisfy. In Messrs. Lindley and Partridge's work on "Mental Automatisms," 81.3% of 495 cases, have counting habits. Some count anything that appeals to the senses, such as telegraph poles, strokes of a bell, ticks of a clock, etc.; some count by "one, two," "one, two," and so on.[33] Some feel troubled if they fail to count all of the desired objects. Riding on cars seems to be most favorable to counting. Perhaps this is due partly to a rhythmical tendency, to the strong presentation of rapid succession; and to states of revery in which the centers are allowed to respond freely to the various series of changes. Mere abstract following of the names of the series is indulged in with great delight by 131 of the 616 returns now before me, and 23 frequently count themselves to sleep. Again counting is often indulged in unconsciously. Just as I have pointed out in a previous article that there are all degrees of number-forms from the most highly complex and elaborate, even of three dimension, to the simple fact that, at least 90% of all children conceive numbers as taking some direction, and nearly all adults have a similar feeling, or conceive large numbers as being "far away"; so the counting period in which all children find pleasure, and indulge to some degree when symbols are furnished, seems to be quite indefinite; but undoubtedly this period is the genesis of such mental phenomena as just described of which the mathematical prodigy is the highest embodiment.

In my article on the "Genesis of Number-Forms" I tried to show that such originate during the period in which the series-idea is being named or the period of spontaneous counting. While the abstract series-idea is being named it is represented by a series of muscular movements as seen in children's counting, but in most cases these muscular movements are suppressed, or partly so at least, before the series is well applied to things, and hence we may expect to find some mental movement corresponding to these muscular movements. The mind struggles to symbolize the series in some way, and on the intellectual side we have some idea of movement given to numbers. This movement may be a mere idea of a vague, indefinite extension in space, or it may become quite definite, complex, fixed, and vivid. It appears then that number-forms have their inception mainly before the series-idea is applied to things, are due to the abstract nature of the series-idea, to suppressed muscular movements and to the long period of development in which the ideas of time, space, and series or number, were so vaguely separated, and of which number-forms stand as a proof.

Much has been said of late about the relation of geometry and numbers. And the tendency is to introduce a kind of "eye-geometry" along with numbers. Even Sylvester said in his address to the British Association: "Whenever I go deep enough I touch a geometrical bottom." If such a relation is shown to exist and has any value it is to be found in the relation of the space concept and the series concept in their nascent state, and the value of such a relation is determined by the degree of dependence yet existing.

## II. The Application of the Series to Things and Impressions

The two steps already considered are the long and gradual formation and development of the series-idea established by an infinite succession of changes produced in consciousness from the beginning of conscious life, and the development of symbols or names representing a series of successions otherwise variously expressed. We have seen that the spontaneity of this period is so great that as soon as any words are arranged in order they are used as a counting machine, and that certain mathematical phenomena that have not, and cannot be co-ordinated in any other treatment, belong here. It next remains to show how these symbols are applied to objects and impressions. Seeing how readily and easily every child learns to count or follow the series even to 100, every teacher and observer must be convinced that its application is the most conscious and difficult step yet reached.

At first the individual thing stands for the number. Two

hundred and ninety-two cases are given where children count objects; as four people, and although all except one may have disappeared, yet if this be the last named it is still called four. In counting chairs, etc., no collection is recognized for sometime. Dogs, chickens, etc., are often counted, each standing for a number and not as a part of a quantity, just as the case already cited where the boy recognized four dogs, Tip as "naught," etc. Many cases of this kind occur in the early counting of children and among savages. Without doubt some of the strange psychological phenomena sometimes called dramatization and individualization of numbers, in which the numbers, sometimes to 20 or more, are invariably associated with, and thought of, as some object or person, finds a satisfactory explanation at this point. Four is a fat duck, 7 a tall man, 8 a pale faced woman, etc. P——. Five is a pig tail, 4 a box, 7 a tall woman, 9 a lazy man, 11 a pair of match horses. S——. I always thought of 7 as my crippled father (one legged), and 8 as my grandmother, and 9 as my tall grandfather. Now it is very natural that the child that called his neighbor's dogs naught, one, two, three, if this association be kept up, will later modify the objects associated with these numbers in accordance with the ease or difficulty in using these numbers. Three may become a mean troublesome dog; two a good puppy trying to make things even; naught an indifferent, easy-going fellow. While I have no direct evidence of this, yet it seems a very natural step in association and a plausible explanation. It further appears that the object is dropped later, or an association based only on some operation in the use of numbers arises. Two is simply a good little figure, 7 is a bad number, 3 is mean and cheats others, 11 is a happy, go-lucky individual, 13 is mean like 3; 25 is a square, round-faced fellow, etc. Then we have a few cases where numbers seem to carry on a continual combat for certain places: thus, 7 tries to get into 14, but is crowded out by 2; it then makes an effort for 28 or 35, but being crowded out, after much difficulty gets into 49, and so on with the various numbers. F——. Four seems disagreeable and devilish, because it turns its back upon every number into which it is put. A child of 6 yrs. says 9 is cranky and you cannot divide it into 2's at all. B——. The figure 4 always seemed so staid and firm to me, until I was told by a teacher that one of his pupils said that she always made the figure 4 to waltz time, and ever since then it has stood apart claiming an air of its own.

While such exceptional cases may seem entirely beyond the explanation given for the simpler forms, yet it is better to seek their explanation in some association in early steps in the development of number than to treat such as entirely outside the ordinary laws of association.

In the application of the series to things is where the child first encounters much difficulty, and this is much increased because the teacher not apprehending the full importance of this step tries to hurry the child over this point entirely too rapidly. It is here that we meet with so many systems and devices for teaching numbers.

It seems necessary, then, that we should first consider the quantitative ratial-idea of numbers, held by Dewey and McLellan, Graham, Speer, and Lefevre, to which reference has already been made. This is entirely different from the series-idea which has so far been under consideration. It is a reasoning process to which the series-idea is applied. The eye-span and ear-span, a summary of which has been given, in so far as they are purely such, are but quantitative relations of groups. In the case of the eye-span where we find the purest, if not the only, examples, in its last analysis, it is the simple recognition of a form. Many cases are reported where animals seem to have a high sense of numbers, such as various fowls that recognize the number of eggs, animals that recognize the number of young, or pigs, sometimes exhibited in shows, capable of playing cards. When a boy, I remember, a turkey hen that always quit her nest if a single egg was removed, even when the nest contained 7 or 8; but after sometime I found she could be thoroughly deceived by removing 3 and putting in 4 hen eggs. It was only necessary to make the general bulk or form appear the same. Such will be found to be the case with most of such examples. The card-playing pig simply recognizes a form, as may be observed by any one who will analyze their own mental operation in playing a game of cards. In order to make clearer the difference between the series-idea and this quantitative ratial-idea, I wish to state some observations made on children. In one of the large kindergartens I observed the children giving the combinations of eight. The lesson was conducted with 8 two-inch cubes by separating them into various combinations. The results were given by the children as if it were an instantaneous recognition of so many numbers. I then asked if other objects could be obtained, and tests were made with various other larger and smaller forms, and objects taken from my pockets; but in every test it was evident that counting was the only guide if any accuracy was reached. Such tests were applied in four different schools to 65 children learning the combinations of 10. The result was such as to make it evident that in most cases the combinations and relations so readily recognized were more a matter of form than of number, and that individual enumeration was resorted to whenever any doubt existed. Again the same thing was found even in a more marked degree when tests were made by presenting dots to the eye. One teacher presented to her children five dots in nine different

arrangements and in every case they were obliged to learn the form
before the number could be recognized as five without counting. The
same thing is found wherever such tests are made. One teacher
states that after teaching the numbers for sometime by dots arranged on cards, she accidentally put some of the numbers on the
board in a different arrangement, and was astonished to find a
hesitancy in recognizing them. She then for the first time realized
that she had been teaching form rather than number. It is fully
believed that a close analysis will show many of the above results
on the eye-span and ear-span to be only the recognition of form, or
that the result is obtained by rapid counting and grouping, which,
occurring so often and so rapidly, gives no conscious mental activity
unless special attention is paid to the operation. There are many
cases where a judgment is immediately given, apparently without
any reflection, and such have been counted *instinctive*; but close
attention to such mental states reveals even to the individual the
steps by which such a judgment was formed.

Mr. Speer's *Primary Arithmetic* is founded on the assumption
that the end of arithmetic teaching is to induce judgments of relative
magnitudes. It is rather curious how much quantitative judgments
are insisted upon. The Dewey and McLellan idea is very much emphasized, and to the entire exclusion of any other side. Here we have
a logical process of reasoning insisted upon to which the series-idea
is applied. "Reasoning in arithmetic establishes equality of relations,
reasoning in any subject equality or likeness of relations."[34] By what
authority can we make the science of numbers co-extensive with all
reasoning? Number in its genesis is independent of any, or all,
quantity, and the science of numbers is essentially the relation of one
number in the series-idea to another. That some form of the series-
idea may be applied to all, or at least, most processes of reasoning,
I admit, but that is quite a different thing.

Dewey and McLellan, with those already mentioned, holding
the same ratial-idea, fail to see that there are two sides to the application of the series to things, the logical analysis to which the series
is applied and a more general comprehension and application of the
series-idea. We are told that, "It requires considerable power of
intellectual abstraction even to count three,"[35] that "the manifestation
of the conscious tendency in a child to count coincides then with
the awakening in his mind of the conscious power of abstraction and
generalization. This also indicates discrimination and relation."[36]

34    *Primary Arithmetic*, p. 35.
35    Dewey and McLellan's *Psychology of Number*, p. 25.
36    Dewey and McLellan's *Psychology of Number*, p. 27.

The truth of such statements can be maintained only by giving counting a false or philosophic meaning not sustained by any of the facts connected with counting. It is a capital error leading to the worst pedagogical blunder to suppose that abstraction and generalization go hand in hand with counting, or to suppose that number has any such meaning. Counting chairs, tallying by beats, etc., are no signs of abstraction and generalization, neither is the power to manipulate the series in the four fundamental relations any sign of such. I have found many children whose number sense was very highly developed, yet very inferior to other children in the power of abstraction and generalization. If this were true, the general intelligence of savage races should go hand in hand with the development of their number concept, but the exceptions are so many and so varied that no one can draw any such a conclusion. Take from the mathematical prodigy the power to *count* and manipulate the relations of the series, and as a rule you have little of any kind of intelligence remaining. They are noted for their general stupidity in other lines. Every one who has lived among the negroes knows how much their number concept is in advance of their general intelligence. They are generally unable to read or write, or to form any abstraction or generalization, but never unable to count and in many cases to perform astonishing calculations. Take Thomas Fuller, the African slave, who died at the age of 80, never having learned to read nor write, and was of very low intelligence, yet his arithmetical calculations are among the wonders of mental phenomena. This philosophical theory is not wide enough to cover all the facts. The ratial-idea is but a part of the philosophy of number and takes in but one part of the application of the series-idea.

In what does the comparison of two quantities differ from the comparison of two leaves? "Quantity is limited quality, and there is no quantity save where there is certain qualitative whole or limitation."[37] To carry out their quantitative ratial-idea, and make number the "rational process" desired is to identify number with all reason. The application of the series-idea to the logical processes of reason no more makes them identical than the giving of motion to a ball makes the ball and the motion identical. Some maintain that mathematical reasoning is different from other reasoning; but there is still a wide difference between the reasoning involved in the fundamental operations with the number-series, and mathematics taken as a whole. This philosophy not only ignores any such difference, but any other that might exist. "*Reasoning in arithmetic establishes equality of relations, reasoning in any subject* equality or likeness of rela-

[37]    *Psychology of Number*, p. 57.

tions." It is true that "all relation is a result of comparison," and we can hardly conceive reasoning that does not involve comparison in some way, and even an application of the series-idea, either definitely expressed or more or less distinctly understood. When a child asserts two leaves to be alike or unlike there may be involved a geometrical comparison and a comparison of the intensity of color; but there is no expression of such on the part of the child, and it is greatly extending the idea of number to call it arithmetic. Even granting there is no strict line of demarcation either between reasoning in general and mathematical reasoning, or between general mathematical reasoning and the simple operations with numbers; yet there are certain marked stages of development and application that no one will think of identifying.

This application of numbers is the latest and most difficult step, and no attempt should be made to push it on the child before the proper time. The most general use of the series does not involve this comprehension and application of numbers. If drill, for the logical reason be the aim, such an application of the series at the proper age is, without doubt, of utmost value; but having seen an advocate of the ratial-idea labor long and hard with no result but confusion on the part of the pupils, I am convinced that it is a step demanding considerable abstraction and generalization, and of a nature not found in the more general or common applications of the series, such as made in ordinary counting and calculation.

## III. Results of Some Original Investigation[38]

This part of the subject will include (1) the examination of 616 returns on the syllabus on Number and Mathematics, (2) the result of 2,043 papers on numbers and arithmetic, collected from the first to the ninth grade inclusive.

The following syllabus was issued:

# NUMBER AND MATHEMATICS

## 1. Psychological and Anthropological

(a) State cases where animals, or children who could not count, have distinguished, *more or less*, objects, as eggs, young, toys, etc. How fine was this discrimination, how shown, and other details?

(b) Describe games of instantaneous guessing of the number

[38]    See also "Genesis of Number Forms," *American Journal of Psychology*, Vol. VIII, pp. 506–527.

of objects in a group, noises in a series, inches, feet or rods in a given distance, surfaces, angles, etc.

(c) Describe cases of tallying by beats or counters, before counting, or before number names are known.

(d) How do children learn number names, and how use them, what changes of order, errors in learning to count things; does the object series or the number series get ahead? Describe fully cases where counting became a passion, and everything must be counted, also cases of school children who use fingers, move toes, nod, etc., or use other counters.

(e) Errors and order in learning figures, making or applying them. Do the figure forms have any moral or personal character, as: 8 looks happy, 7 cross, 4 solid, etc.? Report fully when such associations exist. How different do Arabic and Roman numeral forms seem?

(f) Cases of number forms, *e.g.*, the first 12 numbers being habitually associated with a dial or clock face, the first ten on a line, straight or curved, systems of dots, colors, etc. Do odd seem to you different from even numbers? Draw any number forms. How do you arrange days of the week or month, the musical scale?

(g) Cases of "eye geometry," or automatic puzzling over patterns of carpet, wall paper, bricks on sidewalks, strong fondness for tracing the forms of decorative ornamentation, spontaneous drawing of such patterns or development of them in the use of kindergarten material.

(h) Cases of children exceptionally forward in or fond of mathematics and those exceptionally backward. Describe any physical or mental peculiarities of such children, their other tastes and aversions, and account for this peculiarity. Especially, if you have a prodigy, try to find out just *how* (by what process) each cardinal operation is done; the same of dullards.

(i) Describe any rare case of pupils who associate number processes with personal acts or dispositions, as *e.g.*, four is peaceable, and dwells tranquilly with eight, but with seven it feels and acts out enmity, etc.

(j) Ask children of each grade what part of the year's mathematics they like best and least, and why, letting those of upper grammar and high school grades write out their answers.

(k) What figures or numbers give you, as well as your pupils, most trouble in adding or multiplying?

## II. Pedagogical A. Elementary

(a) Please state how you would teach beginners. Describe your special methods with any phase of the work. Special drills.

(b) What mistakes are most common in—1, notation; 2, numeration; 3, adding (oral and mental); 4, subtracting; 5, multiplying; 6, division; are these more or less if special accuracy is attempted?

(c) If you have tried (1) the Grube method, state its chief merit and defect, (2) the same of Colburn, or much *mental* arithmetic.

(d) When would you begin fractions, and briefly outline your method of (1) beginning, and (2) of teaching common denominator, etc.

(e) Should more intensive methods, a larger or less proportion of time, more mechanical drill of both memory and slate, and less rules and explanations be advised?

(f) Or is this pure form work, abstract and obsolete, and far from the pupil's experience, the traditional application to *values* too commercializing, and should the number relations grow out of observation, facts in zoölogy, botany, physics, astronomy, etc.?

(g) What illustrative or other apparatus would you use for each stage thus far? 1, How long should, *e.g.*, four be illustrated by four girls, tops, apples, etc., before the child understands that it can apply to anything? Would you use any form of abacus, or Russian counters, and if so what, how and how long? Value of associating, *e.g.*, 1, with unicorn; 2, with an ox; 3, with a trefoil; 4, with a quadruped; 5, with a star; 6, an insect, etc.; also value of jointed figure, *e.g.*, 8 joints in the figure 8, etc. Value of toy money, divided spheres, jointed rods, etc., for fractions. Do the marketing, shopping or trading stories, as a setting or motive for the pure number relations, help or hinder; and how, why, instances? Do you know any rhymes, songs, puzzles, or games or any other device that may help some? What charts, or diagrams, or black-board pictures are helpful?

## B. Higher Arithmetic

(a) Of 1, proportion; 2, percentage; 3, roots and powers; which should come first and which last, and briefly, *how would you begin and proceed with each?*

(b) What should be the place of weights, measures, moneys?

(c) Of the business application of the science of pure number relations, as interest and partial payments, exchange and bills, commission and brokerage, banking, taxes, bonds, annuities, or of their application to science, as in mensuration, surveying, longitude and time, geography, astronomy, physics, etc. Which is most important? Which logically first and last, and how would you teach each?

(d) What apparatus would you advise for upper grammar

and high school mathematics, as slates, globes, drawing instruments with verniers, cube root blocks, theodolite, weights and measures, graphic methods and charts, etc., etc.

(e) Name the best text book or books, in your judgment, with the ground of your preference.

## C. Geometry and Algebra, etc.

(a) At what point in arithmetic should geometry be begun and how, and how co-ordinated with arithmetic and algebra?

(b) Name best text book and method for beginners. How far, and if at all how should geometry be based—measurement, drawing, or the data of astronomy or physics?

(c) At what point should algebra begin and how?

(d) Should it be taught abstractly and formally at first or concretely, and if the latter, on what basis? Name best method and text books for beginners.

(e) At what stage of progress, or at what grade or age, would you begin trigonometry? Name best method and text book. How would you connect it with previous mathematical work, and what practical work, observation or experience would you make use of?

(f) At what stage of progress, grade and age would you begin calculus and how? Name best method and text book for beginners. How would you connect this work with (a) previous work, and (b) informal observation and experience?

Something over 800 returns were received, but nearly 200 were found of little value in any way. Nearly all of the returns relate only to the first part of the syllabus, however, about 100 have something to say on the second part, and 13 papers treat it extensively.

Of the 616 reporting on the first part, 235 are men, 319 women, 62 do not designate sex. No further attention is given to sex, since there is no difference of any note in the returns. Seventy-two per cent. are teachers; forty per cent. have taught over five years.

*Animals, or Children who could not Count, Distinguished, More or Less, Objects, etc.* One hundred and thirty-five cases were reported for children; 170 for animals, the nature of which may be seen from the following: G——. A cat with 3 kittens will miss 1 even before they are a day old. R——. Bob used to bring 5 cows; if 1 were missing, would, of his own accord, go back after it. F——. Our guinea always leaves her nest if a single egg is removed. Have tried her time and time again. D——. I have a dog that can count 5. He will bark once if you hold out 1 finger, twice for 2, and so on to 5; he will bark for sticks in the same manner. M——. Bruce, our dog, used to bring the hogs out of the meadow. When in the lot, he would look them over, and, if any were missing, would go back. M——. Thomas, 32, cannot count above 10, yet he can split rails by the hundred and know just how much he has made. H——. I knew a boy, 4, who could play casino before he could count 10. He seemed to know the value of the cards by the arrangement of the spots. C——. Willie, only 3, had 7 blocks with which he played. I took away 2; he observed no difference until he attempted to put them in the usual form. He then cried, saying some one had taken his block; returning 1 did not satisfy him.

These examples are sufficient to make clear the general replies to this question. It will be seen at once that the difficulty encountered here is to determine when it is *form* and when it is *number* that is recognized. That animals have some number sense both as a succession and as a relation between magnitudes cannot well be denied, but, as I have already pointed out, much that passes as such is only the recognition of an individual form; and this is certainly true in nine-tenths of the cases given for both animals and children.

*Games of Instantaneous Guessing of the Number of Objects in a Group, Noises in a Series, etc.* Two hundred and twenty-six cases are given, and 73 different games. Much under this heading bears a close relation to some of the returns on Mental Automatisms,[39] and in some respects to Dr. Lindley's Puzzle Interest. However, he finds guess-games and riddle-making to begin about 3, and culminate from 5 to 8.[40] Only 59 in my returns mention the age of guess-games, and it is generally placed between 6 and 10.

*Of Tallying by Beats before Number Names are learned*, 91 cases are given. H——. Fred will stand by the window and tally as the rain-drops fall. C——. Eddie, only 2, often repeats the strokes of the clock. F——. When I was about 3 I tapped my finger as the rain-drops fell. Also sorted a collection of pictures, making a mark for each one put aside. H——. B., 4, keeps tally by closing one finger as the clock strikes, etc., also by shaking his head when the piano is played. D——. F., 3, was playing "farm"; every now and then he put a stick up the water pipe. E. asked him why he did this. He said: "They will tell me how many times I go to mill." H——. Children follow the series in various ways, sometime before the names are given. F——. A boy, 5, will arrange piles of sticks of different sizes, and then lay aside one larger stick for each of the different piles.

---

39      Lindley and Partridge, *Pedagogical Seminary*, Vol. v.
40      "A Study of Puzzles," *American Journal of Psychology*, Vol. vɪɪɪ, p. 450.

*On Learning Number Names*, 341 give a definite answer; 314 say that children learn them by rote as abstract words; 27, from objects. This is one of the most important topics discussed in the returns. Several cases have already been given in the first part of this article, and only a few need be added here. P——. Children learn number names by imitation or by hearing them used, sometime before they know how to apply them. D——. C. could count 100 long before she could recognize 6 or even 4 objects. M——. They learn number names by hearing them and use them promiscuously, calling objects by number names. It is astonishing how readily, and how many children learn number names even to 100 while they have a very limited knowledge of their application.

*The Application of the Series* formed another very interesting topic to which there were 329 answers; 292 may be classed as cases where they apply them indiscriminately; 37 to objects. Some of the 37 do not seem to understand what is desired. They speak of children applying them to objects, and then state that children designate objects according to their order in the series wherever they may be placed. Practically all substantiate the fact that children apply number names indiscriminately or promiscuously. In this connection are found some of the most important facts for pedagogical treatment or teaching of numbers. R——. C., 2, always uses 2 for everything, if he sees 5 birds he will say "2." H——. When L. was 3 he would press the piano keys and say: "1 key, 4 keys, 8 keys," etc. I have often observed him counting to himself, saying, "1, 5, 8, 10, 20, 3, 9," etc. S——. Sarah will often put blocks in a pile by 2's and count only by ones. M——. Sometimes I have my children count objects they can handle, and, if they have any idea of how many to expect, when the series number begins to get ahead, they will put over two or more at a time.

I am indebted to Miss Shinn for a very accurate, extensive, and valuable record on the observation of a child from the 8th month to the 6th year, a very brief digest of which is presented: First indication of number, observing things in pairs at 8 months; at 16 had an inclination to enumerate similar things, by successively touching them, counted her fingers, but not in correct order; at 17 taking nuts out of a box, etc., one by one, time and time again; at 19 delighted to transfer objects one by one; number above duality was not conceived; "more" has been used, can count, but has no idea of quantity above two. Taking out cards she would say: "De wu" each time, apparently understanding it. At 20 months she understood "all" of any objects. The idea of succession of units was evidently manifested in various ways. At 22 months she tried to count 5; her uncle counted his fingers, she held up hers and counted correctly to 5. Two days later one finger was held before her, she said, "one"; two, she said "three." Being asked to look again, she said: "four," and went mechanically through the list while only 2 were presented. For some time about the 25th month she would call more than 2 "two-three," could count to 10, but did not know 3. At 26 could count without help, if not allowed to count for both taking up and laying down; yet in the 28 month sometimes 2 appeared to mean only more than one. Was proud of her first independent counting, often chanted the numbers; two days later, all alone, trying to count beyond 10, she said 11, 12, 14, 18, 15, 40; do not know how she picked it up. At 35 she could add the combinations to 6, but only subtract one; counted to 19, stumbling on 7 and 17; also counted by repeating names at random. At 4½ years she counted to 50. Four months later Miss Shinn began lessons in number with objects, she cared little for this, and apparently learned little. Her mother, taking her, dropped objects and made it frankly a lesson with a demand on the imagination. The child responded better to this and soon came rapidly into an understanding of numbers. She reduces all to counting, says she does it in her head. Though concrete terms are used, she does not think in such. At 5 years 8 months, could count 1,000. The above is digested from 55 pages.[41]

*Change of Order of Number Names.* One hundred and seventeen such cases were tabulated. A close analysis was made to ascertain if any order was generally hit upon, but such was not found except that 7, 9, 11, and 13 are omitted much more frequently than any other numbers. Eighty-nine, out of the 117 cases reported, omit or misplace one or more of these numbers. Thirteen count almost entirely by using the even numbers, but no general rule prevails. This disregard for order shows that the child cares only for the series of *successions*, and that any suitable words will afford it a counting machine.

*Does the Number Series, or Object Series Get Ahead?* This question was answered by 181; of whom 151 say the number series; 30, the object series. The facts revealed under this head are of the utmost significance. Sufficient cases have been cited in previous parts of the article. In the individual tests made on 66 children, I found that children in the model school and even in the first grade counted with considerable difficulty if they were required to keep the object and the number series equal. It becomes quite a slow process. Mr. S. told me that his children would not get the number series ahead if he

[41]     See page xxxix.

moved the objects over very slowly. The fact that children can hardly go fast enough when following the series only, seems strange, but simply indicates that the number series and its application to things are quite different.

*A Passion for Counting* is strongly emphasized by 131. By 43 it was carried over into adult life; in 88 it was most extreme between 7 and 10, disappearing soon thereafter; 57 first had a passion for following the abstract series, later for counting things. The culmination of this passion between 7 and 10 indicates that it is the period when the number series is applied to the object series. Such may be designated as the counting period which in some is prolonged and highly developed. Dr. Badanes does not specify any age for this counting period, but we infer from his suggestions on teaching numbers that it falls within this period.[42] B——. H., when only 5, could really count 1,000 by 100's, and did count 300 by saying 101, 102, 103, etc. F——. M. could count 100 rapidly when 3. Counted everything she saw when 7 and 8, and often counted time by seconds when alone. T——. Mary, at 8, would stop to count the shutters on houses, count her steps; everything had to be counted or she was not satisfied. One night went to bed very unhappy because she could not count all the stars.

*Counting on Fingers, by Movement of Toes, Head, etc.*, is noted by 260. The reader is referred to what has been given on movements in counting.[43] F——. In a school of 50 children I found that every one counted on their fingers, most of them on the sly, but some unconsciously. G——. I find that when children are forbidden to use their fingers, they will resort to some other movement, tapping the foot, moving the toe, head, or arm, even to any muscular contraction. In some late experiments on counting, involving considerable complexity, Mr. Bohannon found that subjects could not count without making some movement. The motor element plays a large part in nearly all thinking; but any one giving attention to any series of succession will find this tendency stronger than in most other mental activity. The rhythmic nature is perhaps more effective.

*Errors in Making Figures.* One hundred and seventy-two errors are reported; 43 make 3 backward; 52, 9 and 6; 31 confuse 3 and 5; 28, 9 and 6; 18 are miscellaneous. These may furnish minor points of interest for the teacher.

*Individualization or Dramatization of Numbers.* Only 35 cases are given. C——. I always thought of 1 as tall and thin, 3 as cranky, 9 graceful, 7 stubborn. D——. When a child, numbers were always

---

[42]    *Falsity of the Grube Method.*
[43]    See page xli.

some real person to me; 3 a well known carpenter, 4 a heavy woman, 7 a lawyer always prosecuting 9, etc. How this came to be I do not know, and cannot remember when they did not appear so in childhood, even now I am not entirely free from it.

*How Different do Arabic and Roman Numerals seem?* brought forth some rather peculiar answers. Only 4 say they like the Roman numerals; 173 dislike them because they are "stiff," "dignified," "reserved," "vain," "used for state occasions," etc.; 69 detest them because they are of "no use," and cannot see why letters must be used to express numbers. E——. I always thought them grand and stately, and took extra care to make them. G——. Roman numerals seem like something foreign, always thought of Roman soldiers and avoided them when I could. A——. Thought they were meddlesome because they are both letters and numbers. D——. Dignified, always associated them with kings. H——. Always had a great significance to me as I had seen them in the Bible, dreaded to use them. Do not like them now except on the clock. H——. Arabic common; Roman numerals something extraordinary, so brave looking. It would be interesting to relate several more of these returns; the clearness and earnestness with which every one is stated bear conviction that here are some psychological associations, somewhat common, but perhaps unsuspected. They certainly give valuable hints on the laws of association which, if not valuable in themselves, throw light on certain phenomena that seem not to come under any laws of association, such as we have already mentioned, etc.

"*Eye-Geometry*" is indulged in by 150. All of this has been so well worked up in Mental Automatisms to which reference has been made that I deem it unnecessary to present the matter here.

Accounts of 19 children unusually bright in mathematics, and somewhat dull in other branches, are given; and 6 who are quite stupid in mathematics. One boy, 9, can read and write, but cannot learn to count.

*The Likes and Dislikes in Mathematics* are difficult to classify. Seventeen different parts are mentioned as being liked; 21 disliked. Three hundred and fifty-four mention some like or dislike. Since the manner of teaching, etc., modify one's taste so much, I shall cite only the points that seem to be free from this and of most interest. Fifty-five like Interest, none dislike it; while 48 dislike Stocks and Bonds, 2 express a liking for such. Mensuration is liked by 25, disliked by 13; only 1 reporting "eye-geometry" dislikes mensuration; 17 of those who report such like it. The G.C.D. and L.C.M. is detested by 23; 19 like Mechanical work; 12 detest problems; 14 girls and 9 boys hate the whole of arithmetic. Geometry is liked by 36, disliked by 1;

Algebra is liked by 34, disliked by 1; but these nearly all come from a single school. Such are the points of any special interest. The prevailing reason for likes and dislikes was "useful," or "no use."

Besides the above, 260 papers from the 4th and 5th grades, in which children state their likes and dislikes, have been examined. In the 4th grade 38, out of 124, dislike Long Division; 51, G.C.D.; 22, Concrete Problems; 47, Fractions. Sixty-nine like Addition and Multiplication; 62, the Mechanical; 20, Decimals. In the 5th grade 35, out of 136, dislike G.C.D.; 14, Percentage; 19, Fractions; 16, Denominate Numbers. Sixty-two like Interest; 28, Decimals; 18, the whole of Arithmetic.

*What Numbers Give Most Trouble in Adding or Multiplying?* There were 440 returns received; 157 give 7 and 9; 88, 7 and 8; 34, 6 and 7; 42, 7 only; 18, 9 only; 26, 3, 6 and 8. The others were miscellaneous. Seven is found in 327 cases, 9 in 204. Five say 9 is easy, always 1 less than 10.[44]

From the above returns it appears that we may justly conclude that there is a period of number development that precedes conscious counting, quite distinct in children, if not in animals; that tallying by beats, sticks, etc., mark the spontaneous development of the series-idea; that number names are surely learned abstractly, or by rote; that counting first proceeds by following the series names without any regard for the order of the name; that number names are first applied promiscuously to objects in which the *number represents the order of the object in the series and not a collection of objects*; that guess-games and a passion for counting have a considerable place in child-life from 6 to 10, which is, to a great extent, a period of spontaneous counting; that children in their first application of the series to things run the series ahead; that a *muscular movement of some kind is almost unavoidable with children when counting, and not uncommon among adults*; that personalization of numbers may originate in the early application of the number series to things in which the person or thing stands for 4, etc.; that Roman numerals are generally disliked; that a spontaneous habit of forming geometrical figures exists among many; that likes and dislikes of subjects in arithmetic

[44]   On examining the U.S. Census for 1880, it is found that those who guessed at their age, etc., have a decided preference for the fives and tens, also for even numbers. Analysis of ages from 28 to 42 for Ala., Mich., and U.S. as a whole, shows the most striking results. Those giving their age at 30 and 31, being about as 4 to 1 for Ala., as 5 to 2 for U.S.; at 40 and 41, as 5 to 1 for Ala., as 13 to 6 for Mich., as 3 to 1 for U.S.; at 47 and 48, as 4 to 5 for Ala., as 6 to 7 for Mich., as 4 to 5 for U.S., etc. ("Favorite Numbers," *Scientific American Supplement*, March, 1889.) In various curves and diagrams the effect of even numbers is very discernible.

depend in the main, upon the probable degree of usefulness in life, but the word "useful" is not explained by those answering, and this is subject to various modifications of teaching, age, position, etc.

Of the 100 returns bearing on second part of the syllabus, 22 say that mistakes are most common in subtraction; 9 in multiplication (being more of it); 14 say mistakes are more common in oral than in written work; 38, written work.

Twenty know nothing of the Grube Method; 17 have used it to advantage; 28 think that fractions should come earlier; more mechanical drill is urged by 18, and less of it by 28. A., a graduate of Yale, says: "I was taught the numbers as a drill in memory. It was an exercise in which every one wished to excel. We recited our tables until our work with small numbers became almost a reflex action; *never* had any trouble using them." C——. "Drill element is good, but it destroys the higher comprehension of numbers so necessary for development."

Forty-eight think that in the country children's number sense is so developed on entering school that objects are necessary only incidentally; 29 think there is much danger of carrying the objective illustration too far. M. writes that association is best acquired when it is casual and can be dwelt upon until the child will think "5" without thinking "star." Proportion is placed before percentage by 24, after by 56; roots are placed after proportion by 34; last, or with mensuration, by 62. Doubtless much of this depends upon former teaching, books used, etc.

Teachers in different places and schools were requested to give review exercises covering their regular work in arithmetic and to collect the papers for examination. I have examined 2,043 such papers, with the following results:

| Grade. | No. of Papers. | No. of operations or problems. | Total mistakes. | Confusion of operations. | Mistakes in operation. | Mistakes in principle. |
|---|---|---|---|---|---|---|
| I. | 405 | 6264 | 354 | 89 | | |
| II. | 224 | 3815 | 694 | 137 | | |
| III. | 550 | 11976 | 538 | 145 | 66 | 11 |
| IV. | 95 | 272 | 31 | 27 | | |
| | 1274 | 22327 | 1618 | 398 | | |
| V. | 139 | 1604 | 818 | | 15 | 11 |
| VI. | 140 | 847 | 297 | | 47 | 9 |
| VII. | 130 | 1357 | 359 | | 21 | 13 |
| VIII. | 380 | 2251 | 890 | | | |
| | 2043 | 28386 | 3982 | 398 | 149 | 44 |

By confusion of processes is meant that the child's work would have been correct in some other operation as $4 + 4 = 16$, or $7 - 2 = 9$. A large part of the work was not of such a nature as to give this information. Of the 1,618 mistakes made in the first four grades, 409 were of such a nature that it was impossible to tell whether they occurred from a confusion of processes or otherwise. Excluding these, about $33\frac{1}{3}\%$ of all mistakes in these grades are results of the confusion of processes. This confusion appears greatest in 3rd grade, but this is due to the fact that the 409 mistakes belong chiefly to the 1st and 2nd grades. More than 540 papers involved problems, and an effort was made to classify the mistakes on these according to operation and principle. Teachers are fairly well convinced that mistakes in the four operations greatly dominate, even in the 7th and 8th grades. It is very evident that subtraction is more difficult than addition. A teacher of 19 years' experience writes: "Subtraction is the most fruitful source of mistakes even to the 6th grade."

Two hundred and eighty-three papers on multiplication, involving 1,095 problems or multiplications, the majority of which contained three figures in multiplier and four in multiplicand, collected from the 9th grade, are of some interest. Total number of mistakes in these are 691; 186 were made in multiplying by 9; 195, by 8; 199, by 7; 57, by 6; 9, by 5; 15, by 4; 3, by 2. There are certainly some indications that Mr. Walker's charge has a general application. It will be observed in the table that the total mistakes, in all grades, exceed the number of papers by more than one-half. Considerable material in other lines remains to be worked up.

## IV. The Application of Numbers to Arithmetic

Under this heading will be considered, (1) A brief digest of some books and articles on arithmetic, (2) Suggestions on text-book making, (3) The result of the examination of 166 text-books on primary and elementary mathematics.

Brevity may prevent a clear statement of a writer's view; in many cases only a few of the leading points can be mentioned. No classification will be attempted. Reference has already been made to Dewey and McLellan's *Psychology of Number*, in which the Hegelian idea of number as ratio and quantity as limited quality dominates. Number is developed from measurement and measurement arises from the adjustment of activity. The ability to count is made to coincide with the power of abstraction and generalization, requiring ability to hold the mind from being absorbed in the delights of seeing, hearing, etc. Counting trees, etc., can only give the idea of imperfect number since they are not conceived as a vague whole and broken up into parts of *equal units*. Two false methods of teaching numbers are in use, the one teaching numbers as a set of symbols, the other, as a direct property of objects. Neither, they say, takes into account the fact that number arises in and through the activity of mind in dealing with objects. A severe attack is made upon the Grube Method because unity is taken as one thing. In the measuring method unity may be 12, a month, etc. The practical part everywhere shows evidence of an effort to join it to the theoretical, but the difficulty is likewise evident. Much of the practical part is common, and is found in use. The factor idea has its genesis in multiplication, multiplication in addition, division in subtraction; but neither is identical with the other.

Lefevre's *Number and Its Algebra* has as its bottom principle the *Continuity of Number and Mathematics*. Number is *continuous*. Algebra was slowly developed out of the investigation of numbers, and geometry cannot apparently proceed without arithmetic. There is a more primary and essential connection than Euclid made in his Fifth Book. All definitions should be tentative and capable of expansion. The principle of *continuity* makes negatives, zeros, infinities, fractions, and all numbers alike. "Primary number is a discrete magnitude and the product of rational processes." That ten is not a convenient base, that a distinction should be made between pure and applied arithmetic, that all multiplication is not repeated addition (*i.e.*, $\sqrt{2} \times \sqrt{3} = \sqrt{6}$), that long division should be taught first and abbreviated as the mind becomes able, such are but a few of the practical points considered.

Schubert's article on "Monism in Arithmetic" bears on the same line of oneness in mathematics, but is not so clear, deducing the laws of addition and multiplication from algebraic formulas. The substance of Schubert's article on "Notion and Definition of Number" has already been cited. Speer's and Graham's arithmetics have been previously mentioned.

The Committee of Fifteen gives mathematics the second place of all studies. So long as individual differences which are qualitative in so far as they distinguish one part from another are considered, objects cannot be counted. When counted, the distinctions are dropped out of sight as indifferent. Counting is the fundamental operation, all others are devices for speeding this one. Fractions are much more complex than simple numbers, involving three steps instead of one, and comparison or ratio. This is the cause of the child's embarrassment on entering fractions and operations that imply ratio. The pupil descends to the simple and returns to the complex numbers. Decimals are still more difficult, and roots a still further step in ratio. It is an advance to be able to separate or analyze the concrete, whole impression, and consider the quantity apart by itself. But if arrested mental growth takes place here, the result is deplorable. Without doubt such an arrest may take place by the too exclusive training in recognizing numerical relations.

The Committee of Ten recommend that the ordinary course in arithmetic should begin about the sixth year and be completed about the thirteenth; that the course should be abridged by omitting subjects that perplex and exhaust without giving any real mental discipline (that is the practical affords the best means of discipline); that the method of teaching should be thoroughly objective, and, as far as possible, inductive; that the text-book should be subordinated to the living teacher; that quickness and accuracy should be considered of great importance; that child geometry should begin in the kindergarten, and systematic instruction in geometry about the age of ten. The Conference declares that most of the improvements suggested on arithmetic "can be summed up under the two heads of giving the teaching a more concrete *form*, and paying more attention to facility and correctness in work."

Mrs. Hornbrook's *Laboratory Methods* proceeds upon the plan of individual research on different subjects, and she is present during the work to "suggest." Those using this method lay stress on the flexibility of their plan and the previously unperceived differences found among many pupils. A class of 42 in geometry takes a few weeks in concrete work, only a part of the recitation being devoted to class work. The class is divided and inspectors are appointed over each division. She claims that it is related to "self-education," that it enables the mentally acute to advance rapidly, gives the dull ones time, and that the sympathy between pupils and teacher is strengthened. Mrs. Hornbrook has also given us a work on *Concrete Geometry* in which she wishes every beginning in lines, angles, squares, cubes, etc., to be made purely concrete, and to be worked out by the pupils. It is intended for grammar schools.

*A Class in Geometry* by Geo. Iles is a small pamphlet presenting the concrete aspect, and would begin geometry by observation; a house-lot and two fields tell us much geometry. *Go from facts to law.* The work starts off well, but it is difficult to see geometry in all that is said.

Alex. Hogg writes an article, "More Geometry and Less Arithmetic," in which he maintains that arithmetic should not precede, but begin with, geometry. Fractions cannot be taught without geometry, and algebra is but a form of arithmetic, somewhat a connecting link between arithmetic and geometry.

In Jackman's treatment of the "Relation of Arithmetic to Elementary Science," we have a somewhat new view taken. Studies are distinguished as thought studies and form studies. The former exist only logically, but not in ideal educational methods, yet it is impossible to exactly define and distinguish them. The study of number is classed as a *form* study. Arithmetic stands entrenched in the dogmas of the past, it should give us a broader and better outlook into nature. Exactness is necessary but has been greatly neglected, not for want of mathematics, but for want of proper application. Ninety per cent. of all problems in our arithmetics are either abstract or deal with something foreign to the pupil. They should be of things *common* and *comprehensible. Arithmetic must be applied to science, and the mathematical operation made incidental, but by no means accidental.* Arithmetic is not to be the end, but a means to a more accurate end in thought studies, or science. Baldwin's *Industrial Arithmetic* is entirely practical, leads the pupil to discover for himself, follows much in the line of the work above mentioned.

Henry T. Eddy, in his address to the American Association, thinks the past teaching of arithmetic has been a failure largely because of an old idea of *discipline* that does not *discipline.* He insists upon more independent research, such as found in schools of technology, etc. Interest is awakened by use. Mathematical talents are not so rare as supposed. *Much more could and should be done in less time.*

The article on "Two Paths in Arithmetic," by W. D. Mackintosh, first gives a brief presentation of the early development of counting. Multiplication is certainly the domain of counting, but our authors of text-books have referred it to addition. At first with objects the physical operations, addition and subtraction, were the important things; with multiplication, the mental processes. While the world is busy using the original way, the arithmetics go into group counting, requiring too much mental power, or more concentration than the child possesses. The chief point is the relation of one's possessions to himself. Ego is $+$, non-ego is $-$. In this simple fact is the foundation of plus and minus signs.

The falsity of the Grube Method is presented in a thesis by Dr. Badanes. The Grube Method ignores the process of counting, does not avail itself of the advantages of our decimal system of notation; it ignores the serial nature of numbers, begins with deduction instead of induction; it destroys spontaneity, and confuses the child with too many operations with one number; it is a mere mechanism. He maintains that every operation from 1 to 10 reduces necessarily to counting, which is fundamental. Only by real problems demanding solution can we explain the processes in arithmetic.

Directly opposed to this we find Prof. Safford, in his *Mathematics Teaching and Its Modern Methods*, declaring that the Grube

Method is unquestionably the correct method of teaching arithmetic, that the difficulty it presents to teachers is what has caused it to be so little and badly used. "Matter must be digested by the teacher not only in scientific form, but in the form in which it is to be taught." All learning in arithmetic should be by the method of discovery.

The Grube Method as originally given in *Leitfaden für das Rechnen in der Elementarschule, nach den Grundsätzen einer heuristischen Methode* may be briefly stated as follows: The leading idea in Grube's Method is undoubtedly in general use, but not often referred to as such. Saldon is right in saying that the leading principle is *objective illustration*. The second principle presents the four processes with each number before the next higher is taken up. No new number must be taken up until all the possible combinations have been learned. The first year is devoted to numbers from 1 to 10; the second, from 10 to 100; regular work in fractions is introduced in the fourth year. The first step is from the concrete to the abstract, or the universal quantitative character of numbers; the second proceeds from abstraction to application. The child's greatest difficulty is in applied numbers. Multiplication and division are only forms of addition and subtraction. In a way one operation contains all the others. In measuring or comparing numbers pupils must acquire the utmost mechanical skill. The various combinations are familiar to most every teacher.

Doubtless every one is familiar with Mr. Walker's address on Arithmetic in Boston Schools. He claims that the amount of time is in excess of that which should be devoted to arithmetic, while equally important branches demand more attention. He points out that the study is largely pursued by methods supposed to conduce to general mental training, which, in a degree, sacrifices that faculty and accuracy in numerical computation so essential in all the affairs of life; and that the exercises are so difficult and complex as to not only destroy their disciplinary value, but become a positive injury.

Peterson, Supervisor of Boston Schools, differs from the above in his address to the Board in 1887. He claimed that the time should not be reduced; that arithmetic is especially important for developing mental concentration; that it is not an exercise in logic any more than running and eating are exercises in the science of hygiene; that pupils there are not inaccurate in number work; and that since it has been ordered that simple numerical facts must be discovered by the aid of objects, much improvement has followed.

Prof. Newcomb considers arithmetic poorly taught, and suggests that it should be more like the actual lessons of life, and that some lessons be built on the elements of geometry.

Ginn's *Addition Manual* applies the word method to addition and subtraction. He maintains that two-thirds of all errors made are in these processes; that too much number work is given in the first two years; that bad habits are most that is learned; that the child should learn to read the only 45 combinations possible as he would so many words; that $\frac{1}{1}$, $\frac{2}{3}$, etc., are but another expression for 2, 5, etc.; that subtraction should be left until addition is mastered; that the signs $+$ and $-$ are not to be used until later; and that such is superior to the sign method, or the still more complicated Grube Method.

Some valuable hints are given in a pamphlet on *Rapid Addition*, by Sprague. The writer says that it grew out of experience in the counting-room. We do not need to make the teaching of addition easier, but slower. Grouping is the key to rapid addition, and the child should be taught the different combinations as words, and should learn how to break up others; such as $7 + 4 + 7$, where the 4 should be mentally broken into $2 + 2$; in all series, such as $4 + 7 + 10$, $7 + 11 + 15$, etc., the child should be taught that the result is three times the central figure.

Some statistical work has been done which must be considered. D. E. Smith has an article on "Sex in Mathematics," based on 10,518 examination papers. Of the men, 63.6% passed, 59.2% of the women. The average of the men passed was 83.7%; of the women, 83.6%. In arithmetic the men stood noticeably higher in every respect; more of them pass, on the whole, and are better in geometry; the difference in algebra is in favor of the women. The same writer gives us an article on "Arithmetic in Rural Schools," based on 4,000 reports from 19 normal schools. Twenty-six per cent. pronounce number names to themselves, 33% visualize, 12% imagine them written, and 75% were first taught to count by number names. Taste undergoes a marked change in passing from arithmetic to algebra and geometry; on the whole, it is towards a liking for mathematics. About 46% think analysis the greatest difficulty in teaching arithmetic.

Some tests on Children's Ability to Reason have been made by Hancock by sending test problems to the different grades. Mistakes on same problems were almost as common at 14 as at 12. The movement to introduce algebra and geometry earlier is commended; less number work in lower grades and more arithmetic from 9 to 13 is advised. He concludes that practical arithmetic generally means money transactions; that it is doubtful if children can reason beyond their experience and environment; that practical teaching should utilize this fact; and that ability to solve arithmetical problems varies with the rate of growth, in which girls show a decrease at 9 or 10, and 13, boys at 8 and 14.

"A Study of the Mathematical Consciousness," by Miss Calkins, contains some points of interest. It is founded on replies from 87 women and 30 men, Harvard students. She concludes that on the whole the subjects have concrete rather than verbal memories; that the proportion of verbal memories is five times as large among those who do not like mathematics as among mathematicians, and one and two-thirds as great among algebraists as among geometricians; that students who prefer geometry are more likely to be mathematically inclined than those who prefer algebra; that ease in memorizing is at least as common among those who like mathematics as among other students; that classification and reasoning ability is much more strongly developed in the mathematically inclined; that Huxley is wrong in saying that mathematics is an abstract science which knows nothing of experiment, of observation, of induction, and rests on deduction; and that no important distinction is made between men and women.

*Methods of Mind Training* is a small work by Miss Aiken, based chiefly on some short drills in the use of numbers. A revolving blackboard is used on which are placed figures which pupils observe for a few seconds, then reproduce in order, add, extract root, etc. In a few weeks, with five minutes' drill each morning, pupils showed astonishing results. Thirty-two miscellaneous numbers, such as 1789, varying from tens to thousands, arranged in four columns, were repeated after a single glance. Figures with dots, minus or plus signs, etc., were repeated; a group of 20 objects recognized instantaneously. The object of these exercises is to cultivate the power of concentrating attention, to quicken perceptive faculties, to cultivate accuracy in seeing and hearing, and to discriminate by immediately observing similarities and differences. It is claimed that the results have been very marked in awakening dull, slow-moving minds to activity, and causing them to take delight in their newly acquired power; that its effects are seen in reading music and learning poetry; that attention underlies the whole of memory, and this is the sure way to attention. Of course it is claimed that attention to these exercises will strengthen the attention for all and any other, and it is here that the claims will encounter greatest opposition.

The practical dominates in French education. This is quite marked in their text-books and treatises on arithmetic as well as in most of their text-books. As early as 1747 Barrême published *L'Arithmétique ou Le Livre Facile pour Apprendre l'Arithmétique de soi-même, et sans Maître*. One cannot help but be astonished at the comparative excellence of this book. The four fundamental processes are given nearly four times as much attention as other works give, until almost a century later. Division is presented only in the form of cancellation, the arrangement is good, and the explanations and diagrams seem somewhat modern.

Lacroix's *Traité Élémentaire D'Arithmétique*, written in 1811, is well worth considering. It is to some extent both a practical and theoretical treatment of number and its different applications in arithmetic. In the comparison of different objects which fall under our senses, says the writer, we are able to perceive in all, an attribute or quality by which they are capable of being increased or diminished. Such appears, in general, under two forms: as a collection of many particular things, or, of many equally separated parts. (Does not this single sentence contain both the series-idea and the ratial-idea of number?) Soon comes a single whole without distinction of parts, it is as one conceives the distance between two points. The subjects in arithmetic are discussed and it is urged that fractions should be made the key to composite or compound numbers.

Some of the most interesting points from Dr. Scripture's article on "Mathematical Prodigies" have already been mentioned. In many cases of these mathematical prodigies the result is the only thing that seems to come in their minds. Bidder said it came in the short time it took him to announce the result. The velocity of mental processes cannot be adequately expressed. Precocity in counting is from 3 to 10. Their great peculiarity is the visual images of numbers which they always carry about in their minds. Ampère, Bidder, and Mondeux learned their arithmetic from pebbles.

Binet and Henri find that the mnemonic does not retain figures, but substitutes something else, while the calculators retain the figures as such; that the mnemonic is more powerful but slower than the natural memory for figures. More powerful because his substitution allows him to retain a number almost indefinite; slower because he must reproduce all the mnemonic phrases for numbers.

Binet's *Psychologie des Grands Calculateurs et Joueurs D'Échecs* is full of points of interest. Much of it is consumed in the comparison of Inaudi and Diamandi, an account of which I have given in "Genesis of Number Forms."[45] Great calculators are, in general, from unknown or low parentage; they are either slow and dull in learning other things or void of interest in anything else, because they are absorbed in the pleasures and power of great calculations. Their power develops somewhat spontaneously and quite early, without aid and without knowledge of other things. Many of Mondeux's self-developed systems are deduced from algebraic formulas. Many

---

chess-players were questioned; all of them visualize, but only one sees the entire board when playing blind-folded. As a rule, they see only the part where the combat lies.

*The Number Concept: Its Origin and Development*, already referred to, gives us a full treatment of the development of number names and of counting among primitive peoples. Primitive methods, previously mentioned, are thoroughly presented. Even where the concept appears lowest some circumlocution expresses the difference between *one* and *many*. Much uniformity prevails in counting on fingers, nearly always beginning with little finger on left hand. It appears that races lowest in civilization have also the feeblest number sense, but there are many important exceptions. Some savage tribes carry their system to 10,000 or even a million, while in many it is almost entirely absent. Leigh Hunt could not learn the multiplication table, and peasants in Russia have no idea of even a few hundred. The ability to count is always beyond the numerical vocabulary. Counting words are among the very first to appear in any language, yet they change less than any other part of a language. Kinship in tongue, otherwise remote, has been detected by these words. *With the savage the number concept is entirely concrete.* When number in the abstract is reached then reckoning ceases and arithmetic begins. The tables showing from whence savages obtain their numerals are valuable.

Several other valuable articles and books have been reviewed but space forbids a consideration of them here; however, a list of all so far consulted will be found in the bibliography at the close of this paper.

*Suggestions on Text-Book Making.* What is said under this head has grown out of eleven years' experience and the present investigation, and is in no wise intended to be dogmatical. The diversity of human intellects, human needs, human environments, child's spontaneity, psychic activity, and especially *mental phenomena in dealing with number*, demand that neither the teaching nor the text in arithmetic should be dominated by a *single* idea. For general use a text-book should be properly balanced between what is known as the *practical* and *disciplinary* use of arithmetic. It is true that each party claims to accomplish the best results in both; but every one knows that most business men work by rules, tables of interest, etc.; know and care little for the whys. It is possible to find good mathematicians well disciplined, but slow, inaccurate, and void of what is termed "good business sense."

In the presentation of numbers we must allow for the spontaneity of the child, for the knowledge of numbers already possessed on entering school, and for the manner in which it was acquired; begin on the knowledge of the series it already possesses, and make the transition from this to objects. Counting is fundamental and even combinations furnish the first step, hence counting by 2's, 3's, 4's, etc., furnish the first steps in multiplication. The difficulties of subtraction are greater and more lasting than those of addition, hence its introduction on beginning addition must at first be incidental. Care must be taken not to confuse the child by introducing too many processes at once. *Children* do not look at things with adult minds, and it is not necessary to know all about 4 in order to know *any* thing; the processes need not be isolated as they once were, and the simplest fractions may be incidentally introduced quite early, but they involve more relations and hence demand more mental power than the unit. A routine presentation of numbers by the same objects develop *form* rather than number. Problems such as, "How many twenty-sevenths in three-ninths?" were solved by children 5 and 6 in the kindergarten. Ninths and twenty-sevenths were certainly names of some of the little cubes in their toy-box.[46] Such mechanism may prove more detrimental than beneficial.

We must distinguish between a child's ability to perform operations in the relation of numbers and its power to *understand language*. Children often fail because they cannot *read*. A class of 14 failed on a problem concerning a ball with a cavity. Inquiry revealed the fact that only two knew the meaning of *cavity*. I have no statistics of value on which to base it, but my impression from this special study is that children's ability to reason in arithmetic comes later than Hancock concludes; that much of the early work is performed in obedience to a mechanical formula even without the knowledge of the teacher. In the returns, 49 consider the mathematical "insight" a rather sudden innovation; I suppose something like the learning of telegraphy as given by Horter and Bryan.[47] This appears to be true in my own case, but it was certainly due to the manner of teaching and the excessive *help* received. Until further evidence this is a better explanation than to consider it a law of mind growth.

Arithmetical teaching must not be too formal. This is the rock on which our great advocates of analysis stumble. It must not be only an analysis, but a *special* analysis. Only a few days ago an ex-president of the University of West Virginia declared this to be the great evil of modern methods. "My child," said he, "can never understand my solution or see any meaning in it unless cast in a special

[46]   *Grube's Method.* F. Louis Soldan.
[47]   "Studies in Telegraphic Language," *Psychological Review*, Jan., '97.

form. Children's minds are set to a form." The child needs suggestions. Long and formal analysis produces confusion and mechanism. Have you any devices in the use of numbers not given in your book or by your teacher? is a question I put to 1,124 children, receiving 407 replies, including 182 devices or departures from the rules; for example, $3\frac{1}{2} \times 3\frac{1}{2} = 3 \times 4 + \frac{1}{4} = 12\frac{1}{4}$, $19 \times 7 = 20 \times 7 - 7 = 133$. Skipping the 5's in adding, keeping a record of them on fingers; never adding 5 to 27, but 3, then 2; dividing a number like 17 into two parts to multiply it, as $17 \times 6 = 10 \times 6 + 7 \times 6$; never having anything to do with 9, using 10 and subtracting; counting percentage backwards; subtracting a number in parts—these are some of the devices mentioned. An interesting example is given in Miss Shinn's observation already mentioned: "How many 2's in 15?" she was asked when $4\frac{1}{2}$. She replied: "There are three 5's in 15, and two 2's in each 5 and 1 over; that makes six 2's, and 3 over makes one 2 and 1 over; seven 2's and 1 over." A young man who had given up his university education came to me for private lessons in arithmetic. He knew absolutely nothing of the subject in book form, yet he was a good business trader. I have often dictated problems to him, the correct result of which he would announce before he had completed taking it down; he was seldom ever able to tell me how he got the result, often receiving no encouragement of its correctness, and after prolonged effort would report unable to solve it. If not crushed by formalism the mind is almost unlimited in its variation.

Why nearly all advanced arithmetics should devote 60 or 100 pages to the four processes, when such has been preceded by one or two books treating them both oral and written, I fail to see. It is certainly not expected that such voluminous books will be placed in the hands of children. I remember when children used to begin in Ray's Third because it presented all of the primary steps, and both teacher and parent decided it was unnecessary to purchase the first books. This is frequently the practice now in the country. The evil results are readily discernible.

Decimals should grow out of common fractions, and in reading and writing decimals the child should know *exactly* the number of figures necessary for each decimal at least to millionths. This can be learned by proper drill in three recitations; then there will be no stumbling over either reading or writing them. This may be called mechanical, but anything is better than the usual confusion we see in enumerating. Make it rational also, that is all right; but immediate recognition of decimals is necessary. To avoid confusion in division, pointing off should precede the operation. Wentworth is the only one I know of giving both of these points.

Reference has already been made to the fact that the ratial-idea must not be the basis of number in all its development and application, and that as such it cannot explain all of the facts; neither must its value and application be overlooked at the proper time and place. While some base everything upon it, others too much ignore it, even giving proportion a small corner in the last of their text-books. The series-idea undergoes various processes of development in its applications. In its pure mathematical sense, when applied to space and time, the number concept is greatly modified, and differs from its application to familiar tangible objects. In other words exact measure is different from applied numbers. *Number in its first stages of application does not consider equality proper*, but it is only when the idea of continuity is put into number, which is necessary to complete the *oneness* of mathematics, that this equality or ratial-nature is developed. Pure mathematical quantity and number are not identical.[48]

Number is not so simple nor so limited in its application. The *rational process* is preceded by a development which it does not take into consideration. Comparison is a process of reasoning *to which* the number series is applied, rather than *from which* it is developed. This pain is *greater* than that; I enjoy eating *more* than playing; I am fatigued *more* than I was last night, are comparisons of sub-jective states to which the number concept may be applied in a very indefinite manner. But let none of this analysis stand as an argu-ment against the use of the ratial-idea at the proper stage of develop-ment, or even its incidental introduction from the beginning; but it does not appear that children are capable of reasoning accurately or to much extent until 12.

[48]     Since writing the above I have reviewed Russell's article "On the Relation of Number and Quantity," in *Mind*, Vol. VI, pp. 326–341. It is the most masterly treatment of the ratial-conception of number I have seen, and states this difference clearer and stronger than I had conceived it. "Throughout this abstract development of number," says he, "the unit has become gradually more important and explicit. When it is quite ex-plicit we get a third kind of number, which, outside our arithmetic books, is alone of importance. This kind I shall call *applied* number." Again, "the connection of quantity with number—we must conclude—is due partly to motives of convenience, but mainly to a confusion between two fundamentally distinct ways of regarding space and time. It must be maintained, therefore, that quantity applies to contents only when they are regarded as immediate data, and applies then only when such data are not understood. In this it differs from number, for number can, by ab-straction, be applied to material perfectly understood. While things which can be numbered together must have some conception in common, things which can be measured against each other must have no conception not in common, and yet must differ." The idea of the continuum must stand or fall with the relative justification of quantity as against number. Much stress is placed upon the distinction made between intensive and extensive quantity. All quantities must be reduced to spatial equivalents before they can be quantitatively treated.

Having supposed for several years that percentage was quite a blind process to most pupils, in which they closely follow formulas, and that the difficulty lay in the fact that they do not comprehend per cent. as a common fraction, either expressed or understood, I determined to make a test of 224 students, either teachers or preparing to teach. For this purpose 40 problems were prepared involving transactions in gain and loss expressed in common fractions; 81.6% solved all of them; the remainder missed, on an average, over five problems. Later the same problems, the words being changed and the fractions expressed in terms of per cent., were given to 212 of the same students; only 62% solved all, while the average number missed by the others was about 3. It appears that a much more intelligible comprehension can be secured by an interpretation of per cent. in terms of common fractions, such as is well presented in Graham's arithmetic. There ought not to be so much isolation of so many subjects that come under percentage as though they were entirely new subjects. I can hardly account for so many likes for interest and so many dislikes for percentage, especially stocks and bonds.

The rapidly growing use of the Metric System and its exceeding simplicity demand for it more attention than is generally given. It must be remembered that Congress has authorized the use of the Metric System in many departments of the Civil Service.

All of the concrete problems should be followed by sufficient abstract problems to give a more general idea of the application of number. If proficiency and accuracy are to be obtained, the purely drill element cannot all be eliminated from arithmetic. As far as possible problems must grow out of the child's environment.

Upon the suggestions herein outlined a brief review will be made of texts in arithmetic now in circulation and those lately issued, so far as I have been able to ascertain.

The examination of 166 text-books on elementary and secondary mathematics reveals some important points, if they can only be put in a condensed, yet comprehensible form. Nearly all of these are arithmetics, because in arithmetic the application of number is of most interest.

*Earlier Text-Books.* Robert Recorde's *Arithmetic* (ed. 1590 and 1618) reads like a Bible; 260 pages are devoted to the four processes; alligation follows fractions; dots are used for teaching the combinations of numbers; it contains 630 pages, of which fully 500 are consumed in discussion and explanation.

Edward Wingate's *Practical Arithmetick* and *Artificial Arithmetick* (1629) are two books, the latter is written to help the former by borrowed numbers from logarithms. Extensive tables are prepared in interest, etc. All the lower denominations in compound numbers are made out in decimals of the standard. He published another in 1676, in which he first gives the name and number character of all numbers up to 1,000 for English, Greek, and Roman notation.

Cocker's *Arithmetic* (1677) partakes largely of that idea of "sacredness" once attached to mathematics. "By the secret Influence of Divine Providence," says the author, "I have been instrumental to the Benefit of many: And now do with the same wonted Alacrity cast this, my Arithmetical mite into the public Treasury, beseaching the Almighty to grant the like Blessing to these as to my former Labors." The book has many commendable features, and, judging from the fact that there were 48 editions, must have been quite popular. It is largely taken up in discussion.

James Hadder's work (1719) is much like Recorde's. Tracing everything to the four fundamental operations, he makes such the dominant idea; but nearly all is devoted to explanation and discussion. Such is one of the chief characteristics of all the earlier books, perhaps somewhat made necessary by the limited knowledge of the teachers. Probably in this respect the contrast between the old and the new is more striking than in any other.

Gordon and Dobson's *Arithmetic* (1771) contains many very curious problems, rather puzzles. Weights, measures, etc., are introduced just after division. Such is one of the most common qualities of all the old texts. Fractional money frequently follows simple addition, and this is still quite common in English texts. Taken all in all more prominence is given to fractional money, weights, measures, etc., than any other single subject; these nearly always follow the four operations and precede fractions. Temple gives addition of compound numbers on 5th page.

Pike's *Arithmetic* (1793 and 1797) makes one think of their early school days. Many of the rules, almost word for word, can be found in books somewhat modern. The 6% method is used and interest is placed last, save alligation. I cannot understand the prominence given to alligation by so many. In many it is near the middle, following fractions, but in some it precedes. Several books develop *all* rules on the style of the catechism by fixed questions and answers; but never give a summarized statement of the rule. R. C. Smith and several others proceed with each step, as follows: Q. How do you begin to divide? A. As in short division. Q. How many steps are there? A. Four. Q. Name them. Such as this is found on every page.

Walsh (1814) gives no rules, only a few suggestions to the teacher. Motto: *Iter est breve per example.* James Robinson (1825)

introduces long division before short division. In this and other particulars it should be classed with texts of the last decade.

Emerson has the number series and their names to 100 learned
first. Butterworth has the pupil to express first in words, then in
figures, even as high as 6,100,192,204. Porter's *Ready Reckoner*
(1843) applies cancellation to every part and gives *every* rule by
directing what to place on each side of a vertical line. Hilliard's two
volumes are full of devices and short cuts in arithmetic.

Colburn's *Arithmetics* (1849) once had such a wide circulation
and the plan so well understood that little mention need be made
here. This plan objects to explanation on the part of the teacher and
leaves the child to work out his own salvation. Written work is dis-
carded. The later editions have introduced much not found in the
original. Horace Grant's *Arithmetics* (1861) presented in England
the Inductive Method. Mental arithmetic is claimed to be of fundamental importance. Nearly all the work in both books is mental. The
subjects treated are very much reduced; are on the same plan as Colburn's; were once quite popular in England. Walton's *Pictorial Arithmetic* (1866) is full of pictures of all kinds that may be counted; reduces it to object lessons. Burchett's *Practical Geometry* (1855)
holds the lecture method by which the teacher makes drawings on
the board, pupils take notes, and make careful drawings afterwards.
No figures are given.

Leysenne's *La Deuxième Année d'Arithmétique* devotes considerable to compound numbers; square root follows numeration and
decimals. It introduces geometry to a considerable extent, and the
commercial element occupies a prominent place. It is in many respects an excellent book.

The general characteristics of the earlier text-books on arithmetic may be stated as follows: Extensive discussion and explanation which made the volumes comparatively large; the arrangement
by which great prominence is given to fractional money, weights,
etc.; stress laid on proportion being placed before fractions in some
cases; the assignment of interest rather to the last part of the book;
and the peculiar problems, often puzzles. On the other hand, many of
the presentations of primary number, such as Emerson's *Elementary
Lessons*, have not been greatly improved upon; many sets of problems are unsurpassed. The short cuts and devices which business
men use so much are obtained almost entirely from these old books.
The disciplinary idea may be detected in many, yet, on the whole,
the earlier books were dominated by the *practical* idea no less than
those of the present day; but the practical was not so generally accepted.

*Later Text-Books.* Milne's *Standard Arithmetic* introduces many purely number problems in the simplest processes of addition and subtraction, etc. The presentation of decimals is defective; proportion is somewhat slighted; 7 pages of inadequate treatment of the metric system is presented near the close; percentage is likewise defective by not being based on common fractions; mensuration is well treated, and the review problems are excellent. The book aims to be both disciplinary and practical.

White's *New Arithmetic* presents many commendable points. Counting by 4's, 7's, etc., is in strict harmony with the development of the number concept; fractions, decimals, and the metric system are well presented. Percentage seems to be too much wedded to formulas. Proportion precedes roots in its proper place. Problems are practical and well graded.

[49]Moore's *Grammar School Arithmetic* applies the Inductive or Laboratory method throughout. Not a single rule is given, and the pupil is left to devise the definite processes. First the concrete, then the abstract corresponding to it. The simple processes occupy 48 pages, the presentation of which is very good; the treatment of fractions is up to date. The subjects are repeated somewhat on the Spiral-plan. Too much space is devoted to denominate numbers. We can well see how such a book would be all right in the hands of competent teachers, but there is a gap between the subject matter therein presented and the child's knowledge that must be supplied some way. If all teachers were able to properly assist the child in developing the proper manner of procedure, this great objection would disappear, but the majority of teachers are young and inexperienced. I am unable, for example, to see anything to guide the inexperienced teacher and pupil to an understanding of decimals. Whether the book presupposes some knowledge of such, I do not know.

[50]Hewett's *Arithmetics, Primary and Practical*, are on a somewhat new plan, and in every way justify the title *Practical*. The rules are few, suggestions to the point; little distinction of classes or cases problems is made; the pupil is left to sort his problems in percentage, etc., and to make the application as he must do in practical life; all subjects not considered practical are omitted. A better treatment of percentage and interest I have not found. On some points the student is liable to confusion, which is a stumbling-block with all learners; decimals are developed from the unit; the metric system receives but a passing notice of 3 pages as the last subject. In the main the work is too true to a single idea.

---

49     Lately published.
50     Lately published.

[51]E. E. West's *Twentieth Century Arithmetic*, in two parts, presents a few modifications of interest. The second part is the first grammar school text I have found that does not treat extensively the four processes. This opens with as extensive and *complete* consideration of fractions as can be found anywhere. Decimals and percentage might be improved; the metric system is well presented, and the equation of one unknown quantity is introduced in such an incidental manner that it cannot help but be beneficial to the student, and at the same time free from any opposition to those who oppose the logical method. The book is small but comprehensive, and devoted to the practical.

Walsh's work includes a series of three books, on what is called the Spiral-plan, that is taking a little of a subject and returning to it again, perhaps several times. This differs from the frequent review problems in that more subjects are introduced early in the course, and treated less extensively. The practical omission of rules and definitions is noticeable; decimals are well presented; the chapter on geometry adds to the work, for geometry should be introduced incidentally much earlier than it is. The equation is used especially in percentage and interest. Several systems of texts present something of this nature, but I have found nothing that carries this plan so far. If carried out in this form one cannot help but think that it will lead to a lack of organized knowledge, if not confusion on the part of the pupil.

The Venable series subordinates the theoretical and technical to the practical. The Elementary is somewhat on the Grube style; it is good in the presentation of measures. The Practical devotes 63 pages to the four processes; rules are long; the metric system is placed in the appendix.

Sanford's works are old in the presentation of elementary numbers; fractions and compound numbers are well treated; the arrangement is unsatisfactory.

Baldwin's *Industrial Primary Arithmetic* claims to be the natural way of teaching numbers, leads the pupil to discover for himself. Class work and seat work are separated. Everything is presented in the common, practical, business way. Arithmetic must be studied solely for its application to business life. It is the best example of the practical idea, pure and simple, I have seen.

Prince's *Arithmetic by Grades* includes eight small works on the Inductive plan, the most excellent points of which are the treatment of fractions, the introduction of the elements of geometry in the 4th grade which is gradually increased each year, and the excel-

[51]     Lately published.

lently graded problems. There are no rules, but suggestions and diagrams somewhat take their place. If used in graded schools and by experienced teachers no difficulty would be encountered. They also repeat the topics in the grades. In the presentation of primary number some improvement might be made.

Graham's *Common School Arithmetic* has ratio as its fundamental principle, and is founded on the *intensive* or disciplinary idea. The same may be said of Speer's, McLellan and Ames's. Two elementary works by Miss Bacon go with Graham's. His work treats the four operations somewhat differently from most; thus, $2 \times 4 = 8$; $\frac{1}{2} \times 8 = 4$; $4 \times 3 = 12$; $\frac{1}{4} \times 12 = 3$. Tables of such are quite extended, and, without doubt, to *much advantage*, both in multiplication and in fractions. Proportion is treated more than usually and is placed before percentage; the metric system is practically ignored; decimals could be improved. Fractions and percentage are admirably treated. The work is wedded to the idea of ratio and discipline.

Speer's *New Arithmetic*, in two parts, is absolutely devoted to the idea of comparison as a means of developing accurate judgments. A set of blocks of various kinds and sizes go with each book. The Primary begins by having the child find or handle these solids; bring a *larger* or *smaller* one, the largest and smallest. Comparison in colors is introduced at once. Look at four colors, think the colors (eyes closed) from top down, from bottom up. Which is second from top, third from bottom, second from bottom, etc.? Relative magnitudes of all kinds are pointed out, largest solid, smallest solid, tallest boy; compare the height of pupils, largest surfaces of solids, etc.; then an exercise comparing sounds, etc. Show the longest edge of the largest solid, shorter edges. Cut a slip, cut a longer one, shorter one, larger square. Draw a line, one a *little* longer, shorter, etc. Draw a line, separate into equal parts, show one-half of it. By means of such comparisons of blocks, lines, colors, etc., the work proceeds step by step. The Elementary is also accompanied by a *large* collection of blocks illustrating integral and fractional relations. Ratios consume the greater part; interest and percentage are developed from ratio. Much of this kind of work has been done in our best schools, but only in a few instances has it been made the whole of arithmetical training. No other series of text-books follows such a line exclusively. McLellan and Ames's work claims to be founded on the idea of number as measurement, yet both the subject matter and the treatment are entirely different from Speer's. So far as I am able to judge, Miss Walter, of Willimantic Normal Training School, has been practicing Speer's plan for some years in the model school, in about as pure a form as it can be put. Doubtless such work should have a much larger place in our schools. The high value of comparison added to acute attention is of the utmost importance in all reasoning processes whatsoever. The great function of the work above cited, and to some degree of all the other books in this line, is to dress up thought and to make general thinking more acute. No teacher should be blind to its great value, but at the same time such an *exclusive treatment ignores some of the fundamental facts in the nature and application of number.* One may be well trained in all the geometrical and quantitative comparisons and yet be void of good business sense in arithmetic.

[52]McLellan and Ames's *Public School Arithmetic* is based on number as *measurement.* The ordinary drills in the four processes cover the first 74 pages; many of these are pure abstract exercises in numbers, but money value and linear unit play an important part. The four processes are followed by four pages on Comparison of Numbers, and this by square root. How square root to three and even four places is to be made *rational* at this period of development one may well inquire. It must presuppose much more knowledge of arithmetic than the previous treatment indicates. Fractions are handled in an excellent manner; decimals are made to grow out of the dollar and the metric system; however, the metric system is the last chapter in the book. The same difficulty to join the practical to the philosophic idea of number that is evident in The Psychology of Number is made still more evident by this book. One looks in vain to see in this work any great difference from half a score of others. It is by no means as true to the idea as Speer's.

Griffin's *Supplementary Work in Arithmetic* (1893) is a rather large work including lines, areas, volumes, bulk and percentage, and is based, in the main, on the measuring idea. Various figures and drawings are given and many questions concerning their comparison. If judiciously used by the teacher in connection with other work it cannot help but prove of great value. The author appears to have no special method or theory to present, nor does he think of making it the whole of arithmetical training.

*Franklin's New Arithmetic,* by Seaver and Walton, presents no new departure of note, but is none the less pedagogical. The First Book contains several commendable features. The processes are rather incidentally introduced, but not confused, and counting, in various ways, receives attention. The chief points of excellence in the Second Book are found in both the number and character of the problems and the rather incidental introduction of subjects.

The Wentworth series has had such a wide circulation that

[52]    Lately published.

they are doubtless familiar to all teachers. The Primary follows somewhat the Grube method of presentation, and the simplest fractions
are introduced early by use of objects and diagrams. Decimals are
presented and are followed by the most excellent primary treatment
of percentage I have seen anywhere. His Practical Arithmetic contains 372 pages, and presents the usual elementary treatment of numbers in the four processes. That drill in the four processes is the main
thing in arithmetic may be offered as a justification of this practice;
but why children capable of handling this and having had the two
previous ones, should need drill in adding $5 + 8$, etc., in subtracting
$22 - 3$, etc., and in similar simple operations in multiplication and
division, I do not understand. The treatment of decimals, common
fractions, and percentage is not susceptible of much improvement,
save that decimals precede common fractions, and little more prominence might be given to reading and writing decimals according to
the number of figures required. This series is a medium between
the purely disciplinary and the purely practical, between the purely
rational and the purely mechanical in arithmetic, between the thoroughly inductive and the thoroughly deductive. They are neither
dominated by a single idea nor spoiled by method.

Besides the above, *Wheeler's Arithmetic*, *Primary Number
Lessons* and *Advanced Arithmetic*, by the State Board of Education,
California, Ray's series, J. M. White's Oral, Brooks's Mental, Bai-
ley's American, Robinson's series, and Atwood's Graded, arithmetics
are used in different sections of the country, and several others are
quite limited in their circulation. Other books which I have not been
able to secure may be extensively used. On account of necessitated
brevity and lack of space, I have thought it best to confine my review
of later texts to those of this country, although several others have
been examined.

The German books are quite conservative, introducing the
practical, but clinging to the disciplinary. Each step must be thoroughly mastered, and mathematics taught as a unit. The French
make much of the decimal or metric system of measures, etc.;
induction, as presented by Grant and Colburn, has not much place,
books are seldom without some rules, but they are quite exact and
clear. The English texts adhere to deduction in some form. In the
oldest books currency, weights, etc., nearly always follow division,
and occupy much space, and are often introduced with addition;
alligation receives attention. The marks of the *old* are very evident
in all of the *new*.

Among the great diversity of opinions in the articles and
books above reviewed, it is evident that there are four general lines
of thought: (1) Those who hold and treat arithmetic as a system

of logical reasoning, highly suited to develop the mind, and place it more on the plane of pure mathematics; (2) Those who consider arithmetic useful only, or in the main, for practical business life, and would make the shortest cut possible to this end; (3) Those who base all instruction on induction, omitting all rules and explanations, resorting to the laboratory method or method of self-discovery; (4) Those who cling to the old idea of deduction from fixed principles or rules. Omitting some differences in the presentation of primary numbers, nearly all other differences, and many of these, are involved in these points. The first two classes differ concerning the end and the nature of arithmetic; the other two concerning the best means for obtaining the desired end. Those seeking discipline, or development of judgment, may use either the inductive or deductive method; likewise some maintain that the practical is best obtained by memorizing and applying rules; others claim that the most direct and thorough way to secure the practical results is by induction from real transactions. Only a few occupy either of these extreme lines, and there are all grades of compromises, or attempts thereat. Perhaps few would claim to belong to the first or second classes as presented, especially the first, for those who make arithmetic a means to develop accurate judgments also claim to realize the best practical results.

That practice does not always conform to theory and philosophy is manifested in the texts on arithmetic. Notwithstanding the varying theories and methods discussed in prefaces, books, etc., one only needs to put aside about one-half dozen of our latest works, and the differences in the remainder are practically not worth mentioning. The teaching of arithmetic is the most traditional of all subjects; its methods have come down less changed than any other topic, and by many it is thought to be the worst. It is in the presentation of primary numbers that the devices of teaching are so opposite. The mathematical mind was a late development in the race, and so it is in the individual. Too much value is often attached to the abstract manipulation of numbers, and the believer in the concrete often fails to realize the necessity of an intellectual evolution into the higher forms of mathematics. "Skill in computing may be acquired without any intelligent apprehension of arithmetical science, and a profound insight into the truth and principles of arithmetic may be attained without much facility in using numbers."

## v. Conclusion

The main inferences from this work may be briefly summarized as follows:

That the number concept is the outcome of a long process of development marked in the race and in the individual.

That the first step is the formation of a series-idea by the innumerable variety and successive changes in consciousness.

That this develops an abstract idea of succession, manifested in children's desire to follow in various ways any series, and especially in mathematical prodigies.

That prominence *is* given to certain members of the series by the various rhythmic processes as illustrated by the experimental work reviewed, and by the great preference given to certain numbers.

That there is a counting period quite marked in children and to which the mathematical prodigy belongs.

That the number, time, and space concepts are closely related, in their nascent state at least, and this relation gives number a wider application.

That dramatization of numbers, number forms, and prodigies belong to the counting period.

That *some movement* is perhaps unavoidable in the early stages of counting. If the motor element be a necessity of all thought, it is even more so in following an abstract series.

That the application of the series-idea to things is the second and more conscious step, hence the difficulty.

That number as measurement is not the whole of the development of number, but only the complementary side of the series-idea.

That number as measurement can by no means explain all the mental phenomena of numbers.

That the power to manipulate the series bears little or no relation to the development of reason and general judgments.

That number has applications not in a pure mathematical sense as an exact quantity.

That there is a great variety of mental phenomena found among children and adults in connection with numbers.

That the chief lines of discussion concerning number and texts on arithmetic are directed towards either the disciplinary or practical end, the deductive or inductive method of presentation.

That arithmetics and methods of teaching have remained, comparatively speaking, quite constant until the last few years.

That the chief defects in texts are found in the presentation of primary numbers, fractions, decimals, proportion and percentage.

That there is a general tendency in this and other countries to introduce many of the elements of geometry and, at least, the simpler uses of the equation into arithmetic, the former of which, at least, is to be commended.

That the authors of text-books seem to be searching for methods and often ignoring the manner in which the race and the child naturally acquire such knowledge.

That no method should ignore the long psychic and rudimentary stages of development. Yet if allowed to play too great a part, morbid conditions may be developed, such as seen in morbid counters, excessive counting on fingers, etc.

That the great diversity of human intellects, human needs, human environments, child's spontaneity, of mental phenomena in the development and application of number, forbid the exclusive use of any one orthodox method in teaching number and arithmetic. (We have already reached this generalization in teaching reading.)

That practical business training in arithmetic, and preparation for higher mathematics and abstract thinking in general are not identical, nor obtained in the same way.

I must express my great obligation to Drs. Hall, Burnham, and Sanford for valuable assistance—especially to Dr. Hall for suggestions and criticism; to Prof. Luckey, of University of Neb., to Prins. Barnes, of Fairmont Normal, W. Va., Deahl, of West Liberty, W. Va., Miss Williams, of Trenton, N. J., students of these institutions, and others, for valuable returns; to Supt., teachers, and authorities of Worcester schools, for assistance and privileges; to other schools rendering assistance; to different book companies for granting the privilege to examine their publications and for books donated.

# Social Interpretations: A Reply

## JAMES MARK BALDWIN

THE REVIEW of my work by my friend Professor Dewey in the July issue of this *Review*, is worthy of notice both by reason of its careful discussion, and also by reason of the fact that it fails in some degree to see my real point of view. In consequence of what seems a misconception, the detailed criticisms lose the instructiveness which they might have had and also, I am free to say, some of their point. This I aim to show below. As a matter of fact, Professor Dewey has mistaken a knob on my harness for a joint, and aiming at it has, I think, wasted much of his ammunition.[1]

There are two things quite essential to a real understanding of my book: (1) it must be understood that my method is *genetic*, and (2) that the results state empirical generalizations, as all genetic science does, and not metaphysical explanations. I am not attempting to say what either the individual or society is, nor how either of them is possible; I attempt rather to say what the law is of their evolution, and by what relation of fact or of implication of each by the other this law of evolution proceeds. That Professor Dewey fails to realize both of these essentials, it is easy to show. I shall take the second point first, since the great "circle" of contradiction which he finds at the outset illustrates misapprehensions on both of these points.

Professor Dewey says that I am guilty of a fine circle of argument, a circle which he allows I have myself stated "precisely" in the

---

[1]    As I correct the proofs of this, Professor Dewey's article on my book in the *New World* (September, 1898) comes to my hand. I find that article in all respects truer to my meaning, and were I now writing what follows I should be glad to take it for Professor Dewey's mature reading. This I cannot now do. I hope, in case he and the reader find in this "reply" anything but friendly social "give and take," my apologies may be allowed to anticipate their censure; the text was written in bits at various hotels in England! The criticisms made in the *New World* article, I have still to reflect upon, but I have to thank Professor Dewey for all the attention given to the book.

[*First published in* Philosophical Review, VII (*Nov. 1898*), 621–28. *For Dewey's reply, see* The Early Works of John Dewey, v, *p.* 399.]

following quotation:[2] "I do not see in short how the personality of this child can be expressed in any but social terms; nor how, on the other hand, social terms can get any content of value but from the understanding of a developing individual. This is a circle of definition of course, *but that is just my point*. On the one hand, we can get no doctrine of society, but by getting the psychology of the socius with all its natural history; and, on the other hand, we can get no true view of the socius *at any time* without describing the social conditions under which he normally lives, with the history of their action and reaction upon him" (*Soc. Int.*, p. 21). Professor Dewey goes on to say that this "recognition of the circle does credit to the author's candor, but does not eliminate the contradiction" (p. 388).

Now taking Professor Dewey's statement that this quotation "precisely" expresses his point (a fact of which I should not otherwise have been at all sure, even after his explanations), it becomes evident how completely he has misread the theory of my book. I italicize two clauses in the quotation, each of which brings out one of the two essentials stated by me just above. The clause "*but that is just my point*"—and the book is very largely vain if the point be not in the end established—intimates that the "circle" is not a logical one at all; it is a *material* one. So far from falling into a logical circle, I make the material circular process of give and take the subject for my predicates all the way through. I make the growth of the sense of personality (*qua* personality) largely a matter of social absorption and ejective interpretation[3]—a complete circle of fact. And by this very circle of fact, looked at from the objective point of view, society is constituted with its bonds of publicity, etc. To shift one's point of view in considering a process which by its very nature shows two points of view is not to argue in a circle. It is an attempt to establish something material.[4]

<hr/>

[2] The reader of Professor Dewey's review will have noticed that after each statement of a "contradiction" he says: "As usual Mr. Baldwin recognizes all this in another place" (p. 392; see also pp. 387, 398). My reply is made much shorter from this fact—that I have gone over about all the points which Professor Dewey raises. They are things which the genetic point of view as involved in my "dialectic of growth" not only recognizes, but is actually built up on.

[3] Imitative! despite Professor Dewey's fear of the term (p. 390, note). I think most readers readily understand what it is to "read oneself imitatively into others" (though that is Professor Dewey's expression, not mine). It means to think the other by the same content by which the self is thought, with the imitative attitudes which such thinking involves. If I get my self-thought by imitating others, I can reinstate it either as self or as another only by taking on the imitative attitudes over again. See what is said below of the "general" as motor attitude.

[4] The two points of view called by Professor Dewey, I think unhappily, those of process (psychological) and content (sociological),—sub-

Now Professor Dewey's "fundamental" criticism with many of its applications falls of its own weight with this point. Assuming the circle to be a logical one, he attributes to me the distinction between society and the individual which such a circular fallacy presupposes. In other words, I am made an individualist, recognizing individuals independent of society, society over against individuals, and committing the circular fallacy in defining them in terms of each other after such recognition. Nothing could be really more untrue to my position. I nowhere recognize such an individual nor deny sociality to him; I nowhere assume society apart from social individuals; I nowhere fail to protest against just these assumptions. The passage which Professor Dewey quotes as showing "even more explicitly" the "denial of sociality to the individual" is altogether misinterpreted. I say in discussing the child's egoism, not at all in discussing adult reflective action, "the child must grow up to be an individual; that is incumbent upon him at all hazards; what more he may attain in the way of being a good or wise or social individual is based on this first presupposition." What is meant is that it is essential that the child should know how to act in self defense and offense in order to live—it is rather important to his future social career that he should live! So he is provided with organic and spontaneous reactions for personal quasi-egoistic action. But Professor Dewey has understood this to mean that a mature individual exists who is not social, and then has in some way to be made social! On the contrary, such a child is not a person at all, not an individual; I say distinctly that his own self-consciousness is not yet formed. I must say that this reading of my pages seems to me very astonishing.[5]

So also it is not true that I "unconsciously postulate" society

---

jective and objective are much better, for "content" is really psychological —are not only recognized by me, but the great division of my work, into Book I and Book II respectively, is based upon it (disregarding intentional "shifting" in certain chapters). When Professor Dewey asks (p. 387) for "a psychological derivation of the concepts of conscious personality, etc." from the point of view of "content," charging me with its omission, I fail to understand how that is possible. If he means a *sociological*, *i.e.*, anthropological derivation, that I have expressly declined to undertake from lack of competence; and it is not necessary, seeing that I say with sufficient directness that I am seeking light upon society from the *psychological* development of the individual. It would remain for me, were I able, to investigate as to whether the "dialectic of social growth," which I find analogous to and suggested by the "dialectic of personal growth," has really been the method of sociological evolution.

[5]   So on p. 391 he says: "We are simply told that there is an individual who is not social," a statement which is not made and not intimated in the quotation (p. 390) from which Professor Dewey draws it, nor anywhere else in the book! The anti-social people, criminals and lunatics, are expressly excluded.

(p. 389). I expressly and consciously postulate society, in the anthropological or sociological sense, and say that every individual at the stage to which his maturity belongs reflects a society of individuals like himself; all genetic science has so to proceed, as I explain more fully below. When Mr. Dewey says: "Were it not for this unconscious assumption we should have an absolutely numerical individualistic view," I agree, except to say "conscious and necessary assumption"? Things do not grow by leaps, but from earlier stages; yet when Professor Dewey follows that up by attributing to me this: "The thought of the individual in itself is not social; but other individuals come to think in the same way, and then there is society"—I make emphatic demurrer. If he had said, "Then the thought becomes available as social matter in so far as the attitudes which it excites have personal value and reference," he would be true to my exposition in the passage to which he is referring.

Let us take a case from physiology. Here is a writer who is asking how physiological growth takes place. He finds there is an order of changes through which morphological results come about. These changes may be looked at chemically or physically. First, he treats of animal chemistry; then in part II. of his treatise, he treats of functional physiological changes. Now, is he guilty of a *circulum in definiendo* in saying that the functional changes, which can be described only from the physiological point of view, require certain definite chemical changes, and also that the chemical changes in the organ are dependent upon the physiological action of that organ? Can we go on and say that his recognition of the chemical changes makes him an atomist in his morphology, his recognition of the functional changes makes him an organist, and his attempt to unite the two only emphasizes their antagonism? I think his answer would be that any one who knew the real problem of growth, as the facts set it, would see that the development of the organism is actually—materially—a thing of just this sort of higher organization of chemical matter in physiological form. And if any one pressed him with being an atomist he might retort: "Away with you; read me again! And if you, my critic, chance to be a philosopher, I advise you in the meantime to stop lecturing on Aristotle!"

Professor Dewey says: "How a matter which is not itself social (the individual's inventions) can become socialized through a process (imitation) which is not social either, I do not see." But this is just what happens whenever a lower order of fact is built into a higher organization. It is what happens in physiology, and it is what happens here. Imitation is not social unless it be the means of organizing a certain sort of material, and the material is not social unless it be imitatively organized. Self-thoughts imitatively organized are, I contend, the essence of what is social.[6]

Turning to the need of taking the genetic point of view—the other general point—I find Professor Dewey equally wide of the mark.[7] I have italicized a second clause in the sentence which he quotes from my book to prove the fatal circle; I say: "We can get no true view of the socius *at any time* without describing the social conditions under which he normally lives etc." The words "at any time" indicate what the whole book clearly says from preface to back-cover. If we are to assume a ready-made individual, on one hand, and a ready-made society, on the other hand, and an antagonism between them which we are called upon in some way to do away with—all of which I have called (*Soc. Int.*, p. 88) a "hideous un-fact"—then of course we cannot allow ourselves to explain one of these "at any time" or stage of growth as involving elements from the other at some other stage of growth. But if we are studying a progress, an evolution, genetically, and have already determined the essential interdependence of the elements which go into it, it is not only legitimate, it is necessary for attaining truth, that we discover in each stage, "at any time," the part in the whole movement which each of the elements contributes. The individual's growth as a person is as a fact, I think, at once personal and social; and the social situation is, at any time, a reflex of the individual's growth in personality. So a genetic investigation has just to trace out the zig-zag or spiral curve of this one development, now looking toward society from the point of view of the individual and now toward the individual from the point of view of society. It is again a matter of astonishment to me that a member of the Hegelian school should urge for a moment that opposition in the elements of a complex group of phenomena should be considered strictly static—not resolvable into a higher organized unity. To carry out such a point would be to condemn all evolution theory; and—what may sound like a worse penalty to my reviewer—it would destroy Hegel's Philosophy of Mind as well as his Philosophy of Nature.

Space will not suffice for the application of these remarks to all the points of criticism which Mr. Dewey makes. I think the reader will see in most of the instances how the genetic and material points of view relieve the case of all embarrassment.[8] For example,

6    Calling the result of instinctive gregarious coöperation a "company" as opposed to a "society."
7    There is a singular difference, however, between the review and his *New World* article in this respect.
8    I reply to the particular criticisms, however, in various footnotes throughout.

my view of the "publicity" of the ethical sense is said to be contradictory because it is "quantitative" (involving reference to others'
knowledge of the situation) and also "qualitative," *i.e.*, having an
"ideal reference." Waiving matters of fact[9] I see no inconsistency. If
the ideal is a synthesis of ego and alter thoughts *which has been
attained through actual social contact and reciprocal judgment*, then
the ideal reference comes to take the place of the social contact. But
this ideal reference is always confirmable concretely and in terms of
self-attitude only through the original social channels. Private judgment in ethical matters "needs less and less to appeal to an [external]
authority," but its inner authority is always subjected in particular
cases to this appeal. The instance given by Professor Dewey (*i.e.*,
"our surest token that an intention is wrong is our shrinking from
having anybody else know of it") *does* involve the thought of some
one else's knowing of it, and moreover it does not escape the genetic
truth that the judgment of the act has arisen in us through other
experiences in which we had the actual judgment of others. As to
*evidence* of others knowing of the deed, I have taken pains in the
book (pp. 315 f.) to say only of the *negative* case (*i.e.*, in which we
*know the deed to be quite private*) that our ethical competence is
impaired; not that we require evidence in the positive case. In the
negative case, the facts impair the data of moral synthesis; in the
positive case, past experience reinforces the ethical judgment without
such direct evidence.

There are only two points at which I feel Professor Dewey's
remarks take hold upon the matter vitally. One of these (p. 394)
is a point already raised by Professor Tufts in the *Psychological
Review* for May, 1898, and answered by me in the July issue of that
journal (*cf.* also *Soc. Int.*, p. 266, note). It is this: that the general
can be at once unformed and undifferentiated, and also a generalization from concrete thoughts. I hold that there is always in a general
more than the content which stands for the objective class; there is a
forward reach, a prospective reference, a drift which is, in so far, as
yet undifferentiated. In the general self this is just the "projective,"
the unabsorbed balance of personal material which sets imitative

---

[9]     The statements: "Publicity consists in actual possession of the
same content by two or more agents," and "A thought originally not ethical becomes such when one knows somebody else accepts it"—with the
implication of "moral legislation by majorities" (pp. 396–97)—cannot
justly be attributed to me from any "point of view." I should have
thought my meaning would be as plain as "the nose on a man's face" to
Professor Dewey, but it is evident that he sometimes requires a Cyrano de
Bergerac!

copies and, in the higher development, ethical law to the child.[10]

The other point raised by Professor Dewey is whether my doctrine of identity of content in individuals, as necessary to sociality, takes any account of my other "official" doctrine that the general as such is motor attitude. I reply: Certainly it does, though here I might have made further explanations in the text, had I not already (officially!) dealt with the psychology of the general in the earlier book. The identity of content is essential to the identity of motor (*i.e.*, personal) attitudes in which last this general self and the social consciousness consist. I go to the greatest pains to say, in the chapter on Intelligence, that the attitudes are functions of the thought. Given identity of the self-thought, and the attitudes which constitute general and social personality follow—however inadequate the actual content may be to establish sociality. Professor Dewey's criticisms are verbal and logical,[11] and take no account of what to me is the essential fact, *i.e.*, that in thinking himself the individual attains a general and ideal self-attitude with the implication of a social situation. It is not to me the identity of content, as Professor Dewey seems to suppose (pp. 386, 390, 391, 393), that is immediately productive of sociality; but the common attitude which the individual takes up, whether the identical content be determined as ego or as alter-content (see *Soc. Int.*, Appendix D). This consideration and the recognition of the genetic method completely dispose of the criticism on p. 390 of his article. So in the final summary, where Professor Dewey again says that I have myself happily stated the three "contradictory" conceptions of the socius, these are the things to bear in mind. Socius (b)[12] is the content, the identical concrete thought which stands for me and you. It is the socius in so far as that personage has any concrete embodiment. It is the identical content in every concrete self. Socius (a) is the retrospective, historical, psychological self which has experienced pleasures, pains, etc., with other persons. It is not

10    *Cf.* Mr. Dewey's criticism (p. 394) that the ejective process is sometimes stated as giving an alter to practice on, and at another time as resulting in social confirmation. The former is the content considered as concrete and calling out habit merely; the latter is the projective copy for imitation; the latter can be utilized, however, and learned about, only through imitation which now leads to accommodations. Who has not seen a child start out to tyrannize over a playfellow, and then turn in upon himself and reinterpret the whole situation? Both are social, but represent different phases of the genetic process.

11    *Cf.* p. 390, lines 8–10 from top, where the whole point turns on the use of the word "social" in two senses, "social organization" meaning *to the onlooker*, and "social interpretation" meaning *subjective to the individual*, the ambiguity being held up as a confusion of mine! (See also p. 390, second paragraph.)

12    See Professor Dewey's symbols on p. 398 of his review.

content in so far as it is different from (b); but the (b) content is there of course to arouse the (a) attitude. It is the self of habit which dominates over other selves. Socius (c) is the general, *qua* ideal, self which is "projective" and prospective; again not content, since it too is attitude aroused by content (a). Now to say that these three things contradict and annul one another is absurd, save in a faculty psychology. Genetically they are phases in a process upon a content. The thing essential to it all is a social situation which each individual helps on and realizes just by his personal growth. The different passages which discuss it might certainly be better written, but such as they are they do not appear to me inconsistent.

In conclusion, I may say that I do not mean that Professor Dewey has not written with consideration and evident desire to be just, and I regret, indeed, that I do not find his remarks more pertinent. That one of his mind and heart should have so largely, as it seems to me, mistaken my fundamental presuppositions makes me think there must be some radical divergence between his "apperceptive systems" and mine. I make free to add also that at times I find Professor Dewey's writing somewhat unintelligible. For example, the first paragraph on p. 391 of his notice has no glimmer of meaning to me, except that it says, "we are simply told that there is the individual who is not social"—which somebody else must have told him, not I! If this statement refers to the quotation just made from me to the effect that the completely socialized individual—whose rules and sanctions would equate absolutely with those of society—is mythical, it is a singularly wild and uncalled-for misunderstanding. Of course, I mean that there are variations in individuals' sociality—not a hard saying!—and that science has to suppose a mean value; and that conclusions cannot be drawn in concrete cases, since the mean value is seldom or never met with. Where is the assertion of "the individual who is not social"?

So in the note to the same paragraph I am quoted as saying, "society solves it only to renew it," of the "bond between the individual and society." To be frank, this attributes nonsense to me. What I say is: "A final conflict between the individual and society is always possible. It is soluble only by the growth of society . . . and society solves it only to renew it always." It is a part of the task of the book just to show how the progress of society exists by constant solving of the oppositions which the individuals' thoughts produce, and that by producing new thinkers and new thoughts society ever and again renews the opposition on another plane. If Professor Dewey wishes a final adjustment of all oppositions between individuals and society, then I agree with him that my conclusion does not "conclude"; for it is a part of my conclusion that the opposition is itself an essential moment in social progress.

## Discussion.

[Reported by L. H. JONES.]

RICHARD JONES, Albany, N.Y., being called for, explained the experiment now being made by the University of the State of New York in art education. Out of the funds at their disposal the regents of the university have purchased photographs of great works of art, covering architecture, sculpture, paintings, etc. These are divided into groups and are loaned to schools for a definite period. Their use has been intended mainly to stimulate and vivify the work in literature, and this comes directly under my notice as inspector of this study for the state, under direction of the regents. While the matter is to some extent still an experiment, its influence for good is distinctly noticeable.

F. LOUIS SOLDAN, St. Louis, Mo.—A similar experiment has been tried in St. Louis. The Art Committee of the Wednesday Club bought 160 pictures of worthy art subjects and divided them into ten groups, so that each group should contain at least one representation of each kind and each important age. These pictures of a group are held by one school for ten weeks, and they are then exchanged for another group. Superintendents and teachers lecture to pupils, explaining the history of the picture, its motive and artistic significance.

One good effect, in addition to many others, has been to stimulate pupils, teachers, and patrons to buy pictures for the adornment of schoolrooms.

NATHAN C. SCHAEFFER, Harrisburg, Pa.—I wish to propound a question. We have heard much of the value of nature study from a scientific standpoint. We hear little of nature as the home of beauty. What is the comparative place of beauty as we find it in nature, with beauty as we find it in art, as a means of education? I would like to hear from Dr. Harris.

W. T. HARRIS, United States Commissioner of Education.—I smiled at the question of my friend Schaeffer, remembering my controversies with Colonel Parker over the same question. He finds the

[*First published in* Addresses and Proceedings *of the National Educational Association, 1897, p. 346. For Dewey's address, "The Æsthetic Element in Education," see* The Early Works of John Dewey, v.]

source of beauty in nature; I affirm art superior to nature in this respect. Art undertakes to give a manifestation of reason instead of a realization of it. History and nature do the latter. No scene is really worth painting as it really is, but as it is seen by the painter after certain changes which make it fitter to express beauty and reason. Church's Heart of the Andes is highly idealized, and thus expresses the feelings of the artist as no mere reproduction can do. Some pictures are mere photographs. A landscape photograph is not really beautiful, though one may like it for its truth to nature. The true picture is symbolic; has in it the feelings of the artist, expressed by his arrangement and treatment of details. By his arrangement he makes us see or appreciate more than is shown—gives us a vicarious power of the senses, so to speak, enabling one to take the place of others. Nature, by her arrangement of elements, gives us the sense of freedom—freedom from carping care; but art alone puts these elements together so as to preserve this freedom and exhibit perfect reason.

D. L. KIEHLE, Minneapolis, Minn.—I cordially indorse what Dr. Harris has said. In our school work we have approached nature from the scientific side. This I believe to be a mistake—we should seek to lead pupils to love nature.

HENRY SABIN, Des Moines, Ia.—I think we have had no more important subject up for discussion in this Council. The education of the next century is wrapped up in the thesis treated so ably here this afternoon. I would like to ask a question of Miss Nicholson: What would you do if you were principal of a four-room building, each room having dirty walls, with cracked plaster, etc.?

MISS NICHOLSON.—I would have the walls whitewashed (or better, buff-washed), if I had to do it myself. Then I would bring in nature. Plants are the safest form of schoolroom decoration for general use.

W. T. HARRIS.—Photographs of great works of art are safer than poor original pictures.

C. B. GILBERT, Newark, N. J.—The contemplation of great works of art, as contended for in this discussion, is excellent. But this is not all that should be done. There should be a construction side. Drawing should be made to contribute to æsthetic culture, while the child is securing skill in his work. I should like to have Dr. Dewey tell us how this may be done.

JOHN DEWEY, The University of Chicago.—I do not know. I believe drawing should be made to contribute to the end of art education. One of the first principles of art education is that of free self-expression. Drawing should contribute to this end.

S. G. WILLIAMS, Cornell University.—Is not the technical knowledge necessary as a means of developing the art sense?

JOHN DEWEY.—History shows that nations have gained the power to achieve while developing the appreciation of art effects in education. Two interesting experiments in attempting to carry the two hand in hand are those undertaken in Pratt Institute and in Brookline, Mass.

On the request of Mr. Gove, of Colorado, the chair called upon Principal W. H. Smiley, of the Denver High School, to give the plan pursued in his school.

W. H. SMILEY.—The study of the outside world for classification has led us away from the æsthetic study of nature—so our pupils miss the joy they should obtain from such study. The Denver High School has had some help from the public library. We have secured many illustrations from magazines. We advised this in connection with the work in history. The school authorities have bought 100 fine pictures of Seemans, Wandeholde, Leipzig, at a cost of $30.

[N.B. All appendix material is reproduced here in "diplomatic reprint" form, *i.e.*, with minimal correction and change from the original.]

# List of symbols

## A.  Designation of sources

C    Criticisms Wise and Otherwise on Modern Child-Study
CS    Results of Child-Study Applied to Education
E    The Æsthetic Element in Education
EE    Evolution and Ethics
EP    Ethical Principles Underlying Education
ES    *Educational Ethics: Syllabus of a Course of Six Lecture-Studies*
ET    *Education Today*
H    Harris's *Psychologic Foundations of Education*
HS    The Influence of the High School upon Educational Methods
IA    Imagination and Expression
IC    Interpretation of the Culture-Epoch Theory
IR    *Interest in Relation to Training of the Will*
IS    The Interpretation Side of Child-Study
J    Review of *Johnson's Universal Cyclopædia*, Vols. I–V
K    The Kindergarten and Child-Study
KP    E. L. Kellogg Co. pamphlet printing of My Pedagogic Creed
L    Letter to the Editor of the *Chicago Evening Post*
M    The Metaphysical Method in Ethics
MP    My Pedagogic Creed
N    Need for a Laboratory School
NC    Review of Conant's *The Number Concept*
P    The Psychology of Effort
PA    The Psychological Aspect of the School Curriculum
PC    *Philosophy and Civilization*
PE    A Pedagogical Experiment
PF    The Primary-Education Fetich
PN    Psychology of Number
PO    *Plan of Organization of the University Primary School*
PP    *Pedagogy I B 19: Philosophy of Education, 1898–1899—Winter Quarter*
PR    The Philosophic Renascence in America
PS    *Educational Psychology: Syllabus of a Course of Twelve Lecture-Studies*
PU    Pedagogy as a University Discipline

| | |
|---|---|
| PW | Plan for Organization of Work in a Fully Equipped Department of Pedagogy |
| R | Some Remarks on the Psychology of Number |
| RA | The Reflex Arc Concept in Psychology |
| RB | Rejoinder to Baldwin's Social Interpretations: A Reply |
| RC | Report of the Committee on a Detailed Plan for a Report on Elementary Education |
| RS | Remarks on the Study of History |
| S | The Sense of Solidity |
| SC | Review of Bryant's *Studies in Character* and Watson's *Hedonistic Theories from Aristippus to Spencer* |
| SE | Review of Stanley's *Studies in the Evolutionary Psychology of Feeling* |
| SI | Review of Baldwin's *Social and Ethical Interpretations in Mental Development* [*Philosophical Review*] |
| SM | Review of Baldwin's *Social and Ethical Interpretations in Mental Development* [*New World*] |
| SP | *The Significance of the Problem of Knowledge* |
| SS | Review of Sully's *Studies of Childhood* |
| U | The University School |

## B.  Other designations

Page-line number at left is from present edition. All lines of print except running heads and chapter titles are counted.

Reading preceding bracket is from present edition.

Square bracket signals end of reading from present edition, followed by the symbol identifying first appearance of reading.

W means Works—the present edition—and is used for emendations made here for the first time.

The abbreviation *om.* means the reading before the bracket was omitted in the editions and printings identified after the abbreviation.

The abbreviation *rom.* means roman type and is used to signal the omission of italics.

The word *stet* with an edition or printing number indicates a reading retained from an edition subsequently revised; the rejected variant follows the semicolon.

The *asterisk* indicates that a textual note on that emendation follows the tabulation of emendations.

For emendations restricted to punctuation, the wavy dash ∼ means the same word(s) as before the bracket, and the inferior caret ∧ indicates the absence of a punctuation mark.

# Checklist of references

In Dewey's references, titles and authors' names have been corrected and expanded to conform accurately and consistently to the original works. All corrections appear in the List of Emendations in the Copy-Texts. As many of the titles in both the texts and footnotes are in shortened form, full publication information is given in the section that follows.

After each Checklist entry are symbol references to the work in which Dewey mentions or quotes from that entry in the present volume. When Dewey's reference included page numbers, it was possible to identify the edition he used. In other references, among the various editions possibly available to him, the one listed is the most likely source by reason of place or date of publication, or on the evidence from correspondence and other materials, and its general accessibility during the period.

Aber, Mary Rose. *An Experiment in Education; Also, the Ideas Which Inspired It and Were Inspired by It.* New York: Harper and Bros., 1897. (PP)

Adams, Herbert Baxter. *Methods of Historical Study.* Baltimore: Johns Hopkins University, 1884. (PP)

Adams, Sir John. *The Herbartian Psychology Applied to Education.* Boston: D. C. Heath and Co., 1897. (PP)

Adler, Felix. *Moral Instruction of Children.* New York: D. Appleton and Co., 1892. (PP)

Angell, James Rowland, and Moore, Addison W. "Studies from the Psychological Laboratory of the University of Chicago," Part One, Reaction-Time: A Study in Attention and Habit, *Psychological Review*, III (May 1896), 245–58. (RA)

Aristotle. *The Politics of Aristotle.* Trans. J. E. C. Welldon. London: Macmillan and Co., 1883. (PP)

Arnold, Matthew. *Culture and Anarchy: An Essay in Political and Social Criticism.* 2d ed. London: Smith, Elder, and Co., 1875. (PP)

Bain, Alexander. *Education as a Science.* New York: D. Appleton and Co., 1879. (PP)

Baker, James H. "Educational Values," *Educational Review*, X (Oct. 1895), 209–17. (PP)

Baldwin, James Mark. *Handbook of Psychology.* 2 vols. New York: Henry Holt and Co., 1889–91. [Vol. I: *Senses and Intellect*; Vol. II: *Feeling and Will.*] (RA, P, PS, J)

———. *Mental Development in the Child and the Race: Methods and Processes.* New York: Macmillan Co., 1895. (IC, PS, PP, SI)

———. *Social and Ethical Interpretations in Mental Development: A Study in Social Psychology.* New York: Macmillan Co., 1897. (SI, RB, SM)

———. "About Children: A Further Word on Imitation," *Century,* XLIX (Dec. 1894), 308–10. (PS)

———. "Genetic Psychology," III, 712–13; "Genius," III, 715–16; "Habit," IV, 98–99; "Hedonism," IV, 206–7; "Hypnotism," IV, 461–62; "Ideal Feelings, or Emotions," IV, 488–89; "Ideals," IV, 490–91; "Illusion," IV, 502–3; "Imagination," IV, 505–7; "Imitation, or Imitative Suggestion," IV, 508–9; "Impulse," IV, 520; "Innervation," IV, 593; "Insanity," IV, 602–7; "Instinct," IV, 620–21; "Localization," V, 318–20; and "Motive," V, 917–18; in *Johnson's Universal Cyclopædia.* Ed. Charles Kendall Adams. New York: A. J. Johnson Co., 1894. (J)

———. "Social Interpretations: A Reply," in *The Early Works of John Dewey, 1882–1898*, V, lxxvi–xciv. Carbondale: Southern Illinois University Press, 1972. (RB)

Baldwin, Joseph. *School Management and School Methods.* New York: D. Appleton and Co., 1897. (PP)

Barnard, Henry, ed. *Analytical Index to Barnard's American Journal of Ethics* [1855–81]. Washington, D.C.: Government Printing Office, 1892. (PP)

Barnes, Earl. "The Child as a Social Factor," in *Studies in Education,* ed. Earl Barnes, I, 355–60. Stanford: Stanford University Press, 1897. (PP)

———. "Discipline at Home and in the School," in *Studies in Education,* ed. Earl Barnes, I, 26–28, 71–72, 110–11, 149–53, 190–93, 228–29, 270–72. Stanford: Stanford University Press, 1896–97. (PP)

———. "Punishment as Seen by Children," *Pedagogical Seminary,* III (Oct. 1895), 235–45. (PP)

———, and Barnes, Mary S. "Education among the Aztecs," in *Studies in Education,* ed. Earl Barnes, I, 73–80. Stanford: Stanford University Press, 1896. (PP)

———. "Historical Ideals and Methods of Chinese Education," in *Studies in Education,* ed. Earl Barnes, I, 112–18. Stanford: Stanford University Press, 1896. (PP)

Barnes, Mary S. *Studies in Historical Method.* Boston: D. C. Heath and Co., 1896. (PP)

Barnett, Percy Arthur, ed. *Teaching and Organisation, with Special Reference to Secondary Schools: A Manual of Practice.* London: Longmans, Green and Co., 1897. (PP)

Beale, Dorothea, *et al. Work and Play in Girls' Schools.* New York: Longmans, Green and Co., 1898. (PP)

Bolton, Thaddeus L. "Rhythm," *American Journal of Psychology,* VI (Jan. 1894), 144–238. (R)

Bosanquet, Bernard. *A History of Æsthetic.* New York: Macmillan Co., 1892. (SP)

Brown, George P. "Educative Interests," *Public-School Journal,* XV (Feb. 1896), 306–8. (PP)

Browne, George H. "The Educational Value of English," *Educational Review,* IX (Apr. 1895), 377–84. (PP)

Brunetière, Ferdinand. *Éducation et instruction.* Paris: Firmin-Didot et Cie., 1895. (PP)

Bryant, Sophie. *Short Studies in Character* (The Ethical Library, Vol. II, ed. J. H. Muirhead). New York: Macmillan Co., 1894. (SC)

Buisson, Ferdinand Édouard. *Dictionnaire de pédagogie et d'instruction primaire.* 2 pts. in 4 vols. Paris: Hachette et Cie., 1887–88. (PP)

Butler, Nicholas Murray. *The Meaning of Education, and Other Essays and Addresses.* New York: Macmillan Co., 1898. (PP)

———. Editorial, *Educational Review,* VI (Nov. 1893), 410. (PP)

———. Editorial, *Educational Review,* VII (Mar. 1894), 305–6. (PP)

———. Editorial, *Educational Review,* VII (May 1894), 515. (PP)

———. "What Knowledge Is of Most Worth?" *Educational Review,* X (Sept. 1895), 105–20. (PP)

Butler, Samuel. *Unconscious Memory.* London: D. Bogue, 1880. (PS)

Cajori, Florian. *The Teaching and History of Mathematics in the United States.* Washington, D.C.: Government Printing Office, 1890. (PP)

Carpenter, William Benjamin. *Principles of Mental Physiology.* London: H. S. King and Co., 1874. (PS)

Carus, Paul. *Primer of Philosophy.* Chicago: Open Court Publishing Co., 1893. (PR)

———. *The Soul of Man: An Investigation of the Facts of Physiological and Experimental Psychology.* Chicago: Open Court Publishing Co., 1891. (PS)

———. "Ethics and the Cosmic Order," *Monist*, IV (Apr. 1894), 403–16. (EE)

Cattell, James McKeen. "Memory," in *Johnson's Universal Cyclopædia*, ed. Charles Kendall Adams, V, 663–65. New York: A. J. Johnson Co., 1894. (J)

Clarke, Isaac Edwards. *Art and Industry: Education in the Industrial and Fine Arts in the United States*. Washington, D.C.: Government Printing Office, 1885. (PP)

Collins, John Churton. *The Study of English Literature: A Plea for Its Recognition and Organization at the Universities*. London: Macmillan and Co., 1891. (PP)

———. "Language versus Literature at Oxford," *Nineteenth Century*, XXXVII (Feb. 1895), 290–303. (PP)

Conant, Levi Leonard. *The Number Concept: Its Origin and Development*. New York: Macmillan Co., 1896. (NC)

Crane, Walter. *Relations of Art to Education and Social Life*. London: Leek Press, 1893. (PP)

D'Arcy, Charles Frederick. *A Short Study of Ethics*. New York: Macmillan Co., 1895. (M)

Darrah, Estelle M. "Children's Attitude toward Law," in *Studies in Education*, ed. Earl Barnes, I, 213–16, 254–58. Stanford: Stanford University Press, 1896. (PP)

Darwin, Charles Robert. *The Expression of the Emotions in Man and Animals*. New York: D. Appleton and Co., 1873. (PS)

Davis, William M. "The Teaching of Geography," Part One, *Educational Review*, III (May 1892), 417–26; Part Two, *ibid.*, IV (June 1892), 6–15. (PP)

———, King, C. F., and Collie, G. L. "Governmental Maps in Schools," *Educational Review*, VII (Mar. 1894), 232–39. (PP)

De Garmo, Charles. *The Essentials of Method*. Boston: D. C. Heath and Co., 1889. (PP)

———. *Herbart and the Herbartians*. New York: C. Scribner's Sons, 1896. (ES, PP)

———. "German Contributions to the Co-ordination of Studies," *Educational Review*, IV (Dec. 1892), 422–37. (PP)

———. "Is Herbart's Theory of Interest Dangerous?" *Public-School Journal*, XIV (May 1895), 514–15. (PP)

———. "A Working Basis for the Correlation of Studies," *Educational Review*, V (May 1893), 451–66. (PP)

Denison, John H. "Individualism in Education," *Andover Review*, V (June 1886), 589–94. (PP)

Deussen, Paul. *The Elements of Metaphysics: Being a Guide for Lectures and Private Use*. Trans. C. M. Duff. New York: Macmillan Co., 1894. (PR)

Dewey, John. *Outlines of a Critical Theory of Ethics*, in *The Early*

*Works of John Dewey, 1882–1898*, III, 237–388. Carbondale: Southern Illinois University Press, 1969. (M, ES)

————. *Psychology* (*Early Works*, II). (PS)

————. *The Study of Ethics: A Syllabus*, in *Early Works*, IV, 219–362. (RA, ES, PS)

————. "Ethical Principles Underlying Education," in *Early Works*, V, 54–83. (PP)

————. *Interest in Relation to Training of the Will*, in *Early Works*, V, 111–50. (PP)

————. "Intuitionalism," in *Early Works*, IV, 123–31. (J)

————. "My Pedagogic Creed," in *Early Works*, V, 84–95. (PP)

————. "The Psychological Aspect of the School Curriculum," in *Early Works*, V, 164–76. (PP)

————. "The Psychology of Effort," in *Early Works*, V, 151–63. (EE)

————. "The Reflex Arc Concept in Psychology," in *Early Works*, V, 96–109. (P)

————. "The Theory of Emotion," in *Early Works*, IV, 152–88. (PS, SE)

————, and McLellan, James Alexander. *The Psychology of Number and Its Application to Methods of Teaching Arithmetic* (International Education Series, Vol. XXXIII, ed. William Torrey Harris). New York: D. Appleton and Co., 1895. (PA, R, ES, PP, PN)

Dodd, Catherine Isabel. *Introduction to the Herbartian Principles of Teaching*. New York: Macmillan Co., 1898. (PP)

Donaldson, Henry Herbert. *The Growth of the Brain: A Study of the Nervous System in Relation to Education*. London: W. Scott, 1895. (PS)

Droysen, Johann Gustav. *Outline of the Principles of History*. Trans. E. Benjamin Andrews. Boston: Ginn and Co., 1893. (PP)

Dutton, Samuel T. "The Relation of Education to Vocation," *Educational Review*, XII (Nov. 1896), 335–47. (PP)

*Educational Review*. New York: Henry Holt and Co. Indexes in: Vol. II (June–Dec. 1891), Vol. IV (June–Dec. 1892), Vol. VI (June–Dec. 1893), Vol. X (June–Dec. 1895). (PP)

Eliot, Charles William. *Educational Reform: Essays and Addresses*. New York: Century Co., 1898. (PP)

Emerson, Ralph Waldo. "Compensation," in *Essays*, First Series. New and rev. ed., pp. 91–122. Boston: Houghton, Mifflin and Co., 1883. (IR)

*The Encyclopædia Britannica: A Dictionary of Arts, Sciences, and General Literature*. 9th ed. Ed. T. S. Baynes. 25 vols. New York: C. Scribner's Sons, 1878–89. (J)

Exner, Sigmund. *Entwurf zu einer physiologischen Erklärung der psychischen Erscheinungen.* Leipzig: F. Deuticke, 1894. (PS)

Farrar, Frederic William, ed. *Essays on a Liberal Education.* London: Macmillan and Co., 1867. (PP)

Felmley, David. "Discussion," pp. 195–97, in *First Supplement to the Yearbook of the National Herbart Society.* Bloomington, Ill.: Pantagraph Printing and Stationery Co., 1895. (IC)

Findlay, J. J. "The Scope of the Science of Education," *Educational Review,* XIV (Oct. 1897), 236–47. (PP)

Fine, H. B. Review of *The Psychology of Number* by James A. McLellan and John Dewey, in *The Early Works of John Dewey, 1882–1898,* v, xxiii–xxvii. Carbondale: Southern Illinois University Press, 1972. (PN)

Fiske, John. *The Destiny of Man, Viewed in the Light of His Origin.* 19th ed. Boston: Houghton, Mifflin and Co., 1893. (PP)

———. *Excursions of an Evolutionist.* Boston: Houghton, Mifflin and Co., 1884. (PP)

Fitch, Sir Joshua Girling. *The Art of Questioning.* New York: E. L. Kellogg and Co., 1888. (PP)

———. *Lectures on Teaching.* New ed. New York: Macmillan Co., 1891. (PP)

Fitzpatrick, Frank A. "Departmental Teaching in Grammar Schools," *Educational Review,* VII (May 1894), 439–47. (PP)

Foster, Sir Michael. *Physiology.* New York: D. Appleton and Co., 1883. (PS)

Fouillée, Alfred Jules Émile. *Education from a National Standpoint.* Trans. and ed., with a Preface by W. J. Greenstreet; also a Preface by William Torrey Harris. New York: D. Appleton and Co., 1892. (PP)

Frear, Caroline. "Class Punishment," in *Studies in Education,* ed. Earl Barnes, I, 332–37. Stanford: Stanford University Press, 1897. (PP)

Freeman, Edward Augustus. *The Methods of Historical Study.* London: Macmillan and Co., 1886. (PP)

Galbreath, Louis H. "Discussion," pp. 163–65 and 167, in *First Supplement to the Yearbook of the National Herbart Society.* Bloomington, Ill.: Pantagraph Printing and Stationery Co., 1895. (IC)

Galton, Francis. *Inquiries into Human Faculty and Its Development.* London: Macmillan and Co., 1883. (PS)

Garnett, James M. "The Elective System of the University of Virginia," *Andover Review,* V (Apr. 1886), 359–75. (PP)

Geikie, Sir Archibald. *The Teaching of Geography.* London: Macmillan and Co., 1887. (PP)

Gilbert, Charles B. "Practicable Correlations of Studies," *Educational Review,* XI (Apr. 1896), 313–22. (PP)

Gilman, D. C. "The Group System of College Studies in The Johns Hopkins University," *Andover Review*, v (June 1886), 565–76. (PP)

Goodwin, Edward J. "Electives in Elementary Schools," *Educational Review*, x (June 1895), 12–21. (PP)

Goodwin, William W. "The Educational Value of the Ancient Classics," *Educational Review*, IX (Apr. 1895), 335–42. (PP)

Green, Thomas Hill. *Prolegomena to Ethics*. Ed. A. C. Bradley. Oxford: Clarendon Press, 1883. (M)

Grössler, Hermann. *Das gleichschwebende vielseitige Interesse nach Herbart der Zweck des Unterrechts*. Eisleben: E. Schneider, 1883. (IR)

Hailmann, William Nicholas. "Report of Plans to Collect Data concerning Methods and Courses of Work in Elementary Schools," in National Educational Association, *Journal of Proceedings and Addresses, 1897*, pp. 199–208. Chicago: University of Chicago Press, 1897. (RC)

Hall, G. Stanley. "Moral Education and Will Training," *Pedagogical Seminary*, II (1892), 72–89. (PP)

———, ed. *Methods of Teaching History*. Boston: D. C. Heath and Co., 1883. (PP)

———, and Mansfield, John M. *Hints toward a Select and Descriptive Bibliography of Education*. Boston: D. C. Heath and Co., 1886. (PP)

Halleck, Reuben Post. "The Bearings of the Laws of Cerebral Development and Modification on Child Study," in National Educational Association, *Journal of Proceedings and Addresses, 1897*, pp. 833–41. Chicago: University of Chicago Press, 1897. (C)

Ham, Charles Henry. *Manual Training, the Solution of Social and Industrial Problems*. London: Blackie and Son, 1886. (PP)

Hamilton, Sir William. "On the Study of Mathematics, as a Study of the Mind," in *Discussions on Philosophy and Literature, Education and University Reform*, pp. 257–324. New York: Harper and Bros., 1861. (PP)

Hanus, Paul H. "Attempted Improvements in the Course of Study," *Educational Review*, XII (Dec. 1896), 435–52. (PP)

———. "Educational Aims and Educational Values," *Educational Review*, x (Apr. 1895), 323–34. (PP)

Harper, William R. "Ideals of Educational Work," in National Educational Association, *Journal of Proceedings and Addresses, 1895*, pp. 987–98. St. Paul: Pioneer Press Co., 1895. (PP)

Harris, William Torrey. *Psychologic Foundations of Education: An Attempt to Show the Genesis of the Higher Faculties of the Mind* (International Education Series, Vol. XXXVII, ed.

William Torrey Harris). New York: D. Appleton and Co., 1898. (PP, H)

———. "Association of Ideas," I, 373–75; "Generalization," III, 710; "Hegel," IV, 207–9; "Hindu Philosophy," IV, 288; "Idea," IV, 487–88; "Idealism," IV, 489–90; "Identity," IV, 491; "Immortality," IV, 513–14; and "Infinite," IV, 581–82; in *Johnson's Universal Cyclopædia*. Ed. Charles Kendall Adams. New York: A. J. Johnson Co., 1894. (J)

———. "The Church, the State, and the School," *North American Review*, CXXXIII (Sept. 1881), 215–27. (PP)

———. "Herbart's Doctrine of Interest," *Educational Review*, X (June 1895), 71–80. (PP)

———. "In What Does Spiritual Evolution Consist?" *Education*, XVI (Mar. 1896), 413–21. (PP)

———. "The Necessity for Five Co-ordinate Groups of Studies in the Schools," *Educational Review*, XI (Apr. 1896), 323–34. (PP)

———. "Professor John Dewey's Doctrine of Interest as Related to Will," *Educational Review*, XI (May 1896), 486–93. (PA, PP)

———. "The Psychology of the Imitative Functions in Childhood as Related to the Process of Learning," in National Educational Association, *Journal of Proceedings and Addresses*, 1894, pp. 637–41. St. Paul: Pioneer Press Co., 1895. (PP)

———. Reply to De Garmo's "Is Herbart's Theory of Interest Dangerous?" *Public-School Journal*, XIV (June 1895), 575–76. (PP)

———. "Report of Subcommittee on the Correlation of Studies in Elementary Education," in *Report of the Committee of Fifteen on Elementary Education*, pp. 40–99. New York: American Book Co., 1895. (PA, PP)

———. "Report of the Superintendent," in *Eighteenth Annual Report of the Board of Directors of the St. Louis Public Schools, for the Year Ending August 1, 1872*, pp. 13–165. St. Louis: Democrat Printing Co., 1873. (PA, PP, H)

———. "Report of the Superintendent," in *Fifteenth Annual Report of the Board of Directors of the St. Louis Public Schools, for the Year Ending August 1, 1869*, pp. 13–136. St. Louis: Democrat Printing Co., 1870. (PA, PP, H)

———. "Report of the Superintendent," in *Fourteenth Annual Report of the Board of Directors of the St. Louis Public Schools, for the Year Ending August 1, 1868*, pp. 16–102. St. Louis: George Knapp and Co., 1869. (PA, PP, H)

———. "Report of the Superintendent," in *Nineteenth Annual Re-*

port of the Board of Directors of the St. Louis Public Schools, for the Year Ending August 1, 1873, pp. 14–191. St. Louis: Democrat Printing Co., 1874. (PA, PP, H)

————. "Report of the Superintendent," in *Seventeenth Annual Report of the Board of Directors of the St. Louis Public Schools, for the Year Ending August 1, 1871*, pp. 15–191. St. Louis: Plate, Olhausen and Co., 1872. (PA, PP, H)

Hegel, Georg Wilhelm Friedrich. *Die Logik.* Part One of *Encyklopädie der philosophischen Wissenschaften.* 2d ed. Heidelberg: A. Oswald, 1827. (PR)

————. *Werke.* Ed. Philipp Marheineke *et al.* 19 vols. Berlin: Duncker und Humblot, 1832–45, 1877. [Vol. II: *Phänomenologie des Geistes*; Vol. VII, Bk. 2: *Die Philosophie des Geistes*; Vol. VIII: *Grundlinien der Philosophie des Rechts.*] (PR)

Herbart, Johann Friedrich. *The Science of Education.* Trans. Henry M. and Emmie Felkin. Boston: D. C. Heath and Co., 1893. (PP)

————. *A Text-Book in Psychology: An Attempt to Found the Science of Psychology on Experience, Metaphysics, and Mathematics.* Trans. Margaret K. Smith (International Education Series, Vol. XVIII, ed. William Torrey Harris). New York: D. Appleton and Co., 1891. (ES)

Herbart Society. *The First Yearbook of the Herbart Society.* Ed. Charles A. McMurry. [Bloomington, Ill.: Pantagraph Printing and Stationery Co., 1895]. (PP)

————. *The Fourth Yearbook of the National Herbart Society.* Ed. Charles A. McMurry. Chicago: University of Chicago Press, 1898. (PP)

————. *Second Yearbook of the National Herbart Society.* Ed. Charles A. McMurry. Bloomington, Ill.: Pantagraph Printing and Stationery Co., 1896. (PP)

*Herbart und die Herbartianer.* Comp. Wilhelm Rein *et al.* Langensalza: H. Beyer und Söhne, 1897. (PP)

Hering, Ewald. *On Memory and the Specific Energies of the Nervous System.* Chicago: Open Court Publishing Co., 1895. (PS)

Hill, David Jayne. *Genetic Philosophy.* New York: Macmillan Co., 1893. (PR)

Hill, Frank A. "The Educational Value of Mathematics," *Educational Review*, IX (Apr. 1895), 349–58. (PP)

Hinsdale, Burke Aaron. *How to Study and Teach History, with Particular Reference to the History of the United States.* New York: D. Appleton and Co., 1894. (PP)

————. *Studies in Education: Science, Art, History.* Chicago: Werner School Book Co., 1896. (PP)

————. *Teaching the Language-Arts: Speech, Reading, Composition.* New York: D. Appleton and Co., 1896. (PP)

————. "The Laws of Mental Congruence and Energy Applied to Some Pedagogical Problems," *Educational Review*, x (Sept. 1895), 152–71. (PP)

Holman, Henry. *Education: An Introduction to Its Principles and Their Psychological Foundations.* New York: Dodd, Mead and Co., 1896. (PP)

Howison, G. H. "The Harvard 'New Education'," *Andover Review*, v (June 1886), 577–89. (PP)

Huxley, Thomas H. *Evolution and Ethics and Other Essays.* New York: D. Appleton and Co., 1896. ["Prolegomena," pp. 1–45.] (EE)

————. *Science and Education.* New York: D. Appleton and Co., 1896. (PP)

Jackman, Wilbur S. *Nature Study and Related Subjects.* Chicago: Werner School Book Co., 1895. (PP)

————. *Nature Study for the Common Schools.* New York: Henry Holt and Co., 1892. (PP)

————. *Nature Study Record.* Chicago: Werner School Book Co., 1896. (PP)

————. "Correlation of Science and History," *Educational Review*, IX (May 1895), 464–71. (PP)

————. "Mr. Lukens on the Correlation of Studies," *Educational Review*, XI (Jan. 1896), 72–74. (PP)

————. "Relation of Arithmetic to Elementary Science," *Educational Review*, v (Jan. 1893), 35–51. (PP)

————. "Representative Expression in Nature-Study," *Educational Review*, x (Oct. 1895), 248–61. (PP)

————. "The School Grade a Fiction," *Educational Review*, xv (May 1898), 456–73. (PP)

Jacobi, Mary. *Physiological Notes on Primary Education and the Study of Language.* New York: G. P. Putnam's Sons, 1889. (PP)

James, William. *The Principles of Psychology.* 2 vols. New York: Henry Holt and Co., 1890. (RA, P, PS)

Jenks, Jeremiah W. "A Critique of Educational Values," *Educational Review*, III (Jan. 1892), 1–21. (PP)

*Johnson's Universal Cyclopædia.* Vols. I–V. Ed. Charles Kendall Adams. New York: A. J. Johnson Co., 1894. (J)

Jones, Lewis H. "On the Correlation of Studies in Elementary Education," in *Report of the Committee of Fifteen on Elementary*

*Education*, pp. 40–113. New York: American Book Co., 1895. (PF)

Jowett, B., trans. *The Dialogues of Plato*. 4 vols. Boston: Jefferson Press, 1871. [Jowett's Introductions precede each work in all volumes.] (PR)

Kemp, Ellwood Wadsworth. *An Outline of Method in History*. Terre Haute, Ind.: Inland Publishing Co., 1896. (PP)

Kern, Hermann. *Grundriss der Pädagogik*. Rev. ed. Berlin: Weidmann, 1878. (IR)

King, Charles Francis. *Methods and Aids in Geography for the Use of Teachers and Normal Schools*. Rev. ed. Boston: Lee and Shepard, 1895. (PP)

Ladd, George Trumbull. *Elements of Physiological Psychology*. New York: C. Scribner's Sons, 1887. (PS)

———. "Education, New and Old," *Andover Review*, v (Jan. 1886), 1–18. (PP)

Lange, Karl. *Apperception: A Monograph on Psychology and Pedagogy*. Trans. The Herbart Club. Ed. Charles De Garmo. Boston: D. C. Heath and Co., 1894. (ES, PP)

Langl, Josef. *Modern Art Education: Its Practical and Æsthetic Character Educationally Considered*. Trans. S. R. Koehler. Boston: L. Prang and Co., 1875. (PP)

Latham, Henry. *On the Action of Examinations Considered as a Means of Selection*. Boston: W. Small, 1886. (PP)

Laurie, Simon Somerville. *Institutes of Education, Comprising an Introduction to Rational Psychology*. New York: Macmillan Co., 1892. (PP)

———. *Lectures on Language and Linguistic Method in the School*. Cambridge: University Press, 1890. (PP)

———. *Occasional Addresses on Educational Subjects*. Cambridge: University Press, 1888. (PP)

———. *The Training of Teachers, and Other Educational Papers*. London: Kegan Paul, Trench and Co., 1882. (PP)

Lavisse, Ernest. *Études et étudiants*. Paris: A. Colin et Cie., 1890. (PP)

Lombard, Warren P. "Some of the Influences Which Affect the Power of Voluntary Muscular Contractions," *Journal of Physiology*, XIII (1892), 1–58. (P)

Lorenz, Karl. *Der moderne Geschichtsunterricht*. Munich: M. Kellerer, 1897. (PP)

Love, Samuel Gurley. *Industrial Education: A Guide to Manual Training*. New York: E. L. Kellogg and Co., 1887. (PP)

Lukens, Herman T. "The Correlation of Studies," *Educational Review*, X (Nov. 1895), 364–83. (PP)

MacArthur, Arthur. *Education in Its Relation to Manual Industry.* New York: D. Appleton and Co., 1884. (PP)

Mackenzie, John Stuart. *A Manual of Ethics.* 2d ed. London: University Correspondence Press, 1894. (M)

McLellan, James Alexander. *Applied Psychology: An Introduction to the Principles and Practice of Education.* Toronto: Copp, Clark and Co., 1889. (PP)

———, and Dewey, John. *The Psychology of Number and Its Application to Methods of Teaching Arithmetic* (International Education Series, Vol. xxxiii, ed. William Torrey Harris). New York: D. Appleton and Co., 1895. (PA, R, ES, PP, PN)

M'Lennan, S. F. "Emotion, Desire and Interest: Descriptive," *Psychological Review,* ii (Sept. 1895), 462–74. (PS)

McMurry, Charles Alexander. *The Elements of General Method, Based on the Principles of Herbart.* Bloomington, Ill.: Public-School Publishing Co., 1892. (PP)

———. *Special Method for Literature and History in the Common Schools.* 2d ed. Bloomington, Ill.: Public-School Publishing Co., 1894. (PP)

———. *Special Method in Geography for Third and Fourth Grades.* 2d ed., rev. and enl. Bloomington, Ill.: Public-School Publishing Co., 1895. (PP)

———. *Special Method in Reading.* Bloomington, Ill.: Public-School Publishing Co., 1894. (PP)

———. "Correlation of Studies," *Public-School Journal,* xv (1895), 186–88. (PP)

———. "Geography as a School Subject," *Educational Review,* ix (May 1895), 448–63. (PP)

———, and McMurry, Frank M. *The Method of the Recitation.* Bloomington, Ill.: Public-School Publishing Co., 1897. (PP)

McMurry, Frank M. "Concentration," *Educational Review,* ix (Jan. 1895), 27–37. (PP)

———. "Concentration," in *The First Yearbook of the Herbart Society,* ed. Charles A. McMurry, pp. 27–69. [Bloomington, Ill.: Pantagraph Printing and Stationery Co.], 1895. (ES)

———. "Interest: Some Objections to It," *Educational Review,* xi (Feb. 1896), 146–56. (PP)

Malleson, W. *Notes on the Early Training of Children.* 3d ed. Boston: D. C. Heath and Co., 1887. (PP)

Maxwell, William H. "The Grammar School Curriculum," *Educational Review,* iii (May 1892), 472–85. (PP)

Mercier, Charles Arthur. *The Nervous System and the Mind: A Treatise on the Dynamics of the Human Organism.* New York: Macmillan Co., 1888. (PS)

Meyer, Johannes. *Die soziale Frage und die Schule.* Gotha: E. Behrend, 1888. (PP)

Mill, Hugh Robert. *Hints to Teachers and Students on the Choice of Geographical Books for Reference and Reading, with Classified Lists.* London: Longmans, Green and Co., 1897. (PP)

Monroe, Will Seymour. *Bibliography of Education.* New York: D. Appleton and Co., 1897. (PP)

Moore, Addison, and Angell, James Rowland. "Studies from the Psychological Laboratory of the University of Chicago," Part One, Reaction-Time: A Study in Attention and Habit, *Psychological Review*, III (May 1896), 245–58. (RA)

Muirhead, John Henry. *The Elements of Ethics: An Introduction to Moral Philosophy.* New York: C. Scribner's Sons, 1892. (M)

Müller, Friedrich Max. *Three Lectures on the Vedânta Philosophy.* London: Longmans, Green and Co., 1894. (PR)

Münsterberg, Hugo. "The New Psychology," in *The Old Psychology and the New: Addresses before the Massachusetts Schoolmasters' Club*, pp. 14–26. Boston: New England Publishing Co., 1895. (HS)

———. "Psychology and Education," *Educational Review*, XVI (Sept. 1898), 105–32. (PP)

National Educational Association. *Index to Volumes of Proceedings, National Teachers' Association from 1857 to 1870 and the National Educational Association from 1871 to 1897.* Ed. W. M. Griswold. Chicago: University of Chicago Press, 1897. (PP)

———. *Journal of Proceedings and Addresses, 1889.* Topeka: Kansas Publishing House, 1889. (PP)

———. *Journal of Proceedings and Addresses, 1895.* St. Paul: Pioneer Press Co., 1895. (PP)

———. *Journal of Proceedings and Addresses, 1897.* Chicago: University of Chicago Press, 1897. (PP)

———. *Journal of Proceedings and Addresses, 1898.* Chicago: University of Chicago Press, 1898. (PP)

———. *Proceedings of the International Congress of Education of the Columbian Exposition, Chicago, July 25–28, 1893.* New York: J. J. Little and Co., 1894. (PP)

———. *Report of the Committee of Fifteen on Elementary Education.* New York: American Book Co., 1895. (PF, ES, PP)

———. *Report of the Committee of Ten on Secondary School Studies.* New York: American Book Co., 1894. (PP)

Newman, John Henry (Cardinal). *The Idea of a University De-*

*fined and Illustrated*. 4th ed. London: Basil Montagu Picker-
    ing, 1875. (PP)

*New York Teachers' Monographs*, Vol. I, No. 2 (June 1898), 164 pp.
    (PP)

*New York Teachers' Monographs*, Vol. I, No. 3 (Nov. 1898), 132 pp.
    (PP)

Nichols, Herbert, and Parsons, William E. *Our Notions of Number
    and Space*. Boston: Ginn and Co., 1894. (PR)

North Central Association of Colleges and Secondary Schools. *Pro-
    ceedings*. Vols. I–III. Chicago: University of Chicago Press,
    1896–98. (PP)

Norton, Charles Eliot. "The Educational Value of the History of
    the Fine Arts," *Educational Review*, IX (Apr. 1895), 343–48.
    (PP)

Ormond, Alexander Thomas. *Basal Concepts in Philosophy: An
    Inquiry into Being, Non-Being, and Becoming*. New York:
    C. Scribner's Sons, 1894. (PR)

Palmer, George Herbert. *The New Education*. Boston: Little,
    Brown and Co., 1887. (PP)

Parker, Francis Wayland. *How to Study Geography*. New York:
    D. Appleton and Co., 1890. (PP)

———. *Talks on Pedagogics: An Outline of the Theory of Con-
    centration*. New York: E. L. Kellogg and Co., 1894. (ES, PP)

———. "Departmental Instruction," *Educational Review*, VI (Nov.
    1893), 342–50. (PP)

Parsons, William E., and Nichols, Herbert. *Our Notions of Number
    and Space*. Boston: Ginn and Co., 1894. (PR)

Patten, Simon N. "The Educational Value of College Studies,"
    *Educational Review*, I (Feb. 1891), 105–20. (PP)

Paulsen, Friedrich. "Examinations," trans. Alice Nisbet Parker,
    *Educational Review*, XVI (Sept. 1898), 166–76. (PP)

Payne, Joseph. *Lectures on the Science and Art of Education, with
    Other Lectures*. New York: E. L. Kellogg and Co., 1884.
    (PP)

Payne, William Harold. *Contributions to the Science of Education*.
    New York: Harper and Bros., 1886. (PP)

Peirce, Charles S. "The Logic of Mathematics in Relation to Edu-
    cation," *Educational Review*, XV (Mar. 1898), 209–16. (PP)

Phillips, Daniel Edward. "Number and Its Application Psycholog-
    ically Considered," in *The Early Works of John Dewey,
    1882–1898*, V, xxviii–lxxxv. Carbondale: Southern Illinois
    University Press, 1972. (R)

Pickard, Josiah Little. *School Supervision*. New York: D. Appleton
    and Co., 1890. (PP)

Piersol, G. A. "Histology," in *Johnson's Universal Cyclopædia*, IV, 295–315. Ed. Charles Kendall Adams. New York: A. J. Johnson Co., 1894. (J)

Plato. *The Republic*, in *The Dialogues of Plato*, trans. B. Jowett, II, 1–452. Boston: Jefferson Press, 1871. (PP)

*Poole's Index to Periodical Literature.* Rev. ed., 1802–1896. Eds. William Frederick Poole, William I. Fletcher, Franklin O. Poole. 4 vols. Boston: Houghton, Mifflin and Co., 1893–97. (PP)

Preyer, William. *Mental Development in the Child.* Trans. H. W. Brown (International Education Series, Vol. XXIV, ed. William Torrey Harris). New York: D. Appleton and Co., 1893. (SS)

———. *Naturforschung und Schule.* Stuttgart: W. Spemann, 1887. (PP)

Price, Thomas R. "Language and Literature: Their Connection in Practical Education," *Educational Review*, XI (Jan. 1896), 12–28. (PP)

Prince, John T. "The Grading and Promoting of Pupils," *Educational Review*, XV (Mar. 1898), 231–45. (PP)

———. "Report," in *Sixtieth Annual Report of the* [Massachusetts] *Board of Education, Together with the Sixtieth Annual Report of the Secretary of the Board, 1895–1896*, pp. 283–95. Boston: Wright and Potter Printing Co., 1897. (PP)

———. "Report," in *Sixty-First Annual Report of the* [Massachusetts] *Board of Education, 1896–1897*, pp. 275–314. Boston: Wright and Potter Printing Co., 1898. (PP)

Queyrat, Frédéric. *L'imagination et ses variétés chez l'enfant: étude de psychologie expérimentale appliquée à l'éducation intellectuelle.* Paris: F. Alcan, 1893. (PS)

Redway, Jacques W. "Some Applications of Physiography to History," *Educational Review*, VIII (Nov. 1894), 374–81. (PP)

———. "The Status of Geography Teaching," *Educational Review*, VII (Jan. 1894), 33–41. (PP)

———. "Textbooks of Geography," *Educational Review*, V (Feb. 1893), 153–62. (PP)

———. "What Is Physiography?" *Educational Review*, X (Nov. 1895), 352–63. (PP)

Rein, Wilhelm, ed. *Encyklopädisches Handbuch der Pädagogik.* 7 vols. Langensalza: H. Beyer und Söhne, 1895–99. (PP)

———. *Outlines of Pedagogics.* Trans. C. C. and Ida J. Van Liew. London: Swan Sonnenschein and Co., 1893. (PP)

———, Pickel, A., and Scheller, E. *Theorie und Praxis des Volks-*

*schulunterrichts nach Herbartischen Grundsatzen.* 8 vols. Dresden: Bleyl und Kämmerer, 1879–86. (PP)

Ribot, Théodule Armand. *The Diseases of the Will.* Trans. Merwin-Marie Snell. Chicago: Open Court Publishing Co., 1894. (PR)

Rice, Emily J. *Course of Study in History and Literature.* Chicago: F. Flanagan, 1898. (PP)

————. "History in the Common Schools," *Educational Review,* XII (Sept. 1896), 169–79. (PP)

Rosenkranz, Johann Karl Friedrich. *The Philosophy of Education.* Trans. Anna C. Brackett. 2d ed. rev. New York: D. Appleton and Co., 1886. (PP)

Royce, Josiah. "The Imitative Functions, and Their Place in Human Nature," *Century,* XLVIII (May 1894), 137–45. (PS, PP)

————. "Is There a Science of Education?" Part One, *Educational Review,* I (Jan. 1891), 15–25; Part Two, *ibid.,* I (Feb. 1891), 121–32. (PP)

————. "Preliminary Report on Imitation," *Psychological Review,* II (May 1895), 217–35. (PS)

Salmon, Lucy M. "History in the German Gymnasia," *Educational Review,* XV (Feb. 1898), 167–82. (PP)

————. "The Study of History in Elementary Schools," *Educational Review,* I (May 1891), 438–52. (PP)

————. "Unity in College Entrance History," *Educational Review,* XII (Sept. 1896), 151–68. (PP)

Schilling, Hugo K. "The Educational Value of the Modern Languages," *Educational Review,* IX (Apr. 1895), 385–90. (PP)

Schmid, Karl Adolf, ed. *Encyklopädie des gesamten Erziehungs- und Unterrichtswesens.* 2d ed. 10 vols. Leipzig: Fues, 1876–87. (PP)

Schurman, Jacob Gould. *Annual Report of the President of Cornell University,* 1892–3. Ithaca, N.Y.: Cornell University, 1893. (PW)

Search, P. W. "Individual Teaching: The Pueblo Plan," *Educational Review,* VII (Feb. 1894), 154–70. (PP)

Seth, James. "The Educational Value of Examinations," *Educational Review,* XII (Sept. 1896), 133–39. (PP)

————. "The Relation of Knowledge to Will and Conduct," in *The Fourth Yearbook of the National Herbart Society,* ed. Charles A. McMurry, pp. 7–25. Chicago: University of Chicago Press, 1898. (PP)

Shearer, William J. "The Lock-Step of the Public Schools," *Atlantic Monthly,* LXXIX (June 1897), 749–57. (PP)

Shinn, Millicent Washburn. *Notes on the Development of a Child*

(University of California Publications in Education, Vol. I in 2 pts.). Berkeley: University Press, 1893–94. (R, SS)

Small, Albion Woodbury. *Some Demands of Pedagogy upon Sociology*, published with *My Pedagogic Creed* by John Dewey. New York: E. L. Kellogg and Co., 1897. (PP)

Small, Maurice H. "The Suggestibility of Children," *Pedagogical Seminary*, IV (Dec. 1896), 176–220. (PP)

Smith, Goldwin. *Lectures on the Study of History*. London: J. H. and J. Parker, 1861. (PP)

Snedden, David S. "Children's Attitude toward Punishment for Weak Time Sense," in *Studies in Education*, ed. Earl Barnes, I, 344–51. Stanford: Stanford University Press, 1897. (PP)

Speer, William W. *Elementary Arithmetic*. Boston: Ginn and Co., 1897. (R)

———. *Primary Arithmetic; First Year, for the Use of Teachers*. Boston: Ginn and Co., 1896. (R)

Spencer, Frederic, ed. *Chapters on the Aims and Practices of Teaching*. Cambridge: University Press, 1897. (PP)

Spencer, Herbert. *Education: Intellectual, Moral and Physical*. New York: D. Appleton and Co., 1860. (PP)

Stanley, Hiram Miner. *Studies in the Evolutionary Psychology of Feeling*. New York: Macmillan Co., 1895. (SE, PS)

Stephen, Leslie. "Ethics and the Struggle for Existence," *Contemporary Review*, LXIV (Aug. 1893), 157–70. (EE)

Stetson, Charles B. *Technical Education*. Boston: Osgood and Co., 1876. (PP)

Sully, James. *Studies of Childhood*. New York: D. Appleton and Co., 1896. (SS)

———. "The Service of Psychology to Education," *Educational Review*, IV (Nov. 1892), 313–27. (PP)

Thomas, P. F. *La suggestion: son rôle dans l'éducation*. Paris: F. Alcan, 1895. (PP)

Thompson, Anna Boynton. "The Educational Value of History," *Educational Review*, IX (Apr. 1895), 359–67. (PP)

Thurber, Samuel. "Election of Studies in Secondary Schools," *Educational Review*, XV (May 1898), 417–35. (PP)

Tompkins, Arnold. *The Philosophy of School Management*. Boston: Ginn and Co., 1895. (ES)

———. *The Philosophy of Teaching*. Terre Haute, Ind.: Moore and Langen, 1893. (PP)

Tracy, Frederick. *The Psychology of Childhood*. Boston: D. C. Heath and Co., 1893. (PS)

Ufer, Christian. *Introduction to the Pedagogy of Herbart*. Trans.

J. C. Zinser. Ed. Charles De Garmo. Boston: D. C. Heath and Co., 1894. (PP)

Vanderwalker, Nina C. "The Culture-Epoch Theory from an Anthropological Standpoint," *Educational Review*, xv (Apr. 1898), 374–91. (PP)

Van Liew, C. C. "The Educational Theory of the Culture Epochs," in *The First Yearbook of the Herbart Society*, ed. Charles A. McMurry, pp. 70–121. [Bloomington, Ill.: Pantagraph Printing and Stationery Co.], 1895. (IC, ES)

Van Norden, Charles. *The Psychic Factor: An Outline of Psychology.* New York: D. Appleton and Co., 1894. (PR)

Viedt, Ernst. *Darf "vielseitiges Interesse" als Unterrichtsziel hingestellt werden?* Rogasen: Jonas Alexander, 1886. (IR)

Vincent, George Edgar. *The Social Mind and Education.* New York: Macmillan Co., 1897. (PP)

Waldstein, Sir Charles. *The Study of Art in Universities.* London: Osgood and Co., 1896. (PP)

Wallace, William, trans. *Hegel's Philosophy of Mind, Translated from the Encyclopædia of the Philosophical Sciences, with Five Introductory Essays.* New York: Macmillan Co., 1894. (IR, PR)

———. *The Logic of Hegel, Translated from the Encyclopædia of the Philosophical Sciences.* 2d ed., rev. Oxford: Clarendon Press, 1892. (PR)

Walsemann, A. *Das Interesse: Sein Wesen und seine Bedeutung für den Unterricht.* Hannover: C. Meyer, 1884. (IR)

Ward, Lester Frank. *Dynamic Sociology, or Applied Social Science as Based upon Statical Sociology and the Less Complex Sciences.* New York: D. Appleton and Co., 1883. (PP)

Warner, Francis. *A Course of Lectures on the Growth and Means of Training the Mental Faculty.* Cambridge: University Press, 1890. (PS)

Watson, John. *Comte, Mill, and Spencer: An Outline of Philosophy.* New York: Macmillan Co., 1895. (SC)

———. *Hedonistic Theories from Aristippus to Spencer.* New York: Macmillan Co., 1895. (SC)

Whewell, William. *Thoughts on the Study of Mathematics as a Part of a Liberal Education.* Cambridge: J. and J. J. Deighton, 1835. (PP)

White, Emerson Elbridge. *School Management: A Practical Treatise for Teachers and All Other Persons Interested in the Right Training of the Young.* New York: American Book Co., 1893. (PP)

Wickersham, James Pyle. *School Economy: A Treatise on the*

*Preparation, Organization, Employments, Government, and Authorities of Schools.* Philadelphia: J. B. Lippincott and Co., 1865. (PP)

Wilson, W. E. "The Doctrine of Interest," *Educational Review*, XI (Mar. 1896), 254–63. (PP)

Woodhull, John F. "The Educational Value of Natural Science," *Educational Review*, IX (Apr. 1895), 368–76. (PP)

Wundt, Wilhelm. *Lectures on Human and Animal Psychology.* Trans. J. E. Creighton and E. B. Titchener. New York: Macmillan Co., 1894. (PS)

Youmans, Edward Livingston. "Mental Discipline in Education," in *The Culture Demanded by Modern Life*, ed. E. L. Youmans, pp. 1–56. New York: D. Appleton and Co., 1867. (PP)

———, ed. *The Culture Demanded by Modern Life.* New York: D. Appleton and Co., 1867. (PP)

# Textual principles and procedures

These volumes of *The Early Works of John Dewey, 1882–1898* offer a definitive critical text of his published writings arranged in a generally chronological order.

A text may be called "definitive," or "established," (a) when an editor has exhaustively determined the authority, in whole and in part, of all preserved documents containing the work under examination; (b) when the text is then based on the most authoritative documents produced in the work's publishing history; and (c) when the complete textual data of all appropriate documents are recorded, together with a full account of all divergences from the edition chosen as copy-text (the basis for the edited text) so that the student may recover the meaningful (substantive) readings of any document used in the preparation of the edited text.

A text may be called "critical" when an editor does not content himself with faithfully reprinting any single document without modification but instead intervenes to correct the faults or aberrations of the copy-text on his own authority or to alter it by reference to the corrections and revisions of some authoritative edition later than the edition or manuscript chosen as copy-text.[1]

The first step in the establishment of a critical text is the determination of the exact forms of the texts in the early editions and of the facts about their relationship one to another. An important distinction must be made immediately between an "edition" and a "printing" or "impression." Technically, an edition comprises a particular typesetting, without regard for the number of printings made at different times from this typesetting or its plates.[2]

[1]    Various terms used here to describe textual principles and operations are discussed at length in Fredson Bowers, "Established Texts and Definitive Editions," *Philological Quarterly*, XLI (1962), 1–17; and in "Textual Criticism," *The Aims and Methods of Scholarship in Modern Languages and Literatures*, 2d ed., ed. James Thorpe (New York: The Modern Language Association of America, 1970), pp. 29–54.

[2]    In the present edition the use of the bibliographical terms "edition," "impression" (or "printing"), "issue," and "state" follows that recommended in Fredson Bowers, *Principles of Bibliographical Description* (Princeton: Princeton University Press, 1949; offset by Russell and Russell, New York, 1962), pp. 379–426.

Textual variation is most commonly found when for one reason or another a publisher decides to make a new typesetting, since changes are inevitable in the mechanical process of transmitting the words from the copy to the new form. Some of these changes may have authority if the writer himself took the opportunity presented by the new edition to correct or to revise his work; the remaining changes can have no authority since they emanate from publishers' readers or the compositors and may run the gamut from normal house-styling to positive though inadvertent error.

To establish texts for the present edition, all true editions up to Dewey's death in 1952 have been collated, their substantive variants recorded, and a decision made whether on the whole the new editions seem to contain authorial revision, or whether on the whole they represent no more variation than is normally to be anticipated in a series of unattended reprints. When new editions do give every evidence that they were revised by the author, an attempt is thereupon made to distinguish his corrections and revisions from the normal variation of publisher and printer that can have no authority.

Ordinarily, Dewey did not revise his work merely for stylistic felicity but instead to clarify, amplify, and sometimes even to alter his meaning. For this reason, the nature of the changes usually provides sufficient evidence to determine whether or not Dewey had himself revised a new edition.

On the other hand, alterations of various kinds can be made in the plates in preparation for running off more copies to form a new impression, or printing. Often these changes originate with the publisher, whose readers have seen misprints or other actual or fancied errors in the earlier printing and now take the opportunity to correct the plates. Although these corrections may prove to be so necessary or desirable that an editor will wish to accept them, they can have no basic authority, of course, when they were not ordered by Dewey himself. Moreover, it may happen that in the course of resetting a line to conform to the publisher's requested correction the printer may inadvertently make a different error that was not caught by the casual proofreading often adopted for plate-changes. In addition, similar errors may be found when for purely mechanical reasons, such as damage to plates in storage between printings, or an attempt to refurbish excessive wear attacking a plate, the printer without the knowledge of the publisher or author may reset a page in whole or in part to make a new plate or extensively to modify an old one.

Corrections, as distinguished from revisions, made by a publisher's reader are almost impossible to separate from the corrections of an author unless they seem to bring variants into conformity with house-style, in which case their non-authoritative origin is manifest. On the other hand, meaningful revisions such as Dewey ordered made in the plates of both the 1889 and 1891 reprintings of *Psychology* are always recognizable owing to their particular nature or extent.

Not only every new edition but even every printing during an author's lifetime carries within itself the possibility for authorial correction or revision that an editor must take into account. Hence the first step in the establishment of the present text has been the collection of all known editions and impressions of each work, followed by the determination of their order and relationship from the examination of internal as well as external evidence. That is, publishers' markings may indicate the order of separate impressions, as found in the American Book Company's reprints of *Psychology*; but sometimes no external evidence is available, or else (like a failure to change the date on a title page) it is untrustworthy, and then internal evidence based on the wear and deterioration of the plates, combined with their repair, must be utilized to separate one otherwise indistinguishable impression from another and to determine its order in the printing history of the plates.

Such evidence has been gathered by the scrupulous examination of available copies of every known edition on the Hinman Collator, which has enabled the editors to discover the alterations made from time to time in the plates during their printing history, all of which have been recorded so that the evidence may be made available of the total body of facts from which the editors worked. This full stemma, then, of the total number of editions and impressions of any Dewey work, and their order, establishes the necessary physical base for proceeding to the investigation of the complete body of evidence about textual variation and its order of development, a matter that has a crucial bearing upon the determination of the authority of the variants in any given edition or impression.

Modern critics have come to a general agreement about the following propositions for the determination of authority in the process of editing a definitive edition that attempts to establish an author's text, in every respect. For overall authority, nothing can take the place of the manuscript that was used by the printer, because it stands in the closest relation to the author's intentions. In only one respect can the printed edition manufactured from this manuscript exceed the manuscript in authority, and that is in the specific alterations made in proof by the author, which give us his final revised intentions. It is the editor's task to isolate these from other variants such as errors made by the compositor that were overlooked in the proofreading. The distinction between authorial revision in proof and compositorial sophistication of a text is not always easy to make, but informed critical and bibliographical investigation of the corpus of substantive variants between manuscript and printed text will ordinarily yield satisfactory results.

That is, when meaning is involved distinctions can be made. But when meaning is not involved, as in the hundreds and sometimes thousands of variations between manuscript and print in respect to spelling, punctuation, capitalization, and word-division, the inevitable assumption holds that the author has not engaged himself to vast sums of overcharges for proof-corrections, and that the ordinarily expected house-styling has taken place, sometimes initiated by a publisher's reader, but always concluded by the compositors.

A distinction develops, hence, between the words of a text —the "substantives"—and the forms that these words take in respect to their spelling, punctuation, capitalization, or division, what are known as the "accidentals" of a text.[3] Editorial criticism may attempt to assess the authority of the substantives, but one must take it that, as against a printer's-copy manuscript, no printed edition can have full authority in respect to the accidentals.

On the other hand, some authors—and Dewey was often among these—are extremely careless in the typing of the accidentals in their manuscripts since they are relatively indifferent to anomalies and expect the printer to set all right for publication. Thus in some respects it is not uncommon to find that the printed edition's accidentals may be superior to those of the manuscript in matters of consistency and even of correctness. Yet every author whether consciously or unconsciously, and often whether consistently or inconsistently, does use the forms of the accidentals of his text as a method for conveying meaning. For example, Dewey frequently capitalized words he expected to be taken as concepts, thus distinguishing them in meaning

---

[3]    The use of these terms, and the application to editorial principles of the divided authority between both parts of an author's text, was initiated by Sir Walter Greg in "The Rationale of Copy-Text," *Studies in Bibliography*, III (1950–51), 19–36. For an extension and added demonstration, see Fredson Bowers, "Current Theories of Copy-Text," *Modern Philology*, LXVIII (1950), 12–20.

from non-capitalized forms of the same words. That he was not consistent does not alter the fact that he used such a device, which an editor must respect.

It follows that the words of the printed first edition have in general a superior, although not a unique, authority over those of the manuscript form of the text in view of the ever-present possibility that substantive variants in the print can represent authorial revision in proof. On the other hand, the author's accidentals, insofar as they are viable in correctness or consistency, have a superior authority in manuscript from that in the printed form that has undergone the ministrations of copyreaders and compositors.

In these circumstances, a critical text—which is to say an eclectic text—will endeavor to join both authorities by printing each of the two major elements in the text from the form that is uniquely superior in its closeness to the author's own habits or intentions, although either element may be altered as necessary by editorial intervention to restore true authority, or purity.

This editorial principle can be extended logically to the situation when an author's manuscript has not been preserved, or is not available for use. In this circumstance the first edition, which is the only edition set directly from the author's manuscript, must necessarily take the place of the manuscript as the prime authority. If the author has not intervened to alter matters in any subsequent impression or edition, this first edition remains the single authority for both parts of the text and must therefore become the copy-text or basis for the definitive edition, although subject to editorial correction. Later impressions or editions may unauthoritatively alter, and even correct the text, but unless the author has himself ordered such alterations the changes have no authority and may only suggest necessary or advisable corrections to an editor. Indeed, the usual history of a text in these circumstances is one of chronological degeneration into ever more corrupt readings.

On the other hand, when in a later impression or edition the author makes his own revisions and corrections, these represent his altered intentions which must be respected by the editor. Special circumstances may call for special treatment, however, and thus two specific exceptions to the rule will be discussed later. At present it is necessary to remark only that the general principles of editing a single text in critical form call for the editorial acceptance of an author's altered wishes. The earlier readings should be recorded, because they must be made available to the reader concerned to study their historical position in the development of the author's thought; but in the text itself they obviously must be superseded by the author's final intentions in cases when the editor proposes to print only a single combined text. The substantive readings of a revised impression or edition, then, have a general authority superior to those in a preceding form.

Early editors were inclined to take as copy-text the last edition of a work published in the author's lifetime, on the supposition that if he had corrected or revised it this edition would contain the maximum authority. This procedure is no longer current, for in relieving the editor of the necessity to demonstrate that any authorial revision had indeed taken place it usually resulted (in cases when no authoritative intervention had occurred) in an editorial reprint of the most corrupt edition of all. And even when somewhere in the publishing history authoritative revision had appeared, the naïve editorial acceptance of *all* substantive variants in the last edition as necessarily authorial produced an unscholarly mixture of true revisions side by side with the inevitable corruptions of a reprint.

No uncritical acceptance of *all* substantive readings in any edition, whether or not revised, therefore, meets modern standards of scholarly textual criticism. It is the duty of an editor to assess all the variants that have accumulated in a text during its history and to choose on critical and bibliographical evidence those that appear to be authorial while rejecting those that appear to be printers' corruptions.[4]

As suggested above, however, in cases when the manuscript is not available the accidentals of a first edition must necessarily be more authoritative, as a whole, than those of any later reprint. House-styled as in part these first-edition accidentals may be, the fact that they were set directly from the author's manuscript will often have influenced the compositors to adopt the manuscript forms; and in any event, they must necessarily represent a closer approximation of the manuscript accidentals than can any reprint, which is only one printed edition further house-styled and set from another printed edition. What changes in the accidentals may take place in a revised edition at the order of an author are often impossible to isolate, but they must necessarily be fewer than the substantive altera-

---

[4]    As a case-history the first edition of Nathaniel Hawthorne's *House of the Seven Gables* may be cited. In this, scrupulous editorial investigation established that two-thirds of the substantive variants between the manuscript and first edition were unauthoritative in the print and were to be rejected. See the Centenary Edition of Hawthorne, Vol. II (Columbus: Ohio State University Press, 1965), pp. xlvii–lviii.

tions that were the chief reason for his intervention, especially with an author like Dewey.

On the modern textual principle of divided authority, therefore, the copy-text for this edition of Dewey remains stable as the earliest authority closest to the author, usually the first edition;[5] and hence the accidentals for Dewey's texts are established as those of the first editions printed from his manuscripts, when the manuscripts are not available. Whenever it is ascertained that no authorial revision or correction took place in any subsequent impression or edition, the first edition remains the final authority for the substantives as well. On the other hand, when substantive revisions are made in later impressions or editions, and when these are of a nature that permit their incorporation into a single critical text, those variants that the editors believe are authorial are adopted in preference to readings of the first edition, and thus an eclectic text is established that combines the highest authority in respect to the substantives drawn from the revised forms of the text with the highest authority of the accidentals drawn from the edition closest to the manuscript source. In short, in this form of critical text the copy-text remains the first edition, but into the texture of its accidentals are inserted the revised readings that have been selectively ascertained to represent Dewey's altered intentions.

When special circumstances exist, exceptions may be made to this now classic formulation of the principles of copy-text and the treatment of revised editions. First, like some other authors Dewey occasionally revised a work so extensively that it is necessary to print both the original and its rewritten revision

5    Most Dewey manuscripts were not preserved, and those extant are not available for re-editing. Those that have been studied or utilized suggest that the copy given to the printer might vary widely in legibility and in styling. According to his associates, Dewey usually composed on the typewriter with a margin-stop set at the left but seldom at the right, with the result that some words might be typed on the platen instead of on the paper. Customarily the machine was set for triple-spacing; revisions and additions were then typed in so that the final page might look as if it had been single-spaced. Handwritten comments might also be added, as well as handwritten revisions of the typed material.

Dewey was characteristically indifferent about his spelling; punctuation could be sporadic or altogether lacking. Colleagues have told of being asked by Dewey to work over a manuscript and put it into shape for the printer. One of Dewey's long-time editors in Henry Holt and Co. has stated ". . . I tried a number of times to 'improve' his style, but whenever I made a substantial change I found that I also had changed the sense and therefore had to reinstate the original. I did go over many passages with him and he improved them. He permitted us to use our house style, but I kept as close to the original as I could." Letter from Charles A. Madison, 25 June 1964, preserved in the Dewey Center, Southern Illinois University, Carbondale, Illinois.

for the benefit of readers concerned to read each version in its proper historical setting. Matter and idea may be so complexly and thoroughly altered in a revision (as in *Moral Principles in Education*, or *Ethics*, or *How We Think*) as to make impracticable the reader's reconstruction of the earlier form from the conventional list of variants. The two-text principle is sometimes the only answer to otherwise insoluble textual problems. Second, revision may be less thorough than that requiring the printing of both texts, as above, and in all such cases the practical possibility is present, therefore, of contriving the usual eclectic or critical text that would incorporate the revisions in the texture of the original. Yet in special circumstances it may so happen that the revision—usually at a considerably later time—may so blot out the essential ideas or point of view of the original and its corpus of ideas as to create what are, in effect, two independent documents. True, the apparatus list of the rejected earlier readings would still enable a reader to reconstruct the original and its differing content. Nevertheless, the presentation among the early works of such a text based on the revised substantives would occasionally clash sharply with and distort the historical perspective of the development of Dewey's thought gained by the chronological presentation of his works in the present edition. It would be a distinct anomaly, for example, suddenly to come in 1908 upon a developed body of ideas in full flower (as in the revised critical text) that Dewey, in fact, was not fully to formulate until 1932. Whenever this marked ideological difference exists in a revision, the editors have chosen to retain in the present volume the original early version, in its proper context. However, since this second category differs from the first in that a collational apparatus can enable a reader to sift the differences between the two versions, the editors have decided to incorporate in the apparatus for the early text a historical collation of the variant revised readings. A reader of such an early text, therefore, can if he wishes simultaneously investigate the nature of the later revisions.

In the process of editing, the principle has been adopted that each separate work is to be treated as an independent unit in respect to its accidentals. That is, each unit has its own problems of copy-text, with inevitable variation in the nature of the printer's copy and the house-styling given it, ranging from that found in all sorts of journals to that required by different book-publishers. Thus although an attempt has been made to secure uniformity of editorial result within each unit, certain features may vary between independent works within the pres-

ent edition. For example, if the spelling or some other important feature of the accidentals differs within a given work, the
editors attempt to reduce the variation to uniformity according
to Dewey's own style as ascertained from his manuscripts. This
principle has been extended to other spellings (with occasional
forays into capitalization practices) which though uniform
within the unit of the copy-text are demonstrably at odds with
Dewey's own habits as recovered from his manuscripts and
typescripts within the period. Thus when American house-
styling has obscured the known forms of Dewey's own spelling
habits, the editors have emended for authenticity but always
with a record so that the original can be recovered from the
apparatus provided. Except for presumptive error, however, the
copy-text punctuation is ordinarily left untouched, since in most
circumstances no such certainty about the recovery of an author's
exact punctuation can obtain as is possible for his characteristic
spellings.

Except for the small amount of silent alteration listed below, every editorial change in the chosen copy-text has been
recorded, with its immediate source, and the original copy-text
reading has been provided, whether in the substantives or the
accidentals. The complete account will be found in the lists of
emendations.

In most texts that have a reprinting history a certain number of variants will be positive errors or else unnecessary changes
that are unauthoritative and have not been adopted by the present editors. All substantives of this kind have been recorded
whether occurring in new impressions or in new editions.[6] However, when in a new edition the text is reset throughout, the
number of accidentals changes would be too large to list. In
addition, since the editors will have adopted as emendations of
the copy-text all such accidentals variants that seem to be either
authoritative or advisable changes, no useful purpose would be
served by listing the hundreds and hundreds of publishers' or
printers' unauthoritative normalizings of the text on which they
worked.

Since the number of rejected variants of the kind noted
above that qualify for recording[7] is comparatively limited, no
separate list has been made and this group of variants has been
incorporated with the appropriate emendations lists.

[6]    Changes made in the plates that correct errors that would otherwise have been silently made in the copy-text by editorial intervention
(see below) are recorded for the sake of completeness.
[7]    Such rejected readings from editions later than the copy-text are
to be distinguished from copy-text readings rejected in favor of subsequent revision or correction. These are recorded as emendations, of course.

In the emendations lists an asterisk prefixed to the page-line number indicates that the emendation, or the refusal to emend, recorded in this item is discussed in the Textual Notes that follow that list.

In special cases separate lists within the textual material may substitute for part of the Emendations in the Copy-Texts. For example, in the early articles as represented in Volume i the importance of capitalization to indicate concept meanings as distinct from non-concepts called for a certain amount of editorial emendation to correct the required sense from the inconsistent copy-text usage. The importance for meaning of these key words that have been emended is best called to the attention of the student in a separate list, whereas they might be overlooked if buried among a mass of material of other import in the general list of emendations. Similarly, some alterations or revisions in the system of headings in certain texts have seemed to warrant separate lists, as in the reworked headings system of *Psychology*. As explained above on p. cxxv, a new form of list may appear which provides the substantive variants of a later revision when the decision has been made to print the original text in this volume and textual conditions make it possible by such a list to inform the reader of the changes made later. In several volumes, a list of full and correct quotations has also been provided as a supplement to the Checklist of References, as described below.

The editors have made a number of silent alterations in the copy-text. These concern chiefly the mechanical presentation of the text and have nothing whatever to do with meaning, else they would have been recorded.

The most general class of these silent alterations has to do with Dewey's system of references whether within the text, in footnotes, or in lists of authorities that he might append. These references have been checked for accuracy, and the details of capitalization, punctuation, and of bibliographical reference have been normalized for the reader's convenience. When a reference is within the text, its form may be condensed following Dewey's own pattern when the expanded information required by the reader to check the reference will be found in an appended list of authorities. Except for the silent emendations mentioned and changes which appear in the emendations lists, Dewey's footnotes are kept in their original form and position, since their references are completed in the appended Checklist of References.

In most of Dewey's edited texts, quotations have been retained just as he wrote them even though not always strictly accurate, since that was the form on which he was founding his ideas. The section entitled Correction of Quotations gives the correct quotation and will be helpful to the reader in determining from the form of the quotation—whether accurate or sketchy—whether Dewey had the source open before him or was relying on his memory. However, when special circumstances in a specific text require the correction of quotations within the text itself, as in the *Study of Ethics*, special notice will be given the reader.

All references in footnotes or within the text (and also in the rejected readings of the copy-text) that relate to points taken up within the work in question (whether by backward or by forward reference) have had the appropriate pages of the present edition substituted for their original page numbers applying to the copy-text itself.

A second large class of silent alterations concerns itself with the articles that Dewey published in England, wherein the English printer had styled in his own manner the American spellings, punctuation system, and other forms of the accidentals or general presentation such as the formal or typographical features of the punctuation. For the convenience of American readers, and in some part as a means of automatically returning to certain undoubted features of the manuscripts that served as printer's copy, they have chosen instead silently to Americanize the elements in such copy-texts that were styled in the English manner when these run contrary to what can be established as Dewey's own usage. Thus words like "emphasise" have been altered silently to "emphasize," "colour" to "color"; and the position of punctuation in relation to quotation marks has been altered to American usage. However, the case differs for Dewey's works published in American organs that had adopted certain characteristics of English accidentals, for in such circumstances it is impossible to differentiate such anglicizations from other features of the house-styling that in the present edition are normalized to conform to Dewey's own habits, but with a record. Hence the reader of these texts may expect that the English publications will have been silently normalized—in these respects only—to American (and to Dewey's) usage, but that in all texts originating in the United States emendations for normalizing purposes will be recorded.

For the rest, the silent changes are mechanical and concern themselves with correcting typographical errors that could not be mistaken as true readings, making regular some anomalous typographical conventions or use of fonts, expanding most abbreviations, and so on. Typical examples are the removal of periods and dashes after headings, the expansion of "&c." to "etc.," changing syntactical punctuation after roman or italic words (or in italic passages) to follow a logical system, supplying accent marks in foreign words, and normalizing German "ue" to "ü" whether in lower case or capitals. Roman numbers in chapter headings are silently altered to Arabic, as are all references to them.

These remarks concern the general treatment of most texts in the present edition. When unusual features call for unusual treatment, special notice in the respective notes on the texts will be given of modifications or of additions. The intent of the editorial treatment both in large and in small matters, and in the recording of the textual information, has been to provide a clean reading text for the general user, with all the specialized material isolated for the convenience of the student who wishes to consult it.

The result has been to establish in the wording Dewey's final intentions in their most authoritative form divorced from verbal corruption whether in the copy-text or in subsequent printings or editions. To this crucial aim has been added the further attempt to present Dewey's final verbal intentions within a logically contrived system of accidentals that in their texture are as close as controlled editorial theory can establish to their most authoritative form according to the documentary evidence that has been preserved for each work.

*Fredson Bowers*

*20 February 1972*

# A note on the texts

After some nine months away from the University of Chicago, including six months in Europe, John Dewey returned in September of 1895 to the University of Chicago, where he spent the years 1895 to 1904 as Head Professor of Philosophy and Head Professor of Pedagogy.

Of the thirty-nine items in this volume, written and published by Dewey during 1895–1898, six were published separately and thirty-three originally appeared in nineteen different sources. For the thirty-one items which appeared only once and were not revised or republished, the single published version has served as copy-text; the first printing of the eight reprinted items was used for copy-text. Six of these eight have publishing histories and textual problems complex enough to warrant treatment in separate sections of this Note.

In addition to the materials Dewey published, he gave in 1895–1898 a number of addresses which do not survive, and which are reported in University of Chicago publications[2] by title only:

"Psychology and Religion," address to the Christian Union, 26 August 1894;

"Psychology as a University Study," address to the Graduate School of Arts, Literature, and Science, meeting with the Administrative Board of the Graduate School of Arts and Literature, and of the Ogden (Graduate) School of Science, 10 December 1894;

"Responsibilities in the Use of the Mind," address to the Graduate School of Arts, Literature, and Science, 11 December 1895;

1    Although *The Psychology of Number* by James A. McLellan and John Dewey was published in 1895, it is not included in the total of thirty-nine, nor does it appear among *The Early Works of John Dewey, 1882–1898*, because the extent and nature of Dewey's participation in writing the book have not been determined. *The Psychology of Number* is to be republished in a later series.
2    *University Record, University of Chicago Weekly, University Register.*

"Some Points in Froebel's Psychology," address at the Kindergarten Conference, 10 April 1897;

"Education and the Power of Control," address to the Pedagogical Club, 21 April 1897;

"Memorizing," address to the weekly Chapel-Assembly of the Junior Colleges, 3 May 1897;

"The Psychology of Literature Teaching," address to the Conference of English Teachers of the North Central States, 2 July 1897;

"Pedagogical Training for English," round-table discussion under Dewey's leadership, in a series sponsored by the Department of Pedagogy, 14–23 July 1897;

"The Uses of Imagination in Religion (The Presentation of Material for Reflection and Choice)," address in observance of Day of Prayer for Colleges, 27 January 1898.

The content of one similar oral presentation appeared in print at the time, and that report, "The University Elementary School," is included here as an Appendix.

Three printed syllabi for courses given by Dewey during this period are reprinted in this volume. The texts here are based on copies of each original.[3]

Five sets of class lecture notes from Dewey's courses for these years, verbatim transcripts by a stenographer, are extant in full or condensed form. The complete sets are "Psychological Ethics," Winter 1898 (continuation of a previous course; H. Heath Bawden Collection, St. Louis University), 120 pp.; "Political Ethics," Spring 1898 (H. Heath Bawden Collection, St. Louis University; also, Duke University Manuscript Collection), 175 pp. The apparently condensed notes are "Logic of Ethics," Autumn 1895–1896 (H. Heath Bawden Collection, St. Louis University), 48 pp.; Lectures for First Course in Pedagogy, "Philosophy of Education" (Center for Dewey Studies Collection; cf. Arthur Wirth, *John Dewey as Educator* [New York: John Wiley and Sons, 1966], p. 28), 12 lectures, 1896(?); and "Hegel's Philosophy of Spirit," 1897 (H. Heath Bawden Collection, St. Louis University), 103 pp. The authenticity of the documents and the manner in which they were prepared can be

---

[3]  *Educational Ethics: Syllabus of a Course of Six Lecture-Studies* (Chicago: University of Chicago Press, 1895), 12 pp., in the Library of the University of Chicago; *Educational Psychology: Syllabus of a Course of Twelve Lecture-Studies* (Chicago: University of Chicago Press, 1896), 24 pp., in the Library of the University of Minnesota; *Pedagogy I B 19: Philosophy of Education, 1898–1899—Winter Quarter* (Chicago, 1898), 11 pp., in the Columbiana Collection, Columbia University Library.

established by statements from persons who were students in the courses[4] as well as by public announcements for one of the courses in the *University* [of Chicago] *Record* in 1896 and the *School Journal* in 1897.[5]

## The Significance of the Problem of Knowledge

Even though thirteen years elapsed between the original printing of this pamphlet by the University of Chicago and its revision by Dewey for inclusion in *The Influence of Darwin on Philosophy and Other Essays in Contemporary Thought* (New York: Henry Holt and Co., 1910), it was apparently not re-printed during that period. Four copies of the pamphlet were examined on the Hinman Collating Machine and found to be identical. These copies were: Indiana University Library, B21.C47 Vol. 1, No. 3, 388095, which was used as printer's copy; Dewey Center, gift of Pearl L. Weber; State University of Iowa Library, B21 C4, 19746; Cincinnati University Library, 46645, Mar. 23 1908.

Dewey indicated in *The Influence of Darwin* that the essay was reprinted there "with slight change."[6] Many of these changes were indeed formal matters and styling of accidentals, but Dewey also made certain important substantive changes. Inasmuch as these few substantive alterations reflect a different vocabulary, from a different period in Dewey's thinking, they have been listed here separately rather than incorporated as emendations. The revised text can be easily reconstructed from the emendations list and will therefore not be reprinted in its entirety in a later volume of this edition.

---

4      See statements by W. W. Charters and Frederick Eby in *John Dewey, Lectures in the Philosophy of Education: 1899*, ed. Reginald Archambault (New York: Random House, 1966), pp. vii–viii.

5      "The course now being given by Head Professor Dewey in The University on the Philosophy of Education . . . is also offered as a major in the Correspondence Study Department. Students taking it in this way will be furnished type-mimeographed reproductions of steno-graphic reports of the lectures together with bibliographical references and questions for discussion." *University Record*, I (Nov. 1896), 422.

"The University of Chicago has arranged to give correspondence courses in psychology and pedagogy. . . . The correspondence work in pedagogy is undertaken in connection with the lectures now being given at the university by Head Professor John Dewey on 'The Philosophy of Education.' These lectures are reported verbatim, and typewritten in mimeograph form. Copies of the lectures are then sent out to each student registered for the course." *School Journal*, LIV (Feb. 1897), 187.

6      P. 271.

## Ethical Principles Underlying Education

In the *Third Yearbook of the National Herbart Society* (Chicago: The Society, 1897), pp. 7–33, Dewey's essay on "Ethical Principles" appeared for the first time. Using the same plates, the University of Chicago Press then reprinted the article six times between 1903 and 1916 as a separate 34-page pamphlet. In 1909, Dewey substantially revised the content of this essay to make the book *Moral Principles in Education* (Boston: Houghton-Mifflin Co., 1909). Even though there is considerable similarity between parts of the "Ethical Principles" and the *Moral Principles*, both works appear as separate entities in the Works of John Dewey. The revisions, which consisted of rearrangement of the parts, deletion of some material, and rewriting of sections, would have made it difficult for the student to reconstruct either work if the two versions had been merged. Moreover, the continued reprinting of the "Ethical Principles" even after publication of the *Moral Principles* would indicate that the first work exercised its own influence over a period of years and should appear intact.

Copies of the 1903, 1908, 1909, and 1916 reprintings were machine collated against the first printing in the Herbart Society *Yearbook*. This examination showed that a new title page was made for the separate pamphlet publication in 1903, but the original plates—including page numbers and running heads —were used for this text. Dates on the reset title page as well as on the copyright page were changed for subsequent printings, either by resetting the last three lines of type or, as in the 1916 printing, resetting the entire page.

The copies examined were: $I^1$ (1897) Southern Illinois University, 370.6 N2776Y; $I^2$ (1903) Yale University, Lfd 15 903d; $I^4$ (1908) Garrett Biblical Institute, 133044; $I^5$ (1909) New York State Library, 377.2 D51; $I^6$ (1916) State University of Iowa, LC191 D5. The University of Chicago Press listed also on the copyright page of $I^{4-6}$ a "Third Impression, October, 1906" ($I^3$). A copy of that printing was not located for collation.

## My Pedagogic Creed

Dewey's statement of his pedagogical beliefs, now widely known through a number of reprintings and translations, was one in a series of such credos by recognized educators in the *School Journal* in 1897. Despite numerous subsequent appearances during Dewey's lifetime, all reprintings are derived and without authority. The first publication in the *School Journal* has been used here as copy-text; four corrections (87.8, 87.33, 89.20, 92.15) and two substantive emendations (87.10, 88.10) have been adopted from the pamphlet publication by the same publisher the same year (with an essay by Albion W. Small) on the premise that the publisher (or possibly even Dewey himself) exercised more care in correcting proof for this pamphlet than for publication in the journal. The pamphlet, with Dewey's essay and Small's essay, introduced by Samuel Train Dutton, was apparently reprinted in Chicago by A. Flanagan several years later; a copy of this printing has not been located.

All other reprints made during Dewey's life were sight collated to establish the order and authority of the texts. These are: *Educational Creeds of the Nineteenth Century*, ed. Ossian Herbert Lang (New York: E. L. Kellogg and Co., 1898), pp. 5–20; *Journal of the N.E.A.*, XVIII (Dec. 1929), 291–95; *My Pedagogic Creed* (Washington, D.C.: Progressive Education Association, 1929), 17 pp.; *Journal of the N.E.A.*, XXIV (Jan. 1935), 13–16; *Education Today*, ed. Joseph Ratner (New York: G. P. Putnam's Sons, 1940), pp. 3–17; *Fourth Yearbook*, Future Teachers of America (Washington, D.C.: National Education Association, 1944), pp. 8–23.


## The Reflex Arc Concept in Psychology

Though recognized as an important landmark in the history of psychology,[1] Dewey's article on "The Reflex Arc" was

---

[1]    "Modern 'functional' psychology is often said to have begun in . . . 1896, with a paper by Dewey on *The Reflex Arc Concept in Psychology*." J. C. Flugel, *A Hundred Years of Psychology, 1833–1933* (New York: Basic Books, 1964), p. 194.
    "The first important paper in this young Chicago school was Dewey's in 1896. *The Reflex Arc Concept in Psychology*, he called it. . . . In his stress on total coordinations Dewey was anticipating the position of Gestalt psychology. In his insistence that the coordination is adaptive or purposeful, being directed toward success, he was also occupying a position in the history of dynamic psychology." Edwin G. Boring, *A History of Experimental Psychology*, 2d ed. (New York: Appleton-Century-Crofts, 1950), p. 554.
    "From the point of view of the modern psychologist, the greatest contribution of all emerges at this point, his very extraordinary paper on 'The Reflex Arc Concept in Psychology.' . . . It is . . . prophetic of Gestalt and organismic psychology, likewise prophetic of modern conceptions of the indissoluble unity of organism and environment, as taught by Kurt Lewin, prophetic of a social psychology which rejects the old dichotomies of person and social group, and above all I would say, as a student of perception, prophetic of the modern conception that the per-

reprinted without revision only one time after its initial publication in July 1896. The reprinting occurred that same year in the University of Chicago Contributions to Philosophy and is identical with the first printing except for the omission of one end-line hyphen not in a compound. The first printing, in the *Psychological Review*, has been used as copy-text for this volume.

Dewey himself explained in 1914 that he "never reprinted the Reflex Arc thing because of the terminology of the first part. It is too 'subjectivistic'—too 'psychical'—about sensations, etc.— too much the stream of consciousness idea—And I never saw my way to just rewriting the terminology."[2] Nevertheless, he did undertake, apparently, the task of changing some of the terminology in the article for the collection *Philosophy and Civilization*, which was published in September 1931. These changes, characterized by Dewey as "verbal" and made 35 years after publication of the article, appear in a separate list in the present volume; they have not been incorporated as emendations of the original because the revised version properly belongs in the historical perspective of 1931 rather than of 1896.[3]

## Interest in Relation to Training of the Will

Published separately in 1896 as the Second Supplement to the *First Yearbook of the National Herbart Society*, this pamphlet was printed by the Pantagraph Printing and Stationery Company in Bloomington, Illinois. Dewey revised the work considerably in 1899, when it was reprinted by the University of Chicago Press. The 1899 version was reprinted at least six

---

ceptual-cognitive life has its own complex unity, involving continuous modification, growth, together with learning." Gardner Murphy, "Some Reflections on Dewey's Psychology," *University of Colorado Studies in Philosophy*, No. 2 (Aug. 1961), pp. 27, 29.

[2]    Letter to Boyd H. Bode, 12 March 1914, in the Ohio State University Libraries.

[3]    Dewey was not satisfied with his efforts to rework the terminology of the article, even 46 years later. He wrote Arthur F. Bentley in 1943 that the republished article "is in the volume Philosophy and Civilization, with the caption The Unit of Behavior. I think I made a few verbal changes, but probably not enough to straighten out the vocabulary about 'sensations'." *John Dewey and Arthur F. Bentley: A Philosophical Correspondence, 1932–1951*, ed. Sidney Ratner and Jules Altman (New Brunswick, N.J.: Rutgers University Press, 1964), p. 132. In the original letter [Lilly Library, Indiana University], Dewey added that he thought that "sensations" needed work more than "any single one topic."

times thereafter, five for issue in this country and once for issue in Great Britain.

Dewey wrote the material for a round-table discussion by members of the Herbart Society at which he was to have presided. The pamphlet was distributed in advance of the meeting, and the revised second printing noted that Charles De Garmo had led the session because Dewey was not able to attend. For his revisions in 1899, Dewey used the discussants' responses to his first version of the pamphlet along with changes in his own thinking during the three intervening years. The 1896 discussion and Dewey's reactions to it are included in the 1899 revised version and in the present text.

The topical headings supplied by Charles De Garmo for Dewey's 1899 revision have been accepted for the present text because Dewey referred to them in his "Prefatory Note to the Second Edition" as helpful for the reader. A list of references following the article, supplied by Charles McMurry as editor of the 1899 revision, has been omitted. The accidentals of the 1896 printing, which has served as copy-text, have in general been preferred over those of the considerably restyled 1899 version, but the 1899 edition (II) has been noted as the source for the accidentals emendations made here that also appeared in II. The revised substantive readings from the 1899 edition which have been incorporated in the present text appear in the List of Emendations.

On the title page of all printings appears the title "Interest as Related to Will," but Dewey's intention for the title seems to be more clearly established at the head of the article itself where it is "Interest in Relation to Training of the Will." The longer title was also used in running heads in both the 1896 and 1899 versions and has been adopted here in preference to the form shortened for the title page.

Three copies of the 1896 printing (I) collated on the Hinman Machine were identical. Machine collation of fourteen copies of the revised version (II) revealed that there were three printings between 1899 and 1903. The copyright page was reset without change and repairs were made in the plates at 119.11, 121.20, and 143.23 for the second printing (II²); the cover was reset and all of page 112 except the first two lines was reset for II³.

In 1903, the pamphlet was reprinted with the last three lines of the title page reset, the cover and copyright page reset, and the Herbart Society information dropped from the verso of the last page (II⁴).

The 1903 date appeared on two more reprintings (II[5], II[6]). The only change between II[4] and II[5] was in the copyright page which was reset once more and in the advertising matter on the inside back cover, which was updated, indicating that the fifth printing appeared after 1906. For II[6] the cover was reset, as were the title page and page 112. Advertising matter inside the back cover shows this printing to have been after 1908.

Although the last printing of the work carried no date on the title page, it would seem reasonable to assume that it was after 1909, and probably even after 1910, inasmuch as the British issue had advertising matter with that date. Page 112 was reset to eliminate an error which had been introduced in II[6] (112.18, nnder); the cover, title page, and copyright page were reset. The British issue of this book is identical with the last American printing except for the British notice on the inside of the front cover and advertising on the inside back cover. Copies of the pamphlet collated were: I[1a] Dewey Center; I[1b] Cornell University Library, A.119014; I[1c] University of Texas, 370.4 H248P; II[1a] Dewey Center; II[1b] University of California, LB1065 D41899; II[2] University of Minnesota, B370.6 N212 v. 1; II[3a] Ohio State University, LB5 N26 v. 1–3, 1899; II[3b] Indiana University, L13.N2 1895–1900; II[4] McMaster University, 370.15 D519; II[5a] Cornell University, GS 480.20/1/08; II[5b] Illinois State Library, 370.6 N27.7h; II[5c] Yale University Library, L10 N28y, I.1–5; II[6a] State University of Iowa, BF321 D48, c.2; II[6b] Dewey Center; II[6c] Indiana University LB1065.D54; II[7a] Northwestern University, 370.6 N277 v. 1. Sup. 2; II[7b] (British) University of Vermont, 87.995 150 D515.

## Imagination and Expression

Dewey addressed the Western Drawing Teachers' Association meeting in Indianapolis on 30 April 1896 on the subject "Imagination and Expression." In the *Western Drawing Teachers' Association Third Annual Report* (n.p., 1896), his address was printed in part, followed by the note, "The publication committee regrets that on account of Dr. Dewey's absence from Chicago, the remainder of his manuscript could not be obtained in time for this report" (p. 138). In September of the same year, the address appeared in *Kindergarten Magazine*,[7] preceded by the following:

[This address was delivered at the annual meeting of the Western Drawing Teachers' Association in May, 1896 (*sic*). It was later prepared by Dr. Dewey for publication in the annual report of the Association, and partly printed in same. Owing to a protracted absence from Chicago, Dr. Dewey was unable to return the manuscript in time to be completed in the report, and by permission of the publication committee the paper is printed in full in this issue of the *Kindergarten Magazine*. —*Editor.*]

From the editors' notes cited, it would appear that both publications might have stemmed from manuscript. It is probable, however, that the *Western Drawing Teachers' Association Report* printing served as copy for the first part of the *Kindergarten Magazine* printing. Sight collation of the two showed only one change by *Kindergarten Magazine* in either substantives or accidentals from the *Report* version. That change (193.4) has not been adopted as an emendation here because it was apparently made editorially. The original publication of each part of the address has been used in this volume as copy-text and printer's copy: the *Western Drawing Teachers' Association Report* up to 194.30 and *Kindergarten Magazine* from 194.31 to the end.

After publication of the article in *Kindergarten Magazine*, Dewey seems to have reworked the material, abstracting it and dividing it into two parts, one with the title "Imagination and Expression" and another entitled "The Psychology of Drawing." One or both these essays are variously reported to have been included in "the Chicago public school study course,"[8] "the primary drawing books of the Chicago public schools,"[9] and the "Chicago Public Schools, Leaflets for Drawing."[10] No copies of this printing have been located, but a 1919 reprinting of the two shortened sections apparently derives from the

---

7    IX (Sept. 1896), 61–69.
8    Patty S. Hill, comp., *The Psychology of Drawing—Imagination and Expression—Culture and Industry in Education* (Teachers College Bulletin, Ser. 10, No. 10, 1 Mar. 1919 [New York: Teachers College, Columbia University, 1919]), 18 pp.
9    M. H. Thomas, *John Dewey: A Centennial Bibliography* (Chicago: University of Chicago Press, 1962), p. 57.
10   John Dewey, *The Method of the Recitation* [partial report of a course of lectures] (Oshkosh, Wis.: Privately Printed, 1899), p. 59.

Chicago public schools publication.[11] This conclusion is based both on the compiler's statement and on comparison of the 1919 reprints with the first complete printing of the address (*Kindergarten Magazine*); the comparison shows the revisions to be chiefly excisions. Most sentences in the revised versions were taken verbatim from the first publication, but much of the original material was omitted. The abstracted "Imagination and Expression" used material from pp. 192–197.21; "The Psychology of Drawing" is the title assigned to the abstract of pp. 197.22–201. Although on the evidence Dewey was responsible for the changes made, both shortened essays have been omitted in the present volume. The abstracted material was prepared for a specialized audience and includes no content beyond that of the original.

[11]  Cf. Patty Hill, comp., *The Psychology of Drawing*, p. 6n., "Report of an address given before the Western Drawing Teachers' Association in 1896, revised by Dr. Dewey for inclusion in the Chicago public school study course."

# Emendations in the copy-texts

A.    The following kinds of emendations have been made silently throughout the volume:

1. Typographical errors that do not make words have been corrected: "phyiology".

2. Book and journal titles have been put in italic type; articles and sections of books have been put in quotation marks.

3. The form of documentation has been made consistent and complete: "*op. cit.*" has been eliminated and "*ibid.*" is used only when a title is repeated within a single entry; volume and section numbers have been given in Roman, and chapter numbers in Arabic; abbreviations have been regularized; book titles have been supplied and expanded where necessary.

4. Superior numbers have been assigned consecutively throughout an item to Dewey's footnotes; the asterisk has been used only for editorial footnotes.

5. To conform to Dewey's usual pattern, the following have been regularized: "viz.", "*i.e.*", "*per se*", "*e.g.*", and "*cf.*"

6. Ampersands, as in publishers' names and in "&c." have been expanded.

7. Single quotation marks have been changed to double when not inside quoted materials; opening or closing quotation marks have been supplied where necessary.

8. In the three syllabi—*Educational Ethics*, *Educational Psychology*, and *Pedagogy I B 19: Philosophy of Education*—and in the outline section of *Plan of Organization of the University Primary School*, the additional kinds of changes listed below were made silently to eliminate misleading references and confused ordering of headings.

The outline format in each was regularized to follow the pattern for formal matters established in the copy-text: capitalization of words, use of numbers and letters with headings, and punctuation of headings.

In the references, volume numbers were supplied for periodicals, the listing of authors' names was regularized; titles (Dr., Sir, Prof.) were omitted; names were supplied where necessary;

and only the surname was used except in cases where an initial was used to distinguish between authors with the same surname.

Complete information on all references appears in the Check-list of References.

B.   In a number of words, Dewey varied his use of hyphens, so that the same words might be treated as hyphenated compounds, closed-up compounds, or two words. The spelling of these words, whether regular or variable, has been left in its original form. Some examples of such words are: undergraduate, under-graduate; compounds with "over-", such as over-stimulate, overstimulate; common sense, common-sense (n.); common sense, common-sense, commonsense (adj.); thoroughgoing, thorough-going; compounds with "pre-" as in pre-historic, prehistoric.

Spelling of "-ed" and "-ing" forms of such words as label, travel, and model has also been left variable as in the copy-texts.

C.   The following spellings have been editorially altered in this volume to the characteristic Dewey forms, given to the left of the bracket:

although] altho' 29.33

centre] center 7.35, 12.8, 12.13, 65.40, 77.25, 89.15, 89.22, 90.7, 101.16, 101.17, 103.3, 109.4, 147.31, 216.25, 225.6, 236.23, 246.1, 249.21, 249.22, 251.19, 285.4, 286.15, 305.7, 305.20, 438.19, 438.20, 438.38; (-ed) 19.24, 137.23; (-s) 9.29, 88.11, 149.18, 240.31, 282.39, 305.19, 306.28, 309.8, 380.21, 438.27, 439.19

civilization] civilisation 38.27, 39.32

clues] clews 173.27, 173.36

connection] connexion 38.24

criticize] criticise 62.40, 149.25, 288.29, 299.30, 437.5; (-d) 333.23, 333.37, 333.39, 398.33

defense] defence 366.7

enclosure] inclosure 345.23

entrusted] intrusted 377.24

fertilization] fertilisation 37.14

fetiches] fetishes 440.4

fibre] fiber 116.16, 144.26; (-s) 305.20, 308.9

fossilization] fossilisation 48.12

fulfill] fulfil 347.21, 365.27; (-ment) 158.12, 394.11

fullness] fulness 157.5

generalization] generalisation 39.32

insure] ensure 327.32

italicized] italicised 39.2

organizing] organising 47.23
realizing] realising 48.24
reflection] reflexion 34.22
repellent] repellant 126.14, 127.26
skillful] skilful 261.1
socialized] socialised 37.5
spatial] spacial 198.5, 322.4
though] tho 457.9
through] thru 453.4, 453.8, 453.30, 454.9, 454.30, 456.4, 456.36, 463.35; (-out) 462.37
utilize] utilise 52.2; (-d) 48.24; (-s) 38.1

D.  The following abbreviations were editorially expanded to characteristic Dewey forms, given to the left of the bracket:
Massachusetts] Mass. 358.1
President] Pres. 434.1
Professor] Prof. 247.9, 250.9, 348.7, 348.8, 349.35, 350.3, 353n.1, 354.26, 424.20, 425.17, 426.21, 427.16

E.  The following examples of word division and hyphenation have been editorially altered in this volume to the known Dewey forms, given to the left of the bracket:
child development] child-development 249.6
child life] child-life 195.22, 245.13, 249.39, 253.4, 261.5, 369.17
child-study] child study 207 (title), 209 (title), 209.1, 209.6, 209.20, 209.23, 210.7, 210.8, 210.13–14, 210.20, 210.25, 210.26, 248.8–9, 368.25, 445.15, 446.19
co-education] coeducation 272.34
co-existence] coexistence 316.28–29
culture-epoch] culture epoch 333.23, 336.19, 340.28; (-s) 335.14–15, 335.27
dust-cloths] dust cloths 240.5
fountainhead] fountain head 22.18
give-and-take] give and take 414.21, 418.8
interaction] inter-action 220.8
language study] language-study 254.8, 257.23
law-suit] lawsuit 114.17
mid-air] mid air 34.13
nature study] nature-study 199.29, 205.32, 267.17, 268.9–10, 268.24, 296.11, 296.18, 296.37–38
organic circuit] organic-circuit 305.31–32
race development] race-development 249.6
ready-made] ready made 16.22, 232.5
reflex action] reflex-action 306.38–39, 349.17–18

reflex arc] reflex-arc 305.31
reinforce] re-enforce 377.31
           re-inforcing 197.22
school life] school-life 254.11–12, 256.15, 264.16, 292.29
school work] school-work 233.5–6
self-determination] self determination 29.22
self-development] self development 331.17
self-expression] self expression 229.31
sense-activity] sense activity 305.34
              sense activities 310.10
sense-organ] sense organ 305.23, 305.26; (-s) 304.30
so-called] so called 49.35, 50.5, 331.36, 376.32
starch-cell] starch cell 243.7
subject-matter] subject matter 284.21, 284.23–24, 287.28, 297.28,
    329.16–17, 331.40, 333.14, 343.24, 443.16, 443.20
text-books] textbooks 198.40
thought-content] thought content 405.22
thread-winder] thread winder 242.13
today] to-day 35.22–23, 41.14, 47.23, 171.7, 220.31, 255.36, 257.17,
    257.23, 259.8, 269.1, 377.16
tomorrow] to-morrow 41.15
twofold] two-fold 389.33

# List of emendations

## *The Significance of the Problem of Knowledge*

[Copy-text is SP: University of Chicago Contributions to
Philosophy, Vol. I, No. 3. See Special Emendations List,
1, *The Early Works of John Dewey*, v.]

10.31    *Æsthetic*] W;   *Æsthetics* SP
18.16    of] W;   or SP

## The Metaphysical Method in Ethics

[Copy-text is M: *Psychological Review*, III (Mar. 1896),
181–88.]

25.6    content] W;   contents M
25n.2    1895] W;   1895–96 M

31.9      we] W;    We M
33.34     a] W;    *om.* M


## Evolution and Ethics

[Copy-text is EE: *Monist*, VIII (Apr. 1898), 321–41.]

35.25     Lecture] W;    lecture EE
36.33     20] W;    *om.* EE
*43.7     initiative] W;    initiation EE
44.19     (p. 41).] W;    (p. 41), EE
*51.30    Nature] W;    nature EE
52.25     Nature] W;    nature EE


## Ethical Principles Underlying Education

[Copy-text is EP: *Third Yearbook of the National Herbart Society*, 1897, pp. 7–33. See A Note on the Texts, *The Early Works of John Dewey*, v.]

70.32     stand] W;    stands EP
78.32     organizes] W;    organize EP


## My Pedagogic Creed

[Copy-text is MP: *School Journal*, LIV (Jan. 1897), 77–80. Six emendations are from E. L. Kellogg pamphlet publication (KP), 1897. See A Note on the Texts, *The Early Works of John Dewey*, v.]

87.9      playground] KP;  play-ground MP
87.11     forms that] KP;   or that MP
87.34     background] KP;  back-ground MP
88.11     that moral] KP;   that the moral MP
89.16     of] W;   on MP
89.20     so-called] KP;   ~∧~ MP
92.16     nine-tenths] KP;   ~∧~ MP
94.35     science] W;   service MP


## The Reflex Arc Concept in Psychology

[Copy-text is RA: *Psychological Review*, III (July 1896), 357–70. Emendations adopted from *Philosophy and Civilization* (New York: Minton, Balch and Co., 1931), pp.

233–48 (PC), also appear in Special Emendations List, 2, *The Early Works of John Dewey*, v, *q.v.*]

| | |
|---|---|
| 96.17 | criticizing] PC;    criticising RA |
| 98.23 | affair] PC;    affairs RA |
| 98.37 | seeing-of-a-light] PC;    ~–~–~–~ₐ~ RA |
| 100.28 | precedes] PC;    proceeds RA |
| 101.4 | mono-ideism] W;    mono-ideaism RA |
| 102n.4 | maintenance] PC;    maintainance RA |
| 102n.5 | maintenance] PC;    maintainance RA |
| 104.29 | peck] PC;    pick RA |
| 107.2–3 | is doubt] W;    is to doubt RA |
| 107.29 | stimulus] PC;    ~, RA |
| 108.18 | becomes] PC;    become RA |
| 108.35 | are minor] PC;    are to minor RA |

## Interest in Relation to Training of the Will

[Copy-text is the 1896 edition (I); substantive emendations have been adopted from the 1899 revised edition (II).]

| | |
|---|---|
| 113.7 | the very problem] II;    the problem I |
| 113.7 | in the guise of] II;    under cover of I |
| 113.24 | help] II;    to help I |
| 114.5 | interest] II;    Interest I |
| 114.6 | from] II;    on I |
| 114.7 | interest. At] II;    interest in its relation to the other factors and aspects of volition. At I |
| 114.10 | shall] II; may with more promise of success I |
| 114.14 | matter with more] II;    matter. We may restate and re-interpret the part played by interest in instruction with deeper insight and more I |
| 114.17 | *Interest* vs. *Effort—an Educational Law-suit*] W;    Interest *vs.* Effort—an Educational Law-suit. [*at side*] II;    *om.* I |
| 114.20 | contradiction in] II;    contradiction sometimes expressed, more often latent, in I |
| 114.21 | regarding this] II;    regarding precisely this I |
| 114.22 | doctrine] II;    school which insists I |
| 114.30 | *versus*] II;    *rom.* I |
| 114.35 | that,] II;    ~ₐ I |
| 115.1 | that,] II;    ~ₐ I |
| 115.2 | interest,] II;    ~ₐ I |
| 115.3 | fact,] II;    ~ₐ I |
| 115.12 | task,] II;    ~ₐ I |
| 115.25 | "Compensation,"] W;    *Compensation,* II; Compensation, I |
| 115.27 | that,] II;    ~ₐ I |

115.31    have, at some future time, a] II;    have a I

115.32    interests—that] II;    interests at some future time;—that I

116.8    must] II;    have to I

116.22    appeal even in childhood days] II;    appeal in childhood days even I

116.23    is,] II;    ~∧ I

117.17    *The Verdict*] W;    The Verdict. [*at side*] II;    *om.* I

117.22    behalf] II;    ~, I

118.3    growth,] II;    self-expression∧ I

118.3    is,] II;    ~∧ I

118.6    will,] II;    ~∧ I

118.8    *Divided Attention*] W;    Divided Attention. [*at side*] II;    *om.* I

118.16    product, he] W;    product, that he I–II

118.20    cannot] II;    can not I

119.12    realization of his own impulses] II;    self-expression I

119.12    cannot] II;    can not I

119.24–25    well-disciplined] II;    ~∧~ I

120.3    It would not be wholly palatable] II;    I do not think it would be well for us I

120.7    cease teaching in sheer disgust] II;    be discouraged from all future endeavor I

120.11    *Making Things Interesting*] W;    Making Things Interesting. [*at side*] II;    *om.* I

120.14    interesting,] II;    ~∧ I

120.16    object,] II;    ~∧ I

120.19    other] II;    rather I

120.32    interesting,] II;    ~∧ I

120.37    *Division of Energies*] W;    Division of Energies. [*at side*] II;    *om.* I

121.1    mechanical] *stet* I;    ~, II

121.2    time,] II;    ~∧ I

121.16    *Summary*] W;    Summary. [*at side*] II;    *om.* I

121.33–122.4    But when we . . . concerned throughout.] II; Self-expression in which the psychical energy assimilate material because of the recognized value of this material in aiding the self to reach its end, does not find it necessary to oppose interest to effort. Effort is the result of interest, and indicates the persistent outgo of activities in attaining an end felt as valuable; while interest is the consciousness of the value of this end, and of the means necessary to realize it. I

122.6    *The Psychology of Interest*] W;    The Psychology of Interest. [*at side*] II;    *om.* I

122.8    preceding] II;   preceeding I

122.30   *inter-esse*] II;   *rom.* I

122.32–33   the person . . . his action] II;   subject and object I

122.34   union.¹ ¹It is true . . . motive.] II; [*in text*] I
and 122n.1–123n.5

123.2–4   mentioned: [¶] *The Propulsive Phase of Interest* [¶] (1)
The active] W;   mentioned: The Propulsive Phase of Interest. [*at side*] [¶] 1. The active II; mentioned. (1) First,
the active I

124.12   *The Objective Side of Interest*] W;   The Objective Side
of Interest. [*at side*] II;   om. I

124.13   (2) Every interest] W;   2. The objective side of interest.
Every interest II; (2) Second, the objective side of interest. Every interest I

124.20–21   feeling. [¶] Error begins] II;   feeling. [¶]The question of psychological import is the relationship existing
between activity and idea or object. The object arises as the
definition or interpretation of the impulsive activity. The
objects exhibit the bringing to consciousness of the quality
of the impulsive activity. [¶] Error begins I

124.25–35   save as they stimulate . . . intrinsic interest.] II;   they
set before him, in objective shape, some capacity which
he already possesses and of whose mode of translation into
action he is thereby made conscious. The object, in other
words, transfers the impulsive activity into intellectual
terms. The impulse itself is blind. This only means that
it does not know what it wants, what it is after. But as it
finds outlet and expression, it reveals itself. The object of
interest is that which gives the spontaneous activity filling
or content. The object which supplies means and ends to
an impulse brings it to consciousness and thus transforms
it into an abiding interest. I

124.36   *Emotional Phase of Interest*] W;   Emotional Phase of Interest. [*at side*] II;   om. I

125.2    worth.] II;   ∼∧ I

*125.3–4   purely individual] *stet* I; purely important, individual II

125.4    worth,] II;   ∼∧ I

125.8–9   activity . . . tendencies. If we examine] II;   activity. If
we examine I

125.17–19   felt value. [¶] *Mediate* vs. *Immediate Interest—Work*
vs. *Drudgery* [¶] There are cases] W;   felt value. Mediate *vs.* Immediate Interest—Work *vs.* Drudgery. [*at side*]
[¶] There are cases II;   felt value. [¶] At this point, it
is necessary to distinguish two typical phases into which

the one activity of self-expression, at the basis of all interest, differentiates itself, as this differentiation gives us also
two types of interest. These two types of self-expression
arise according as the end and means of expression do, or
do not, coincide in time. In the former case we have immediate interest, in the latter mediate. It is all-important
to carry our analysis over into an examination of these
points, because it is in the matter of mediate interest that
the one-sided theories arise, which, on one side (isolating
the emotional phase), identify pleasure with interest; or,
on the other (isolating the intellectual or ideal phase),
deny interest and identify volition with effort. [¶] There
are cases I

125.27      take] *stet* I;    takes II

126.8–128.16    On the other hand . . . take a case of artistic construction.] II;    But when the object or end exists in idea
or symbol, then the end, the object to be reached and the
means, the energies at command for reaching it, fall apart.
A period of adjustment is required. We do things in which
we would not be interested if they were ultimates; in which
we are interested because they are conceived as necessary
to an end.

It is a mistake, however, to suppose that we regard
these intermediates *merely* as means;—as *lacking* in interest. In a case of sheer drudgery we feel that we have to go
through things merely in order to reach a final end. But
these intermediate steps are not recognized as in any sense
*really* means; and hence interest in the end is never transferred over into them. If we felt they were in reality means
to the end, we should feel them so organically bound up
with the end as to share in its value. The fact that they
are repulsive indicates that we do not consider them intrinsically connected with the desired end. They are necessary
evils, accidentally and externally attached to something
we want, so that we can't get one without the other. They
are not regarded as in the same process of self-expression
as is the end. If we take the example of a man doing a
day's work utterly repulsive to him simply for the sake of
getting his wage, it is obvious that the day's task is to him
only incidentally, accidentally, not intrinsically, a means
to the end. The wage is an end simply in the sense that it
comes last or afterwards; it is a physical, not a psychical,
end. So the day's work is a means simply in the sense that
it must precede getting pay, not in the sense that it organically aids in realizing the end.

The all-important point then in the consideration of
mediate interest or voluntary attention is the kind of relationship which exists between the putting forth of energy
considered as means, and the idea or object to be reached
considered as end. If the two fall apart, if the means are
not identified with the end, interest is not really mediated.
The intervening steps are regarded simply as necessary
evils to be gotten over with as soon as possible for the sake
of the final outcome.

Here self-contradiction emerges. If the interest is
wholly in the end and not at all in the means, there is nothing to insure attention being kept upon the means, and
hence no way to guarantee the reaching of the end. The
mind is not really on the work. The agent is not taken up
with what he is doing. He is not psychically, but only externally, engaged. Hence, so far as he is concerned, it is a
mere accident whether or not the end be reached. The
break in interest between means and end marks, in other
words, a break in the self.

On the other hand, if the means are recognized truly
as means, if they are felt to be simply the way in which
the end presents itself at the particular moment, then the
full interest in the end is at once transferred to the so-
called means. For the time being that becomes the end. As
we illustrated the other case by an instance of drudgery,
we may illustrate this by one of artistic construction. I

127.30    it] W;    is II

*127n.1    heard] W;    *om.* II

128.33    *Relation of Interest to Desire and Effort*] W;    Relation of
Interest to Desire and Effort. [*at side*] II;    *om.* I

128.36–37    mediated interest] II;    this mediated interest I

129.15    desire,] II;    ~∧ I

129.26–28    desire. [¶] *Impulse, Emotion* [¶] We often speak] W;
desire. Impulse, Emotion. [*at side*] [¶] We often speak II;
desire. [¶] According to the previous account, there is absolutely one and the same psychical process at the basis of
both desire and effort. The distinction is not in the facts
themselves, but simply in the attitude which the psychologist or observer takes toward the facts. Both desire and
effort are phases of self-expression arising whenever it becomes so complex that the end, the self to be expressed, and
the powers at hand, the means of expression, do not directly coincide with each other. The errors previously discussed on the educational side arise from abstracting either
desire or effort from the active process of self-expression.

Separated from activity, one may be set over against the other. For the sake of dealing with these educational errors at their root, it becomes necessary, accordingly, to discuss both desire and effort somewhat more in detail. [¶] We often speak I

129.38    power,] II;    ~∧ I

130.12    defense] II;    defence I

130.22    realization] II;    self-expression I

130.31    ends,] II;    ~∧ I

130.38    commonplace] II;    common-place I

131.9    *Function of Emotion*] W;    Function of Emotion. [*at side*] II;    *om.* I

131.25    weak] II;    week I

131.32–33   blind feeling. [¶] *Function of Desire* [¶] Desire cannot] W;   blind feeling. Function of Desire. [*at side*] [¶] Desire cannot II; blind feeling. [¶] Desire is a phase of this excitation or disturbance in the adjustment of active impulses or habits as means to an object considered as end or ideal. Desire cannot I

132.14    ideas] II;    ideals I

132.24    over-hastiness] II;    overhastiness I

132.25    over-hasty] II;    overhasty I

132.28–30   into being. [¶] *Relation of Pleasure to Desire* [¶] We thus get] W;   into being. Relation of Pleasure to Desire. [*at side*] [¶] We thus get II;   into being. [¶] The question, in other words, is whether the desire is made to contribute to the realization of the end, whether it has held strictly to its function as instrument, or whether the end gets subordinated to the desire. In the latter case we have self-indulgence. The end is thought of in order to get the impulses into play; but the moment this is secured the end is dropped or pushed out of sight, and the satisfaction got out of the excitation is substituted for it. The object, end, in other words, is prostituted to be an instrument of excitation only. Its claim to direct the powers which it has stimulated is ignored or willfully denied. Hence, the contradiction involved in the immoral use of emotion and desire. The end, the ideal, cannot be entirely absent from consciousness, as it is in the case of purely brute appetite. The end or aim has to be in consciousness to stir up or reinforce the active tendencies. It must be admitted, therefore, as end, but no sooner has it done the work of stimulation than it is denied to be an end and is reduced purely to the place of means. [¶] We thus get I

133.7     *Bearing of Desire on Interest*] W;    Bearing of **Desire** on
          Interest. [*at side*] II;    *om.* I
133.9     this:] II;    ∼. I
133.26    cannot] II;    can not I
133.35–37 instrumental powers. [¶] *Analysis of Ends* [¶] So far
          we] W;    instrumental powers. Analysis of Ends. [*at side*]
          [¶] So far we II;    instrumental powers. [¶] We are thus
          able to see the error in those theories which hold that
          pleasure is the end of desire. As is well known, these
          theories divide themselves into two types. On one hand,
          one school of moralists holds that since pleasure is the
          object of desire it is the ideal and standard of conduct. The
          other school, accepting the same theory of the relation of
          pleasure and desire, holds that, on this very account, desire
          must be eliminated from the moral will; that the presence
          of desire in the motivation of conduct indicates a purely
          selfish or pleasure-seeking factor. Once recognize, how-
          ever, that pleasure marks the satisfaction taken in the ideal
          of self-expression, and we see the falsity of both these
          theories. The real object of desire is not pleasure, but self-
          expression. The presence of desire marks simply the tension
          in the stage of self-expression reached. The pleasure felt is
          simply the reflex of the satisfaction which the self is an-
          ticipating in its own expression. [¶] The fundamental mis-
          take, in other words, lies in considering desire as a process
          prior to or outside of volition. It marks one stage in the
          development of volition—that stage in which the end, the
          purpose, the ideal, is sufficiently present to arouse and
          reinforce active impulses, and when there is still enough
          conflict within the self, as ideal on one side and as actual
          on the other, to make it a problem whether the end will
          succeed in directing the active powers as well as in ex-
          citing them. The development of desire into interest marks
          the happy solution of this problem. [¶] So far we I
134.15–16 possible realization] II;    objective self-expression I
134.22    terms,] II;    ∼∧ I
134.28    *Conflict of Ideals*] W;    Conflict of Ideals. [*at side*] II;
          *om.* I
134.34    motive,] II;    ∼∧ I
135.11    *Meaning of Normal Effort*] W;    Meaning of Normal
          Effort. [*at side*] II;    *om.* I
135.16    itself; it] *stet* I;    itself; its II
135.33    show overwhelming] II;    show such overwhelming I
136.1     *Effort as Strain*] W;    Effort as Strain. [*at side*] II;
          *om.* I

136.22    *Summary*] W;    Summary. [*at side*] II;    *om.* I
136.30    commonplace] II;    common-place I
136.34    reached] II;    reaced I
137.3      undirected,] II;    ~∧ I
137.9      riotous,] II;    ~∧ I
137.12    movement or outlet] II;    expression I
137.12–14    direction, and that consequently . . . desirable end.]
            II;    direction; that, therefore, the effort to realize an end
            where such interest is wanting means necessarily a division
            of the self. On one side, its natural tendency to self-expres-
            sion cannot be got rid of by being ignored. On the other,
            external circumstances force it to utilize some of its energies
            in ways which to it are valueless. I
137.21    *Kantian* vs. *Herbartian Theories of Desire and Will*] W;
            Kantian *vs.* Herbartian Theories of Desire and Will. [*at
            side*] II;    *om.* I
137.22    Current] II;    The current I
138.32    knowledge,] II;    ~∧ I
138.36    psychological,] II;    ~∧ I
138.37    represent,] II;    ~∧ I
138.40–139.1    animating and intended aim] II;    goal I
139.2      activity.] II;    ~, I
139.5–6    unified whole. [¶] Moreover, when we] II;    unified whole.
            [¶] When Kant comes to the account of how the moral
            ideal can become a motive, how it can become an actual
            working power, he of necessity contradicts himself. All
            interest must be ruled out from motive as selfish. But if
            the abstract and formal idea of reason does not interest, if
            it does not arouse the emotional side, how is it to get work-
            ing force? Kant is obliged to hold that there is one sort of
            feeling, one sort of interest, which is not selfish but dis-
            tinctly moral; that through the wakening of the feeling
            one's consciousness of moral law may get executive force.
            [¶] This, of course, is self-contradiction. Feeling having
            been ruled out as non-moral or immoral in order to set a
            pure end of reason, Kant has no right to fall back on feel-
            ing as a moral motive when he desires to get his law of
            reason into operation. The principle he sets up at one time
            he is bound to hold to at another, not shifting to meet the
            conveniences of his question. If interest in one form may
            be a moral motive, then interest *per se* cannot have an
            immoral quality. But if interest as such is selfish, then
            interest in any possible guise must be ruled out. [¶] More-
            over, when we I

139.12    an] II;    and I

139.18–19    is not] II;    is I

139.24–25    temptation. [¶] We find] II; temptation. [¶] Not only
does Kant contradict himself, then, in admitting interest
at all, but he contradicts the needs of education in admitting interest only in its most finished and complete
form, ignoring completely the earlier and more concrete
interests which are necessary to produce the highly generalized form of interest called reverence. [¶] I think we
also find a contradiction in Herbart's account of interest
and its relation to moral education. I do not see how the
psychology and pedagogy of interest among the Herbartians can possibly be made to square with each other.
[¶] If we take the pedagogy of interest we find I

139.25    things:] II;    ~. I

139.26    interest] II;    it I

140.7    view,] II;    ~ₐ I

140.14    cannot] II;    can not I

140.17    *Vorstellung*] II;    vorstellung I

140.26    demand,] II;    ~ₐ I

140.26    *Vorstellung*] II;    *vorstellung* I

140.30    activity.] II;    activity.† †At this point an ambiguity comes
here. This junction having been once effected and the "ap-
perception-mass" established, what is the meaning in the
idea of a *repetition* of the process of junction. And in what
sense can there be said to be any "new" element the second
time? I

140.30    activity.] II;    activity.† †At this point an ambiguity comes
out. Psychologically this can mean only repetition of the
previous activity; but in its pedagogical application, the
Herbartians always assume that it is not bare repetition,
but the *outgoing* of this old activity to assimilate still more
new material. But when the transition? Psychologically,
this new fusion must be independent of interest, depending
wholly on the mechanism of ideas. I

140.33    interaction] II;    inter-action I

140.35–36    apperceived. [¶] The weakness] II; apperceived. [¶] It
follows at once that psychologically all interest is dependent upon desire; is, indeed, one form of desire. Desire
is simply the consciousness of the striving of one of the
inhibited ideas against its counteracting ideas. When the
desire is directed towards no special idea, but towards
the repetition of the apperceptive powers, we have interest.
        Just why the repetition is desired is a point upon

which (so far as I have investigated) Herbartians are not clear. At times their statements imply it is because of the pleasures of "ease" and let up of strain involved in the fusion of old and new—the attaining of harmony. If this view is accepted, immediate (*i.e.* pure) interest, is an impossibility. The repetition of the pleasure is the real object of interest. Another alternative would be that there is a mechanism of apperceptive processes striving against each other. The doctrine of "apperception-masses" might fairly be taken to indicate this. But in this sense, interest can not be said to be a motive, or influence in effecting one apperception rather than another; it is simply a passive attendant upon the pull and haul of the respective apperceptive processes striving to get to the top, attaching itself to which ever comes out ahead.

Herbartianism seems then to be in this dilemma. If interest is a modifying force, it is as love of the repetition of a certain pleasure—*i.e.*, impure. If it is not a desire for pleasure, then it does not determine apperception, but waits upon it, apperception being mechanically determined by the respective force of ideas.

Summing up, we get the following: The development of a certain equilibrated, many-sided interest is the end of education. Wherever we have this interest we have a character good within and effective without. But now comes the question how to obtain this end. How shall this interest be developed? The answer at first sight seems clear and serviceable. Since feeling, since interest follows upon ideas and upon the apperceptive relations of ideas, instill through instruction the right sort of ideas, and in their right relationships, and the end is gained. Yes, but once more comes the question: *How?* When and how are we to get the leverage necessary to get some ideas rather than others in the child's consciousness, and, as active forces, in his sub-consciousness? Still more, how are we to get the right chains and complexes of ideas established—the right apperceptive organs? How, in a word, is the idea in the educator's mind, in the book, in the material of observation, or experiment, to get over into the pupil's mind? What is the instrument of transfer?

The sole answer is: Interest. Appeal to the child's interests so that he shall attend to and assimilate the ideas required to build up the proper type of character. Very good, as a practical, pedagogical reply. But none the less it contradicts the fundamental Herbartian psychological assumption that feeling, that desire, etc., is a product of the mechanical interworking of ideas. Ideas, in their reciprocal interactions, produce feelings, which are simply states (Zustände) of ideas. But when it is a question of producing the *right* interests, that depend upon the *right* combination of ideas, we cannot trust to this mechanism. We must have some means of loading down certain ideas, of giving them additional weight, in order that they may prevail in the struggle for psychical existence; and this instrument is interest. Interests, in a word, have to be assumed as primitive in order to give ideas their proper function in building up final interests.*

* In a word, it is a question of mediating interests, not of producing them.

I should have no interest in convicting Herbartians of inconsistentcy, did it not (like the Kantian self-contradiction) point to a truth of decided practical import. The weakness I

140.37 seems to me to lie just here—in] II;   is its I

140.40–141.1 impulses and the activity that results from them] II; the process of self-expression I

141.6 ends, out of] II;   ends, whether as to generality or definiteness, out of I

141.6 action] II;   self-expression I

141.8 the instinctive tendencies to action] II;   this native self-expression I

141.11 nation] II;   nature I

141.27 direct experience] II;   self-expression I

141.30 natural tendencies] II;   self-activity I

141.31–32 interest. [¶] We are not] II;   interest. [¶] But, to return to a comparison of Kant and Herbart, it is a case of heads or tails as to the merits of their respective doctrines of freedom. If Herbart puts the actual self in a complexus of ideas and apperceptive masses, Kant equally places the individual self, the Tom, Dick, or Harry, butcher, baker, or candle-stick maker, in a historical, empirical process and product. The individual self, in both theories, is an object, a phenomenon; and in both cases, I venture to assert, because of neglect of the intrinsic, universalizing value found in primitive impulse. If Kant asserts the necessity of a transcendental unity of apperception, back of actual combinations of ideas, so does Herbart assert a real, simple supersensuous substance as the source and bearer of all

ideas. Kant gives his transcendental self more to do in the
process of experience than Herbart ascribes to his metaphysical essence; but, by way of revenge, Herbart ascribes
definite and substantial existence to his soul, while Kant's
self is not a substance, but only a logical function of unity.

Herbart denies freedom of the will, on psychological
grounds, but Kant also denies what is ordinarily understood as freedom of the will, viz.: contingent liberty of
choice. Kant asserts freedom as an ethical attainment,
the conformity of conduct to the universal principles of
reason; but equally Herbart recognizes freedom in the senses
of agreement between apperception—complexes and the
substantial interests, scientific, aesthetic, social, and religious of life. Kant is so far from allowing any interference
of will with the environment that he expressly holds that
it is always possible to account for any and every occurrence, psychical as well as physical, upon the basis of
causal necessity. If Kant be credited still with a doctrine of
freedom in a transcendental sense, outside of time and
space and all order of phenomena, including psychical
events, it is only charity to give Herbart the benefit of his
belief in freedom as attained in a proper development and
distribution of interests. [¶] But we are not I

141.34    psychological,] II;    ~∧ I
142.9    *interest*] II;    *Interest* I
142.12–13    from the educational side the whole discussion.] II;    the
outcome of the whole discussion upon the educational
side. I
142.14–146.34    INTEREST IN RELATION . . . reasoned insight.] II;
[¶] The child is a self-expressing being. In this self-expression he, subjectively, finds satisfaction; and objectively
effects something—presents objects to himself in the form
of ideas and through the medium of sensations.

The teacher is not there either to submit to the special
mode of self-expression reached in a given case as a finality,
as the ultimate law of his own work, nor is he there to suppress, ignore, or arbitrarily deflect it. It is blindness to
suppose there is no alternate save either to surrender to this
special mode of interest, to humor the child, devoting one's
self to stimulating it and keeping it going till the child get
self-conscious of the pleasure involved, and proceeds to
make that his aim; or else to set up some foreign ideal,
whether of future work and needs, or of success, or of attainment of moral perfection, and demand of the child that
he put forth his efforts towards these ideals irrespective of

his sense of their value—his interest. The teacher is there to utilize any special mode of self-expression, to make it function, to make it an instrument in bringing the child to consciousness of new and further ends, and to re-direct his activity, through the accomplished end as means to the new end.

The teacher is there with his knowledge of the future and the remote, not to set up the future and the remote as ideals to be striven for, but through the wider and deeper knowledge to *interpret* the present, to see what it really, and not simply superficially means, and to furnish the conditions under which the child may come to the same intepretation of himself, and thereby pass on to new activities of larger import.

In a word, the teacher is there for indirect, not for direct, purposes—for the indirect service of vitally furnishing the conditions which shall mediate present interest into future interests, not for the direct service either of amusing or of stirring up by immediate appeal the child's will power, so called.

The educator is supposed to know, to be able to anticipate, that world of social activities and relations which is, in its main lines, the objective expression of the child's own impulses. If the educator has any business at all, it is first—himself to interpret the child's present interests in the light of this objective reason and will, and then to provide the child with such material and means of expression for his present interests that he may come to identify his own interests with the interests of this social whole, and its interests with his own interests—to find himself his own value.

I cannot close without calling attention to the great practical contradiction involved in existing education on the moral side. We preach *to* the teacher; we expect *of* the teacher, that all instruction and discipline shall make for character. We then surround that teacher with conditions which absolutely necessitate that a very conconsiderable part of instruction shall make simply for the accumulation of information. We deprive the teacher of the materials and the tools for *securing* to the child that active expression and construction which shall make for character. Then we cap the matter by holding the teacher, or else the original badness of the boy responsible when the desired training does not come about.

We insist, as a prime condition of morality, that the

right act shall be done for its own sake, from the motive of intrinsic affection. We then carefully set up conditions which necessitate that the teacher shall, for the most part, appeal to the child on the side of future rewards or successes, of present affection for the teacher, of dislike to bothering or trying her, of a so-called wholesome dread of her. Just because we refuse or neglect to furnish the positive materials and instruments of self-expression, and thus permitting and occasioning an activity in which the child shall be interested in and of itself, finding his motivation in his work, we make it an absolute necessity for the teacher to resort to all these factitious and external "moral" stimuli—motives which theoretically we condemn as inconsistent with true morality. Then once more we blame the teacher or the child.

Again, we profess the doctrine of self-activity as the essence of all education. Then we organize our schools on a basis and with methods which require self-activity only in the most transcendental, or Pickwickian, sense. Self-activity becomes the motto of the book on pedagogy and of the teachers' institute, and learning enough information to pass to the next grade becomes the practice of the schoolroom. Why? Is it due to the stupidity of the teachers, their frivolity, the fact that they are not suitably prepared for ther work, that they are teaching simply to make money, to fill in a gap before getting married? About one part of all this put together, in my judgment, to nine parts of the simple fact that we fail to organize our curriculum and to equip our schools on the basis of opportunity and demand for specific, concrete expressions of self-activity. A self-activity which is manifested mainly in absorption is a contradiction in terms. And, once more, we wonder why all the pains we take with our educational systems, all the money we put into buildings and books and teachers turn out morally so disproportionate a result, and tend to lead us to believe that our teachers are incompetent, or our boys and girls largely infected with original sin.

Is it not time that we devoted less attention to ethical ideas and to exhorting our teachers to give more thought and earnestness to the moral welfare of those under their charge? Is not the day ripe to ask ourselves and ask the community whether the ultimate responsibility is not to provide the school with the *materials and instruments* for utilizing the child's present interests in outgo, in construction, in expression, that he may attain to the deeper and more permanent interests? Is not any other course to demand bricks without straw? I

149.39–150.7    References [¶] "The best . . . without interest."] II; *om.* I

150.1    Viedt] W;   Vieth II

## The Psychological Aspect of the School Curriculum

[Copy-text is PA: *Educational Review*, XIII (Apr. 1897), 356–69.]

176.4    mind and kind] W;   kind and mind PA

## Some Remarks on the Psychology of Number

[Copy-text is R: *Pedagogical Seminary*, V (Jan. 1898), 426–34.]

178.5    that "the] W;   "That the R
178.23    when] W;   When R
179.18    "Eeny, meeny, miny, mo,"] W;   "Eeny, meney, mony, mi," R
184.16    163 to 165] W;   163, 165 R
186.33–34    is, the] W;   ~∧ ~ R
189.29    has] W;   have R

## Imagination and Expression

[Copy-text is IA: *Third Report of the Western Drawing Teachers' Association*, pp. 136–38, and *Kindergarten Magazine*, IX (Sept. 1896), 64.4–69. See A Note on the Texts, *The Early Works of John Dewey*, V.]

193.29    physical] W;   ~, IA
193.30    mental,] W;   ~∧ IA
*196.28–29    consciousness] W;   conscious IA
*197.30    simply] W;   simple IA
*199.22    makes] W;   make IA
199.39    reproductions,] W;   ~∧ IA
199.39    marks] W;   mark IA

## The Kindergarten and Child-Study

[Copy-text is K: N.E.A. *Addresses and Proceedings*, 1897, pp. 585–86.]

*207.30   to] W;   of K

## The Interpretation Side of Child-Study

[Copy-text is IS: *Transactions of the Illinois Society for Child-Study*, II (July 1897), 17–27.]

213.2     Oriental and Western] W;   oriental and western IS
219.35    attention.] W;   ~? IS

## *Plan of Organization of the University Primary School*

[Copy-text is PO: pamphlet printing, Chicago (?), 1895.]

225.29    powers] W;   power PO
229.21    that is] W;   that if PO
230.8     they (1)] W;   (1) they PO
239.35    "Wood-Work."] W;   "Wood-work." PO
240.1     *Geography, Geology and Mineralogy*, as in "Wood-Work."]
          W;   Geography, geology, mineralogy, as in "Wood-work."
          PO
240.26–27   "Wood-Work."] W;   wood-working. PO
240.29    "Wood-Work."] W;   wood-work. PO
241.5     "Wood-Work"] W;   "Building" PO
241.16    "Wood-Work."] W;   "Buildings." PO
242.2     towels] W;   towel PO
242.2     dust-cloths] W;   dust-cloth PO
242.18    trees] W;   tree PO

## A Pedagogical Experiment

[Copy-text is PE: *Kindergarten Magazine*, VIII (June 1896), 739–41.]

244.1     Department] W;   department PE
244.3     Street] W;   street PE
244.4     University] W;   university PE
244.6–7   University] W;   university PE
244.9     Department] W;   department PE
245.19    University] W;   university PE

246.12    made] W;   making PE
246.25    University] W;   university PE
246.34    University] W;   university PE

## Interpretation of the Culture-Epoch Theory

[Copy-text is IC: *Public-School Journal*, xv (Jan. 1896), 233–36. The Herbart Society reprinting is derived and without authority.]

250.10    pp. 195–96] W;   p. 195 IC

## The Primary-Education Fetich

[Copy-text is PF: *Forum*, xxv (May 1898), 315–28. The *Education Today* (New York: G. P. Putnam's Sons, 1940, pp. 18–35) reprinting is derived and without authority. Three emendations adopted for the present text also appeared in *Education Today* (ET), which is noted as the source.]

261.1     surround] W;   surrounds PF
263.9     Readers"] ET;   ~," PF
269.29    school] ET;   ~, PF
269.31    ultimately] ET;   ~, PF

## The Influence of the High School upon Educational Methods

[Copy-text is HS: *School Review*, iv (Jan. 1896), 1–12.]

272.38    ladies'] W;   ladies HS
275.27    Conclusion:] W;   ~_∧ HS
279n.2    Schoolmasters'] W;   Schoolmaster's HS

## Pedagogy as a University Discipline

[Copy-text is PU: *University* [of Chicago] *Record*, i (Sept. 1896), 353–55, 361–63.]

282.26    university] W;   University PU
284.15    pursued,] W;   ~; PU
284.27    in in an] W;   in an PU
*286.13   question] W;   questions PU
287.3     greater, force] W;   ~_∧ ~ PU

## Educational Ethics

[Copy-text is ES: Syllabus (Chicago: University of Chicago Press, 1895).]

292.25   give] W;   gives ES
295.12   13] W;   12 ES
298.13   *First Yearbook of the Herbart Society*, articles] W;   Herbart Year Book; Articles ES
299.35   from 2] W;   from to 2 ES

## Educational Psychology

[Copy-text is PS: Syllabus (Chicago: University of Chicago Press, 1896).]

311.1   adjustments. Significance] W;   adjustments significance PS
311.19   *Psychology of Childhood*] W;   Child Psychology PS
311.21   *Seminary*] W;   Seminar PS
311.24   *Psychological Review*] W;   Educational Review PS
311.32   boys' or girls'] W;   boy's or girl's PS
313.6   constitutes] W;   constituted PS
315.12   *Study*] W;   Syllabus PS
*320.36   Define] W;   Defines PS
*320.37   Are adaptation] W;   Is adaptation PS
323.11   Illustrations] W;   Illustration PS
324.35   with in] W;   within PS
325.36   *Emotions*] W;   Emotion PS
327.35   50] W;   51 PS

## Pedagogy I B 19: Philosophy of Education

[Copy-text is PP: Syllabus (Chicago: University of Chicago, 1898).]

328.13   *Psychologic*] W;   Psychological PP
328.15   1894] W;   1895 PP
329.3–4   *Fourth Yearbook of the National Herbart Society*] W;   Herbart Year Book, Fourth Year PP
329.18–19   faculties; and *vs.*] W;   Faculties; *vs.* PP
329.32–33   "Social Factors in Popular Education in the United States,"] W;   Social Factors U.S. Education, PP
329.34   *soziale*] W;   Sociale PP
329.35–36   "My Pedagogic Creed"] W;   Pedagogical Creed; PP
329.37   *The*] W;   Some PP
330.11–12   St. Louis Superintendent's Annual Report for 1871] W;   St. Louis Reports, '70–'71 PP

330.14   *as a Science*] W;   as Science PP
330.21   On *School Discipline*] W;   *School Discipline* PP
330.31   213] W;   212 PP
331.7    *as a Science*] W;   as Science PP
332.10   *of a University*] W;   of University PP
332.21   Promoting of Pupils,"] W;   Promotion PP
332.23   Pickard] W;   Packard PP
333.1–2  St. Louis Superintendent's Annual Report for 1873] W;
         St. Louis Reports for '72–'73 PP
333.4    515] W;   516 PP
333.11   VII] W;   V PP
334.5–6  *Education as a Science*] W;   Science of Education PP
334.7    *Institutes of Education*] W;   Institutes PP
334.33–34  *Education as a Science*] W;   Science of Ed. PP
334.34   on Sequence] W;   Sequence PP
334.38–39  *Report of* [Mass.] *Board of Education*] W;   Mass.
         Board of Education PP
335.9    *Practices*] W;   Practice PP
335.13   *Curriculum, Herbartian*] W;   ~∧ ~ PP
335.14   *Volksschulunterrichts*] W;   Volkschulunterrichts PP
335.18   VIII] W;   VII PP
335.19   96] W;   97 PP
335.20–21  *Herbart and the Herbartians*] W;   Herbart PP
335.32–33  St. Louis Superintendent's Annual Reports] W;   St.
         Louis School Reports PP
335.35–36  *First Yearbook of the Herbart Society* and *Second Year-
         book of the Herbart Society*] W;   Herbart Year Book,
         Years I and II PP
336.2    323] W;   322 PP
336.10   451] W;   450 PP
336.14–15  464; Hinsdale] W;   464 and XI, 72; Hinsdale PP
336.18   correlation] W;   Correlation PP
336.18   isolation] W;   Isolation of PP
336.20–21  *First Yearbook of the Herbart Society* and *Second Year-
         book of the Herbart Society*] W;   Herbart Year Book, I
         and II PP
336.26   *Education as a Science*] W;   Science of Education PP
336.27–28  "The Value of the Classics"] W;   classics PP
336.34   *Method for*] W;   Methods in PP
336.35   54] W;   45 PP
336.36   *Special Method in Reading*] W;   in Reading PP
336.36–37  *Lectures on Language and Linguistic Method in the
         School*] W;   Lectures on Language Teaching PP
337.1    *Teachers'*] W;   Teacher's PP
337.6    *as a Science*] W;   as Science PP

337.10  Peirce] W;  Pierce PP
337.18  *moderne*] W;  modern PP
337.20  *Lectures on Teaching*] W;  on Teaching PP
337.28–29  *Course of Study in History*] W;  Course in History PP
337.30  *Education as a Science*] W;  Science of Education PP
337.31  *Study*] W;  Studies PP
337.34–36  *Art and Industry: Education in the Industrial and Fine Arts in the United States*] W;  American Education in Fine and Industrial Art PP
337.40  417] W;  117 PP
338.6  *Lectures on Teaching*] W;  on Teaching PP
338.7  on Nature Study] W;  Nature Study PP
338.14  *Method*] W;  Methods PP
338.18  Vols. III and IV] W;  May, '92, Jan. '92 PP
338.20  Vol. V] W;  Jan. '93 PP
338.25–26  *Fourth Yearbook of the National Herbart Society*] W;  Herbart Year Book, Fourth Year PP
339.39  Vol. XVI] W;  March, '95 PP
341.18  Bibliographies] W;  Biographies PP
341.27  Schmid's] W;  Schmidt's PP


## The Philosophic Renascence in America

[Copy-text is PR: *Dial*, XVIII (Feb. 1895), 80–82.]

342n.18–19  C. Scribner's Sons] W;  D. Appleton & Co. PR
343.39–40  Open Court Press] W;  "Open Court" press PR
347.11–12  Introduction] W;  introduction PR


## Review of *Johnson's Cyclopædia*

[Copy-text is J: *Psychological Review*, II (Mar. 1895), 186–88.]

348.29  Feelings, or Emotions,] W;  Feelings (Emotion), J
349.1  Memory] W;  memory J
349.3  Memory] W;  memory J
349.21  Feelings] W;  Feeling J


## Review of Bryant and Watson

[Copy-text is SC: *Psychological Review*, III (Mar. 1896), 218–22.]

350.20  *Aristippus*] W;  *Antippus* SC
350.22  essays] W;  Essays SC
351.4–5  My Neighbor] W;  thy Neighbor SC

351.23   of] W;   or SC
353.25   led] W;   lead SC

### Review of Conant

[Copy-text is NC: *Psychological Review*, III (May 1896), 326–29.]

358.3   fingers] W;   finger NC

### Review of Stanley

[Copy-text is SE: *Philosophical Review*, v (May 1896), 292–99.]

358.24   recourse] W;   resource SE

### Review of Sully

[Copy-text is SS: *Science*, n.s. IV (Oct. 1896), 500–502.]

370.10   phenomena] W;   phenomenon SS

### Review of Harris

[Copy-text is H: *Educational Review*, XVI (June 1898), 1–14.]

372.15   Preface] W;   preface H
373.35   Method] W;   method H
373.36   System] W;   system H
373.36   Foundations] W;   foundations H
378.35   Church] W;   church H

### Reviews of Baldwin and Dewey's Rejoinder

[Copy-texts are SI: *Philosophical Review*, VII (July 1898), 398–409; RB: *Philosophical Review*, VII (Nov. 1898), 629–30; and SM: *New World*, VII (Sept. 1898), 504–22.]

392n.6      102] W;   101 SI
393.11      *Mental Development*] W;   his earlier book SI
393.15–16   *Mental Development*] W;   former book SI
395.15      34] W;   43 SI
397.4       he] W;   "~ SI
397.5       "the] W;   ∧~ SI
397.10      535] W;   534 SI
400.12–13   writing,] W;   ~∧ RB

402.22     475] W;   474 SM
403.34     moments] W;   momenta SM
415.30     in] W;   on SM
418.31–32     *Mental Development*] W;   his previous volume SM

## Letter to *Chicago Evening Post*

[Copy-text is L: *Chicago Evening Post*, 19 Dec. 1895.]

423.3     Normal School] W;   normal school L

## Need for a Laboratory School

[Copy-text is N: typewritten signed document, Manuscripts Collection, University of Chicago.]

433.4     Pedagogy] W;   pedagogy N
433.9     staffs] W;   staff N
433.15     Pedagogy] W;   pedagogy N
433.21     university] W;   University N
433.26–27     institution] W;   Institution N
434.4     Pedagogy] W;   pedagogy N

## The University School

[Copy-text is U: report of Dewey's address in *University* [of Chicago] *Record*, 1 (Nov. 1896), 417–19.]

436.4     Avenue] W;   avenue U
436.18     women's] W;   woman's U

## Plan for Organization of Work in a Fully Equipped Department of Pedagogy

[Copy-text is PW: typewritten document, Manuscripts Collection, University of Chicago.]

443.25     systems] W;   system PW

## Report of the Committee on a Detailed Plan for a Report on Elementary Education

[Copy-text is RC: N.E.A. *Addresses and Proceedings, 1898*, pp. 335–43.]

448n.1     N.E.A. *Proceedings, 1897*] W;   *Milwaukee Report*, 1897 RC

457.25    Specific Methods to Be Employed] W;    *om.* RC
463.39    individual,] W;    ~_∧ RC
464.22    the] W;    he RC


## TEXTUAL NOTES

43.7      initiative] In the parallel discussion at 79.3–4, Dewey lists
          "initiative, insistence, persistence, courage and industry"
          as characteristics of "force of character". The word "in-
          itiation" here identifying one of the "forms of self-
          assertion" seems to be a typographical error rather than a
          clear statement of his thought.

51.30     Nature] Both uses of "nature" emended in the copy-text
          (51.30, 52.25) seem to depart by oversight from Dewey's
          intention to capitalize the word when he used it as a per-
          sonification, as he indicated at 50.26 and 50.29.

125.3–4   purely individual] Apparently an author's or an editor's
          note "important" was picked up by the typesetter and in-
          corporated into the sentence at the time revisions were
          being made for the new edition of *Interest in Relation to
          Training of the Will.*

127n.1    heard] This word has been supplied to complete the sense
          of the sentence, correcting the omission which probably
          occurred in the printing process.

196.28–29  consciousness] By analogy with "unconscious" in the
          same sentence, the last syllable of this word seems to have
          been unintentionally omitted.

197.30    simply] Though the original reading "simple" is possible
          within the meaning of this sentence alone, the context of
          the discussion requires the emendation to "simply".

199.22    makes] The subjunctive verbs immediately preceding (re-
          flect, define) seem to have been erroneously carried on into
          the form "make" which has been changed to continue the
          sense of the main verb "makes".

207.30    to] The careless placing of the word "both" seems to have
          resulted in a misleading use of "of". The word "to" has
          been substituted to restore Dewey's characteristic separa-
          tion of "principles" and "facts".

286.13    question] "Another type of questions" might be considered
          an acceptable phrase, but the "is" following makes it ap-
          parent that the plural was not Dewey's intention for the
          sentence.

320.36  Define, Are adaptation] Following the parallel plural verb
320.37  used to introduce "means", the two verbs (defines, is)
have been changed to make the outline and the series
consistent.

# Special emendations list, 1
## *The Significance of the Problem of Knowledge*

In the list below, the readings to the right of the bracket are the substantive changes made in "The Significance of the Problem of Knowledge" when it was republished in *The Influence of Darwin on Philosophy and Other Essays in Contemporary Thought* (New York: Henry Holt and Co., 1910, pp. 90–98). Changes in accidentals, and changes in formal matters, such as the use of "e" for "æ" in "mediæval" and the styling of book titles, have been omitted.

| | |
|---|---|
| 4.7–8 | 200 years] SP;   two centuries |
| 4.11–12 | seems often] SP;   often seems |
| 5.8 | knowledge] SP;   science |
| 5.19 | evening[1]] SP;   evening |
| 5.28 | reality] SP;   substance |
| 5.29 | which] SP;   that |
| 5.33 | stating] SP;   statement |
| 5.33–34 | question, rather than the question itself.] SP;   question. |
| 5n.1–2 | [1]This . . . Michigan.] SP;   *om.* |
| 6.4 | formulæ] SP;   formula |
| 6.4 | and of practical] SP;   and practical |
| 6.5–6 | life, and which] SP;   life, conflicts which |
| 6.11 | for] SP;   of |
| 6.40 | there] SP;   therein |
| 7.16 | habit] SP;   custom |
| 7.21 | which] SP;   that |
| 7.26 | everyone] SP;   every one |
| 7.27 | Christian] SP;   Protestant |
| 7.34 | anyone] SP;   any one |
| 8.4 | for the time remote from] SP;   remote for the time being from |
| 8.6–7 | someone] SP;   some one |
| 8.34 | the truth] SP;   truth |
| 8.34 | in] SP;   by |
| 8.39 | would] SP;   could |

9.4        thousand devious] SP;   thousand and devious
9.5        philosopher] SP;   philosophers
9.8        they spread] SP;   they were spread
9.15       the social] SP;   social
9.16       disintegration going on.] SP;   disintegration.
9.29       which] SP;   that
9.30       gulf] SP;   span
9.34       dim, it was the ideas] SP;   dim, the ideas
9.35       which served] SP;   served
9.38       which] SP;   a view that
10.19      which] SP;   that
10.39      This] SP;   There
11.7       the truths] SP;   truths
11.21      digested, be transformed] SP;   digested, it be transformed
12.19      which] SP;   that
12.39      consciousness] SP;   civilization
13.4       make] SP;   makes
13.26      the] SP;   a
13.32      and of forms] SP;   and forms
13.32      which] SP;   that
13.35      Hence it is that the] SP;   Hence the
13.37      are] SP;   were
14.11      sound to say it, the] SP;   sound, the
14.14–15   often seeming] SP;   seeming often
14.20      direct] SP;   to direct
14.20      become] SP;   to become
14.29      belief] SP;   faith
15.1       knowledge] SP;   science
15.10      not] SP;   it is
15.32      reality which is got] SP;   reality got
16.21      very] SP;   supposed
16.27      formulæ] SP;   formula
16.29      is] SP;   gives
16.31      is] SP;   supplies
17.11      which] SP;   that
17.15      which] SP;   that
17.23      insert] SP;   find
17.35      which] SP;   that
17.38      which] SP;   that
18.22      is] SP;   lies in
18.24      association] SP;   associations
18.31      which] SP;   that
18.35–36   reason then that] SP;   cause, then, why
18.37      each one abstracts] SP;   each abstracts

18.39–40   positions] SP;   position
19.1       which] SP;   that
19.9       which] SP;   that
19.25      find its outlet] SP;   find outlet
19.26      remark] SP;   problem
20.1       which] SP;   that
20.1       fulfill] SP;   fulfil
20.3       is] SP;   lies
20.5       which] SP;   that
20.17      which] SP;   that
20.26      but] SP;   and
20.26      *only*] SP;   alone
20.28      spiritual] SP;   moral
21.3       of the] SP;   to the
21.3       value] SP;   values
21.21      the judgment] SP;   judgment
21.22      he] SP;   it
21.24      he] SP;   it
21.24      himself.] SP;   itself.
21.32      business which] SP;   business that
22.12      the truth] SP;   truth
22.39–40   epistemologist, knowing that the future is with him.
           It is with him, because the whole cause] SP;   episte-
           mologist. The cause
23.3       conscious] SP;   individual
23.14–18   Psychology . . . actualized.] SP;   *om.*
23.19      the inclusive] SP;   inclusive
23.21      it rather attempts] SP;   it attempts rather
23.22      which] SP;   that
23.27      But] SP;   Yet
23.31      an inquiry of] SP;   inquiring as to
23.32      which] SP;   that
23.32      everyone] SP;   every one
23.33      of] SP;   as to
23.33      shall render] SP;   render
24.3       fulfillment] SP;   fulfilment
24.4       which] SP;   that
24.11–12   the final] SP;   a better

# Special emendations list, 2
## The Reflex Arc Concept in Psychology

In the list below, the readings to the right of the bracket are the substantive changes made in "The Reflex Arc" when it was republished in *Philosophy and Civilization* (New York: Minton, Balch and Co., 1931, pp. 233–48) with the title "The Unit of Behavior." Changes in accidentals, and changes in formal matters, such as the substitution of double for single quotation marks or the use of a hyphen for a diæresis (co-operation), have been omitted except for the use of italics, the use of hyphens to create compounds, and the use of quotation marks where none originally appeared.

96.5      cumulation] RA;   accumulation
96.6      that also] RA;   which
96.11     than any] RA;   than has any
96.20     urge] RA;   show
97.11     psychical unity] RA;   unit
97.11–12  react into and] RA;   be consistently employed to
97.12     constitutive] RA;   constructive
97.14     be viewed, not] RA;   not be viewed
97.18     What is the reality so designated? What shall we term]
          RA;   But what can we properly *term*
97.20     but which is primary; which] RA;   but which
97.21     psychical] RA;   mental
97.23     reality] RA;   more inclusive process
97.30     There is, of course, no] RA;   No
97.30     that] RA;   this
97.31     process] RA;   seeming course of events
97.33     begin] RA;   *begin,*
97.39     act] RA;   *act*
98.11     sight] RA;   light
98.23     affairs] RA;   affair
98.34     *to*] RA;   to
98.34     is *into*] RA;   is, so to speak, *into*
98.37     seeing-of-a light] RA;   ~-~-~-~

99.7    that we] RA;   we
99.15   defective in] RA;   defective, first, in
99.16   psychical] RA;   mental
99.18   reconstituting] RA;   reconstructing
99.26   or in the] RA;   or the
99.28   arc] RA;   "∼"
99.28   virtually] RA;   actually
99.28   circuit] RA;   *circuit*
100.1   it still] RA;   still
100.16  sound] RA;   noise
100.23  or the] RA;   or to the
100.27  psychical] RA;   mental
100.28  proceeds] RA;   precedes
100.36  within the] RA;   within a
100.37  sound] RA;   hearing
101.4   mono-ideaism] RA;   *mono-idealism*
101.7–8  admission to consciousness. Or, to speak more truly in the metaphor, the] RA;   admission, so that the
101.23  The muscular] RA;   Muscular
101.24  is involved in this as well as sensory stimulus] RA;   as well as sensory stimulus is involved
101.25  definite set of the motor] RA;   definite motor
101.36  value] RA;   quality
101.41  constitutes that, which finally becomes] RA;   develops the original nervous shock into
102.7   this] RA;   *this*
102.9   The motor] RA;   No one thinks that the motor
102.10  is, once more, into, not merely to,] RA;   is a separate, disconnected event, but neither is it to be regarded as merely reaction to
102.11–12  to get rid of it. The resulting quale] RA;   or more exactly, to develop the suggested experiences which make the sound really significant. The movement
102.13  is] RA;   *is*
102.26  reached] RA;   attained
102n.5  as far] RA;   so far
102n.7  the 'repetition'] RA;   "repetition"
102n.8  the] RA;   a
103.13  as the] RA;   as are the
103.28–29  visual-heat-pain-muscular-quale] RA;   ∼-∼-∼-∼∧∼
103.29–30  visual-touch-muscular-quale] RA;   ∼-∼-∼∧∼
103.36  is not] RA;   is now not
104.4–13  We ought . . . assumption.] RA;   *om.*
104.15  a reconsideration] RA;   reconsideration

104.15    idea, of] RA;    idea, and
104.24    case] RA;    stage
104.29    pick] RA;    peck
104.39    such an orderly] RA;    an orderly
105.6     Regarding such cases] RA;    Cases
105.6     viewed as] RA;    which
105.9     each] RA;    either
105.9     and] RA;    or
105.15    the above case] RA;    this stage
105.20    act] RA;    *act*
105.24    such cases] RA;    cases
105n.6    series] RA;    succession
105n.8    of a] RA;    to a
105n.8    to] RA;    of
106.14    given] RA;    desired
106.32–33  a bright] RA;    bright
106.39    sensation or conscious] RA;    conscious sensation of a
107.2–3   It is to doubt] RA;    Uncertainty
107.3     no, which gives] RA;    not, gives
107.17    possible] RA;    *possible*
107.17    as conscious] RA;    or conscious
107.21    and will] RA;    and it will
107.29    stimulus,] RA;    $\sim_\wedge$
107.33    used] RA;    directed
108.1–2   time, fixing attention, holding] RA;    time, holding
108.5–6   the response] RA;    response
108.7     quales] RA;    qualities
108.9     quales] RA;    qualities
108.18    become] RA;    becomes
108.25    regarded as simply] RA;    regarded simply as
108.33    existences] RA;    physical existences
108.35    are to minor] RA;    are minor
108.36    positions to the] RA;    positions the
109.7     circle] RA;    circuit
109.9     reconstitution] RA;    reconstruction
109.22    then only] RA;    only then
109.23    To attain either] RA;    Attainment of either
109.33–34  psychical evolution] RA;    mental development
109.35    and the] RA;    and to the

# Special emendations list, 3
## The Results of Child-Study Applied to Education

In the list below, the readings to the right of the bracket are the substantive changes made in "The Results of Child-Study Applied to Education" when it was reprinted in Dewey's "The Theory of the Chicago Experiment," Appendix II of *The Dewey School* by Katherine Camp Mayhew and Anna Camp Edwards (New York: D. Appleton-Century Co., 1936), pp. 474–76. Changes in accidentals and in formal matters have been omitted.

204.6    which] CS;    that
204.10   consideration] CS;    a consideration
204.11–12   which the application of results of Child-Study] CS; which child study
204.13   teacher] CS;   the teacher
204.14   child] CS;   the child
204.15   Applications] CS;   Application
205.2    are always] CS;   always are
205.11–12   coloring,—moral (personified characters, dramatized deeds and situations) and æsthetic] CS;   coloring—personal, characteristic, dramatic deeds and situations, moral, and esthetic
205.29   for purposes of] CS;   in
205.29   and hence] CS;   hence
205.30–31   either with] CS;   with
205.31   with the] CS;   the
205.38   Kindergarten] CS;   kindergarten
206.2    and function, what they will do.] CS;   and function.
206.4–6   *the school is to the child and teacher the social institution in which they, for the time, live,*] CS;   the school is to the child and to the teacher the social institution in which they live,
206.6    mere means for] CS;   means to

# Correction of quotations

Dewey represented source material in varying ways, from memorial paraphrase to verbatim copy, sometimes citing his source fully, in others mentioning only authors' names, and in still others, omitting documentation altogether. Because his form of citation varied also, quotation marks in the original did not necessarily signal a direct or precise quotation.

All material enclosed in quotation marks, except when the device is obviously used for emphasis or restatement, has been searched out, and the documentation has been verified and emended when necessary. Emendations in documentation are described in Textual Principles and Procedures, but the editors have considered Dewey's variations from the original quotations of sufficient importance to list them.

Except for corrections required by special circumstances and noted in the lists of emendations, all quotations have been retained as they were first published. The variable form of quotation suggests that Dewey, like many scholars of the period, was unconcerned about precision in matters of form, but many of the changes in cited materials may have arisen in the printing process. For example, comparing Dewey's quotations with the originals reveals that some journals house-styled the quoted materials as well as Dewey's own. Such variations are not listed here. Three changes in accidentals (178.5, 178.23, and 397.4–5) which apparently occurred in the printing process have been restored and are included in the List of Emendations.

The most frequent alteration Dewey made in quoted material was to change or omit punctuation. He also often failed to use ellipses or to separate quotations to show that material had been left out. No citation of the Dewey material or of the original appears if the changes were only of this kind—omitted or changed punctuation, including ellipses. In the case of omitted ellipses, attention is called to short phrases; if, however, a line or more has been left out, no attention has been called to the omission.

Italics have been considered accidentals. When Dewey omitted those used in his source, the omission is not noted, though Dewey's added italics are listed. If changed or omitted accidentals have substantive implications, as in the capitalization of some concept words, the quotation is noted. Quotations from Dewey as well as from his source appear in a form designed to assist the reader in determining whether Dewey had the book open before him or was relying on his memory.

Page references to D. E. Phillips, "Number and Its Application," and to J. M. Baldwin, "Social Interpretations: A Reply," have been keyed to the present volume.

Notations in this section follow the formula: page-line numbers from the present text, followed by the text condensed to first and last words or such as make for sufficient clarity, then a square bracket, followed by the symbol identifying the Dewey item. After a semicolon comes the necessary correction, whether of one word or a longer passage, as required. Finally, in parentheses, the author's surname and shortened source-title from the Checklist of References are followed by a comma and the page-line reference to the source.

10.25  are] SP; was (Bosanquet, *History of Æsthetic*, 146.26)

10.26  theory. The] SP; theory. What we justly stigmatise as the (Bosanquet, *History of Æsthetic*, 146.28)

10.28  welfare. Its essence is] SP; welfare, . . . the essence of scholasticism is (Bosanquet, *History of Æsthetic*, 146.30–33)

26.14  of the] M; to the (D'Arcy, *A Short Study of Ethics*, 8.1)

29.11–12 experience. Self-determination] M; experience. It may seem that it ought to be evident directly that self-determination (D'Arcy, *A Short Study of Ethics*, 28.1–2)

30.5  is] M; as (D'Arcy, *A Short Study of Ethics*, 58.27)

30.6  Self, unless] M; Self, like a despot, dominates the whole realm of experience, and, unless (D'Arcy, *A Short Study of Ethics*, 59.2–3)

30.18–19 God himself would be simply one unit in a multitude and isolated] M; If God were merely Personal, we should be constrained to think of Him as isolated (D'Arcy, *A Short Study of Ethics*, 47.11–13)

30.19  his] M; His (D'Arcy, *A Short Study of Ethics*, 47.13)

30.20  But it is] M; It is (D'Arcy, *A Short Study of Ethics*, 47.20)

30.20–21 multitude] M; multiplicity (D'Arcy, *A Short Study of Ethics*, 47.20–21)

30.27  persons] M; Persons (D'Arcy, *A Short Study of Ethics*, 102.19)

30.27   naturally] M;   mutually (D'Arcy, *A Short Study of Ethics*, 102.19)

30.28   one in] M;   One in (D'Arcy, *A Short Study of Ethics*, 102.20)

30.29   Hence the good] M;   Hence the Good (D'Arcy, *A Short Study of Ethics*, 102.21)

30.30   true good] M;   True Good (D'Arcy, *A Short Study of Ethics*, 102.22)

30.30–31.1   common good] M;   Common Good (D'Arcy, *A Short Study of Ethics*, 102.23)

31.1    absolute good] M;   Absolute Good (D'Arcy, *A Short Study of Ethics*, 102.23)

32.14–15   circumstances has] M;   circumstances which can be a field for action has (D'Arcy, *A Short Study of Ethics*, 108.16–17)

32.15   good is perfectly individualized.] M;   good is always one. It never conflicts with itself. It is found in the concrete act, and is, therefore, perfectly individualised. (D'Arcy, *A Short Study of Ethics*, 109.18–20)

32.16   It is no] M;   The ethical principle is therefore no (D'Arcy, *A Short Study of Ethics*, 111.17)

36.15   who happen] EE;   who may happen (Huxley, *Evolution and Ethics*, 81.24)

36.16   exist] EE;   obtain (Huxley, *Evolution and Ethics*, 81.26)

36.17   best. The practice] EE;   best. [¶] As I have already urged, the practice (Huxley, *Evolution and Ethics*, 81.27–28)

36.18   which] EE;   what (Huxley, *Evolution and Ethics*, 81.29)

36.21–22   ends. The imitation by] EE;   ends; if the imitation of it by (Huxley, *Evolution and Ethics*, 83.9)

36.23   ethics. Let] EE;   ethics; what becomes of this surprising theory? [¶] Let (Huxley, *Evolution and Ethics*, 83.11–12)

36.31–32   strictly speaking, is part of the general cosmic process, just] EE;   To this extent the general cosmic process begins to be checked by a rudimentary ethical process, which is, strictly speaking, part of the former, just (Huxley, *Evolution and Ethics*, 115.15–18)

36.32   governor] EE;   "governor" (Huxley, *Evolution and Ethics*, 115.19)

38.25–26   macrocosm is pitted against the microcosm; that man is subduing nature] EE;   microcosm against the macrocosm and to set man to subdue nature (Huxley, *Evolution and Ethics*, 83.16–17)

38.26–27   that the history] EE;   The history (Huxley, *Evolution and Ethics*, 83.24)

38.27     we] EE;   men (Huxley, *Evolution and Ethics*, 83.25)

38.29     that there lies] EE;   there lies (Huxley, *Evolution and Ethics*, 83.28)

38.29     man] EE;   him (Huxley, *Evolution and Ethics*, 83.28)

39.1     *exist*] EE;   obtain (Huxley, *Evolution and Ethics*, 81.26)

39.1     to the survival] EE;   but (Huxley, *Evolution and Ethics*, 81.26)

39.13     might leave us with nothing] EE;   might bring about, in the vegetable kingdom, a population of more and more stunted and humbler and humbler organisms, until the "fittest" that survived might be nothing (Huxley, *Evolution and Ethics*, 80.29–81.2)

33.14     diatomes] EE;   diatoms (Huxley, *Evolution and Ethics*, 81.2–3)

33.15     that] EE;   those (Huxley, *Evolution and Ethics*, 81.3)

33.20     with] EE;   in (Huxley, *Evolution and Ethics*, 81.25)

33.20     to] EE;   of (Huxley, *Evolution and Ethics*, 81.25)

42.29     involves] EE;   repudiates (Huxley, *Evolution and Ethics*, 82.9)

46.4     man] EE;   he (Huxley, *Evolution and Ethics*, 52.20)

46.5     the axe] EE;   axe (Huxley, *Evolution and Ethics*, 52.22)

46.6     *former*] EE;   *rom.* (Huxley, *Evolution and Ethics*, 52.21)

51.4     of the needs] EE;   of the conditions to the needs (Huxley, *Evolution and Ethics*, 13.21–22)

177.14     series idea; number] R;   series-idea. [¶] That number (Phillips, "Number and Its Application," lxxxiv.24–25)

178.6     the application] R;   its application (Phillips, "Number and Its Application," xliii.24)

180.17     the constant] R;   the most constant (Phillips, "Number and Its Application," xxxviii.13)

182.7–8     *movements*] R;   *rom.* (Phillips, "Number and Its Application," xxxi.33)

182.16     *adjustment of activity*] R;   adjustments of activity (Phillips, "Number and Its Application," xxxiv.10)

183.8     The child] R;   he (McLellan and Dewey, *Psychology of Number*, 30.4)

183.10     *implicitly*] R;   *rom.* (McLellan and Dewey, *Psychology of Number*, 30.6)

183.10     *the ideas*] R;   *rom.* (McLellan and Dewey, *Psychology of Number*, 30.6)

184n.6     relation.] R;   *relations*, (Phillips, "Number and Its Application," li.42)

349.40     efforts] J;   movement (Baldwin, "Genetic Psychology," 713:1.6)

349.40     an] J;   another (Baldwin, "Genetic Psychology," 713:1.6)

356.22   used] NC;   taken (Conant, *Number Concept*, 48.19)

356.28   *other* hand] NC;   other (Conant, *Number Concept*, 53.1)

359.5   of feeling] SE;   of a feeling (Stanley, *Evolutionary Psychology of Feeling*, 6.22–23)

359.17   being any more] SE;   being more (Stanley, *Evolutionary Psychology of Feeling*, 12.18)

363.20   how cognition] SE;   how mere cognition (Stanley, *Evolutionary Psychology of Feeling*, 102.1–2)

367.3   will-effort] SE;   will effort (Stanley, *Evolutionary Psychology of Feeling*, 376.26)

370.34   imagery] SS;   images (Sully, *Studies of Childhood*, 31.25)

371.10   eyes] SS;   eye (Sully, *Studies of Childhood*, 31.29)

372.16   *educational factors*] H;   *rom.* (Harris, *Psychologic Foundations of Education*, x.11)

387.12   requisite to] SI;   requisite is to (Baldwin, *Social and Ethical Interpretations*, 13.16)

387.12   is] SI;   in (Baldwin, *Social and Ethical Interpretations*, 13.16)

388.24   socius] SI;   "~" (Baldwin, *Social and Ethical Interpretations*, 21.24)

388.24   its] SI;   his (Baldwin, *Social and Ethical Interpretations*, 21.24)

388.25   socius] SI;   "~" (Baldwin, *Social and Ethical Interpretations*, 21.25)

390.34   situations] SI;   situations of life (Baldwin, *Social and Ethical Interpretations*, 542.22)

392.25   thing] SI;   action which (Baldwin, *Social and Ethical Interpretations*, 104.27)

392n.5–6   *situation* [italics mine] instruct] SI;   situation operate to instruct (Baldwin, *Social and Ethical Interpretations*, 102.19–20)

394.30   *one*] SI;   *rom.* (Baldwin, *Social and Ethical Interpretations*, 80.28)

396.13   is] SI;   are (Baldwin, *Social and Ethical Interpretations*, 315.26)

397.8   *are to have*] SI;   *rom.* (Baldwin, *Social and Ethical Interpretations*, 535.19)

400.28–30   while the passages might be better expressed, there is essentially no inconsistency in these three aspects of development.] RB;   The different passages which discuss it might certainly be better written, but such as they are they do not appear to me inconsistent. (Baldwin, "Social Interpretations," xciii.9–11)

412.17–18   thoughts, intellectual states, such as imaginations, knowledges and informations.] SM; *thoughts; by which is meant all sorts of intellectual states, such as imaginations, knowledges, and informations.* (Baldwin, *Social and Ethical Interpretations,* 487.17–19)

448.10 purpose] RC; purpose-life (Hailmann, N.E.A. *Proceedings,* 1897, 202.5)

# Word-division list

Word-division at the end of a line in the copy-texts may present something of a problem for editorial decision whether Dewey's own general custom (insofar as it coincides with the style of the copy-texts themselves) requires certain words to be treated as hyphenated or as unhyphenated compounds. The editors have decided the form of clear-cut cases silently. However, all doubtful examples, or examples that need emphasis, have been listed here, according to the formula

37.30   Over-sight

The reader should observe that in the present edition (W), all end-of-the-line hyphenations are the modern printer's unless specific record is made of those hyphenated compounds within the line in the copy-texts that are ambiguously broken and hyphenated at the end of the line by W, which are recorded as in the formula

155.9   psycho-|physical

I.   Compounds, or possible compounds, broken at the end of the line in the copy-texts occurring internally in W:

| | |
|---|---|
| 37.26 | two-edged |
| 37.30 | Over-sight |
| 62.40 | standpoint |
| 70.5 | interactions |
| 77.39 | subject-matter |
| 84.20 | standpoint |
| 85.13 | haphazard |
| 97.8 | patchwork |
| 98.19 | seeing-for-reaching |
| 98.37 | seeing-of-a-light-that-means-pain-when-contact-occurs |
| 100.6 | extra-experimental |
| 105.20 | sensori-motor |
| 106.19 | onlooker |
| 135.37 | second-handed |
| 143.26 | book-keeping |
| 148.22 | toothache |
| 157.26 | extra-psychical |

| | |
|---|---|
| 159.19 | extra-sensational |
| 166.33 | subject-matter |
| 169.8 | wrought-out |
| 172.35 | subject-matter |
| 174.28 | interaction |
| 190.1 | one-sided |
| 198.19 | visual-touch-action |
| 199.2 | standpoint |
| 237.8 | Water power |
| 239.35 | "Wood-Work." |
| 251.34 | half-barren |
| 269.12 | subject-matter |
| 279.20 | text-book |
| 280.17 | would-be |
| 288.20 | text-book |
| 293.33 | subject-matter |
| 297.2 | standpoint |
| 324.30 | child-study |
| 329.32 | *Standpoint* |
| 331.23 | life-process |
| 335.28 | Formal Stages |
| 343.13 | long-time |
| 347.8 | thorough-going |
| 360n.2 | James-Lange |
| 367.6 | will-effort |
| 367.8 | will-effort |
| 369.31 | well-defined |
| 371.15 | standpoint |
| 371.24 | overplus |
| 376.7 | child-study |
| 383.37 | interrela-\|tion |
| 399.15 | well-worn |
| 407.23 | give-and-take |
| 413.13 | give-and-take |
| 428.15 | *standpoint* |
| 429.18 | today |
| 456.20 | everyday |

II.      Compounds that are broken and hyphenated at the end of the line in W but appear as hyphenated compounds within the line in the copy-texts:

| | |
|---|---|
| 15.16 | Græco-\|Roman |
| 18.1 | one-\|sided |
| 32.10 | non-\|existent |

| | |
|---|---|
| 41.5 | non-\|moral |
| 72.2 | culture-\|epoch |
| 90.26 | subject-\|matter |
| 97.1 | sensori-\|motor |
| 97.19 | sensation-followed-by-idea-followed-by-\|movement |
| 103.28 | visual-heat-pain-muscular-\|quale |
| 103.29 | visual-touch-muscular-\|quale |
| 116.18 | over-\|reliance |
| 116.27 | sugar-\|coated |
| 119.24 | well-\|disciplined |
| 144.33 | half-\|consciously |
| 146.18 | man-\|made |
| 149.2 | Will-\|training |
| 152.2 | non-\|sensational |
| 155.9 | psycho-\|physical |
| 156.23 | one-\|hundredths |
| 163.19 | on-\|looker |
| 240.26 | "Wood-\|Work." |
| 259.11 | dwelling-\|place |
| 263.10 | language-\|forms |
| 272.31 | twenty-\|five |
| 275.24 | non-\|professional |
| 277.36 | text-\|book |
| 297.29 | "Culture-\|Epoch" |
| 370.30 | sense-\|experience |
| 372.11 | subject-\|matter |
| 390.8 | thought-\|material |
| 393.18 | content-\|identity |
| 415.18 | eye-\|activity |
| 429.25 | so-\|called |
| 453.30 | day-\|by-day |

III. Compounds, or possible compounds, broken at the end of the line in the copy-texts and in W:

| | |
|---|---|
| 123.22 | cross-\|eyedness |
| 171.28 | back-\|ground |
| 217.2 | stand-\|point |
| 217.31 | play-\|thing |
| 269.13 | language-\|studies |
| 430.21 | "filling-\|in," |

# Index

# Index

Abstraction: Phillips's use of term, 182; early emphasis on, 261; essence of, 261; dangers in, 383

Academy: as preparatory school, 271

Accidentals: authority of, cxxi–cxxii; treatment of, cxxv–cxxvi; English, treatment of, cxxviii

Act: relation of, to content by Baldwin, 416

Action: as union of percept and concept, 21; importance of, in theory of knowledge, 21–22; in sensori-motor circuit, 97; and emotion, 324; and volitional consciousness, 361

Active: and passive in child development, 91

Activity: mechanical external, 121; random internal, 121; direct, in elementary education, 144; indirect, in secondary education, 144; modes of human, 231; psychological aspect of, 439

Adjustment: as adaptation to environment, 51

Æsthetic element: combination of law and freedom in, 202; significance of, 202

Æsthetic interest: use of, in teaching drawing, 200; in kindergarten, 207; in child-study, 215–17

Agassiz, Louis: mentioned, 265

Agricultural instinct: in education, 250–51

Apperception: theory of, 297

Appetite: relation to energy, 129

Aristippus: mentioned, 352, 353

Aristotle: and thought, 8; and philosophy, 8–9; mentioned, 141, 212, 213, 400

Arithmetic: Fine's views on, 427

Art in education: union of, with science, 95; references on, 337

Artistic expression: teaching of, 192–201

Attention: exercise of will manifest in, 118; division of, 118, 119, 120; external, 119; simulation of, 119–20; and effort, 163; sense of, 163; and interest, 320–21; and emotion, 323

Balance and rhythm: in æsthetic experience, 202

Baldwin, James Mark: incompleteness of his theory, 100; on reactive consciousness, 100; quoted on effort, 160; on motive, 348; his work on *Johnson's Cyclopædia*, 348–49; his position criticized, 385–99; his sociological approach, 386; on personality, 387–89,

activities, 204; errors in treating, in school, 204; as social being, 205, 226; as foundation for social life, 213; as element in political organization, 213–14; as source of better life, 216–17; as symbol to adult, 217; as key to nature of growth, 217–18, 249; nature of, 226; as end in himself, 451–52

Child development: epochs of, 298–99

Childhood: idealization of, 218

Child life: movements of interest in, 215–16

Child psychology: study of, 206

Child-study: principles established by, 204–6; criticism of, justified, 209; as one direction of general physiology, 210; isolation of, from sciences, 210; questions concerning, 211; three sources of interest in, 212; as determined by political ends, 215; æsthetic interest in, 215–17; interest in, during Renaissance, 215–17; three movements in, 219–20; scientific approach to, 219–21; Sully on interest in, 368–69; in educational psychology, 445

Christianity: development of, in Roman Empire, 9, 10, 11

Circuit: sensori-motor, 98; organic, 317

Clothing: activities in study of, 240; principles in study of, 240; study of botany in, 240; study of zoology in, 240–41; study of arith-

metic in, 241; study of history in, 241; study of physics in, 241

Co-education: in Western colleges, 272

College: changes in policy and curriculum in, 272

Communication: role of, in constructive activity, 231

Community life: its influence on education, 94

Conant, Levi Leonard: his book chiefly on counting, 355; on controversy about numerical judgments, 355; his work as useful to philologist, 355–56; psychological points in his work, 356–58

Concept: function of, in judgment, 323

Conception: adjustment of, with perception in judgment, 321

Conditions of life in U.S., 59–60

Conduct: principles of, as same in life and in school, 54; in individual, 55; in society, 55; two points of view on, 55; as mode of individual activity, 55–56; as social, 56; psychological view of, 56

Conflict: as necessary factor in moral life, 45–46

Consciousness: individual in modern, 15, 16; in man, 53; discussed by Stanley, 359–62

Constructive activities: as basis of unity in studies, 230; psychological opportunities in, 230–31; analysis of, 231; social opportunities in, 231; study of social aspects of, 231

Content: value and form in